Reconstructing Atrocity Prevention

In the two and a half decades since the end of the Cold War, policymakers have become acutely aware of the extent to which the world today faces mass atrocities. In an effort to prevent the death, destruction, and global chaos wrought by these crimes, the agendas for both national and international policy have grown beyond conflict prevention to encompass atrocity prevention, protection of civilians, transitional justice, and the Responsibility to Protect. Yet, to date, there has been no attempt to address the topic of the prevention of mass atrocities from the theoretical, policy, and practicing standpoints simultaneously. This volume is designed to fill that gap, clarifying and solidifying the present understanding of atrocity prevention. It will serve as an authoritative work on the state of the field.

SHERI P. ROSENBERG (1967–2015) was a scholar, professor, and human rights advocate focusing on issues of law and mass atrocity. She was Associate Clinical Professor of Law and Director of the Cardozo Law Institute on Holocaust and Human Rights (CLIHHR) and the Human Rights and Atrocity Prevention Clinic. Her publications include "Genocide by Attrition: Efficient and Silent," in *Genocide Matters* (2013) and "Responsibility to Protect: A Framework for Prevention" in the journal *Global Responsibility to Protect* (2009).

TIBI GALIS is a political scientist. He is the Executive Director of the Auschwitz Institute for Peace and Reconciliation, a New York-based NGO that helps governments prevent genocide worldwide.

ALEX ZUCKER is an editor and a translator of Czech literature. He has received an English PEN Award for Writing in Translation, a National Endowment for the Arts Literature Fellowship, and the ALTA National Translation Award. He currently serves as co-chair of the PEN America Translation Committee.

Reconstructing Atrocity Prevention

Edited by

Sheri P. Rosenberg
Cardozo Law School

Tibi Galis
Auschwitz Institute, New York

Alex Zucker
Independent Scholar

CAMBRIDGE
UNIVERSITY PRESS

CAMBRIDGE
UNIVERSITY PRESS

32 Avenue of the Americas, New York, NY 10013-2473, USA

Cambridge University Press is part of the University of Cambridge.

It furthers the University's mission by disseminating knowledge in the pursuit of education, learning, and research at the highest international levels of excellence.

www.cambridge.org
Information on this title: www.cambridge.org/9781107094963

© Cambridge University Press 2016

First published 2016

A catalog record for this publication is available from the British Library.

Library of Congress Cataloging in Publication Data
Reconstructing atrocity prevention / [edited by] Sheri P. Rosenberg, Cardozo Law School, Tiberiu Galis, Auschwitz Institute, New York, Alex Zucker, Independent Scholar.
    pages cm
Includes bibliographical references and index.
1. Atrocities – Prevention.   2. War crimes – Prevention.
3. Genocide – Prevention.   I. Rosenberg, Sheri P., editor.   II. Galis, Tiberiu, editor.   III. Zucker, Alex, editor.
HV6322.R43   2016
363.32–dc23   2015012308

ISBN 978-1-107-09496-3 Hardback

In memory of Sheri Rosenberg, scholar, colleague, mentor, friend. Sheri dedicated her life to the prevention of mass atrocities and to helping the people affected by them. Her knowledge, passion, and humor were an inspiration to us all, and her vision lives on in this volume.

Contents

Foreword

Roméo Dallaire

Retired generals rarely write prefaces to nonmilitary books, but this is a rare book on a topic of crucial importance. The United Nations provided me with no serious briefing, scholarly or journalistic, before posting me to Rwanda in 1993. Major Brent Beardsley, my excellent assistant, scoured libraries and bookstores before our departure and put together a few basic facts. Only when we reached Kigali was he even able to purchase at a local shop a map of the city of Kigali and our areas of immediate responsibility. Such cavalier attitudes toward the needs of peacebuilding staff members permeated the UN system in the early 1990s, but, as later developments in Rwanda made clear, the success of UN peace operations requires rigorous and early input from experienced scholars and practitioners.

When "spoilers" undermined implementation of the Arusha Accords and the Rwanda genocide against Tutsi unfolded in spring 1994, most member states, especially those with seats on the UN Security Council, retreated to the narrowest notions of their core self-interests and mustered no comprehensive vision of genocide prevention or any recognition that protecting civilian lives was a vital responsibility of national leaders and the UN system itself. Neither the provisions of the UN Genocide Convention nor the concept of "human security" sufficed to mobilize states against mass atrocities aimed at destroying an entire human group. Only the desperate postgenocide discovery of sovereignty as responsibility, a concept pioneered by Francis Deng with Roberta Cohen at the Brookings Institution,[1] lit the way toward concrete implementation of the concept of "Never Again," a legacy of the Holocaust and World War II that, until the late 1990s, was honored rhetorically, but never in practice.

As a Canadian, I am proud that farsighted leaders and public servants such as Lloyd Axworthy and Don Hubert spearheaded the campaign to create the

---

[1] See Roberta Cohen and Francis M. Deng, "Normative Framework of Sovereignty," in Francis M. Deng, Sadikiel Kimaro, Terrence Lyons, Donald Rothchild, and I. William Zartman (eds.), *Sovereignty as Responsibility: Conflict Management in Africa* (Washington, DC: Brookings Institution Press, 1996), 1–33.

International Commission on Intervention and State Sovereignty (ICISS), whose December 2001 report, *The Responsibility to Protect*, embodies the enduring ideas discussed in this volume. But I am also forced to admit that theirs was a minority effort within the government of Canada and that we would not be discussing the responsibility to protect (R2P) today were it not for the commitment and intellectual energy of Gareth Evans, the formidable foreign minister of Australia from 1988 to 1996 and president of the International Crisis Group from 2000 to 2009.

Why had no concrete mechanism and guidelines for preventing genocide emerged before Kosovo in 1999 and R2P in 2001? As Frank Chalk and my colleagues at Concordia University's Montreal Institute for Genocide and Human Rights Studies found in their interview-based comparative research, in the wake of the Rwanda genocide, "the United States' experience with Milosevic's brutal record in the Balkans, and its perceived national interest in securing Europe" played major roles.[2] Unlike the Rwandan crisis, "the geopolitical importance of the Balkans to the U.S. and its NATO allies constituted a powerful impetus for action against Milosevic."[3] The Racak massacre of forty Kosovar Albanians in January 1999 and the failure of the Rambouillet Peace Talks in February of that year compelled President Clinton to explore the military option.[4] Chalk and our team concluded in their 2009 study that "Ultimately, the NATO intervention was motivated by a confluence of narrowly perceived U.S. national interests, moral imperative, and the desire to demonstrate NATO's continued military prowess and prestige."[5]

In the aftermath of Kosovo, a strong consensus on what governments should do to organize themselves to prevent future mass atrocities emerged. It is crystallized in *Mobilizing the Will to Intervene: Leadership to Prevent Mass Atrocities*, the book I co-authored with Chalk, Kyle Matthews, and others in 2010, and in *Preventing Genocide: A Blueprint for U.S. Policymakers* (2008), an important study piloted by Madeleine K. Albright and William S. Cohen.[6] Enabling leadership, enhancing coordination, building capacity, and ensuring knowledge are the central tasks. That means presidents and prime ministers who make preventing mass atrocities a national priority for their governments

---

[2] Romeo Dallaire, Frank Chalk, Kyle Matthews, Carla Barqueiro, and Simon Doyle, *Mobilizing the Will to Intervene: Leadership and Action to Prevent Mass Atrocities* (Montreal: Montreal Institute for Genocide and Human Rights Studies, Concordia University, 2009), 105. A book version of this study is available as *Mobilizing the Will to Intervene: Leadership to Prevent Mass Atrocities* (Montreal: McGill-Queen's University Press, 2010). Page numbers referred to in this Preface refer to the 2009 version, cited above.

[3] Ibid., 106.

[4] Ibid., 106 and 108.

[5] Ibid., 109.

[6] Madeleine K. Albright and William S. Cohen, eds. *Preventing Genocide: A Blueprint for U.S. Policymakers* (Washington, DC: United States Holocaust Memorial Museum, American Academy of Diplomacy, and the Endowment of the United States Institute of Peace, 2008).

and appoint a focal point person to lead the genocide prevention agenda across the government. It means permanent legislative committees to serve as watchdogs ensuring that the executive branch of government is given the necessary resources and follows through on its commitment. It also means overcoming the tendency to seal off vital intelligence on looming mass atrocities by creating an atrocities prevention board to share information across the government, galvanize diplomacy, craft carefully targeted foreign aid, and, if necessary, deploy military resources in mass atrocity response operations. And, finally, it means civil society groups and media focused on mass atrocity prevention and implementing "the responsibility to report."[7]

Most political leaders still don't understand that their nation's self-interest is tied to preventing mass atrocities against other human beings, especially while they are haunted and intimidated by the specters of Iraq and Afghanistan at election time. President Obama's Atrocity Prevention Board is a very important step in the right direction, but even it, in practice, is not yet the dynamo needed to energize the U.S. government's prevention efforts. Interests and perceptions matter, and it may take disasters like the Ebola epidemic and its worldwide ramifications for public health to highlight for political leaders the indirect connections between atrocity prevention in faraway lands and the national security of their citizens. Dr. Jay Keystone, head of the Tropical Disease Unit at the Toronto General Hospital, tied these threads together in our 2009 study, when he wrote: "Preventing genocide and crimes against humanity are front line tasks in our fight to maintain public health security right here in North America. Our politicians and public health officials need to lead in this area."[8]

Ebola

I like this book. I like the editors' recognition that we still have a lot to learn and that it will take a truly interdisciplinary approach to learn it. I like their focus on viewing prevention through the lenses of theory, policy, and practice. And I like the fact that it is a book written with students, our future preventers, in mind. The greatest challenge we will face is to convince political leaders to wisely use the insights and recommendations developed by these authors. And that will not be easy when we consider the hurdles they face, even those with the best will in the world. As political scientist René Lemarchand recently wrote: "we need to remind ourselves that it is in states where poverty is rife, political institutions are failing and human rights are abused that we should expect the greatest amount of turmoil."[9] But no one ever said the job would be easy!

---

[7] *Mobilizing the Will to Intervene*, 17–63.
[8] Ibid., 12.
[9] René Lemarchand, "The Arc of Instability in Africa," unpublished paper, July 2014, 9–10.

I believe that priority should be given to a carrot-and-stick approach, encouraging and harnessing a broader idea of national self-interest to counter political leaders' fears about backlashes after intervention and the costs to their states of foregoing the lures of profits earned from arms sales and resource control. One useful approach is for international institutions like the World Bank, the European Union, the Organization for Security and Cooperation in Europe, and the UN to provide compensation to the smaller nations for the direct and indirect costs of prevention and to recognize more vigorously the sacrifices that taxpayers in wealthier countries make when their leaders undertake peace diplomacy. Once national leaders grasp the practical importance of R2P, renewing their commitment to financing growing expertise that improves operational understanding of other cultures, languages, and histories is the next crucial step. The convergence of national interests and mass atrocity prevention will one day be obvious to all, but we have a long way to go – the transition from noble words to practical action is essential.

Contributors

ELAZAR BARKAN is Professor of International and Public Affairs and the Director of the Human Rights Concentration at Columbia's School of International and Public Affairs. His research interests focus on human rights and on the role of history in contemporary society and politics and the response to gross historical crimes and injustices. His books include *Choreography of Sacred Spaces: State, Religion and Conflict Resolution* (2014); *No Return, No Refuge: Rites and Rights in Minority Repatriation* (2011); *The Guilt of Nations: Restitution and Negotiating Historical Injustices* (2000); *Taking Wrongs Seriously: Apologies and Reconciliation* (2006); and *Claiming the Stones/Naming the Bones: Cultural Property and the Negotiation of National and Ethnic Identity* (2003).

ALEX J. BELLAMY is Professor of Peace & Conflict Studies and Executive Director of the Asia Pacific Centre for the Responsibility to Protect at the University of Queensland, Australia. He is also Non-Resident Senior Adviser at the International Peace Institute, New York; Fellow of the Academy of Social Science in Australia; and Secretary of the High Level Advisory Panel on the Responsibility to Protect in Southeast Asia. His most recent book is *The Responsibility to Protect: A Defense* (2015), and he is currently editing *The Oxford Handbook on the Responsibility to Protect* with Tim Dunne.

KELLY BONNER is an attorney with White & Case LLP. Prior to joining White & Case, she worked with the Committee on the Administration of Justice in Northern Ireland, advising the Consultative Group on the Past as to legal strategies for addressing the legacy of the Troubles. She is a graduate of New York University and Fordham Law School.

BRIDGET CONLEY-ZILKIC is an assistant research professor at Tufts University's The Fletcher School and Research Director of the World Peace Foundation, where she leads a project, "How Mass Atrocities End." Previously, she worked at the United States Holocaust Memorial Museum Holocaust Memorial Museum on issues related to contemporary genocide, with responsibility for developing the institution's research and educational projects on ongoing threats of genocide. She helped frame the museum's position regarding ongoing violence, produced films, conducted training workshops, and curated an exhibition, *From Memory to Action: Meeting the Challenge of Genocide Today.* She has a PhD in Comparative Literature from Binghamton University.

ROMÉO DALLAIRE is a retired lieutenant-general, retired senator, and celebrated humanitarian. In 1993, L.Gen Dallaire was appointed Force Commander for the UN Assistance Mission for Rwanda (UNAMIR), where he witnessed the country descend into chaos and genocide leading to the deaths of more than 800,000 Rwandans. Since his retirement, he has become an outspoken advocate for human rights, genocide prevention, mental health, and war-affected children. He founded the Roméo Dallaire Child Soldiers Initiative, an organization committed to ending the use of child soldiers worldwide, and is the author of two best-selling books.

ANDREW FEINSTEIN is a former ANC Member of Parliament in South Africa where he introduced the first-ever motion on Holocaust remembrance. He is the author of the best-selling political memoir *After the Party: A Personal and Political Journey Inside the ANC* and the critically acclaimed *The Shadow World: Inside the Global Arms Trade*, which the *Washington Post* describes as "the most complete account [of the trade] ever written." He is Executive Director of Corruption Watch UK based in London. He appears regularly in a wide range of international print and broadcast media.

TIBI GALIS is a political scientist. He is the Executive Director of the Auschwitz Institute for Peace and Reconciliation, a New York-based nongovernmental organization (NGO) that helps governments prevent genocide worldwide.

ELISA VON JOEDEN-FORGEY is Assistant Professor of Holocaust and Genocide Studies at the Richard Stockton College of New Jersey. Prior to this, she was a visiting scholar and lecturer in the Department of History at the University of Pennsylvania, where she earned her PhD degree in modern German and African history. She has taught courses on the Holocaust, genocide, human rights, war, and imperialism. Her current research on gender and genocide has appeared in several journals and collected volumes. She is currently completing a book on gender and the prevention of genocide, which will be published by the University of Pennsylvania Press.

MICHAEL T. KLARE is the Five College Professor of Peace and World Security Studies, a joint appointment at Amherst, Hampshire, Mount Holyoke, Smith College, and the University of Massachusetts at Amherst. He has written widely on U.S. defense policy, international peace and security, and global resource politics. He is the author of fourteen books, including *Resource Wars* (2001), *Blood and Oil* (2004), *Rising Powers, Shrinking Planet: The New Geopolitics of Energy* (2008), and *The Race for What's Left: The Global Scramble for the World's Last Resources* (2012). He is also the defense correspondent of *The Nation* and a contributing editor of *Current History*.

JENNIFER LEANING is the Director of the François-Xavier Bagnoud Center for Health and Human Rights at Harvard University, the FXB Professor of the Practice of Health and Human Rights at Harvard School of Public Health, Associate Professor of Medicine at Harvard Medical School, and a member of the faculty in the Department of Emergency Medicine at Brigham and Women's Hospital. Her research, field investigations, and publications focus on public health, medical ethics, and early warning in response to war, disaster, and mass atrocities. She has written widely on these issues in the peer-reviewed literature.

GEORGE A. LOPEZ serves as vice president at the United States Institute of Peace and Hesburgh Professor of Peace, Emeritus, at the University of Notre Dame. He has been involved in sanctions research and policy since 1992, having co-written or edited six books and more than forty articles and book chapters on economic sanctions. He has advised international agencies and governments regarding sanctions issues, especially on limiting humanitarian impact and the design of targeted financial sanctions. From October 2010 to July 2011, he served on the UN Panel of Experts for monitoring and implementing UN Sanctions on North Korea.

DR. DANA ZARET LUCK is a licensed psychologist who specializes in clinical neuropsychology and serves as the managing partner of the Mattis and Luck Center for Neuropsychological Services, LLP. By viewing R2P through a psychological lens, she seeks to draw attention to the devastating impact of atrocity crimes on individuals and groups and to raise the level of awareness in the R2P and policy-making communities of how the trauma and recovery process for victims, perpetrators, humanitarian workers, and others who have been exposed to atrocity crimes should factor into policy and practice.

EDWARD C. LUCK A scholar, practitioner, and author, Dr. Edward C. Luck served as the UN's first Special Adviser on the Responsibility to Protect, at the Assistant Secretary-General level, from 2008 to 2012. He was responsible for its conceptual, political, and operational/institutional development and was the architect of the Secretary-General's three-pillar strategy for implementing R2P. He has held a wide range of leadership positions in academia, nonprofit organizations, think tanks, and the UN.

DR. DEBORAH MAYERSEN is a historian and Vice-Chancellor's Postdoctoral Research Fellow at the Institute for Social Transformation Research, the University of Wollongong, Australia. Her most recent publications include *On the Path to Genocide: Armenia and Rwanda Reexamined* (2014) and the edited volume (with Annie Pohlman) *Genocide and Mass Atrocities in Asia: Legacies and Prevention* (2013).

OWEN C. PELL is a litigation partner at White & Case in New York. He handles complex commercial matters, including cases involving the extraterritorial reach of U.S. law, securities and RICO claims, claims against foreign sovereigns, and reparation claims under the U.S. Alien Tort Statute. He also represented Peru in gaining the return of artifacts taken from Machu Picchu. He gave a TED talk ("Diplomacy 2.0") on how companies and NGOs are changing how international legal norms are formed, and he formulated a proposal, endorsed by the European Parliament, for a title-clearing system to address Holocaust-looted art claims.

DWIGHT RAYMOND Colonel (Retired) Dwight Raymond is a peace operations specialist at the Peacekeeping and Stability Operations Institute at the U.S. Army War College, where he also teaches a course on Humanitarian Intervention. A West Point graduate, his military awards include the Bronze Star Medal; Combat Infantryman's Badge; and Airborne, Ranger, and Pathfinder qualification badges. He is one of the primary authors of the *Mass Atrocity Response Operations (MARO) Military Planning Handbook*, the *Mass Atrocity Prevention and Response Options (MAPRO) Policy Planning Handbook*, the *Protection of Civilians Military Reference Guide*, and military doctrinal publications regarding stability and peace operations.

RAMIRO RIERA is a lawyer and a professor of legal sciences. He has a BA in philosophy from the University of Buenos Aires and an MA in human rights from the National University of La Plata. He is a PhD candidate in International Law at the University of Buenos Aires. He teaches graduate and postgraduate courses on matters of criminal law, human rights, and international law at the University of Buenos Aires, Salvador University, and the University of National Defense. Outside academia, he has served at the Human Rights and International Humanitarian Law Direction of the Ministry of Defense of Argentina.

SHERI P. ROSENBERG (1967–2015) was a scholar, professor, and human rights advocate focusing on issues of law and mass atrocity. She was Associate Clinical Professor of Law and Director of the Cardozo Law Institute on Holocaust and Human Rights (CLIHHR) and the Human Rights and Atrocity Prevention Clinic. Her publications include "Genocide by Attrition: Efficient and Silent," in *Genocide Matters* (2013) and "Responsibility to

Protect: A Framework for Prevention" in the journal *Global Responsibility to Protect* (2009).

ASHAD SENTONGO is Director of African Programs at the Auschwitz Institute for Peace and Reconciliation. His research work focuses on power-sharing and ethnic conflict in Africa. He previously worked with the Genocide Prevention Program as Program Officer on Genocide Prevention at the International Conference on the Great Lakes Region, and he helped to establish the Regional and National Committees in Member States. He worked as consultant on dialogue in oil-producing communities in the Delta State of Nigeria, Research Associate at the National Defense University, Program Assistant on transitional justice at Coexistence International, and Program Assistant at Mercy Corps on Conflict Management in Kosovo, Guatemala, Indonesia, and Ethiopia.

SCOTT STRAUS is Professor of Political Science and International Studies at the University of Wisconsin, Madison. He is the author most recently of *Making and Unmaking Nations: War, Leadership, and Genocide in Modern Africa* (2015) and *Fundamentals of Atrocity Prevention* (2015). He has also written widely on Rwanda, including *The Order of Genocide: Race, Power, and War in Rwanda* (2006), and published in various academic journals, including the *American Journal of Political Science, Perspectives on Politics, World Politics, Foreign Affairs*, and *African Affairs*.

DR. EKKEHARD STRAUSS qualified as judge in Germany and holds a doctoral degree in international law and human rights from the University of Potsdam in Germany. Following experience in academia, government, and the private sector, he served with the OSCE and the UN OHCHR since 1998. Throughout his career, he published extensively on protection of minorities, prevention of human rights violations, postconflict peacebuilding, and the prevention of mass atrocities. At the time of writing, he worked as an independent researcher and consultant. He is an associate professor with the Asia Institute at Griffith University.

JOHANNA RAY VOLLHARDT is Assistant Professor of Psychology at Clark University, where she also directs the doctoral program in social psychology and is affiliated with the Strassler Center for Holocaust and Genocide Studies. She is a co-founding co-editor of the *Journal of Social and Political Psychology* and serves on the editorial boards of the *Journal of Social Issues* and *Politische Psychologie*. From 2012 to 2015, she served on the governing council of the International Society of Political Psychology. She has been working with the NGO Radio LaBenevolencija, which produces edutainment radio reconciliation programs in Rwanda, Burundi, and Eastern DRC, since 2005.

JENNIFER M. WELSH is Professor and Chair in International Relations at the European University Institute and a Fellow of Somerville College, University of Oxford. She is a co-director of the Oxford Institute for Ethics, Law and Armed Conflict, and, since July 2013, has served as Secretary-General Ban Ki-moon's Special Adviser on the Responsibility to Protect. She is the author and editor of several books and articles on the responsibility to protect, humanitarian intervention, the UN Security Council, and the principle of sovereignty. From 2014, she is directing a five-year research project, funded by the European Research Council, on the "individualization of war."

KERRY WHIGHAM is a doctoral candidate in New York University's department of Performance Studies. His research examines memory practices and activism in postgenocidal societies, with a focus on Argentina, Germany, and the United States. His work has been published in a number of journals, including the *Journal of Latin American Cultural Studies*, *Tourist Studies*, *Memory and Society*, and *Material Culture*. He is also the managing editor of *e-misférica*, a biannual, trilingual journal on performance and politics in the Americas published by the Hemispheric Institute.

ALEX ZUCKER is an editor and a translator of Czech literature. He has received an English PEN Award for Writing in Translation, a National Endowment for the Arts Literature Fellowship, and the ALTA National Translation Award. He currently serves as co-chair of the PEN America Translation Committee.

Introduction

Sheri Rosenberg, Tibi Galis, and Alex Zucker

In February 2013, the Benjamin N. Cardozo School of Law Program in Holocaust, Genocide, and Human Rights Studies and the Auschwitz Institute for Peace and Reconciliation, a New York City–based nongovernmental organization, convened a two-day conference, "Deconstructing Prevention: The Theory, Policy, and Practice of Mass Atrocity Prevention," at Cardozo Law School in Manhattan. The aim of the conference was to reflect on the state of atrocity prevention today and to consider strategies for meeting new challenges and moving forward. Day One brought together twenty-three researchers and policy practitioners in closed session to discuss topics ranging from transitional justice, arms control, data mapping, resource conflicts, and economic sanctions to civilian protection, the use of force, international law, corporate social responsibility, and performance studies – all considered from the perspective of how they contribute to the theory, policy, or practice of atrocity prevention. Day Two, open to the public and attended by more than 250 policymakers, students, scholars, and advocates, began with a keynote address by Roméo Dallaire, leader of the United Nations peacekeeping mission that was forced to watch powerlessly as the 1994 genocide unfolded in Rwanda, followed by four panel discussions. The first featured the three former UN special advisers on prevention of genocide sharing insights into the institution's evolution, while the remaining three featured prominent government officials and scholars, from the United States and abroad, discussing transitional justice, crisis mapping, and how to organize national governments to deal with mass atrocities.[1]

The most important outcome of the conference is the volume you are reading now, intended as an authoritative, enduring work on atrocity prevention. To date, there has been no attempt made to address this topic from the theoretical, policy, and practicing standpoints simultaneously. The existing literature has not caught up either with the realities of

---

[1] A report on the conference, including the text of Dallaire's keynote address, is available at www.auschwitzinstitute.org/_content/Deconstructing-Prevention-Conference-Report.pdf. Videos of Dallaire's address and all four panel discussions are available at www.youtube.com/playlist?list=PLuzaPqT98VixVzDPhbwyuXyTG7JrBpH6F.

contemporary atrocities or practical prevention work as it has developed over the past decade and a half. This volume therefore has three main goals: to solidify the current understanding of mass atrocity prevention, to define its parameters, and to help clarify its relationship to related disciplines and agendas. In addition, from an academic standpoint, one of its aims is to reorient the emerging field of atrocity prevention from its current multidisciplinary approach to an interdisciplinary one. At the same time, however, we are acutely aware that, at bottom, this issue is not a theoretical or conceptual one, but a real, immediate, and practical one for the hundreds of thousands of human beings whose very existence is threatened by mass atrocities.

Since the conference in 2013, international events have rocked the world. Already when we began work on this volume, the Arab Spring that blossomed in December 2010 was looking more like the reign of Robespierre in some countries, with the Responsibility to Protect (R2P) appearing to have morphed into the Responsibility to Talk About Protecting. Now, as of this writing, in April 2015, the group known as the Islamic State of Iraq and the Levant (ISIL), or simply the Islamic State, is responsible for the atrocities that dominate the headlines. Meanwhile, appalling crimes have not ceased in Syria, Sudan, South Sudan, Burma, and Nigeria, just to name a few. As countless atrocities unfold around the globe, it often feels as if there is nothing the rest of the world can do but sit and watch in horror. As we write this introduction, we are struck by the overwhelming sense of fragility and vulnerability populations are experiencing across the globe. We are also struck by the dissonance between communities that have traditionally resonated with one another. Human rights organizations interpret events through a relatively absolutist lens, calling out abuses and violations regardless of the scale of violence; the conflict prevention community is focused on bringing parties to the table to end conflict, as opposed to assigning blame or identifying potential perpetrators of international criminal law to stop atrocities; and, meanwhile, amid the horror, humanitarian agencies carry on, despite their fatigue, to ameliorate suffering. This moment, right now, vividly illustrates the challenges facing the anti-atrocity community. Yet there will always be moments like these. Whenever there seems to be progress, the machinations of *Realpolitik* remind us of the limitations that still exist when it comes to preventing mass atrocities.

I.1.   A Brief History of Atrocity Prevention

"Never again." According to Holocaust historian Raul Hilberg, the phrase first appeared on signs put up by prisoners in the Buchenwald concentration camp

[Handwritten margin notes: "conflicts perspective"; "- human rts expose (abuses)"; "- conflict prevention (bring parties to the table)"; "- humanitarian (ameliorate suffering)"]

after it was liberated at the end of World War II.[2] In the decades since, the phrase has come to serve as a slogan and a rallying cry not only for those combating anti-Semitism, but for all who seek to prevent human beings from being singled out for persecution, violence, or killing on the basis of their identity. In 1948, owing largely to the tireless efforts of Raphael Lemkin, the UN adopted the Convention on the Prevention and Punishment of Genocide. Yet, while the 1960s saw the birth of Holocaust studies as an academic field, soon giving rise to Holocaust and genocide studies (as well as genocide studies tout court), with academic departments housing scholars who teach and conduct research and journals dedicated to scholarship on the topic, actual policy to prevent genocide seemed nowhere to be found.

In policy circles, following the end of the Cold War, discussion of the broader topic of conflict prevention got a shot in the arm in 1994, when the Carnegie Corporation of New York established the Carnegie Commission on Preventing Deadly Conflict "to address the looming threats to world peace of intergroup violence and to advance new ideas for the prevention and resolution of deadly conflict." Meanwhile, the more specific goal of genocide prevention also took on a new life, primarily in reaction to the occurrence of two highly visible genocides – in Rwanda (1994) and the former Yugoslavia (1995) – in rapid succession, with around-the-clock television coverage providing updates on the horrors to viewers worldwide. In 2001, the International Commission on Intervention and State Sovereignty (ICISS) issued its report *The Responsibility to Protect*. The ICISS had been established in response to then Secretary-General Kofi Annan's plea to the UN General Assembly in 1999, and again in 2000, to find a way to stop mass atrocities. In particular he asked: "If humanitarian intervention is, indeed, an unacceptable assault on sovereignty, how should we respond to a Rwanda, to a Srebrenica, to gross and systematic violations of human rights that affect every precept our common humanity?"[3] The report was intended as a direct response to not only the genocides of Rwanda and Yugoslavia, where there had been no "external military intervention for human protection purposes,"[4] as the authors put it, but also to events in Somalia (1993) and Kosovo (1999), where there was military intervention but questions abounded regarding both its effectiveness and legality, as well as the process by which the

---

[2] "Is There a New Anti-Semitism? A Conversation with Raul Hilberg," *Logos: A Journal of Modern Society and Culture*, 6.1–2 (Winter–Spring 2007), www.logosjournal.com/issue_6.1–2 /hilberg.htm.

[3] United Nations General Assembly, *We the Peoples: The Role of the United Nations in the Twenty-First Century: Report of the Secretary-General*, A/54/2000 (March 27, 2000), www.un.org/en /ga/search/view_doc.asp?symbol=A/54/2000.

[4] Foreword, *The Responsibility to Protect*, Report of the International Commission on Intervention and State Sovereignty (Ottawa: International Development Research Centre, 2001), vii, http://responsibilitytoprotect.org/ICISS%20Report.pdf.

interventions were conceived. In any case, given the timing of the ICISS report, mere weeks after the world-shaking events of 9/11, the implications of R2P for the prevention of mass atrocities were not fully realized until several years later. 2004 was another landmark year in the history of atrocity prevention, with the Fourth Stockholm International Forum, "Preventing Genocide: Threats and Responsibilities," leading to, among other things, the establishment of a special adviser for genocide prevention at the UN in New York. In 2005, Member States of the UN endorsed a version of R2P as defined in the World Summit Outcome Document.[5] R2P marked the shift away from genocide prevention to the prevention of genocide, crimes against humanity, and war crimes. This evolution was a result of a growing frustration, among policy and advocacy circles alike, at the inability to identify genocide in time to prevent it, as well as, for some, the belief that for the purpose of prevention there is no qualitative difference between the mass loss of innocent lives due to genocidal intent and the mass loss of life due to violence without regard for identity. The focus on prevention, moreover, was key in cementing a consensus in favor of R2P among UN Member States, many of which had serious misgivings about approving any norm, principle, statement, or document that allowed the use of armed force for humanitarian purposes.[6] Since 2005, efforts to solidify R2P conceptually and operationally have focused primarily on prevention. However, the avoidance of meaningful discussion on military intervention to prevent genocide or the other acts covered under R2P meant that when Libyan leader Moammar Gaddafi responded to protests against his regime with violence and inflammatory rhetoric in February 2011 and the UN Security Council in Resolution 1973 authorized "all necessary measures" to protect civilians in Libya – including, in the event, the removal of Gaddafi himself – there was a tidal wave of confusion and pushback, not only from states and civil society organizations that had been opposed to R2P all along, but even from those who had been strong supporters of the concept.

As Louise Arbour of the International Crisis Group stated, at that point in time, R2P advocates had been assiduously touting and working on early to mid-term prevention to solidify support for the norm while pointedly ignoring

---

[5] "Responsibility to protect populations from genocide, war crimes, ethnic cleansing and crimes against humanity," para. 138–140, UN General Assembly, *World Summit Outcome*, A/RES/60/1 (October 24, 2005), 31–32, www.un.org/en/ga/search/view_doc.asp?symbol=A/RES/60/1.

[6] Article 2(7): "Nothing contained in the present Charter shall authorize the United Nations to intervene in matters which are essentially within the domestic jurisdiction of any state or shall require the Members to submit such matters to settlement under the present Charter; but this principle shall not prejudice the application of enforcement measures under Chapter VII." United Nations, *Charter of the United Nations*, 1 UNTS XVI (October 24, 1945), www.un.org/en/documents/charter/index.shtml.

conflict prevention
int'l criminal law
R2P atrocities prevention
prot. of civilians PK
IHR

the question of military intervention.[7] The consequences of this are both clear and predictable.

I.2. Atrocity Prevention Today: Challenging Fundamental Assumptions

Today, the agenda for national and international policy alike has grown beyond conflict prevention, genocide prevention, and R2P to encompass the concepts of transitional justice (born in the early 1990s out of efforts to address the legacies of dictatorships in Latin America and Eastern Europe), protection of civilians (in armed conflict; dating back to 1999), and, with the creation of the International Criminal Court under the Rome Statute in 2002, the concept of "mass atrocities" or "atrocity crimes" and, along with it, atrocity prevention. At the same time, the atrocity prevention agenda has sometimes been conflated or confused with these and other related agendas. Similarly, the strategies and tactics of atrocity prevention both complement and are in tension with related agendas, including conflict prevention, protection of civilians, and the protection of human rights.

In spite of, or perhaps because of, these challenges, the current debate on atrocity prevention – in the public sphere as well as in domestic and international policy circles – is lively and urgent, yet at times seems lacking in coherence and direction. The rapid evolution of policy response and civil society advocacy has left little time for critique and self-reflection. In particular, the underlying assumptions of this still-young field, as well its goals and its ability to achieve its stated objectives, have remained for the most part underexamined and undertheorized. One prominent example of such an assumption is the enduring belief that atrocities – and especially genocide – tend to unfold sequentially, in steps or phases that lead, in logical order, from one to the next. This idea derives from the model put forth by Raul Hilberg in his pioneering study of the Holocaust, *The Destruction of the European Jews*, first published in 1961. Hilberg identified four steps in the process by which the Nazi Germans undertook to destroy European Jews.[8] Decades later, in 1996, Gregory Stanton, who is today recognized as one of the pioneers of genocide studies, drafted a briefing paper for the U.S. State Department while working in the Foreign Service.[9] The paper identifies eight stages common to every

tendency to adopt a sequenced approach

---

[7] Louise Arbour, "Address to the Stanley Foundation Conference on the Responsibility to Protect, New York" (January 18, 2012), www.r2p10.org.

[8] Raul Hilberg, "Definition, Expropriation, Concentration, Annihilation," in *The Destruction of the European Jews*, revised hardcover edition (New Haven, CT: Yale University Press, 2003), 53–54.

[9] Gregory H. Stanton, "The 8 Stages of Genocide" (1996), www.genocidewatch.org/images/8StagesBriefingpaper.pdf. In the paper, Stanton also notes, "A full strategy for preventing genocide should include attack on each of genocide's operational processes," and elsewhere, "The strongest antidote to genocide is justice."

genocide. Although Stanton himself has described the stages as "predictable but not inexorable," being careful to emphasize that "the process is not linear" and that while "logically, later stages must be preceded by earlier stages, ... all stages continue to operate throughout the process,"[10] the clarity of his model – the very quality that makes it so powerful – has, over the years, had the unfortunate effect of policymakers (and anti-genocide advocates) adopting it as a reductive template for understanding and recommending action on a range of potentially genocidal situations, with too little attempt made to understand the specific dynamics. This sequential approach (one might even be tempted to call it teleological) has also carried over into discussions and – again – policy on prevention of the broader category of mass atrocities or atrocity crimes under the aegis of R2P.[11] Although these "stages" are broad enough to encompass most genocides, a single prototypical process of genocide (or other mass atrocity scenarios) does not exist. Rather, genocide and mass atrocities are flexible concepts that do not follow one particular developmental path. There are variable types of genocide that unfold based on their own internal logic. The differences across cases may include bureaucratic efficiencies, stage of economic and political development, technological sophistication, geographic variances, and the threat (or lack thereof) of significant violence by the victim group. Linear models cannot capture these variances. Rather, genocide (and other forms of mass atrocity) must be understood as a complex, systems-based phenomenon that unfolds slowly. In fact, many deaths that occur during genocide are the result of attrition pursued through intentional acts of starvation, enslavement, displacement, and sexual violence and can be captured through the concept of "genocide by attrition." Genocide by attrition refers to the slow and complex process of annihilation that reflects the unfolding phenomenon of mass murder of a targeted group, rather than the immediate unleashing of violence and death.[12] We believe that although, intellectually, dividing a mass atrocity into stages may help after the fact to clarify what happened, from the point of view of understanding how atrocities evolve and, most crucially, how to prevent them from originating or escalating, there are serious limitations to this conceptualization, and those limitations can have devastating consequences for the people who suffer the atrocities.

---

[10] Gregory H. Stanton, "The 8 Stages of Genocide" (1998), Genocide Watch, www.genocide watch.org/genocide/8stagesofgenocide.html.

[11] See, for instance, "Ban Calls for Three-Pronged Strategy to Implement 'Responsibility To Protect,'" UN News Centre (January 30, 2009), www.un.org/apps/news/story.asp? NewsID=29732.

[12] Sheri P. Rosenberg and Everita Silina, "Genocide by Attrition: Silent and Efficient," in *Genocide Matters: Ongoing Issues and Emerging Perspectives*, edited by Joyce Apsel and Ernesto Verdeja (New York: Routledge Press, 2013), 106, 109–110.

6 for friction = attrition slow death

Another assumption common in the field of atrocity prevention is that it can be practiced above or outside of politics, as a technical matter, without regard for relations of power – whether among actors within the country where there is a risk of atrocities, or between actors within that country and other states or outside actors. We believe it is impossible to practice effective atrocity prevention without a keen understanding of the political dynamics of each individual situation – and the same holds for economic relations as well, particularly when it comes to trade. Of course, this complicates rather than simplifies the formulation of policy, but the reality is that policy based on a simplistic understanding of atrocities may satisfy the urge to take a moral stand but rarely succeeds in preventing atrocities and, on top of that, may lead to a formidable variety of unintended and undesirable consequences. Blockage in responding to mass atrocities, especially on the international level, offers a bitterly clear example of why politics must be taken into account when assessing approaches to atrocity prevention and is also the reason why we feel strongly that domestic and regional prevention policies may often be preferable to higher level action.

A third and particularly thorny issue is the question of what we actually mean when we use the term *prevention*. Some definitions are so expansive as to include everything – economic development, institution building, rule of law – whereas others insist on a definition so narrow, it limits prevention strategies and tactics. One way that some have sought to address this problem is to disaggregate the concept into "structural" versus "proximate" or "operational" prevention. Yet theoretical conceptions of structural and proximate prevention no longer accurately describe the circumstances under which preventive actions are taken. Rather, we must develop a deeper concept of mid-term prevention and conceptualize what this means in practical terms. In other words, we need to know what engagement points are available beyond structural assistance, but before the tipping point of direct killings has been reached. It is that sweet spot of engagement that remains undertheorized and underdeveloped.

often comes too late if this is neglected

structural v. operational prevention

A fourth assumption has been that atrocity prevention as a policy area is enacted apart from other matters, as well as that it is *only* a matter of policy, exclusively by governments and other institutions, as opposed to something enacted by society as a whole. Although, because of the scale of mass atrocities, it is essential for governments to have policy on preventing them and to devote time and resources to doing so, there are numerous arenas of social interaction that already prevent mass atrocities and contribute to the well-being and peaceful participation of groups within society: human rights protection systems, anti-discrimination systems, civilian protection institutions, conflict and crisis management systems, and more. The use of an "atrocity prevention lens," as suggested by Alex Bellamy in his chapter for this volume, may be helpful not only in the formulation of policy, but also for individuals and societal institutions as a whole. Mass atrocity prevention, contrary to many of our past assumptions, is a lens facilitating decisions rather than a set of policy options or structural choices that enduringly protect groups from becoming victims of mass atrocities.

On a societal level, atrocity prevention needs to be a continuous effort to integrate concern for the protection of groups, however they define themselves or are defined by others. Integrating an atrocity prevention lens within our interactions means that societal actors conceive of their actions by naturally making sure they will not have negative consequences on groups, along with making sure they do not break other societal rules. In a governmental context, the application of an atrocity prevention lens means that all parts of government integrate within their normal policy development procedures an analysis of the atrocity prevention dimension of those policies. The creation of special bodies tasked with prevention (as is happening now in the Great Lakes Region of Africa, as well as in Latin America, Denmark, and the United States) should be focused on making sure this process of analysis and self-reflection becomes second nature to all governmental bodies, regardless of their immediate foci. In addition, this internal change agent, the national mechanism for mass atrocity and genocide prevention, needs to have its own domestically professionalized bureaucracy that can act as a bureaucratic habit changer within governments.

A final assumption we seek to question in this volume is that atrocity prevention is exclusively or primarily a matter for the "international community" (usually used as a synonym for the UN and its agencies), a set of policies and practices formulated outside the countries or societies where there is a risk of atrocities and implemented or applied inside a country or society from the outside. In fact, there has been an important shift in recent years toward the domestic dimension of prevention. This is reflected by the attention given to the development of national structures and policies for prevention, often in the context of regional organizations such as the International Conference on the Great Lakes Region (ICGLR) or the Latin American Network for Genocide and Mass Atrocity Prevention.[13] This shift of focus, in our opinion, reflects the move from the discursive commitment to prevention to attempts to operationalize prevention in very different societies. It also reflects a reality check on the international community's capacity to engage in prevention beyond crisis management.

The domestication of prevention is not an invitation to international apathy. On the contrary, systematic atrocity prevention in the case of donor countries requires their development agenda to go beyond the requirement of "do no

---

[13] See www.icglr.org/index.php/en/genocide-prevention and www.auschwitzinstitute.org/latin-american-network-for-genocide-and-mass-atrocity-prevention/.

harm" and to integrate atrocity prevention as a priority. Furthermore, the crisis management aspects of prevention unavoidably involve a robust international component. But the newly affirmed domestic focus on prevention opens the door to a genuine localization of the prevention agenda in very diverse societies around the world, and this localization necessarily reflects the diversity of experiences regarding inclusion and exclusion of certain groups in those societies. Consequently, a preventive focus looks one way in Latin America (a focus on rights protection coupled with robust transitional justice, sometimes in a tense human security environment), another in Africa's Great Lakes Region (a focus on diversity management and on resource management, 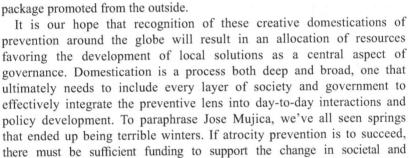 sometimes in a situation of high risk of atrocities), and yet another in the United States or Canada (a focus on incipient transitional justice processes for indigenous populations and on national levers for supporting prevention through foreign policy). This diversity of application of an "atrocity prevention lens" only deepens through practice, creating layers of expertise that respond to local realities in a manner more beneficial than could be achieved by any policy package promoted from the outside.

It is our hope that recognition of these creative domestications of prevention around the globe will result in an allocation of resources favoring the development of local solutions as a central aspect of governance. Domestication is a process both deep and broad, one that ultimately needs to include every layer of society and government to effectively integrate the preventive lens into day-to-day interactions and policy development. To paraphrase Jose Mujica, we've all seen springs that ended up being terrible winters. If atrocity prevention is to succeed, there must be sufficient funding to support the change in societal and governmental behavior. Half- or, more accurately, twentieth-hearted support will result in the concept and practice of prevention being undermined.

I.3.   Reconstructing Atrocity Prevention: Concepts, Policies, Practices

With the ideas just described providing the backdrop for our inquiry, *Reconstructing Atrocity Prevention* is divided into three parts. The first, Fluidities, is the most conceptual, drawing out the diversity of perspectives and disciplines that can be brought to bear on the prevention of mass atrocities. The second, Above Chronology, presents viewpoints that either directly contest or operate outside of the customary practice of conceiving of – and enacting – atrocity prevention as a sequential chronological process. The third, Acting Out Prevention, examines the surprisingly broad range of technologies, tools, and institutions – societal and governmental, many typically overlooked – that may be engaged in the prevention of mass atrocities.

As noted earlier, in our critique, one enduring challenge of atrocity prevention has been reaching a consensus on the scope and definition of the concepts of both "atrocity" and "prevention." Definitional debates can be stymieing. But definitions matter. They matter for research and for attempts to understand the causes, actors, and dynamics of an unfolding series of events. Definitions also matter for policy. The prevention community needs a working definition of the class of events it is trying to prevent. A lack of conceptual clarity results in conceptual confusion and muddled strategies. Scott Straus opens this volume with a useful proposal to group what are currently most often termed "mass atrocities" or "atrocity crimes" under the broader rubric of "large-scale, systematic violence against civilian populations."

This addresses the question of what constitutes an atrocity but still leaves open the question of what is prevention. Following Straus's contribution, Bridget Conley-Zilkic examines how the dominant understanding of "prevention" has become synonymous with "military intervention." This has resulted from a highly selective choice of past cases for "lessons learned," an emphasis on prevention from outside, and a failure to take into account the changed nature of violent conflict in the years since the paradigmatic cases took place. Throughout, moreover, there has been a persistent habit of ignoring the tension between goals that this perspective has so often produced. Next, Alex Bellamy uses the concept of an "atrocity prevention lens" to suggest the many ways in which prevention can be augmented on all levels – international, national, regional, and civil society – without the creation of new institutions, which in times of budgetary constraints can seem an insurmountable obstacle to building effective atrocity prevention policy. Jennifer Welsh, in her important chapter, considers the consequences of situating the R2P doctrine within a criminal framework. In particular, she argues that because conflict resolution operates on a principle of impartiality, it can run counter to tools used for R2P, which aim at deterring or punishing individuals. Furthermore, Welsh draws attention to the uneasy relationship between the collective responsibility of the international community and the collective nature of mass atrocities, given individualistic approaches to atrocity crime prevention and response.

One of the factors most frequently cited as a driver of atrocities, particularly when they involve the targeting of a group of people based on their identity (as in genocide), is hate speech. There is still a disturbing – and mistaken – tendency to attribute such crimes simply to "evil" or "hatred" without any examination of the role political power plays in creating and manipulating human emotion and inciting people to carry out heinous and gruesome acts against their fellow human beings. Social psychology research, however, demonstrated a long time ago that situation and circumstances have as much to do with what drives these acts as individual human psychology. Psychologist Johanna Vollhardt, in her contribution to this volume, explains how the human tendency to categorize other individuals as part of a group and assign particular characteristics to that group that may be negative enough to elicit a violent response exists along a continuum, and she describes how these same categorization processes, once understood, may be used to develop media interventions that reduce the likelihood of intergroup violence in general and mass atrocities in particular. Finally, in reconceptualizing the approach to preventing atrocities, Elisa von Joeden-Forgey, in a particularly original approach, contributes the concept of "life force atrocities," an extreme type of sexualized violence targeting the deep human bonds that hold together not only families but society as a whole, and offers evidence to suggest that where perpetrators are committing such acts, there is almost surely genocidal intent as well, with clear implications for both monitoring and early warning in atrocity prevention efforts, whether in times of war or in peace.

Part II, Above Chronology, offers a closer look at some policy areas and approaches that have, up to now, been overutilized, underutilized, or entirely left out of atrocity prevention and can be fruitfully incorporated far in advance of the outbreak of mass killing (or any violence whatsoever), thus challenging the dominant mindset of prevention as crisis management. Sheri Rosenberg opens this part by urging a critical reflection on the role of international criminal law (ICL) in the atrocity prevention agenda. She argues that "there is an unexplored orthodoxy about the preventive effects of ICL. This orthodoxy has lead to 'box ticking' exercises, in which stakeholders routinely call for Security Council referrals to the ICC as one of several atrocity prevention activities that is routinely checked off a list, without examining the underlying merits or implications of pursuing ICL as an atrocity prevention strategy in a particular situation." Rosenberg's chapter explores deterrence rationales in the ICL context, arguing for a move from deterrence in the national sense to a broader concept of atrocity prevention captured best through an expressive account of ICL atrocity prevention, which will aid the prevention community in determining when and how to pursue ICL as a prevention strategy.

Scholar Elazar Barkan examines the impact of historical narratives on shaping national identity, in particular narratives regarding suffering and the violation of human rights, which, as he notes, lie "at the heart of many contemporary conflicts," including ones with major episodes of mass atrocities. Next, Andrew Feinstein exposes how the global arms trade, with its lack of regulation and rampant corruption, fueled the Rwandan genocide of 1994, and will continue to contribute to mass atrocities in the future unless there is a concerted effort to bring this deadly commerce into check. Edward Luck, former Special Adviser to the UN Secretary-General on the Responsibility to

Protect, and Dana Luck, psychologist, offer a creative angle on R2P, suggesting that individuals may also have a responsibility to prevent mass atrocities and proposing "to identify critical groups of decision makers and to develop more effective means of influencing their decisions."

The role of natural resources in financing rebel groups that commit mass atrocities has often been in the headlines in recent years. Michael Klare, in his chapter, describes the changing face of contemporary conflict, with increased targeting of civilians and the trafficking of commodities to fund armed groups, and he gives an overview of the successes as well as the limitations of sanctions – both by the UN and, as a result of consumer advocacy campaigns, by corporations – to choke funding for atrocity-prone groups in ongoing conflicts. Next, Deborah Mayersen explores the role of factors in a society that inhibit genocide, even in situations when significant risk is present, highlighting the importance of studying cases not only where atrocities have taken place, but also where they have not. The military tends to be viewed almost exclusively in terms of use of force and only after atrocities or other types of violence have already broken out, but, as Dwight Raymond explains, military means (national, regional, or international) can be employed well in advance of atrocities, "to shape a preventive environment and deter would-be perpetrators from committing atrocities," and are in fact most effective when used in conjunction with nonmilitary efforts.

The volume's third part, Acting Out Prevention, digs deeper into the nuts and bolts of atrocity prevention, domestically, regionally, and on the international level. First, Kerry Whigham gives us an inspiring chapter on the ways in which individuals, as members of civil society, can and do help prevent atrocities through public activism, as well as contributing to healing in the aftermath. Next, Jennifer Leaning draws on the extensive work in public health surveillance to suggest that the "Big Data" available thanks to today's rich social networks may be gleaned and combed for patterns of escalation to produce more effective early warning for mass atrocities. George Lopez has been immersed for decades in the study of economic sanctions for human rights protection, as well as having experience in designing sanctions himself. In his chapter, he proposes applying sanctions not only to top leaders but to lower-level supporters of regimes committing or likely to commit atrocities, as well as applying controls to processes (such as trade and financial transactions) that may enable the perpetrators of atrocities. Looking at the role of multinational corporations, Owen Pell and Kelly Bonner suggest that government regulations and industry-imposed transparency initiatives, together with existing compliance regimes, may be effective means to decrease the likelihood of corporate aiding and abetting of atrocity crimes. Ever since the Genocide Convention was adopted in 1948, the UN has been at the center of most debates over atrocity prevention. Ekkehard Strauss examines the historical, political, and legal hurdles the UN has faced in its efforts to prevent mass atrocities over the past six and a half decades, and argues for both a stronger theoretical understanding of atrocities at the UN and a broader strategy for risk mitigation based on a fresh legal interpretation of the Genocide Convention. Turning to the practice of atrocity prevention by policymakers themselves, Ashad Sentongo explains the regional structures created for early warning and response in the Great Lakes Region of Africa and reviews their successes and shortcomings based on their use so far in Kenya, South Sudan, and the Democratic Republic of the Congo. Finally, Ramiro Riera, from the Argentinean Ministry of Defense, describes the genesis of his country's National Mechanism for the Prevention of Genocide, comparing and contrasting it with similar initiatives in other countries and providing a blueprint of its bureaucratic structure and procedures.

I.4.   Atrocity Prevention in the Future: Looking Ahead

The past few decades have offered many lessons about the opportunities and pitfalls of preventing the crimes now known as mass atrocities. Perhaps the most important thing to keep in mind is that although the human emotions that drive these horrors – fear, hatred, insecurity, and, yes, the lust for power – are constant, the way atrocities unfold is never exactly the same from one time to the next. This means that the study of just a few signal cases, however powerful they may be, is not enough. There have been dozens of mass atrocities over the years that do not fit the patterns of the "canon" so often referred to – Armenia, the Holocaust, Rwanda, Bosnia (and, sometimes, Cambodia). These need to be studied no less exhaustively, as do those cases where no atrocities occurred despite all expectations. As our knowledge advances, so must our willingness to question the approaches used so far; to be honest about what is working and what is not and to commit to discarding old thinking when it has proven ineffective or, in fact, even harmful. We have made some progress. There is still a long way to go. Force of habit may be humankind's greatest enemy. In order to move forward, one must avoid the rut of old patterns. Scholars, policymakers, advocates, and individuals must harness the lessons of the past in a systematic way while remaining flexible enough to apprehend the fluid, chaotic, and idiosyncratic reality of the process of mass atrocities and the contexts in which they emerge.

Part I

Fluidities

1 What Is Being Prevented? Genocide, Mass Atrocity, and Conceptual Ambiguity in the Anti-Atrocity Movement

Scott Straus

1.1. Introduction

In recent years, a significant conceptual shift has taken place in the anti-atrocity policy-making, academic, and activist world. Whereas in the 1990s the conceptual focus was almost exclusively on preventing and responding to "genocide," the dominant conceptual framework in the 2000s and beyond has become either "mass atrocities" or "atrocities."[1] The prevention of "mass atrocities" or "atrocity crimes" is now the conceptual rudder within the United Nations system and the broader Responsibility to Protect (R2P) community. Within the U.S. government, with the advent of the Atrocities Prevention Board in the early 2010s, that concept now anchors policy efforts. The nongovernmental world varies, but, increasingly, the bedrock concept is "mass atrocities."

The conceptual shift away from the concept of genocide has merit, as I discuss in this chapter. However, the new standard raises the question of what a "mass atrocity" is and, further, the difference between an "atrocity" and a "mass atrocity." Neither "mass atrocity" nor "atrocity" has definition in international law.

The most common operationalization of "mass atrocities" is reference to the four crimes listed in the 2005 World Summit document that endorsed the R2P doctrine. Those crimes are "genocide," "crimes against humanity (CAH)," "war crimes," and "ethnic cleansing." However, as I discuss in this chapter, although those four crimes have an important degree of overlap, they also cover

---

[1] An early version of this paper was written while the author was a Winnick Fellow at the Center for Genocide Prevention at the U.S. Holocaust Memorial Museum. The author thanks the Museum for support of this project. The paper has benefited from excellent comments by Mike Abramowitz, Bridget Conley-Zilkic, Sheri Rosenberg, Beth Van Schaak, participants at two presentations at the Museum in 2011 and 2012, and an authors' workshop for this volume. A much shortened version of this essay appears in *Fundamentals of Genocide and Atrocity Prevention* (United States Holocaust Memorial Museum, forthcoming 2015).

a large and diverse range of acts. The shift to an expansive, elastic standard may eventually be the purposeful policy choice. But in many anti-atrocity circles, the move to "mass atrocities" and "atrocities" has been driven primarily by a desire to find a powerful substitute for "genocide." Relatively little explicit discussion of the boundaries of "mass atrocity" has taken place. Similarly, relatively little explicit discussion of the merits of a medium-broad versus an expansively broad standard has occurred.

No one likes definitional debates. Disagreement about what constitutes "genocide" has plagued scholarship on genocide (May 2009, Straus 2001). But definitions matter. They matter for research and in trying to understand causes and dynamics. Scholars often have different definitions of what they are explaining, ranging from genocide (Midlarsky 2005) to mass killing – defined variously as 1,000 civilian deaths per year (Ulfelder and Valentino 2008) to 5,000 total civilian deaths (Bellamy 2011) – to one-sided killing (Eck and Hultman 2008). Those differences in conceptualization of the dependent variable of interest has limited the field's ability to generate cumulative findings (Finkel and Straus 2012).

Definitional debates also matter for policy. The atrocity prevention community should have a working definition of the class of events it is trying to prevent. A strict framework of any atrocity defined as a crime against humanity or war crime would include dozens of situations in a given year. In the early 2010s, those cases would include Afghanistan, Bahrain, the Central African Republic, China, Côte d'Ivoire, the Democratic Republic of Congo, Egypt, Iraq, Kenya, Kyrgyzstan, Libya, Mali, Myanmar, Nigeria, Somalia, South Sudan, Sudan, Syria, and Yemen. The policy objective may be to prevent and respond to such a wide range of violence against civilians, but, if so, that standard should be clarified.

This chapter has three objectives. First, the chapter puts the conceptual question into focus. Practitioners and scholars will disagree among and between themselves about the what the class of events to study and prevent should be. There are good arguments in favor of narrow, medium-broad, and expansively broad definitions. But scholars and practitioners should not sidestep the conceptual confusion that often exists.

Second, the chapter analyzes the four main constituent crimes – genocide, CAH, ethnic cleansing, and war crimes – with an eye toward seeing whether they have a core zone of overlap.

Third, based on that analysis, the chapter proposes a rubric – large-scale, systematic violence against civilian populations – as that which defines the scholarly and policy field of "mass atrocities." That proposition is not likely to end debate. But, hopefully, the claims in the chapter will contribute to a more self-conscious discussion of the conceptual framework that unifies the field of atrocity prevention.

1.2. The Concept of "Genocide"

Within the academic literature, the definition of genocide has been the subject of great debate. Nonetheless, I would argue that the core meaning of "genocide" is "intentional group destruction." As such, genocide has three component parts: extensive violence (large-scale, sustained, widespread, systematic violence), group-selective (targeted at groups), and group-destructive (designed to destroy groups in particular territories under perpetrators' control).

To make that claim, I start with two of the most important and lasting conceptualizations, those by Raphael Lemkin and the UN Convention on the Prevention and Punishment of Genocide, known as the Genocide Convention (UNGC). In 1944, Lemkin coined the term "genocide" by combining the Greek word for race, nation, or tribe (*genos*) with the Latin word for killing (*cide*). In an efficient conceptualization of the term, Lemkin wrote that genocide is the "destruction of a nation or of an ethnic group" (Lemkin 1944: 79). He also referred to genocide as the "destruction of human groups" (Lemkin 1947: 147). Elaborating, he claimed:

> Generally speaking, genocide does not necessarily mean the immediate destruction of a nation, except when accomplished by mass killings of all members of a nation. It is intended rather to signify a coordinated plan of different actions aiming at the destruction of essential foundations of the life of national groups, with the aim of annihilating the groups themselves. The objectives of such a plan would be the disintegration of the political and social institutions, of culture, language, national feelings, religion, and the economic existence of national groups, and the destruction of the personal security, liberty, health, dignity, and even the lives of the individuals belonging to such groups. Genocide is directed against the national group as an entity, and the actions involved are directed against individuals, not in their individual capacity, but as members of the national group. (Lemkin 1944: 79)

Similarly, Lemkin wrote:

> The crime of genocide involves a wide range of actions, including not only the deprivation of life but the prevention of life (abortions, sterilizations) and also devices considerably endangering life and health (artificial infections, working to death in special camps, deliberate separation of families for depopulation purposes and so forth). All these actions are subordinated to the criminal intent to destroy or to cripple permanently a human group. The acts are directed against groups, as such, and individuals are selected for destruction only because they belong to these groups. In view of such a phenomenon the terms previously used to describe an attack upon nationhood are not adequate. Mass murder or extermination wouldn't apply in the case of sterilization because the victims of sterilizations were not murdered, rather a people was killed through delayed action by stopping propagation. Moreover, mass murder does not convey the specific losses to civilization in the form of the cultural contributions which can be made only by groups united through national, racial, or cultural characteristics. (Lemkin 1947: 147)

There is a great deal of insight in these passages. They are quoted at length to emphasize the ways in which groups are essential to Lemkin's original conceptualization. Lemkin's core vision of genocide is *group-destructive* violence. Violence is "directed against groups," and individuals are targeted because of the groups to which they ostensibly belong, Lemkin argues. Genocide is a "coordinated plan … aiming at … the destruction … of national groups."

If one takes Lemkin's original definition seriously – and most who work in genocide studies do – then one has to recognize that genocide is distinguished by group-oriented and, more specifically, group-destructive violence. Indeed, etymologically, the term "genocide" almost requires a focus on groups: *geno*-cide is the killing (destruction) of groups.

A number of ambiguities remain in Lemkin's formulation, and, in his writing, he tends to reify human social groups (which are in reality more constructed and fluid than Lemkin tends to acknowledge). Lemkin also refers to a range of forms of destruction, ones that are beyond simply killing. Nonetheless, his central idea is to define genocide as a form of violence that leads to the destruction of groups.

Although the definition changed in the 1948 UNGC, the core meaning remains group destruction. After rounds of negotiations, in which a number of political forces came to bear on the exact wording (Schabas 2000), the final language of the Convention defines genocide as the "intent to destroy, in whole or in part, a national, ethnical, racial, or religious group, as such." The Convention in turn specifies five acts of genocide: (1) killing members of the group, (2) causing serious bodily or mental harm to members of the group, (3) deliberately inflicting on the group conditions of life calculated to bring about its physical destruction in whole or in part, (4) imposing measures intended to prevent births within the group, and (5) forcibly transferring children of the group to another group.

A number of scholars remain unsatisfied with the Convention definition: on the one hand, it is arguably too restrictive in limiting genocide to four specific groups; on the other, it is arguably too open-ended in referring to group destruction "in part." I discuss these and other concerns in the next section. Nonetheless, the core meaning in the Convention resonates with Lemkin's original formulation, and, indeed, Lemkin was central to the passage of the Convention (Power 2000).

A fair bit of ink has been spilled about how to conceptualize and define genocide since the UNGC was passed. Nonetheless, intentional group destruction remains central to how most courts and scholars understand genocide's core. For example, in a number of landmark and complex decisions handed down by the International Criminal Tribunals for Rwanda and the former Yugoslavia, the focus on group destruction is central (Schabas 2006: 99). Although both tribunals affirmed the Convention's restriction to ethnic, racial, religious, and national groups (i.e., groups to which ascription is presumed to be stickier and less mobile than political or economic groups), the tribunals strongly affirmed group destruction or substantial group destruction as the benchmark for adjudicating genocide. Similarly, if one considers other prominent reworkings of the definition – for example, those by Frank Chalk and Kurt Jonassohn (1990), on the one hand, and Helen Fein (1990), on the other – one sees a similar focus on genocide as the destruction of groups (or collectivities).

Working from this core meaning, I disaggregate the concept into three constitutive parts. First is group-selective violence. That is, genocide is not indiscriminate violence but rather violence in which those from particular social groups are selected for violence. Group-selective violence necessarily implies that civilians are targeted. If social groups are the object of violence, then such violence will entail violence against individuals not involved in combat.

Second is extensive violence. The concept of group destruction implies large-scale violence. No specific numerical threshold exists for genocide. But as group-destructive violence, the term implies a scale that threatens the survival of the target group. A helpful guiding logic for conceptualizing scale is spelled out in the appeals court decision from the International Criminal Tribunal for the former Yugoslavia (ICTY) in the *Krstić* case. In that decision, the court delineated a standard of "substantiality" to determine how much of a part of a group needed to be destroyed to qualify as genocide (Schabas 2006). The large scale in group destruction also implies that the violence is sustained and widespread. Violence in genocide is repeated not only over time but also over space; it is systematic – repeated, regular, organized, and coordinated.

Third is group-destructive violence. Much political violence conforms to a coercive logic: it is designed to change the behavior of specific audiences (Kalyvas 2006). But the hallmark of genocide is that it exceeds a strictly coercive logic; it is designed to destroy groups (Straus 2015).

1.3.   The Limits of Genocide

Since the early 2000s, scholars and practitioners have expressed increased concern with genocide as the main concept around which to build a preventative policy. Why? One reason is that genocide is a specific, somewhat rare, form of violence. Building a policy around such a specific form of violence is overly limiting to some.

A second reason is that the legal definition of genocide emphasizes the importance of ascertaining intent. In international law, the perpetration of genocide is distinguished by demonstrating that a "special intent" to destroy groups in whole or in part exists. However, special intent is difficult to show clearly while a process of violence is ongoing. More importantly, by the time a special intent to destroy groups in whole or in part may be visible, the process of violence is likely to be quite advanced. That renders the idea of prevention moot and can render response quite difficult. In short, waiting until the special intent to destroy groups in whole or in part is evident may be too long to wait to contain the violence (Scheffer 2006).

A third reason is that the concept of genocide is inherently contested or ambiguous. Consider the question of protected groups. Earlier, I offered a capacious interpretation, arguing simply that genocide is about intentional group destruction. However, the UNGC specifies that the protected groups are only national, ethnic, religious, and racial in nature. That formulation is partly a product of political negotiations when the UNGC was being drafted, notably objections from the Soviet Union, which did not wish to have "political" or "economic" groups included, given that country's political history (Kuper 1981, Schabas 2000). But, in reviewing the preparatory materials for the Convention, the recent international tribunals found a substantive justification for the Convention's focus on "permanent" groups; such groups are bound by relatively inflexible, ascriptive identifies rather than by elective, more mobile identities (Schabas 2006). Indeed, the concept of more permanent identities structured by lineage and descent is implied etymologically in the concept of "genocide." *Genos* is about precisely that.

However, a focus on the four listed groups is quite objectionable to many. Such a focus excludes some major cases: Indonesia in 1965 where the focus was on killing communists; a good portion of the violence under the Khmer Rouge, which was focused on killing "new" people and those associated with the former regime; and the anti-Kulak violence under Stalin in the former Soviet Union. If the ultimate goal is protection of groups, there is no compelling reason to exclude protection of other types of groups, such as political, gender, regional, and sexuality-based groups.

By the same token, it is not clear why *groups* as such should be the object of special international protection. Ethnic, national, religious, and other kinds of groups are socially and historically constructed. They are not inherent groups, and, even if they were, it is not clear why, from a policy perspective, group-ness should enjoy a special dispensation.

The threshold for group "destruction" is also ambiguous in genocide. Perpetrators never achieve total group destruction. Even the Nazis did not. The Convention implicitly acknowledges this point by referring to group destruction "in part." However, that standard creates ambiguity about how much partial group destruction is needed to qualify as group destruction. A "part" could be construed as dozens of civilians, even if dozens is not the standard most observers have for genocide.

As argued earlier, when examining this issue, the ad hoc tribunals have concluded that a "substantial" portion of a group must be killed for "genocide" to occur. The most extensive discussion occurs in an appellate decision from the ICTY when ruling in the *Krstić* case. There, the tribunal was faced with a decision as to whether the murder of about 8,000 men in Srebrenica constituted genocide. The trial chamber concluded that genocide did occur, and, on appeal, that decision was confirmed. The appeals chamber argued, after reviewing the Convention in detail, that the standard was whether or not a "substantial" portion of the group was destroyed. That decision has been affirmed in the International Court of Justice ruling on *Bosnia v. Serbia* as well. Even so, "substantiality" remains a relative term, one without a clear threshold.

Other, though less common, disagreements exist. One is whether the state is a necessary perpetrator of genocide. Some scholars argue it is (Harff and Gurr 1998), but, in practice, nothing in the original or legal conceptualization of genocide requires state involvement. Tribunals appear to have upheld that interpretation (Schabas 2006). In practice, however, and as argued earlier, genocide implies substantial group destruction. But nothing conceptually limits genocide to states.

In sum, genocide is a powerful word. It grabs attention. It has a widely ratified international convention behind it. However, for building a prevention policy, the term has significant limits. The concept is narrow: it is group-selective violence, it requires evidence of a special intent to destroy groups in whole or in part, it is legally focused on four groups, and it focuses on group destruction. But the concept is also contested and ambiguous: what is a group, why limit prevention to groups and to only four groups, what counts as "partial" group destruction?

1.4.   Atrocities and Mass Atrocities

These various problems with genocide have led scholars, advocates, and policymakers to search for an alternative framework. In 2006, David Scheffer, a former U.S. official in charge of war crimes, proposed the idea of "atrocity crimes." Over time, the concept has morphed into a focus on "mass atrocities" or simply "atrocities," as in the Atrocities Prevention Board. Others retain the concept of "atrocity crimes."

Although mass atrocities and atrocities have no formal, legal definition, they usually refer to genocide, CAH, war crimes, and ethnic cleansing. Those four crimes define mass atrocities in some leading works on atrocity prevention, notably Gareth Evans's (2008: 11) book on R2P and the Mass Atrocities Response Operations handbook (Sewell et al. 2010: annex A). Most importantly, these four crimes are listed in the World Summit's 2005 statement on R2P (as discussed later). All but ethnic cleansing are listed in the International Criminal Court's Rome Statute. The question remains how to operationalize the commonality among these four concepts.

1.4.1. Crimes against Humanity

Although there is not an international treaty defining and prohibiting CAH, the standard contemporary definition comes from the Rome Statute. Article 7 defines CAH as a set of acts "committed as part of a widespread or systematic attack directed against any civilian population." The specific acts listed in the Statute include murder, extermination, enslavement, deportation, imprisonment, torture, rape (and other gender or sex crimes), group-based persecution, enforced disappearance, apartheid, and "other inhumane acts of a similar character intentionally causing great suffering, or serious injury to body or to mental or physical health."

Like genocide, CAH concern large-scale or organized violence directed against civilian populations. Acts of violence will rise to the level of CAH when they are committed either on a "widespread" or a "systematic" basis. CAH also concern sustained violence. The Rome Statute refers to CAH as "the *multiple* commission of acts ... against any civilian population" (emphasis added). CAH are also organized. They are "systematic" and the product of "State or organizational policy," according to the Rome Statute. And like genocide, with its focus on group destruction, CAH are defined by whom the violence targets, in this case civilians.

At the same time, CAH is much broader than genocide. Unlike genocide, CAH are not limited to group-oriented violence. Although some specific types of CAH are group-based (e.g., "extermination" and "apartheid"), CAH do not require that groups be the targets. Torture, slavery, sexual violence, forced disappearance, and other acts listed as CAH are not necessarily group-selective violence. In sum, the central idea of CAH is the idea of widespread or systematic attacks against civilians, and groups are not fundamental to that conceptualization.

1.4.2. Ethnic Cleansing

Ethnic cleansing has no formal definition in international law and is not defined as an international crime per se. In general, however, ethnic cleansing refers to the forced removal of an ethnic group from a territory. It is thus a form of forced migration and mass population displacement; in this case, it is forced migration on a large scale targeted against ethnic groups.[2]

Ethnic cleansing and genocide are thus similar. Both are forms of group-selective violence; as group-selective violence against populations defined by ethnicity, ethnic cleansing targets civilians, as does forced migration (Leaning 2011).

Like genocide, ethnic cleansing implies significant scale. To change the ethnic composition of territory, the violence is likely to be extensive (organized, widespread, sustained, and systematic). The central difference between the two terms concerns the purpose of the violence. In genocide, the purpose is group destruction; in ethnic cleansing, the purpose is group removal. Cleansing may be a part of genocide – that is, terrorizing and removing a group may be a part of a process of group destruction – but the two concepts are not synonymous.

Ethnic cleansing and CAH overlap. Both concern large-scale, organized violence against civilians. But ethnic cleansing is necessarily group-selective violence, whereas CAH are not. The idea of ethnic cleansing also implies a specific purpose – changing ethnic demography – whereas CAH have no such requirement of intent.

In sum, the commonality among all three terms concerns extensive (large-scale, systematic, organized, widespread, sustained) violence against civilians. The central ways in which they differ are (1) the role of groups and (2) the purpose of the violence.

1.4.3. War Crimes

War crimes are arguably the broadest of the four crimes. As outlined in Article 8 of the Rome Statute, war crimes refer to a large number of different types of acts. The Rome Statute lists some fifty separate instances of war crimes. Some are explicitly violations of the Geneva Conventions, such as the improper treatment of prisoners of war and hostage-taking. Others are violations of general customs and laws associated with conflict, such as attacks on civilian towns, on objects used for humanitarian assistance, or on any buildings that do not have a military purpose.

Taken together, the long list of types of war crimes includes categories of violence of a quite different character from the other three atrocity crimes. War crimes do not imply a large or extensive scale. Moreover, war crimes are uniquely committed during war, whereas the other three categories of atrocity may occur in either wartime or peacetime. And, unlike genocide and

---

[2] For an excellent analysis of forced migration as a potential element in crimes against humanity, see Leaning 2011.

ethnic cleansing, war crimes are not group-selective. In short, war crimes stand somewhat apart in terms of scale and character from the other three types of atrocity typically listed as component parts of "mass atrocity."

What, then, do war crimes have in common with the other forms of mass atrocity? Underlying the premise of most war crimes is the idea of protecting civilians or soldiers removed from combat. War crimes are about shielding noncombatants from the violence of war. In that focus on the protection of civilians or noncombatants, war crimes share an important commonality with the other three types of atrocity – and that should be a basis for seeking a common standard.

Defined by the four constituent crimes, the core of "atrocities" is the deliberate infliction of violence and harm against civilians and other noncombatants. Explicit in genocide and ethnic cleansing, and implicit to the conceptualization of CAH, is the idea of scale and systematicity. The concept of "*mass* atrocities" also implies violence against civilians on a large scale; the policy is driven by a desire to prevent and respond to a distinctive and odious class of events.

Putting these elements together, I propose that the core conceptualization of mass atrocities be large-scale, systematic (extensive, organized, widespread, sustained) violence against civilians and other noncombatants. The notion of scale reflects a preference for a medium-broad standard that underlies the policy field. Too broad a standard – too low a threshold – will make it difficult to generate the collective will and mobilization necessary to make atrocity prevention a priority. At the same time, the standard here is flexible enough to cover a lot of different types of large-scale violence against civilians. The standard may not make sense from a research standpoint where a more disaggregated categorization is valuable. The proposed standard also does not imply either group-selective or group-destructive violence.

1.4.4.   R2P and the 2005 World Summit

The idea that atrocities are committed against civilians and noncombatants is central to the four crimes typically covered under mass atrocities. However, when the UN General Assembly gathered for the 2005 World Summit and agreed to endorse the principle of R2P, the language did not focus on civilians or noncombatants per se. The two key paragraphs of the summit's Outcome Document frame the discussion in this way:

138. Each individual State has the responsibility to protect its populations from genocide, war crimes, ethnic cleansing and crimes against humanity . . . .

139. The international community, through the United Nations, also has the responsibility to use appropriate diplomatic, humanitarian and other peaceful means, in

accordance with Chapters VI and VIII of the Charter, to help protect populations from genocide, war crimes, ethnic cleansing and crimes against humanity.

The focus in these paragraphs is on *populations*, not civilians. Since 2005, within the UN system and within the nongovernmental community focused on the UN, the concept of protecting "populations" has been central.[3]

"Populations" is a broader and vaguer concept than "civilians." "Populations" could conceivably include combatants, as in the idea of military populations. Furthermore, the concept of "populations" is not central in the legal language that defines genocide, CAH, and war crimes, at least as defined in the Genocide Convention and the Rome Statute.

The question then becomes how to reconcile the focus on populations within the UN and the R2P community with the argument I have made about the prominence of civilians and noncombatants in the legal statutes of the component parts of atrocity crimes. The synthesis that I propose is that of "large-scale, systematic violence against civilian populations," with the understanding that "civilians" here could include combatants removed from fighting, such as the wounded and prisoners war.

1.5.   Other Umbrella Concepts

Before moving to a conclusion, it is important to consider other alternative concepts. "Mass atrocities" is not the only proposed substitute to "genocide." One prominent alternative is the concept of "mass killing." In his academic work, Benjamin Valentino (2004) argues that mass killing is organized violence that claims at least 50,000 civilian deaths in a five-year period. In later work, Jay Ulfelder and Valentino (2008) relax the numerical threshold to 1,000 civilian deaths in a single-year interval.

Mass killing and the synthetic notion of mass atrocities just proposed overlap. Both concern large-scale, systematic violence against civilians. Mass killing is precise about how much violence; as operationalized, the concept typically has a numeric threshold attached to it. However, in contrast to mass atrocity, mass killing is exclusively about killing rather than a range of violence including starvation, attacks on shelter or water supplies, sexual violence, and other forms of violence. Both the four constituent crimes in R2P and the general gist of the policy community has been to include a range of violence beyond simply killing. In sum, mass killing makes very good sense in an explicitly research-oriented context. Such a concept allows for clearer measurement and comparison. However, the focus on killing is unlikely to make it a consensus concept to replace "genocide" in the practitioner world.

---

[3] I thank Ed Luck and Jennifer Welsh, contributors to this volume, for emphasizing this point.

A second term is "mass violence." Christian Gerlach (2010: 1) defines mass violence as "widespread physical violence against non-combatants, that is, outside of immediate fighting between military or paramilitary personnel. Mass violence includes killings, but also forced removal or expulsion, enforced hunger or undersupply, forced labor, collective rape, strategic bombing, and excessive imprisonment." In this definition, mass violence is very similar to the synthetic conception of mass atrocity proposed earlier. The terms may be considered synonymous, and they reinforce the idea that there is a conceptual zone of consensus around the idea of large-scale, systematic violence against civilians.

A final umbrella concept is "democide," a term coined by the scholar R. J. Rummel (1994). The term means "the murder of any person or people by a government," and the term includes genocide, "politicide" (discussed later), and mass killings. Democide is perhaps the broadest possible category of violence around which those in the atrocity prevention community would wish to mobilize. At the same time, the term is limited to violence by governments and to murder (rather than other forms of nonlethal violence). Thus, although the term has appeal in a research context for considering a wide range of state violence, the term is likely too narrow as a reference category for those in the atrocity prevention policy community.

In addition to these concepts, some others are in use, such as "politicide," "classicide," and "gendercide." In the main, "politicide" refers to the destruction of political groups in the way that genocide in the Convention refers to the destruction of ethnic, racial, national, and religious groups (Harff and Gurr 1988). Coined by Michael Mann (2005: 17), "classicide" refers to the "intended mass killing of social classes." Invented by Adam Jones (2004), "gendercide" refers to systematic destruction of one gender.

These latter three concepts are parallel concepts to genocide. They essentially seek to include groups that the UNGC did not. However, if the prevention community looks for a broader, not-group-selective framework, none of these concepts accomplishes that objective. At the same time, each of these concerns large-scale, systematic violence against civilian populations. In that sense, the synthetic conception of mass atrocities proposed earlier has significant overlap with these terms.

1.6.   Conclusion

Conceptual analysis remains vitally important for identifying the class of events that the atrocity prevention community seeks to prevent. The move away from genocide as the exclusive basis for preventative and responsive action is likely to persist. The concept of "mass atrocities" is potent enough, and it sets a potentially high enough threshold to serve as an alternative and more flexible alternative standard. The key then is to be transparent about what "mass atrocities" is.

Based on a conceptual analysis of mass atrocities, I have proposed a standard of large-scale, systematic violence against civilian populations. The idea of large-scale, systematic implies that the violence is organized, repeated over time and space in a regular fashion, coordinated, widespread, and sustained. Violence includes killing but also includes other forms of deliberate harm being inflicted, such as rape, starvation, and population removal. As conceptualized here, *civilians* means noncombatants and combatants removed from conflict (e.g., prisoners of war).

Furthermore, I have argued that this conception of mass atrocities shares a conceptual zone of overlap with other concepts in use, such as mass killing, mass violence, democide, politicide, classicide, and gendercide, among others.

Some readers may dislike the proposed standard. They may wish for a broader or narrower standard. They may wish for a standard that focuses on group-selective violence. Whatever the case may be, the ultimate purpose of the chapter is to stimulate a debate about core conceptualization in the field of atrocity prevention. Debating definitions may strike some as not focused enough on "action," but being clear about the class of events being prevented will, in the long run, help to build a stronger anti-atrocity policy.

Bibliography

Bellamy, Alex. 2011. "Mass Atrocities and Armed Conflict: Links, Distinctions, and Implications for the Responsibility to Protect." Stanley Foundation. Available at www.stanleyfoundation.org/resources.cfm?ID=445.

Chalk, Frank, and Kurt Jonassohn. 1990. *The History and Sociology of Genocide: Analyses and Case Studies*. New Haven, CT: Yale University Press.

Evans, Gareth. 2008. *The Responsibility to Protect: Ending Mass Atrocity Crimes Once and for All*. Washington, DC: Brookings Institution.

Fein, Helen. 1990. "Genocide: A Sociological Perspective." *Current Sociology* 38: 1–126.

Finkel, Evgeny, and Scott Straus. 2012. "Macro, Meso, and Micro Research on Genocide: Gains, Shortcomings, and Future Areas of Inquiry." *Genocide Studies and Prevention* 7(1): 56–67.

Gerlach, Christian. 2010. *Extremely Violence Societies: Mass Violence in the Twentieth-Century World*. Cambridge: Cambridge University Press.

Harff, Barbara, and Ted Robert Gurr. 1988. "Toward Empirical Theory of Genocides and Politicides: Identification and Measurement of Cases since 1945." *International Studies Quarterly* 32: 359–71.

International Criminal Tribunal for the former Yugoslavia (ICTY). 2004. *Prosecutor vs. Radislav Krstic*, Appeals Chamber Judgment, Case Number IT-98-33-A, April 19.

Jones, Adam, ed. 2004. *Gendercide and Genocide*. Nashville: Vanderbilt University Press.

Kalyvas, Stathis. 2006. *The Logic of Violence in Civil War*. New York: Cambridge University Press.

Kuper, Leo. 1981. *Genocide: Its Political Use in the Twentieth Century*. New Haven, CT: Yale University Press.

Leaning, Jennifer. 2011. "Enforced Displacement of Civilian Populations in War: A Potential New Element in Crimes against Humanity." *International Criminal Law Review* 11: 445–62.

Lemkin, Raphael. 1944. *Axis Rule in Occupied Europe*. Washington, DC: Carnegie Endowment for International Peace.

Lemkin, Raphael. 1947. "Genocide as a Crime under International Law." *The American Journal of International Law* 41: 145–51.

Mann, Michael. 2005. *The Dark Side of Democracy: Explaining Ethnic Cleansing*. New York: Cambridge University Press.

May, Larry. 2009. *Genocide: A Normative Account*. New York: Cambridge University Press.

Richardson, Louis. 2006. *What Terrorists Want: Understanding the Enemy, Containing the Threat*. New York: Random House.

Rummel, R. J. 1994. *Death by Government*. New Brunswick, NJ: Transaction.

Schabas, William. 2000. *Genocide in International Law: The Crime of Crime*. Cambridge: Cambridge University Press.

Schabas, William. 2006. "'The Odious Scourge': Evolving Interpretations of the Crime of Genocide." *Genocide Studies and Prevention* 1(2): 93–106.

Scheffer, David. 2006. "Genocide and Atrocity Crimes." *Genocide Studies and Prevention* 1(1): 229–50.

Sewell, Sarah, Dwight Raymond, and Sally Chin. 2010. *Mass Atrocity Response Operations: A Military Planning Handbook*. Cambridge, MA: Carr Center for Human Rights Policy/US Army Peacekeeping and Stability Operations Institute.

Straus, Scott. 2001. "Contested Meanings and Conflicting Imperatives: A Conceptual Analysis of Genocide." *Journal of Genocide Research* 3(3): 349–75.

Straus, Scott. 2015. *Making and Unmaking Nations: The Dynamics of Genocide in Contemporary Africa*. Ithaca, NY: Cornell University Press.

Ulfelder, Jay, and Benjamin Valentino. 2008. "Assessing the Risks of State-Sponsored Mass Killing." Washington, DC: Political Instability Task Force.

Valentino, Benjamin. 2004. *Final Solutions: Mass Killing and Genocide in the Twentieth Century*. Ithaca and London: Cornell University Press.

2 The Pistol on the Wall: How Coercive Military Intervention Limits Atrocity Prevention Policies

Bridget Conley-Zilkic

2.1. Introduction

In the late 1800s, Russian playwright Anton Chekhov famously introduced a principle that would later come to be known as "Chekhov's gun": "if in the first act you have hung a pistol on the wall, then in the following one it should be fired. Otherwise don't put it there."[1] Chekhov thereby succinctly illustrated the principle of "foreshadowing": inclusion of a pistol on stage orients the audience's expectations throughout the performance. It is not a matter of firing or not firing the weapon; its very presence organizes a framework for understanding how events are perceived and what actions might therefore follow. His principle goes further, instructing his fellow playwrights on the art of focusing only on what is necessary and irreplaceable. Although the artistry of rhetoric is undeniably reduced in the texts of international institutional discourse, in the realm of policy on atrocity prevention and response, "Chekhov's gun" applies.

There has been significant discussion about the inclusion of coercive military intervention into the so-called toolbox for responding to atrocities. Advocates argue that even noncoercive response or prevention measures require a threat of military action in order to succeed. Critics have countered that coercive military action in the name of halting atrocities suffers from fatal flaws: it is of limited practical effect because it is too reliant on consensus to be a realistic deterrent. represents a neo-imperial invitation to intervene wherever great powers select to do so, it underestimates the problem of distinguishing Realpolitik and humanitarian interventions, or it lowers the bar for intervention by attempting to legislate the exception.[2] Furthermore,

---

[1] Ilia Gurlyand, 1904, "Reminiscences of A. P. Chekhov," in *Teatr i iskusstvo* 1904, 28: 11, 521.

[2] See Aidan Hehir, "The Responsibility to Protect: 'Sound and Fury Signifying Nothing'?" *International Relations* 24: 218–239 (2010); Mahmood Mamdani, "Responsibility to Protect or Right to Punish?" *Journal of Intervention and Statebuilding* 4:1, 53–67 (2010);

as Michael Newman[3] argued in 2009, debate and discussion on the place of coercive armed intervention consumes attention to the detriment of focus on the relationship between atrocities, on one side, and development and human security issues, on the other.

But there has been less discussion of the ways that coercive military intervention – regardless of whether it is deployed – organizes the framework for mass atrocities *prevention*. This point is even more salient in light of the fact that, for many, there is no clear division between practices of prevention and response, as explored more in the next section. The dominant approach to mass atrocities revolves around certain principles that maintain the possibility for coercive military action *even when interventions are not being considered*, and it does so in ways that have limited the capacity of the field to envision a coherent prevention strategy.

Maintaining the "pistol on the wall" as a prevention and response tool has oriented the conception of atrocity prevention within a framework marked by four key characteristics. First, work on atrocities is locked into a mindset of the permanent emergency. Second, prevention lessons at odds with military action from even the canonical cases are forgotten; the dominant framework assumes that these cases *required* military action, and therefore subsequent policies needed to legitimize it. Third, *triage*, attempting to identify the greatest risks and tailoring policy tactics (the "toolbox") to engage them, is the best model for prevention. Fourth, consensus on principles supporting civilian protection is worth risking in order to enable coercive action, rare as it might be.

The idea of coercive military intervention to end atrocities has effects that expand well beyond its practices. In the case of prevention, it invisibly polices the borders of what is considered relevant. At stake is the prevention imagination. What other insights, cases, and practices might become apparent if we took the pistol off the wall?

2.2.   The Dominant Prevention Paradigm

A brief review of the dominant anti-atrocities paradigm is in order. In this chapter, "mass atrocities" refers to widespread and systematic violence against civilians, but the challenging fluidity of definitions will also be addressed. One

David Chandler, "The Responsibility to Protect? Imposing the 'Liberal Peace,'" *International Peacekeeping* 11:1, 59–81 (2004); Alex de Waal, "R2P in Theory and Practice," *African Arguments Blog* (2009). Accessed July 10, 2014. Part I, May 20. http://africanarguments.org /2009/05/20/r2p-in-theory-and-politics-1/; Part II, May 21. http://africanarguments.org/2009/05 /21/r2p-in-theory-and-politics-2/; Part III, May 22. http://africanarguments.org/2009/05/21/r2p- in-theory-and-politics-2/.

[3] Michael Newman, "Revisiting the 'Responsibility to Protect,'" *The Political Quarterly* 1: 92–100 (2009).

of the more politically salient and compelling places to witness how the assumptions embedded in prevention and response is through the work on Responsibility to Protect (R2P) at the United Nations. Research and policy development on systematic violence against civilians predates R2P[4] and is undertaken today by numerous actors and within diverse institutions. However, a combination of factors – the struggles to find international common ground on the principles at stake in R2P policies, the UN's role in sanctioning (or not) military intervention, and its institutional investment in a dedicated office on R2P – makes it a particularly rich ground for studying the policies, assumptions, and challenges of the work of preventing mass atrocities.

The intellectual progenitor of R2P can be found in the writings and practices of Sudanese diplomat and scholar, Francis Deng, in conjunction with his work on internally displaced persons. As early as 1993, he argued that sovereignty confers not only rights but also responsibility, and he elaborated these ideas in depth in *Sovereignty as Responsibility: Conflict Management in Africa* (1996), co-authored with Sadikiel Kimaro, Terrence Lyons, Donald Rothchild, and I. William Zartman.[5] Although some themes in this original conceptual development resonate with later efforts to transform the idea into policy guidelines for the international community, the orientation of his work was fundamentally different from the articulation of "responsibility to protect" in the International Commission on Intervention and State Sovereignty (ICISS) report and subsequent interpretations of the principle. Deng et al. were foremost concerned with analysis of the national and regional ramifications of conceptualizing sovereignty differently during a time of decreasing international strategic concern with African countries; it was not oriented toward international military intervention.

Whereas Deng's intellectual and diplomatic work provided the foundation for the ICISS that formulated a principle of R2P, Kosovo was its catalyst. As will be discussed further, intervention in Kosovo sparked a debate about legitimizing military intervention to protect civilians. It was this question that the ICISS was designed to grapple with. For example, the first sentence of the ICISS report is: "This report is about the so-called 'right of humanitarian intervention': the questions of when, if ever, it is appropriate for states to

---

[4] The anti-atrocities agenda, although it draws on legal developments as codified by the Geneva Conventions and religious and other moral traditions about when violence can be sanctioned, takes shape in its current form at the end of the Cold War, particularly beginning with responses to Somalia, Bosnia, and Rwanda in 1990s and subsequent developments in research, policy, and activism.

[5] Francis Deng, Sadikiel Kimaro, Terrence Lyons, Donald Rothchild, and I. William Zartman, *Sovereignty as Responsibility: Conflict Management in Africa* (Washington, DC: The Brookings Institute, 1996).

take coercive – and in particular, military – action, against another state for the purpose of protecting people at risk in that other state."[6]

Global leaders at the 2005 UN World Summit offered a limited embrace of the ICISS report. They affirmed the basic idea that states have a responsibility to protect their populations and that the international community also has a stake in this work. In 2008, Secretary-General Ban Ki-moon appointed Edward Luck as the first Special Adviser on the Responsibility to Protect, initially a part-time position, which was later merged with that of the Special Adviser on the Prevention of Genocide, headed at the time by Francis Deng. Subsequent development of the principle of R2P at the UN elaborated three pillars describing the relationship between sovereignty and responsibility: state sovereignty includes a responsibility to protect populations from systematic violence, specifically from acts of genocide, mass atrocities, ethnic cleansing, and war crimes. The international community has a responsibility to assist states in this endeavor. The third pillar of R2P further asserts that when a state manifestly fails to protect its populations or is itself the perpetrator of violence, the international community has a responsibility to employ strong measures, including potential collective use of force through the UN Security Council (UNSC).

The knowledge base informing today's policy paradigm for preventing and responding to atrocities typically divides engagement into three major phases. First, is address of root causes or structural risk factors that render certain states more prone to mass violence. This is not early warning of impending violence, but rather an assessment of the core conditions understood to correlate with a potential risk of atrocities. Second is proximal or direct prevention, which addresses factors that might trigger mass violence and attempts to articulate anti-escalatory actions. The goal of activities under this heading is to target a place hovering on the brink of or already experiencing violence and to de-escalate the crisis. Third, is response to ongoing widespread and systematic violence against civilians.

However, these phases do not necessarily correspond with the three R2P pillars described earlier, nor are actions to engage at any one of these phases – particularly phases two and three – categorically understood as either prevention or response. For instance, a report from the UN Secretary-General of July 25, 2012, argues that prevention activities under all three pillars can also be understood as response: "Some may consider that

---

[6] International Commission on Intervention and State Sovereignty (ICISS). 2001. "Report of the International Commission of State Sovereignty and Intervention: The Responsibility to Protect." Ottawa: International Development Research Center, vii.

prevention and response are at opposite ends of the spectrum. In practice, however, the two often merge."[7] The report further argues that even coercive action can be understood as prevention because it aims to form "the beginning of a period of social renewal and institutional capacity-building aimed at making future violence less likely."[8]

The cases that form the foundation for both policy and research on atrocities invoke the extremes: the Holocaust, Bosnia, Rwanda, Kosovo and Darfur, Sudan. Each of these instances of violence offered vivid and terrifying examples of how national and international systems permitted systematic brutality of civilian populations. Within this framework, international responses, however varied, valuable or harmful, are deemed failures until the point when military action occurs, or complete failures if such action did not take place. This narrative of "failure" coupled with a powerful ethical imperative to ward off future calamities animates the current approach to prevention and response.

These are, in very brief outline, the key ingredients of the dominant paradigm for prevention of atrocities. The overall approach is already treated as largely self-evident in its framework and core practices. Structural prevention, as Alex Bellamy[9] points out, looks very much like conflict prevention, except that location of effort is guided by a list of countries that manifest indicators of likelihood for atrocities. Prescriptions include promoting economic equality and growth, building public institutions, diffusion of power, strengthened judiciary, lessened corruption, strengthened rule of law, increasing human rights legal protections, supporting intercommunity dialogue, strengthening civil society, and the like.[10] Proximate prevention, often merging into response, is often presented as the work of applying a range of discrete measures (the toolbox) to countries as they approach known triggering events or as violence unfolds. The focus today is on refining the knowledge base that informs identification of at-risk countries and the precision of tools to influence leaders' decisions. As reflected in comments from Jonathon Prentice, Senior Policy Adviser at International Crisis Group, in a speech of May 12, 2011, the work that remains is often understood to be increasing the consistency of implementation or refining around the edges:

---

[7] United Nations, Security Council (UNSC). 2012a. *Responsibility to Protect: Timely and Decisive Response: Report of the Secretary-General*, A/66/874 (July 25, 2012), available from undocs.org/A/66/874, para. 11.

[8] UNSC 2012a, para. 15.

[9] Alex Bellamy, "Mass Atrocities and Armed Conflict: Links, Distinctions, and Implications for the Responsibility to Protect," Stanley Foundation Policy Brief (2011). Accessed July 7, 2014. www.stanleyfoundation.org/publications/pab/bellamypab22011.pdf

[10] Bellamy 2011.

The so-called toolbox is by now pretty well known. And pretty full, constituting, at its core, early warning, whether by NGOs [nongovernmental organizations], the media, UN offices, civil society and grass-roots peace work; institution-building; reducing economic inequities; security sector reform; strengthening legal protections; developing inclusive means of governance; and so on.

It may be that there is little more that can be added to it (though the existing tools could perhaps be further refined), just as perhaps our normative human rights framework – the articulation of our rights and the corresponding obligations of states – is by now pretty well fleshed out. What's needed is their effective implementation.[11]

Prentice downplays the significance of military intervention in the concept of R2P – a shift in focus that is reflected across the field, particularly at the UN since 2011. My concern is that although this particularly robust tool is rarely deployed, it cannot be so easily bracketed. What is more, there may be more work to do than merely editing around the edges of the atrocities prevention paradigm. One reason it has been difficult to imagine this additional work, let alone undertake it, is that the inclusion of coercive military action in the atrocity response toolbox has produced a limited yet hegemonic way of imagining prevention.

Through an examination of four key characteristics of today's atrocities framework, we can see the specific ways that the idea of coercive military intervention limits prevention strategies. Tensions between prevention and response may, in the end, be unavoidable. But this does not mean that they should be unexamined. In examining the core assumptions of the atrocities agenda, it is also possible to see the contours of a different, principled approach that might reinvigorate the debate about how best to contribute to preventing systematic violence against civilians.

2.3.   Four Organizing Principles of Atrocities Prevention

2.3.1.   *The Permanent Emergency*

Resolute cries of "never again," "not on my watch," or "enough!" may seem to the cynic who watches example after example of atrocities as the naïve self-importance of youthful activists. But what the upstart anti-atrocities revolutionary and the jaded "realist" share is a selective historical narrative that bounces from emergency to emergency, summarizing world events as a series of tragic disappointments. Their responses are characterized by both

---

[11] Jonathon Prentice, "Prevention of Genocide and Mass Atrocities (2011)," delivered at Identifying and Overcoming Obstacles to Preventive Action: From Early Warning to Policy Options to Response. Brussels, May 12. Accessed February 12, 2014. www.crisisgroup.org/en /publication–type/speeches/2011/prevention-of-genocide-and-mass-atrocities.aspx.

distrust in systems and a commitment to powering through events by threat of force in the name of a higher good.[12]

As an approach to atrocities prevention, this historical narrative inherits a model of case selection from the discourse of genocide studies, which precedes and becomes the foundation for atrocity prevention and response. The crime of genocide, as Paul Boghossian argues, is treated in research and policy as a distinct phenomenon that is morally wrong and distinctively heinous.[13] This view presents political violence as existing within a moral hierarchy, whereby genocide sits at the apex – or perhaps only just beneath the particular example of the Holocaust – and atrocities reside just below "genocide." Embedded within the logic of this hierarchy is an assumption that exceptional forms of violence require exceptional responses.

The problem with this approach is twofold. First, "genocide" was never a clear-cut or absolute concept, and this shortcoming is more pronounced in terms of "atrocities." In addition to the challenges of applying the concepts to discrete cases at any one moment – always a politically fraught endeavor – there is also historical variation in how violence is perceived. Standards have, thankfully, changed. There is no question, for instance, that dropping a nuclear bomb on a city would today count as an atrocity, regardless if it failed the test for a legal case of genocide or occupies a place of national pride for some who argue it decisively and expeditiously ended a war that was rife with horrors. By comparison, a case where 1,000 people had died would not rise to historic levels of "exceptional" violence, as some claimed in relation to Libya in 2011,[14] let alone the few hundred killed by the Lord's Resistance Army each year for the last six years.[15] These are not anecdotes: these are, in fact, emblematic of the reality. The normative changes that value human lives more and accept massive intentional loss of life less are to be applauded; we should also appreciate the fact of these historical changes.

Second, even if a more uniform definition could be applied to today's examples of violence, it does not follow that identifying and denouncing

---

[12] There are continuities between the militarism embraced by the anti-atrocity agenda field and those of the neo-conservative and liberal hawks, for more on this, see Mahmood Mamdani, *Saviours and Survivors: Darfur, Politics and the War on Terror* (New York: Doubleday, 2009).

[13] Paul Boghosian, "The Concept of Genocide," *Journal of Genocide Research* 12: 1–2, 69–80, 73 (2010).

[14] Gareth Evans, "No Fly Zone Will Help Stop Gaddafi's Carnage," *Financial Times* (February 27, 2011). Accessed May 3, 2014. www.ft.com/intl/cms/s/0/8ac9d1dc-4279-11e0-8b34-00144fea bdc0.html#axzz1v8yz3hYa.

[15] See the statistics on LRA activity produced by Invisible Children, an organization that promotes a military solution to the violence. Their "Crisis Tracker" reports that, since 2008, more than six years of data collection, 2,328 people have been killed by the LRA. Available at www.lracrisis tracker.com/ (accessed February 17, 2014).

such violence as exceptionally heinous immediately converts into an equivalent clarity for the response measures that might be deployed. There are limits to what military interventions can achieve, and these limits are often met at exceptional risk for both the interveners and, in more acute ways, for those who suffer intervention. Violence against civilians in Iraq following the U.S. invasion, which continues today, and the post-Gaddafi violence in Libya ought to quickly dispel the idea that coercive action magically transforms a situation of violence. In short, identifying the problem does not make the solution self-evident.

Nonetheless, too often, the anti-atrocity paradigm draws on a selective presentation of the variety of contexts and patterns of past cases, paired with a constant drumbeat about the exceptional nature of today's threats. Thereby, history appears as a series of endless emergencies of the most compelling ethical nature. This reflects a logic of the enduring emergency, the effects of which pervade work on atrocities and genocide, even in its preventionary aspects. Certainly, those who work on prevention can point to a number of initiatives designed to engage before the crisis moment appears; but early engagement of the crisis is not the same thing as exiting a crisis mindset.

The emergency is characterized, as Craig Calhoun has described it, as a way of looking at the world that has lost faith in systems of change (economic and political) and instead yearns for an instant remedy, one beyond all reproach: "something good to do without waiting for progress, even if you have doubts that progress will ever come. The emergency has become the definitive because it is understood to pose immediate moral demands that override other considerations."[16] An emergency framework is oriented by the task of warding off the worst eventuality. When action is demanded, it is based on ethical arguments that a priori exclude certain measures in favor of stark options that produce either doom or salvation. The narrative is mythical: these options do not really exist.

Furthermore, emergency action is understood as launched from the exterior, that is, from a place of neutrality into a well-contained, ethical field. Hence, the work of crafting prevention and response measures has been imagined as a toolbox. It aims to tinker around edges, engaging only when violence surpasses a certain level, unconcerned with a critique of existing structural and habitual practices. The sum result is not a world laid bare for interventions everywhere in a neo-imperial fashion. Instead, it is one where emergency frameworks predetermine the nature of debates about policy choices such that policy

---

[16] Craig Calhoun, "The Idea of Emergency: Humanitarian Action and Global (Dis)order," in *Contemporary States of Emergency: the Politics of Military and Humanitarian Interventions*, edited by Didier Fassin and Mariella Pandolfi (New York: Zone Books, 2010), 45.

itself is transformed into emergency management.[17] Atrocity prevention participates in this process and is symptomatic of its very nature by holding that a key aim of policy ought to make sure that the *worst does not occur.*

But, oriented toward the worst of the worst, the work of prevention has, as yet, been unable to grapple with larger historical trends of significant declines in violence and the changes in public policy and society that have contributed to those trends. Although the "global war on terror" and events of the Arab Spring have produced an uptick in violence, neither has (yet) altered the overall momentum of this decline. By excluding most historical cases and then jumping to the present, where a rhetoric of superlatives is applied to what are very different levels of violence, the field of atrocities prevention flattens history out into a selective narrative of exceptional cases whose continued existence requires extrasystemic, emergency address.

Search again, and, against the litany of horrors that composes the canon of genocide and atrocities, one can discover another historical arc. The twentieth century witnessed unparalleled capacity for destruction and remarkable global effort to counter the most extreme forms of violence. In neither category was vulnerability, blame, failure, or success evenly distributed. The numbers tell a story of cataclysm: an estimated 20 to 30 million civilians killed in World War II, including 6 million Jews killed in the Holocaust; 20 million civilians killed under Stalin's regime; and 40 million Chinese under the regime led by Mao Tse-tung. These numbers make even the horrific post-World War II events pale: 500,000 people killed during the partition of India, tens to hundreds of thousands of Algerians killed in the Algerian Revolution and similar numbers in the Nigerian Civil War, more than a million people killed during the war for Bangladeshi independence, and 2 million people killed under the Khmer Rouge in Cambodia. If one were to chart the magnitude of lethal violence against civilians, the mid-twentieth century would appear as a spike of destruction at apocalyptic levels.

But this narrative only tells half of the past century's story. Even including these massive upheavals, Steven Pinker suggests that if we place recent decades into the longer span of human civilization, a different story emerges. Although the raw magnitude of twentieth century capacity to inflict violence is perhaps unique, its proportional impact demonstrates an overall decline in violence. Citing evidence covering a broad array of aspects of life from war,

---

[17] This approach is not limited to the anti-atrocities agenda, but marks an orientation toward global problems that is characterized by what David Chandler refers to as "anti-foreign policies": policies based on large, bland statements of what the issuers are against, rather than political engagement with states. David Chandler, "The Security–Development Nexus and the Rise of 'Anti-foreign Policy,'" *Journal of International Relations and Development* 10: 362–386 (2007).

Pinker's theory / overall decline in violence

to domestic abuse, to crime, he argues that our time period may be "the most peaceable era in our species' existence."[18]

However, one does not need to speculate about the entirety of human history, nor to belittle the cataclysms of violence that mark the twentieth century, to bear witness to fundamental changes in the use of systematic violence against civilians in more recent decades. The very century that began with a burgeoning international peace movement only to produce World War I also witnessed a widespread, consistent, and largely unremarked decline of violence that began in the 1970s and showed further significant reductions following the end of the Cold War.

Of the cases that sparked the anti-atrocity agenda from the 1990s and since, *only* the 1994 Rwandan genocide is anywhere near the scale of killing that marked the earlier cases. Barbara Harff has argued that, in the period of 1948–2010, there has been a 90 percent decline in genocide and politicides.[19] The decrease in lethality is also apparent in larger conflict trends, a fact that is significant since atrocities frequently (although not always) correlate with conflict. Significantly, in terms of the scale of violence wrought by contests between major powers, none has fought each other in more than fifty years.[20] The Human Security Report asserts that the average international conflict in the 1950s killed 20,000 people a year on the battlefield; in the 1990s, that average had declined to 6,000 and since has halved again.[21] The number of ongoing armed conflicts per year has remained fairly steady over recent years, in the low thirties, as compared to an average of fifty per year during the Cold War; although this number has risen steadily over the past six years, the number remains low for the entire post-1946 period. Conflicts claiming 1,000 or more lives have declined 50 percent since the 1990s.[22] The most lethal conflicts, like that in Syria, tend to produce a significant proportion of deaths; since 2005, there has been a slow, steady increase in battlefield deaths, but not such that threaten the overarching trend of historic decline.[23] Furthermore, the Minorities at Risk project documents that, between 1991 and 2004, the

---

[18] Steven Pinker, *The Better Angels of Our Nature: Why Violence Has Declined* (New York: Penguin Group, 2011), xxi.

[19] Birger Heldt, "Mass Atrocities Early Warning Systems: Data Gathering, Data Verification and Other Challenges" (March 25, 2012). Accessed February 12, 2014. http://papers.ssrn.com/sol3/papers.cfm?abstract_id=2028534, 15.

[20] Joshua S. Goldstein. *Winning the War on War: The Decline of Armed Conflict Worldwide* (New York: Dutton/Plume, 2011).

[21] There has been a recent uptick in violence due to the various conflicts of the war on terror, but even with these, the overall trend remains downward. Human Security Report Project, *Human Security Report 2009/2010: The Causes of Peace and The Shrinking Costs of War* (New York: Oxford University Press, 2010).

[22] Lotta Themner and Peter Wallensteen, "Armed Conflicts, 1946–2013." *Journal of Peace Research* 51:4, 541–554, at 547 (2014).

[23] Themner and Wallensteen 2014, 544.

number of minority groups being victimized by governments dropped from seventy-five to forty-one.[24]

Take, for example, the case of East Asia. During the first two-thirds of the twentieth century, the region was exceptionally bloody. The civilian tolls from civil war in China, World War II, the second phase of the Chinese civil war, anticolonial conflicts in Indochina, Mao's reign, the Korean War, the Vietnam War, and the Khmer Rouge in Cambodia, among other smaller conflicts, arguably rendered the region the world's most dangerous location for civilians for decades. All this began to change following the death of Mao and declined again in the mid- to late 1970s.

Since that time, war in this region has today dropped to negligible numbers, and those conflicts tend to be highly localized and contained with low casualty numbers – including low numbers of civilian deaths. Multiple factors seem to have played a role in the East Asian decline in violence: the death of Mao Tse-tung and the pragmatism of his successor, Deng Xiaoping, is no doubt significant not only for state-sponsored violence inside China, but for also the role that the country plays in the wider region. Other contributing factors include the defeat and withdrawal of foreign forces, notably changes in interventions by the USSR and the United States; the subsequent preference in the region for noninterference; an emphasis on economic growth and development; the growing number of democracies; and the general approach of the "ASEAN way."

Amitav Acharya characterizes the "ASEAN way" as "associated with a high degree of discreteness, informality, pragmatism, expediency, consensus building, and non-confrontational bargaining styles which are often contrasted with adversarial posturing and legalistic decision-making procedures in Western multilateral negotiations."[25] It is distinct from the liberal human rights models that shape the dominant approach to ending atrocities, and yet – although such an approach may be only a part of the explanation – violence in East Asia has witnessed astonishing reductions. Such dramatic declines should be taken seriously by scholars and at least provoke questions about the assumption that interventions and liberal human rights models are necessary to achieve declines in atrocities.[26]

Most parts of Africa have also experienced a comparable decline in violence. Scott Straus points out that "in the early 2000s there were on average eight to ten wars in any given year, which is about half the number of wars in

[24] As cited in Human Security Report 2010, 77.
[25] Amitav Acharya, "Culture, Security, Multilateralism: The 'ASEAN Way' and Regional Order," *Contemporary Security Policy* 19:1, 55–84, at 58 (1998).
[26] See also Alex Bellamy, "The Other Asian Miracle?: The Decline of Atrocities in East Asia," *Peace & Security* 26:1, 1–19 (2013).

sub-Saharan Africa in the early-to-mid 1990s."[27] Furthermore, he argues that the duration of conflicts has also declined and that there has been an overall decline in the frequency of atrocities, even if the cruel nature of their perpetration has not been altered: "the peak of large-scale mass killing episodes in sub-Saharan Africa was the 1980s, with a decline in the 1990s and 2000s."[28]

There is no single accepted explanation for the global downward trend. Among the major theories put forward are increased democratization, the end of Cold War interventions, economic development and interdependence, and the growth of international mechanisms and organizations, as well as the spread of attitudes that view armed conflict and other large-scale use of violence as illegitimate. What these explanations share, notably, is that each describes systemic change in international relations that can be shaped into coherent and consistent policies, in contrast to the exceptionalism that has marked policies intended to directly "prevent" atrocities.

None of the data documenting historical change minimizes the horror of those atrocities that nonetheless still occur. Atrocities are no less atrocious if they occur with overall lessening frequency. One might logically argue that special measures are necessary to address those cases that stand outside the global trend. Nonetheless, the work of *preventing* atrocities needs to grapple with the implications of global changes. Across the globe, large-scale, systematic violence against civilians is in decline, and the downward trend predates the emergence of an anti-atrocity policy agenda in the post-Cold War era and as captured in the principles and practices associated with R2P. Failing to place its goals and policy recommendations into the context of this global trend, anti-atrocities advocates have not assessed how threats might be changing. They have also not seriously engaged the questions of what new tools and modes of engagement might need to be developed. The trap to avoid is continuing to prepare for another Holocaust or Rwanda and thereby miss today's challenges altogether.

The assumption that exceptional response mechanisms are needed, including coercive intervention, inhibits the field's ability to place its work in the larger global context. The field has emphasized extrasystemic measures – special positions to address atrocities (focal points) and license for different kinds of international discussion and approaches when atrocities are concerned. Few of the policymakers and scholars have contextualized their proposals in light of the historical trend. Those concerned with developing policies designed to prevent atrocities would be remiss to ignore the fact that *something is*

---

[27] Scott Straus, "Wars Do End! Changing Patterns of Political Violence in Sub-Saharan Africa," *African Affairs* 11: 443, 179–201, at 184 (2012a).
[28] Straus 2012a, 187–188.

working in the system. Reinforcing and expanding this trend should be on the agenda for atrocities prevention, even as it continues to examine the places that remain outside the trend.

The field must be prepared to inquire along two paths simultaneously. First, to query the impact of legitimizing coercive armed intervention for any reason (even atrocities response) on the forces, particularly the delegitimization of violence, that have made such historic gains.[29] And second, to forge stronger understanding of exactly why certain places have not participated in the larger trend of decline in violence – there may be reasons that elude the standard toolbox. In short, a changing international environment needs to be acknowledged both to appreciate improvements and to discern variation in causes of harm.

2.3.2. *Prevention Lessons Yet to Be Learned*

The tension that I am drawing out between prevention and response is not new. It was inherent even in the analysis of cases that informed the development of R2P, but it was completely overshadowed by efforts to legitimize military action. Take one of the key examples: Kosovo.

In 1999, Kosovo was a largely Albanian-populated province of Serbia in Yugoslavia[30] when a NATO-led bombing campaign was launched to protect Kosovar Albanians from a Serbian military offensive. Yugoslavia began to disintegrate in 1991 as several of its former republics declared independence, with varying results. Kosovo suffered another fate: political subordination to Serbia, the dominant republic in what remained of Yugoslavia. Kosovar Albanian leaders pursued a campaign of nonviolent resistance while wars raged elsewhere. Then, four years after the conclusion of the bloody war in Bosnia (1992–1995), Kosovo went up in flames.

Picking up from where Bosnia left off, international negotiators embarked on a round of intensive diplomacy backed by threats of coercive action against

---

[29] Both the United States and Russia have invaded countries deploying arguments, even if not readily believable, that the interventions were justified by civilian protection principles. The United States did so in Iraq, also citing the "war on terror," and Russia did so in Ukraine, annexing Crimea and setting off armed conflict between the country's western and eastern halves. Whether these interventions would have happened anyway is unclear, but any agenda that provides fuel for military interventions must grapple with how that justification will be misused, because it will. The initial ICISS report tried to contain this problem by establishing criteria to cage the beast of military intervention. For a discussion of the challenges of operationalizing the criteria, see Alex Bellamy, "Responsibility to Protect and the Problem of Military Intervention," *International Affairs* 84: 615–639 (2008).

[30] Kosovo was an autonomous constituent part of the Yugoslav republic of Serbia following World War II. The 1974 Yugoslav constitution changed its status to an autonomous province, increasing its autonomy. However, following 1989, Serbian leader Slobodan Milosevic significantly reduced the province's political rights.

Yugoslavia (Serbia and Montenegro). Informed by hastily arrived at lessons from Bosnia,[31] where more than 30,000 civilians were killed, international negotiators assumed that Slobodan Milosevi, the leader of Serbia, would only respond to diplomacy backed by credible threats of force, and that, facing force, he would back down quickly. When negotiations failed, the threat of force was realized in the form of a NATO intervention launched against Serbian forces in Kosovo (1999) and expanding to targets in Serbia proper and Montenegro.[32] The goal of the action was to coerce the Serbian leadership to make concessions on Kosovo's status and allow a NATO-led peacekeeping force on the ground, which it did on June 11, 1999.

Reviewing this conflict was the Independent International Commission on Kosovo, created in August 1999 and funded by the government of Sweden, co-chaired by Richard Goldstone and Carl Tham, with eleven additional members, and endorsed by UN Secretary-General Kofi Annan. Their report, published in 2000, included often-overlooked insights on how the crisis might have been prevented. It described several turning points at which the international community failed to capitalize on opportunities to de-escalate the situation. Among these were the failure to articulate any international principles regarding the nonviolent resolution of the impasse between Kosovar Albanian and Serb demands and the subsequent failure to support those within the region who were advocating for nonviolent change and political compromise. It cited specific opportunities lost in 1992, 1995, and 1996–97[33] to include discussion of Kosovo and potential nonviolent resolutions to its political impasse on the international agenda. The report also emphatically noted that 1998, the year before the violence broke into headlines, was the last period during which the best, least violent options remained open.[34] As the situation became increasingly lethal, international options for response narrowed – a process aggravated by multiple and divergent goals among the international actors and diplomacy based on coercion in violation of the UN Charter.[35]

In terms of prevention, the crucial insight from this report is the need for principled commitment to support nonviolent political change: "the failure to

---

[31] Bridget Conley-Zilkic and Alex de Waal, "Setting the Agenda for Evidence Based Research on Atrocity Endings," *Journal of Genocide Research* 16: 1, 55–76 (2014).

[32] Montenegro was targeted several times despite the fact that its leader at the time, Milo Đukanović, was not a supporter of Serbia's leader, Slobodan Milosevic.

[33] Independent International Commission on Kosovo. *The Kosovo Report* (Oxford: Oxford University Press, 2000), 48, 50, 59, and 50–51.

[34] Thereafter, the long-running, nonviolent protests by Kosovar Albanians were set aside in favor of a strategy led by the Kosovo Liberation Army (KLA). The KLA was "woefully ill-prepared for war" and favored a strategy of armed provocations of the Serbian authorities with the goal of prompting a crackdown at a level that would force international attention (Independent International Commission on Kosovo, 2000), 52.

[35] Independent International Commission on Kosovo, 2000, 1.

take more seriously the demands of the non-violent movement at an early stage led to the conclusion that violence produces results and is a more effective political strategy. This had profound implications for the post-conflict political culture."[36] This was not to be. The prevention insights of the report made no impact. Likewise, the signature reports that analyzed international responses to key events that formed the consciousness of the anti-atrocities agenda – reports on Rwanda, Srebrenica, and Sri Lanka, for example – included important insights about what could have and should have been done to avoid military action. Again, like the Kosovo Report, these insights took a back seat to the privileged place afforded coercive military action.

Stealing headlines at the time and ever since were two different arguments made by the report's authors. The first was a recommendation of "conditional independence" for Kosovo.[37] The second was the description of NATO's intervention as "illegal but legitimate."[38] On the latter point, the authors argued that the Kosovo experience "suggests the need to close the gap between legality and legitimacy."[39]

It was this gap that became the starting point for subsequent efforts, such as the R2P philosophy that most significantly shaped the atrocities prevention and response policy agenda. Henceforward, prevention would be addressed as a challenge that existed along a continuum, with the more coercive measures guiding response at the far end. Rather than witnessing inherent tensions between creating a coherent and principled *prevention* agenda, as suggested by the prevention lessons from Kosovo, subsequent efforts have ignored tensions and instead envision all responses as existing on a single plane defined by the imminent emergency.

2.3.3. The Limits of Triage: How the Search for Greatest Risk Can Sideline the Potential for Greatest Benefit

Atrocities prevention has sought to increase predictive knowledge about where atrocities will occur in the hopes of drawing attention to the greatest imminent threat and deploying specialized response measures to that threat. It is prevention as anticipatory triage. Driving the need to single out the most extreme threat is the implicit understanding that exceptional measures might be necessary for these cases and these cases alone. However, there is a serious impediment to such an approach: the knowledge base informing risk assessment and early warning is simply not refined enough to guide such an approach. Whereas additional research will likely improve the record, there are

[36] Ibid., 61.
[37] Ibid., 9.
[38] Ibid., 4.
[39] Ibid.,10.

limits to this approach. Among them are the changing nature of what is classified as "atrocities" and changes in the longer term trends about the greatest risks to civilians. Together, these challenges suggest that prevention activities based on the goal of distinguishing the greatest threats of mass atrocities will miss the protection mark.

Sudan has long been among the signature examples of a place at risk for atrocities and genocide. But it also provides an object lesson in the limits of triage. Almost no one outside of Sudan was paying attention to events taking place in the country's western area of Darfur in Spring 2003. Understandably, international diplomatic attention focused on negotiations to end the two-decade-long war between the north and south. There, the dominant approach to Sudan saw the Muslim northerners as perpetrators of violence against the Christian, southern victims.

Given this narrative, the greatest threat (imminent emergency) was solely located at the point where these two groups met. There was no effort to apply a consistent set of principles to identifying risk within northern or southern communities. But once the scale of violence became apparent in Darfur in 2004, on the western region of northern Sudan, the anti-genocide movement quickly developed around this one case as the most exceptional threat.[40]

Henceforward, new identities of victimhood would dominate; no longer southern Christians against northern Muslims – now it was Africans versus Arabs. This had ramifications for engagement in Darfur on issues related to the north-south process, as well as confirming a pattern that would forget to assess vulnerabilities within South Sudan. The identity of the conflict in Darfur became fixed within genocidal terms of perpetrator and victim rather than on the analysis of the conditions under which certain people became vulnerable. So, even after the conflict shifted, the atrocities response community was still arguing over whether or not Darfur was genocide in 2009.[41] At that point, Arab tribes previously largely left out of the conflict were drawn in, increasing the vulnerability of a new group in the region.[42]

---

[40] This is partially explained by the fact that new organizations intending to engage the public and policymakers in the United States were created specifically in response to the crisis in Darfur. Groups that preexisted this crisis tended to pay more attention to Darfur while it was at its highest crisis point although not entirely abandoning issues that stemmed from other conflicts within Sudan. For example, from 2004 to 2007, International Crisis Group published twice as many reports about Darfur as Sudan (counting reports that include portions on the North/South peace process in addition to Darfur). This changes for ICG in 2007, when North/South issues again begin to dominate. Enough, however, issued its first report on Darfur in March 2007 and continued to focus heavily on Darfur through 2008, at which point conflict broke out in the area of Abyei (between north and south Sudan).

[41] Alex de Waal, Chad Hazlett, Christian Davenport, and Joshua Kennedy, "The Epidemiology of Lethal Violence in Darfur: Using Micro-data to Explore Complex Patterns of Ongoing Armed Conflict," *Science and Social Medicine* 1–10 (2014).

[42] de Waal, Hazlett, Davenport, and Kennedy 2014.

When conflict flared in hotspots along the north-south border, like Abyei (2007–2008), and in advance of the July 2011 referendum on southern independence, attention pivoted back to the north-south issues. Again, within the logic of seeking the greatest threat, the South Sudan government's patterns of patrimonialism, militarism, corruption, and anti-democratic governance were downplayed, neither taken as seriously nor condemned as thoroughly as threats from the north. As a collective, the "south" was the victim; this status, as has happened in many other cases, thus conferred on the leadership immunity against serious reckoning with their policies. Therefore, in 2013, when fighting splintered factions in the South Sudan government again, early warning had failed to rivet the necessary attention. Within weeks, the conflict resulted in 10,000 casualties[43] and the displacement of 702,000 people, including some 123,000 estimated to be refugees in neighboring Uganda, Kenya, Ethiopia, and even Sudan.[44]

There are a few insights about prevention that emerge from this example. The knowledge base informing early warning remains imprecise, particularly at the subnational level. It points to the way that conflict narratives and expectations misdirect attention and the search for policies to protect civilians. It also suggests that even if improvements in data-driven warning systems could be achieved, the model of triage might still fail to guide policy. In chasing the greatest risk, the work of atrocities prevention may overlook strategies to reinforce the greatest protection.

Work on early warning or risk assessment for atrocities has grown considerably over recent years, but it remains imprecise. A key contribution of work in this area has been to debunk or at least challenge some of the assumptions that the field of atrocities prevention inherited from genocide studies about the conditions ripe for systematic violence. For instance, whereas early work on genocide learned much from the examples of fascism and communism to emphasize strong states with well-articulated ideologies, later work has noted that atrocities today often occur in "anocracies" – that is, in states whose governance model exists somewhere between autocracy and democracy.[45] State-sponsored exclusionary ideologies remain important factors, but the nature of the ideology and how it maps onto other social

---

[43] Nicholas Kulish, "New Estimate Sharply Raises Death Toll in South Sudan," *New York Times* (January 9, 2014). Accessed February 12, 2014. www.nytimes.com/2014/01/10/world/africa/new-estimate-sharply-raises-death-toll-in-south-sudan.html

[44] UN Office for the Coordination of Humanitarian Affairs, "Under-Secretary-General for Humanitarian Affairs and Emergency Relief Coordinator, Valerie Amos Press Remarks on South Sudan – Juba, 29 January 2014." Accessed July 10, 2014. http://reliefweb.int/report/south-sudan/under-secretary-general-humanitarian-affairs-and-emergency-relief-coordinator

[45] Jay Ulfelder and Benjamin Valentino. "Assessing Risks of State-Sponsored Mass Killing" (2008). Social Science Research Network, February 1. Accessed October 23, 2013. http://dx.doi.org/10.2139/ssrn.1703426

schisms is significant.[46] Hate, often identified with genocide, has proved less salient an explanation, as work on perpetrators reveals a much broader mix of motivations.[47]

Nonetheless, those who work on atrocity prevention recognize that advances in research have not yet translated into finely honed and specific systems for preventing atrocities. Much of what is known about atrocities prevention emerges from the field of conflict prevention, even though these two related phenomenon are not the same. Further distinguishing an atrocities prevention agenda remains a goal of the field. Currently, there are various strategies for achieving this goal, but generally they follow the approach as presented by Rieke, Sharma, and Welsh (2013), which calls for specifying atrocities and testing tools in order to fine-tune the toolbox for policy:

> there is to date very little knowledge of the conditions under which particular tools might be effective, and the specific capacities (national, regional and international) that are required to deliver them. We argue that more focused atrocity prevention capacity needs to be built at these three levels, which can then be tailored to particular circumstances.[48]

In this case, the authors argue that crafting these atrocity-distinct mechanisms will require a more limited field of inquiry, one shifting away from root causes and structural risk and toward a model borrowed from criminology and focused on identifying perpetrators, victims, and permissive environments. Others are working on increasing the knowledge base about what differentiates a predilection for atrocities among a range of societies that demonstrate similar conditions, but few of which actually experience such violence. Important work is also being done to improve early warning systems and to elaborate concepts of social resilience or inhibitory factors.[49] Such efforts will undoubtedly move the field forward by further specifying what is unique to atrocities.

---

[46] Scott Straus, "Retreating from the Brink: Theorizing Mass Violence and the Dynamics of Restraint." *Perspectives on Politics* 2: 343–362 (2012b).

[47] James Waller, *Becoming Evil: How Ordinary People Commit Genocide* (New York: Oxford University Press, 2002); Stathis Kalyvas, *The Logic of Violence in Civil War* (New York: Cambridge University Press, 2006); Lee Ann Fujii, *Killing Neighbors: Webs of Violence in Rwanda* (Ithaca, NY: Cornell University Press, 2009).

[48] Rubin Reike, Serena Sharma, and Jennifer Welsh, "A Strategic Framework for Mass Atrocity Prevention" (2013). Australian Government, Australian Civil-Military Centre Paper 03/201. https://www.acmc.gov.au/wp-content/uploads/2014/09/3-2013-A-Strategic-Framework-for-Mass-Atrocity-Prevention1.pdf. Accessed April 10, 2015.

[49] Jay Ulfelder, "Making a Case for (Imperfect) Statistical Modeling as the Basis for Genocide Early Warning" (2011). U.S. Holocaust Memorial Museum. Accessed February 12, 2014. www.ushmm.org/m/pdfs/20111021-ulfelder-early-warning.pdf; Stephen McLoughlin and Deborah Mayersen, "Risk and Resilience to Mass Atrocities in Africa: A Comparison of Rwanda and Botswana," *Journal of Genocide Research* 13:3, 247–269 (2011); Scott Straus, "Retreating from the Brink," 343–362.

However, it remains a point of contention whether further specializing research should be the sole strategy for atrocity prevention. It may not be possible. As Charles Tilly asserted more than a decade ago: "a fairly small number of causal mechanisms and processes recur throughout the whole range of collective violence."[50] David Cunningham and Douglas Lemke took up this point recently in the context of the most studied form of organized violence: civil war. They argue that much of what is currently presented as distinct to civil war relates to broader and more diverse forms of violence: "We have shown that several correlates of civil war incidence are also correlates of less violent forms of sub-state conflict. What we believe we know about civil war thus also informs what we know about sub-state violence."[51] While most researchers are focused on increasingly specific studies of factors related to civil war, Cunningham and Lemke propose that the field might do well to query a broader range of violence:

The commonalities across these many types of sub-state violence offer intriguing possibilities for expanding the study of civil war to include lesser forms of violence, and for refining the study of civil war in hopes of developing better theory about when civil wars will plague states.[52]

A similar strategy might contribute to a principled and systemic approach to atrocities prevention.

Added to the knowledge base challenge is an additional one for atrocities prevention: the definition of what "counts" as an atrocity is historically and politically contingent, as noted previously. Furthermore, as the authors of *The Global Burden of Armed Violence*[53] point out, civilians increasingly are threatened from violence in scenarios that do not adhere to the examples of genocide from history. Considerably more civilians are at risk from situations that are endemic, involve a multitude of non-state actors, and blur the lines between political and criminal violence. Additionally, whereas governments tend to be responsible for the highest spikes in violence against civilians, nongovernmental groups tend to commit violence against civilians in greater numbers.[54] Those high spikes have declined in parallel as more governments become democracies, but there is also a stubborn trend of countries locked

[50] Charles Tilly, *The Politics of Collective Violence* (New York: Cambridge University Press, 2003), xi.
[51] David Cunningham and Douglas Lemke, "Beyond Civil War: A Quantitative Analysis of Sub-state Violence" (2011). Social Science Research Network, August 1. Accessed February 12, 2014. http://papers.ssrn.com/sol3/papers.cfm?abstract_id=1900695, 27.
[52] Cunningham and Lemke 2011, 27.
[53] Geneva Declaration (2011), *The Global Burden of Armed Violence 2011*. Accessed February 12, 2014. www.genevadeclaration.org/measurability/global-burden-of-armed-violence/global-burden-of-armed-violence-2011.html
[54] Kristine Eck and Lisa Hultman, "One-Sided Violence against Civilians in War: Insights from New Fatality Data," *Journal of Peace Research* 44:2, 233–246 (2007).

somewhere between autocracy and democracy – countries where civilians too often suffer from remarkably robust patterns of low-level violence.[55]

The tools of the field of atrocities prevention that attempt to weaken and even, in rare cases, overthrow governments committing violence may be producing the very circumstances that are ripe for other forms of systematic violence against civilians. In short, even if research reveals stronger ways of differentiating widespread and systematic targeting of specific civilian groups, the vulnerabilities to violence may be shifting to a situation characterized by weak states and the increasing significance of transnational actors, where violence may be endemic and diffuse rather than concentrated and overwhelming. The tools for response designed for the former may not be effective for the latter; what is more, they may even be counterproductive for civilian protection within these conditions.

Even where violence does follow patterns that can readily be identified as mass atrocities, as noted in the example of Darfur, violence shifts in its nature, victims, and perpetrators. Although the study of armed violence makes conceptual divisions between organized and interpersonal violence, conflict and criminal contexts, state-sponsored and non-state actors, systematic versus incidental, and so forth, distinct situations rarely conform to these distinctions.[56] Different forms of violence can exist at the same time: "armed violence can have multiple and overlapping motives; different political, economic, identity-based, ideological, and other motives."[57] Even if one form of violence dominates at a certain point, it often evolves over time. Any labels applied to a conflict must be understood as time- and context-specific. One example: in 2010, more people were murdered in Juarez, Mexico, related to the activities of criminal gangs than in all of Afghanistan or Darfur, Sudan.[58] The picture of global threats to civilians posed by lethal violence may suggest a

---

[55] Jay Ulfelder, 2012, "Forecasting Onsets of Mass Killing," Social Science Research Network, May 4. Accessed July 7, 2014. http://dx.doi.org/10.2139/ssrn.2056306, 10.

[56] Recognizing that correlates and patterns are often misconstrued when violence is studied within only one framework (armed conflict), the field of conflict studies is seeking ever more micro-level data collection. See Clionadh Raleigh, Andrew Linke, Havard Hegre, and Joakim Karlsen, "Introducing ACELD: An Armed Conflict Location and Event Dataset: Special Data Feature," *Journal of Peace Research* 47: 651–660 (2010).

[57] Geneva Declaration 2011,15.

[58] In 2010, murders in Ciudad Juarez surpassed 3,000; civilian deaths in Afghanistan were recorded at 2,777 and in Darfur, Sudan, at 2,321. See, in order: Nick Valencia, "Juarez Counts 3,000th Homicide of 2010" (2010). CNN, December 15. Accessed July 7, 2014. www.cnn.com/2010/WORLD/americas/12/15/mexico.juarez.homicides/index.html; United Nations Assistance Mission for Afghanistan and Afghanistan Independent Human Rights Commission, "Afghanistan: Annual Report 2011 on Protection of Civilians in Armed Conflict," Kabul, Afghanistan (March 2011). Accessed July 7, 2014. http://unama.unmissions.org/Portals/UNAMA/human%20rights/March%20PoC%20Annual%20Report%20Final.pdf; Agence France Presse, "Darfur Death Toll Mounts amid New War Fears" (January 19, 2011). Accessed July 7, 2014. http://reliefweb.int/node/381345

more varied landscape than the static picture presented by the atrocities lens. In failing to acknowledge such variations, both analytical knowledge and policy options are stovepiped. The authors of the *Global Burden of Violence* warn: "the most important types of violence may be neglected due to the policy predispositions or orientations of major donors and stakeholders."[59]

In trying to anticipate where the worst of the worst might occur and to focus exceptional tools on responding to such threats – including the most invasive – atrocities prevention has unnecessarily isolated itself from study and prevention of violence per se and therefore from the prevention and protection innovations that emerge from other approaches to violence. Although there are undoubtedly improvements in atrocities prevention that can and will be made, it is also unlikely that atrocities prevention will ever be a science. This limit of the knowledge base must be further appreciated as the application of the term "atrocities" is applied to a wider range of cases. Better, perhaps, would be a strategy of reinforcing and further developing knowledge about the broader phenomenon of how civilians become vulnerable to a range of threats of violence. This would be more feasible if the term "atrocities" were not so married to a particular suite of exceptional response measures.

2.3.4.   Does Political Will to Take Coercive Action Unravel Protection Consensus?

In the aftermath of the Libya intervention (2011), controversies about the decision to pursue regime change splintered support for R2P and catalyzed efforts at the UN to create firewalls between R2P and civilian protection practices. Whether one was a supporter of the Libya intervention or a critic, the fallout discussion regarding the place of civilian protection and R2P is important. Assessments of the war diverge sharply: was it a successful example of the international community acting with speed and focus to protect civilians whose government was preparing to massacre them? Or was it an international alliance to remove a nasty rogue government with minimal Western casualties, justified by the demand to protect Libyan civilians from their own government's violence?

Supporters like Jon Western and Joshua Goldstein argue that Libya provides cause for celebrating the principles of R2P and humanitarian intervention. For them, the narrative is straightforward: the violence, which hardly needs to be revisited, constituted a clear case of R2P crimes – termed "an imminent slaughter." The shift from civilian protection to a military goal of regime change is barely addressed, and then only in terms of the value of hastening

---

[59] Geneva Declaration 2011, 18.

an end to the civil war.[60] On the opposite side of the debate is, for instance, Hugh Roberts, who was the North Africa director for International Crisis Group, an organization that Western and Goldstein cite as proof of international consensus in favor of quick UN action while glossing over what appropriate actions were recommended. Roberts provides a scorching critique of the interventionist logic in Libya. Whether one liked it or not, the Libyan government had a right, he argued, to put down a rebel threat. Acknowledging that this right is subject to higher laws about treatment of civilians, Roberts points out that the facts about atrocities in the case of Libya were stretched: "the invocation of rules (e.g. no genocide) can go together with a cynical exaggeration and distortion of the facts by other states. There are in fact no reliable rules."[61] When the terms for intervention leave so much room for interpretation, then the decision to intervene is based in the hands of the major powers.[62]

At the UN, the aftermath was marked by a concerted effort to distinguish civilian protection and R2P both conceptually and pragmatically. Before the Libya intervention, the Security Council treated protection of civilians and R2P as compatible activities. For instance, UNSC Resolution 1894 (2009) adopted on November 11, 2009, reaffirmed the 2005 World Summit Outcome document "regarding the protection of civilians in armed conflict, *including* paragraphs 138 and 139 thereof regarding the responsibility to protect populations from genocide, war crimes, ethnic cleansing and crimes against humanity."[63] But on May 22, 2012, UN Secretary-General Ban Ki-moon noted that the intervention in Libya went beyond civilian protection, potentially causing harm to the idea of protecting civilians. Then he issued a call for subordinating interventions to principles of civilian protection, a point that previously might have been considered redundant in any R2P context. After Libya, the principle of civilian protection needed protection itself, as Ban stated:

However, the extent to which its [UNSC Resolution 1973] implementation was perceived to go beyond the protection of civilians raised concerns among some Member States that continue to colour the Council's discussions on the protection of civilians and related issues in other situations. It may also have had the unintended effect of undermining the protection of civilians agenda, including as a framework for

---

[60] Jon Western and Joshua Goldstein, "Humanitarian Intervention Comes of Age: Lessons from Somalia to Libya," *Foreign Affairs* (November/December 2011). Accessed February 12, 2014. www.foreignaffairs.com/articles/136502/jon-western-and-joshua-s-goldstein/humanitarian-intervention-comes-of-age

[61] Hugh Roberts, "Who Said Gaddafi Had to Go?" *London Review of Books* 33: 8–18 (2011). Accessed February 17, 2014. www.lrb.co.uk/v33/n22/hugh-roberts-who-said-gaddafi-had-to-go

[62] Roberts 2011.

[63] United Nations, Security Council, 2009, Resolution 1894/2009, S/RES/1894 (November 11, 2009), available from undocs.org/S/RES/1894. Accessed February 12, 2014.

action in future crises. In the future, in addition to complying scrupulously with international humanitarian law and human rights law, the implementation of such decisions must be limited to promoting and ensuring the protection of civilians.[64]

The Brazilian ambassador to the UN went further by pointedly asserting that there is a responsibility "while protecting" that imposes limitations to the coercive approach. In a letter to the UN General Assembly, Ambassador Antonio de Aguiar Patriota, Minister of External Relations of Brazil, wrote: "There is a growing perception that the concept of the responsibility to protect might be misused for purposes other than protecting civilians, such as regime change. This perception may make it even more difficult to attain the protection objectives pursued by the international community."[65]

The debate raged from the end of 2011 through 2012. The UNSG Ban signaled which side the UN was on, not only by engaging the debates but also in declaring 2012 the "Year of Prevention." Reflecting this change, the UNSG's report on R2P, released in July 2013,[66] was entirely a prevention report. It focused on the evolving knowledge base and core principles that ought to inform prevention. It addressed risk factors, triggers and permissive environments, national resilience, democratization, transitional justice, security sector reform, distribution of resources, governance issues, and human rights. It approached specific measures targeted to atrocities in terms of creating governmental focal points on atrocities, education, commemoration, and fora addressing regional cooperation on prevention.

Had understanding of R2P turned a corner? Implementing a policy of coercive military intervention was never designed to be the central tenet of R2P. But it was always there, dominating the imagination of how atrocities end. Having witnessed this policy in Libya to controversial ends, would the time come not only to downplay it, but to reject it altogether? Would war in the name of protection be banished, thus allowing a different approach altogether to develop? It is not clear if the shift that appeared to have happened was a tactical avoidance of the controversy or a new opening to rethink atrocities prevention and response. Ideally, the latter would be true, but it would have required confronting the major powers that have increasingly militarized their foreign policy, as well as the vocal contingent of advocates who have placed so much

---

[64] United Nations, Security Council, 2012b, "Report of the Secretary General on the Protection of Civilians in Armed Conflict," S/2012/376 (May 22, 2012), available from undocs.org/S/2012 /376. Accessed February 12, 2014, para. 19.

[65] United Nations, General Assembly, 2011, Letter dated November 9, 2011, from the Permanent Representative of Brazil to the United Nations addressed to the Secretary-General, A/66/551 (November 11, 2011), available from undocs.org/A/66/551. Accessed February 12, 2014; para. 10.

[66] United Nations, Security Council, 2013, State Responsibility and Prevention: *Report of the Secretary-General*, A/67/929 (July 9, 2013), available from undocs.org/A/67/929. Accessed February 12, 2014.

trust in the exertion of force. However, only thus would a coherent prevention agenda become possible.

Another benefit of rethinking civilian protection and use of coercive military force is the accruing evidence supporting the contributions of UN peacekeeping missions for decreasing the killing of civilians. Response to failures of peacekeeping missions to protect civilians in the devastating cases of the 1990s catalyzed not only the atrocities response model, but also reforms within traditional peacekeeping. Since 1999, the UN is increasingly likely to send peacekeeping missions to places where civilians have been attacked (as opposed to conflicts with low targeting of civilians) rather than deploying under the illusion of best-case scenarios. In further contrast to the peacekeeping missions to Bosnia and Rwanda, since 1999, with the UN Mission in Sierra Leone (UNAMSIL), almost all peacekeeping missions have included a civilian protection mandate.

Although much work remains to improve civilian protection practices,[67] the shift in mandate has already made an impact overall in the record of how peacekeeping missions impact the level of violence directed at civilians. In a study that analyzed peacekeeping missions 1991–2008, including force level changes over the course of a mission and how these changes correlate with instances of violence against civilians, Lisa Hultman, Jacob Kathman, and Megan Shannon[68] found strong evidence that UN peacekeeping can play an important role in decreasing the level of violence against civilians. The factors that made a difference included deployments at significant size and inclusion of a strong policing capacity. This research gains greater saliency when paired with evidence of patterns of violence against civilians in cases of mass atrocity. Mass atrocities do not occur evenly throughout a conflict; they often spike to very high levels close to onset and then decline, until or unless there are significant power or capacity shifts.[69] International interventions rarely, if ever, match this pacing and so tend to be out of step with the most acute killing incidents. When international interventions do occur – or are threatened – they raise the stakes for all those involved in the crisis. Another challenge is that those perpetrating systematic violence may accelerate assaults in advance or immediately following military intervention.

[67] Victoria Holt and Glyn Taylor, with Max Kelly, *Protecting Civilians in the Context of UN Peacekeeping Operations* (New York: United Nations, UN Department of Peacekeeping Operations/Office for the Coordination of Humanitarian Affairs, 2009). Accessed July 7, 2014. http://reliefweb.int/sites/reliefweb.int/files/resources/B752FF2063E282B08525767100751 B90-unocha_protecting_nov2009.pdf.

[68] Lisa Hultman, Jacob D. Kathman, and Megan Shannon, "United Nations Peacekeeping and Civilian Protection in Civil War," *American Journal of Political Science* 57: 875–891 (2013).

[69] Ulfelder and Valentino 2008.

This latter point has been cited as a limitation of peacekeeping missions as well as coercive action. But, over time, as Jacob Kathman and Reed Wood assert, impartial interventions do more to decrease atrocities than do partial interventions on the side of a perpetrating government *as well as* those on the side of victims.[70] At a minimum, studies like this point to a need to understand intervention as a long-term commitment rather than a short-term fix, and one where the strongest results emerge from impartial interventions.[71] Although some debate remains about whether peacekeeping results in less decisive endings to conflicts – and how these types of endings may produce different sorts of subsequent challenges – the record of peacekeeping's contributions to lessening war resumption and likely hastening endings is supported by cross-case data.[72] As Hultman, Kathman, and Shannon conclude: "UN peacekeeping is seemingly better at reducing human suffering than more biased forms of intervention."[73]

A fuller analysis of this and other data would be necessary to conclude that peacekeeping has a definitively better track record in protecting civilians than does coercive action. I raise the issue here not to try to make an impeachable case, but to point to the fact that the record on the effectiveness of coercive military interventions over that of peacekeeping missions is far from proved. Furthermore, as argued throughout this chapter, inclusion of this extreme response mechanism – even when it is not used – skews the prevention agenda. It orients the paradigm toward an extrasystemic approach, commands attention to the detriment of crafting principled prevention policies, stovepipes research on atrocities and policies related to them, and erodes political consensus on civilian protection.

The work of developing a strong prevention agenda will require precisely the international consensus that military response withered. It may be time to draw a line between the two. As if shifting focus could cure the schisms that military intervention in Libya had produced, suddenly, not only did "prevention" steal the focus the UN, but it also influenced the larger conversation as well. But a change in emphasis may not be enough if the overall paradigm is, as I have argued, organized by the "pistol on the wall."

---

[70] Jacob Kathman and Reed Wood, "Managing Threat, Cost, and Incentive to Kill: The Short- and Long-Term Effects of Intervention in Mass Killings," *Journal of Conflict Resolution* 55:5, 735–760 (2011).

[71] Kathman and Reed 2011, 754.

[72] Page Fortna, "Inside and Out: Peacekeeping and the Duration of Peace after Civil and Interstate Wars," *International Studies Review* 5:4, 97–114 (2003).

[73] Fortna 2003, 15.

2.4.   Conclusion: Toward Atrocities Prevention as a Stand-alone Set of Principles

The dominant paradigm for atrocities prevention today requires recalibration in light of the facts that a historical decline in atrocities predates the atrocities prevention agenda, that the knowledge base informing identification of risk of atrocities and the effectiveness of tools is still weak and imprecise, and that the "tool" most specifically honed to respond to atrocities is politically and practically compromised. Prevention is not best undertaken from an emergency mindset, may contain principles that are at odds with coercive action, might learn from a broader knowledge base concerning violence against civilians, and can find powerful tools to support less controversial international practices.

For those whose aim is to prevent atrocities, the answer is not a better toolbox; it is to articulate principles that will strengthen the momentum against the use of violence as a legitimate tool for addressing political contestation and in favor of policies that bolster resilient societies and prioritize civilian protection. Such a prevention agenda embraces principles that might have profound implications for doing business differently, rather than merely implementing a new toolbox.

In fact, this approach would not be at odds with how R2P has most frequently functioned politically. Scrutinizing the cases in which R2P principles were invoked, Alex Bellamy has argued that the primary effect of the principle is not that it determines a course of action, but rather how it instills what he calls "habits of protection." He writes: "Habits of protection mean that the Council gives consideration to RtoP related issues as a matter of routine, but they do not determine particular courses of action."[74] If we can accept Bellamy's assessment – and he has been one of the closest watchers of how the principles of R2P have played out at the UN – then we must acknowledge that the contributions of the "atrocity prevention lens" and the "toolbox" are not what they might seem at first. In recognizing this fact, the next steps require focusing attention on strengthening the real contributions of the principle rather than whittling away the emergent consensus by requesting that it embrace the most controversial and less proven response measures.

The innovation of genocide and atrocities prevention was to catalyze international consensus on the principle that violence against civilians is not only unnecessary, it is reprehensible and unacceptable. Its ethical insight translates into policies that centralize international concern on crafting habits of protection. But its (self-)critical acumen must also be developed, so that the principles that guide its response engagement do not erode its prevention potential.

---

[74] Alex Bellamy, "R2P: Added Value or Hot Air?" *Cooperation and Conflict* 1–25, 3 (2014).

Bibliography

Acharya, Amitav. 1998. "Culture, Security, Multilateralism: The 'ASEAN Way' and Regional Order." *Contemporary Security Policy* 19:1, 55–84.

Agence France Presse. 2011. "Darfur Death Toll Mounts amid New War Fears." January 19. Accessed July 7, 2014. http://reliefweb.int/node/381345

Bellamy, Alex. 2008. "Responsibility to Protect and the Problem of Military Intervention." *International Affairs* 84: 615–639.

Bellamy, Alex. 2011. "Mass Atrocities and Armed Conflict: Links, Distinctions, and Implications for the Responsibility to Protect" Stanley Foundation Policy Brief. Accessed July 7, 2014. www.stanleyfoundation.org/publications/pab/bellamy pab22011.pdf

Bellamy, Alex. 2013. "The Other Asian Miracle?: The Decline of Atrocities in East Asia" *Peace & Security* 26:1, 1–19.

Bellamy, Alex. 2014. "R2P: Added Value or Hot Air?" *Cooperation and Conflict* 1–25.

Boghosian, Paul. 2010. "The Concept of Genocide." *Journal of Genocide Research* 12: 1–2, 69–80.

Calhoun, Craig. 2010. "The Idea of Emergency: Humanitarian Action and Global (Dis)order." In *Contemporary States of Emergency: The Politics of Military and Humanitarian Interventions* edited by Didier Fassin and Mariella Pandolfi, 29–58. New York: Zone Books.

Chandler, David. 2004. "The Responsibility to Protect? Imposing the 'Liberal Peace.'" *International Peacekeeping* 11:1, 59–81.

Chandler, David. 2007. "The Security–Development Nexus and the Rise of 'Anti-foreign Policy.'" *Journal of International Relations and Development* 10: 362–386.

Conley-Zilkic, Bridget, and Alex de Waal. 2014. "Setting the Agenda for Evidence Based Research on Atrocity Endings." *Journal of Genocide Research* 16: 1, 55–76.

Crawford, Timothy, and Alan Kuperman. 2006. *Gambling on Humanitarian Intervention: Moral Hazard, Rebellion and Civil War*. New York: Routledge.

Cunningham, David, and Douglas Lemke. 2011. "Beyond Civil War: A Quantitative Analysis of Sub-state Violence." Social Science Research Network, August 1. Accessed February 12, 2014. http://papers.ssrn.com/sol3/papers.cfm?abstract_id=1900695

de Waal, Alex. 2009. "R2P in Theory and Practice." *African Arguments Blog*. Accessed July 10, 2014. Part I, May 20. http://africanarguments.org/2009/05/20/r2p-in-theory-and-politics-1/; Part II, May 21. http://africanarguments.org/2009/05/21/r2p-in-theory-and-politics-2/; Part III, May 22. http://africanarguments.org/2009/05/21/r2p-in-theory-and-politics-2/.

de Waal, Alex, Chad Hazlett, Christian Davenport, and Joshua Kennedy. 2014. "The Epidemiology of Lethal Violence in Darfur: Using Micro-data to Explore Complex Patterns of Ongoing Armed Conflict." *Science and Social Medicine* 1: 1–10.

de Waal, Alex, Jens Meierhenrich, and Bridget Conley-Zilkic. 2012. "How Mass Atrocities End: An Evidence-Based Counter-Narrative." *The Fletcher Forum of World Affairs*, January 31. Accessed November 29, 2013. www.fletcherforum.org/2012/01/31/dewaal-etal/

Deng, Francis, Sadikiel Kimaro,Terrence Lyons, Donald Rothchild, and I. William Zartman. 1996. *Sovereignty as Responsibility: Conflict Management in Africa.* Washington, DC: The Brookings Institute.

Eck, Kristine, and Lisa Hultman. 2007. "One-Sided Violence Against Civilians in War: Insights from New Fatality Data." *Journal of Peace Research* 44:2, 233–246.

Evans, Gareth. 2011. "No Fly Zone Will Help Stop Gaddafi's Carnage." *Financial Times*, February 27. Accessed May 3, 2014. www.ft.com/intl/cms/s/0/8ac9d1dc-4279-11e0-8b34-00144feabdc0.html#axzz1v8yz3hYa. Retrieved May 13, 2013.

Fortna, Page. 2003. "Inside and Out: Peacekeeping and the Duration of Peace after Civil and Interstate Wars." *International Studies Review* 5:4, 97–114.

Fujii, Lee Ann. 2009. *Killing Neighbors: Webs of Violence in Rwanda.* Ithaca, NY: Cornell University Press.

Geneva Declaration. 2011. *The Global Burden of Armed Violence 2011.* Accessed February 12, 2014. www.genevadeclaration.org/measurability/global-burden-of-armed-violence/global-burden-of-armed-violence-2011.html

Goldstein, Joshua S. 2011. *Winning the War on War: The Decline of Armed Conflict Worldwide.* New York: Dutton/Plume.

Gurlyand, Ilia. 1904. "Reminiscences of A. P. Chekhov." *Teatr i iskusstvo* 28(11): 521.

Hehir, Aidan. 2010. "The Responsibility to Protect: 'Sound and Fury Signifying Nothing'?" *International Relations* 24: 218–239.

Heldt, Birger. 2012. "Mass Atrocities Early Warning Systems: Data Gathering, Data Verification and Other Challenges." March 25. Accessed February 12, 2014. http://papers.ssrn.com/sol3/papers.cfm?abstract_id=2028534

Holt, Victoria, Glyn Taylor, with Max Kelly. 2009. *Protecting Civilians in the Context of UN Peacekeeping Operations.* New York: United Nations, UN Department of Peacekeeping Operations/Office for the Coordination of Humanitarian Affairs. Accessed July 7, 2014. http://reliefweb.int/sites/reliefweb.int/files/resources/B752F F2063E282B08525767100751B90-unocha_protecting_nov2009.pdf

Hultman, Lisa. 2013. "UN Peace Operations and Protection of Civilians: Cheap Talk or Norm Implementation?" *Journal of Peace Research* 50(1): 59–73.

Hultman, Lisa, Jacob D. Kathman, and Megan Shannon. 2013. "United Nations Peacekeeping and Civilian Protection in Civil War." *American Journal of Political Science* 57: 875–891.

Human Security Report Project. 2010. *Human Security Report 2009/2010: The Causes of Peace and The Shrinking Costs of War.* New York: Oxford University.

Independent International Commission on Kosovo. 2000. *The Kosovo Report.* Oxford: Oxford University Press.

International Commission on Intervention and State Sovereignty. 2001. "Report of the International Commission of State Sovereignty and Intervention: The Responsibility to Protect." Ottawa: International Development Research Center.

Kathman, Jacob, and Reed Wood. 2011. "Managing Threat, Cost, and Incentive to Kill: The Short- and Long-Term Effects of Intervention in Mass Killings." *Journal of Conflict Resolution* 55:5, 735–760.

Kalyvas, Stathis. 2006. *The Logic of Violence in Civil War.* New York: Cambridge University Press.

Kulish, Nicholas. 2014. "New Estimate Sharply Raises Death Toll in South Sudan" *New York Times*, January 9. Accessed February 12, 2014. www.nytimes.com/2014/01/10/world/africa/new-estimate-sharply-raises-death-toll-in-south-sudan.html

Laub, Karin. 2011. "Libyan Estimate: At Least 30,000 Died in the War." Associated Press, September 8. Accessed February 14, 2014. www.theguardian.com/world/feedarticle/9835879

Mamdani, Mahmood. 2009. *Saviours and Survivors: Darfur, Politics and the War on Terror*. New York: Doubleday.

Mamdani, Mahmood. 2010. "Responsibility to Protect or Right to Punish?" *Journal of Intervention and Statebuilding* 4:1, 53–67.

McLoughlin, Stephen, and Deborah Mayersen. 2011. "Risk and Resilience to Mass Atrocities in Africa: A Comparison of Rwanda and Botswana." *Journal of Genocide Research* 13:3, 247–269.

Newman, Michael. 2009. "Revisiting the 'Responsibility to Protect.'" *The Political Quarterly* 1: 92–100.

Pinker, Steven. 2011. *The Better Angels of Our Nature: Why Violence Has Declined*. New York: Penguin Group.

Prentice, Jonathon. 2011. "Prevention of Genocide and Mass Atrocities." Delivered at Identifying and Overcoming Obstacles to Preventive Action: From Early Warning to Policy Options to Response. Brussels, May 12. Accessed February 12, 2014. www.crisisgroup.org/en/publication-type/speeches/2011/prevention-of-genocide-and-mass-atrocities.aspx.

Raleigh, Clionadh, Andrew Linke, Havard Hegre, and Joakim Karlsen. 2010. "Introducing ACELD: An Armed Conflict Location and Event Dataset: Special Data Feature." *Journal of Peace Research* 47: 651–660.

Reike, Rubin, Serena Sharma, and Jennifer Welsh. 2013. "A Strategic Framework for Mass Atrocity Prevention." Australian Government, Australian Civil-Military Centre Paper 03/201. Accessed April 10, 2015. www.acmc.gov.au/wp-content/uploads/2014/09/3-2013-A-Strategic-Framework-for-Mass-Atrocity-Prevention1.pdf

Roberts, Hugh. 2011. "Who Said Gaddafi Had To Go?" *London Review of Books* 33: 8–18. Accessed February 17, 2014. www.lrb.co.uk/v33/n22/hugh-roberts/who-said-gaddafi-had-to-go

Straus, Scott. 2012a. "Wars Do End! Changing Patterns of Political Violence in Sub-Saharan Africa." *African Affairs* 11: 443, 179–201.

Straus, Scott. 2012b. "Retreating from the Brink: Theorizing Mass Violence and the Dynamics of Restraint." *Perspectives on Politics* 2: 343–362.

Themner, Lotta, and Peter Wallensteen. 2014. "Armed Conflicts, 1946–2013." *Journal of Peace Research* 51:4, 541–554.

Tilly, Charles. 2003. *The Politics of Collective Violence*. New York: Cambridge University Press.

Ulfelder, Jay. 2011. "Making a Case for (Imperfect) Statistical Modeling as the Basis for Genocide Early Warning." U.S. Holocaust Memorial Museum. Accessed February 12, 2014. www.ushmm.org/m/pdfs/20111021-ulfelder-early-warning.pdf

Ulfelder, Jay. 2012. "Forecasting Onsets of Mass Killing." Social Science Research Network, May 4. Accessed July 7, 2014. http://dx.doi.org/10.2139/ssrn.2056306

Ulfelder, Jay, and Benjamin Valentino. 2008. "Assessing Risks of State-Sponsored Mass Killing." Social Science Research Network, February 1. Accessed October 23, 2013. http://dx.doi.org/10.2139/ssrn.1703426

United Nations Assistance Mission for Afghanistan and Afghanistan Independent Human Rights Commission. 2011. "Afghanistan: Annual Report 2011 on Protection of Civilians in Armed Conflict." Kabul, Afghanistan, March. Accessed July 7, 2014. http://unama.unmissions.org/Portals/UNAMA/human%20rights/March %20PoC%20Annual%20Report%20Final.pdf

United Nations, General Assembly. 2011. Letter dated November 9, 2011, from the Permanent Representative of Brazil to the United Nations addressed to the Secretary-General, A/66/551 (November 11, 2011). Available from undocs.org/A/66/551. Accessed February 12, 2014.

United Nations Office for the Coordination of Humanitarian Affairs. 2014. "Under-Secretary-General for Humanitarian Affairs and Emergency Relief Coordinator, Valerie Amos Press Remarks on South Sudan – Juba, 29 January 2014." Accessed July 10, 2014. http://reliefweb.int/report/south-sudan/under-secretary-general-huma nitarian-affairs-and-emergency-relief-coordinator

United Nations, Security Council. 2009. Resolution 1894/2009, S/RES/1894 (11 November 2009). Available from undocs.org/S/RES/1894. Accessed February 12, 2014.

United Nations, Security Council 2012a. *Responsibility to Protect: Timely and Decisive Response: Report of the Secretary-General*, A/66/874 (July 25, 2012), Available from undocs.org/A/66/874.

United Nations, Security Council. 2012b. "Report of the Secretary General on the Protection of Civilians in Armed Conflict," S/2012/376 (May 22, 2012). Available from undocs.org/S/2012/376. Accessed February 12, 2014.

United Nations, Security Council. 2013. *State Responsibility and Prevention: Report of the Secretary-General*, A/67/929 (July 9, 2013). Available from undocs.org/A/67/ 929. Accessed February 12, 2014.

Valencia, Nick. 2010. "Juarez Counts 3,000th Homicide of 2010." CNN, December 15. Accessed July 7, 2014. www.cnn.com/2010/WORLD/americas/12 /15/mexico.juarez.homicides/index.html

Valentino, Benjamin. 2004. *Final Solutions: Mass Killing and Genocide in the Twentieth Century*. Ithaca, NY and London: Cornell University Press.

Waller, James. 2002. *Becoming Evil: How Ordinary People Commit Genocide*. New York: Oxford University Press.

Western, Jon, and Joshua Goldstein. 2011. "Humanitarian Intervention Comes of Age: Lessons from Somalia to Libya." *Foreign Affairs*, November/December. Accessed February 12, 2014. www.foreignaffairs.com/articles/136502/jon-western-and-joshua-s-goldstein/humanitarian-intervention-comes-of-age

3 Operationalizing the "Atrocity Prevention Lens": Making Prevention a Living Reality

Alex J. Bellamy

In his closing remarks to the 2012 informal interactive dialogue of the United Nations General Assembly on the Responsibility to Protect (R2P), UN Deputy Secretary-General, Jan Eliasson called for the prevention of genocide and mass atrocities to be made a "living reality." Three years earlier, in his first report on implementing R2P, the Secretary-General had described "the ultimate purpose of the responsibility to protect" as being "to save lives by preventing the most egregious mass violations of human rights."[1] Indeed, since the adoption of R2P at the 2005 World Summit, there have been many generic calls for a focus on the prevention of genocide, war crimes, ethnic cleansing, and crimes against humanity (hereafter *genocide and mass atrocities*). This is unsurprising, given that the world's commitment to R2P included a specific call for the *prevention* of these crimes. Since 2009, UN Member States of all types and from every region have voiced their support in the General Assembly for the prevention of genocide and mass atrocities, recognizing that it not only saves lives but also reduces the need for enforcement further down the line. This sentiment echoes views expressed in the academy, which largely agrees that prevention is far better than cure.[2]

But although there is broad agreement about the normative and practical imperative of preventing genocide and mass atrocities, much less is understood about how this might be achieved in practice. Although work examining the incorporation of genocide and mass atrocity prevention into US foreign and defense policy has progressed apace,[3] relatively little attention has been paid to the question of how to implement the preventive

---

[1] Ban Ki-moon, *Implementing the Responsibility to Protect. Report of the Secretary-General*, A/63/677, January 12, 2009, para. 67.

[2] Eli Stamnes, "Speaking R2P and the Prevention of Mass Atrocities," *Global Responsibility to Protect*, 1(1):71 (2009); and Lawrence Woocher, "Developing a Strategy, Methods and Tools for Genocide Early Warning, Report for the Office of the Special Adviser to the UN Secretary-General on the Prevention of Genocide," September 26, 2006.

[3] Genocide Prevention Task Force, *Preventing Genocide: A Blueprint for US Policymakers* (Washington, DC: US Holocaust Museum and US Institute of Peace, 2008) and Bruce Jentleson, "The Obama Administration and R2P: Progress, Problems and Process," *Global Responsibility to Protect* 4(4) (2012).

aspects of R2P more generally and less still to the specific role played by pivotal international organizations such as the UN.[4] To date, academic work on the UN's role has tended to focus, understandably, on early warning and assessment,[5] although an emerging body of work examines the role of the system's human rights mechanisms in helping to prevent genocide and mass atrocities.[6] Thus far, the UN itself has focused on developing its mandate and capacity for early warning and assessment, as well as on the establishment of a convening authority designed to facilitate timely advice in crisis situations. The UN has also begun preliminary work, under the auspices of the Framework Team's Experts Reference Group on Prevention, on system-wide approaches to genocide and mass atrocity prevention.[7]

This chapter outlines one potential practical approach to prevention that might be adopted by organizations with protection mandates or individual states that are committed to implementing R2P: the mainstreaming of an "atrocity prevention lens." By "atrocity prevention lens," I mean the infusion of atrocity-specific analysis and perspective into existing policy frameworks and the tailoring of existing policies and activities to address causes of risk and escalation, support sources of resilience, and prepare policymakers and field missions for future crises and contingencies. This might be done by national governments,[8] regional or subregional arrangements, the UN, and nongovernmental organizations.

The central argument offered in this chapter is that the atrocity prevention lens provides a feasible way of improving the international community's capacity to prevent genocide and mass atrocities that overcomes some of the principal limitations and obstacles that have tended to confront prevention in practice up to now. It proceeds in two parts. The first briefly examines some of the key limitations and obstacles to the successful prevention of genocide and mass atrocities. The second part outlines the principal elements of the

---

[4] Exceptions include Stamnes, "Speaking R2P" and Lawrence Woocher, "The Responsibility to Prevent: Towards a Strategy," in W. Andy Knight and Frazer Egerton (eds.), *Routledge Handbook on the Responsibility to Protect* (London: Routledge, 2012).

[5] Ban Ki-moon, *Early Warning, Assessment and the Responsibility to Protect, Report of the Secretary-General*, A/64/864, July 14, 2010; Woocher, "Developing a Strategy."

[6] Jacob Blaustein Institute for the Advancement of Human Rights, *Compilation of Risk Factors and Legal Norms for the Prevention of Genocide* (New York: Jacob Blaustein Institute, 2011).

[7] Alex J. Bellamy, "United Nations Action in Sri Lanka and the Responsibility to Protect," Global Centre for the Responsibility to Protect Occasional Paper, 2013.

[8] The U.S. Atrocity Prevention Board is a good example, and ideas about potential roles for national "R2P Focal Points" are another. See Jentleson, "Obama Administration and R2P"; Global Centre for the Responsibility to Protect/Stanley Foundation. "Preparatory Workshop for the Second R2P Focal Points Meeting," Policy Memo, March 12, 2012; and Alex J. Bellamy, "The Responsibility to Protect: Towards a Living Reality," report for the UN Association of the UK, 2013.

atrocity prevention lens and describes how this approach relates to, or overcomes, the issues identified in the first part.

3.1.   Operationalizing Prevention: Limits and Obstacles

"The perfect is the enemy of the good." Attempts to bridge the gap between the theory and practice of atrocity prevention need to be realistic about the practical limitations and obstacles that they confront. Some of the most significant are created by the twin realities of a world of sovereign states and an age of financial austerity.

The international community is comprised of sovereign states that pursue their own interests (however defined), privilege domestic over foreign concerns, and generally cherish their legal right to determine their own affairs. As Edward Luck pointed out, "in the nation-state era there will be limits to both the practicality and the wisdom of formally breaching the proper boundaries of sovereignty."[9] Practical approaches to prevention have to take this reality as their starting point. In the foreseeable future, states are not likely to endorse limits on their sovereignty. Nor are they going to become cosmopolitans or "good international citizens" overnight. Nor are they likely to reconcile their different interests and perspectives. It is imperative, therefore, to understand and work with the norms, politics, interests, rules, priorities, values, and institutions of the world as it is. Putative "remedies," such as reforming the Security Council, establishing a UN army, restructuring the world economy, persuading states to risk an unlimited number of their citizens and money in protecting strangers from potential future harm may (or may not, each is highly contestable) be laudable goals in themselves, but they are unlikely to make a positive contribution to preventing genocide and mass atrocities any time soon. Progress in the here and now should not be made hostage to potential future reforms to the very structure of international relations.

It is also difficult to overestimate the significance of financial austerity. Many major donors to the UN have cut their own national budgets and imposed austerity measures on their own populations. Unsurprisingly, the UN is also expected to cut its budget – by around $100 million in 2013. The Secretary-General has asked the whole system to find savings, principally through cuts to personnel. He has also significantly reduced the budget for Special Political Missions. Within the peacekeeping field, it is widely understood that the UN has reached its capacity in terms of the number of personnel it can financially support. The harsh financial reality, therefore, is that, in the near term, the

---

[9] Edward C. Luck, "Sovereignty, Choice and the Responsibility to Protect," *Global Responsibility to Protect* 1(1): 20–21 (2009).

prevention of genocide and mass atrocities will have to be relatively cost-neutral. Practical strategies for prevention therefore need to focus on making better use of existing capacities.

A third generic limit is the relatively limited influence that outsiders have on the conflicts that give rise to genocide and mass atrocities. Although concerted international action can sometimes prevent mass atrocities (e.g., Cote d'Ivoire, Kenya, Libya), the primary reason as to why some countries with relatively high levels of risk avoid such crimes typically rests within the country itself.[10] International efforts can facilitate prevention where there is genuine local will and some degree of capacity, but the so-called structural or root causes of genocide and mass atrocities are often deeply ingrained in societies, economies, and national institutions. Although outsiders can play important enabling and facilitative roles, foreign assistance cannot by itself achieve structural change except through massive interventions that are rarely contemplated.[11] Well-targeted programs can sometimes support local sources of resilience to genocide and mass atrocities, but they cannot manufacture resilience out of thin air.

At the later stages of a crisis, when genocide and mass atrocities are imminent or have already been committed, international actors may provide mediation or might attempt to influence events on the ground by using punishments and incentives to change the local leadership's assessment of the likely costs and benefits of different courses of action. Mediation and diplomacy are often very challenging at this late stage of a crisis, and the international community has sometimes found it difficult to credibly communicate its resolve.[12] Typically, armed groups turn to atrocities only after other means have been tried and found wanting.[13] In such situations, where groups have tried and failed to satisfy their interests, even exceptionally skilled mediators will find it difficult to succeed until a mutually hurting stalemate is reached.[14] The failed international response to the escalating crisis in Syria in 2011–12 provides one recent example where international mediation was stymied by the fact that the government and, to some extent, elements of the rebel movement believed that they could satisfy their interests

---

[10] Stephen McLoughlin and Deborah Mayersen, "Reconsidering Root Causes: A New Framework for the Structural Prevention of Genocide and Mass Atrocities," in Bert Ingelaere, Stephan Parmentier, Jacques Haers, and Barbara Segaert, eds., *Genocide, Risk and Resilience: An Interdisciplinary Approach* (Basingstoke: Palgrave).

[11] See Paul Collier, *War, Guns, & Votes: Democracy in Dangerous Places* (London: The Bodley Head, 2009).

[12] Alex J. Bellamy, *Massacres and Morality: Mass Atrocities in an Age of Civilian Immunity* (Oxford: Oxford University Press, 2012).

[13] Daniel Chirot and Clark McCauley, *Why Not Kill Them All? The Logic and Prevention of Mass Political Murder* (Princeton, NJ: Princeton University Press, 2006).

[14] I. William Zartman, "The Timing of Peace Initiatives: Hurting Stalemates and Ripe Moments." *Global Review of Ethnopolitics* 1(1): 8–18 (2001).

better through violence than through negotiations and where international efforts failed to alter those calculations.

At least two important points flow from this. First, modesty about the capacity of international actors to prevent genocide and mass atrocities is required. "Ending mass atrocities once and for all" is a task that will be achieved primarily *within* states and societies themselves, albeit with international assistance, and not within a short space of time. Second, and as a result of this, prevention should be attuned to local conditions. International actions should be guided by detailed understandings of local conditions, including local sources of resilience to underlying risk. To paraphrase Alex de Waal in a different context, prevention needs to operate through the local "political marketplace."[15] Those who are in the business of preventing genocide and mass atrocities "ignore vernacular politics, to the detriment of the countries they leave at the end of their contracts."[16]

In addition to these generic limitations – state sovereignty, fiscal austerity, and limited influence – the practice of genocide and mass atrocity prevention confronts some of its own inherent challenges. Perhaps the most fundamental is the question of comprehensiveness – the problem that preventive action could be interpreted to mean almost anything, thus making it almost impossible to translate into a practical strategy.

According to Edward Luck, the UN Secretary-General's first Special Adviser on R2P, prevention confronts a "dilemma of comprehensiveness." The dilemma stems from the fact that the prevention agenda is so broad that it "appears as if the advocates of prevention have tried to make it be all things to all people; but in the process it could end up meaning very little to anybody."[17] The problem may actually be more profound than this because it is not so much that advocates have made the requirements of prevention *appear* so wide and comprehensive as that scholarship has demonstrated a bewildering range of structural and direct *causes* of violent conflict and thus genocide and mass atrocities. One report, for example, identified fifty root causes of war.[18] Some of the most significant factors associated with heightened risk of civil war, genocide, and mass atrocities are deep social structures. For example, countless statistical studies have demonstrated that economic wealth and inequality are related to the risk of armed conflict, genocide, and mass atrocities. Likewise, regime type and past histories of genocide and mass atrocities are also related statistically to the risk of these

---

[15] Alex de Waal, June 24, "Dollarised," *London Review of Books*, 32(12) (2010).

[16] de Waal, "Dollarised."

[17] Edward Luck, "Prevention: Theory and Practice," in Fen Osler Hampson and David Malone, eds., *From Reaction to Conflict Prevention: Opportunities for the UN System* (Boulder, CO: Lynne Rienner, 2001), 256.

[18] Hague Agenda, *The Hague Appeal for Peace*, 1999.

crimes being committed again.[19] That being so, a comprehensive approach to prevention would seem to demand a political and economic commitment to a potentially vast experiment of social engineering. As Benjamin Valentino has pointed out, advocates of prevention may be right to argue that prevention is cheaper than reaction when judged from the perspective of individual conflict-ridden countries (as argued by the Carnegie Commission in 1997[20]), but when one factors in the need to do prevention *everywhere* because we do not know in advance where genocide and mass atrocities will occur, then the economic cost associated with a comprehensive approach to prevention becomes very great indeed.[21]

Given this, it is not surprising that the better-established theory and practice of *conflict* prevention is suffused with uncertainty about the field's limits. For diplomats and those focused on current crises, conflict prevention tends to be associated with early warning, preventive diplomacy, and crisis management – the "direct preventers" aimed at tackling the immediate causes of conflict. Even here, though, conflict prevention can involve coercive diplomacy, economic considerations such as sanctions, trade, humanitarian and financial aid, military measures such as deterrence, embargoes, peacekeeping, and a variety of legal measures.[22] Proponents of this "narrow" view of prevention are quite critical of broader conceptions. Gareth Evans, for example, argues that atrocity prevention should be narrowly construed to distinguish it from the UN's other thematic agendas (conflict prevention, human rights, protection of civilians, etc.).[23] For Evans, "if too much is bundled under the R2P banner, we run the risk of diluting its capacity to mobilize in the cases where it is really needed."[24] However, whereas "narrow" prevention can reduce imminent escalation to violent conflict, it cannot by itself prevent the emergence of violent disputes in the first place and is not likely to succeed in

[margin note: not every conflict. mother advertise? murder]

---

[19] Barbara Harff, "No Lessons Learned from the Holocaust? Assessing Risks of Genocide and Political Mass Murder Since 1955," *American Political Science Review* 97(1): 57–73 (2003); and Barbara Harff, "How to Use Risk Assessment and Early Warning in the Prevention and De-Escalation of Genocide and Other Mass Atrocities," *Global Responsibility to Protect*, 1(4).

[20] Carnegie Commission on Preventing Deadly Conflict. *Preventing Deadly Conflict – Final Report* (Washington, DC: Carnegie Commission on Preventing Deadly Conflict, 1997).

[21] Benjamin Valentino, "The True Costs of Humanitarian Intervention: The Hard Truth about a Noble Notion," *Foreign Affairs* (November/December 2011).

[22] See Carnegie Commission, *Preventing Deadly Conflict*, Peter Wallensteen, ed., *Preventing Future Conflicts: Past Record and Future Challenges* (Uppsala: Uppsala University, 1998), and I. William Zartman, *Preventive Negotiation* (Lanham, MD: Rowman and Littlefield, 2001).

[23] Gareth Evans, "The Responsibility to Protect and International Affairs: Where to From Here?" keynote lecture at the Australian Catholic University, Melbourne (November 27, 2009). Also International Peace Institute. 2009. "Conflict Prevention and the Responsibility to Protect," IPI Blue Papers, No. 7.

[24] Evans, "The Responsibility to Protect and International Affairs."

every case.[25] Meeting these challenges requires action to address the "structural" factors that give rise to violent disputes resulting in genocide and mass atrocities.[26] Economic development and inequality reduction, good governance, human and minority rights, security sector reform, and the rule of law are seen as crucial components of this agenda.[27]

An additional problem for genocide and mass atrocity prevention is that there is little clarity about its relationship to existing work on conflict prevention, economic development, democratization, rule of law, human rights, peacebuilding, transitional justice, and other issues. Critics complain that "the atrocity and genocide prevention agendas do not offer appreciably new approaches to established response agendas outside of a rationale for armed intervention."[28] As a result, "instead of infusing an atrocities-prevention lens into pre-existing development and democratization programs, these and other efforts to promote early action to prevent atrocities or genocide have unleashed a new and ill-defined paradigm for military intervention."[29]

I have written elsewhere about the dangers of conflating conflict prevention with genocide and mass atrocity prevention. The principal concerns are that (1) conflict prevention and atrocity prevention have different purposes. Whereas the former tries to find a mutually agreeable settlement, the latter is focused on dissuading an actor from committing atrocities. (2) Conflict prevention strategies are sometimes unsuited to the prevention of mass atrocities, for example, when the former dictates that perpetrators and victims be treated similarly. (3) Conflict prevention may encourage atrocities by groups wanting to "earn" a seat at the table.[30] Moreover, not every episode of genocide and mass atrocity occurs within a context of armed conflict (postelection violence in Kenya, communal violence in Kyrgyzstan, and the early atrocities

---

[25] Genocide Prevention Task Force, *Preventing Genocide*; David A. Hamburg, *Preventing Genocide: Practical Steps Toward Early Detection and Effective Action*, revised edition (New York: Paradigm Publishers, 2010); Harff, "No Lessons Learned"; Harff, "How to Use Risk Assessment"; Office of the Special Advisor for the Prevention of Genocide, "Analysis Framework," UN (2011); Ervin Staub, *Overcoming Evil: Genocide, Violent Conflict and Terrorism* (Oxford: Oxford University Press, 2011); I. William Zartman, "Preventing Identity Conflicts Leading to Genocide and Mass Killings," report for the International Peace Institute in cooperation with the UN Office of the Special Adviser on the Prevention of Genocide (2011).

[26] See, for instance, Paul Collier et al., *Breaking the Conflict Trap: Civil War and Development Policy* (Oxford: Oxford University Press/World Bank, 2003).

[27] Hugh Miall, "Global Governance and Conflict Prevention," in Fergal Cochrane, Rosaleen Duffy, and Jan Selby, eds., *Global Governance, Conflict and Resistance* (Houndmills: Palgrave, 2003), 59–77.

[28] Alex de Waal, Jens Meierhenrich, and Bridget Conley-Zilkic, "How Mass Atrocities End: An Evidence Based Counter Narrative," *Fletcher Forum of World Affairs* (January 31, 2012).

[29] Ibid.

[30] Alex J. Bellamy, "Mass Atrocities and Armed Conflict: Links, Distinctions and Implications for the Responsibility to Protect," Policy Brief for the Stanley Foundation.

in Syria are recent cases in point), and not every armed conflict triggers genocide or mass atrocities (the decade-long civil war in Nepal is a good recent example).

But although genocide and mass atrocity prevention is not synonymous with conflict prevention, it is not entirely separate either. Although these crimes sometimes occur outside a context of armed conflict, most are committed in the course of such conflicts.[31] Thus, even traditional conflict prevention can contribute to the prevention of genocide and mass atrocities by reducing the incidence of armed conflict. The same might be said of the other thematic agendas listed in the previous paragraph. Even without self-consciously addressing genocide and mass atrocities, these agendas contribute to prevention by addressing some of the factors associated with heightened risk. Given this, and the political and financial constraints described earlier, it would make little sense to advocate an approach to prevention that stood entirely apart from this existing work. Indeed, the degree of overlap has led some analysts, including the UN Secretary-General's current Special Adviser on R2P Jennifer Welsh to question the added value of extending the genocide and mass atrocity prevention lens into these areas.[32]

Rather than understanding the overlap between genocide and mass atrocity prevention and other areas of work as a sign of weakness, however, the atrocity prevention lens approach takes it as a practical foundation on which to build. There are at least four reasons for this. First, an atrocity prevention perspective cannot be dispensed with because, as I noted earlier, existing frameworks are unsuited to the prevention of genocide and mass atrocities and may sometimes prove counterproductive. Second, precisely because there is overlap between atrocity prevention and other areas of work, international actions might inadvertently create or exacerbate the risk of genocide and mass atrocities or undermine local sources of resilience. An atrocity prevention lens is critical to the task of reducing these unintended consequences. Third, by not developing an atrocity-specific perspective, organizations would limit the preventive potential of their existing work. As the UN Secretary-General has made clear, it is important for policymakers to understand that they have a broad range of options available to them and that they have the flexibility to utilize them in ways appropriate to specific contexts.[33] In most cases involving the prevention of genocide and mass atrocities, policymakers are presented with only limited options. Expanding the range of potential options would increase

---

[31] Bellamy, "Mass Atrocities."

[32] Jennifer Welsh, Ruben Reike, and Serena Sharma, "Operationalizing the Responsibility to Protect," Ethics, Law and Armed Conflict Policy Paper (Oxford: Oxford University Press, 2012).

[33] Ban, *Implementing the Responsibility to Protect*, 2.

the likelihood of determined preventive action and the world's capacity to tailor responses to particular circumstances. Fourth, the fact that there is overlap means that there is no need to overlay new large bureaucracies to support the prevention of genocide and mass atrocities. This is especially important given the contemporary politics of austerity mentioned earlier.

In the introduction, I observed that there was a gap between the rhetoric and practice of genocide and mass atrocity prevention. That gap may, in part, be due to the limits and obstacles described in this section. On the one hand, there are generic factors that limit what might be realistically achieved – an international community of sovereign states, an economic context of austerity, and the limited capacity of outsiders to influence events within countries. On the other hand, the prevention of genocide and mass atrocities faces a series of specific obstacles relating to the "dilemma of comprehensiveness" and the relationship between genocide and mass atrocity prevention and other international policy agendas. With these conditions in mind, the next section outlines an atrocity prevention lens approach to developing the prevention of genocide and mass atrocities.

3.2.   The Atrocity Prevention Lens

The atrocity prevention lens is an approach that focuses on injecting atrocity prevention considerations into existing policies, programs, and capabilities and, when necessary, "convening" or "coordinating" these assets for prevention purposes. Here, I have in mind something along the lines of the "convening authority" granted to the UN's Office on Genocide Prevention and R2P in 2010, but not necessarily that specific configuration because there are other ways of achieving the same effect. The lens might be thought of as establishing an atrocity prevention "seat" at the policy table to ensure that the atrocity prevention perspective is included in deliberations about how to engage with a particular country. It should not be expected that the atrocity prevention voice will always prevail in complex discussions about how to set and pursue an organization's priorities, but it is imperative that the perspective is aired and taken into account by decision makers. In some circumstances, where genocide and mass atrocities are imminently apprehended, it may indeed be necessary to prioritize atrocity prevention. For this reason, the "lens" should be infused with some form of "convening" or "coordinating" capability.

In physical terms, the atrocity prevention lens is essentially an analytical and convening capability. It aims to maximize the positive contribution of an organization's existing work to genocide and mass atrocity prevention, identify and monitor potential risks, plan for future contingencies, and convene "whole-of-organization" responses to imminent dangers. The additional direct resources needed to operationalize the "lens" are very modest – either the appointment of a single person in a mission or office charged with providing the atrocity prevention perspective, the establishment of a small office capable of providing this perspective across missions and departments, or – perhaps more likely in large organizations – a combination of both. Ideally, the atrocity prevention lens would be the responsibility of a designated official or office and not simply one of many responsibilities assigned to an official or office. This is important because, for the model to work, it is imperative that a clear and unadulterated atrocity prevention perspective is brought to the policy table. It is worth noting in this respect that a number of recent studies and reports, including that of the Secretary-General's Internal Review Panel on the UN's actions in Sri Lanka, have shown that the combination of several responsibilities under a single bureaucratic roof – so-called *double-hatting* – can dilute understandings of responsibility and confuse lines of authority.[34]

For the atrocity prevention lens to work most effectively, those given carriage of it must feel a strong sense of ownership and a professional obligation to tell others within the organization what they *need* to hear about the relevant risks, not what they *want* to hear.[35] The enduring problem of diffused responsibility for protection was one of the central themes of the 2012 report of the Secretary-General's Internal Review Panel on the UN's actions in Sri Lanka. The report found that because the UN relied on the cooperation of the Sri Lankan government for humanitarian access, among other things, it was reluctant to publish information about civilian casualties caused by government actions or voice concerns about the government's actions. In a context of mounting civilian casualties and abundant evidence of noncompliance with International Humanitarian Law, no part of the UN Country Team in Sri Lanka assumed responsibility for protection. The Panel concluded that, "there was a continued reluctance among UN Country Team institutions to stand up for the rights of the people they were mandated to assist. In Colombo, some senior staff did not perceive the prevention of killing of civilians as their responsibility" (para. 76). One of the principal purposes of the atrocity prevention lens is to ensure that *somebody* within an organization that has a mandate or interest in protection has a clearly understood responsibility for the prevention of genocide and mass atrocities.

---

[34] *Report of the Secretary-General's Internal Review Panel on United Nations Action in Sri Lanka* (November 2012). More broadly, see Victoria Metcalfe, Alison Giffen, and Samir Elhawary, "UN Integration and Humanitarian Space: An Independent Study Commissioned by the UN Integration Steering Group," Stimson Center/Humanitarian Policy Group (December 2011).

[35] This, of course, had been one of the central arguments of the 2000 Brahimi report on UN peacekeeping. The UN's 2012 Internal Review Panel on Sri Lanka also made this point.

Because the atrocity prevention lens focuses on working through existing programs and activities rather than developing wholly new ones, the approach emphasizes the importance of *tailoring* existing work to individual situations. In other words, the atrocity prevention lens finds ways of utilizing ongoing forms of engagement and assistance to strengthen the prevention of genocide and mass atrocities.

What, precisely, would an atrocity prevention lens look like? Although the precise practical configuration of the approach depends on the bureaucratic setting in which it is employed and will thus vary from organization to organization, we can sketch out the approach's parameters in necessarily broad terms. Doing so, we might usefully distinguish two modes of action. The first relate to "normal" country situations, where the risk of genocide and mass atrocities is not thought to be imminent although some of the risk factors are present. The second comes into play in situations of imminent danger. In these situations, a "convening" or "coordinating" capacity is added to the normal analytical and advisory work of the lens.

Before explaining in more detail how the atrocity prevention lens might work in practice, it is worth briefly reflecting on how even these modest changes might impact on policy. Consider, for example, the case of Rwanda in 1994. Taking one step back, the atrocity prevention lens could have advised negotiators at Arusha who mediated the peace accord that led to Rwanda's ill-fated power-sharing deal about some of the pitfalls of their approach and on the need to introduce safeguards.

Between the Arusha accords and the genocide, there was ample evidence of preparation, including publicly broadcast hate speech and incitement as well as embedded practices of discrimination and abuse and a recent history punctuated by mass atrocities. On the basis of this publicly available information alone, any office given carriage of the atrocity prevention lens would have been alerting others of the risks in Rwanda and watching developments there closely. It could also have provided advice on how the UN peacekeeping mission and various other organizations in Rwanda might have shaped their policies to address the risks of genocide more directly. Any such "atrocity prevention" office within the UN system would have established information channels to gather information from the organization's mission in the field, UN Assistance Mission for Rwanda (UNAMIR). Thus, before the situation began to deteriorate, officials at both UN headquarters and in the field mission would have been more sensitized to the risks. In that context, the arrival of General Dallaire's famous cable to UN headquarters that detailed a specific threat of genocide would have created much more of a stir. An office charged with the prevention of genocide and mass atrocities, whose analysts were already advising of heightened risk in Rwanda and were communicating regularly with the field mission, would have received a copy of the cable and given it a very different interpretation to the one it was given by the Department of Peacekeeping Operations (DPKO). In such a situation, it might be expected that those with carriage of the lens would have communicated their advice directly to the Secretary-General. This may have resulted in Dallaire being given different instructions. It may also have resulted in the Secretary-General deciding to share the intelligence with members of the Security Council.

Even if no different action had been taken at this point, perhaps because decision makers had decided to privilege the DPKO's assessment over that of the atrocity prevention lens, once the genocide began, it would have done so in a context of a UN system, including the Secretary-General and possibly members of the Security Council, sensitized to the threat of genocide in Rwanda. In this context, the UN Secretariat could be expected to have been much quicker to identify what was happening in Rwanda as genocide. For their part, hesitant Member States would have had much less scope for obfuscation and activist Member States much more ammunition with which to argue the case for a timely and decisive response.

In short, then, the atrocity prevention lens could have changed things in Rwanda at any or all of the three stages in the crisis: at the Arusha peace accords, by highlighting some of the problems and advising on safeguards; prior to the genocide, by advising on how UNAMIR and others could better direct their activities to genocide prevention and by sensitizing UN officials and Member States to the risks; and in the first few days of the genocide, by helping to clarify what was actually happening and providing analysis and information to support activist states. Of course, none of these might have prevented the genocide outright, but they may well have encouraged a more sensitive approach to the Arusha accords and their implementation and a swift response to the genocide.

3.2.1.   *"Normal" Mode: Analysis and Support for Country Engagement*

In "normal" situations, where there is no immediate risk of genocide and mass atrocities but where some of factors associated with underlying risk may nevertheless be present, the principal role of the atrocity prevention lens would be to provide advice relating to how an organization's engagement with the country might be used to further the prevention of genocide and mass atrocities, usually by helping to reinforce local sources of resilience. In these contexts, international engagement is likely to be development-led, led by humanitarian concerns, led by trade and diplomatic concerns, or led by some combination of the three. In these situations, the lens would fulfill four primary functions.

First, it would *provide o-going assessment of the situation with regards to the risk of genocide and mass atrocity*. The first responsibility of the atrocity prevention lens is to provide other members of the organization with a detailed and current understanding of the situation in which they are operating from the perspective of genocide and mass atrocities prevention. Because the atrocity prevention lens focuses on adapting existing policies and activities to local needs and circumstances, the starting point must be a clear and detailed understanding of the local situation. Country assessments based on rigorous frameworks should be employed to identify local sources of risk, but these should be sufficiently flexible to accommodate the specific circumstances of individual countries. As the UN Secretary-General noted in his 2010 report on "Early Warning and Assessment," analysis of country situations needs to provide a "moving picture," not a one-off snapshot.[36] Being a moving picture, assessments need not always emphasize the *prediction* of future genocide and mass atrocities. Instead, their principal purpose is to build situational awareness and identify specific sources of risk and potential sites of escalation. In some conditions, however, such as prior to an election or at the onset of civil strife, assessments might examine the likely trajectory of events as a guide to policy and contingency planning.

To ensure that information is transmitted to senior decision makers in a timely fashion, it is imperative that officials with responsibility for atrocity prevention have the capacity to communicate threats and warnings *directly* to the organization's leadership. Of course, such access should be used very sparingly. The credibility and legitimacy of the atrocity prevention lens rests on the accuracy of its advice, and few things would be more damaging that sounding the alarm at the highest levels without excellent cause.

Second, it would *identify local sources of resilience that policies and programs might impact upon or support*. To date, early warning assessments have tended to focus only on the sources of risk.[37] They have not identified the local factors that might help to mitigate these risks. As a result, analysts have been hard pressed to explain why some countries that exhibit underlying risk succumb to mass violence whereas others that exhibit an equal or sometimes greater level of risk appear to avoid mass killing, thus leading the UN Secretary-General to call for further research on this topic.[38] Situational assessments provide only part of the picture if they focus only on risk and not on the local sources of resilience. Evidence deduced from observations in

---

[36] Ban, *Early Warning and Assessment*.

[37] Mcloughlin and Mayersen, "Reconsidering Root Causes." This idea originated in McLoughlin's doctoral thesis.

[38] Leading the Secretary-General to call for more research on precisely this question. Ban, *Implementing the Responsibility to Protect*.

some of those countries suggests that a diverse range of factors might foster national resilience to genocide and mass atrocities. These include:

- Extreme authoritarianism (which inhibits the emergence of organized opposition, as in North Korea);
- The fragmentation of political authority (which makes it difficult to build a coalition in support of atrocities, as in Iran);
- The pursuit of equality between ethnic groups at the expense of social goods such as economic efficiency (which prevents the emergence of striking horizontal inequalities, as in Tanzania);
- Strong and relatively independent judiciaries (which can sometimes prevent or stymie the worst abuses by state officials, as in Botswana);
- Opposition groups that have dedicated themselves to nonviolence (which makes it difficult for governments to justify widespread open violence, as in the case of Zimbabwe);
- Inspired political leadership willing to sacrifice narrow self-interest in order to avoid violent conflict (as in the case of Zambia's transition to democracy).

Given my earlier points about the limited influence wielded by external actors, international efforts in support of prevention are likely to be both more efficient (delivering more added value for equal or less investment) and effective (better able to prevent genocide and mass atrocities) if they are directed wherever possible to supporting local sources of resilience. The focus on local resilience implies a different ethos to that of more traditional conceptions of structural prevention. The latter has tended to assume that outsiders know which deep structures give rise to violent conflict and which do not in any given society and to foster interventions that support the former. By contrast, a focus on resilience starts with an understanding of the *local* institutions, dynamics, groups, individuals, and other factors that provide bulwarks against genocide and mass atrocities and asks what can be done to support these already existing sources of strength in a way that does not impose particular prevention templates on individual situations.

If the first job of the atrocity prevention lens is to inform policymakers on where and what the relevant risks are, the second is to advise them about the local people, groups, institutions, and factors that help mitigate those risks and that may benefit from external support. This information could be used to adjust existing work to improve its contribution to prevention, as well as informing a more holistic understanding of the context that might prove significant should a crisis emerge.

Third, it would *identify and provide advice about the potential or actual unintended consequences of programs and policies*. The atrocity prevention lens should be double-faced, looking outward to situations containing risk and inward at the organization's own policies and actions. External actors need to ensure that they do not inadvertently increase the risks associated with genocide and mass atrocities or undermine local sources of resilience. Unfortunately, history offers up several cases in which international actions have inadvertently increased risk: in the late 1980s, international demands for debt repayment sent Yugoslavia into an economic decline from which it never recovered; in the early 1990s, structural economic reforms increased inequalities in Rwanda, sharpening ethnic divisions there, and a poorly supported power-sharing agreement paved the way to genocide; international relief efforts in eastern Zaire after the Rwandan genocide helped sustain that country's *genocidaires* and provoked a Rwandan intervention that triggered a continental calamity in what soon became the Democratic Republic of the Congo (DRC); an internationally brokered referendum in East Timor triggered a wave of killing and ethnic cleansing by pro-Indonesia militia; and, most recently, the internationally assisted collapse of the Gaddafi regime in Libya facilitated the flow of arms and fighters to the Tuareg rebellion in Mali.

Harm mitigation is an important part of atrocity prevention, and it is imperative that organizations with prevention mandates not exacerbate already existing risks through the unintended consequences of their actions. This requires a form of "due diligence" of the type already employed by some organizations operating in conflict situations. Known as "conflict sensitivity," some government programs that deliver aid in conflict settings (e.g., USAID and the UK's Department for International Development) employ frameworks to assess the impact of their aid on the social environment. It is important that such work is done on a systematic basis and, owing to the differences between conflict and atrocity prevention described earlier, that it utilize an atrocity-specific framework.

Unintended negative consequences are not, however, limited exclusively to effects on sources of risk. External actors might also inadvertently weaken local sources of resilience. This, too, should be factored into any analysis. Potential examples include internationally sponsored economic strategies that prioritize growth but increase horizontal inequalities, conflict resolution strategies that give armed groups a seat at the table but that exclude and marginalize peaceful groups, coercive inducement strategies that target states but that politically weaken local moderates, and bureaucratic or legal reform strategies that inadvertently concentrate political authority. Although advice stemming from this analysis should be forward looking, it should also be informed by careful assessments of the consequences of past policies and actions. Ideally, both aspects of this analysis should be undertaken on an ongoing basis.

Fourth, it would *provide information about factors that could trigger or escalate a crisis that may give rise to genocide and mass atrocities and conduct preliminary planning for potential contingencies.* That the 2007 elections in Kenya gave rise to communal violence and atrocities came as little surprise to experts on the country.[39] In 2010, it was widely understood among those conversant with the situation in Sri Lanka that the resumption of armed conflict would trigger war crimes and ethnic cleansing. Indeed, in 2007, the Special Representative of the Secretary-General on the Human Rights of Internally Displaced Persons had reported as much.[40] Despite evident understanding of both the underlying risks of mass atrocities and the likely triggers, in neither of these cases was contingency planning conducted to ensure that relevant organizations knew how best to respond should the risks become manifest. In the Sri Lankan case, this left the UN responding to a major protection crisis with a Country Team configured for economic development and without expertise in relation to either protection or conducting operations in a conflict environment.[41] As well as events within the country itself, potential triggers could come from exogenous sources, as in the case of the escalation of the Tuareg rebellion in Mali, which was facilitated to some extent by the downfall of Gadhafi's regime in Libya.

The atrocity prevention lens should sensitize decision makers to the fact that certain "events" might cause an escalation toward genocide and mass atrocities. That is not to say that these events (e.g., elections) ought to be avoided outright, but it does mean that organizations in the business of atrocity prevention need to develop and implement strategies to help a country navigate the event without triggering conflict and escalation. International actions prior to and during the 2011 South Sudanese referendum on independence and the 2013 elections in Kenya – both of which were identified in advance as potential triggers for violence – provide examples of the sort of multifaceted approaches needed to achieve this effect.

When used outside a context of imminent emergency, therefore, the atrocity prevention lens is primarily concerned with building situational awareness in relation to the sources of risk of genocide and mass atrocities and resilience to them and with providing advice on the situation and context, the likely impact of policies and programs, ways in which engagement might be tailored to better serve prevention goals, and potential future triggers of escalation and contingencies. The overarching purposes of this analysis and advice are to (1) strengthen the capacity of existing programs of work in areas such as development, peacebuilding, human rights, rule of law, political rights,

---

[39] See Serena K. Sharma, "The 2007–08 Post Election Crisis in Kenya: A Success Story for the Responsibility to Protect?" in Julia Hoffmann and Andre Nollkaemper, eds., *Responsibility to Protect: From Principle to Practice* (Amsterdam: Pallas Publications, 2012).
[40] Internal Panel on the UN Action in Sri Lanka, para. 7.
[41] *Internal Review Panel Report on UN Action in Sri Lanka.*

bureaucratic organization, and humanitarianism as appropriate to the country and to make a positive contribution to the prevention of genocide and mass atrocities; (2) reduce the likelihood of unintended negative effects as a result of actions by outsiders; (3) sensitize decision makers to the sources of risk and resilience within a particular country or region; and (4) sensitize decision makers to future risks and triggers, potential contingencies that might arise, and appropriate responses if, or when, they do. In this mode, the atrocity prevention lens provides a voice for atrocity prevention in policy planning, execution, and evaluation that can help tailor existing programs to prevention needs.

When crises erupt in which genocide and mass atrocities are committed or are imminently apprehended, this essentially analytical and advisory approach becomes insufficient. It should therefore be augmented with a bureaucratic system in which the atrocity prevention lens becomes the principal organizing concept for a process capable of marshaling a whole-of-organization response to the crisis. As the UN's reports on its failed responses to genocides in Rwanda (1994) and Srebrenica (1995) and the more recent internal report on its actions in Sri Lanka (2010) show, good policy in the face of the threat or commission of mass atrocities requires a clear-eyed assessment of the situation and a response that privileges the protection of human life.[42] These reports show that, prior to the genocide in Rwanda, the UN pursued a path of conflict prevention and resolution when evidence from the field was pointing to a clear and present danger of genocide: in Srebrenica, the UN privileged impartiality and conflict resolution over the protection of human life; in Sri Lanka, the UN Country Team traded its protection concerns for largely illusory promises of humanitarian access. The addition of a "convening" or "coordinating" capacity to the atrocity prevention lens would help organizations avoid these problems.

In the face of imminent risks, organizations that have a mandate for preventing genocide and mass atrocities require a capacity for privileging prevention considerations over other concerns. In these contexts, organizations need to ensure the rapid transmission of atrocity prevention advice to senior decision makers, generate multidimensional whole-of-organization strategies for prevention, and coordinate their effective implementation. These are the main purposes of the second aspect of the atrocity prevention lens – the convening or coordinating mechanism.

---

[42] Kofi Annan (November 15, 1999), *Report of the Secretary-General Pursuant to General Assembly Resolution 53/35: The Fall of Srebrenica*, A/54/549; *Report of the Independent Inquiry into the Actions of the United Nations during the 1994 Genocide in Rwanda*, December 16, 1999; *Internal Review Panel Report on United Nations Action in Sri Lanka*, December 2012.

Ideally, the convening or coordinating mechanism should operate under the highest administrative authority available to the organization and should enjoy a direct line of communication to the leadership. To function effectively, three important imperatives must be incorporated into its design. First, it is imperative that the heads of all the major relevant departments participate in the mechanism (for instance, the U.S. Atrocity Prevention Board includes representatives from the Departments of State, Defence, Treasury, Justice, and Homeland Security, as well as the Joint Staff, USAID, the U.S. Mission to the UN, the Office of the Director of National Intelligence, the CIA, and the Office of the Vice President). Second, individual departments within the organization that is establishing the atrocity prevention lens must ensure that their own policies and actions are consistent with the strategy determined by the leadership. Third, it is important that – until it is determined otherwise by the leadership – once invoked, the mechanism be the organization's primary coordinating framework and that there is no duplication of this role.

The convening or coordinating mechanism should take the form of a series of regular meetings of the organization's principal officials, with the pace and frequency of meetings determined by the situation. The mechanism might also develop working groups or other working-level processes to contribute to the principals' deliberations and/or lead on the coordination of actions aimed at implementing its decisions. Wherever possible, the mechanism should be administered and chaired by the office or officials responsible for the atrocity prevention lens. This is necessary to ensure that deliberations are focused primarily on protecting populations from the apprehended threats and are largely (although not exclusively) driven by atrocity-specific analysis and situational understanding.

The convening or coordinating mechanism has three principal purposes. First, to *provide consolidated advice to the leadership on the situation at hand*. The mechanism should act as a repository for information and analysis about the situation drawn from across the organization. It should assist the principals to develop a shared understanding of the situation and to communicate this to the leadership. Because crisis situations are especially fluid, this should be a dynamic process informed by all the relevant information and analysis that the organization can gather.

Second, the mechanism has the purpose to *develop integrated policy advice and guidance on what strategy should be pursued to prevent genocide and mass atrocities*. The mechanism should produce advice to the leadership on the strengths and weaknesses of various policy options and a multifaceted strategy that ought to be pursued. This should include advice on matters such as the composition and configuration of the organization's presence in the country concerned, ways in which its existing policies and programs might be amended to mitigate risks and support local sources of resilience, messaging and communications, engagement and cooperation with other partners and/or with political decision makers, and potential contingencies. The process should aim to provide leaders with as many options as possible and propose strategies that utilize all of the organization's relevant capabilities. Given the fluidity of crisis situations in which potential opportunities close and others open, this should be a dynamic process through which past assumptions and strategies are questioned and, where appropriate, new ones developed.

Third, once the leadership has set an initial strategy, the mechanism should *coordinate the whole-of-organization implementation* of that strategy. This would involve the mechanism acting as a forum through which individual entities would report their activities, a central body that could provide support to teams in field, and a process for ensuring coherent public communications and engagement with potential partners. The mechanism would be able to gather information about the situation itself and the organization's policies and actions. Armed with this information, it could provide a vehicle for reviewing and modifying implementation of the organization's strategy.

The convening or coordinating mechanism should remain in place until either the leadership determines it is no longer necessary because the crisis has passed or until an alternative framework is established for coordinating policy.

Conclusion

This chapter has detailed the atrocity prevention lens approach to the prevention of genocide and mass atrocities. The atrocity prevention lens provides a way of tailoring existing work to the needs of preventing genocide and mass atrocities and of identifying specific areas where augmentation of that work would contribute to prevention goals. It does so by prioritizing specific situational understanding, reducing the chances of unintended negative consequences, identifying local sources of resilience, and facilitating strategies to achieve particular goals in particular settings. The lens should provide early warning of imminent dangers, analysis of triggers and sources of escalation, and forward thinking about contingencies. It should also include a mechanism to convene and coordinate whole-of-organization responses to imminent threats and crises. As such, this approach does not sit apart from other thematic agendas such as conflict prevention, conflict resolution, and peacebuilding, but rather works through these agendas to achieve its goals.

The atrocity prevention lens is a practical way of closing the gap between the theory and practice of genocide and mass atrocity prevention. The "lens" is a self-avowedly modest approach that tries to utilize existing policies, programs, and frameworks as much as possible for the purpose of preventing these grave crimes. Mindful of the world's limited resources, the approach focuses on tailoring and targeting existing capacities to address specific sources of risk and resilience. It rests on the premise that international activities such as foreign aid, capacity building, peacebuilding, human rights promotion, rule of law assistance, and conflict prevention can all contribute to the prevention of genocide and mass atrocities and that the tailoring of these activities to address local sources of risk while supporting sources of resilience can enhance these contributions. In other words, rather than adding to the list of international policy frameworks, the atrocity prevention lens tries to achieve its goals *through* them. In "normal" or noncrisis situations, the atrocity prevention lens focuses on the gathering and assessing of information about risks and resilience, advising on how external engagement might strengthen prevention goals, and reducing the likelihood of unintended consequences. The lens calls for this analysis to be incorporated into the day-to-day practice of organizations and for it to guide their programs and planning. In crisis situations involving the imminent risk of genocide and mass atrocities, the approach calls for the creation of a convening or coordinating mechanism that would oversee a whole-of-organization response.

The atrocity prevention lens could be criticized as too incremental in its response to the urgent challenge of genocide and mass atrocity prevention. In response, it might be argued that nothing here prevents the adoption of more far-reaching structural reforms. What the atrocity prevention lens contributes is a way of thinking that can be translated into modest first steps as organizations strengthen their capacity to contribute to the prevention of genocide and mass atrocities. It is a small step in the direction of making the prevention of these crimes "a living reality."

4   The "Narrow but Deep Approach"
     to Implementing the Responsibility to Protect:
     Reassessing the Focus on International Crimes

Jennifer M. Welsh

In the commentary on states' endorsement of the Responsibility to Protect (R2P) at the 2005 World Summit,[1] the decision to focus the principle's application on four specified acts – genocide, war crimes, crimes against humanity, and ethnic cleansing – has generally been praised.[2] The narrow scope of R2P is welcomed not only because it enhances the prospects for political consensus, but also because it is believed to give the principle, in the words of United Nations Secretary-General Ban Ki-moon, greater "operational utility."[3] Whereas the original report of the International Commission on Intervention and State Sovereignty (ICISS) had conceptualized the application of R2P to those grave and rare circumstances where there was "serious and irreparable harm occurring to human beings, or imminently likely to occur,"[4] it left unclear whether this included only intentional violence or killing or other forms of humanitarian emergency, such as, for example, natural disasters. The Summit Outcome Document, by contrast, avoids linkage to the extent of humanitarian catastrophe and makes clear that R2P concerns only those acts that the international community, as a whole, has stigmatized as international *crimes*.[5]

The views expressed in this chapter are those of the author and not of the United Nations Joint Office of the Special Advisers on the Prevention of Genocide and the Responsibility to Protect.

[1] "2005 World Summit Outcome," UN doc. A/Res/60/1 (September 16, 2005), para. 138 and 139.

[2] See, for example, Alex J. Bellamy, *Global Politics and the Responsibility to Protect: From words to deeds* (New York: Routledge, 2011), 83; and Gareth Evans, *The Responsibility to Protect: Ending Mass Atrocity Crimes Once and for All* (Washington: Brookings Institution Press, 2008), 64–69.

[3] *Implementing the Responsibility to Protect: Report of the Secretary General*, UN doc. A/63/677 (January 12, 2009), par. 10b.

[4] *The Responsibility to Protect*, Report of the International Commission on Intervention and State Sovereignty (Ottawa: International Development Research Centre, 2001), xii. The Commissioners appear to have had in their minds Michael Walzer's notion of acts "which shock the conscience of mankind." See *Just and Unjust Wars: A Moral Argument with Historical Illustrations*, 3rd ed. (New York: Basic Books, 2000), 107.

[5] Ethnic cleansing is not defined as an international crime per se, but is most commonly subsumed under either genocide or crimes against humanity. For a discussion of ethnic cleansing's status,

I generally share the positive view of the "narrow but deep approach" to the implementation of R2P as elaborated in the 2009 report of the Secretary-General ("narrow" referring to R2P's scope and "deep" to the range of instruments available to prevent and respond to the four acts).[6] However, this chapter also argues that it is critical to assess the consequences – some intended and some not – of situating R2P within a criminal framework. The first section provides a general overview of the phenomenon of criminalization in international relations and demonstrates how the international crimes to which R2P applies individualize criminal responsibility for the four acts. Section 2 argues that although the narrowing of the scope of R2P to this particular set of crimes was designed to forge a greater consensus around the extraordinary situations that might justify invoking the international community's responsibility to protect, contestation has lingered over the trigger point for activating international responsibilities to act, particularly under so-called Pillar III. In the third section, I demonstrate how a criminal framework has significant implications for how we address what is still the most common context in which genocide, war crimes, crimes against humanity, and ethnic cleansing occur – namely, the context of armed conflict.[7] Attempts to prevent or resolve conflict, which often employ the principle of impartiality (equal treatment of *parties*), can seemingly run counter to commonly discussed tools for implementing R2P, which aim at deterring or punishing *individuals*. Furthermore, some approaches to atrocity crime prevention risk simplifying the nature of conflict and applying overly rigid categories of "victim" and "perpetrator." In the concluding section, I reflect more broadly on the often-uneasy relationship between the "collective" – the collective responsibility of the international community to protect and the collective nature of the violence R2P was designed to address – and more individualistic approaches to atrocity crime prevention and response.

4.1.   Defining Criminalization

The criminalization of a transgression can be defined as the authoritative process that establishes the legal possibility of criminal proceedings against

---

see David Scheffer, 2008, "Atrocity Crimes Framing the Responsibility to Protect," *Case Western Reserve Journal of International Law* 40 (1): 128–129.

[6] *Implementing the Responsibility to Protect*, para. 10c.

[7] Whereas some of the international crimes identified in the Summit Outcome Document can be committed in contexts of peace as well as war, the presence of an armed conflict remains one of the main risk factors for atrocity crimes. As Scott Straus argues, the empirical connection between genocide and war is particularly robust. See "'Destroy Them to Save Us': Theories of Genocide and the Logics of Political Violence," *Terrorism and Political Violence*, Vol. 24 (2012).

agents suspected of that particular transgression.[8] This process is essentially additive because it seeks not to create a new offence, but instead to affix penal sanctions to a transgression that *already exists* in the law.[9] In other words, criminality and illegality are distinct notions, with the latter embracing both crimes proper and civil delicts and the former expressly specifying a punishment, rather than a restitutive injunction, for its commission.[10] Applying this distinction to a concrete example, we can therefore say that although there was a prohibition against aggressive war by the 1920s (set forth in the Kellog-Briand Pact), criminalization of aggressive war only followed in 1945, when the London Agreement (LOAC) instituted individual criminal responsibility for violations of the Kellog-Briand rule.[11]

The growing importance of criminality in contemporary international relations is the consequence of two closely related developments in the international legal order: first, the emergence of international crimes (as opposed to transnational crimes, such as counterfeiting, money laundering, drug or arms trafficking, or the financing of terrorism[12]) as a distinct legal category in international law, and, second, the international legal principle of individual criminal responsibility. The former has created a set of crimes that are deemed to threaten values considered vital to the international community as a whole, transforming those who commit them into what Mark Drumbl calls "enem[ies] of all humankind."[13] Consequently, there is both a universal interest in repressing them and distinct mechanisms for holding perpetrators

---

[8] See, for example, Glanville L. Williams, *Learning the Law*, 11th ed. (London: Stevens, 1982), 3. The definition deployed here is also compatible with the definition of "crime" used in Michael R. Gottfredson, "Some Advantages of a Crime-Free Criminology," in Mary Bosworth and Carolyn Hoyle, eds., *What Is Criminology?* (Oxford: Oxford University Press, 2011), 36.

[9] See, for example, Edwin H. Sutherland and Donald R. Cressey, *Principles of Criminology*, 5th ed. (Chicago: J.B. Lippincott Company, 1955), 8–13. This definition implies that the process of criminalization is complete at the point of the institution of sanctions, rather than at the point of their initial application against a particular felon. I am grateful to Anatoly Levshin for directing me to this literature and to these definitions.

[10] Sutherland and Cressey, *Principles of Criminology*, 3–24.

[11] See, for example, Ian Brownlie, *International Law and the Use of Force by States* (Oxford: Clarendon Press, 1963); and Cornelius A. Pompe, *Aggressive War: an International Crime* (The Hague: Martinus Nijhoff, 1953). Robert Jackson made a similar distinction in his discussion of the Nuremberg Trials: "it is clear that by 1939 the world had come to regard aggressive war as so morally wrong and illegal that it *should be treated as criminal if occasion arose.*" See "Nuremberg in Retrospect: Legal Answer to International Lawlessness," reproduced in Gueanael Mettraux (ed.), *Perspectives on the Nuremberg Trial* (Oxford: Oxford University Press, 2008), 369.

[12] Transnational crimes have been codified in international conventions so that states can control forms of criminal activity having transboundary effects. They do not create individual criminal accountability under international law.

[13] Mark Drumbl, *Atrocity, Punishment, and International Law* (Cambridge: Cambridge University Press, 2007), 4. See also Ruti Teitel, *Humanity' Law* (Oxford: Oxford University Press, 2011), 199–201.

of such crimes accountable at the international level.[14] In instances where such acts have been committed or are imminent, states have thus accepted the legitimacy of international interference in a key prerogative of sovereignty: the right to decide whether and when to criminally punish one of their own citizens.[15]

The second and related innovation in international law involves the creation of individual perpetrators of international crimes; this despite the scale of violence that is generally involved in the perpetration of genocide, crimes against humanity, and war crimes. Prior to Nuremberg, warring states were obliged to prevent their officials from committing the acts prohibited by the LOAC. If and when officials committed transgressions, the state to which the errant officials belonged was responsible under international law; the question of whether individuals would then be held accountable for their behavior was left to the discretion of the domestic courts. This principle was elaborated in the judgment of the Nuremberg tribunal, which stated that "[c]rimes against international law are committed by men, not by abstract entities, and only by punishing individuals who commit such crimes can the provisions of international law be enforced."[16]

But, as I suggest later, this "individualized" mode of facilitating responses to international crimes in some ways runs counter to the criminological nature of those crimes as widespread and systematic acts of mass or collective violence.[17] As the International Criminal Tribunal for the former Yugoslavia (ICTY), at the conclusion of its first case, explained: "most of the crimes [before us] do not result from the criminal propensity of single individuals," but rather "constitute manifestations of a collective criminality" in which members of a group act together with a common objective.[18] Whereas in domestic law punishment of criminals is often justified by pointing to their work as autonomous agents who are thus capable of having criminal intent, in the case of the atrocity crimes to which R2P applies, perpetrators are frequently overseeing a group or operating within a group that is following norms perceived to be acceptable within that particular collective context (even if the behavior deviates from international standards). As I suggest later, the

---

[14] Antonio Cassesse, *International Criminal Law*, 2nd ed. (Oxford: Oxford University Press, 2008), 11–12.

[15] Larry May, *Crimes Against Humanity: A Normative Account* (Cambridge: Cambridge University Press, 2005), 3.

[16] International Law Commission, "Principles of International Law Recognized in the Charter of the Nuremberg Tribunal and in the Judgement of the Tribunal, with Commentaries," 374.

[17] Larry May, *Genocide: A Normative Account* (Cambridge: Cambridge University Press, 2010), 12; and Tallgren "The Sense and Sensibility of International Criminal Law," 565–566.

[18] Cited in Mark Osiel, *Making Sense of Mass Atrocity* (Cambridge: Cambridge University Press, 2011), 6.

tension between the collective and systematic nature of atrocity crimes[19] and the focus in individual criminal law on holding individual perpetrators accountable for these acts has implications for both the responsive and preventive dimensions of the responsibility to protect.

4.2. Criminalization and Norm "Precision"

One of the primary outcomes of criminalization, it is often argued, is the provision of greater precision around society's conception of acceptable and unacceptable behavior.[20] Similarly, it is commonplace within international relations literature, both rationalist and constructivist, to see institutionalization and legalization as important steps toward facilitating compliance with norms. According to this view, the specificity provided by the 2005 Summit Outcome Document should have dampened disagreement around the scope of R2P and brought states' expectations about appropriate behavior into greater alignment.[21] During the difficult negotiations over the text in Articles 138 and 139, states concerned about creating a pretext for widespread military intervention succeeded in forging agreement around a conception of R2P that was limited to those crimes that had been identified in both the 1998 Rome Statute and the 2001 Constitutive Act of the African Union and that therefore reflected definitions that states had already accepted as legitimate.[22]

More specifically, the formulation of R2P's scope in the Summit Outcome Document succeeded in adding greater precision to the original ICISS notion of "large scale loss of life" that is "actual or apprehended."[23] As I have demonstrated elsewhere, this narrower reading of R2P quickly became the settled interpretation within the UN system.[24] Following Cyclone Nargis,

---

[19] Larry May refers to them as collective or group-based crimes. See *Crimes Against Humanity*, 21. To date, the international criminal justice system has addressed this tension partly by focusing criminal prosecution on the architects of mass violence. See, for example, Scott Straus, *The Order of Genocide: Race, Power, and War in Rwanda* (Ithaca: Cornell University Press, 2007); and Drumbl, *Atrocity*.

[20] I would agree with May, however, that such agreement could and should precede criminalization as well. As he argues: "we need to move beyond the simple claim that a crime is merely an act that a society has agreed to call a crime." *Crimes Against Humanity*, 22. In May's case, the grounding for international crimes such as genocide is found in a combination of what he calls the "security principle," "the international harm principle," and *jus cogens* norms.

[21] Martha Finnemore and Kathryn Sikkink, "International Norm Dynamics and Political Change," *International Organization* 52 (4): 887–917 (1998); Ann Florini, "The Evolution of International Norms," *International Studies Quarterly* 40 (3): 363–389 (1996); and Kenneth W. Abbott, Robert O. Keohane, Andrew Moravcsik, Anne-Marie Slaughter, and Duncan Snidal, "The Concept of Legalization," *International Organization* 54 (3): 401–419 (2000).

[22] For an overview of the diplomacy leading to the endorsement of R2P, see Bellamy, *Global Politics and the Responsibility to Protect*, 21–25.

[23] *The Responsibility to Protect*, xii.

[24] Jennifer M. Welsh, "Norm Contestation and the Responsibility to Protect," *Global Responsibility to Protect* 5 (4): 365–396 (2013).

which wreaked widespread devastation in Myanmar in 2008, some mounted an argument that the government's slow provision of humanitarian assistance constituted a crime against humanity. However, this interpretation was strongly contested by – among others – China, which resisted moves to coerce states into accepting humanitarian assistance.[25] Critics also insisted that R2P, as defined in the Summit Outcome Document, was not applicable to natural disasters – a view shared by many high-level officials within the UN, including Secretary Ban Ki-Moon, who (as suggested earlier) worried about stretching the concept beyond operational utility.[26]

By focusing the application of R2P on what are viewed as the most serious and conscience-shocking actions in international society, the Summit Outcome Document did provide greater precision around the scope of the principle. As Gareth Evans famously argued, if R2P "is to be about protecting everybody from everything, it will end up protecting nobody from anything."[27] Given that the demanding notion of *responsibility* is at the heart of this principle – including international responsibility – it is logical and appropriate that it is focused on criminal acts that violate *jus cogens* norms.[28] Nevertheless, the employment of a crimes framework has not ended the debate over the threshold that should activate international action, particularly coercive measures[29] under Pillar III. This is so for two main reasons.

First, some of the crimes outlined in the Outcome Document require further specification if they are to guide implementation of R2P. This is particularly true of war crimes, which is a broad category that includes random acts committed by a single soldier or member of a rebel group. The origins of the principle of R2P indicate that it was designed to address more widespread and systematic instances of violence or persecution.[30] On the other hand, R2P was purposely framed to include criminal acts beyond genocide – given the latter's demanding requirement of proof of discriminatory intent. Thus, for example,

---

[25] M. Bernard Kouchner, "Burma," *Le Monde*, May 20, 2008. For the views of two ICISS Commissioners on this case, see Ramesh Thakur, "Should the UN Invoke the 'Responsibility to Protect'?" *Globe and Mail*, May 8, 2008; and Gareth Evans, "Facing Up to Our Responsibilities," *The Guardian*, May 12, 2008.

[26] *Implementing the Responsibility to Protect*, paragraph 10b. For further discussion of the issue of "stretching" R2P, see Joanna Harrington, "R2P and Natural Disasters," in Andy W. Knight and Frazer Egerton, eds., *The Routledge Handbook of the Responsibility to Protect* (New York: Routledge, 2012), 141–151.

[27] Evans, *Responsibility to Protect*, p. 65.

[28] For a more in-depth discussion of how international crimes violate *jus cogens* norms, see May, *Crimes Against Humanity*, chapter Two.

[29] By "coercive" I mean not only the use of military force, but also the application of sanctions.

[30] See, for example, Don Hubert and Ariela Blatter, "The Responsibility to Protect as International Crimes Prevention," *Global Responsibility to Protect* 4: 33–66 (2012). Their efforts to further specify the scope of R2P are similar to those that have been taken by the International Criminal Court to determine levels of "gravity" when considering the crimes under its jurisdiction that it will seek to prosecute.

the acts committed by Janjaweed militia against civilians in Darfur, although not initially found to constitute genocide, did satisfy the requirements of crimes against humanity and were clearly viewed as being within the scope of R2P.[31]

Some have taken this logic a step further and argued that, from the perspective of prevention or timely response, it may not always be possible or desirable for the international community to wait for situations to fully satisfy legal criteria of criminality. This point of view has formed part of the ongoing discussions over the French government's proposal to develop a voluntary "code of conduct" restricting the use of the veto by the permanent members of the UN Security Council (UNSC) in cases of "mass atrocities."[32] But, given that the umbrella term "mass atrocities" does not have the same standing in international law as the four acts specified in the Summit Outcome Document, it has given rise to a certain degree of analytical confusion that some fear could undermine the credibility of those advocating early action to implement the responsibility to protect.[33] It is partly this concern that has motivated states responding to the French proposal to stress the need for an "authoritative and respected entity" that can bring ongoing or imminent instances of international crimes to the attention of the Security Council.[34]

A second reason for continued debate is that, even if R2P is based on existing and well-known legal standards, it faces a challenge common to many principles or emerging norms: the tendency to generate contestation *as it is used*.[35] Contestation over a principle's scope can persist beyond its institutionalization, particularly as new circumstances and crises arise that differ from those surrounding its origins.[36] One current example in the case of R2P is the issue of non-state actors and the degree to which the principle can or should seek to address them in terms of seeking to encourage their

---

[31] Report of the International Commission of Inquiry on Darfur to the UN Secretary General (Geneva: January 25, 2005).

[32] This proposal was first articulated publicly by then the French Minister for Foreign Affairs and International Development, Laurent Fabius. See "A Call for Self-Restraint at the UN," *The New York Times*, October 4, 2013, www.nytimes.com/2013/10/04/opinion/a-call-for-self-restraint-at-the-un.html?_r=2& (accessed October 24, 2014).

[33] Scott Straus, "Identifying Genocide and Related Forms of Mass Atrocity," Working Paper, U.S. Holocaust Memorial Museum (Washington, DC, October 2011).

[34] See, for example, the Statement by H. E. Dr. Aurelia Frick, Minister of Foreign Affairs of the Principality of Liechtenstein to the Ministerial Side-Event, "Regulating the Veto in the Event of Mass Atrocities," September 25, 2014, https://storify.com/GCR2P/a-responsibility-not-to-veto (accessed October 24, 2014). The representative of Lichtenstein spoke on behalf of eleven countries that collaborate on issues of Security Council working methods reform: Australia, Chile, Costa Rica, Estonia, Hungary, Ireland, Norway, Saudi Arabia, Slovenia, Switzerland, and Lichtenstein.

[35] This second issue is addressed more fully in Welsh, "Norm Contestation."

[36] For further discussion, see Antje Weiner, "Enacting Meaning-in-Use: Qualitative Research on Norms and International Relations," *Review of International Studies* 35 (1): 175–193 (2009); and Mona Krook and Jacqui True, "Rethinking the Cycles of Norms," *European Journal of International Relations* 18: 103–127 (2010).

compliance with international humanitarian law or of assisting states to deal with non-state actors that commit or threaten to commit atrocity crimes.

But contestation over R2P also runs deeper, especially in those instances in which it is the state that is actively committing or facilitating one or more of the four acts specified in 2005. The debate can take a variety of forms. In the case of Sri Lanka, in the spring of 2009, the controversy was around how to characterize a situation involving the threat or commission of atrocity crimes. Was this a case in which the international community had to take collective action to fulfill its role in implementing the responsibility to protect, as argued by, among others, the nongovernmental organization Global Responsibility to Protect?[37] Or, were the actions of the Sri Lankan government both necessary and proportionate, given its engagement in a battle with terrorists that had threatened all its citizens for decades?[38] In other cases, such as Syria, the controversy relates more to the question of who is responsible for committing atrocity crimes and on reaching agreement on the answer while "timely response" is still feasible. When it issued its initial report, the Independent International Commission of Inquiry on the Syrian Arab Republic could not yet definitively establish responsibility for the May 2012 massacre at Houla, in which more than 100 people (half of them children) were killed.[39] Two months later, when it did point fingers at Syrian government forces and militia backed by state officials at the highest levels,[40] it was much more difficult to galvanize a collective response in the Security Council.

Aside from the intense political debate that accompanied both of these high-profile examples, particularly concerning whether and how outside actors should respond, we come back to the question of whether a *criminal law* definition of the acts specified by R2P can always serve as the *policy*

---

[37] Open Letter from the Global Centre for the Responsibility to Protect to the UN Security Council, April 15, 2009. The letter was signed by, among others, the former UN Coordinator for Humanitarian Affairs, Jan Egeland, and the former Special Advisor on the Prevention of Genocide, Juan Mendez.

[38] This was the argument of Ramesh Thakur, one of the original members of the International Commission on Intervention and State Sovereignty. See "West Shouldn't Fault Sir Lankan Government Tactics," *Daily Yomiuri*, June 12, 2009.

[39] Oral Update of the Independent International Commission of Inquiry on the Syrian Arab Republic, UN doc. A/HRC/20/CRP.1 (June 26, 2012). The Commission was not able to visit the site of the killings before issuing this update and therefore relied on interviews with witnesses, information provided by governmental and nongovernmental sources, and satellite imagery. Although media reports at the time tended to blame the incident on local militia operating with or under the orders of Syrian government security forces, the Commission outlined two other sets of potential perpetrators that it could not yet rule out: anti-government forces trying to escalate the conflict and to punish those not supporting the rebellion and foreign fighters with an unknown affiliation.

[40] Report of the Independent International Commission of Inquiry on the Syrian Arab Republic, UN doc. A/HRC/21/50 (August 15, 2012).

definition as well.[41] In time-sensitive situations where policymakers want to act preventively, it may be that criminal definitions cannot always be authoritative and that political and moral considerations must also come into play.[42]

4.3.   Atrocity Crime Prevention and Conflict Resolution

Thus far, I have argued that while the narrowing of R2P's scope has contributed to greater clarity around its application, the criminal framework in which it is now situated has important conceptual and practical implications. Some of these affects are only now becoming clearer as states and international organizations seek to clarify the policy options for fulfilling their responsibility to protect populations from atrocity crimes.

With respect to the "sharp end" of the spectrum of policy options, the focus on criminality has the potential to change the very nature of interventions for humanitarian purposes. As Brad Roth argues, military interventions under the banner of humanitarianism have in the past often been depicted and justified as "stop gap" measures designed to "avert impending humanitarian catastrophe, not as recourse against wrongdoing as such."[43] But if there is now a clear linking of international criminal justice and the international law of peace and security, then there is also a firmer embrace of punishment as a motive for collective action.[44] This is particularly challenging for a body such as the UN, which is committed in many contexts to a stance of impartiality.

---

[41] David Luban and Henry Shue, writing in the context of the torture debate, usefully refer to this as the "forensic fallacy": the tendency to equate the narrowness and precision of criminal categories with the defining features of the wrong in question. See "Mental Torture: A Critique of Erasures in U.S. Law," *The Georgetown Law Journal* 100: 823–863 (2012), 850–55.

[42] For a discussion of this dilemma in the Libya case, see Jennifer M. Welsh, "Responsibility to Protect and the Language of Crimes," in Don Scheid (ed.), *The Ethics of Armed Humanitarian Intervention* (Cambridge: Cambridge University Press, 2014), 209–223. In Resolution 1970, the Security Council referred the situation in Libya to the International Criminal Court and requested the Chief Prosecutor to determine whether war crimes and crimes against humanity had been committed. UN doc. S/Res/1970, February 26, 2011. The Council passed Resolution 1973, authorizing the "use of all necessary means" to protect the civilians and civilian populated areas, before the Prosecutor came back with his findings. UN doc. S/Res./1973, March 17, 2011.

[43] Brad Roth, *Sovereign Equality and Moral Disagreement* (Oxford: Oxford University Press, 2011), 164.

[44] Although Chapter VII of the Charter empowers the Security Council with the right to identify those who threaten the peace and to mobilize the efforts of Member States to respond to affronts to international order, in reality the Council has operationalized this power to punish in only a handful of cases. The most prominent examples include the UN responses to the North Korean invasion of South Korea in 1950 and the Iraqi invasion of Kuwait in 1990.

More generally, the policy options for addressing potential or actual criminals may not be identical to those for addressing conflicts. Take, for example, the tool of mediation. Impartiality – the imperative to treat parties even-handedly – is considered one of the hallmarks of effective mediation.[45] However, in situations where there are ongoing atrocity crimes committed by individuals, it is more difficult for international mediators to adopt a stance whereby any outcome, as long as it is agreed to by negotiating parties, would be acceptable. Indeed, as some analysts argue, the assumptions that guide a human rights or rule of law approach, which involves "naming and shaming" and the pursuit of accountability, often appear at odds with the assumptions guiding mediation.[46] Whereas the drive for accountability largely follows its own "judicial logic" independent of microlevel politics, mediation and conflict resolution tack more closely to local political developments and opportunities. This tension was evident throughout February and March 2011, during the crisis in Libya, where an early referral to the International Criminal Court (ICC) in UNSC Resolution 1970 made a political resolution of the crisis increasingly less likely.

Those who caution against an instrumental use of justice mechanisms as tools of coercive diplomacy and/or atrocity prevention point out that the selectivity and politicization that have accompanied such efforts could inflict serious damage on the broader project of international justice.[47] They also remind us that there is still very little empirical evidence that the introduction of such mechanisms into an ongoing conflict can deter further atrocity crimes.[48] It is worth noting that even those involved in prosecution and the prevention of atrocity crimes doubt some of the expansive claims made about the impact of criminal justice mechanisms.[49] In reality, the relationship between international justice and the dynamics of conflict is both complex and variable.

---

[45] United Nations, *Guidance for Effective Mediation* (New York: September 2012), www.un.org/wcm/webdav/site/undpa/shared/undpa/pdf/UN%20Guidance%20for%20Effective%20Mediation.pdf

[46] Eileen F. Babbitt, "Mediation and the Prevention of Mass Atrocities," in Monica Serrano and Thomas G. Weiss, eds., *The International Politics of Human Rights: Rallying to the R2P Cause?* (New York: Routledge, 2013), 29–47, at 30; and Anthony Dworkin, "International Justice and the Prevention of Atrocity," European Council on Foreign Relations (October 2014), 15.

[47] Louise Arbour, Address to the Stanley Foundation Conference on the Responsibility to Protect, New York, January 18, 2012, www.r2p10.org.

[48] Dworkin, "International Justice," p. 34; and Dan Saxon, "The International Criminal Court and the Prevention of Crimes," in Serena Sharma and Jennifer Welsh, eds., *The Responsibility to Prevent* (Oxford: Oxford University Press, forthcoming 2015). http://ukcatalogue.oup.com/product/9780198717782.do

[49] Juan Mendez, then the Special Adviser on the Prevention of Genocide to the United Nations Secretary General, observed in 2004 that the idea that criminal punishment plays a role in the prevention of crimes was "an act of faith." See Martin Mennecke, "Punishing Genocidaires: A Deterrent Effect or Not?" *Human Rights Review* 8(4): 319–339 (2007), 319.

The Libya case, as I have previously suggested[50], vividly shows the practical difficulties of attempting deterrence through threats of criminal prosecution. Aside from the question of whether the Security Council's referral of the situation to the ICC actually deterred high-level members of the Gaddafi regime from continuing their attacks or planning is the issue of the coherence of the Council's approach. On the one hand, as part of its coercive diplomacy, it imposed targeted sanctions (such as asset freezes and travel bans) on particular members of the Gaddafi regime. These sanctions were made conditional on "better behavior" from the target: meeting the demands of the Council could have led to the lifting of such measures. On the other hand, however, ICC referrals and indictments are inherently unconditional; they cannot be retracted once they are initiated. The fact that the Security Council combined both of these measures simultaneously reveals ambiguity over whether it really wanted to deal with perpetrators by involving them in a political settlement or whether it believed their behavior was not subject to modification and that they should be handed over for criminal prosecution.[51]

In addition to posing challenges for how policymakers employ traditional conflict prevention or resolution tools, an atrocity crime perspective can engender (whether consciously or not) a simplified view of conflict and of those who participate in it. Crimes are most often understood as acts committed *by* perpetrators *against* victims. Within some "late stage" atrocity crime prevention strategies, perpetrators are depicted as shrewd calculators of costs and benefits, who can be denied the means to commit their crimes or deterred through sanctions or threats of punishment, and victims are viewed as weak, vulnerable, and in need of both protection and deliberate assistance from third parties.

The use of these fixed categories, however, can limit policymakers' appreciation of the fluid identities of actors within some conflict situations. It has often been remarked, particularly within the community of scholars working on peacebuilding and transitional justice, that today's victims can quickly morph into tomorrow's perpetrators.[52] Russian diplomats at the UN leveled a similar kind of charge over the crisis in Syria, criticizing the language of blame and confrontation that they believed underpinned the

---

[50] Welsh, "The Responsibility to Protect and the Language of Crimes."

[51] Leslie Vinjamuri, "Deterrence, Democracy, and the Pursuit of International Justice During Conflict," *Ethics and International Affairs* 24(2): 191–211 (2010).

[52] In addition, as Drumbl has argued, the blanket term "perpetrator" simplifies the very different motives and standing of those who resort to mass violence. Atrocity crime situations, he demonstrates, usually involve at least three different categories of perpetrator: so-called conflict entrepreneurs (who are the commanders of violence), intermediaries (who receive orders but also exercise some authority over others), and actual killers ("ordinary" people who are conforming to perceived social expectations or, in some cases, committing crimes under duress). See *Atrocity*, 25–35.

strategy of Western members of the Security Council. In the Russian view (which is undoubtedly also heavily influenced by geostrategic factors), it is incumbent upon the international community to pursue an even-handed dialogue that does not treat one of the parties as a criminal outlaw, but rather criticizes both parties for war crimes and accommodates both as part of any political settlement.[53]

More fundamentally, approaches to atrocity crime prevention that treat perpetrators as rational calculators whose choices to commit violent acts can be changed or deterred by altering perceived costs and benefits, frequently overlook the degree to which conflict is both unpredictable and transformative.[54] Some instances of atrocities might indeed be best understood as "joint criminal enterprises,"[55] led by strategic figures at the top of the pyramid who use atrocity crimes as a way to ensure military victory, political power, or economic wealth. In such cases (and South Sudan may prove to be an illustration), the judicious use of carrots and sticks may reduce overall levels of violence by incentivizing individuals to restrain those belonging to their faction. More often, however, episodes of violence against civilians are not unilateral acts stemming from rational individual choices but rather the product of interaction between an armed actor, his or her group, a developing context of conflict, and deeper political and social conditions. As Randall Collins advises, we should speak less of "violent individuals" and more of "violent situations."[56]

Conclusion

This chapter has accepted, but then problematized, the narrow scope of R2P as encompassing a specific set of international crimes. Although this specificity was crucial in achieving the 2005 consensus and creating a platform to operationalize the principle, it also carries with it a series of

---

[53] Russian views were expressed during the Council debate surrounding the vetoed resolution of July 2012. See UN doc. S/PV.6810, July 19, 2012.

[54] Examples of a rational choice approach to conflict include Stathias Kalyvas, *The Logic of Violence in Civil War* (Cambridge: Cambridge University Press, 2006); and Benjamin Valentino, "Why We Kill: The Political Science of Political Violence against Civilians," *Annual Review of Political Science* 17(10): 89–103 (2014). Recent work in the phenomenology of war criticizes the individualist methodology underpinning rational choice and emphasizes the transformative and generative nature of conflict. See, for example, Tarak Barkawi and Shane Brighton, "Powers of War: Fighting, Knowledge, and Critique," *International Political Sociology* 5(2): 126–143 (2011); Randall Collins, *Violence: A Micro-Sociological Theory* (Princeton, NJ: Princeton University Press, 2008); and Stefan Klusemann, "Massacres as Process: A Micro-Sociological Theory of Internal Patterns of Mass Atrocities," *European Journal of Criminology* 9(5): 468–480 (2012). I am grateful to Christian Fastenrath for pointing me to this literature.

[55] Roth, *Sovereign Equality*, 164–165.

[56] Collins, *Violence*, 1.

challenging implications – both conceptual and practical. These can be addressed, but they will require resisting the temptation to focus too heavily on what criminologist call the immediate "situational" context for crime in which individuals operate and to pay greater attention to the underlying "social" context of their actions.[57]

This brings us back to the tension between the collective nature of atrocity crimes and the individualization of responsibility under international criminal law.[58] This problem has long been recognized and was at the heart of the UK government's refusal to participate in the drafting of the Genocide Convention in 1948.[59] Legal scholars and practicing lawyers have often addressed it by depicting an individual's act as a *political* act, with an intentional connection to the action or plans of a state or other group.[60] But this approach does not address the deeper critique that the pursuit of individual legal responsibility fails to invoke the sense of collective responsibility needed for societies to truly recover.[61] Nor does it give sufficient recognition to the possibility that it may be the broader "criminal state"[62] (to borrow David Luban's phrase) that provides the context and backing for individual acts that amount to atrocity crimes.

From the more specific perspective of the responsibility to protect and its preventive dimension, this problem calls for a re-emphasis on the second half of the implementation imperative set out in the Secretary-General's 2009 Report: *deep* as well as narrow. The fact that individuals have committed or threaten to commit an atrocity crime points to wider issues within a state that limit its capacity to protect its population; as a consequence, the tools for protection must extend beyond those related to establishing criminal responsibility. But this does not necessarily mean, as some critics contend,

---

[57] I am grateful to Ruben Reike for suggesting these criminological categories. For further discussion of situational approach, see Ronald Clarke, "Situational Crime Prevention: Theory and Practice," *British Journal of Criminology* 20(0): 139–143 (1980); and Daniel R. Lee, "Understanding and Applying Situational Crime Prevention Strategies," *Criminal Justice Policy Review* 21(3): 264 (2010).

[58] For further discussion of this tension, see Kirsten Ainley, "Individual Agency and Responsibility for Atrocity," in R. Jeffery, ed., *Confronting Evil in International Relations* (Basingstoke: Palgrave Macmillan, 2008).

[59] William A. Schabas, *Genocide in International Law* (Cambridge: Cambridge University Press, 2000), 79.

[60] See, for example, May, *Crimes Against Humanity*, 164–176. As May notes, although this strategy still prosecutes an individual for something a collective has done, he or she can be held accountable only for his or her role in that crime. We would thus speak of "shared" rather than "sole" responsibility (p. 172).

[61] Mark Drumbl, "Collective Responsibility and Postconflict Justice," in Tracy Isaacs and Richard Vernon, eds., *Accountability for Collective Wrongdoing* (Cambridge: Cambridge University Press, 2011), 23–60.

[62] David Luban, "State Criminality and the Ambition of International Law," in Isaacs and Vernon, *Accountability*, 61–91.

that R2P then becomes "about everything" and gets lost in a sea of efforts to address so-called root causes.[63]

Research and experience have revealed that there are a set of specific "inhibitors" to atrocity crimes that can address or even reverse the dynamics that can lead to these acts.[64] Although in some cases these inhibitors will work directly against potential perpetrators, in others, they will address broader institutional weaknesses and build up indigenous capacity for dialogue and conflict resolution. One area of strategic focus for preventive efforts could be the power configurations within a state that maintain systematic political and economic inequality along group or collective lines.[65] This would require both the willingness and the creativity to adjust mechanisms from R2P's "deep toolbox" to directly address intercommunal tensions. More traditional international agendas, such as economic development and the promotion of human rights, have only in rare instances managed to touch this delicate but important terrain. By more consciously incorporating an atrocity crime perspective, perhaps they could do so more frequently in the future.

---

[63] Rama Mani and Tom Weiss, "Introduction," in *Responsibility to Protect: Cultural Perspectives in the Global South* (New York: Routledge, 2011), 4; and Thomas G. Weiss, *Humanitarian Intervention* (Cambridge, MA: Polity Press, 2007), 104.

[64] These inhibitors are outlined in the 2014 Report of the Secretary General, *Fulfilling Our Collective Responsibility: International Assistance and the Responsibility to Protect*, UN doc. A/68/941, July 11, 2014, para. 43–58.

[65] For an in-depth and comparative analysis of how these inequalities can lead to violence and atrocity crimes, see L. Cederman, K. S. Gleditch, and H. Buhaug, *Inequality, Grievances, and Civil War* (Cambridge: Cambridge University Press, 2013).

5   The Role of Social Psychology in Preventing Group-Selective Mass Atrocities

Johanna Ray Vollhardt

5.1.   Introduction

Mass atrocities and their prevention are not a primary area of research within the field of social psychology, which is concerned with the ways in which the social situation influences individuals' thoughts, feelings, and behaviors (Allport, 1985). Yet genocide and mass atrocity prevention have captured the interest and attention of social psychologists (e.g., Suedfeld, 2000). Although social psychological field research in societies that have recently undergone genocide and other mass atrocities is scarce, some social psychologists have investigated these topics by drawing on archival data and scholarship about mass atrocities from other disciplines. These scholars have developed theoretical models and (less frequently) obtained some empirical evidence of social psychological mechanisms that contribute to the evolution of mass atrocities and that, in turn, may be used to derive strategies for mass atrocity prevention. In this chapter, I review social psychological theories and practical contributions that social psychologists have made to our knowledge about mass atrocity prevention. I discuss social psychological processes that are relevant within societies where mass atrocities do or may take place, as well as relevant processes in third-party or bystander nations. Because of the disciplinary focus of this chapter, it addresses primarily the role of individual group members in mass atrocities and their prevention.

5.1.1.   The Scope and Limitations of Social Psychological Theorizing and Research on Mass Atrocity Prevention

At the onset of this chapter, it is important to state what I mean by mass atrocities and by genocide and why I often refer to them together. Following Straus's conceptualization (Straus, 2011), I use *genocide* to mean "a form of extensive, group-selective violence whose purpose is the destruction of that group in a territory under the control of a perpetrator" (Straus, 2011, 4).

In contrast, the term *mass atrocities* includes not only genocide but also crimes against humanity, war crimes, and ethnic cleansing – in other words, widespread attacks against civilians, although not necessarily group-selective (Straus, 2011). It will become apparent in this chapter that social psychological expertise related to genocide and mass atrocity prevention is, to a large extent, based on the analysis of processes related to group and intergroup relations. Therefore, I only discuss those mass atrocities that are "group-selective" in nature, that is, "target[ing] groups and individuals for their membership in groups" (Straus, 2011, 4). This includes various socially construed groups, such as race, ethnicity, religion, and nationality, but also class, political ideology or affiliation, or other group identities that may be targeted for attack (Straus, 2011). Because my use of the term *mass atrocities* differs from the broader definition put forward by Straus, I refer to "group-selective mass atrocities" throughout the chapter to clarify the nature of the events under discussion.

Additionally, I discuss research related to genocide and other group-selective mass atrocities together, without always distinguishing which specific type of atrocity (e.g., genocide, smaller-scale mass killing, or ethnic cleansing) was being considered. This is in following with other social psychologists studying these issues, who generally have made little distinction between genocide and other group-selective mass atrocities (e.g., Staub, 1992). Although the distinction is obviously crucial for legal analyses and decisions regarding policy response, it has some disadvantages when it comes to prevention because the distinction can often be made only at a later stage, at which point it is too late for prevention, and intervention may not be feasible for a variety of reasons, ranging from moral to political to logistical (Straus, 2011; see also Staub, 1992, 2011). Moreover, from a psychological point of view, the individual-level cognitive processes that accompany genocide and group-selective mass atrocities are presumably shared: social psychological processes related to group-selective killing, complicity in mass atrocities, or the experience of victimization through genocide or mass violence are assumed to be– with the exception of specific genocidal ideologies – largely the same (Vollhardt and Bilewicz, 2013). For example, moral exclusion, dehumanization, or desensitization to violence are relevant in all cases of group-selective mass atrocities, whether or not they constitute genocide owing to the fact that they are "extensive (... of a large scale, ... sustained over time and across space, ... organized and systematic" (Straus, 2011, 4) and "group-destructive (designed to destroy groups in particular territories under perpetrators' control)" (Straus, 2011, 5). The latter two criteria are determined mostly through a societal or state level of analysis (e.g., how many people were killed in which territory), rather than the level of the individual and group and therefore are mostly irrelevant for a social psychological analysis. In other words, the distinction between experiencing group-selective mass atrocities in general and genocide in particular tends to be negligible from a psychological point of view.

In addition, it is important to note several caveats. Although social psychology as a discipline focuses heavily on empirical research, most social psychological work on genocide and other group-selective mass atrocities, as well as their prevention, is theoretical. The desire to understand and prevent genocide and other group-selective mass atrocities has stimulated some famous social psychological studies, including the Milgram experiments (see Berkowitz, 1999; Blass, 2002; Miller, 2004), as well as research on dehumanization (Bandura, 1999) and on social identity and intergroup discrimination (Tajfel and Turner, 2001; see also Billig, 2002). However, the overwhelming majority of this research has been conducted among college students in times of relative peace. So although reviews of social psychological theories and discussions about their utility for explaining and preventing group-selective mass atrocities may be compelling (e.g., Newman and Erber, 2002; Staub, 1992, 2011; Waller, 2007), given the lack of empirical validation in relevant contexts, we do not know whether the predictions and explanations that the authors put forward in these works hold up in the reality and complexity of group-selective mass atrocities (e.g., Berkowitz, 1999; Billig, 2002).

To a great extent, these limitations are due to the methodological approach favored by many social psychologists – focusing on individual-level analysis and on experiments or (somewhat less commonly) surveys, typically conducted in a laboratory setting rather than in the field. Thus, the present nature of most social psychological research is not likely to generate findings that have direct relevance for understanding or preventing ethnic conflict and group-selective mass atrocities (see Bar-Tal, 2004; Glick and Paluck, 2013; Paluck and Green, 2009a; Vollhardt and Bilewicz, 2013). However, some social psychologists who study political violence, including genocide and other group-selective mass atrocities, have used historical data (e.g., Klein and Licata, 2003; Reicher, Cassidy, Wolpert, Hopkins, and Levine, 2006; Volpato, Durante, Gabbiadini, Andrighetto, and Mari, 2010) or corroborated findings from laboratory research with historical case studies (Glick, 2002; Staub, 1992; see also Bilewicz and Vollhardt, 2012; Vollhardt and Bilewicz, 2013). This integrative approach increases the likelihood that their conclusions may be relevant and valid in real-world settings as well. Moreover, some social psychologists have conducted or evaluated interventions aimed at reconciliation and the prevention of violence in postconflict and postgenocide settings (e.g., Bilali and Vollhardt, 2013; Bilewicz and Jaworska, 2013; Paluck, 2009a, 2010; Paluck and Green, 2009b; Staub, Pearlman, Gubin, and Hagengimana, 2005), and others have addressed the effects of societal-level mechanisms of transitional justice and their repercussions (Gasparre, Bosco, and Bellelli, 2010; Kanyangara, Rimé, Philippot, and Yzerbyt, 2007; Rimé, Kanyangara, Yzerbyt, and Paez, 2011).

5.1.2.   Chapter Overview

In the remainder of this chapter, I review the social psychological processes that contribute to group-selective mass atrocities, with a particular focus on implications for interventions aimed at their prevention. One example is discussed in greater detail, a psychology-based mass media intervention in the Great Lakes region of Africa (Burundi, the eastern provinces of the Democratic Republic of Congo, and Rwanda), where there have been a series of interrelated group-selective mass atrocities in recent decades (Lemarchand, 2009). Rather than focusing on leaders, I primarily discuss the role of ordinary citizens because they are typically the subjects of social psychological research (with some exceptions, e.g., Klein and Licata, 2003; Mandel, 2002; Reicher et al., 2006). I begin by describing social psychological processes within societies at risk of group-selective mass atrocities, including those in which atrocities have taken place in the past and could recur due to unresolved grievances or deep-seated perceptions of groups as threatening or hostile. I then address social psychological processes that either promote or reduce awareness of group-selective mass atrocities among third parties (or what one may refer to as *bystander nations*: Staub, 2011), as well as support and activism for interventions aimed at halting or preventing group-selective mass atrocities in other countries.

5.2.   Social Psychological Processes in Societies at Risk of Group-Selective Mass Atrocities

Most of the social psychological work relevant to the prevention of group-selective mass atrocities has focused on understanding processes that fall within the first three stages of Stanton's eight-stage model of genocide (1998): classification (differentiating between "us and them" based on a socially construed group distinction), symbolization (marking outgroup members through symbols, clothing, etc.; see also Straus, 2011), and dehumanization (denying the humanity of the targeted group). Relevant research includes more fine-grained analyses of social categorization processes, scapegoating, delegitimization, and moral exclusion and inclusion, as well as passivity in the face of injustice and violence directed against outgroups. Staub (1992, 2011) has argued that understanding these mechanisms will allow us to raise awareness and develop interventions that reduce support for violence among the general population, thereby helping to prevent mass atrocities. This body of research also provides information about psychological and societal phenomena that may serve as early warning signs, indicating the need to take preventive action rather than waiting until a later stage to intervene. Of course, this assumes that people do not wish to harm others and that they can be persuaded to resist violence, which is not always the case and may not apply to certain segments of the population (e.g., ideological extremists).

5.2.1.   Classifying and Depicting the Perceived Enemy Group

One of social psychology's main contributions to the study of intergroup relations is, arguably, social identity/categorization theory (e.g., Tajfel and Turner, 2001). Simply put, this theory posits that, as humans, we have a natural tendency to classify both the physical and the social world into categories in order to reduce cognitive complexity and make sense of our surroundings. Mentally, in the context of the social world, we divide people into ingroups and outgroups based on categories such as gender, religion, nationality, and ethnicity, as well as into smaller social units such as neighborhoods or even sports teams. We also tend to exaggerate the similarities *within* each group as well as the differences *between* groups, a phenomenon that helps explain some aspects of social discrimination. In addition, social identity/categorization theory argues that we have a tendency to derive self-esteem from our identification with these groups, meaning that we favor those groups that we see ourselves as belonging to (ingroups) while perceiving those that we do not see ourselves as a part of (outgroups) in a less positive light.

Although many scholars and popular writers have used social identity/ categorization theory to explain the occurrence of violence between ethnic and religious groups (e.g., Ashmore, Jussim, and Wilder, 2001; Chirot, 2011; Moshman, 2011; Peacock, Thornton, and Inman, 2007), in fact social identity/ categorization theory in and of itself is not sufficient to explain extreme prejudice and violence (e.g., Billig, 2002; Hewstone, Rubin, and Willis, 2002). At most, social categorization is a starting point, a necessary but not sufficient condition for one group's derogation and maltreatment of another. It is obvious from everyday observation that social categorization occurs all the time without necessarily resulting in violence between groups. In short, social identity processes are not mechanistic determinants of group-selective mass atrocities. Brewer (1999) has famously argued that ingroup love (i.e., favoring one's ingroup) is not equal to outgroup hatred; rather, these are two independent processes that are not inevitably tied to one another. Moreover, studies in postconflict settings suggest that the specific identity content matters. For example, a survey study in Northern Ireland revealed that only antagonistic identity content (i.e., when the adversarial relationship with an outgroup is an essential part of the individual's group identity) predicts support for hostile behaviors toward outgroups; it is not the case for social identities that do not entail antagonistic beliefs about the relationship with the outgroup (Livingstone and Haslam, 2008). Similarly, the tendency to glorify the ingroup and perceive it as superior is associated with more hostile intergroup attitudes, as well as less willingness to acknowledge atrocities committed by ingroup members, whereas mere attachment to the ingroup is not associated with these negative intergroup attitudes (Bilali, 2013; Doosje, van den Bos, Loseman, Feddes, and Mann, 2012; Leidner, Castano, Zaiser, and Giner-Sorolla, 2010; Roccas, Klar, and Liviatan, 2006).

Yet even these more polarizing categorization and identity-related processes cannot explain the extremity of outgroup derogation that contributes to group-selective mass atrocities. Other psychological mechanisms also need to be taken into account, including destructive ideologies and emotions, the specific content of stereotypes of the targeted outgroup, scapegoating in light of perceived threat, and processes related to the moral exclusion and delegitimization of the targeted outgroup.

5.2.1.1.   Destructive Ideologies and Emotions   Ideology is a crucial component in explaining how social categorization can feed into violent conflict, even leading as far as group-selective mass atrocities (Billig, 2002; Cohrs, 2012). Specifically, destructive ideologies make it more likely that violence toward outgroups will be supported and favored. Two in particular that have been heavily investigated by social psychologists are right-wing authoritarianism (Altemeyer, 1996)[1] and social dominance orientation (Pratto, Sidanius, Stallworth, and Malle, 1994).

Right-wing authoritarianism is characterized by three features: authoritarian submission, authoritarian aggression, and conventionalism. Those who subscribe to this view tend to agree with statements such as "Our country

---

[1] Although there has been considerable debate regarding the relationship between left-wing and right-wing authoritarianism (for reviews, see, e.g., Altemeyer, 1996; van Hiel, Duriez, and Kossowksa, 2006), there has been very little empirical research into left-wing authoritarianism, whereas research into the right-wing variety is abundant. An initial study in the context of Western Europe suggests that left-wing authoritarianism may be less mainstream, limited to more radical party members and activists (van Hiel et al., 2006). It also suggests that the structure of left-wing authoritarianism is similar to that of the right-wing variety in its reliance on submission to leaders, although it tends to be characterized by more aggression directed toward "the establishment" than is right-wing authoritarianism. Moreover, in postcommunist Eastern Europe a few years after the transition, authoritarianism was associated with a preference for left-wing economic principles (Duriez, Van Hiel, and Kossowska, 2005).

desperately needs a mighty leader who will do what has to be done to destroy the radical new ways and sinfulness that are ruining us," or "Our country will be great if we honor the ways of our forefathers, do what the authorities tell us to do, and get rid of the 'rotten apples' who are ruining everything" (Altemeyer, 1996). Agreement with these statements is clearly linked to support for societal-level repression and violence and possibly even group-selective mass atrocities. So far, though, the available empirical evidence has tended to focus on societies in times of relative peace or on approval of war in general, rather than on specific group-selective atrocities. Nevertheless, data gathered from samples in the United States and several European countries shows that right-wing authoritarianism predicts diverse outcomes linked to intergroup violence, including support for war, deportations of Muslims and immigrants after 9/11, moral disengagement from ingroup harmdoing in the Iraq war, and legitimization of torture (e.g., Jackson and Gaertner, 2010; Larsson, Björklund, and Bäckström, 2012; Skitka, Bauman, Aramovich, and Morgan, 2006). ②

Similarly, social dominance orientation has been shown to predict not only prejudice but also support for torture and war, as well as less concern about the loss of human life in war (Larsson et al., 2012; McFarland, 2005). Generally, social dominance orientation is characterized by the view that there are legitimate group hierarchies and that superior groups should dominate inferior groups – through violence if necessary – and is measured by agreement with statements such as "It's OK if some groups have more of a chance in life than others" or "Inferior groups should stay in their place" (Pratto et al., 1994). More general research on these attitudes with regard to intergroup prejudice (the context in which most of this research has been conducted) has shown that while both right-wing authoritarianism and social dominance orientation predict support for negative intergroup attitudes, they operate through different motivational processes: right-wing authoritarianism through a perceived threat to the established social order by deviants and social dominance orientation through perceived competition with other groups over power and status (Duckitt, 2006). However, it remains to be tested whether the same cognitive and motivational processes hold true in more violent intergroup contexts, including the perpetration of group-selective mass atrocities.

threat v. competition

In addition to destructive ideologies, destructive emotions have also been discussed as crucial for intergroup violence, ranging from armed conflict to genocide. In particular, hatred is seen as an important factor in mobilizing violence against other social groups (Halperin, 2011; Reicher, 2010; Sternberg, 2003). Other researchers have also discussed the role of humiliation (e.g., Lindner, 2006), although the empirical evidence here is more mixed (e.g., Ginges and Atran, 2008).

5.2.1.2. Stereotype Content Another reason why prejudice and stereotyping resulting from social categorization cannot by themselves explain the occurrence of intergroup conflict, let alone group-selective mass atrocities, is that stereotypes vary in their intensity and valence (Billig, 2002). Not all stereotypes are negative, and not every negative stereotype is held intensely enough to motivate harm toward other groups. The stereotype content model (Cuddy, Fiske, and Glick, 2007; Fiske, Cuddy, Glick, and Xu, 2002) provides a way to differentiate stereotypes and determine which ones are more (or less) likely to feed into violence. In this model, each stereotype toward a group is located along two axes: warmth (whether or not the group or person is perceived as friendly, sincere, etc.) and competence (whether or not the group or person is perceived as capable, skilled, etc.). Plotting group stereotypes along these dimensions (high in warmth and competence; low in warmth and competence; high in warmth but low in competence; low in warmth but high in competence) consequently allows predictions of affective and behavioral responses with particular relevance for intergroup conflict and violence. Thus, according to this model, when a group is stereotyped as low in warmth and low in competence (such as homeless people or drug addicts), it gives rise to prejudice that is characterized by *contempt*. Groups stereotyped as low in warmth but high in competence (e.g., successful minorities) are viewed with *envy*, whereas groups stereotyped as high in warmth but low in competence (e.g., the elderly or disabled) are perceived with *pity*. The stereotype of high warmth and high competence, which gives rise to *admiration*, is usually reserved for the ingroup (Cuddy et al., 2007; Fiske et al., 2002). This classification of stereotypes has been demonstrated not only for contemporary outgroups in numerous countries (Cuddy et al., 2009), but also in historical analyses of propaganda images used by Italian fascists during World War II (Durante, Volpato, and Fiske, 2010).

"Contemptuous prejudice" (i.e., prejudice characterized by contempt: low warmth, low competence) appears to have the most severe implications for tendencies to exclude or harm other groups. Unlike other forms of prejudice, it has been shown (in neuroimaging studies) to activate regions of the brain associated with disgust (Harris and Fiske, 2006). Moreover, people asked to describe how other people in society behave toward groups characterized in this way report significantly higher levels of both passive harm (exclusion and demeaning) and active harm (attacking and fighting) (Cuddy et al., 2007). "Envious prejudice" (i.e., prejudice characterized by envy: low warmth, high competence) gives rise to greater levels of reported active harm, whereas pity increases passive but not active harm. In other words, the two forms of prejudice based on perceptions of low warmth are those that lead to harmful treatment of other groups.

envy (↓ warmth) ⇒ scape-
↑competence goating

5.2.1.3. *Scapegoating in the Context of Threat*

The classification of stereotypes has also proved useful in archival research and theoretical work on scapegoating in the context of group-selective mass atrocities. *Scapegoating* has been defined as an extreme form of prejudice in which people blame an outgroup for having caused their ingroup's misfortunes (Glick, 2002, 2008). Glick argues that some groups are more likely to be singled out as scapegoats, particularly those perceived to be high in competence but low in warmth – in other words, groups viewed with envy. Using several historical examples, such as witch hunts, the Armenian genocide, and the Holocaust, Glick demonstrates that it is minority groups that are successful (rather than weak) who are the ones most at risk of being designated as scapegoats and targeted for group-selective mass atrocities. Scapegoating serves very specific psychological functions in times of threat and misfortune, above all restoring a sense of control (Frey and Rez, 2002; Rothschild, Landau, Sullivan, and Keefer, 2012). In times of crisis, moreover, scapegoating provides a way to explain how the crisis came about and a course of action to resolve it, namely by restricting the rights of or, in the extreme case, even eliminating the group designated as scapegoat (Glick, 2002, 2008; Staub, 1992).

explain Crisis

5.2.1.4. *Moral Exclusion, Dehumanization, and Delegitimization*

In addition to stereotypes of the outgroup as cold and hostile and presenting a threat to the well-being of the ingroup, another social psychological phenomenon that characterizes group-selective mass atrocities is the exclusion of the outgroup from the realm of those to whom moral considerations apply (Opotow, 1990, 2011). This may happen, for example, if the outgroup is perceived as having violated moral norms and values, and therefore as undeserving of equal treatment (Bar-Tal and Hammack, 2012). It may also happen if the outgroup is dehumanized, a phenomenon that has been documented in many genocides, with the victim group labeled or portrayed, for example, as lice, rats, snakes, cockroaches, or dogs (e.g., Hagan and Rymond-Richmond, 2008; Haslam, 2006; Kelman, 1973; Staub, 1992). Dehumanization reduces restraints on violence and allows for "sanctioned massacres" to be carried out (Kelman, 1973). It is one of several mechanisms of moral disengagement that enable people to commit atrocities while preserving a positive self- and group image (Bandura, 1999).

5.2.1.5. *Propaganda*

All the elements mentioned so far are often used in propaganda and hate speech by political leaders to gain support among the (nontargeted) population for policies supporting group-selective violence and mass atrocities (Herf, 2006). Studying propaganda is therefore essential, both after the fact to understand the elements of destructive propaganda and

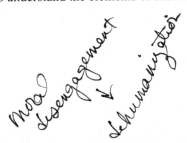

moral disengagement ↓ dehumanization

hate speech and in real time to allow early detection of group-selective violence and, ideally, to prevent it (Bilewicz and Vollhardt, 2012; Durante et al., 2010; Volpato et al., 2010). For example, depictions of Jews in Nazi propaganda magazines such as *Der Stürmer* included not only blatant dehumanization of the Jews but also a stereotypical portrayal of them as wealthy, sly, and influential (Bilewicz and Vollhardt, 2012; Herf, 2006). Thus, *more subtle mechanisms of delegitimization and derogation are equally important to be aware of and must be taken seriously as early warning signs.*

5.2.1.6. Implications for Prevention of Group-Selective Mass Atrocities

Whereas social psychological research on interventions that could improve intergroup relations has focused on strategies to include other groups in shared, superordinate, or cross-cutting social categories (e.g., Crisp and Hewstone, 2007; Dovidio, Gaertner, and Saguy, 2009; Gaertner and Dovidio, 2000; Riek, Mania, Gaertner, McDonald, and Lamoreaux, 2010), an early-warning approach to atrocity prevention based on social psychological principles of categorization should also involve monitoring the *content* of stereotypes and *specific portrayals* of groups at risk of being targeted. Above all, *depictions of a group as "cold" and hostile should be of concern, as should any attempts to blame certain groups for economic, political, or other problems within a society.* Furthermore, *the delegitimization of certain groups by way of assertions that they do not deserve the same rights or treatment as others should be considered an early warning sign.* Building on historical case studies and analyses of propaganda in the context of violent conflict, sensitization and education programs may be developed to inform the population (e.g., in schools and the media) about destructive ideologies, scapegoating, and mechanisms of delegitimization and moral exclusion. Based on our knowledge about the social psychological processes that accompany mass atrocities, scholars and activists together should develop criteria to detect destructive propaganda and hate speech and prevent it from spreading and contributing to escalating violence (e.g., Vollhardt, Coutin, Staub, Weiss, and Deflander, 2007). Raising public awareness may also help people realize that others in society do not necessarily share the distorted views expressed in hate speech, thereby preventing what social psychologists refer to as "pluralistic ignorance" (i.e., the false belief that others, unlike oneself, accept a certain norm or attitude). This is a crucial step for prevention because pluralistic ignorance is one of many factors that contribute to the evolution of group-selective violence into mass atrocities (see Newman, 2002).[2]

---

[2] The term "evolution of violence" goes back to the work of Ervin Staub (1992).

[Marginal note: pluralistic ignorance → false belief that others accept a norm or attitude]

grievance
historical memory

5.2.2. Grievances and Victim Beliefs

Just as social psychological processes may contribute to the categorization, perception, and delegitimization of an outgroup in a way that increases the likelihood of group-selective mass atrocities, ingroup perceptions and interpretations of history that produce a sense of collective victimhood may pose a risk. To date, few social psychological analyses of mass atrocities have addressed the role of victim beliefs (e.g., Staub, 2011), yet we know from historical studies of several genocides and group-selective mass atrocities (including Bosnia, Rwanda, and the Holocaust) that a sense of collective victimhood and vulnerability among the perpetrators – whether real or imagined – has contributed to cycles of violence (Lemarchand, 2009; MacDonald, 2002; Mamdani, 2001; Robins and Jones, 2009). The social psychological mechanisms through which this occurs presumably include a desire for revenge as well as intense emotions, such as fear of a recurrence of past victimization (Bar-Tal and Antebi, 1992a, b; Bar-Tal, Chernyak-Hai, Schori, and Gundar, 2009; Vollhardt, 2012a). As a result, violence against the perceived victimizer is justified in the perpetrators' eyes, construed as legitimate self-defense or preemptive violence (Bar-Tal and Antebi, 1992a, b; Bar-Tal et al., 2009; Bilali, 2013; Bilali, Tropp, and Dasgupta, 2012; Wohl and Branscombe, 2008). Similarly, a sense of grievance can obstruct the effectiveness of violence prevention programs and interventions (Paluck, 2010).

By contrast, when people do not perceive their group's victimhood as unique *shared* *victimhood* and instead can recognize similarities in its experience with other victim groups, it may reduce the likelihood of destructive consequences and ⬇ contribute to positive attitudes toward other victim groups or even toward the other party in a conflict. For example, among some members of groups targeted *empathy* for genocide and other mass atrocities, the realization that other groups in the world have been targeted in similar ways has led to peace activism and *forgiveness* prosocial actions on behalf of other victim groups (Klar, Schori-Eyal, and Klar, 2013; Vollhardt, 2012b). Similarly, an experimental study among Israelis and Palestinians in which participants were made to think about similar ways in which the other side has suffered from the conflict led to increased forgiveness by both groups toward the other (Shnabel, Halabi, and Noor, 2013).

5.2.2.1. Implications for Mass Atrocity Prevention Drawing on social psychological research regarding perceptions of ingroup victimization (for reviews, see Bar-Tal et al., 2009; Noor, Shnabel, Halabi, and Nadler, 2012; Vollhardt, 2012a), interventions designed to promote inclusive ways of thinking about past victimization could contribute to the prevention of

group-selective mass atrocities. Reducing a victim group's sense of unique suffering while fostering recognition of experiences it has in common with other victim groups may help to decrease support for group-selective violence and promote more prosocial relations between groups. This may be accomplished through dialogue groups (Adwan, Albeck, and Bar-On, 2002; Bar-On and Kassem, 2004), peace education (Salomon, 2004), or mass media-based projects disseminating real or fictional accounts of other groups' experiences (Bilali and Vollhardt, 2013) or speeches of leaders discussing the similarities between the victimization of the ingroup and other groups, thereby making this position normative and validating the importance of such narratives (Vollhardt, 2012b, 2015). At the same time, however, in any such undertaking it is crucial to acknowledge the particularities of the ingroup's experience as well, in order to avoid backlash against such comparisons and generalizations (Vollhardt, 2013).

5.3.   Collective Action, Active Bystandership, and Resistance

Government policy aside, early action among ordinary citizens can be crucial in preventing all types of mass atrocities. Ervin Staub has stressed the importance of active bystandership (Staub, 1992, 2011); that is, members of society who are not directly targeted speaking out against injustice and violence against others. Like others in the field of atrocity prevention, he emphasizes that it is crucial to do so early on, before the situation has become too dangerous to intervene as an individual. One important way for ordinary citizens to engage to prevent atrocities is collective action against injustice and societal exclusion of minorities or other groups targeted for persecution. Collective action is a well-studied area in social psychology, with research in this field focusing primarily on the role of a politicized collective identity, anger, and perceived collective efficacy to achieve change as crucial factors that motivate collective action (e.g., Stürmer and Simon, 2004; Tausch et al., 2011; Thomas and Louis, 2013; van Zomeren, Leach, and Spears, 2012). However, most of the research has examined collective action in the context of democratic societies at times of relative peace and therefore may not be applicable to situations around the world today where group-selective mass atrocities have occurred or are ongoing.

Collective action aimed at reducing, halting, or preventing oppression and even mass atrocities in more repressive and extreme environments has been studied to a lesser extent by social psychologists. This form of collective action, perhaps more appropriately termed *resistance*, becomes more relevant at a later stage, when violence has already erupted or repression is severe. It may originate either among victim groups or among bystanders, in each instance involving a different set of social psychological mechanisms.

Social psychological research on resistance among victim groups has examined the role of collective identity and social cohesion, as well as the importance of leadership (Haslam and Reicher, 2012). In addition, studies of Jewish resistance during the Holocaust found that knowledge and awareness of the nature of the mass killings were crucial predictors of overall engagement in resistance. Although many Jews had little access to information about the extent of the atrocities or did not believe the information was true, to the extent they were aware of it and believed it, it made resistance more likely (Einwohner, 2009; Tiedens, 1997). Thus, a crucial part of the Holocaust resistance fighters' work was spreading information in the ghettos about massacres that occurred in other ghettos and in forests in the countryside, as well as about what was happening in the death camps (Tec, 2013). Likewise, in line with the findings of the more general literature on collective action, information about uprisings and other acts of resistance in ghettos or concentration camps provided a sense of collective efficacy that was crucial in motivating acts of resistance (Maher, 2010).

Resistance among bystander groups includes rescuing or aiding members of a targeted group. The best-known social psychological research on this topic is based on interviews with Christian rescuers of Jews during the Holocaust. In a famous study of several hundred such rescuers (and a control group of nonrescuers, too), Oliner and Oliner (1988) found that rescuers were often approached by others and asked to help. Moreover, more than half of their sample was motivated by ingroup norms – in other words, ingroup members (e.g., relatives, priests, others with authority) conveying the idea or role-modeling that helping Jews (and others in need) was in line with their norms and values. Other predictors of rescuing behavior were previous contact with Jews and diverse networks in general, as well as a sense of social responsibility expanding beyond the immediate social ingroup, which Oliner and Oliner refer to as "extensivity." Similarly, other researchers identified values of universalism (Suedfeld and de Best, 2008) and perceptions of a shared, superordinate identity with the Jews (e.g., "we are all fellow Bulgarians": Reicher et al., 2006) as factors that motivated rescuing behavior. In line with Oliner and Oliner's findings regarding the importance of ingroup norms, an analysis of the arguments used to persuade Bulgarians of the importance of saving Bulgarian Jews from deportation also revealed that it was stressed at the time how this act was normative for Bulgarians – that is, in line with their identity and shared national values (Reicher et al., 2006). Nor did those who supported the rescue of the Jews hesitate to point out the harm it would cause Bulgarian society to lose its Jewish members.

5.3.1. Implications for Mass Atrocity Prevention

Obviously, more research on this topic is needed before any conclusions for mass atrocity prevention can be drawn. In general, though, we can say that the psychological processes leading to resistance in times of group-selective mass atrocities are much less understood than collective action to combat structural violence (i.e., inequalities in society that are not [yet] accompanied by direct violence). However, collective action and resistance lie on a continuum, and collective action against injustice, exclusion, and destructive policies early on may help prevent group-selective mass atrocities down the line. Collective action is promoted by a sense of collective efficacy (meaning the idea that groups of people have the ability to bring about social change) based on a politicized collective identity, one that enables and encourages individuals to act "as a mindful and self-conscious collective" on behalf of a political cause (see Simon and Klandermans, 2001, p. 323). It is crucial to keep in mind, however, that collective action can also be violent and destructive. Therefore, it is equally important to promote inclusive social identities and extensivity (Oliner and Oliner, 1988) to avoid collective action being used against other groups. Likewise, inclusive and tolerant ingroup norms and values are crucial (see also Paluck, 2009a, b). To this end, in any resistance effort aimed at preventing and halting group-selective mass atrocities, it is important that authorities and respected community members show support for such inclusive identities, as well as for prosocial norms of helping outgroup members. Of course, the feasibility of each of these strategies depends on the stage of violence and the level of repression in society. Likewise, in the aftermath of group-selective mass atrocities, sharing stories about how members of different groups helped each other can promote reconciliation and help build an ingroup norm of cross-group helping that can be activated in times of crisis (Bilewicz and Jaworska, 2013; Broz, Hart, and Elias-Bursac, 2004; Conway, 2011).

The social psychological literature seems to suggest that in order to increase resistance among the targeted group, it is crucial to disseminate information about the exact nature of the crimes, leaving no illusion about the victims' chances of survival. This is supported by recent uprisings in the Middle East and elsewhere, in which social media and other means of sharing information about violence and grievances have played an important role in mobilizing protest (e.g., Breuer, 2012).

5.4.   Using Mass Media to Prevent Mass Violence: The Example of Radio La Benevolencija

One example of how social psychological theories have been used in the aftermath of group-selective mass atrocities and genocide to attempt to promote reconciliation and prevent cycles of violence is the radio dramas produced by the Radio La Benevolencija/Human Tools Foundation, in the Great Lakes region of Africa.[3] This mass-media intervention is based on the principles of "edutainment" (i.e., educational entertainment) that have been used successfully in various contexts to promote positive social change (Singhal, Cody, Rogers, and Sabido, 2004). The theoretical foundation comes from Albert Bandura's social cognitive theory of mass communication and his ideas about the role of vicarious experiences and observational learning in bringing about behavior change (Bandura, 2002). Accordingly, edutainment drama serials embed educational messages into entertaining soap operas in which the characters, created in a way that a large segment of the population can identify with them, enact and role-model positive behaviors. Edutainment programs have been used extensively and successfully in South America, Asia, and Africa to promote literacy, family planning, equal rights for women, and other social and public health issues (Singhal et al., 2004). The radio dramas produced since 2005 by Radio La Benevolencija in Rwanda, Burundi, and eastern Democratic Republic of Congo (DRC) (Paluck, 2012; Staub, Pearlman, and Bilali, 2010) represent a rare attempt to base edutainment interventions on social psychological theories about the evolution of group-selective mass atrocities and its prevention (based on Staub, 1992, 2011), as well as clinical theories about trauma healing after mass violence (Pearlman, 2013). Underpinning them is the idea that understanding and healing from the psychological wounds of past violence can contribute to the prevention of future violence and that early prevention is important because the nature of group-selective mass atrocities is to evolve from more subtle to more blatant forms (Staub, 1992, 2011). Accordingly, the role of active bystanders and their willingness to speak out and act against injustice at an early stage is given particular attention in the messages and programming, as is citizens' ability to detect hate speech and manipulation by leaders (Vollhardt et al., 2007). All radio dramas in these series revolve around fictional ethnic groups that are in conflict with each other over land, power, or resources. The groups are also shown to have a history of grievances against each other that has erupted in cycles of violence. The radio dramas portray how negative dynamics evolve into violence, as well as the positive behaviors across group lines that counteract this, with characters discussing and role-modeling how to intervene and counteract derogation and violence in one's community safely, taking precautions to reduce the risks involved. Programs also offer ideas for constructive collective action by ordinary community members faced with hardships and a lack of resources.

[handwritten margin note: early prevention Key]

---

[3] http://www.labenevolencija.org/

An initial evaluation of the programs in Rwanda, utilizing a controlled and randomized field-experimental design, revealed positive effects of the radio drama on important intergroup attitudes (Paluck, 2009a). Specifically, listeners (compared to a control group of nonlisteners) reported greater support for their children intermarrying with members of other groups, higher levels of trust, and more willingness to speak out when witnessing problematic ingroup behaviors. Compared to the control group, listeners also reported a higher perceived importance of discussing trauma, more cooperative behavior, and a greater tendency to dissent to authoritarian structures in ingroup discussions (for similar findings, see also Paluck and Green, 2009b). Overall, the results suggest that the programs were more effective in changing perceived community norms around intergroup relations and other social issues than they were in changing personal beliefs (Paluck, 2009b).

A follow-up evaluation was conducted after several years of broadcasting of the radio drama in Rwanda, implementing a priming paradigm. It found that listeners who were reminded of the radio drama were more likely than nonlisteners (or listeners who were not reminded of the radio drama) to report historical perspective-taking in the context of the violent conflict (Bilali and Vollhardt, 2013). In other words, listeners who were reminded of the radio drama were more likely to report that one should learn about the other group's perspective on the history of mass violence, try to understand their perspectives, and the like. Listeners also reported more inclusive victim beliefs and less competitive victimhood.

In Burundi, using the same methodology, the programs were also found to have a positive effect on several important intergroup attitudes, including less ingroup superiority, less social distance, less mistrust toward the outgroup, and less competitive victimhood, as well as higher levels of inclusive victim beliefs (Bilali, Vollhardt, and Rarick, invited resubmission under review). In contrast, the findings in eastern DRC were less positive, displaying mixed results or, in some cases, even negative effects (Bilali and Vollhardt, invited resubmission under review). This is in line with earlier findings in the same region, where a year-long field experiment revealed that a talk show implemented after the radio drama led to less tolerant beliefs and less willingness to aid unliked outgroup members compared to a control group in which only the radio dramas were broadcast. It was observed that listeners who also had a chance to reflect on and talk about the programs (in the context of the talk show) drew parallels to their own situation and focused more on their grievances, which could explain the negative effects (Paluck, 2010). Taken together, these findings reveal the difficulties of conducting such interventions in the midst of ongoing violence and insecurity. Under such conditions, people' s mindsets and psychological needs are different than in times of relative security in the aftermath of violence. The stage of conflict and the level of threat are essential to take into account. Interventions must be tailored to the population's psychological needs given the stage of conflict, violence, or reconciliation and must address any unresolved grievances that exist.

5.5.   Social Psychological Processes among Third Parties and in Bystander Nations

In addition to considering the social psychological processes that contribute to atrocity prevention within a society at risk, it is also important to examine how awareness of mass atrocities can be raised among external bystanders (i.e., third parties in other countries; e.g., Staub, 2011), including what motivates their interest in supporting interventions and advocating on behalf of targeted groups (as opposed to remaining disinterested and passive). While political scientists study whether activism by civilians who are outsiders to group-selective mass atrocities is effective, social psychologists can address the question of *why* people become active on behalf of other groups that are being targeted.

Mirroring some of the findings reported earlier on rescuing behavior among bystanders in societies where genocide and mass atrocities occur, social psychological research has shown that universal values (Cohrs, Maes, Moschner, and Kielmann, 2007; Spini and Doise, 1998) and a global orientation referred to as "identification with all humanity" (McFarland and Mathews, 2005; McFarland, Webb, and Brown, 2012; McFarland, 2010) are important predictors of positive attitudes toward international human rights in times of relative peace. Similar to Oliner and Oliner's "extensivity" (again, a sense of social responsibility that extends beyond the group or groups that one belongs to), "identification with all humanity" means a person reports identifying with "people all over the world" rather than just "people in my community" and "Americans" (McFarland et al., 2012). Other predictors of support for international human rights are education and knowledge of human rights issues (Cohrs et al., 2007; McFarland and Mathews, 2005; Stellmacher, Sommer, and Brähler, 2005), as well as dispositional empathy (McFarland, 2010; McFarland and Matthews, 2005). In contrast, and in line with the research summarized earlier in this chapter, social dominance orientation, right-wing authoritarianism, and ethnocentrism as well, are all associated with decreased concern for international human rights (Cohrs et al., 2007; McFarland, 2010; McFarland and Matthews, 2005).

In addition to these findings concerning favorable attitudes toward human rights in general (a rather abstract notion), some social psychological research has examined the question of which factors increase or reduce people's support for military intervention in concrete instances of mass atrocities, or support for providing aid to targeted groups in other countries. First, socially shared prototypes of genocide and mass atrocities, shaped by well-known instances in the past, influence the perception of cases in the present. For example, support for military intervention in Bosnia in the 1990s was fueled by images of emaciated Bosnian Muslims behind barbed wire that evoked associations with the Holocaust (Power, 1999). Similarly, Gadaffi's call to attack protesters he labeled as "cockroaches" in 2012 alarmed the international community because of its close resemblance to language used during the Rwandan genocide and presumably contributed to support for the intervention in Libya (ICRtoP, 2012). This phenomenon can be explained with the help of prototype theory (Rosch, 1975; see also Mazur and Vollhardt, invited resubmission under review); that is, the idea that people have certain cognitive structures and prototypes of objects and social categories in their minds that influence how quickly they recognize and process exemplars of these categories depending on how closely they resemble the prototype. Two studies among students and a community sample in the United States revealed a culturally shared prototype of genocide (Mazur and Vollhardt, invited resubmission under review). This prototype included specific cases that were associated with genocide more readily than others (e.g., the Holocaust and the 1994 genocide in Rwanda were much more readily associated with genocide than were the Cambodian and Armenian cases), as well as certain terms (e.g., "racism," "innocence," "large-scale," "systematic," "war") that were more commonly and more readily associated with genocide than other terms (e.g., "disease," "loss of identity," "child soldiers," "refugees"). Moreover, when a fictional case of group-selective mass atrocities was presented using terms that were central to the prototype, participants perceived the case as more urgent and severe, and they were also more likely to support military intervention (Mazur and Vollhardt, invited resubmission under review, study 4).

In addition to the way in which specific cases of mass atrocities are portrayed in the media, the depiction of victim groups also influences bystander groups' empathy and willingness to help. Specifically, there is a "collapse of compassion" as the number of victims depicted increases (Cameron and Payne, 2011; see also Slovic, 2007). In other words, when people see a greater number of victims, instead of experiencing more empathy and willingness to help, they become less sensitive. One of the psychological processes underlying this effect is the tendency to regulate one's emotions to reduce the increased distress that comes with seeing a greater number of victims depicted. In one experiment, when participants were told beforehand that they would be asked to donate money to aid victims of mass atrocities in Darfur, they were actually more likely to exhibit a collapse of compassion (Cameron and Payne, 2011).

Another study, comparing aid offered to victims of the 2004 tsunami in Asia versus aid offered to victims of mass atrocities in Darfur, found that participants were more willing to donate to those afflicted by natural disaster than to those harmed by human-caused atrocities due to a tendency to blame the victims in Darfur (Zagefka, Noor, Brown, de Moura, and Hopthrow, 2011).

Finally, reactions among bystanders may also vary depending on whether their own group has been victimized by genocide and mass atrocities in the past. As described earlier in this chapter, inclusive victim beliefs among historically victimized groups – that is, perceived similarities between their own victimization and the victimization of present-day groups – may motivate some people to take action on behalf of groups currently being subjected to mass atrocities (Vollhardt, 2012a, 2012b, 2015). For example, the U.S. Jewish community played a major role in the "Save Darfur" campaign, driven by the perception of a moral obligation to prevent other groups from suffering the same fate as Jews (and others) did during the Holocaust (Vollhardt, 2012b; see also Vollhardt, 2013). Importantly, these self-perceived responsibilities should not be confused with externally imposed moral obligations assigned by third parties to historically victimized groups (Warner and Branscombe, 2012).

5.5.1.   Implications for Mass Atrocity Prevention

The social psychological research on bystander group responses to mass atrocities in other parts of the world has several practical implications for prevention. First, human rights education and awareness of mass atrocities is important to disseminate. But *how* these events – and the victim groups – are portrayed is critical. Initial research suggests that to maximize bystander support for any action, national or international, aimed at preventing, mitigating, or halting group-selective mass atrocities, the events may need to be portrayed in a manner consistent with the culturally shared prototype of genocide. Also, depictions of individual victims are likely to be more effective than images of multiple victims, which will emotionally overwhelm the viewer. In addition, *any information that could lend itself to victim blaming* (e.g., reports about targeted individuals refusing to leave behind their house or belongings) *should be avoided*; otherwise, it is likely to activate the viewer's natural tendency to blame the victim, thereby inhibiting the willingness to help.

Finally, it is crucial to create a sense of common humanity and identification with the victim group and to reinforce global-mindedness and universal values. Different strategies may be necessary to achieve this, depending on whether the bystander group has its own history of collective victimization. In an experimental study, the inclusive and universal description of the Holocaust as a "crime against humanity" (as opposed to a "crime against Jews" or "a crime against Jews and other targeted groups") was most effective in eliciting support for victims in Darfur (e.g., signing petitions urging government leaders to take action) among people who did not identify with a historical genocide (Vollhardt, 2013). The results were somewhat different for Jewish participants, for whom acknowledging the distinct fate of Jews during the Holocaust, in addition to portraying the Holocaust as a crime against humanity involving the targeting of several groups, elicited the highest level of prosocial attitudes and behavior toward the victim group facing mass atrocities in Darfur.

5.6.   Conclusion: Social Psychological Recommendations for Mass Atrocity Prevention

Social psychological research suggests that mass atrocity prevention can and should start very early on, with the promotion of societal values and ideologies that emphasize personal and social responsibility to prevent others from suffering and to take action when others are disparaged and excluded. These values should be taught to leaders and citizens alike, beginning with education in schools and branching out to all levels of society. Civic education should also contribute to the building of inclusive social identities and categories based on commonalities (including ingroup experiences of collective victimhood) across group lines. At the same time, however, it is crucial to acknowledge the distinctiveness of each group to avoid backlash and the other risks that come with creating broad, shared identities (Crisp, Stone, and Hall, 2006; Dovidio et al., 2009; Hornsey and Hogg, 2000a, 2000b). For example, focusing on commonality may have the result of appeasing disadvantaged groups, thereby reducing the likelihood that they will seek to engage in collective action against injustice (Dixon, Levine, Reicher, and Durrheim, 2012; Saguy, Tausch, Dovidio, and Pratto, 2009). Policymakers and nongovernmental organizations planning projects with these aims in mind must consider these risks very seriously and take steps to avoid them.

Obviously, in some cases, inclusive and shared identities are not realistic or feasible, such as in societies that are already divided or under the yoke of severe oppression. In these instances, communicating ingroup norms related to helping other groups and portraying them as important ingroup values and virtues is crucial. Although leaders in power are obviously unlikely to take part in the effort, other respected and influential community members − religious leaders, public intellectuals, community activists, even celebrities − may help spread and popularize such norms. In addition, mass media, literature, and popular stories told by community members can also play an important role in promoting inclusive identities and social categories, disseminating knowledge about mass atrocities in a way that utilizes familiar prototypes without being emotionally overwhelming, and communicating ingroup norms of cross-group helping and social responsibility. Although these social psychological principles cannot prevent group-selective mass atrocities once violence has broken out, they may help keep it from reaching that point in the first place.

Bibliography

Adwan, S., Albeck, J. H., and Bar-On, D. (2002). "Dialogue Groups: TRT's Guidelines for Working through Intractable Conflicts by Personal Storytelling in Encounter Groups. *"Peace and Conflict: Journal of Peace Psychology*, 8: 301–322.

Allport, G. W. (1985). "The Historical Background of Social Psychology." In *The Handbook of Social Psychology* (3rd ed., vol. 1), edited by G. Lindzey and E. Aronson, 1–46. New York: McGraw-Hill.

Altemeyer, B. (1996). *The Authoritarian Specter*. Cambridge, MA: Harvard University Press.

Ashmore, R. D., Jussim, L. J., and Wilder, D. (Eds.). (2001). *Social Identity, Intergroup Conflict, and Conflict Reduction*. New York: Oxford University Press.

Bandura, A. (1999). "Moral Disengagement in the Perpetration of Inhumanities." *Personality and Social Psychology Review*, 3: 193–209.

Bandura, A. (2002). "Social Cognitive Theory of Mass Communication." In *Media Effects: Advances in Theory and Research* (2nd ed.), edited by J. Bryant and D. Zillmann, 121–153. Mahwah, NJ: Lawrence Erlbaum.

Bar-On, D., and Kassem, F. (2004). "Storytelling as a Way to Work through Intractable Conflicts: The German-Jewish Experience and Its Relevance to the Palestinian-Israeli Context." *Journal of Social Issues*, 60: 289–306.

Bar-Tal, D. (2004). "The Necessity of Observing Real Life Situations: Palestinian-Israeli Violence as a Laboratory for Learning about Social Behaviour." *European Journal of Social Psychology*, 34(6): 677–701.

Bar-Tal, D. and Antebi, D. (1992a). "Beliefs about Negative Intentions of the World: A Study of the Israeli Siege Mentality." *Political Psychology*, 13(4): 633–645.

Bar-Tal, D., and Antebi, D. (1992b). "Siege Mentality in Israel." *International Journal of Intercultural Relations*, 16: 251–275.

Bar-Tal, D., Chernyak-Hai, L., Schori, N., and Gundar, A. (2009). "A Sense of Self-Perceived Collective Victimhood in Intractable Conflicts." *International Review of the Red Cross*, 91(874): 229–258.

Bar-Tal, D., and Hammack, P. L. (2012). "Conflict, Delegitimization, and Violence." In *The Oxford Handbook of Intergroup Conflict*, edited by L. R. Tropp, 29–52. New York: Oxford University Press.

Berkowitz, L. (1999). "Evil Is More than Banal: Situationism and the Concept of Evil." *Personality and Social Psychology Review* 3(3): 246–253.

Bilali, R. (2013). "National Narrative and Social Psychological Influences in Turks' Denial of the Mass Killings of Armenians as Genocide." *Journal of Social Issues* 69(1): 16–33.

Bilali, R., Tropp, L. R., and Dasgupta, N. (2012). "Attributions of Responsibility and Perceived Harm in the Aftermath of Mass Violence." *Peace and Conflict: Journal of Peace Psychology* 18(1): 21–39.

Bilali, R., and Vollhardt, J. R. (2013). "Priming Effects of a Reconciliation Radio Drama on Historical Perspective-Taking in the Aftermath of Mass Violence in Rwanda." *Journal of Experimental Social Psychology* 49(1): 144–151.

Bilali, R., and Vollhardt, J. R. (under review, invited resubmission). "Can Mass Media Interventions Effectively Promote Peace in Contexts of Ongoing Violence? Evidence from Eastern Democratic Republic of Congo." *Peace and Conflict: Journal of Peace Psychology.*

Bilali, R., Vollhardt, J. R., and Rarick, J. R. D. (under review, invited resubmission). "Assessing the Impact of a Media-Based Intervention to Prevent Intergroup Violence and Promote Positive Intergroup Relations in Burundi." *Journal of Community and Applied Social Psychology.*

Bilewicz, M., and Jaworska, M. (2013). "Reconciliation through the Righteous: The Narratives of Heroic Helpers as a Fulfillment of Emotional Needs in Polish-Jewish Intergroup Contact." *Journal of Social Issues* 69(1): 162–179.

Bilewicz, M., and Vollhardt, J. R. (2012). "Social Psychological Processes Underlying Genocide and Mass Killing." In *Social Psychology of Social Problems. The Intergroup Context*, edited by A. Golec de Zavala and A. Cichocka, 280–307. New York: Palgrave Macmillan.

Billig, M. (2002). "Henri Tajfel's 'Cognitive Aspects of Prejudice' and the Psychology of Bigotry." *British Journal of Social Psychology* 41(2): 171–188.

Blass, T. (2002). "Perpetrator Behavior as Destructive Obedience: An Evaluation of Stanley Milgram's Perspective, the Most Influential Social-Psychological Approach to the Holocaust." In *Understanding Genocide: The Social Psychology of the Holocaust*, edited by L. S. Newman and R. Erber, 91–109. New York: Oxford University Press.

Breuer, A. (2012). "The Role of Social Media in Mobilizing Political Protest: Evidence from the Tunisian Revolution." *SSRN Electronic Journal.* doi:10.2139/ssrn.2179030

Brewer, M. B. (1999). "The Psychology of Prejudice: Ingroup Love and Outgroup Hate?" *Journal of Social Issues* 55(3): 429–444.

Broz, S., Hart, L. K., and Elias-Bursac, E. (2004). *Good People in an Evil Time: Portraits of Complicity and Resistance in the Bosnian War.* New York: Other Press.

Cameron, C. D., and Payne, B. K. (2011). "Escaping Affect: How Motivated Emotion Regulation Creates Insensitivity to Mass Suffering." *Journal of Personality and Social Psychology* 100(1): 1–15.

Chirot, D. (2011). *Contentious Identities: Ethnic, Religious, and Nationalist Conflicts in Today's World.* New York: Routledge.

Cohrs, J. C. (2012). "Ideological Bases of Violent Conflict." In *The Oxford Handbook of Intergroup Conflict*, edited by L. R. Tropp, 53–71. New York: Oxford University Press.

Cohrs, J. C., Maes, J., Moschner, B., and Kielmann, S. (2007). "Determinants of Human Rights Attitudes and Behavior: A Comparison and Integration of Psychological Perspectives." *Political Psychology* 28(4): 441–469.

Conway, P. (2011). "Righteous Hutus: Can Stories of Courageous Rescuers Help in Rwanda's Reconciliation Process?" *International Journal of Sociology and Anthropology* 3 (7): 217–223.

Crisp, R. J., and Hewstone, M. (2007). "Multiple Social Categorization." In *Advances in Experimental Social Psychology* (vol. 39), edited by M. P. Zanna, 163–254. San Diego, CA: Elsevier.

Crisp, R. J., Stone, C. H., and Hall, N. R. (2006). "Recategorization and Subgroup Identification: Predicting and Preventing Threats from Common Ingroups." *Personality and Social Psychology Bulletin* 32(2): 230–243.

Cuddy, A. J. C., Fiske, S. T., and Glick, P. (2007). "The BIAS Map: Behaviors from Intergroup Affect and Stereotypes." *Journal of Personality and Social Psychology* 92(4): 631–648.

Cuddy, A. J. C., Fiske, S. T., Kwan, V. S. Y., Glick, P., Demoulin, S., Leyens, J. -P., . . . Ziegler, R. (2009). "Stereotype Content Model across Cultures: Towards Universal Similarities and Some Differences." *British Journal of Social Psychology* 48(1): 1–33.

Dixon, J., Levine, M., Reicher, S., and Durrheim, K. (2012). "Beyond Prejudice: Are Negative Evaluations the Problem and Is Getting Us to Like One Another More the Solution?" *Behavioral and Brain Sciences* 35(06): 411–425.

Doosje, B., van den Bos, K., Loseman, A., Feddes, A. R., and Mann, L. (2012). "'My In-Group Is Superior!': Susceptibility for Radical Right-Wing Attitudes and Behaviors in Dutch Youth: Determinants of Radicalization." *Negotiation and Conflict Management Research* 5(3): 253–268.

Dovidio, J. F., Gaertner, S. L., and Saguy, T. (2009). "Commonality and the Complexity of 'We': Social Attitudes and Social Change." *Personality and Social Psychology Review* 13(1): 3–20.

Duckitt, J. (2006). "Differential Effects of Right Wing Authoritarianism and Social Dominance Orientation on Outgroup Attitudes and Their Mediation by Threat from and Competitiveness to Outgroups." *Personality and Social Psychology Bulletin* 32(5): 684–696.

Durante, F., Volpato, C., and Fiske, S. T. (2010). "Using the Stereotype Content Model to Examine Group Depictions in Fascism: An Archival Approach." *European Journal of Social Psychology* 40(3): 465–483.

Duriez, B., Van Kiel, A., and Kossowska, M. (2005). "Authoritarianism and Social Dominance in Western and Eastern Europe: The Importance of the Sociopolitical Context and of Political Interest and Involvement." *Political Psychology* 26(2): 299–320.

Einwohner, R. L. (2009). "The Need to Know: Cultured Ignorance and Jewish Resistance in the Ghettos of Warsaw, Vilna, and Łódź." *Sociological Quarterly* 50(3): 407–430.

Fiske, S. T., Cuddy, A. J. C., Glick, P., and Xu, J. (2002). "A Model of (Often Mixed) Stereotype Content: Competence and Warmth Respectively Follow from Perceived Status and Competition." *Journal of Personality and Social Psychology* 82(6): 878–902.

Frey, D., and Rez, H. (2002). "Population and Predators: Preconditions for the Holocaust from a Control-Theoretical Perspective." In *Understanding Genocide: The Social Psychology of the Holocaust*, edited by L. S. Newman and R. Erber, 188–221. New York: Oxford University Press.

Gaertner, S. L., and Dovidio, J. F. (2000). *Reducing Intergroup Bias: The Common Ingroup Identity Model*. Philadelphia: Psychology Press.

Gasparre, A., Bosco, S., and Bellelli, G. (2010). "Cognitive and Social Consequences of Participation in Social Rites: Collective Coping, Social Support, and Post-Traumatic Growth in the Victims of Guatemala Genocide." *Revista de Psicología Social* 25: 35–46.

Ginges, J., and Atran, S. (2008). "Humiliation and the Inertia Effect: Implications for Understanding Violence and Compromise in Intractable Intergroup Conflicts." *Journal of Cognition and Culture* 8: 281–294.

Glick, P. (2002). "Sacrificial Lambs Dressed in Wolves' Clothing: Envious Prejudice, Ideology, and the Scapegoating of Jews." In *Understanding Genocide: The Social Psychology of the Holocaust*, edited by L. S. Newman and R. Erber, 113–142. New York: Oxford University Press.

Glick, P. (2008). "When Neighbors Blame Neighbors: Scapegoating and the Breakdown of Ethnic Relations." In *Explaining the Breakdown of Ethnic Relations*, edited by V. M. Esses and R. A. Vernon, 121–146. Oxford, UK: Blackwell Publishing.

Glick, P., and Paluck, E. L. (2013). "The Aftermath of Genocide: History as a Proximal Cause." *Journal of Social Issues* 69(1): 200–208.

Hagan, J., and Rymond-Richmond, W. (2008). "The Collective Dynamics of Racial Dehumanization and Genocidal Victimization in Darfur." *American Sociological Review* 73(6): 875–902.

Halperin, E. (2011). "The Emotional Roots of Intergroup Aggression: The Distinct Roles of Anger and Hatred." In *Human Aggression and Violence: Causes, Manifestations, and Consequences*, edited by P. R. Shaver and M. Mikulincer, 315–331. Washington, DC: American Psychological Association.

Harris, L. T., and Fiske, S. T. (2006). "Dehumanizing the Lowest of the Low: Neuroimaging Responses to Extreme Out-Groups." *Psychological Science* 17(10): 847–853.

Haslam, N. (2006). "Dehumanization: An Integrative Review." *Personality and Social Psychology Review* 10(3): 252–264.

Haslam, S. A., and Reicher, S. D. (2012). "When Prisoners Take Over the Prison: A Social Psychology of Resistance." *Personality and Social Psychology Review* 16(2): 154–179.

Herf, J. (2006). *The Jewish Enemy Nazi Propaganda during World War II and the Holocaust*. Cambridge, MA: Harvard University Press.

Hewstone, M., Rubin, M., and Willis, H. (2002). "Intergroup Bias." *Annual Review of Psychology* 53(1): 575–604.

Hornsey, M. J., and Hogg, M. A. (2000a). "Subgroup Relations: A Comparison of Mutual Intergroup Differentiation and Common Ingroup Identity Models of Prejudice Reduction." *Personality and Social Psychology Bulletin* 26(2): 242–256.

Hornsey, M. J., and Hogg, M. A. (2000b). "Intergroup Similarity and Subgroup Relations: Some Implications for Assimilation." *Personality and Social Psychology Bulletin* 26(8): 948–958.

ICRtoP. (2012). "*The Crisis in Libya.*" Retrieved from www.responsibilitytoprotect.org/index.php/crises/crisis-in-libya

Jackson, L. E., and Gaertner, L. (2010). "Mechanisms of Moral Disengagement and Their Differential Use by Right-Wing Authoritarianism and Social Dominance Orientation in Support of War." *Aggressive Behavior* 36(4): 238–250.

Kanyangara, P., Rimé, B., Philippot, P., and Yzerbyt, V. (2007). "Collective Rituals, Emotional Climate, and Intergroup Perception: Participation in 'Gacaca' Tribunals and Assimilation of the Rwandan Genocide. *Journal of Social Issues* 63 (2): 387–403.

Kelman, H. C. (1973). "Violence without Moral Restraint: Reflections on the Dehumanization of Victims and Victimizers." *Journal of Social Issues* 29(4): 25–61.

Klar, Y., Schori-Eyal, N., and Klar, Y. (2013). "The 'Never Again' State of Israel: The Emergence of the Holocaust as a Core Feature of Israeli Identity and Its Four Incongruent Voices: The Never Again State of Israel." *Journal of Social Issues* 69(1): 125–143.

Klein, O., and Licata, L. (2003). "When Group Representations Serve Social Change: The Speeches of Patrice Lumumba during the Congolese Decolonization." *British Journal of Social Psychology* 42(4): 571–593.

Larsson, M. R., Björklund, F., and Bäckström, M. (2012). "Right-Wing Authoritarianism Is a Risk Factor of Torture-Like Abuse, but So Is Social Dominance Orientation." *Personality and Individual Differences* 53(7): 927–929.

Leidner, B., Castano, E., Zaiser, E., and Giner-Sorolla, R. (2010). "Ingroup Glorification, Moral Disengagement, and Justice in the Context of Collective Violence." *Personality and Social psychology bulletin* 36(8): 1115–1129.

Lemarchand, R. (2009). *The Dynamics of Violence in Central Africa.* Philadelphia: University of Pennsylvania Press.

Lindner, E. (2006). *Making Enemies: Humiliation and International Conflict.* Westport, CT: Praeger Security International.

Livingstone, A., and Haslam, S. A. (2008). "The Importance of Social Identity Content in a Setting of Chronic Social Conflict: Understanding Intergroup Relations in Northern Ireland." *British Journal of Social Psychology* 47(1): 1–21. doi:10.1348/014466607X200419

MacDonald, D. B. (2002). *Balkan Holocausts? Serbian and Croatian Victim-Centered Propaganda and the War in Yugoslavia.* Manchester, UK: Manchester University Press.

Maher, T. (2010). "Threat, Resistance, and Collective Action: The Cases of Sobibór, Treblinka, and Auschwitz." *American Sociological Review* 75: 252–272.

Mamdani, M. (2001). *When Victims Become Killers: Colonialism, Nativism, and the Genocide in Rwanda.* Princeton, NJ: Princeton University Press.

Mandel, D. R. (2002). "Instigators of Genocide: Examining Hitler from a Social-Psychological Perspective." In *Understanding Genocide: The Social Psychology of the Holocaust*, edited by L. S. Newman and R. Erber, 259–284. New York: Oxford University Press.

Mazur, L., and Vollhardt, J. R. (invited resubmission under review). "The Prototypicality of Genocide: Implications for International Intervention." *Analysis of Social Issues and Public Policy*.

McFarland, S. (2010). "Personality and Support for Universal Human Rights: A Review and Test of a Structural Model." *Journal of Personality* 78(6): 1735–1764.

McFarland, S., and Mathews, M. (2005). "Who Cares about Human Rights?" *Political Psychology* 26(3): 365–385.

McFarland, S., Webb, M., and Brown, D. (2012). "All Humanity Is My Ingroup: A Measure and Studies of Identification with All Humanity." *Journal of Personality and Social Psychology* 103(5): 830–853.

McFarland, S. G. (2005). "On the Eve of War: Authoritarianism, Social Dominance, and American Students' Attitudes toward Attacking Iraq." *Personality and Social Psychology Bulletin* 31(3): 360–367.

Miller, A. G. (2004). "What Can the Milgram Obedience Experiments Tell Us about the Holocaust? Generalizing from the Social Psychology Laboratory." In *The Social Psychology of Good and Evil*, edited by A. G. Miller, 193–239. New York: Guilford Press.

Moshman, D. (2011). "Identity, Genocide, and Group Violence." *Handbook of Identity Theory and Research*, edited by In S. J. Schwartz, K. Luyckx, and V. L. Vignoles, 917–932. New York: Springer.

Newman, L. S. (2002). "What Is a 'Social-Psychological' Account of Perpetrator Behavior? The Person versus the Situation in Goldhagen's Hitler's Willing Executioners." In *Understanding Genocide: The Social Psychology of the Holocaust*, edited by L. S. Newman and R. Erber, 43–67. New York: Oxford University Press.

Newman, L. S., and Erber, R. (Eds.). (2002). *Understanding Genocide: The Social Psychology of the Holocaust*. New York: Oxford University Press.

Noor, M., Shnabel, N., Halabi, S., and Nadler, A. (2012). "When Suffering Begets Suffering: The Psychology of Competitive Victimhood between Adversarial Groups in Violent Conflicts." *Personality and Social Psychology Review*.

Oliner, S. P., and Oliner, P. M. (1988). *The Altruistic Personality: Rescuers of Jews in Nazi Europe*. New York: Free Press.

Opotow, S. (1990). "Moral Exclusion and Injustice: An Introduction." *Journal of Social Issues* 46(1): 1–20.

Opotow, S. (2011). "How This Was Possible: Interpreting the Holocaust." *Journal of Social Issues* 67(1): 205–224.

Paluck, E. L. (2009a). "Reducing Intergroup Prejudice and Conflict Using the Media: A Field Experiment in Rwanda." *Journal of Personality and Social Psychology* 96(3): 574–587.

Paluck, E. L. (2009b). "What's in a Norm? Sources and Processes of Norm Change." *Journal of Personality and Social Psychology* 96(3): 594–600.

Paluck, E. L. (2010). "Is It Better Not to Talk? Group Polarization, Extended Contact, and Perspective Taking in Eastern Democratic Republic of Congo." *Personality and Social Psychology Bulletin* 36(9): 1170–1185.

Paluck, E. L. (2012). "Media as an Instrument for Reconstructing Communities Following Conflict." In *Restoring Civil Societies*, edited by K. J. Jonas and T. A. Morton, 284–298. Chichester, UK: Wiley.

Paluck, E. L., and Green, D. P. (2009a). "Prejudice Reduction: What Works? A Review and Assessment of Research and Practice." *Annual Review of Psychology* 60: 339–367.

Paluck, E. L., and Green, D. P. (2009b). "Deference, Dissent, and Dispute Resolution: An Experimental Intervention Using Mass Media to Change Norms and Behavior in Rwanda." *American Political Science Review* 103(04): 622.

Peacock, J. L., Thornton, P. M., and Inman, P. B. (Eds.). (2007). *Identity Matters: Ethnic and Sectarian Conflict*. New York: Berghahn Books.

Pearlman, L. A. (2013). "Restoring Self in Community: Collective Approaches to Psychological Trauma after Genocide." *Journal of Social Issues* 69(1): 111–124.

Power, S. (1999). "To Suffer by Comparison?" *Daedalus* 128(2): 31–66.

Pratto, F., Sidanius, J., Stallworth, L. M., and Malle, B. F. (1994). "Social Dominance Orientation: A Personality Variable Predicting Social and Political Attitudes." *Journal of Personality and Social Psychology* 67(4): 741–763.

Reicher, S. (2010). "The Mobilizing of Intergroup Hatred." In *The Dynamics of Intergroup Communication* (vol. 8), edited by H. Giles, S. Reid, and J. Harwood, 167–177. New York: Peter Lang.

Reicher, S., Cassidy, C., Wolpert, I., Hopkins, N., and Levine, M. (2006). "Saving Bulgaria's Jews: An Analysis of Social Identity and the Mobilisation of Social Solidarity." *European Journal of Social Psychology* 36(1): 49–72.

Riek, B. M., Mania, E. W., Gaertner, S. L., McDonald, S. A., and Lamoreaux, M. J. (2010). "Does a Common Ingroup Identity Reduce Intergroup Threat?" *Group Processes and Intergroup Relations* 13(4): 403–423.

Rimé, B., Kanyangara, P., Yzerbyt, V., and Paez, D. (2011). "The Impact of Gacaca Tribunals in Rwanda: Psychosocial Effects of Participation in a Truth and Reconciliation Process after a Genocide." *European Journal of Social Psychology* 41(6): 695–706.

Robins, N. A., and Jones, A. (Eds.). (2009). *Genocides by the Oppressed: Subaltern Genocide in Theory and Practice*. Bloomington: Indiana University Press.

Roccas, S., Klar, Y., and Liviatan, I. (2006). "The Paradox of Group-Based Guilt: Modes of National Identification, Conflict Vehemence, and Reactions to the In-Group's Moral Violations." *Journal of Personality and Social Psychology* 91(4): 698–711.

Rosch, E. (1975). "Cognitive Representations of Semantic Categories." *Journal of Experimental Psychology: General* 104: 192–233.

Rothschild, Z. K., Landau, M. J., Sullivan, D., and Keefer, L. A. (2012). "A Dual-Motive Model of Scapegoating: Displacing Blame to Reduce Guilt or Increase Control." *Journal of Personality and Social Psychology* 102(6): 1148–1163.

Saguy, T., Tausch, N., Dovidio, J. F., and Pratto, F. (2009). "The Irony of Harmony: Intergroup Contact Can Produce False Expectations for Equality." *Psychological Science* 20(1): 114–121.

Salomon, G. (2004). "Does Peace Education Make a Difference in the Context of an Intractable Conflict?" *Peace and Conflict: Journal of Peace Psychology* 10(3): 257–274.

Shnabel, N., Halabi, S., and Noor, M. (2013). "Overcoming Competitive Victimhood and Facilitating Forgiveness through Re-categorization into a Common Victim or Perpetrator Identity." *Journal of Experimental Social Psychology* 49(5): 867–877.

Simon, B., and Klandermans, B. (2001). "Politicized Collective Identity: A Social Psychological Analysis." *American Psychologist* 56: 319–331.

Singhal, A., Cody, M. J., Rogers, E. M., and Sabido, M. (Eds.). (2004). *Entertainment-Education and Social Change: History, Research, and Practice.* Mahwah, NJ: Lawrence Erlbaum Associates.

Skitka, L. J., Bauman, C. W., Aramovich, N. P., and Morgan, G. S. (2006). "Confrontational and Preventative Policy Responses to Terrorism: Anger Wants a Fight and Fear Wants 'Them' to Go Away." *Basic and Applied Social Psychology* 28(4): 375–384.

Slovic, P. (2007). "'If I Look at the Mass I Will Never Act': Psychic Numbing and Genocide.' *Judgment and Decision Making* 2: 79–95.

Spini, D., and Doise, W. (1998). "Organizing Principles of Involvement in Human Rights and Their Social Anchoring in Value Priorities." *European Journal of Social Psychology* 28(4): 603–622.

Stanton, G. (1998). "The Seven Stages of Genocide." Working Paper, Yale Program for Genocide Studies. New Haven, CT: Yale University.

Staub, E. (1992). *The Roots of Evil: The Origins of Genocide and Other Group Violence.* New York: Cambridge University Press.

Staub, E. (2011). *Overcoming Evil: Genocide, Violent Conflict, and Terrorism.* New York: Oxford University Press.

Staub, E., Pearlman, L. A., and Bilali, R. (2010). "Understanding the Roots and Impact of Violence and Psychological Recovery as Avenues to Reconciliation after Mass Violence and Intractable Conflict: Applications to National Leaders, Journalists, Community Groups, Public Education through Radio, and Children." In *Handbook on Peace Education*, edited by G. Salomon and E. Cairns, 269–285. New York: Psychology Press.

Staub, E., Pearlman, L. A., Gubin, A., and Hagengimana, A. (2005). "Healing, Reconciliation, Forgiving and the Prevention of Violence after Genocide or Mass Killing: An Intervention and Its Experimental Evaluation in Rwanda." *Journal of Social and Clinical Psychology* 24(3): 297–334.

Stellmacher, J., Sommer, G., and Brähler, E. (2005). "The Cognitive Representation of Human Rights: Knowledge, Importance, and Commitment." *Peace and Conflict: Journal of Peace Psychology* 11(3): 267–292.

Sternberg, R. J. (2003). "A Duplex Theory of Hate: Development and Application to Terrorism, Massacres, and Genocide." *Review of General Psychology* 7(3): 299–328.

Straus, S. (2011). "Identifying Genocide and Related Forms of Mass Atrocity." Working paper, United States Holocaust Memorial Museum. www.ushmm.org/m/pdfs /20111219-identifying-genocide-and-mass-atrocity-strauss.pdf

Stürmer, S., and Simon, B. (2004). "Collective Action: Towards a Dual-Pathway Model." *European Review of Social Psychology* 15(1): 59–99.

Suedfeld, P. (2000). "Reverberations of the Holocaust Fifty Years Later: Psychology's Contributions to Understanding Persecution and Genocide." *Canadian Psychology/ Psychologie canadienne* 41(1): 1–9.

Suedfeld, P., and de Best, S. (2008). "Value Hierarchies of Holocaust Rescuers and Resistance Fighters." *Genocide Studies and Prevention* 3(1): 31–42.

Tajfel, H., and Turner, J. (2001). "An Integrative Theory of Intergroup Conflict." In *Intergroup Relations: Essential Readings*, edited by M. A. Hogg and D. Abrams, 94–109. New York: Psychology Press.

Tausch, N., Becker, J. C., Spears, R., Christ, O., Saab, R., Singh, P., and Siddiqui, R. N. (2011). "Explaining Radical Group Behavior: Developing Emotion and Efficacy Routes to Normative and Nonnormative Collective Action." *Journal of Personality and Social Psychology* 101(1): 129–148.

Tec, N. (2013). *Resistance: Jews and Christians Who Defied the Nazi Terror.* New York: Oxford University Press.

Thomas, E. F., and Louis, W. R. (2013). "Doing Democracy: The Social Psychological Mobilization and Consequences of Collective Action." *Social Issues and Policy Review* 7(1): 173–200.

Tiedens, L. Z. (1997). "Optimism and Revolt of the Oppressed: A Comparison of Two Polish Jewish Ghettos of World War II." *Political Psychology* 18(1): 45–69.

Van Hiel, A., Duriez, B., and Kossowska, M. (2006). "The Presence of Left-Wing Authoritarianism in Western Europe and Its Relationship with Conservative Ideology." *Political Psychology* 27(5): 769–793.

Van Zomeren, M., Leach, C. W., and Spears, R. (2012). "Protesters as 'Passionate Economists': A Dynamic Dual Pathway Model of Approach Coping with Collective Disadvantage." *Personality and Social Psychology Review* 16(2): 180–199.

Vollhardt, J. R. (2012a). "Collective Victimization." In *The Oxford Handbook of Intergroup Conflict*, edited by L. R. Tropp, 136–157. Oxford: Oxford University Press.

Vollhardt, J. R. (2012b). "Interpreting Rights and Duties after Mass Violence." *Culture and Psychology* 18(1): 133–145.

Vollhardt, J. R. (2013). "'Crime against Humanity' or 'Crime against Jews'? Acknowledgment in Construals of the Holocaust and Its Importance for Intergroup Relations." *Journal of Social Issues* 69(1): 144–161. doi:10.1111/josi.12008

Vollhardt, J. R. (2015). "Inclusive Victim Consciousness in Advocacy, Social Movements, and Intergroup Relations: Promises and Pitfalls." *Social Issues and Policy Review* 9(1): 86–115.

Vollhardt, J. R., and Bilewicz, M. (2013). "After the Genocide: Psychological Perspectives on Victim, Bystander, and Perpetrator Groups." *Journal of Social Issues* 69(1): 1–15.

Vollhardt, J., Coutin, M., Staub, E., Weiss, G., and Deflander, J. (2007). "Deconstructing Hate Speech in the DRC: A Psychological Media Sensitization Campaign." *Journal of Hate Studies* 5: 15–36.

Volpato, C., Durante, F., Gabbiadini, A., Andrighetto, L., and Mari, S. (2010). "Picturing the Other: Targets of Delegitimization across Time." *International Journal of Conflict and Violence* 4(2): 269–287.

Waller, J. (2007). *Becoming Evil: How Ordinary People Commit Genocide and Mass Killing* (2nd ed.). New York: Oxford University Press.

Warner, R. H., and Branscombe, N. R. (2012). "Observer Perceptions of Moral Obligations in Groups with a History of Victimization." *Personality and Social Psychology Bulletin* 38(7): 882–894.

Wohl, M. J. A., and Branscombe, N. R. (2008). "Remembering Historical Victimization: Collective Guilt for Current Ingroup Transgressions." *Journal of Personality and Social Psychology* 94(6): 988–1006.

Zagefka, H., Noor, M., Brown, R., de Moura, G. R., and Hopthrow, T. (2011). "Donating to Disaster Victims: Responses to Natural and Humanly Caused Events." *European Journal of Social Psychology* 41(3): 353–363.

6 Gender, Sexualized Violence, and the Prevention of Genocide

Elisa von Joeden-Forgey

In the past two decades, sexualized violence during conflict has gained the attention of international judicial bodies, policymakers, and international organizations. The world is beginning to recognize publicly both the scope and the seriousness of the crime, as well as the long-term physical and psychic trauma it causes survivors and their families and communities. Although case studies of sexualized violence in conflict are still woefully inadequate, those that do exist are shedding light on the causes, patterns, and the extent to which men and boys are also victimized. More recently, people working in genocide prevention have begun to appreciate that gender-based violence, including sexualized violence, is an integral element of genocidal processes and can help us in identifying these processes early on within a conflict. Less well understood is what these specifically genocidal patterns can tell us about the longer term prevention of genocide. This chapter examines the implications of the study of sexualized violence and genocide for our short-term prevention strategies and sketches out what the implications may be for the longer term.

Throughout this chapter, I use the term "sexualized violence" because, unlike "sexual violence," it places the emphasis on perpetrator agency and his or her active sexualization of power and of harm. Particularly during times of genocide, when sexualized violence is employed as part of an intent to destroy a group of people, the decision made by perpetrators to use this particular torture needs to be highlighted, for reasons I discuss at greater length later. "Sexualized violence" has the added benefit of calling into question the extent to which the violence of rape and other gender-based crimes can be considered to be "sexual" at all.[1] As Ruth Siefert has observed, rapes in conflict "are acts of extreme violence implemented, of course, by

---

[1] For an example of the use of the term "sexualized violence" in current atrocity prevention initiatives, see the web-based mapping and documentary project "Women Under Siege," www.womenundersiegeproject.org/.

sexual means."[2] When we look at sexualized violence in genocide and think about its implications for short- and long-term intervention and prevention, it is important that we recognize in the language that we use that it is neither natural nor static; it plays multiple roles in conflict, none of which has much to do with sexuality as such.[3]

In international law, sexualized violence during conflict can be a war crime, a crime against humanity, and a crime of genocide. Legally, a single act can be categorized as one of these or as a combination, depending on the circumstances.[4] Sexualized violence during conflict is the result of a variety of decision-making processes, perpetrators, and circumstances. It can include rape, the threat of rape, sexual assault, ritualized sexual torture, mutilation, sexual slavery, forced prostitution, forced maternity, forced nudity, the forced termination of pregnancy, forced participation in pornography, trafficking, and inappropriate and intrusive searches, exams, and medical procedures. It can be committed against men and boys as well as women and girls, although women and girls constitute the majority of its victims and therefore are particularly vulnerable to it.[5] Similarly, it can be committed by both men and women, although the vast majority of perpetrators are men. Although the work of Elisabeth Wood has shown that sexualized violence is not the "natural" or the inevitable consequence of conflict, it is a common and widespread characteristic of warfare that only threatens to get worse in the twenty-first century as the dividing line between battle front and home front, soldier and civilian, continues to blur.[6]

---

[2] Ruth Siefert, "War and Rape: A Preliminary Analysis," in Alexandra Stiglmayer, ed., *Mass Rape: The War against Women in Bosnia-Herzegovina* (Lincoln/London: University of Nebraska Press, 1994), 55.

[3] For a short overview of sexualized violence against women in conflict, see Jeanne Ward and Mendy Marsh, "Sexual Violence against Women and Girls in War and Its Aftermath: Realities, Responses, and Required Resources: A Briefing Paper" (UNFPA, 2006), https://www.unfpa.org /emergencies/symposium06/docs/finalbrusselsbriefingpaper.pdf, last accessed February 20, 2014; Charlotte Lindsey, "Rape and Other Forms of Sexual Violence," in Marie Vlachová and Lea Biason, eds., *Women in an Insecure World: Violence against Women, Facts, Figures and Analysis* (Geneva, Switzerland: Geneva Center for the Democratic Control of Armed Forces, 2005), 113–129.

[4] For an overview of the development of international law with respect to rape and sexualized violence, see Rhonda Copelon, "Toward Accountability for Violence against Women in War: Progress and Challenges," in Elizabeth D. Heineman, ed., *Sexual Violence in Conflict Zones: From the Ancient World to the Era of Human Rights* (Philadelphia: University of Pennsylvania Press, 2011), 232–256.

[5] For an overview and bibliography of the research on sexual violence against men in conflict, see W. Russel, A. Hilton, M. Peel, L. Loots, and E. Darnell, "Care and Support of Male Survivors of Conflict-Related Sexual Violence," Briefing Paper (Pretoria, South Africa: Sexual Violence Research Initiative, 2011), www.svri.org/CareSupportofMaleSurviv.pdf, last accessed September 12, 2013.

[6] Elisabeth Jean Wood, "Rape in Not Inevitable During War," in Kathleen Kuehnast, Chantal de Jonge Oudraat, and Helga Hernes, eds., *Women and War: Power and Protection in the 21st Century* (Washington, DC: US institute of Peace, 2011), 37–64.

Sexualized violence during warfare has multiple and complex causes. Although the roots of sexualized violence will vary with the history, culture, and regional specificity of each conflict, it is generally agreed that sexualized violence in war is a continuation of patriarchal traditions and gender-based violence in peacetime.[7] Peacetime violence against women and girls sets the stage for their violation at times of conflict, it can influence the willingness of soldiers to commit sexualized violence during war, it produces forms of masculinity that lend themselves to widespread atrocity, and it also defines the social conditions according to which the victims of sexualized violence will experience the short- and long-term repercussions of their victimization. Furthermore, patterns of sexualized violence that extend across long stretches of history – and across what for women and girls is a very blurry boundary between "peacetime" and "war" – can often link the shape of one conflict to the shape of another. A case in point is the genocide in Guatemala from 1981 to 1983, where the form of sexualized violence used systematically by the U.S.-trained Guatemalan Army against Mayan villagers echoed centuries of violation of indigenous women and indigenous families. The rampant and brutal sexualized violence of the genocide has carried over into present-day violence against women. "When one traces the antecedents of recent Guatemalan incidents of strategic rape and femicide," writes Roselyn Costantino, "it becomes evident that although the perpetrators and circumstances may morph along the time and space continuum of patriarchal social organization, neither the conditions that encourage femicide nor the perpetrators disappear."[8]

Because sexualized violence is in part an expression of the normative patriarchal control over women's bodies, mass rape in wartime need not always be coordinated from above. It may be committed by individual soldiers or small groups on an opportunistic and uncoordinated basis during conflict. It is also often committed by noncombatant men during conflict for similar reasons. As we are beginning to recognize, however, sexualized violence may also be used instrumentally – as a "weapon of war" – by armed forces to achieve various goals: to force people to flee an area that is rich in resources or that holds a specific symbolic importance to the perpetrators, to terrorize a population into submission, to punish a population for past wrongs or for resistance, to forcibly extract information from the victim or from somebody close to him or her, to forcibly impregnate women in order to change the demographic makeup of a territory, to entice men to serve as

---

[7] The path-breaking articulation of this was Susan Brownmiller's *Against Our Will: Men, Women and Rape* (New York: Fawcett Books, 1975).

[8] Roselyn Costantino, "Guatemaltecas Have Not Forgotten: From Victims of Sexual Violence to Architects of Empowerment in Guatemala," in Carol Rittner and John K. Roth, eds., *Rape: Weapon of War and Genocide* (St. Paul, MN: Paragon House, 2012), 121.

soldiers, to sow confusion among targeted communities, to destroy the reproductive capacity of a group, or to create strong martial bonds between the soldiers committing sexualized atrocities. Sexualized violence is often committed by all parties to a conflict, including peacekeeping forces, although usually for different reasons and in different forms. In regions where sexualized violence has been pronounced and conflict is entrenched, environments of impunity can arise where sexualized violence becomes a norm of everyday gender relations.

The long-term individual and societal impact of sexualized violence is beginning to be better understood and appreciated. On an individual level, the victims of sexualized violence often die from the sequelae of physical trauma, and they face permanent physical damage, infection with HIV and other sexually transmitted diseases, unwanted pregnancy, anxiety, depression, post-traumatic stress disorder (PTSD), thoughts of suicide, communal and familial ostracism, social isolation, inescapable poverty, and further sexual exploitation. In postconflict societies or refugee camps where public services are compromised or nonexistent, the victims of sexualized violence will be forced to suffer alone and in silence, without the necessary medical or social services to address their trauma. The scant evidence we have of the social effects of conflict-related sexualized violence on male survivors suggests that they suffer similar fates.[9] Surviving family members also suffer deeply as secondary victims of sexualized violence.[10] In many cases, they were forced to watch rapes of their loved ones that were very brutal and very public, and yet few resources exist to help them. In fact, secondary victimhood may help explain some of the harmful responses of spouses and communities to the rape victims. Whatever the case, mass sexualized violence can create severely traumatized societies in which the persons most entrusted with the raising of the next generation and the provision of life-sustaining resources for families and communities are weakened and vulnerable.

Moreover, sexual violence does not end with the end of war, as Ann Jones points out in her aptly titled book on the subject, *War Is Not Over When It's Over.* "Even when a conflict officially ends," she writes, "violence against women continues and often grows worse."[11] One only need watch Joshua Oppenheimer's brilliant documentary film, "Act of War," to see the open misogyny and rape fantasies that continue in the leadership of the Pancasila

---

[9] Will Storr, "The Rape of Men: The Darkest Secret of War," *The Observer*, Saturday, July 16, 2011, www.theguardian.com/society/2011/jul/17/the-rape-of-men (last accessed August 5, 2014).

[10] For a discussion of secondary victims, see D. Christiansen, R. Bak, and A. Alklit, "Secondary Victims of Rape," *Violence Victimization* 27(2): 246–262 (2012).

[11] Ann Jones, *War Is Not Over When It's Over* (New York: Metropolitan Books, Henry Holt and Company, 2010), 8.

Youth paramilitary organization, which was one of the principal death squads responsible for the mass murder of people labeled as "communists" in the 1960s. Studies have shown that women and girls in regions marred by conflict are still vulnerable to sexualized violence long after the cessation of hostilities.[12] The reasons for this include the breakdown of local and national security institutions, the incorporation of known war criminals into national armed forces and police, the widespread militarization of masculinity, the desensitization of demilitarized soldiers to rape and sexual violence, the structural vulnerability of war widows and their children, PTSD among male veterans, feelings of collective shame that result in the punishment of women for having been raped, the dislocations and insecurity of displaced person and refugee camps, and the destabilizing effects of conflict on traditional gender relations within society and the family.

Despite the continued threat of sexualized violence after armed conflict and its impact on survivors and their families, domestic and international funding is still woefully inadequate for widespread and effective postconflict trauma interventions, social healing at the family level, and anti-rape programs. In Rwanda, for example, where so many of the women survivors of sexual violence during the genocide were intentionally infected with HIV by Hutu perpetrators, early treatment was only made publicly available to these perpetrators in prison as well as to the few women who testified against them. Most women have been abandoned to their own fates, living on the margins of society and caring for their own children – some of whom were born as a consequence of rape – as well as for orphans.[13] Ironically, the negligence shown by the Rwandan government and the international community to the needs of women survivors of genocide and rape may be an unintended consequence of rape's new *visibility* in international law. Doris Buss has argued that the treatment of a crime against the individual (rape) as a crime against the group (genocide) can have the long-term unintended effect of rendering invisible the importance of legal and economic justice for the individual women survivors.[14]

It is hard to overestimate the importance to long-term peace of intervening effectively into the social dislocations caused by sexualized violence during conflict. Not only are victims and their families traumatized, but entire communities are compromised by sexual violence, which can make

---

[12] Jones, *War is Not Over*, 102; Dara Kay Cohen and Ragnhild Nordås, "Sexual Violence in Armed Conflict: Introducing the SVAC Dataset, 1989–2009," *Journal of Peace Research* 51: 418–428 (2014); Tilman Brück and Marc Vothknecht, "Impact of Violent Conflicts on Women's Economic Opportunities," in Kuehnhast et al., eds., *Women and War*, 87.

[13] Anne Marie de Brouwer (ed.), *The Men Who Killed Me: Rwandan Survivors of Sexual Violence* (Vancouver/Toronto/Berkeley: Douglas & McIntyre, 2009), 146–147.

[14] Doris E. Buss, "Rethinking 'Rape as a Weapon of War,'" *Feminist Legal Studies* 17: 145–163 (2009).

households and the wider social order economically and socially unsustainable, leading to transgenerational vulnerability to poverty, conflict, and further environmental degradation.[15] This is particularly the case when conflict and widespread sexualized violence have created refugee communities – often decades old – where resources are few and security is compromised. Furthermore, memories of sexualized violence against loved ones is often fuel for future conflict, contributing to the revenge cycles of pogroms, ethnic cleansing, and genocide that can poison intercommunal relationships for generations.[16]

6.1.   Genocidal Sexualized Violence

The literature on genocide and mass rape has made clear that the systematic use of rape and other forms of sexualized violence can be in and of itself an intentional form of group destruction. The International Criminal Tribunal for Rwanda's judgment in *Prosecutor v. Akayesu* in 1998 recognized sexualized and other forms of gender-based violence as a core component of the Hutu Power genocidal project.[17] Despite this new visibility, many scholarly and public definitions of genocide continue to underestimate sexualized violence as a tool of genocide, emphasizing the murderous aspect above all else. This is a mistake. Defining genocide as mass murder ignores the very specific processes of torture, humiliation, and desecration that end up in mass murder and coincide with it but that often happen well before large-scale massacres. These atrocities can offer us evidence of a hidden genocidal policy organizing the early-stage violence. Focusing solely on mass murder also ignores the experiences of vast numbers of women and girls during genocide, experiences that should certainly inform our definition of the crime. Furthermore, if we continue to treat mass rape as something that happens separate from genocidal killing, we empower perpetrators to use rape as a tool of genocide. Theoretically at least, perpetrators could pursue genocidal aims solely through the use of sexualized violence, for it has proved

---

[15] For a moving report on the transgenerational conflict caused by rape during the Rwandan genocide, as well as creative efforts to address this problem, see Sue Montgomery, "Rape Divides Mothers, Children," *The Calgary Herald* (March 31, 2014), B2.

[16] Although rape is rarely explicitly discussed in the historical literature on these revenge cycles, initial examination of the documents from the nineteenth and early twentieth centuries in the Caucasus, Southeastern Europe, and the Mediterranean shows rape – and the collective memory of it – to have been a pronounced feature of group destruction, as it has been in the cycles of violence and revenge that have characterized the Great Lakes region in Africa since independence. Ben Liebermann, *Terrible Fate: Ethnic Cleansing in the Making of Modern Europe* (Chicago: Ivan R. Dee, 2006); Rene Lemarchand, *The Dynamics of Violence in Central Africa* (Philadelphia: University of Pennsylvania Press, 2009).

[17] For a discussion of the myriad issues raised by the Akayesu case, see Chile Eboe-Osuji, "Rape as Genocide: Some Questions Arising," *Journal of Genocide Research* 9(2): 251–273 (2007).

itself to be a cheap and effective means of destroying a group by destroying, but not necessarily always killing, the bodies and the essential relationships of members of groups. A policy of genocide-through-sexualized violence offers genocidaires the opportunity to avoid an indictment for genocide in an international world where the relationship between rape and genocide is poorly understood and poorly appreciated.

We must recognize that historically sexualized violence has almost always been part of the genocidal effort to destroy a group as such, although it has not always been ordered from above or part of a clearly articulated genocidal strategy, and it is not always reducible to what we call "rape." There are many cases in which rape has indeed been a "weapon of war." In cases where, as in Bosnia-Herzegovina, sexualized violence was a core part of official military policy, rape's power to destroy families and communities was well understood by military leaders. One of the official documents related to Serb strategies during the Bosnian war, for example, directly linked sexualized violence to the goal of group destruction. According to a Slovene newspaper, the so-called RAM Plan, designed by psychological operations specialists inside the Serbian Army in the early 1990s, found that Bosniaks' (Bosnian Muslims) "morale, desire for battle, and will could be crushed more easily by raping women, especially minors and even children, and by killing members of the Muslim nationality inside their religious facilities."[18] The plan reasoned that:

Our analysis of the behavior of the Muslim communities demonstrates that the morale, will, and bellicose nature of their groups can be undermined only if we aim our action at the point where the religious and social structure is most fragile. We refer to the women, especially adolescents, and to the children. Decisive intervention on these social figures would spread confusion . . . , thus causing first of all fear and then panic, leading to a probable retreat from the territories involved in war activity. In this case, we must add a wide propaganda campaign to our well-organized, incisive actions so that panic will increase. We have determined that the coordination between decisive interventions and a well-planned information campaign can provoke the spontaneous flight of many communities.[19]

It is, of course, in Bosnia-Herzegovina where a specific type of "genocidal rape" was identified: an explicit policy of forced maternity with the intent of changing the demographic makeup of the victim community.[20]

---

[18] Todd A. Salzman, "Rape Camps as a Means of Ethnic Cleansing: Religious, Cultural, and Ethical Responses to Rape Victims in the Former Yugoslavia," *Human Rights Quarterly* 20(2): 356 (May 1998). See also Beverly Allen, *Rape Warfare: The Hidden Genocide in Bosnia-Herzegovina and Croatia* (Ithaca: University of Minnesota Press, 1996), 56–60.

[19] M. Cherif Bassiouni and Marcia McCormic, *Sexual Violence: An Invisible Weapon of War in the Former Yugoslavia* (1996), 21, n. 4; Allen, *Rape Warfare*, 57.

[20] Allen, "Genocidal Rape," in *Rape Warfare*, 62–66.

All genocides will not operate with the same clear intention and apparently comprehensive preplanning to use sexualized violence against those group members who are also deep symbols of a group's existential potential. As Baaz and Stern point out, in situations of mass rape, there is often no hard and direct line of intent that links the architects of genocide, to the leadership of armed forces, to the foot soldiers: various actors act in accordance with separate but interrelated intents and motives.[21] In some cases, perpetrators seem almost instinctually to devise genocidal strategies that instrumentalize sexualized violence to degrade and humiliate cherished group members and symbols of group continuity once a genocidal policy is unleashed. During the Holocaust, for example, sexualized violence was rampant but improvised at mass grave sites, in ghettos, during deportations, and in concentration and death camps.[22] As in other cases of genocide, sexualized violence in the Holocaust was maximally brutal, often leading to death; it was often public and coordinated with other tortures, such as the killing of infants and children in front of their parents. But it appears not to have been a strategic part of the genocide. In other cases, rituals devised on the periphery in an improvised fashion end up becoming more coordinated and systematized over time and through a process of invention, institutionalization, and radicalization. The spread of genocidal rape rituals across various fighting forces in the Democratic Republic of the Congo seems to follow this pattern.

With or without the existence of a coordinated state plan, sexualized violence, when it occurs in a genocidal context, tends to take on certain forms that I have called "life force atrocities," which I break down into two groups: inversion rituals and ritual desecrations.[23] The goal of these ritualized atrocities is to debase and then completely annihilate the generative force that perpetrators implicitly believe to be responsible for the existence of the group. These atrocities are surprisingly consistent across conflicts and can help us identify the genocidal potential within a conflict before genocide takes the shape we usually associate with the term. A key feature of these atrocities is the perpetrators' instrumentalization of deep human bonds and symbols of love and mutual responsibility among their victims through the use of various crimes including public rape, especially in front of family or community members; rape as murder; rape with implements of torture; mutilation,

---

[21] Maria Eriksson Baaz and Maria Stern, "Why Do Soldiers Rape? Masculinity, Violence, and Sexuality in the Armed Forces in the Congo (DRC)," *International Studies Quarterly* 53: 495–518 (2009).

[22] Sonia M. Hedgepeth and Rochelle G. Saidel (eds.), *Sexual Violence against Jewish Women during the Holocaust* (Lebanon, NH: Brandeis University Press, 2010).

[23] Elisa von Joeden-Forgey, "The Devil in the Details: "Life Force Atrocities" and the Assault on the Family in Times of Conflict," *Genocide Studies and Prevention* 5(1): 1–19 (2010).

especially of genitals and breasts; the evisceration of pregnant women; the separation of the sexes and of family members; and the use of particularly tortuous cruelties against children. Frequently, these atrocities are committed as atrocity sets: following a general pattern of inversion rituals, some victims will be killed, others will be forced to watch or to participate, others will be violated through sexualized violence. Very often, there are no survivors, so the spectacle was for the consumption of the perpetrators and victims alone. What makes these atrocity sets genocidal is that they betray the strong possibility of genocidal intent: in and of themselves, these atrocities are highly correlated with known genocides and their internal logic strongly suggests that the person committing them views his or her victims as representatives of or stand-ins for a larger group that they wish to destroy.

I have argued elsewhere that, in the context of genocide, sexualized violence and especially public rape, can function as an "anchor crime": the person who is raped (and often left for dead) stands as audience and witness to the murder, torture, and pillage that effect the complete destruction of family and community that is organized around or culminates with her rape. To cite an example, a survivor of sexualized violence in the Democratic Republic of Congo, Nadine, told in 2007 how unidentified soldiers attacked her village.[24] First they killed the chief and his family; they then they tried to force Nadine's brother to rape her. When he refused, he was killed. After this, they began to kill Nadine's children, one by one, casting her infant daughter to the ground. Nadine was then gang raped, publicly and so viciously that her organs were ruptured. She was kidnapped and forced into sexual slavery, where the soldiers continued their ritualized atrocities against their captives. Before escaping, Nadine witnessed the soldiers eviscerating a pregnant woman and cooking her unborn baby: this child was then given to Nadine and the other women, who were forced to eat it.

Nadine's initial rape here is an anchor crime in that the other atrocities appeared to have been organized around it and derive a narrative meaning and tempo from it: murder, torture, humiliation, inversion rituals, ritual desecrations, strategically patterned killing of local notables. Although it is unlikely that things were consciously organized in this way, even mayhem can have a logic to it. The logic of the mayhem unleashed against Nadine's small village seems to suggest that, for one reason or another, the roots of her community were being targeted for destruction along with the branches. Additionally, some of the sequencing – demanding that her brother rape her, his murder upon his refusal, the murder of her children before her rape – appear to derive their meaning to the perpetrators from the fact that the tortures would

---

[24] The pattern of the violence suggests that the perpetrators were ex-Interahamwe and/or members of the FDLR, who had committed identical atrocity sets in Rwanda during the genocide.

culminate in a brutal, public gang rape. That her tormenters continued to use life force atrocities after her capture and sexual enslavement indicates the extent to which this logic had become an organizing principle of their fighting lives. This can tell us a great deal about their commitments, their worldview, and their perceived goals.

Nadine's story was retold by Eve Ensler as a story of rape, and it is indeed that. But her story is also a story of community destruction and the torture and murder that comes with it. We must find ways to catalogue all of these crimes together in a meaningful way. Sensitivity to sexualized violence early on in a conflict, and good research and reporting strategies while a conflict is under way, will often lead us to "life force atrocities" like the ones described by Nadine. When we see life force atrocities in a conflict, it is an indication that something "worse than war" is occurring. The job then becomes to determine why they are being committed, who is ultimately responsible, and, based on these things, how they might develop into genocide down the road. It is important that we pay attention to sequencing of atrocities and the identities (real and symbolic) of the victims and take note of atrocities that suggest a genocidal logic, such as reports by witnesses and survivors of inversion rituals as well as physical evidence of ritual desecrations, such as the disembowelment of pregnant women, the killing of infants and small children, and the mutilation of sexual organs and of women's breasts. A consistent pattern of life force atrocities, no matter how small, tells us that potentially genocidal processes are in the works. At the very least, such a pattern suggests that a conflict will be brutal and long, with a very high potential for cumulative radicalization leading to mass murder. The harm committed by life force atrocities is so extreme that preventing them should be a core part of any genocide prevention strategy, even if, in the long run, they may not have developed into a classic case of the crime.

6.2.   Sexualized Violence and Flexible Genocide

In several articles, Catherine MacKinnon has called attention to the fact that genocides are sexualized (and often so pornographic) for a reason. In her analysis, perpetrators use sexualized violence as a tool of domination of groups of men and women because it has worked so well for so long in enforcing domination of men over women. "Sexual abuse," she writes, "is a perfect genocidal tool. It does to ethnic, racial, religious, and national groups as such what has been done to women as such from time immemorial in one of the most effective systems of domination-to-destruction in history."[25] Rape,

---

[25] Catherine A. MacKinnon, "Genocide's Sexuality," in *Are Women Human?* (Cambridge, MA: Belknap Press, 2006), 233.

especially as an intentional form of torture or an "anchor crime" around which other atrocities cluster, lends itself to the genocidal project because the form of domination it expresses is so all-encompassing; just as perpetrators of genocide frequently encircle villages and encircle their victims before pressing in and murdering them, the rapist is able to encircle every aspect of his or her victim by (subjectively) penetrating the interior world of the victim – the invisible space inside where life and spirit reside – and robbing the victim of agency and bodily integrity, often for extensive periods of time. Rape provides a model for genocide in its perceived ability to destroy both the outer and inner dimensions of human life.

What we call "rape" – in peacetime and in war – is therefore not only a crime, but also a framework for and a mode of attack involving encirclement, total domination, and the extinguishing of the individual will and personal autonomy of the victim in what is usually a drawn-out act of humiliation and debasement. This may be why genocides seem to be characterized by higher rates of male rape and sexualized violence against men and boys than we see in other conflicts or in peacetime. As a framework for attack, rape can be applied to many things, including but not limited to female bodies. Its generalization during genocide therefore makes a great deal of sense. In times of genocide, when peacetime rape models show up as organizing principles of violence against target groups, they take on a much more pronounced and directed social dimension. Genocidal rapes send messages – to the victim, to the victim's family, to the victim's community, and, ultimately, to the intangible and abstract identity that the victim is believed to personify. This transposition of a crime against women to a crime against the group is what accounts for the clustering of life force atrocities around sexualized violence. The obsessive, time-consuming, psychologically trying attention that perpetrators invest in the degradation of the symbols of the life force of the group, and especially the instrumentalization of family bonds (and other intangibles) as a form of torture, therefore can be considered to be a "congealment" of genocidal intent, of the will to communal destruction. It is what intent looks like on the ground level. Whether ordered from above or improvised from below, life force atrocities tell us that somebody in a conflict is pursuing genocidal ends.

Rape, rather than being a sideshow to genocidal destruction, provides a powerful roadmap for the destruction of groups, one that is shared between the leadership and many of the foot soldiers simply by virtue of living in systems of male domination. When we suggest that perpetrators act according to a rape model, however, we are not suggesting that this is either natural or explicitly intentional. In fact, this approach to rape requires that we call into question both the older "biological" or evolutionary arguments that treat both wartime rape and genocide as integral parts of male sexuality and human nature, respectively, and more recent rational actor arguments that overstate the logical and pragmatic decision-making processes involved in setting upon a policy of genocide and the use of "rape as a weapon of war."[26] These "essentialist" and "rational actor" explanatory systems both suffer from a static and unitary view of intent that does not account for the rapidly shifting nature of conflict. To account for war's "messiness," Janie L. Leatherman has suggested we take a constructivist approach to sexualized violence in conflict that explores "systemic factors like hegemonic masculinity and how it links up with situational factors in conflict to produce other masculinities that are subordinate, violence laden and catastrophic."[27] In her approach, sexualized violence is a "runaway norm" that contributes to the moral collapse of a society into torture, ethnic cleansing, and genocide.[28] In other words, sexual violence is an important radicalizer in conflict; its presence is therefore also an important indicator of a potential near-term radicalization.

To fully understand the particular relationship between sexualized violence and genocide, we also need to unpack some abiding assumptions about genocide. In particular, we need to interrogate the static approach to genocide that views the crime principally as top-down mass murder arising out of state-based policies and initiatives. Although states tend to be the institutions most suited to the commission of genocide, because of their immense pre-existing military and administrative resources as well as because of their ideological underpinnings, the genocidal impulse exists separately from the emergence of the modern state system. Whether we understand the genocidal impulse politically, socially, historically, psychologically, theologically, or philosophically, it unquestionably finds its home within individual human beings. The impulse becomes mediated through institutions, which define opportunities, set limits, and therefore determine some of the diversity of forms of genocide that we see expressed across time and space, but it exists always in the human realm, and specifically in the realm of individual minds and spirits. Genocide becomes a collective project and an official policy and strategy, but it must first be a thought. This is important because, when we think in these terms, it helps us lift genocide out of the procrustean and static bed of "systematization" and "coordination" and think a bit about its early, more mobile, and uncoordinated expressions.

---

[26] For a trenchant analysis and critique of the "rape as a weapon of war" narrative, see Maria Eriksson Baaz and Maria Stern, *Sexual Violence as a Weapon of War? Perceptions, Prescriptions, and Problems in the Congo and Beyond* (London/New York: Zed, 2013).

[27] Janie L. Leatherman, *Sexual Violence and Armed Conflict* (Cambridge, UK: Polity Press, 2011), 4.

[28] Leatherman, *Sexual Violence*, 36.

A flexible approach to genocide allows us to cast our net both more broadly (as we incorporate violence that is not yet clearly part of a genocidal project) and more specifically (as we home in on potentially genocidal gender-based violence). A flexible approach allows us to read backward from the behavior of perpetrators to the world that helped facilitate it. It allows us to interrogate genocide as something in addition to a pragmatic problem-solving option available to dictators. We can speak of "genocidal violence" that, if generalized, would become "a genocide." A flexible approach may even help us pinpoint the "near-term indicators, triggers and accelerators" that have proved to be so elusive in genocide prevention.[29] For example, just before the 1992 Prijedor massacre that began what eventually became a genocide in Bosnia-Herzegovina, the local Serbian Democratic Party (SDS), which had taken control of the town, started a propaganda campaign that, among other things, accused a Bosniak politician of injecting drugs into Serb women that rendered them incapable of bearing male children. Bosniaks were also accused of forcing Serb women to have abortions if they were carrying boys and of castrating Serbian male infants.[30] These accusations betray a genocidal logic within the minds of those making them and could have been a tip-off that the "civil war" was going to be something much more extreme indeed.

A flexible approach to genocide can certainly help us integrate theories about sexualized violence into our genocide prevention mechanisms. Sexualized violence, because it is a prevalent feature of peacetime life, offers an important bridge between the preconflict world and the specific time and space of genocide.[31] This bridge connects both patterns of gender-based violence in peacetime and war as well as societal acceptance of such patterns and ideological support for them. A key example is pornography, which was, as Catherine MacKinnon has argued quite convincingly, an important framework though which Bosnian Serb soldiers understood their violence against Bosniak women and men.[32] It is fair to assume that certain patterns of sexualized violence, as well as widespread social acceptance of them and ideological speech that supports them, can make a society at once more vulnerable to the

---

[29] Madeleine Albright and William Cohen, "Preventing Genocide: A Blueprint for U.S. Policymakers" (Washington, DC: United States Institute of Peace, December 2008), 21.

[30] International Criminal Tribunal for the Former Yugoslavia, *Judgment*, Prosecutor v. Milomir Stakj (July 31, 2003) 26–30, www.icty.org/x/cases/stakic/tjug/en/stak-tj030731e.pdf, last accessed March 3, 2014.

[31] On the high incidence of sexualized violence in most societies across the globe, see: Valerie M. Hudson et al. (eds.), "The Heart of the Matter: The Security of Women and the Security of States," in *Sex and World Peace* (New York: Columbia, University Press, 2012): 95–118.

[32] Catharine A. MacKinnon, "Turning Rape into Pornography: Postmodern Genocide," *Ms.* 4(1): 24–31 (July/August 1993).

growth of genocidal ideologies as well as more primed for the commission of genocidal atrocities at home and abroad.

It is equally important that we pursue a "flexible approach" to rape and sexualized violence because it can also be helpful to genocide prevention. For example, it is crucial that we recognize that rape is a mode of attack that can take different forms and can serve different purposes. Identifying those forms that are most closely related with the development of genocide is critical. One of the forms that has a particularly serious genocidal potential is life force atrocity. Others include widespread rape of women and girls alongside the separation, detention, and massacre of men and boys, as well as assaults that are directed specifically against children. An example of the latter is the murder and mutilation of thirteen-year-old Hamza Ali al-Khateeb in Syria in April and May 2011, ostensibly for participating in anti-government rallies. When his body was returned to his parents, he was covered in bruises and cigarette burns, his kneecaps and jaw has been smashed, he had three gunshot wounds, and his genitals had been cut off.[33] The sorts of sexualized violence that can be identified as genocidal and highly potentially genocidal all betray a preoccupation among perpetrators with the "reproductive arenas" of the groups they are targeting. They can involve systematic campaigns of rape and sexualized violence against women and girls coordinated from the top and aimed at destroying the biological reproductive capacity of a group; they can involve forced maternity, under the mistaken notion that women will bear children of the perpetrator group; they can involve the sexual brutalization and mutilation of men and boys in detention; and they can involve sustained torture campaigns aimed at the annihilation of smaller groups that fall into the perpetrator's ambit, campaigns that will target family and community members in accordance with their rank and role in the biological and social reproductive hierarchy.

In examining the development of sexual violence in conflict, it is therefore critical that we consistently ask ourselves what the perpetrators are expressing through the sexualized violence they are committing. Even mass sexualized violence that appears to have its genesis in conditions that are not genocidal – in the breakdown of security during conflict and the opportunism of soldiers, for example – can be taken up by superiors and directed toward genocidal purposes as the conflict develops. Furthermore, genocidal violence can exist in a military or political leadership even in the absence of clear genocidal plans. Genocidaires can continue to use genocidal atrocities in situations that are no longer a part of the initial genocide, as when they cross borders and move on to new targets, for example. Equally, sexualized violence that emerges on the

---

[33] Liz Sly, "Apparent Torture of Boy Reinvigorates Syria's Protest Movement," *The Washington Post* (May 29, 2011).

periphery of a conflict can have a decidedly genocidal color to it and can potentially spread – along with the genocidal concepts and urges that gave rise to it – thus posing a specific security problem of its own: "rogue genocide" innovated from below.

Nevertheless, breaking down how we interpret and talk about sexualized violence is not an easy task. Even talking about rape's different roles in conflict can raise ethical concerns regarding the potential for certain forms of rape to be treated more seriously than others. Rhonda Copelon gave voice to this concern early on in the debates about "genocidal rape." She argued that "what is going on in the many places in the world where women are being raped, whether it be for booty, whether it be to move people off their land, whether it be for genocide, whether it be to terrorize the population, whether it be random or systematic, it is of comparable terribleness. The gender dimension of these crimes must be recognized. That is why distinctions between genocidal rape and other types of rape are wrong. By treating genocidal rape differently, one is in effect saying that all these other terrible abuses of women can go forward without comparable sanction."[34] I propose that, rather than speak of genocidal rape in contrast to or in competition with other forms of rape, we recognize rape's inherent annihilative power. The difference becomes the goal and the ultimate target of that annihilation. All rape, in and of itself, has a genocidal dimension to its logic and can offer us clues to the development of genocidal thinking and ideologies.

6.3. Genocide, the "Reproductive Arena," and Long-Term Prevention

The discussion thus far points to the gendered nature of genocide and the role that sexualized violence can play in genocidal destruction. Without taking gender patterns seriously and incorporating them into our core definitions and understandings of the crime, we end up defining the crime as mass killing, which distorts genocidal processes to fit a conceptualization of genocide that is much too restrictive. Treating genocide as mass killing also excludes some of the primary ways in which women and girls experience the crime, and risks seriously underestimating the long-term individual and communal harm that results from sexualized violence. Moreover, it hampers our ability to identify potentially genocidal violence before murder takes on a massive scale. Although not all incidents of mass rape will be genocide, and not all rapes within a conflict will be genocidal, there are specific patterns and expressions of sexualized violence that are strongly suggestive of the presence

---

[34] Rhonda Copelon, "Women's Rights as International Human Rights: Women and War," *St. John's Law Review* 69:67 (1995).

of genocidal intent, and these need to be taken seriously for their forensic and evidentiary value.

To understand how sexualized and gender-based violence may help us with long-term prevention of genocide and mass atrocities, it is necessary to go beyond these patterns and crimes and examine the world that they destroy during genocide: what R. W. Connell calls the "reproductive arena."[35] The reproductive arena is one of the most underresearched subjects in the modern social sciences. Often viewed as a natural phenomenon, taken for granted, and gendered female as "domestic life," the "reproductive arena" is conceptualized, if at all, to be a space acted upon by conflict but not itself to be a factor within it. However, as we have begun to understand the importance of the "home front" in times of war, as civilians have again become the targets of war on a mass scale, and as women and girl soldiers and perpetrators of genocide have become a subject of scholarly curiosity, this space, which was assumed to be ahistorical, passive, unimportant to larger events and long-term history, has found a place on center stage.

It is important to underscore that most of the sexualized violence committed during genocide also can be characterized as "reproductive violence" because its aim is to destroy the ability of a group to reproduce itself as a strong historical agent in the future. When the rape model is used for generalized destruction of a group, rape becomes means of invading and dominating a group's reproductive autonomy, its body politic, its sovereign realm. So the rape, in case of genocide, is not aimed just at harming women or humiliating men, as it is often described; it is a totalizing form of violence that aims at reducing the target community to utter powerlessness, to historical nonexistence. The intended destruction of this invasion is not merely physical; it is also cultural, emotional, psychic, and spiritual. Sexualized violence, precisely because it is so intimate, so invasive, and so disruptive of human relationships, destroys individuals, families, and communities on every conceivable level of their existence.

To achieve this scale of destruction, perpetrators target the entire "reproductive arena" of individual family units: men and women, boys and girls, the born and the unborn, the elderly and the very young. Family units are targeted in time as well as in space. As we know, perpetrators do not limit themselves to the physical killing of individual bodies, but also seek to destroy a group's past and future, using a variety of techniques. In some cases, perpetrators may burn down religious or intellectual institutions; in others, they may be limited to destroying family photographs or everyday objects. The goals in each case are similar: the erasure of the temporal power of the

---

[35] R. W. Connell, "Globalization and Men's Bodies," *The Men and the Boys* (Berkeley: University of California Press, 2001), 57–66.

reproductive arena being targeted. In societies where cousins are particularly important, we often find that life force atrocities exploit that relationship. Perpetrators also target the reproductive arena of the wider community, in concentric circles, from individual, to family, to community, to the larger socially constructed and abstracted group identity by destroying the institutions of familial, social, political, economic, intellectual, and cultural reproduction. Rapes of single individuals can effect large-level destruction: by raping the daughter of an important religious leader in public, for example, perpetrators can cause deep harm that ripples throughout a community. The desecration that often occurs during rape can also be directed at symbols of a group's historical power: religious texts defamed with bodily fluids, family members' nakedness and humiliation filmed to create pornographic photographs and videos, and so forth. The rupture and extinguishing of individual autonomy that we see in the rape of individual people becomes the rupture and extinguishing of the autonomy of collectivities in genocide: families, communities, and abstract "groups."

The reproductive arena must be examined for the potential insights it can offer into genocidal processes. Here, I offer some provisional thoughts on how we might do this. Connell defines the reproductive arena as the space in which bodies are defined by gender differentiation and given socially constructed meaning.[36] In using the term here, I mean it to represent the biological, social, cultural, political, and symbolic space in which human beings work to continue and ensure the survival of the species and of specific groups and cultures within it. Especially when applied to genocide prevention, the reproductive arena should not be understood in biological terms. Instead, it should be understood as the space in which all groups, including social or political groups, are formed or in which perpetrators believe groups are formed. So, for example, genocidal processes against political groups will tend to target personal networks, membership groups (such as unions), certain professions (such as teachers or the clergy), and other social spaces that appear to play a role in regenerating the group being targeted. The reproductive arena is not synonymous with concepts like the nuclear family, nor limited to persons who are gender differentiated or biologically related. More than anything else, the reproductive arena is a socially constructed space of vital but tense dynamics related to the production of history, culture, power, and existential meaning through small groups that are socially related to a wider community.

The gendered patterns of genocidal violence demonstrate, I think quite clearly, that perpetrators are expressing hostility to the reproductive arena in general while targeting specific groups on which they perform that hostility.

---

[36] R. W. Connell, *Gender: In World Perspective* (Cambridge: Polity Press, 2014), 11.

Hatred of the group may emerge out of personal and social frustrations originating in the reproductive arena that create existential crises. While seeking to shore up and exert maximum control over their own reproductive arenas through forms of plunder and state control of the reproductive resources, perpetrators certainly appear to imagine reproductive arenas within their victim groups and methodically exploit them to exert maximum harm. Common cruelties enacted against reproductive arenas during genocide include the torture and then murder of all but one member of a family; killing the male members (sons, fathers, grandfathers, husbands) while raping the female members (daughters, mothers, grandmothers, wives); torturing an entire family and community with drawn-out life force atrocity rituals that prey on deep symbols of existential meaning; forcing family and community members to commit atrocities against one another; forcibly separating family members, often along gendered lines; and the forced removal of children. In North America and Australia, some of the most painful genocidal policies involved the kidnapping of children from their families and their relocation to residential schools, where they were forbidden from speaking their native language or having contact with their home communities and where they were subjected to harsh conditions and punishments, often leading to death.[37] Even when apparently "social" or "political" groups are targets of genocidal violence, perpetrators betray a desire to defile the reproductive arena of their targets, which suggests that, in the case of genocide, these groups are imagined by perpetrators to have a quasi-biological basis.[38]

If perpetrators imagine their targets as reproductive units, then genocide becomes a reproductive justice issue. Certain patterns would seem to support this possibility. For example, apart from the direct destruction of people within reproductive arenas, perpetrating cadres may appropriate people from the target community to create alternative reproductive arenas in the perceived absence or weakness of their own: women and girls can be taken as slaves or concubines, boys and girls as soldiers and forced laborers, infants to replenish the perpetrator group in the future. We have seen this latter pattern in Argentina, where it is estimated that more than 500 children of political prisoners were kidnapped and adopted by military families from the period between 1976 and 1983.[39] We see the former two patterns in the Lord's Resistance Army (LRA)

---

[37] A. Dirk Moses (ed.), *Genocide and Settler Society: Frontier Violence and Stolen Indigenous Children in Australian History* (New York/Oxford: Berghahn Books, 2005); The Truth and Reconciliation Commission of Canada, *They Came for the Children* (Winnipeg, Manitoba, 2012), www.trc.ca/websites/trcinstitution/index.php?p=580, last accessed March 3, 2014.

[38] For an example of the naturalization of political groups in perpetrator ideology, see Daniel Feierstein, "Political Violence in Argentina and Its Genocidal Characteristics," *Journal of Genocide Research* 8(2): 149–168 (2006).

[39] Michael L. Lazzara, "Kidnapped Memories: Argentina's Stolen Children Tell Their Stories," *Journal of Human Rights* 12(3): 319–332 (July 2013).

and the Revolutionary United Front (RUF), both militarized alternative societies reliant on appropriating resources – including human beings – to reproduce themselves.[40] In these cases, the genocidal violence involves a partial consumption of the target community, frequently accompanied by massive destruction, including murder, sexualized violence, and life force atrocities committed against the remaining community members. The appropriation of part of the group alongside the laying waste to the rest should be considered a form of genocide.

The dynamic of appropriation and destruction that characterizes most genocidal processes point to the revolutionary nature of most genocidal movements. Generally speaking, they wish to oust traditional male elites or, when the genocidal leadership is already in power, to refashion manhood around martial ideas that transgress deep moral and ethical codes that are have been reaffirmed within patriarchal families and communities. So, sexualized violence during genocidal processes is a refashioning rather than a simple extension of patriarchal norms of violence and control. To replace the patriarchal order, many genocidal regimes usurp the position of patriarchs and set themselves up as the "parent" of the group they believe they are protecting through genocide. Both the Nazi Party and the Committee of Union and Progress (under Talaat Pasha) in the Ottoman Empire sought to extend state powers over family life; the Hitler Youth and League of German Girls were aimed at completely undermining parental authority.[41] In Cambodia, the Khmer Rouge abolished family life while claiming to be the "father-mother" of the Khmer people.[42] The first three instructions of the "Hutu Ten Commandments" involve the proper construction of Hutu families and the proper comportment of male and female family members.[43]

Appreciating this centrality of the reproductive arena can help us think in greater depth about the ways that gendered social relations are bound up in genocidal processes. The long-term prevention of genocide is a project as much about gender dynamics as about ethnic or other communal-based conflict. It is possible that the intersection of the two is ultimately crucial to our ability to

---

[40] For an interesting look at LRA kidnapping as a form of resource exploitation, see James Bevan, "The Myth of Madness: Cold Rationality and 'Resource' Plunder by the Lord's Resistance Army," *Civil Wars* 9(4): 343–358 (December 2007).

[41] For an extended discussion of the particularly revolutionary nature of "genocidal masculinity," see Elisa von Joeden-Forgey, "Genocidal Masculinity," in Adam Jones, ed., *New Directions in Genocide Research* (New York: Routledge, 2011), 76–95.

[42] Eric D. Weitz, *A Century of Genocide: Utopias of Race and Nation* (Princeton, NJ: Princeton University Press, 2003), 163.

[43] The original commandments, printed in the Hutu Power newspaper, *Kangura*, in December 1990, can be found at https://repositories.lib.utexas.edu/bitstream/handle/2152/9315/unictr_kangura_006a.pdf, last accessed May 7, 2014.

identify peacetime patterns that are most likely to result in genocide should open conflict or crisis emerge. The *specific* peacetime institutions that might inadvertently contribute to the emergence and spread of genocidal ideologies still need to be identified. How might ideological and social approaches to it in peacetime contribute to those thought processes and social conflicts that can later become expressed through genocide? It is possible that reducing gender conflict and gendered social pressures will be as important as reducing intercommunal tensions in our efforts to prevent genocide over the longue durée. In fact, we will need to begin to consider the intersection of gender with several factors when devising local approaches to long-term prevention, including the way that group identity is socially constructed, the way states instrumentalize the reproductive arena in the allocation of resources, the state's gendered approach to group definition, the role played by group categories in political ideologies, and so forth, all of which are very gendered projects. We have seen that in situations that threaten to develop into genocide, many of the tensions that exist between groups begin to be understood and expressed ideologically with reference to the reproductive arena.[44]

Looking at the long-term prevention of genocide through the centrality of the reproductive arena to genocidal ideology and practice leads us to some provisional thoughts. One clear implication is that policies and efforts geared toward reducing conflict within and around the reproductive arena and supporting the creation of family systems that dignify the individuality and the worth of each member should be front and central to long-term efforts to reduce a society's vulnerability to genocide. One of the clearest paths to dehumanization is the depiction of a person or a group as existing outside of stable family life. The Nazis, for example, depicted Jewish men as predators who targeted respectable girls and families.[45] The Hutu Power extremists represented Tutsi women as highly sexualized agents of Tutsi aggression sent to disrupt Hutu life.[46] The Roma-Sinti in Europe have been historically stereotyped as unfit parents. Similarly, Native Americans in the United States were commonly defamed as sexually licentious and having no family life at all.[47] Policies that recognize the importance of the relative autonomy of reproductive realms – women's bodies, families, and autonomous cultural spheres – vis-à-vis state power should be encouraged in order to arrest the

---

[44] Joeden-Forgey, "Genocidal Masculinities," 76–95.

[45] Marion Kaplan, *Between Dignity and Despair* (New York/Oxford: Oxford University Press, 1999).

[46] Christopher C. Taylor, *Sacrifice as Terror: The Rwandan Genocide of 1994* (Oxford: Berg, 1999), 155.

[47] Andrea Smith, *Conquest: Sexual Violence and American Indian Genocide* (Cambridge, MA: South End Press, 2005), 7–33.

development and the currency of such stereotypes. Ideologies that would usurp the rights of men and women to form families (through forced sterilizations, state control over access to abortion or reproductive technologies, or high-levels of state-mandated removal of children) send up red flags. State penetration into the autonomous realms of families can normalize forms of executive power that can easily radicalize into overt violence in times of social stress and conflict.

State policies that consistently undermine the cohesion and welfare of the reproductive arena of a particular group set a dangerous precedent. The criminal justice system in the United States, for example, which disproportionately incarcerates young black men, usually for nonviolent crimes, has had a devastating effect on black family life, an effect that is accepted and legitimated by dominant society.[48] A similar destabilization of black family life has occurred through the widely accepted reality of high rates of female and male rape within the prison system.[49] In a similar fashion, policy discourses that betray an obsession with the reproductive arena of subdominant groups bear within themselves a pronounced genocidal potential. An example of this is the discourse on "anchor babies" and "welfare queens" in the United States, which not only demonstrates an obsession with the reproductive habits of groups but also a desire to defame and humiliate them.[50] The high levels of forced child removal in Native American families that continue to this day are not only a continuation of genocidal patterns that treated Native American communities, families, and bodies as "open," porous, and without protection, but also a potentially dangerous precedent that could be transposed to other populations and that encourage a more general dehumanization of minority and vulnerable populations.[51]

More generally, certain approaches to sexualized violence and the reproductive realms within political ideologies seem particularly primed for genocide, such as those that imagine brutal sexual hierarchies within the reproductive arena, that utilize rape imagery as a sign of state or party power, and that betray a preoccupation with the sacredness and impregnability of the

---

[48] Rose M. Brewer, "Imperiled Black Families and the Growth of the Prison Industrial Complex in the U.S.," *Council on Crime and Justice Newsletter*, n.d., www.crimeandjustice.org/counci linfo.cfm?pID=58, last accessed February 1. 2014.

[49] Joanne Mariner et al., "No Escape: Male Rape in U.S. Prisons" (New York: Human Rights Watch, 2001); Dorothy Q. Thomas et al., "All too Familiar: Sexual Abuse of Women in U.S. State Prisons" (New York: Human Rights Watch, 1996).

[50] Emily Kendall, "Amending the Constitution to Save a Sinking Ship? The Issues Surrounding The Proposed Amendment of the Citizenship Clause and 'Anchor Babies,'" *Berkeley La Raza Law Journal* 22:350 (2012); Nazneen Mehta, "Opposing Images: 'Third World Woman' and 'Welfare Queen,'" *Women's Policy Journal of Harvard* 7: 65–70 (2010).

[51] On the historical development of the construction of Native communities as "open" for violence, see Andrea Smith, *Conquest: Sexual Violence and American Indian Genocide* (Cambridge, MA: South End Press, 2005).

ideologue's own reproductive arena, casting perceived enemies as agents of sexual or moral contagion who would illegitimately penetrate this sacred realm. This helps explain why the victims of genocides are so often represented in perpetrator propaganda as sexual deviants and rapists who are intent on defiling the perpetrator's reproductive arena or why those who may be planning future genocides often allege that their victims are plotting or actually causing the annihilation of their own group. This also helps explain why genocidaires so frequently pursue the "decapitation" of the target group by killing, humiliating, and sexually mutilating perceived patriarchs – it is seen to be an existential as well as a practical means of accessing the inner sanctum, a form of rape of the familial and collective body that is meant to neutralize the supposed sexual threat posed by this group.

Because access to the reproductive arena has such high-stakes consequences for men and for women, our gendered efforts to reduce the risk of genocide in the long term will need to be sensitive not only to women's systematic exclusion, disempowerment, and dehumanization in peacetime, but also specifically to social processes that exclude men, and especially young men, from the reproductive arena. For example, in situations such as the ethnoregional conflict in the Great Lakes, where population pressures make land acquisition and hence marriage and social status beyond the pale for many young men, genocide prevention will need to focus on opening up routes for meaningful participation and engagement for men The problem goes well beyond the lack of economic resources; as Adam Jones has pointed out for Rwanda, the problem is often nothing short of an existential crisis.[52] In North and South Kivu of the Democratic Republic of the Congo, some of the worse life force atrocities have occurred in situations in which one group has lost land to another.[53] Similarly, during the election-related violence in Kenya in 2007, many of the most clearly potentially genocidal atrocities were committed against Kikuyu in the Rift Valley, where the Kikuyu were broadly understood to be recent settlers who had monopolized the land.[54] The inclusion of men and boys, the recognition of their worth and dignity, and access to the reproductive arena must go hand-in-hand with efforts to reduce gender-based violence and improve the lives of women.

By way of conclusion, it is important to point out that some of the longest lasting effects of genocide occur in the reproductive realm of groups.

---

[52] For the dynamics of the existential crisis in Rwanda, see Adam Jones, "Gender and Genocide in Rwanda," *Journal of Genocide Research* 4:1 (2002), 67.

[53] On the dynamics of land pressure in these regions, see René Lemarchand, *The Dynamics of Violence in Central Africa* (Philadelphia: University of Pennsylvania Press, 2009), especially pp. 13–15.

[54] Karuti Kanyinga, "The legacy of the White Highlands: Land rights, Ethnicity and the Post-2007 Election Violence in Kenya," *Journal of Contemporary African Studies* 27(3): 325–344 (July 2009).

The patterns of atrocity that characterize genocide deprive survivors of their family members. Often, these survivors witnessed terrible spectacles involving the people most dear to them. The patterns of atrocity also make the formation of families in the future more difficult. Sexualized violence can compromise the emotional and biological ability of women and men to bear and raise children. When children are conceived through genocidal rape, these difficulties can be amplified, a result that is often intended by the rapists. Furthermore, in cases where the perpetrating group or society is left intact after the genocide, structural patterns forged through genocide can create a situation in which the survivors of genocide are treated as eternally "open" people whose right – and therefore whose ability – to create well-defined and sovereign autonomous social entities called families is consistently undermined and questioned. Examples of the latter include the high rates of referral to foster care of Native American children in South Dakota, for example, and similar patterns in American cities with high densities of African-American families.[55] The intimacy and the depth of the harm caused by genocidal violence is the reason that we must keep using the term "genocide" and understand it for the insidious and gendered process that it is.

Working effectively over longer periods of time with the risk of genocide in the front of one's mind requires that we question not just those peacetime dynamics and norms that appear to have the most direct relationship to genocide, such as those promoting intercommunal hostility, but also those less obvious traditions that could inadvertently contribute to the growth of genocidal thinking within the population. Some of the most dangerous framings are also deeply gendered ones, tied to existential crises about who has transcendent resources and who does not. Looking at the gendered nature of genocide – its ideology and its patterns – can help us pin-point some of the less obvious historical red flags and perhaps even the historical triggers for genocide.

The link between gender-based violence in peacetime and conflict is clear, although the specific routes traveled need to spelled out with more precision. What needs further study is the way in which peacetime forms of gender-based violence influence the shape of violence during mass atrocity and genocide, which would require a longitudinal analysis of perpetrators of atrocities: their cultural and historical contexts, their gender identities, their peacetime lives, their training, and the dynamic interplay between military hierarchy and individual creativity that results in gendered genocidal atrocities. Of specific

---

[55] Jeff Armstrong, "Lakota to File UN Genocide Charges against US, South Dakota," *Counterpunch* (May 19, 2013), www.counterpunch.org/2013/05/29/lakota-to-file-un-genocide-charges-against-us-south-dakota/, last accessed March 5, 2014.

importance to our understanding of long-term prevention are the forms of gender-based violence in peacetime that have the greatest potential to influence the decision of political and military leaders to commit genocide, the willingness of soldiers to implement genocide, and the potential that soldiers will engage in life force atrocity and other forms of genocidal violence independently of any explicit order. Rather than being simply the consequence of or corollary to genocidal intent, sexualized violence can be important to genocide's initial formulation, its acceptance, and the shape it takes once implemented.

Part II

Above Chronology

7   Audacity of Hope: International Criminal Law, Mass Atrocity Crimes, and Prevention

Sheri P. Rosenberg

7.1.   Introduction

Over the past two decades, there has been a proliferation of international criminal tribunals empowered to punish perpetrators for genocide, crimes against humanity, and war crimes (hereinafter, "atrocity crimes"[1]). Since the establishment of the ad hoc tribunals in the 1990s and the permanent International Criminal Court (ICC) in 2002, with its broad jurisdiction over atrocities occurring in the territory of any state party to the Rome Statute, international criminal tribunals have found a prominent place in the global atrocity prevention agenda.

The central justifications propounded by international criminal justice advocates and international judges for prosecuting individuals who commit atrocities are retribution and deterrence.[2] Retribution posits that inflicting punishment on perpetrators of crimes corrects the moral imbalance to the extent that punishment is what the criminal deserves.[3] For the retributivist,

---

[1] In this chapter, "atrocities" refer to the set of crimes within the jurisdiction of, and as defined by, the ICC. These crimes are war crimes, crimes against humanity, and genocide. To date, the crime of aggression has not been defined. See Rome Statute of the International Criminal Court, Preamble, July 12, 1998, 2187 U.N.T.S. 900 (hereinafter "Rome Statute").

[2] *Prosecutor v. Stakic*, Case No. IT-97-24-A, para. 402 (ICTY Appeals Chamber, March 22, 2006) (stating that "[t]he Appeals Chamber notes that the jurisprudence of the Tribunal and the ICTR consistently points out that the two main purposes of sentencing are deterrence and retribution."); *Prosecutor v. Rutaganda*, Case No. ICTR-96-3, para. 456 (ICTR Trial Chamber, December 6, 1999); and David S. Koller, "The Faith of the International Criminal Layer," *International Law and Policy* 40: 1025 (2008). Other justifications include establishing a historical record of past events, promoting national peace and reconciliation, and re-establishing the rule of law. See Office of the Secretary-General, *The Rule of Law and Transitional Justice in Conflict and Post-conflict Societies*, Report of the Secretary-General, para. 32, delivered to the Security Council, U. N. Doc. S/2004/616 (August 23, 2004) (hereinafter *Rule of Law Report*); Laurel Fletcher and Harvey Weinstein, "Violence and Social Repair: Rethinking the Contribution to Reconciliation," *Human Rights Quarterly* 24: 573 (2002).

[3] Robert D. Sloane, "The Expressive Capacity of International Punishment: The Limits of the National Law Analogy and the Potential of International Criminal Law," *Stanford Journal of International Law* 43(39): 77 (2007).

punishment must reflect a balance between the gravity of the offence and the degree of the offender's responsibility.[4] Deterrence theory posits that the purpose of prosecution and punishment is to dissuade individuals from committing crimes.[5] From a deterrence perspective, punishment is pursued for the utilitarian, consequentialist effect of the punishment – namely, reducing its recurrence. Whereas retributivist theory is backward looking, deterrence rationales are forward looking and are analogous to the prevention goals of the broader atrocity prevention community.

The deterrence rationale currently plays the most prominent role in justifying international criminal law (ICL) and has been a central purpose of ICL since its inception.[6] In fact, the language of deterrence was ubiquitous at the Rome conference in the summer of 1998, where national delegates negotiated the terms of the new ICC. Delegates and advocacy groups attending the conference insisted that an independent and effective international court would deter serious violations.[7] And support for a permanent court, as opposed to the ad hoc tribunals of the 1990s, rests on the argument that a permanent international criminal court will be more likely to deter future atrocity crimes.[8] Although the sentencing judgments of the ad hoc tribunals cite primarily to the twin goals of retribution and deterrence in their sentencing considerations,[9] the preamble to the Rome Statute provides that signatories "are determined to put an end to impunity for the perpetrators of these crimes and thus to contribute to the prevention of such crimes."[10]

---

[4] *Prosecutor v. Akayesu*, Case No. ICTR-96-4-S, para. 40 (I.C.T.R. Trial Chamber, October 2, 1998) ("[A] sentence must reflect the predominant standard of proportionality between the gravity of the offence and the degree of responsibility of the offender.").

[5] Robert D. Sloane, "The Expressive Capacity of International Punishment: The Limits of the National Law Analogy and the Potential of International Criminal Law," *Stanford Journal of International Law* 43(39): 77 (2007).

[6] William A. Schabas, "International Sentencing: From Leipzig (1923) to Arusha (1996)," in *International Criminal Law* (2nd ed., vol. 3), edited by M. Sherif Bassiouni (1999), 171, 173–174 (noting statements justifying international punishment by reference to its deterrence value); see, e.g., David J. Scheffer, "War Crimes and Crimes Against Humanity," *Pace International Law Review* 11(319): 328 (1999). ("As instruments of deterrence, the tribunals are formidable partners that cannot be lightly ignored in the future.")

[7] Julian Ku and Jide Nzelibe, "Do International Criminal Tribunals Deter or Exacerbate Humanitarian Atrocities?" *Washington University Law Review* 84: 777, 789 (2006); UN Diplomatic Conference of Plenipotentiaries on the Establishment of an International Criminal Court, 2d plen. Mtg. ¶ 81, U.N. Doc. A/CONF.183 (vol. II) (June 15, 1998). A representative example includes a statement by the South Korean Representative: "Bringing to justice the perpetrators of crimes of international concern would serve as an effective deterrent." *Id.*

[8] Jan Klabbers, "Just Revenge? The Deterrence Argument in International Criminal Law," *Finnish Year Book of International Law* 12: 249, 251 (2001) (citing deterrence as perhaps the main justification for creating the ICC).

[9] Allison Marston Danner, "Constructing a Hierarchy of Crimes in International Criminal Law Sentencing," *Virginia Law Review* 87: 415, 444, n.109 (2001).

[10] Rome Statute, *supra* note 1, at Preamble.

Indeed, in public statements from inside the ICC, prevention is a recurring theme. The prosecutor and other senior court officials have claimed, on several occasions, that the Court has already had a preventive impact on situations ranging from Colombia to Sri Lanka, and on actors in countries in between.[11] Outside observers have also identified situations in which they believed the Court, or at least awareness of the Court, had a preventive effect.[12]

Prevention claims, however, are anecdotal, with little empirical evidence to support them. In fact, research on the preventive impact of ICL mechanisms in general is limited. ICL is still in its infancy, and any methodical attempts to test its preventive impact have only begun in the past five to ten years.[13] Furthermore, some argue that the deterrent effect of international criminal justice is empirically indeterminate; it cannot be proved or disproved in a methodologically sound way.[14] In fact, it is that very indeterminacy that may,

---

[11] For example, the Prosecutor of the ICC has claimed that the cases it pursued on child soldiers in Africa have had a deterring impact in Colombia and Sri Lanka. See Luis Moreno-Ocampo, Address to the Assembly of States Parties, Eighth Session, 3 (November 18, 2009). Crimes by the LRA in northern Uganda "have dramatically decreased" as a result of the ICC indictment and the group's recruitment efforts "dried up almost instantly after indictments." Hans-Peter Kaul, Second Vice-President of the Int'l Criminal Court, *Peace Through Justice? The International Criminal Court in The Hague* 15 (November 2, 2009). "In 2003 an Australian military pilot conducting operations in Iraq realized that if he executed the order received, he could be prosecuted in accordance with the Rome Statute. He returned to his base without dropping the bombs." Luis Moreno-Ocampo, *Remarks at the Qatar Law Forum on the Role of International Judicial Bodies in Administering the Rule of Law* 7 (May 30, 2009).

[12] Observers from outside the Court, including Human Rights Watch have also shared anecdotes of deterrence. *Course Correction: recommendations to the ICC Prosecutor for a More Effective Approach to "Situations under analysis."* Human Rights Watch Report, June 2001, p. 2, fn. 2 (stating that rebel leaders in the Democratic Republic of Congo and the Central African Republic told researchers that they did not want to end up in the ICC like Lubanga).

[13] Elana Balylis, "Reassessing the Role of International Criminal Law: Rebuilding National Courts Through Transnational Networks," Boston College Law Review 50: 1 (2009) (examining the impact of ICL in Congolese courts); Sheri P. Rosenberg, "What's Law Got to Do with It? The Bosnia v. Serbia Decision's Impact on Reconciliation," *Rutgers Law Review* 61: 131 (2008) (examining the impact of the ICTY and ICTJ genocide decision on reconciliation in Srebrenica, and arguing that the impact is negligible in the short term).

[14] Tomer Broude, "Prevention Debate – How Can the ICC Maximize Its Crime Prevention Impact?" UCLA Law Forum, Topic for October 2011 – February 2012, at p. 1, http://uclalaw forum.com/prevention (last accessed October 10, 2014) (arguing that crime prevention should remain an ancillary goal of the ICC because, in the international criminal realm, deterrence is empirically intangible); David Scheffer, "Should the United States Join the International Criminal Court," *University of California Davis International Law and Policy* 9: 45, 51 (2002) (arguing for a possible deterrent effect from the ICC because it is as factually improvable to say there will not be a deterrent effect as there is to say there will not be a deterrent effect). A similar argument is made concerning deterrence theory in national criminal law as well. See Dan Kahan, "The Secret Ambition of Deterrent Theory," *Harvard Law Review* 113: 416 (1999) (arguing that deterrence claims are inherently and empirically speculative).

in fact, cause the ICC to point to the attainment of prevention in certain circumstances in the absence of tangible convictions and the significant numbers of indictees at large. In this way, a turn to prevention serves a pragmatic and instrumental function for the ICC.

Thus, the question remains: can an international tribunal deter the commission of systematic crime by authoritarian regimes, armies, or violent non-state groups? The debate over whether ICL prevents mass atrocity crimes should continue because undue attention or reliance on ICL for this purpose impacts decision making within the tribunals and the ICC concerning which cases to pursue, which crimes to indict, and which procedures to follow during sentencing. Furthermore, and most importantly from an atrocity prevention perspective, undue attention or reliance on ICL for this purpose distracts from prophylactic strategies to take action in the face of impending atrocities. With this in mind, further research and reflection is necessary to understand how ICL fits into an overall atrocity prevention strategy. Presently, there is an unexplored orthodoxy about the preventive effects of ICL. This orthodoxy has led to "box ticking" exercises in which stakeholders routinely call for Security Council referrals to the ICC as one of several atrocity prevention activities[15] that is routinely checked off the list, but without examining the underlying merits or implications of pursuing ICL as an atrocity prevention strategy in a particular situation.[16]

This chapter adds to this conversation by exploring deterrence rationales in the ICL context and arguing for a move from deterrence in the national sense to a broader sense of atrocity prevention captured best through an expressive account of ICL atrocity prevention. It argues that conscious attention to the expressive function of ICL and prevention will best allow judges and prosecutors to work in a manner that supports the goals of prevention by encouraging less fragmentation and supporting ICL's legitimacy, thereby adding to the credibility of the tribunals and Court, which is crucial to the prevention project. An expressive account of ICL will also aid stakeholders in the prevention community when determining when and how to pursue ICL as a prevention strategy.

---

[15] Activities undertaken in the effort to prevent or arrest escalation of atrocities include naming and shaming, diplomatic pressure, economic sanctions, and commissions of inquiry.

[16] See, e.g., U.N.S.C. Res. 1593, 31 March 2005 (referring the situation in Darfur to the ICC); UNSC Res. 1970, February 26, 2011 (referring the situation in Libya to the ICC after the failure of the Gaddafi regime to protect its population). Efforts to secure a Security Council referral of the situation in Syria to the ICC have been vetoed on more than one occasion. For a discussion of the challenges of the SC referral of the Libya situation to the ICC, see Carsten Stahn, "Libya, the International Criminal Court and Complementarity: A Test for 'Shared Responsibility,'" *International Criminal Justice* 10: 325–349 (2012).

7.2.   Deterrence Rationales

Assuming crime deterrence can be proved or disproved, whether ICL prevents mass atrocities cannot be answered in the near future because deterrence rationales rely on the certainty and severity of punishment.[17] *Certainty* captures the notion that the individual is likely to be arrested, convicted, and punished for his misdeeds. *Severity* of punishment refers to the depth of the punitive quality of the punishment.[18,19] The ICL regime is simply too new to make definitive comments about certainty and severity, and as stated earlier, arguments are made both ways on this point. Furthermore, the answer to that question depends on how one views history. Certainly international criminal punishment is more likely now than it was in 1950. Whether the certainty is enough to tip the balance of calculation away from atrocity crime for a would-be perpetrator is unknown.[20]

In any event, the central challenge to conceptualizing the role of deterrence in the ICL context is not whether certainty of punishment will develop over time. Rather, the central challenge to understanding the role of mass atrocity crime prevention has been the uneasy extrapolation of national law justifications for criminal punishment to the international context.[21] The ICL context has a number of extraordinary features that distinguish it from the national law context. These features include the complexity of the crimes, the diversity and numbers of criminal actors, and the multiplicity of stakeholders. Mass atrocity crimes generally take place in the context of complete societal breakdown,[22] where social norms have been turned upside down and all of society has been caught up in the crimes in one way or another. Generally, there are high-level perpetrators, those who foment hatred and orchestrate the widespread and extreme violence, and low-level perpetrators who have been indoctrinated into what Payam Akhavan has called an "aberrant context of

---

[17] Julian Ku and Jide Nzelibe, "Do International Criminal Tribunals Deter or Exacerbate Humanitarian Atrocities?" *Washington University Law Review* 84: 777, 792 (2006).

[18] Ibid.

[19] Elana Balylis, "Reassesing the Role of International Criminal Law: Rebuilding National Courts Through Transnational Networks," *B. C. Law Review* 50: 1 (2009)(examining the impact of ICL in Congolese courts); Sheri P. Rosenberg, "What's Law Got to Do with It?" (examining the impact of the ICTY and ICTJ genocide decision on reconciliation in Srebrenica, and arguing that the impact is negligible in the short term).

[20] Beth Simmons and Allison Danner, "Credible Commitments and the International Criminal Court," *International Organization* 64(2): 225–256 (2010) (using a methodical analysis, the authors argue that under certain circumstance the ICL deters).

[21] Sloane, *supra* note 3, at p. 45.

[22] Alex J. Bellamy, "Mass Atrocities and Armed Conflict: Links, Distinctions, and Implications for the Responsibility to Prevent," *The Stanley Foundation Policy Analysis Brief* (February 2011) (arguing that not all conflicts give rise to mass atrocities, and not all atrocity crimes occur during armed conflict).

inverted morality."[23] In this context, criminal law is not punishing deviant behavior. In fact, it is punishing conduct that, in the time and place it was committed, was in conformity with social norms.[24] Furthermore, in the international context where the interests served are national and the figurative, international deterrence rationales also depend not only on certainty of punishment, but also on related concepts of capability, commitment, and credibility or legitimacy.[25] For these reasons, deterrence rationales, born in national contexts, may be too narrow a theoretical frame for analyzing the prevention capacity of ICL.

The deterrence rationale takes two forms. First, ICL will prevent international crimes through immediate deterrence, which posits that the threat of criminal punishment will deter a specific individual or a group of individuals from committing a future criminal act. Second, ICL will prevent atrocities in the long term through general deterrence. General deterrence provides that the threat of criminal punishment generally will dissuade others from committing crimes, knowing that criminal punishment awaits them. General deterrence is subdivided into categories of complementarity (passive or proactive) and norm proliferation (i.e., the creation of a normative environment where extraordinary crimes, as described in the Rome Statute, are no longer tolerated).

Both forms of deterrence, immediate and general, rely on what former Prosecutor for the International Criminal Tribunal for Yugoslavia (ICTY) Louise Arbour calls the "entrenched culture of impunity" thesis.[26] This view operates on the assumption that international criminal justice – and ICC justice in particular – can deter future atrocities by ending the culture that allows perpetrators to escape sanctions for their crimes.[27] Realizing that an ICC prosecution is possible, perpetrators will be more likely to refrain from committing atrocities.[28]

---

[23] Payam Akhavan, "Beyond Impunity: Can International Criminal Justice Prevent Future Atrocities?" *American Journal of International Law* 95: 7, 10 (2001). (Specifically, Akhavan was examining the context that formed the work of the Yugoslav and Rwanda tribunals where he argued that political elites created the "aberrant context of inverted morality in which dehumanization and violence against members of the 'enemy' group were legitimized s purported acts of self-defense.")

[24] Mark A. Drumbl, *Atrocity, Punishment and International Law* (Cambridge: Cambridge University Press, 2007), 8.

[25] Christopher Rudolf, "Constructing an Atrocities Regime: The Politics of War Crimes Tribunals" *International Law Organization* 55: 655, 684 (2001).

[26] Louise Arbour, "The Prosecution of International Crimes: Prospects and Pitfalls," *Washington University Journal of Law and Policy* 1: 13, 23 (1999).

[27] Ku and Nzelibe, *supra* note 7, at 797.

[28] See, for example, similar ICTY and ICTR deterrence justifications. *Prosecutor v. Rutaganda*, Case No. ICTR-96-3-T para. 45 (ICTR Trial Chamber, December 6, 1999), aff'd on appeal; *Prosecutor v. Rutaganda*, Case No. ICTR-96-3-A (ICTR Appeals Chamber, May 26, 2003)

7.2.1.   Immediate Deterrence

Immediate deterrence refers to attempts by courts to dissuade specific individuals or groups within society from committing international crimes. International tribunals and the ICC engage in this activity in several ways. First, the *ad hoc* tribunals are explicitly mandated to stop the commission of international crimes. For instance, during the ethnic conflict and genocide in Bosnia & Herzegovina, which began in 1991, the Security Council authorized Resolution 827 establishing ICTY in 1993. Therein it pronounced that the creation of the ICTY would ensure that "violations are halted and effectively redressed" as part of the Security Council's mandate to promote international peace and security.[29] The opening of investigations and issuance of arrest warrants in Darfur and Libya in the midst of ongoing conflict established that the ICC is not solely acting as an *ex post facto* mechanism, but also as an instrument to constrain ongoing violence and atrocity crimes.

Second, tribunals put war criminals on notice of prosecution and punishment through attempts to bring them before the court. Currently, the ICC seeks to dissuade specific individuals in particular situations from committing atrocity crimes by issuing indictments and arrest warrants. Initially, the Court may have expected or hoped that the arrest warrant would be accompanied by detention of the individual. However, at this point, where more indictees remain at large than are arrested and detained, the notion is that the likelihood of prosecution will deter them from further criminal activity regardless of detention. At the time of this writing, October 2014, there are more than thirty-five indictments, the majority of which remain unenforced. Most well known are the outstanding arrest warrants for Sudanese president Omar al-Bashir and Lords Resistance Army Commander Joseph Kony. Interestingly, on October 10, 2014, Uhuru Kenyatta, the president of Kenya who was indicted by the ICC in 2012, has appeared in the Court in 2014 to argue for the dismissal of his case.[30]

(stating that punishment "dissuade(s) forever ... others who may be tempted in the future to perpetuate such atrocities. ...); *Prosecutor v. Stakic*, Case No. IT-97-24-A, para. 402 (ICTY Appeals Chamber, March 22, 2006) (stating that "the Appeals Chamber notes that the jurisprudence of the Tribunal and the ICTRY consistently points out that the two main purposes of sentencing are deterrence and retribution).

[29] UNSC Resolution 827 U.N.S.C. Res. 827, S/Res/827 (1993) at Preamble.

[30] See David Bosco, "President Kenyatta's Trial: How to Destroy the ICC from Within," *Horn Affairs*. Available at http://hornaffairs.com/en/2014/10/11/president-kenyattas-trial-how-to-de stroy-the-icc-from-within/ (last visited October 30, 2014). In fact, commentators have speculated that he appeared before the Court because the Prosecution is having a difficult time obtaining evidence from Kenya. As a result, the Prosecutor may not be able to make her case. President Kenyatta, aware of this, appeared at the Court to argue for a dismissal and for show. The case was dismissed on December 5, 2014, without prejudice.

Third, immediate deterrence may also take the form of signals and direct warnings. During the preliminary investigation phase, the Office of the Prosecutor (OTP) might seek to prevent a particular set of atrocities through issuing public statements and warnings directed at public or ethnic leaders. For example, when violence broke out in Cote d'Ivoire after a disputed election, the Prosecutor publicly warned one individual that his incitements to violence might be prosecuted.[31] In situations where conflict has broken out abruptly, the OTP signaled to combatants that it is scrutinizing events in an attempt to alter the course of hostilities and prevent atrocities. When fighting erupted between Georgian and Russian forces in August 2008, the Court released a statement indicating that it was analyzing alleged crimes committed during combat operations.[32]

Fourth, in its strategy document, the OTP incorporated the goal of prevention through public monitoring. It states that the office will "make preventive statements noting that crimes possibly falling within the jurisdiction of the Court are being committed [and] make public the commencement of a preliminary examination at the earliest possible stage through press releases and public statements."[33]

7.2.2.   *General Deterrence*

To balance state prerogatives to prosecute with the ICC's effectiveness, states parties to the Rome Statute created a unique jurisdictional scheme that adheres to and builds on the principles of complementarity under international law. Under the complementarity system, the ICC may not exercise jurisdiction over a case if it "is being investigated or prosecuted by a State which has jurisdiction over it, unless the State is unwilling or unable genuinely to carry out the investigation or prosecution."[34] Thus, a state may shield its citizens from ICC prosecution by a sufficient show of investigation or prosecution. Complementarity has been interpreted – and

---

[31] See Press Release, ICC, "Statement by ICC Prosecutor Luis Moreno-Ocampo, on the Situation in Cote d 'Ivoire" (December 21 2010), http://www.icc-cpi.int/NR/exeres/EB76851B-C125-4E70-8271-D781C54E2A65 (last visited August 24, 2014).

[32] See Press Release, ICC, "ICC Prosecutor Confirms Situation in Georgia Under Analysis" (August 20, 2008), www.icccpi.int/menus/icc/press%20and%20media/press%20releases/press%20releases%C20%c282008%/icc%20prosecutor%C20confirms%C20situations%C20in%C20georgia%C20under%20analysis. It is interesting to note that the OTP has not issued any comments on the situation in Syria where a bloody conflict between Bashir Al-Asaad and insurgents has been raging since 2011. More than an estimated 191,369 people died in the conflict from March 2011 to April 2014. "Human Rights Analysis Group, Updated Statistical Analysis of Documentation of Killings in the Syrian Arab Republic," 1 (2014), www.ohchr.org/Documents/Countries/SY/HRDAGUpdatedReportAug2014.pdf

[33] Office of the Prosecutor, Prosecutorial Strategy 2009–2012, para. 39 (February 1, 2012).

[34] Rome Statute, *supra* note 1.

pursued – more robustly than simply as a negative restraint in which the ICC relinquishes jurisdiction to a national court. Indeed, commentators and the ICC prosecutor have interpreted complementarity as a positive force for empowering national courts.[35] According to some, complementarity might encourage states to "aggressively and fairly pursue domestic prosecutions of international crimes so as not to trigger the jurisdiction of the ICC over the case and invite the glare of the eyes of the international community."[36]

Legal scholar William Burke-White has gone further and proposed a system of "proactive complementarity" in which the ICC would "encourage, and perhaps even assist" with prosecutions in national courts.[37] Proactive complementarity rests on the view that complementarity should encourage shared responsibilities and relationships between national courts and the ICC, with a view toward enhancing the Court's general deterrent effect through building the deterrent potential of national courts. Burke-White's proposal is one among several recent scholarly theses pointing toward shifting the burden of accountability back to national governments. This shift comes from the perception that claims that would end impunity for atrocities have been overblown and the fact that the accomplishments of the ad hoc tribunals and the ICC have been limited and inconsistent.[38]

Finally, Luis Moreno-Ocampo, the former ICC prosecutor, has recognized the power of leveraging complementarity. He stated on more than one occasion that an absence of trials in the ICC, if a consequence of the regular functioning of national courts, would signal a major success for the ICC.[39] To date, there is very little empirical evidence to support whether ICL has in fact encouraged genuine national prosecutions. There is some evidence to suggest that Sudan and the Democratic Republic of Congo have pursued investigations to head off ICC justice.[40] And some argue that the

---

[35] International Criminal Court Office of the Prosecutor, "Report on Prosecutorial Strategy," at 5 (September 14, 2006), www.icc-cpi.int/library/organs/otp/OTP_Prosecutorial-Strategy-20060 914_English.pdf (noting how this system encourages national resolution of cases and fosters international cooperation).

[36] Mark S. Ellis, "The International Criminal Court and Its Implication for Domestic Law and National Capacity Building," *Florida Journal of International Law* 15: 215, 223 (2003).

[37] William W. Burke-White, "Proactive Complementarity: The International Criminal Court and National Courts in the Rome System of International Justice, *Harvard International Law Journal* 49: 53, 57–58 (2008).

[38] Elena Baylis, "Reassessing the Role of International Criminal Law: Rebuilding National Courts Through Transnational Networks *B. C. Law Review* 50: 1, 2 (2009).

[39] See Luis Moreno-Ocampo, "Statement to the Assembly of States Parties to the Rome Statute of the International Criminal Court" (April 22, 2003), www.iccnow.org/documents/MorenoOca mpo22Apr03eng.pdf (last visited October 30, 2014).

[40] Elena Baylis, "Reassessing the Role of International Criminal Law."

mainstreaming of criminal justice in international relations in general has created an incentive in some instances for "preemptive" national proceedings.[41]

Whereas ICL enthusiasts and ICL judges and lawyers continue to rely on and extol the deterrent effects of ICL, the deterrent justification has more than its share of skeptics. The skepticism, I suggest, rests primarily on the imperfect fit between national and international theories of criminal punishment. The deterrence rationale for ICL is transposed from the role that criminal punishment plays in national settings to international settings.

But it is not a perfect shift, and the critiques of this transposition generally fall into three categories. First, deterrence theory in national settings rests on two key elements: the certainty and severity of punishment,[42] with most agreeing that the certainty of criminal punishment plays a more dominant role in deterrence than the does severity of the punishment.[43] Thus, deterrence theory requires a credible threat of prosecution, which ICL currently lacks. The ICL regime does not have its own police force, relies on state cooperation for evidence and witnesses, and enforces the law sporadically, selectively, and inconsistently at best.[44]

Second, whereas the rational actor model is suspect in the national context, it is even more so in the international context where war or other large-scale violence distorts the cost-benefit analysis on which the rational-actor theory relies. The common argument is that perpetrators do not act rationally because they are often motivated by nationalist fervor, revenge, or ethnic or religious animosity stirred up by ethno-nationalist leaders hungry for power. Scholars who subscribe to this view argue that individuals who commit atrocity crimes are "unlikely to behave as rational actors, deterred by the risk of punishment."[45]

---

[41] Ibid.

[42] Johannes Andenaes, "The General Preventive Effects of Punishment," *University of Pennsylvania Law Review* 114: 949, 960, 964 (1964) (stating that the risk of detention coupled with severity of punishment affect deterrence).

[43] Christopher W. Mullins and Dawn L. Rothe, "The Ability of the International Criminal Court to Deter Violations of International Criminal Law: A Theoretical Assessment," *International Criminal Law Review* 10: 771, 773 (2010) (stating that empirical research has shown that the main variable in general deterrence is certainty); Cesare Beccaria, "On Crimes and Punishments (1764)," in *Readings in Jurisprudence and Legal Philosophy*, edited by Morris R. Cohen and Felix S. Cohen (1951), 346, 349; *Prosecutor v. Furundzija*, Case No. IT-95-17/1-T, Para. 290 (December 10, 1998). ("It is the infallibility of punishment, rather than the severity of the sanction, which is the tool for retribution, stigmatization, and deterrence.")

[44] David S. Koller, "The Faith of the International Criminal Lawyer," 1021, 1028.

[45] Martha Minow, *Between Vengeance and Forgiveness: Facing History after Genocide and Mass Violence* (1998), 50. Cf., Stathis Kalyvas, "Wanton and Senseless? The Logic of Massacres in Algeria," *Rationality and Society* 11: 245 (1999) (arguing that the decision to commit seemingly wanton atrocities can been seen to follow a rational strategy).

Third, mass atrocity crimes are almost always collective in nature. Atrocities that fall within the ambit of the international criminal tribunals, although embodying different elements, share a common core of characteristics: namely, they are large scale, systematic, and target large numbers of individuals usually based on their actual or perceived membership in a particular group.[46] They are generally widespread and systematic, encompassing multiple levels of perpetrators, victims, bystanders, and a vacillating mélange of persons who flow endlessly between perpetrator and victim. The collective nature of ICL means "group think," in which individuals often want to be part of the violent groups and find comfort therein. In stable societies, criminal acts are considered outside the norm and deviant. In times of mass atrocities, such behavior is normalized – in fact, obedient.[47] Furthermore, many perpetrators of mass atrocity crimes believe they are acting for the collective good. High-level perpetrators, the masterminds, often act to obtain or hold onto power, whereas lower level perpetrators, research has shown, act for myriad reasons, including personal gain or survival. This complex collective nature of mass atrocities further challenges and stretches the deterrence rationale.

According to Ku and Nzelibe, who engaged in a thorough study of economic models of deterrence to analyze whether potential perpetrators of mass atrocities would likely be deterred by the risk of future persecution found that, taking into account certainty of prosecution and severity of punishment, as well as a particular individual's preference for risk, international criminal justice is unlikely to deter its most frequent targets and, in fact, may exacerbate the situation in some instances.[48]

Of course, we should not overstate the influence of these critiques, just as we should not overstate the claims that ICL deters future atrocity crimes. The critiques do not establish that, for ICL, deterrence does not work. Similarly, statements that ICL deters atrocity crimes does not establish that deterrence does work. In fact, some suggest that if the challenge is certainty of punishment, then the solution lies in more resources and persecutions. Thus, the problem is not inherent to ICL, but rather a functional problem that can be resolved over time. Moreover, as discussed earlier, perpetrators of mass crimes are not monolithic. Each has his own set of incentives for committing such crimes. Thus, one cannot simply assume that deterrence will never work in ICL. The limits of deterrence theory, however, in the ICL context does establish that we must seek a transformative theory of the role

---

[46] Mark A. Drumbl, *Atrocity, Punishment and International Law*, 4.

[47] Ibid., 8.

[48] Julian Ku and Jide Nzelibe, "Do International Criminal Tribunals Deter or Exacerbate Humanitarian Atrocities?" *Washington University Law Review* 84: 777–833 (2006). Available at http://openscholarship.wustl.edu/cgi/viewcontent.cgi?article=1186&context=law_lawreview (accessed June 20, 2015).

of ICL in atrocity prevention if we are to understand its place in the atrocity prevention agenda.

7.3.   Toward an Expressive Theory of ICL and Prevention of Atrocity

An expressive account of criminal law, I argue, best captures the role that ICL plays in the prevention agenda. Drawing on sociology, anthropology, philosophy, and psychology, expressivism is a theoretical frame outlining the perceived social meaning of law.[49] Law, like other forms of communication, manifests a state of mind, including beliefs and attitudes. Therefore, law has social meaning; ultimately, laws express a society's values, what it prefers and what it abhors. Through the communication of laws, social relationships or understandings among people are created and particular attitudes and norms become internalized. For example, laws in the United States that provided for racial segregation sent the message that African Americans were second-class citizens or a kind of social pariah. Once a majority of people shared an understanding that segregation laws express contempt for minority populations, the laws constituted such minorities as a stigmatized group.[50] Although still undertheorized, a number of scholars have turned to expressive theory to explain the meaning of the crime of genocide and ICL prosecutorial and sentencing processes.[51]

Particularly relevant in the criminal context, "punishment is not only to deter crime or exact a debt to society, but it is a special social convention that signifies moral condemnation."[52] The expressive function has special meaning in criminal law. Unlike other forms of law, criminal punishment often exerts the harshest of penalties; a deprivation of a criminal's very liberty, thus signaling

---

[49] Elizabeth S. Anderson and Richard H. Pildes, "Expressive Theories of Law: A General Restatement," *University of Pennsylvania Law Review* 148:1503 (2000).

[50] Ibid., 1503, 1529.

[51] Payam Akhavan, "Beyond Impunity," 7, 13 (2001) (arguing that, over time, international criminal law will instill a new reality of "habitual lawfulness"; Diane Marie Amann, "Group Mentality, Expressivism, and Genocide," *International Criminal Law Review* 2: 93, 95 (2002) (arguing that the expressive function of law has special force in international criminal law); Drumbl, *Atrocity, Punishment and International Law*, 173–176 ("Expressivism theories extol the messaging value of punishment to affirm respect for law, reinforce a moral consensus, narrate history and educate the public"); Robert D. Sloane, "The Expressive Capacity of International Punishment: The Limits of National Law Analogy and the Potential of International Criminal Law," *Stanford Journal of International Law* 43: 39 (2007) (defending an expressive account of punishment by international criminal tribunals); Margaret M. deGuzman, "Choosing to Prosecute: Expressive Selection at the International Criminal Court," *Michigan Journal of International Law* 33: 265 (2012) (arguing that the International Criminal Court should turn to an expressive agenda in its case selection decisions).

[52] Dan M. Kahan, "What Do Alternative Sanctions Mean?" *University of Chicago Law Review* 63: 591, 599 (1996).

the strongest of societal opprobrium. Expressive accounts of criminal theory posit that criminal punishment manifests society's abhorrence to behavior that thwarts normatively held values that the wrongdoer's behavior denies.[53] Punishment expresses attitudes of disapproval on the part of the punishing authorities and, ultimately, signals that the behavior is outside the bounds of societal acceptance and deserving of society's moral condemnation.[54] As one of the leading scholars of international criminal law explains, "[t]he pursuit of justice and accountability fulfills fundamental human needs and expresses key values necessary for the prevention and deterrence of future conflicts."[55]

Law is important for the understandings it creates among members of society about attitudes toward myriad categories of people and objects. Expressive theory underscores that a significant function of law is the way it shifts social norms and meanings.[56] This influence is particularly seen in areas of equality and norms involving dangerous behavior.[57] Social meaning of the law is about communication, and communication is by definition contextual. Individuals understand words and acts as mediated through their social contexts. Thus, expressivism dwells not as much on the intended meaning of the law, but rather on the meaning understood by the hearers; that is, the social meaning of the law.[58]

A number of theorists advocate for expressivism as a justification for criminal punishment. These theorists "view crime as an expressive act and consider punishment justified when it counters the wrongful expression inherent in the criminal act."[59] As Payam Akhavan has argued, even if prosecutions fail to deter culpable individuals from committing further crimes, prosecutions will nonetheless reinforce applicable international norms and will contribute to the establishment of a political culture that considers the commission of atrocities unacceptable.[60] Over time, international criminal justice will operate to prevent

[53] Kahan, "The Secret Ambition of Deterrence," 413.
[54] Joel Feinberg, "The Expressive Function of Punishment," in *Doing and Deserving: Essays in the Theory of Responsibility* (Princeton, NJ: Princeton University Press, 1974), 95, 98; and Kahan, "What Do Alternative Sanctions Mean?" 591, 599. ("Punishment is not just a way to make offenders suffer; it is a special social convention that signifies moral condemnation.")
[55] M. Cherif Bassiouni, "Justice and Peace: The importance of Choosing Accountability over Realpolitik," *Case Western Reserve Journal of International Law* 35: 191, 192 (2003).
[56] Cass R. Sunstein, "On the Expressive Function of Law," *University of Pennsylvania Law Review* 144: 2029–2033 (1996).
[57] Ibid., 2033, 2043.
[58] Anderson and Pildes, "Expressive Theories of Law," 1503, 1513, 1523–1525, 1550 (explaining the importance of "socially constructed meaning").
[59] deGuzman, "Choosing to Prosecute," 265, 313 (citing Dan M. Kahan, "The Anatomy of Disgust in Criminal Law," *Michigan Law Review* 96: 1622, 1641 (1998)) (claiming that "an expressively effective punishment must make clear that we are in fact disgusted with what the offender has done").
[60] Payam Akhavan, "Justice in The Hague, Peace in the Former Yugoslavia?" *Human Rights Quarterly* 20: 743, 751 (1999).

atrocities by instilling "unconscious inhibitions against crime" or "a condition of habitual lawfulness" in society.[61] Thus, what the courts express over time will lead to the general deterrence of individuals considering committing atrocity crimes.

An example of the ICC making an "expressive" choice in prosecution includes the choice of crimes to pursue in the eastern Congo. The ICC's choice of indictments related to the conflict in eastern Congo reflect the OTP's choice to enhance the Court's preventive impact by selecting the prosecution against Thomas Lubanga on three counts of crimes against humanity, all of which involve the use of child soldiers. By choosing this theme, the Prosecutor may have decided to help stigmatize a practice that is accepted as normal in some places. The Prosecutor's opening statement to the Court underscores the point: "The Lubanga case, beyond the guilt or innocence of Mr. Lubanga, is also a clear message to perpetrators of crimes against children such as enlisting them as soldiers, are very grave and will be prosecuted."[62]

An expressive account best captures the ICL context for an additional reason. Crimes motivated by discriminatory animus, as most atrocity crimes are, have something special to say about bias-motivated crimes. As Kahan asks: "What do they mean and what should the law say about them?" Proponents of hate crime legislation believe that hate crimes have a distinct social meaning worthy of particular social condemnation. Hate crimes are an affront to the dignity not only of the victim, but also to those who share their defining characteristics, such as identity, race, and ethnicity. In the end, hate crime laws affirm the value of equality.[63] Many, if not most, atrocity crimes are hate crimes on a large scale. They are often perpetrated in the context of collective perpetrators committing atrocity crimes against a collective victim group identified often on the basis of immutable characteristics, including race, religion, or sexual identity. Thus, not only does ICL express condemnation of certain criminal acts, it also affirms the value of equality.

But laws express attitudes only insofar as they take on a particular social meaning.[64] In the context of ICL, there are multiple stakeholders and interests and therefore differentiated contexts in which social meaning becomes absorbed and assimilated. International criminal tribunals serve the interests of the figurative international community and the community of victims in a given situation. For this reason, the expressive theory of

---

[61] Payam Akhavan, "Beyond Impunity," 7, 12.

[62] *Prosecutor v. Thomas Lubanga Dyilo*, Case No. ICC-01/04–01/05, Opening Statement, 29 (January 26, 2009).

[63] Kahan, "The Secret Ambition of Deterrent Theory," 416, 420.

[64] Ibid.

prevention in ICL must transcend expressive theory in national criminal law systems. Whereas punishment in national legal systems generally can be appraised in terms of the objectives of a single community, communal interests in the ICL context are diffuse. At times, we refer to the interests of the individual victims who are harmed by international crimes, seeking to remedy their individual harms. At other times, we emphasize the interests and values of the illusive "international community," either as a political notion of a "community of states" or a metaphysical notion of a "community of mankind."[65]

Also, atrocity crimes are almost always collective crimes. They are generally widespread and systematic, encompassing multiple levels of perpetrators, victims, bystanders, and participants who are both perpetrator and victim. The challenge, then, is for ICL to find a way to apprehend the collective within a consciously individualist paradigm of criminal punishment originating from the liberal tradition to capture the web of individuals involved in mass atrocities.

Whereas the expressive function of ICL likely has a secondary deterrence value as a form of a norm that expresses what society is unwilling to accept, "[e]xpressivism strikes an intermediate path between the deontological road of retribution and the consequentialist road of deterrence."[66] It does so by consciously focusing simultaneously on the immediate instrumental value of trials and on punishment as a tool of both retribution and deterrence on the rational-actor model because its overarching concern is the normative expressive value served by ICL.[67] This balance and long-term view makes expressivism a particularly useful frame for understanding ICL's contribution to the atrocity prevention agenda. Ultimately, ICL's ability to contribute to the atrocity prevention agenda relies on its legitimacy and credibility as authoritative expression.[68] The result of utilizing a variant of expressive theory of national criminal law to understand and pursue the preventive capacity of ICL is to counsel more attention to the judicial process and ensure that not only the laws, but also how the courts function and what they communicate aim consciously toward enhancing both the likelihood of prosecution and punishment as well as the integrity and credibility of the courts themselves.

---

[65] Mark Osiel, "The Banality of Good: Aligning Incentives Against Mass Atrocity," *Columbia Law Review* 105: 1751, 1756 (2005) (emphasizing the disconnect between the interests of the local participants to conferences on ICL focused on historical grievances and the those of the more "cosmopolitan" academic consultants bent on drawing abstract inferences).

[66] Amann, *supra* note 50, at 120.

[67] Sloane, *supra* note 3, at 71 (arguing, however, that expressivism focuses less on retribution and deterrence and "more on long term normative values served by any system of criminal law").

[68] Sloane, *supra* note 3, at 70.

7.4.   Legitimacy, Fragmentation, and the Expressive Capacity of ICL

The relationship between the individual to the group is central to the entire ICL project. This is true as concerns the interests served: namely, the collective (figurative) "international community" and the individual victim and the collective, systematic crime juxtaposed to individual guilt.

To capture the collective nature of atrocity crimes, the ad hoc tribunals developed modes of liability, including for example, joint criminal enterprise and aiding and abetting liability. These modes enable the court to assess the culpability of the web of individuals who work together in one capacity or another to pursue the goals of a particular crime. Because deterrence theory rests primarily on a sense of certainty of punishment, the state of the law on these modes of liability is relevant to this discussion. Criminal responsibility in ICL can arise not only when a person physically commits the crime in question, but also when individuals who are not the direct perpetrators are otherwise involved in criminal conduct.[69]

International crimes are committed on such a large scale that it is difficult to conceive of a single individual being held criminally culpable. Rather, these crimes result from groups of individuals acting in pursuit of a "common criminal design."[70] The concept of "system criminality"[71] concerns a group of offenders and also assumes an "intellectual perpetrator."[72] The intellectual perpetrator can be one person or a group of people in a political or military structure (command structure). In such cases, the participation and contribution of group members is often vital in committing the crimes in question, and the moral culpability of intellectual perpetrators is often equal to those who actually carry out the acts.[73]

System criminality, however, poses interesting challenges for criminal law, mainly in confronting the principle of personal culpability.[74] Specifically, the question is: in the web of actors required to turn an ordinary crime into an extraordinary crime (mass crime), when and at what point does liability begin?

---

[69] Antonio Cassese et al., *International Criminal Law*, 3rd ed., revised. (2013), 161.

[70] *Prosecutor v. Tadić*, Case No. IT-94-1-T, Judgment, ¶ 191 (July 15, 1999) (Appeals Chamber) ("Most of the time these crimes do not result from the criminal propensity of single individuals but constitute manifestations of collective criminality: the crimes are often carried out by groups of individuals acting in pursuance of a common criminal design. Although only some members of the group may physically perpetrate the criminal act . . . , the participation and contribution of the other members of the group is often vital in facilitating the commission of the offense in question").

[71] Elies van Sliedregt, "Modes of Participation," in *Forging a Convention for Crimes Against Humanity* (edited by Leila Nadya Sedat (2010), 223 (citing Roling).

[72] Ibid.

[73] *Prosecutor v. Tadić*, Case No. IT-94-1-T, Judgment, ¶ 191 (July 15, 1999) (Appeals Chamber).

[74] van Sliedregt, "Modes of Participation," 224.

Where crime is highly organized and carried out on a massive scale, individual responsibility concepts have expanded in both domestic and international law frameworks. Examples include accessory liability theories of (1) joint criminal enterprise (better known as JCE), which addresses the criminal liability of participants in a common plan; (2) command responsibility or superior responsibility, which imposes criminal liability on supervisors who fail to prevent or punish criminal activities of their subordinates; and (3) aiding and abetting, which comprises giving practical assistance to the principle perpetrator.

Individual legal liberalism, the philosophy or political worldview through which ICL is expressed, however, does not coexist easily with the collective nature of mass atrocity crimes. ICL embodies core elements of liberalism, including, "locat[ing] the individual as the central unit of analysis for purposes of sanctioning violations."[75] Since Nuremberg, international tribunals have gone back and forth between holding on to orthodoxies of individual agency to embracing and punishing collective agency.[76] As Laurel Fletcher notes, ICL is deeply embedded in liberal legalism defined as "the legal principles and values that privilege individual autonomy, individuate responsibility, and are reflected in criminal law of common law legal systems."[77] The tension between liberal legalism and the reality that mass atrocities are, by definition, group crimes in which the individual can only be defined in relation to the collective remains vexing to the courts. To illustrate the point, one can turn to the inchoate development of the jurisprudence on the mode of accomplice liability in ICL called "aiding and abetting liability" and the recent bait and switch of the tribunals.

7.4.1.   Accomplice Liability and ICL's "Specific Direction" Detour

Accessory liability is not new to ICL. Early ad hoc tribunal decisions relied on Nuremberg trials' case law, which provides an inconsistent, patchwork of laws on aiding and abetting liability.[78] And this patchwork of laws reflects the national criminal jurisdictions' fragmentation on this issue of accomplice liability.

The ad hoc international criminal tribunals and the ICC have therefore been trudging along in an attempt to clearly and consistently apply the law to aiders

---

[75] Laurel E. Fletcher, "From Indifference to Engagement: Bystanders and International Criminal Justice," *Michigan Journal of International Law* 26: 1013, 1031 (2005).

[76] Drumbl, *Atrocity, Punishment and International Law*, 39; see also, Andrew Clapham, "Extending International Criminal Law beyond the Individual to Corporations and Armed Opposition Groups," *Journal of International Criminal Justice* 6: 899, 900 (2008) (arguing that international criminal law is developing obligations that go beyond the individual).

[77] Fletcher, "From Indifference to Engagement," 1013, 1031.

[78] *Prosecutor v. Tadić*, Case No. IT-94-1-T, Opinion and Judgment, ¶ 679 (May 7, 1997).

and abettors of mass atrocity crimes. Generally, aiding and abetting is defined in ICL as giving practical assistance, encouragement, or moral support knowing that it assists a perpetrator in the commission of a crime. The *actus reus* (act) of aiding and abetting in ICL requires that the assistance, encouragement, or moral support have a "substantial effect" on the perpetration of the crime. Recently, however, the ICTY abruptly broke away from this line of jurisprudence in an attempt to narrow the scope of individual criminal liability in aiding and abetting under ICL.[79] In particular, in *Prosecutor v. Perišić*, the ICTY departed from its previous case law[80] and that of other international precedent by adding – and then soon after rejecting – a requirement to the *actus reus* of aiding and abetting that the prosecution must prove that the defendant "specifically directed" his or her assistance to the organization's criminal acts.[81]

The defendant, Momčilo Perisić, was the highest ranking officer of the Yugoslav Army (VJ) and provided extensive military and logistical assistance to the Army of the Republika Srpska (VRS) from 1993 to 1995.[82] Although the Bosnian Serbs would not have been able to commit mass atrocity crimes on the scale they did without the aid that Perisić gave the VRS, the military leader escaped conviction given his remoteness from the actual operations and the general nature of the aid he provided.[83] Indeed, the *Perišić* Court found that, although the evidence needed to prove that the accused "specifically directed" his assistance must be determined on a case-by-case basis, "evidence establishing a direct link between the aid provided . . . and the relevant crimes committed by the principal perpetrators is necessary."[84] In other words, the prosecution must draw a straight line from the accused's conduct to the criminal acts. Therefore, general assistance to an organization that engages in criminal activity, even with the intent to assist the criminal behavior, was not enough.[85] Nor would evidence providing "general assistance

[79] Beth Van Schaack, "Charles Taylor Verdict Today: New Standard of Liability for Aid to Rebel Forces?" Just Security (September 26, 2013), http://justsecurity.org/2013/09/26/charles-taylor-verdict-today-standard-liability-assistance-rebel-forces/ (last visited May 14, 2014).

[80] *Prosecutor v. Mrkšić and Šljivančanin*, Case No. IT-95-13/1-A, Judgment (May 5, 2009). The Appeals Chamber explicitly found that "specific direction" was not an element of the *actus reus* of aiding and abetting liability in international criminal law. *Id.* at ¶ 159.

[81] *Prosecutor v. Momčilo Perišić*, Case No. IT-04-81-A, Judgment, ¶¶ 32–36 (February 28, 2013). Notably, Perišić was not charged under the theory of Joint Criminal Enterprise. See Marko Milanovic, "The Limits of Aiding and Abetting Liability: The ICTY Appeals Chamber Acquits Momcilo Perišić," EJIL Talk!, www.ejiltalk.org/the-limits-of-aiding-and-abetting-liability-the-icty-appeals-chamber-acquits-momcilo-perisic/ (last visited December 4, 2013).

[82] *Prosecutor v. Momčilo Perišić*, Case No. IT-04-81-A, Judgment, ¶ 2 (February 28, 2013).

[83] *Prosecutor v. Momčilo Perišić*, Case No. IT-04-81-A, Judgment, ¶¶ 20, 51, 53, 57, 71, 73–74 (February 28, 2013).

[84] *Prosecutor v. Momčilo Perišić*, Case No. IT-04-81-A, Judgment, ¶ 44 (February 28, 2013).

[85] See Jens David Ohlin, "Why Did the ICTY Acquit Stanisic and Simatovic?" Lieber Code, www.liebercode.org/2013/06/why-did-icty-acquit-stanisic-and.html (June 1, 2013).

which could be used for both lawful and unlawful activities" suffice.[86] Such proof of "specific direction," therefore, raised the standard for proving accomplice liability in ICL.[87]

Scholars, including Manuel Ventura, argue that the legal analysis in the *Perišić* judgment was "manifestly" flawed reasoning.[88] Coco and Gal conclude that the specific direction requirement "blurs the lines between aiding and abetting – an accessorial mode of liability – and forms of principle perpetration" and "undermines the hierarchy of modes of participation by making it easier to prove principle participation than accessorial aiding and abetting."[89] The *Perišić* court relied on the reasoning in previous case law in *Prosecutor v. Tadić*. Read in context, however, the *Tadić* court was contrasting aiding and abetting with JCE. In fact, the language used to discuss aiding and abetting was *dicta* (not central to the judgment) given that accomplice liability was not even an issue in the *Tadić* case.[90] Thus, as Ventura and Stewart point out, citing to *Tadić* to prove that "specific direction" was an element of aiding and abetting liability was legally flawed.[91]

After the *Perišić* decision came out, an unidentified source leaked a letter from ICTY Judge Harhoff claiming that President Meron pressured the ICTY judges to adopt the "specific direction" standards to appease the American and Israeli militaries.[92] Additionally, the ICTY Trial Chamber, in *Stanisic and Simatovic*, applied the "specific direction" standard and acquitted the defendants on that basis.[93]

In September 2013, the Special Court for Sierra Leone (SCSL) Appeals Chamber in *Prosecutor v. Charles Taylor* affirmed Taylor's convictions and

---

[86] *Prosecutor v. Momčilo Perišić*, Case No. IT-04-81-A, Judgment, ¶ 44 (February 28, 2013).

[87] Van Schaack, "Charles Taylor Verdict Today."

[88] Manuel J. Ventura, "Farewell 'Specific Direction': Aiding and Abetting War Crimes and Crimes Against Humanity, in Perišić, Taylor, Sainović et al., and US Alien Tort Statute Jurisprudence," in *The War Report*, edited by S. Casey-Maslen (2014), Ch. 13, 2, http://papers.ssrn.com/sol3/papers.cfm?abstract_id=2435515 (last visited May 15, 2014).

[89] Antonio Coco and Tom Gal, "Losing Direction: The ICTY Appeals Chamber's Controversial Approach to Aiding and Abetting in Perišić," *Journal of International Criminal Justice* 12: 345, 348, 364 (2014), http://jicj.oxfordjournals.org/content/early/2014/03/22/jicj.mqu010.full.pdf+html (last visited May 15, 2014).

[90] Ventura, "Farewell 'Specific Direction,'" Ch. 13, 11.

[91] Ibid.; James G. Stewart, "Guest Post: The ICTY Loses Its Way on Complicity – Part 1," Opinio Juris, http://opiniojuris.org/2013/04/03/guest-post-the-icty-loses-its-way-on-complicity-part-1/ (last visited November 30, 2013). See also James G. Stewart, "Specific Direction Is Unprecedented: Results from Two Empirical Studies," EJIL Talk (September 4, 2013), www.ejiltalk.org/specific-direction-is-unprecedented-results-from-two-empirical-studies/#more-9258 (last visited May 14, 2014).

[92] Van Schaack, "Charles Taylor Verdict Today" (citing to Original Private Letter Judge Frederik Harhoff, www.vaseljenska.com/english/orginal-private-letter-judge-frederik-harhoff/), http://justsecurity.org/2013/09/26/charles-taylor-verdict-today-standard-liability-assistance-rebel-forces/ (last visited May 14, 2014)).

[93] *Prosecutor v. Stanisic & Simatovic*, Case No. IT-03-69-T, Judgment (May 30, 2013).

unanimously rejected the ICTY's "specific direction" standard for aiding and abetting liability found under *Perisić*.[94] In a concurring opinion, Justices Fisher and Winter provided a more scathing critique of the "specific direction" standard, finding that the idea "that the Judges of this Court would be open to the argument that we should change the law or fashion our decisions in the interests of officials of States that provide support for this or any international criminal court is an affront to international criminal law and the judges who serve it."[95] As a result, after expressing serious condemnation for the ICTY's decision in *Perisić*, the SCSL Appeals Chamber opted to return to previous ICL precedent. Commentators assert that the SCSL Appeals Chamber accused the *Perišić* Appeals Court of acting in bad faith when the *Taylor* court claimed that the ICTY judges ignored their mandate by failing to apply customary international law principles.[96] In addition, other scholars have found that such direct conflict between two ad hoc international criminal tribunals' jurisprudence leads to further fragmentation of ICL with regard to aiding and abetting liability,[97] which continues to uproot legal certainty at a time of critical reflection on the ICL project as a whole.

In January 2014, the ICTY Appeals Chamber in *Prosecutor v. Sainović et al.* "unequivocally rejected" the *Perisić* Appeal Chamber's finding that "specific direction" is an element of aiding and abetting liability under customary international law.[98] In a 4-to-1 majority, the Appeals Chamber analyzed de novo ICTY and ICTR jurisprudence and customary international law with regard to this issue and concluded that aiding and abetting's *actus reus* "consists of practical assistance, encouragement, or moral support which has

---

[94] *Prosecutor v. Charles Ghankay Taylor*, Case No. SCSL-03–01-A (September 26, 2013). Interestingly, the facts of the *Taylor* case were legally identical to those in *Perisić*. c Manuel J. Ventura, "What the ICTY Appeal Judgment in Perisić means for the SCSL Appeals Chamber" in *Spreading the Jam: International Law, International Criminal Law, Human Rights and Transitional Justice*, edited by Taylor, http://dovjacobs.com/2013/03/11/guest-post-what-the-icty-appeal-judgment-in-perisic-means-for-the-scsl-appeals-chamber-in-taylor/ (last visited May 15, 2014); see also Manual J. Ventura, "Guest Post: Specific Direction a la Perisić, the Taylor Appeal Judgment and what it could mean for the ICTY Appeals Chamber in Sainović et al. – Part I," *Spreading the Jam: International Law, International Criminal Law, Human Rights and Transitional Justice*, http://dovjacobs.com/2014/01/08/guest-post-specific-direc tion-a-la-perisic-the-taylor-appeal-judgment-and-what-it-could-mean-for-the-icty-appeals -chamber-in-sainovic-et-al-part-i/ (last visited May 13, 2014).

[95] *Prosecutor v. Charles Ghankay Taylor*, Case No. SCSL-03-01-A, ¶ 717 (September 26, 2013).

[96] Kevin Jon Heller, "The SCSL's Incoherent – and Selective – Analysis of Custom," Opinio Juris, http://opiniojuris.org/2013/09/27/scsls-incoherent-selective-analysis-custom/ (last visited May 13, 2014).

[97] Marko Milanovic, "SCSL Appeals Chamber Affirms Charles Taylor's Conviction," Ejil: Talk! (September 26, 2013), www.ejiltalk.org/scsl-appeals-chamber-affirms-charles-taylors-convic tion/ (last visited May 14, 2014).

[98] *Prosecutor v. Sainović et al.*, Case No. IT-05-87-A, Judgment, ¶¶ 1617–51, 1650 (January 23, 2014).

a *substantial effect* on the perpetration of the crime."[99] In rejecting the *Perisić* "specific direction" standard, the Court relies on both ICTY precedent as well as the SCSL Appeals Chamber's reasoning in *Taylor*.[100] Furthermore, the *Sainović* Court affirms the *Blaskic* Appeal Judgment by finding that the required *mens rea* of aiding and abetting is "the knowledge that these acts assist the commission of the offense."[101] The Appeals Chamber upheld the *Sainović* Trial Chamber's decision, which found one of the defendants, Lazarević, guilty of aiding and abetting the crimes of deportation and other inhumane acts of forcible transfer as crimes against humanity.[102] Specifically, the Appeals Chamber decided that the Trial Court correctly applied the law in finding that his "acts and omissions provided a *substantial contribution* to the commission of the crimes."[103] Notably, the Trial Court did not determine whether these acts and omissions were "specifically directed" to assist in the commission of these crimes, and the Appeals Chamber determined as a preliminary matter that the Trial Court was not required to do so.[104] The majority decided that the *Perišić* holding was "in direct and material conflict with the prevailing jurisprudence . . . and with customary international law."[105] This decision came less than one year after the ICTY Appeals Chamber's *Perišić* decision[106] and was a clear departure from its own previous ruling as opposed to following precedent or at least an attempt at harmonization, a common judicial practice.[107]

In light of the *Sainović* decision, the ICTY OTP, in an unprecedented move, filed a motion for reconsideration of the *Perisić* appeal judgment.[108] The OTP

---

[99] *Prosecutor v. Sainović et al.*, Case No. IT-05-87-A, Judgment, ¶¶ 1618–48, 1649 (January 23, 2014) (emphasis added).

[100] *Prosecutor v. Sainović et al.*, Case No. IT-05-87-A, Judgment (January 23, 2014); see Marko Milanovic, "The Self-Fragmentation of the ICTY Appeals Chamber," EJIL Talk! (January 23, 2014), www.ejiltalk.org/the-self-fragmentation-of-the-icty-appeals-chamber/ (last visited May 14, 2014) (arguing that "the case law of the ICTY remains in a state of flux and fragmentation on the specific direction issues – so much so that the guilt or innocence of specific accused will very much depend on which judges get assigned to their Appeals Chamber").

[101] *Prosecutor v. Sainović et al.*, Case No. IT-05-87-A, Judgment, ¶ 1649 (January 23, 2014).

[102] *Prosecutor v. Sainović et al.*, Case No. IT-05-87-T, Trial Judgment, vol. III, ¶¶ 930, 935, 1211.

[103] *Prosecutor v. Sainović et al.*, Case No. IT-05-87-T, Trial Judgment, vol. III, ¶ 926.

[104] *Prosecutor v. Sainović et al.*, Case No. IT-05-87-A, Judgment, ¶¶ 1617, 1651 (January 23, 2014).

[105] *Prosecutor v. Sainović et al.*, Case No. IT-05-87-A, Judgment, ¶¶ 1649–50 (January 23, 2014).

[106] Notably, two of the five judges were the same judges who sat on the *Perišić* appeal.

[107] Sergey Vasiliev, "Consistency of Jurisprudence, Finality of Acquittals, and Ne Bis In Idem," Center for International Criminal Justice (February 3, 2014), 3, 5, http://cicj.org/?page_id=1608 (last visited May 14, 2014) (arguing that "[i]n the struggle for the law at the ICTY, the law itself may have been lost, and the judicial dialogue seems to have reached its lowest point").

[108] See "Statement of Prosecutor Serge Brammertz" in relation to the motion for reconsideration submitted by the Prosecution in the *Perišić* case, The Hague (February 3, 2014), www.icty.org /sid/11447 (last visited May 14, 2014); Dov Jacobs, "The Return of the Sequel to the Specific Direction Saga: Prosecutor Files for Reconsideration of Perisic Appeals Judgment," Spreading

argued that the Court was required to "rectify the manifest miscarriage of justice" resulting from its reversal of the *Perisić* Trial Court's ruling.[109] (Interestingly, such use of the concept of miscarriage of justice is, in this case, being used against the accused rather than to protect the rights of the accused, as it is generally used in criminal law principles.[110]) The Appeals Chamber denied the motion on March 20, 2014.[111]

The *Perisić* judgment, unless resurrected in future case law, may be seen as a short-lived departure from customary international law principles. The question remains, however, about the consequences of such flawed and disordered jurisprudential reasoning. Given that the international tribunals' rulings – at least at the ICTY Appeals Chamber – seem to be unsettled and inchoate, rather than based upon settled case law and legal principles, the ICL project (and legal certainty, judicial consistency, and predictability) seems to be suffering as a result. Although recent decisions have been an attempt to steer the ship back on course, the fragmentation left in its wake has quite possibly shaken whatever confidence there had been in the fairness and impartiality of international criminal tribunals as a whole.

Indeed, the resulting jurisprudential melee between the SCSL and the ICTY pulled the ICTY's judicial decision making back into line; however, arguably, the damage to the preventive and deterrence efforts with regard to aiders and abettors had been done. What is more troubling is what the courts expressed through this jurisprudential tug of war: that the international criminal tribunals may not be above political pressure and that the international community is not certain about who should be punished and deterred from aiding and abetting international crimes in the future. The unfortunate accusations among judges within and between ad hoc tribunals, combined with the continued legal uncertainty over who may be indicted as an accomplice, communicates loudly and clearly ICL's continued discomfort with attributing individual criminal responsibility to systems crimes. The result is a weakening of ICL's capacity to prevent crimes because both certainty of punishment and ICL's

the Jam (February 3, 2013), http://dovjacobs.com/2014/02/03/the-return-of-the-sequel-to-the-specific-direction-saga-prosecutor-files-for-reconsideration-of-perisic-appeals-judgment/ (last visited May 14, 2014); Vasiliev, "Consistency of Jurisprudence."

[109] *Prosecutor v. Momčilo Perišić*, Case No. IT-04-81-A, Motion for Reconsideration, ¶¶ 2–4, 5 (February 3, 2014), www.scribd.com/doc/204236558/Perisic-Motion-Submitted-by-Prosecution#download (last visited May 14, 2014); *Prosecutor v. Momčilo Perišić*, Case No. IT-04-81-A, Decision on Motion for Reconsideration (Mar. 20, 2014) (citing to the Motion, at para. 5, 2–4), www.icty.org/x/cases/perisic/acdec/en/140320.pdf (last visited May 14, 2014).

[110] For a discussion of this issue, see Jacobs, "The Return of the Sequel to the Specific Direction Saga."

[111] *Prosecutor v. Momčilo Perišić*, Case No. IT-04-81-A, Decision on Motion for Reconsideration (March 20, 2014), www.icty.org/x/cases/perisic/acdec/en/140320.pdf (last visited May 14, 2014).

legitimacy and credibility have been damaged in the wake of the *Perisić* debacle.

A consciously expressive theory of the preventive role of ICL counsels more attention to judicial process than has been seen in the aiding and abetting jurisprudence to date. The approach to this ever-present tension between individual criminal accountability and collective crime requires not rote adoption of national criminal laws, procedures, and theories, but rather a transformative approach that envisions an expressivist theory of ICL in all of its particularities.

7.5.   Conclusion

The connection between international prosecutions and the prevention of future atrocities is at best a plausible assumption. Actual experience with these efforts is not encouraging. Beginning in 1941, the United States and the United Kingdom issued a series of highly publicized warnings that violations of the law of wars would be punished. Allied radio and press explicitly warned the German population that there would be criminal trials for the "systematic murder of the Jews of Europe."[112] Similarly, in the former Yugoslavia, atrocities continued in spite of international criminal prosecutions. The expanding field of atrocity prevention and international criminal punishment together, however, is promising. The interrelationship of the varying preventative methods, together with greater certainty of prosecution by a permanent court, increases the preventive potential of the Court.

Central challenges, however, to the developing field of ICL remain, conceptually, politically, and practically. Cumulatively, these challenges confront the meta-question: what is the *essential* relationship between ICL and prevention? And they uncover the normative question: what role should the ICC and other international tribunals play in atrocity prevention? Although it is too soon tell what kind of preventive impact tribunal and ICC justice is having or will have, we do know that tribunal and ICC justice has and may have the potential to allow member states of the United Nations to avoid their responsibility to protect populations facing atrocity crimes by engaging in their responsibility to prosecute, as witnessed by the fact that crimes under the jurisdiction of the Court were referred to the ICC two years after the conflict in Darfur, Sudan, broke out. To meet the prevention challenges we face, we must strategically evaluate the preventive role of ICL within the broader atrocity prevention agenda. The first step in this process is to conceptually reimagine the role of ICL in the atrocity prevention agenda. Although

---

[112] Benjamin Ferencz, "International Criminal Courts: The Legacy of Nuremberg," *Pace International Law Review* 10: 203, 210 (1998).

deterrence theory plays a role in ICL, deterrence and mass atrocity prevention are not the same phenomena. The idea of deterring crime through certainty and severity of punishment overlaps with preventing mass atrocities, but they are not the same in concept or practice. As this chapter has shown, a move toward an expressive theory of ICL atrocity prevention provides the clearest frame in which to conceptualize the preventive role of ICL in the context of an overarching strategy of mass atrocity prevention.

An expressive account of ICL prevention best approximates the systemic multistakeholder and systems process of ICL within the totality of the atrocity prevention agenda. Ultimately ICL, as one component of the atrocity prevention agenda, should assist in developing a bourgeoning worldwide culture that renders atrocity crimes beyond the realm of the politically or morally acceptable.

8   Historical Dialogue and the Prevention of Atrocity Crimes

Elazar Barkan

8.1.   Prevention

Prevention refers conventionally to short-term or immediate action in the face of imminent danger. In many cases, prevention fails. Syrians, notwithstanding the global commitment to Responsibility to Protect (R2P), are suffering horrific violence because current attitudes to prevention and conflict resolution are at times appallingly inadequate, whether for political or doctrinal shortcomings. The elaborate explanation of why it is complicated to support one extreme faction of the opposition as opposed to the others or the power-play in the United Nations Security Council are no doubt critical from the UN perspective, yet it is less helpful to the refugees and civilians who are battered daily. Inaction is not an option, as the widening of the conflict to Iraq patently proves. Yet, it is very much a reality.

Part of the problem of failed prevention is its time horizon. Prevention is often thought about more like putting out fires than as structural realignment to bring the sides to minimize their differences before violence erupts. The purpose of this chapter is to explore the potential role for historical dialogue as a new mechanism to be employed in conflict prevention and resolution fields or even in peacebuilding, which will necessitate a new paradigm for how to approach brewing conflicts that can result in mass atrocities. This must take place as an ongoing effort among antagonistic groups in order to build and strengthen civil society and political commitments to counter conflict, not as a last-minute intervention. It is meant as an additional tool, one that does not negate existing mechanisms, which should be evaluated on their own terms. This contrasts with the existing conflict prevention paradigm that focuses exclusively on the future. It largely approaches the challenge from a rational choice perspective by trying to bring the two sides to focus on their achievable goals and to ignore the past and the memory of previous grievances. This lack of recognition of historical violence, fears, and animosity avoids acknowledgment and respect and does not address the systematic root causes

175

of identity. The claim of "let bygones be bygones" is voiced frequently but is often unpersuasive to the protagonists and is especially rejected by victims. Consequently, there is no accepted methodology among international conflict resolution professionals that would address historical violence and would provide for or assist in prevention when the conflict is reignited.

A good example of the paradigmatic approach for prevention was the report by the Carnegie Commission on Preventing Deadly Conflict, released in the 1990s, which examined the role of incentives in international relations, concerning issues as diverse as countering weapons proliferation in regional conflict resolution and the role of international financial institutions.[1] The Commission focused primarily on economic incentives, as well as on political and security ones, underscoring the various factors that play a critical role in ending or preventing numerous conflicts from developing. The dilemma of whether to foster prevention through fear of sanctions or even a threat of war or whether to provide economic incentives has always been at the heart of international relations. The international community would certainly prefer to incentivize regimes to prevent conflict, but the historical evidence could point in either direction. In 1938, *appeasement* (or incentives) led to World War II, whereas fifty years later, incentives facilitated the end of the Cold War with no violence between the superpowers. For our purpose, it is worth noting that the Commission did not pay attention to the historical aspects of conflicts. The identity of the stakeholders and their fears and animosity toward each other was viewed, if at all, as obstacles to overcome, not to engage.

Engaging history as a conflict resolution methodology should be viewed first as an advocacy project responding to the need to face the structural mythologies that drive nationalist propaganda and xenophobia by raising awareness among activists, scholars, and intellectuals. Involving public intellectuals in the conversation would be a prerequisite to changing national perspectives and to facilitating a new attitude toward the (former) enemy. It is not offered as a quick solution or a short-term intervention. Although, given political constraints, a medium-term intervention and the installation of a mechanism for dialogues ought to be initiated, the long-term goal is to change attitudes and group perceptions. The goal of historical dialogue and of writing shared history is to provide a methodology and practice of addressing the root causes of a conflict through a dialogue between the different sides in that conflict. Where history is the subject of national dispute, it has to be addressed through historical research and writing in a preventive manner, in order to facilitate goodwill and shared empathy among peoples.

---

[1] David A. Hamburg (Author), Cyrus R. Vance (Editor), "Preventing Deadly Conflict" (1997), www.dtic.mil/dtic/tr/fulltext/u2/a372860.pdf

8.2.   The Role of History

History is at the center of national identity. The self-perception of nations shapes and determines the scope of national ambitions and the policies of the state. In this context, a national identity that is informed by fear, hate, and animosity toward its neighbors is prone to instigate conflict and fall prey to nationalist propaganda. The role of history in politics has been increasing since the end of the Cold War, although it has always played a critical role. The less that conflicts are shaped by global politics (proxy wars) and more by local animosities, regional considerations, popular myths, and ethnic interests, then the more apparent is the role of history in the conflict. Engaging past national violence and injustices has become a core component of contemporary identity in numerous nations and is a critical aspect of the discourse of rights and ethics in public culture. Within the past generation, history has become a turf for conflict among politicians both within and among countries. It would not be an exaggeration to say that, today, history is at the heart of many national conflicts around the world. Because history is closely tied to national identity and because historical animosity can linger for a long time, it is imperative to recognize that leaving history unaddressed overshadows any presumption of success in conflict prevention. Indeed, any such illusion can easily be swept away by nationalist propaganda.

The denial of a historical narrative of gross violations of human rights and suffering is often an affront to national identity and is a sure prescription for inciting conflict. History also lies at the heart of many contemporary conflicts. The numerous examples come from the most volatile regions of the world, including Israel–Palestine, Turkey–Armenia, and the former Yugoslavia, as well as Darfur, Rwanda, and Afghanistan to mention a few of the places less widely recognized as obvious historical conflicts. History also plays a major role in relations among countries that are on friendly terms but occasionally regress into a public dispute over history – with critical political implications. In northeast Asia, tension among Japan, Korea, and China is multifaceted, but the reciprocal public animosity between Japan and its neighbors is grounded in memories of Japanese violence and distorted history, a situation that politicians are only too happy to stir up to advance their own agendas and domestic support. Similarly, East Central Europe provides many examples of discourse on historical injustices and atrocities, including Poland–Ukraine, the Czech Republic–Germany, and the Baltic States, even though these are currently not subject to active conflict. Russia has been exploiting historical propaganda in raising tensions for a decade or more, especially in its relations with the Baltic States and Ukraine, where conflict exploded in 2014. What began as primarily internal Ukrainian historical disputes destabilized the nation and escalated into a conflict with

Russia, in which Putin exploited historical memories to justify in part the invasion of Crimea and the claims for Novorossiya.

The past informs the protagonists of these conflicts and their understanding of the goals and legitimacy of their struggle. Although the historical context of conflicts is often acknowledged, the need to address the historical legacy as a tool of prevention is not recognized. History as a methodology does not engage conflict resolution professionals. History is treated as a past that cannot be changed, and therefore recognition of its ability to aggravate animosities or as a propaganda tool of nationalists is not viewed as a space of prevention. I would like to propose that history is a critical long-term line of defense against genocide and other identity-based atrocities. I believe that there are ways to counter nationalist histories in order to draw the fangs of hatred. The inclusion of historical dialogue in its multivariant forms could be a new and important prevention tool, one that extends the scope of prevention from emergency into a steady-state policy. The process of historical dialogue will aim to change cultural and historical identities that are etched in public memory, and this is, by necessity, a long-term process. The magnitude of the task may be overwhelming, but the first stage is to recognize the need.

8.3.   Transitional Justice

Transitional justice is a field of expertise that comes closest to engaging with the past within the context of conflict. Indeed, its rationale is to counter future conflicts and crimes of atrocity by emphasizing accountability. The discourse of transitional justice views peace and justice as mutually reinforcing and, indeed, argues not only that the two are complementary, but also that they cannot stand on their own. This is evident, for example, in the statement of Fatou Bensouda, the Prosecutor of the International Criminal Court (ICC), that there is no distinction between justice and peace: "Peace and justice are two sides of the same coin. The road to peace should be seen as running *via* justice, and thus peace and justice can be pursued simultaneously" (*New York Times*, March 19, 2013). This represents the conventional view among practitioners – namely, that the distinction is false, and the topic is no longer controversial. Whether the two go hand in hand or whether there are situations when peace and justice conflict and may have to be prioritized is, in part, an empirical matter, but it is also true that the beliefs of practitioners create a reality of their own. The title of the UN Special Rapporteur for the promotion of "truth, justice, reparation and guarantees of non-recurrence" describes the method by which the transitional justice field believes it can achieve prevention. This raises difficult questions concerning each of the four categories – truth, justice, reparation, and guarantees – and their reciprocal relations. Let us begin by exploring the methodology of transitional justice, its time scale, and the type of conflicts addressed by it.

Transitional Justice has become, over the course of the past generation, the central tool and methodology for addressing past violence and gross violations of human rights. It does that primarily through truth commissions and trials, in national and international courts and through ad hoc tribunals. The impact of transitional justice is important, if controversial. In most cases, it is initiated by official governmental acts (often legislation), run by formal institutions, or sponsored by international organizations (e.g., the UN). Transitional justice is employed mostly in a national, not an international context, the Former Yugoslav Republic notwithstanding. In addition to the difficulties of reaching an agreement about the specifics of a formal mechanism and an official agreement to initiate a process of transitional justice, the cost proves sometimes a deterrent and, during the process, an impediment that constrains even the best of intentions. Although in the immediate aftermath of a political transition there is often widespread support to facilitate these mechanisms, this is not the case in postconflict situations, in which there is often opposition to it from various stakeholders. The regional truth commission in the former Yugoslavia never came into being, and opposition to it is not limited to the perpetrators' perspective. Transitional justice so far has been employed more often during democratizations than in conflict resolution.

Transitional justice's focus on accountability means that it privileges addressing recent violence, primarily those violations in which the responsible perpetrators are still alive and can be brought to justice. It is less concerned with longer term violence and atrocities, those we may call historical. It primarily focuses on living perpetrators and survivors; that is, on the immediate past. Older historical issues are generally excluded even when formally declared to be part of the mission of a truth commission. There are no good examples of truth commissions that addressed historical issues going further back in time than the immediately preceding violent period. This is in contrast to historical commissions, in which the emphasis is on telling the historical narrative in an authoritative manner, preferably through agreement by all commission members, who are supposed to represent the point of view of the various stakeholders (sides) in the conflict. These commissions are probably best known in investigating the legacy of World War II in many countries or in several investigations (too few) of the violence of colonialism.

An attempt to include history as part of the mandate of a truth commission was evident in the work of the Guatemala Commission for Historical Clarification, which included several reports by individual historians on historical violence, but these reports were neither integrated into the analysis nor influenced the writing of the rest of the report. Another example of attempt to investigate several decades of violence informed the establishment of the truth commission in Kenya. Its goal was to investigate the atrocities occurring since independence. Although the commission failed for other reasons, it also did not have the capacity or methodology to historically investigate these atrocities.

A second limitation of transitional justice's capacity to address historical crimes is the lack of distinction between atrocities perpetrated under an authoritarian regime or during a conflict situation. Even when the differentiation is made, there are no distinct methodologies employed to address these two dramatically diverse types of violence. Experts' discussion of best practices or the studies of the impact and efficacy of truth commissions do not distinguish between the two kinds of transitions. This is particularly important when the conflict involves two or more identity groups: religious, ethnic, racial, or national. In those cases, when the conflict may have ceased its violent phase but the groups have not gone through a fundamental reconciliation process, the memory of the violence and animosity remain. Such regions are likely to be prone to renewed hostilities, even following a successful conflict resolution and a peace process. In the Balkans, the memory of World War II and the Battle of Kosovo were two memories among others that were exploited in instigating the wars in the 1990s. When distrust prevails, any historical issue can provide a space for conflict, as in the commemorations of the centenary of the outbreak of World War I. Raw sectarian memories are immediately transformed into tensions among countries in the region.

A third critical distinction is the focus on judicial truth. This is related to the role of victims in transitional justice and prevention. Although the need of victims to be recognized is well documented, and the field has indeed focused its attention on victims' dignity, this does not necessarily cohere with peacebuilding. The focus on individual crimes in times of political transition and during or after conflict may divert attention from the political and other structural causes that led to the outbreak of violence at the macrosocietal level. If a crime or mass atrocity cannot be attributed to individuals and proved in the court beyond a reasonable doubt (i.e., if criminal liability cannot be established), then it is less likely to receive adequate public attention. That is, if the crime could not be addressed by a court even if it is likely to be part of a truth commission's hearings, it raises the fear of impunity. Furthermore, in breaking up the "truth" into individual instances and seeing the world through the prism of the victims' perspectives, transitional justice often strives to reach a homogenous truth, one that aims to narrate a similar story in the court room, in the public, and in the scholarly arena. It focuses on the micro (horrific as it often is) at the expense of the macro reality, which is likely to produce a more complex history. In addition, those various regimes of knowledge production (judicial, public discourse, scholarly) construct various versions of the truth that are likely to collide and present a need to contextualize these within a dialogue. This is even more problematic and explicit in cases where different national identity groups view the history of the conflict in diametrically opposed ways.

This is well illustrated in Northern Ireland, where there is a general consensus that each side of the conflict has its own truth. Although there is intensive work of reconciliation, conflict resolution, and judicial inquiries, these efforts do not extend to bridging the historical narratives, but continue to allow sectarian perspectives to dominate the public sphere. An inquiry into the specifics of Bloody Sunday took years to complete and produced an exemplary report about the details of the violence and the crimes. Yet there is no attempt to scale up the conversation to structural historical analysis, to attempt to achieve an agreed-upon history. Concurrently, Belfast is saturated with sectarian images, most clearly manifested by the murals on each side of the divide. Seemingly, one could argue that engaging the sectarian history is unnecessary since peace has been achieved. My sense is that, although this is currently true (despite the slight tremor caused by the arrest of Gerry Adams in April 2014), the tense relations between the communities are such that – notwithstanding the economic vested interests in peace – sectarian violence could be renewed, thus reawakening historical animosities. This continues to be a distinct possibility in each community.

Victims have a special standing in today's society, and respect for their suffering saturates not only every discussion of atrocities, but even of day-to-day existence. As such, victims are the main protagonists whose perspective is embraced in transitional justice mechanisms. Victims' suffering is often the object of justified empathy, and redressing the rights of victims, who hold the high moral ground, is the explicit goal of advocates in the field. Yet their pain is also often the source of politics of revenge and hatred. Much more must be said about the role of victims in conflict instigation and prevention, but, for the moment, I must underscore that this is a topic that is not publicly discussed. Who is included or excluded from the category of victims? In Ireland, the recognition of paramilitary members as victims is a very contentious point, but, in general, we have no moral yardstick, let alone political experience, by which to measure our response to victims' real or exploited pain that instigates hatred and conflict.

Skepticism by advocates and experts of the role that transitional justice plays in postconflict societies has recently been explored in a report entitled

"Can Truth Commissions Strengthen Peace Processes?" (2014).[2] The report focuses on commissions that were established as a part of a peace process, not postauthoritarian commissions or those that were constituted in a postconflict situation but were not part of the peace negotiations. The report is critical of the high expectations imposed on truth commissions, and it highlights the various failures of commissions such as in Nepal, Congo, and Kenya. "The mandates of truth commissions have continued to expand in recent decades, as they have been required to cover an ever-wider range of violations and carry out a greater number of functions. This is a source of increasing concern for experts in the field" (p. x). The report is a deflating text that emphasizes the limitations of commissions, the lack of best practices, the dependency on local conditions, and the significance of emphasizing competence at the expense of representativeness of the various groups. In short, the extensive recognition is that "Peace negotiators should avoid thinking of a truth commission as the only means of securing victims' right to truth. Parties should identify other measures that can contribute practically to this right, such as providing better access to official records and taking urgent action to determine the fate of those who were forcibly disappeared during the conflict" (p. ix).

Truth commissions are expected to reconcile society and, even more specifically, to reconcile individual victims and perpetrators in the short term, a goal that advocates and experts worry leads commissions to neglect the rights of victims. This concern assumes that when victims' rights and peace are in tension, the process should clearly privilege accountability. The critique underscores the unrealistic expectations that reconciliation, or peacebuilding, is a short-term proposition and that by "the time the truth commission's work is completed, the country will be reconciled, and that reconciliation is directly linked to forgiveness, which victims may be expected to grant." The language is of impending failure, not a celebration of the potential of truth commissions' contribution to peace. The report, however, recognizes an alternative, one that moves away from criminal accountability to macro analysis and explores the historical context.[3]

8.4.   Historical Dialogue

This is where historical dialogue comes in. Conflict between groups is often transgenerational, and the historical animosity remains if it is not addressed. Fear and desire for revenge often linger and inform the policies of the groups

---

[2] "Can Truth Commissions Strengthen Peace Processes?" (2014) The report was issued by the International Center for Transitional Justice (ICTJ) and the Kofi Annan Foundation.

[3] The disillusion is most evident in the piece by Eduardo González, "Set to Fail? Assessing Tendencies in Truth Commissions Created after Violent Conflict."

involved, and are prone to be awakened by nationalists and fundamentalists as carriers of xenophobia. Historical dialogue aims to diffuse such hatred by engaging government and civil society in conversations about history and introducing empathy and even sympathy toward the other. Historical dialogue takes place directly and explicitly when two sides are engaged in joint historical writing, such as through a bilateral commission (or at least through one that has representatives from all sides), joint civil society projects, or other ways of producing historical knowledge. But historical dialogue also takes shape indirectly when historians and others are engaged in the re-evaluation of their own histories and contribute to the re-examination of national beliefs.

This is particularly important in cases of histories of atrocities and war crimes because a re-evaluation of injustices and crimes that had been self-justified can lead to opening conversations between sides. Perhaps as likely is a nationalist backlash against historical reinterpretation that casts shadows and, at times, against the historians involved. In this aspect, historical dialogue is very much a mirror image of human rights advocacy. Although the methodology is scholarly or scientific (the distinction often reflects cultural terminologies, especially in countries where history utilizes the language of science), the larger discourse is political. In this sense, whether the historian is explicitly political, her work clearly has political resonance. The short-term reward for delving into the dispute may be notoriety and even possibly widespread rejection.

Consider, for example, the attitudes in Poland to Polish complicity in the Holocaust. In the immediate aftermath of the Nazi occupation of Eastern Poland in 1941, there was extensive violence against Jews by the local population, which has become part of the story of the Holocaust. In the small town of Jedwabne, a pogrom carried out by the Polish population killed and burned hundreds of Jews, their "neighbors," most of the local population. After the war, several trials took place and individuals were punished, but the event disappeared from national memory. It was as a result of the writings by Jan Gross that, in 2000, the case of Jedwabne captured first Polish public opinion and later received wide international attention. The case has transformed the attitudes of Poles to their own history. It has led to extensive public discussion, formal investigations and commissions, presidential apologies, further ongoing investigations of the extent of similar events, the complicity of the Poles in the Holocaust, and further discussions over anti-Semitism in general. Some right-wing nationalists and anti-Semites remained vocal, but, generally speaking, Poland acknowledged its historical responsibility and is eager to examine its own history. Anti-Semitism has never been a secret in Poland, and many Jews have always viewed Poland as being responsible for much Jewish suffering before and during the Holocaust. But it is only the Polish self-examination as a result of the controversy over Jedwabne that allows for a greater reconciliation between the two peoples. It is not the horrific event that is the catalyst, but the willingness of Poland to take ownership of it that enabled better relations between the two sides.[4]

Israel's conventional history of its War of Independence, which views the Palestinians as the aggressors and the Palestinian refugees as wholly responsible for their own fate, is another example of a changing national historical self-perception, even if it has not had a perceptible impact on the peace process. In the 1980s, Israeli historians began using Israeli and British archives to uncover the role of Israel in the Palestinian displacement, and the story of the refugees became more complex. In the generation following Independence, at least in part of the Israeli public, there is empathy for the Palestinians' suffering, not only condemnations. The historical narrative is far from complete, and the Palestinians and even Israeli progressive historians are yet to reach a shared history. But the national positions are no longer exclusively polarized, and there is an initial process of bridging these histories together. From the Israeli perspective, the new narrative has transformed the national perspective of the War of Independence, which is critical for understanding the Israeli willingness to view the conflict as a national conflict and the Palestinians not merely as aggressors but as victims as well. The Israeli responsibility for the refugee problem was never previously publicly acknowledged in Israel; historical research provided new knowledge that has a direct impact on the Israeli approach to possible solutions to the conflict. There has not been a similar move among Palestinian scholars.

Historical dialogue is not bartering for truth; it is not compromising and covering up unpleasant facts in order not to offend. The fear that dialogue or shared historical narratives is meant to avoid the truth and create parity between perpetrators and victims is a frequent complaint of human rights advocates.[5] The polarized misconception has been dispelled even within the transitional justice discourse. The goal of the dialogue, no matter the form it takes, is to see the events, the crimes, and the violence from multiple perspectives. Understanding obviously does not mean condoning, and including the perspective of the perpetrators does not mean excusing or justifying. Yet the risk that this process might be viewed as such and the fact that it raises resistance among advocates and the group that suffered is understandable and

---

[4] Jan Gross, *Neighbors* (Princeton, NJ: Princeton University Press, 2001); Antony Polonsky and Joanna Michlic (eds.), *The Neighbors Respond* (Princeton, NJ: Princeton University Press, 2004); Elazar Barkan, Elizabeth A. Cole, Kai Struve, *Shared History – Divided Memory. Jews and Others in Soviet Occupied Poland, 1939–1941* (Leipzig: Leipziger Universitätsverlag, *Leipziger Beiträge zur jüdischen Geschichte und Kultur*, 2008), 5.

[5] Robert I. Rotberg and Dennis Thompson (eds.), "Truth v. Justice: The Morality of Truth Commissions," 2000; Naomi Roht-Arriaza and Javier Mariezcurrena (eds.), *Transitional Justice in the Twenty-First Century: Beyond Truth versus Justice*, 2006.

should be taken into account. One way to address this is to present cases in which the dialogue did not lead to whitewashing but rather to greater awareness and acknowledgment of the violence.[6]

Historical dialogue can contribute to prevention by engendering better relations between groups and demythologizing old hatred when it is built on false history. Historical dialogue can build a reservoir of goodwill toward the Other, the group, and the nation. This clearly is not a matter of only telling a truth, but also of political and cultural processes. It is never too late to reawaken nationalist myths and hatred, to instigate old conflicts. Historical dialogue therefore has to be ongoing and practiced on numerous levels (including education and popular culture). In this sense, historical dialogue is a living process, not one that is likely to come to a conclusion before reconciliation is part of the consensus.

A clear example of an old conflict reignited is seen in the case of the former Yugoslavia, where the old Battle of Kosovo provided a rallying cry for Milosevic in the late 1980s to rally Serb nationalists. Furthermore, when the wars were raging on in the 1990s, both Croats and Serbs took to the images and rhetoric of World War II to both castigate each other and to reaffirm the old alliances of the nation, connecting them to the legacy of the Chetniks (Serbs) and Ustaša (Croats). Notwithstanding four decades of being part of one country and a great deal of interaction, including the use of the same language, the fact that contentious history was never addressed meant that it served as kindling for the fire of nationalist politicians. Similarly, in Rwanda, the racial colonial legacy of confronting the Hutu and the Tutsi as an ancient rivalry based on exploitation served as a ready-made ideology for genocide. Eastern Europe is particularly rife with similar examples.

8.5.   Commissions

Most often, the transitional justice goal of establishing truth is approached by creating a truth commission, which depends mostly on the testimonies of primarily victims, as well as supporting research from specific criminal cases. The most famous among the several dozen commissions is the South African Truth and Reconciliation Commission (TRC). Although the structure and mission of these commissions vary, few truth commissions are charged with exploring historical issues that cannot be addressed (or resolved) by testimonies or that are not victim-centered, no matter how good the testimonies and the work of the commission. Because the immediate goal of

---

[6] See Elazar Barkan, "AHR Forum: Truth and Reconciliation in History, Introduction: Historians and Historical Reconciliation," *American Historical Review* 114(4): 899–913 (October 2009) and the articles that followed in the Forum.

a truth commission is to bring solace to victims, their testimonies are at the heart of the process.

Historical commissions are a related mechanism. They have operated over the years in various countries but are not part of the transitional justice space. There is some overlap with transitional justice, but it is rather minimal. Instead, historical commissions operate both as formal and semiformal settings. Many of these commissions addressed Holocaust and World War II culpability and were most popular in the 1990s. These led to some redress mechanisms, and had some success in rewriting historical narratives and bridging gaps between conflicting perspectives. Quite a number of commissions were established in cooperation with Germany or were initiated by Germany and led to reparations to German victims, greater disclosure of various corporations that were implicated by benefiting from Nazi policies, and bridging and healing relations with neighbors, such as the Czech Republic and Poland.

A relatively successful experience of historical commissions took place in Switzerland in the 1990s, and the studies transformed the country's view of its neutrality role during World War II. As a result of pressure from victims, two commissions were appointed (Bergier, Volcker), and their work exposed the historical complicity of Switzerland with Nazi Germany, as well as the callous attitudes of its institutions, foremost the banks, toward Holocaust survivors. It also led to reparations and payments to victims and heirs. This is obviously not an example of violent conflict or the potential for one, but rather of constructing frameworks to rework histories, the result of which influences not only the specific goal (redress) but also the identity of the protagonists.

The situation is very different between Turkey and Armenia. The aspiration for normalization and peace between the two countries faces several obstacles, none greater than the recognition of the 1915 Armenian genocide. In 2009, following extended negotiations, the countries reached an agreement ("the Protocols") that soon afterward broke down. One component of the agreement was the establishment of a historical commission. This was a moment on a continuum of Turkish sentiments of growing legitimacy for the Armenian demand that Turkey acknowledge responsibility for the genocide. There were previous civil society attempts to reach an agreement on the historical narrative (see below), and, whereas a decade ago even mentioning the genocide was a criminal offense, it has become commonplace today. There may still be a historical commission, but there is little doubt that agreeing on the historical narrative is critical to any conflict resolution between the two countries.

Other commissions, such as the Australian Commission "Bringing Them Home: The 'Stolen Children'" (Report 1997) or the ongoing Indian Residential

Schools Truth and Reconciliation Commission in Canada, addressed indigenous issues. Historical and truth commissions are varied enough within each category that the use of the term has to be understood as an *ideal type*, not a rigid classification. Politically, there is some overlap between historical and truth commissions, and several are intentionally formulated to serve both roles. The role of historical commissions as a mechanism of conflict resolution has not yet been well explored, let alone implemented.

Historical commissions investigate past violence as a key way to acknowledge human rights abuses at the macro level and reconcile inter- or intrastate conflicts. There have been and are numerous historical commissions worldwide. These diverse fora include commissions that are more like truth commissions and others that are bilateral, national, commercial, nongovernmental, informal, or academic. Some commissions work to establish a national claim, others to resolve a bilateral conflict. These commissions share an engagement with a controversial past, conduct investigations, and frequently issue a report, the substance of which reframes critical aspects of the national history. At times, the commissions are influential; in other cases, they are ignored or receive little notice by the public or politicians. A critical issue is whether the commissions come into being after a political transition or political compromise, what part of the history is open for investigation, and the political culture within which their work is done.

8.6.   Truth

The delineation between a truth commission and a historical commission is often unclear. To a certain degree, it parallels the relation of judicial truth to historical truth. Both aim to establish a record and to acknowledge the past. Judicial truth aims to resolve very specific micro cases, it is subject to specific evidentiary procedures, and the decision is reached by a court within a clear and predetermined hierarchy, with only the final outcome being considered the truth. For example, a court's decision may be overturned eventually by a Court of Appeals. The judicial truth is about an outcome, not the process. The indicted person is either guilty or not guilty of specific crimes. The data of the trial may be interesting for historical purposes but become irrelevant at the end of the trial. What remains is the verdict. Its reliance on procedure, argument, and adversarial approach means that the specific outcome depends on numerous variables. The final decision of a court is definitive.

Historical truth is very different. It is interested more in the macro truth even when it engages and studies the micro. It is not primarily about punishing, its evidentiary findings are subject to revision, and it is more likely to be based on textual and inanimate evidence than on testimony. Truth commissions, for example, have been relying more heavily on oral testimony, although there is extensive overlap between the two truths. Most importantly, all historians recognize that future historians will write a revised history, so, in this sense, the conclusions of historical studies by individuals or commissions are always provisional and subject to re-evaluation.

Judicial truth is imposed, and although it is better when judicial truth is persuasive, justice ultimately relies on force and the power of the state to impose its conclusions. In contrast, historical truth depends almost exclusively on its persuasive power to be accepted, and, if it fails – for example if a commission produces a narrative that is not persuasive – it has no power to impose it as historical truth. Its power is in its rich description and data, its construction of the identity of the protagonists and of the national memory. This memory is impacted in turn by trials, commissions, and other forms of narration and testimony that are more free-flowing. In this free market of ideas and memories, the competition is subject to much politics and manipulation. The historical narrative has to be persuasive and be able to build a strong political support in order to contribute to conflict resolution.

Historical commissions therefore are particularly important in cases of historical conflict, when historical memory overshadows contemporary politics. Japan's colonialism and legacy in its relations with China and Korea provide a prominent example. Turkey obviously faces the challenge of integrating its history into productive contemporary international and domestic politics.

8.7.   The Ambivalence of Kenya

Consider the case of Kenya, which, in the spring of 2013, experienced a peaceful election process despite a seemingly failed transitional justice process during the previous four years. Kenya suffered contentious elections in 2007 that led to violence and an international effort, headed by UN General-Secretary Kofi Annan, to stop the killings. The effort to contain the mass violence invoked the R2P doctrine and seemed initially (by 2009) to prove a case of successful mass atrocity prevention and conflict resolution. The uncertainty of the following three to four years, however, marred by occasional political violence and killings, raised fears domestically and internationally as a growing number of reports showed the failure of the transitional justice mechanism. Most troubling was the impunity of perpetrators. Even though violence was avoided during the 2013 election and its aftermath, there is little doubt that transitional justice mechanisms were lagging behind political events, failing to bring to justice those responsible for the violence and with the truth commission publishing its final report only after the election. Notwithstanding his impending trial in the ICC, Uhuru Kenyatta was elected president. Even if, in the long run, the court will have its say, in real time the trials proved no hindrance for the candidates; if anything, they may have energized the electorate to vote against international interference in Kenyan affairs. Yet, if the goal was to avoid violence, then the process could be said to have succeeded. Was peace preferred by Kenyans over justice? Clearly, the relative failure of the truth commission had minimal immediate negative repercussions. The slogan "no peace without justice" did not materialize. Instead of initiating a galvanizing process, the truth commission itself became mired by questions of integrity, incompetence, and responsibility. To the degree that it has received attention over the past four years, it has been mostly for its record of failure. The work of the commission and its report deserve extensive analysis.[7] The rationale for transitional justice as prevention in 2009 was to establish a mechanism to avoid ethnic violence in the build-up to the 2013 election. The horizon for prevention was four long years.

Although none of the mechanisms was successful, large-scale violence was averted.[8] That can mean at least one of two things. First, that prevention worked despite the failure of transitional justice mechanisms. The long shadow of trials and even the ineffective truth commission created an appearance of accountability, dominated the public sphere, and established a norm of restraint. Experts justify the demands for trials by arguing that impunity leads to new violence – that there is no peace without justice. Leaders responsible for the violence have to be brought to trial. Indeed, the argument is that perpetrators who remain free present a clear danger and are not only an affront to the victims, but also become the embodiment of impunity. How did this unfold in Kenya? The winners in the presidential elections were the leading accused perpetrators of the violence, according to the ICC indictment; their freedom indicated impunity and a failure of prevention. Yet, it is also possible that the indictments themselves had a calming effect and contained the level of propaganda and ethnic hatred during the campaign. It is possible that an atmosphere of aspiring accountability may have itself served as prevention. If that were true, it challenges the general belief that the presence of reputed criminals who are responsible for mass atrocities and yet continue to participate in politics is bound to lead to more violence and distrust in the system. In Kenya, it did not. An alternative interpretation is that the impending violence was overstated. All of this leaves open the question of the transitional justice

---

[7] "The Final Report of The Truth Justice and Reconciliation Commission of Kenya," http://tjrcke nya.org/index.php?option=com_content&view=article&id=573&Itemid=238; Elena Naughton, "Kenya a Case Study" in *Can Truth Commissions Strengthen Peace Processes?* (2014). The report was issued by the International Center for Transitional Justice (ICTJ) and the Kofi Annan Foundation.

[8] The ethnic violence seems often to be on the verge of erupting; see www.csmonitor.com/World /Africa/2014/0708/Kenyans-fear-fresh-cycle-of-violence-as-ethnic-reconciliation-falters-video

paradigm of prevention. The mandate of the Kenyan Truth Commission included a historical inquiry going back to 1963. The commission had neither the methodology nor the mechanism to engage in the intensive and comprehensive historical investigation with which it was charged. Yet, in selective cases, it addressed historical disputes over mass violence, provided what information it could gather through documentation and testimonies, and, despite a lack of resources, showed that its mandate to address history as a tool of prevention should be pursued further.

8.8.   History as a Tool for Prevention

Genocide is distinguished from other conflicts because, at its heart, is identity hatred. Although there are many causes for conflicts, in identity conflicts protagonists are viewed as members of homogenous and hateful groups, and one group is intent on destroying the other in part or in whole. The distinguishing mark of the conflict is group identity. Such group rivalry does not have to be grounded in real, empirical historical animosity or fear, but it is certainly presented as such. The Jews never endangered Germany or even presented anything that could remotely be seen as rivalry, yet the Nazi Party presented the Jews as engaged in a struggle for world domination. Genocide means for perpetrators that the survival of their own group necessitates the destruction of their enemies. This view is grounded in historical memory and mythology that recalls past violence and suffering as a critical factor in instigating the new phases of old conflicts. Empirical veracity is unnecessary, but the narrative and the fear are foundational to one or both sides. A nationalist ideology can inflame hatred based on real or mythological narratives of the recent or more distant past. In Rwanda, these mythologies included the racial makeup of migrating groups, as well as recent invented conspiracies. There are obviously many identity conflicts that never deteriorate into atrocities or genocide but continue to simmer. More importantly, the conflicts that do turn into genocides have such genealogies. Histories of conflicts are a critical prerequisite and a cause in many cases of conflict that degenerate into genocides.

The definition of genocide has at least two polarized meanings: the legal and the public. In the public perception, it is the crime of crimes, it applies to every case of horrific violence, and victims are offended if their suffering does not rise to the level of genocide. Somehow not naming it genocide disrespects victims' suffering. It is divorced from intent and even from group specificity. The legal definition, however, applies only where intent can be proved concerning the destruction of an identity group, in whole or in part. This can include the removal of children, even if no killing takes place. The dissonance is clear. The struggle over the naming of historical and more recent genocides animates national conflicts.

Given the central role of history in fomenting the most horrific violence, the question is whether scholars and intellectuals could engage in historical dialogue that produces new perspectives among groups in conflict and whether this could provide a more amiable context for prevention. If histories are the nonfictional narratives we tell about the past, could these be used to minimize hate?

Historical dialogue includes various mechanisms that can contribute to a public discourse. It is not limited to explicit engagement between sides. Some of its manifestations, such as collaboratively producing shared historical narratives that provide reliable facts and analysis for public debate and discussion on contentious violent histories, involve explicit dialogue; others, such as civil society organizations and individuals using different methodologies to counter nationalist myths and popular misconceptions, present a nuanced national identity that recognizes the humanity of the Other, and acknowledge the nation's responsibility for various historical injustices, are done unilaterally and contribute to an implicit dialogue. These manifestations take the form of traditional historical writings, reports, commemorations, memorials, old and new media, dramatic and documentary movies, and exhibitions. Each provides a space for discussion and engagement, and, if receiving wide public attention, can shape the identity of the nation. The purpose of historical dialogue is to demythologize nationalist narratives in order to provide a framework, one based on nuanced history, for better mutual understanding of the identity of the nation and its ethnicities. Other mechanisms include education curriculum, museums, and media (including documentaries), all of which have cumulative impact on public identity. Numerous practitioners and a growing number of scholars in various academic fields are engaged in these activities, but the approach is yet to receive recognition or be widely understood, and it is yet to be recognized as a specific field.

Faced with the horrific violence occurring in many parts of the world, there is widespread recognition that the stakes for peace cannot be higher. Because historical conflicts are tied closely to violations of human rights, peace, and security, it is imperative that historical narratives and attending to historical conflicts become essential elements of global diplomacy in the pursuit of conflict resolution and prevention. Although much of historical dialogue has become part of transitional justice, historical conflicts do not belong exclusively to this category. In the best cases, the response to gross violations of human rights takes various forms of redress, from retributive justice (punishing perpetrators) to restorative policies, from truth commissions to financial reparation and compensation, restitution, apologies, and historical commissions. Each of these mechanisms has evolved and expanded over the past generation. Truth commissions have become a conventional practice, so much so that it sometimes seems a precondition for any peace settlement, both in countries that emerge from a period of political violence and in those that emerge from a dictatorship. Historical commissions also should become part of this repertoire.

For historical dialogues to be meaningful, new norms will have to be evolved, similar to human rights norms or transitional justice. The international community and civil society will have to provide leadership in sponsoring and advocating for demythologizing nationalist narratives and opening a more empathetic public sphere in societies and countries in conflict.

8.9.   Shared Narratives

To hold promise for conflict resolution, historical narratives that acknowledge past violence and suffering must be written by scholars from all sides of a conflict who show empathy and are interested in utilizing their knowledge to counter popular misconceptions and historical myths.

Numerous textbooks commissions involving Germany and its neighbors (although not exclusively) have been organized by the Georg Eckert Institute for International Textbook Research. Among its notable achievements are the Franco–German Textbook Commission on Controversial Issues in European History, a German–Polish Textbook Commission, and an Israeli–Palestinian Textbook "project" (not quite a commission).[9] In East Asia, multiple efforts have been made to move toward greater cooperation on historical narratives. These include multilateral conferences and joint publications, both of which are largely a post-Cold War phenomenon (although there were a few earlier precedents). There have also been atypical historical commissions, such as a governmentally initiated commission set up by Japan and Korea as the Joint Committee to Promote Historical Research in Japanese and Korean History.[10] Civil society cooperation has occurred between Armenians and Turks, such as the Workshop for Armenian/Turkish Scholarship (WATS) that coordinated joint meetings initiated at the University of Michigan, met internationally (including a controversial meeting in Istanbul, in 2005), and contributed greatly to the formation of a bridging discourse between Armenian and Turkish scholars.[11] This initiative was largely scholarly but had significant political reverberations. A more explicitly political effort was a track-two diplomacy effort, the Turkish Armenian Reconciliation Commission, which

---

[9] www.gei.de/fileadmin/bilder/pdf/Institut/gei-past-present-future.pdf

[10] Daqing Yang, "A Noble Dream?" Shared History and Asia Pacific Community," http://web.iss .u-tokyo.ac.jp/kyoten/asnet/0511_5.doc

[11] Ronald Grigor Suny, Fatma Müge Göçek, and Norman M. Naimark (eds.), *A Question of Genocide. Armenians and Turks at the End of the Ottoman Empire* (Oxford: Oxford University Press, 2011).

engaged semiofficial representatives under informal American sponsorship in an attempt to reach a shared view of the 1915 conflict. Outsourcing it to lawyers did not prove fruitful.[12] There have been quite a number of small efforts at informal joint historical writings between Palestinian and Israeli scholars, with the odd success but admittedly little political impact at this stage.[13]

The writing of shared narratives in these examples at times brought new evidence and knowledge based on archival research. When this is possible, the significance of producing new data and knowledge should not be underestimated. However, much good work also has been done not by illuminating new complex historical narratives or new methodological innovations, nor not even by unearthing new evidence that had been hidden from public view, but by rewriting from within a dialogue a new narrative that shows greater openness to the Other – a rewriting of history with an empathetic perspective. Major conflicts are often shaped by fundamental historical misunderstanding. More precisely, numerous misconceptions inform politicians – even those who are engaged in conflict resolution – and shape the political process. These reinforce prejudices and stereotypes. Famously, the intervention in the Bosnia war was delayed for three years because the United States viewed the war as part of the Balkan's culture – a force of nature. It is up to scholars to correct these misperceptions and thereby create new space for political negotiations. Although their political impact is indirect and possibly long term, these examples of shared historical narratives show potential, one that is feasible and, if it becomes widespread, may lead to results.

A caveat is in order: national conflicts involve a lot more than historical misconceptions. There is real suffering, and at times the question of redress is itself painful, volatile, and not easily agreed upon. Mere acknowledgment is not enough. What is suggested here is not that a new historical narrative will be a magic wand for solving national animosities, but that there are instances where a new historical understanding can provide an opportunity for politicians and the public to re-examine particular beliefs that inform those animosities, and thus historical narrative can facilitate a new approach to the conflict. Furthermore, this approach is built on the assumption that once a person or a group is confronted by authoritative data that challenges particular beliefs, they will be more open to re-examine similar and analogous knowledge. Although this is not a universal characterization, and there are those who hold strongly (even stubbornly) to their beliefs, the process suggested here could apply to

---

[12] David L. Phillips, *Unsilencing the Past: Track Two Diplomacy and Turkish-Armenian Reconciliation* (Berghahn, 2005).

[13] Rafi Nets-Zehngut, "Palestinians and Israelis Collaborate in Addressing the Historical Narratives of Their Conflict." *Quest: Issues in Contemporary Jewish History* 5: 232–252 (2013).

those who are susceptible to persuasion. Thus, although national conflicts are based on extensive real animosity, the shared history is likely not one of undifferentiated hostility. The combination of countering prejudicial stereotypes with recognition of a group's own responsibility for certain aspects of the conflict may provide for new perspectives and better understanding of the Other in a way that could contribute to resolution.

This possibility is particularly appealing in cases where history is central to the conflict. By working with prominent scholars, respected human rights advocates, and community leaders, the goal is to develop an approach to address the conflict by commissioning negotiated historical narratives that are written by stakeholders from both sides of the conflict. It aims to bring together scholars from opposing sides of these historical conflicts to collaborate on joint research and write common histories. Since this is both a public and a scholarly effort, the task is to establish a community of discourse that would represent both levels; that is, that would be both scholarly sound and represent a national narrative.

"Representing the national narrative" is a phrase that needs explication. Critics of national narratives may see "representing" as propaganda, not scholarship. And it is with this critique in mind that the goal must be to establish a community discourse that does not practice propaganda and that represents not national (or governmental) policies but rather *national identity*. As an essential part of practical realism, representing means taking seriously the phobias and concerns that exist in a national history and engaging with the real beliefs that inform the public (or at least major segments of it) without dismissing the national history as merely nationalistic, ignorant, or propaganda-mongering. The aim is not to support any particular governmental position and certainly not to accept any set of beliefs that conflict with empirical historical research. It does mean giving a fair hearing to alternative narratives and examining the degree to which conflicting positions can coexist. As long as we recognize that identity is a significant component in the writing of history and that subjectivity has its place, such representation becomes necessary. Yet, subjectivity is not relativism. Not all positions are equal, and narratives are not about assertions and power. Rather, the construction of joint narratives requires patience and a readiness to examine and engage the other side's perspective, especially in cases when such positions seem initially offensive. It means engaging the best possible research with the recognition of a political end. Historical truth works on a different time-scale from political truth.

Historical claims vetted by experts aim to become "practical truth" and noncontroversial in the public arena. This takes time and work. Demythologizing national beliefs includes controversial conclusions that might be innovative, interesting, and challenging but unlikely to achieve the status of truth until embraced by the profession and later the public. It is plausible that this might be viewed as giving a veto power to nationalist propagandists who often populate the profession and may maintain xenophobic narratives. Although nationalist historians often have a powerful voice, given time, empirical evidence, and advocacy, the pragmatic truth might emerge and be accepted by increasing segments of the professional community and, eventually, the public.

International professional historians in today's world do shape the alternative narratives that are accepted by their profession. This, in itself, creates pressure on the domestic professional historian community, which, for its own professional needs, seeks international approbation. Taking into account the impact of international professionals, it is likely that each community of discourse will, as a rule, eventually approximate practical pragmatic truth – even when that truth conflicts with the traditional nationalist narrative. It is both at the time of the construction of an international consensus and at the time when the national professional community comes to accept the critique of the nationalist narratives that historians can have some impact on reconciliation. For example, many countries in Eastern Europe have internally conflictual approaches to Nazi and Soviet crimes, as well as conflicts concerning their own legacy of anti-Semitism, and these conflicting beliefs are motivated in part by the need to adapt to European Union norms. The role of the Holocaust as a foundational event in European history confronts local nationalist homogenous views of the nation, and, although it is not clear in what direction the next generation will evolve, nationalist bravado faces serious challenges in places like Poland. In other countries, the nationalist narrative is more vehement. Although there are relatively few Jews living in these countries, and no conflict is likely to emerge, the struggle with the historical truth takes place over the national identity.

Transitional justice is currently unable conceptually or methodologically to deal with historical animosity. If it is agreed that historical animosity can instigate crimes of atrocity, then it should become clear that there is a need to develop methodology to confront these dangers. In this, there is room for existing professional communities of conflict resolution and peacebuilding, as well as transitional justice practitioners, to connect with historians and other scholars to initiate historical dialogue as a form of mass atrocity prevention and as a way of translating the right to truth from an individual event to a peacebuilding tool.

9   Through the Barrel of a Gun: Can Information
     from the Global Arms Trade Contribute
     to Genocide Prevention?

Andrew Feinstein

9.1.   Introduction

This chapter considers whether information gleaned from research and investigations on the global arms trade can meaningfully assist active work aimed at the prevention of genocide. In addition to attempting to provide a preliminary answer to the question, it also aims to identify further work that might be required to furnish a more comprehensive response. The argument is based on my investigations and research into the global arms trade over the past decade and a half, which is reflected in my book *The Shadow World: Inside the Global Arms Trade* (2011).

9.2.   Context of the Arms Trade

Global military expenditure totaled about $1.74 trillion in 2013, equal to $248 for every person on the planet.[1] On average, between $60 and $110 billion is spent every year on conventional weapons alone.[2] The trade in small arms is worth about $4–5 billion a year[3] but has an impact far beyond this value because small and light weapons are relatively cheap, easy to transport, use, and maintain, and are so abundantly available. Between 2008 and 2012, the period of the current and ongoing economic crisis, international arms transfers increased by 17 percent over the preceding five years.[4]

The United States, Russia, the United Kingdom, France, Germany, Sweden, Holland, Italy, Israel, and China are regularly identified as the largest producers

---

[1] Siemon T. Wezeman and Pieter D. Wezeman, *Trends in International Arms Transfers, 2013*, SIPRI Fact Sheet, March 2014, http://books.sipri.org/product_info?c_product_id=475.
[2] Andrew Feinstein, *The Shadow World: Inside the Global Arms Trade* (New York: Farrar, Straus & Giroux, 2012), xxii.
[3] Ibid.
[4] *Trends in International Arms Transfers, 2013*.

196

and traders of weapons and matériel.[5] The arms trade is clearly a crucial component of national defense and foreign policy, both overt and covert. But spending on arms has profound impacts on the world beyond this: from the enabling, fueling, and perpetuation of conflict and repression, to the corrosion of democracy in both buying and selling countries and massive socioeconomic opportunity costs.

Arms deals stretch across a continuum of legality and ethics from the official, or formal trade, to the gray and black markets. In practice, the boundaries between the three markets are fuzzy. They are often intertwined and dependent on each other. With bribery and corruption commonplace, there are very few arms transactions that do not involve some illegality, most often through middlemen or agents who operate across the licit and illicit markets.

In extraordinary work based largely on confidential information gleaned from national treasuries and intelligence agencies around the world, Joe Roeber, working with Transparency International, concluded that, up to the end of 2003, the trade in weapons accounted for around 40 percent of all corruption in global trade.[6] More recently, Transparency International has estimated that bribes of around $20 billion are paid in the trade every year.[7] Corruption and illegality are built into the structure, the very DNA, of the arms business, where you often have contracts worth billions of dollars being decided on by a very small number of people, all taking place behind a veil of national security-imposed secrecy.

There are a range of national laws governing the export of weapons, as well as some regional and multilateral agreements, for example, the European Union (EU) Common Position on Arms Exports.[8] But they are very seldom fully implemented or complied with. For instance, if the Common Position were enforced, as well as domestic guidelines in a range of EU countries and the United States, weapons deals with Saudi Arabia, a country that has been identified as committing human rights abuses, would not be legal.

Transgressors are very seldom brought to book, since the defense companies and arms dealers have close relationships with governments at the highest levels and with defense and foreign ministries, political parties, and the military and intelligence agencies. There is a continuous revolving door of people among these entities. Of an estimated 502 recorded violations of United

---

[5] *Shadow World*, xxiii.
[6] Joe Roeber, "Hard-wired for Corruption," *Prospect*, August 28, 2005.
[7] Government Defence Anti-Corruption Index, Transparency International, www.defenceindex.org.
[8] "Council Common Position 2008/944/CFSP of 8 December 2008 Defining Common Rules Governing Control of Exports of Military Technology and Equipment," *Official Journal of the European Union*, December 13, 2008, http://eur-lex.europa.eu/LexUriServ/LexUriServ.do? uri=OJ:L:2008:335:0099:0103:EN:PDF.

Nations arms embargoes since their inception in 1990, two have resulted in legal action, one of which ended in conviction.[9] It should therefore come as no surprise that the trade in weapons is less regulated than the trade in bananas![10]

In this parallel legal universe, corruption, poor decision making, and outright criminality, as well as the efforts to conceal them, undermine the rule of law, distort the market, and pollute the business environment, the political process, and the functioning of the state. In late 2006, for instance, then British prime minister Tony Blair personally intervened to close down a detailed investigation into the biggest and most corrupt arms deal in history, the Al Yamamah deal, in which the United Kingdom sold Saudi Arabia more than £43 billion of weapons. £6 billion in commissions were paid, including more than a billion pounds paid into the accounts of the Saudi ambassador to the United States, who was the son of the country's defense minister at the time. Mark Thatcher, son of British prime minister Margaret Thatcher who had negotiated the deal with the Saudis, was paid £12 million on the deal.[11] And this is the cleaner, government-to-government trade in arms. This corruption is always an important, and sometimes crucial, driver of arms deals, including deals that result in the perpetration of atrocities.

The illicit trade, which is illegal in conception and execution, is inextricably intertwined with this formal trade. This symbiosis occurs in multiple ways but primarily through the economics and individuals involved. The value of weapons produced by large manufacturers is significantly increased at point of sale in the knowledge that they will be used repeatedly not only in formal conflicts by the original buyer, but also in multiple other conflicts into which they are on-sold illegally. Most crucially, many known illicit arms dealers are used by the large manufacturers, their governments, and intelligence agencies, both overtly and covertly. For example, on a highly corrupt deal with South Africa in 1998–99, BAE Systems, a British multinational defense, security, and aerospace company headquartered in London, utilized arms dealer John Bredenkamp, who was on EU and U.S. financial sanctions lists as a crony of Zimbabwe's president Robert Mugabe and has been active in the Democratic Republic of Congo

---

[9] *Shadow World*, xxix.

[10] "What's the Deal with Bananas and the Global Arms Trade?" The Politics of Poverty: Ideas and analysis from Oxfam America's policy experts, June 26, 2012, http://politicsofpoverty.oxfamamerica.org/2012/06/comparing-bananas-to-the-global-arms-trade/.

[11] The BAE files, Part 6: "Secrets of al-Yamamah," *The Guardian*, n.d., www.theguardian.com/baefiles/page/0,,2095831,00.html; and Mark Hollingsworth and Paul Halloran, *Thatcher's Fortunes: The Life and Times of Mark Thatcher* (Edinburgh: Mainstream, 2005), 217.

(DRC), where mass atrocities have been ongoing to varying degrees since 1993.[12]

The hypocritical use of illegal dealers by the world's governments is best illustrated by the career of Russian Viktor Bout, known as the "merchant of death," who sold to most sides in the Angolan Civil War (1994–98), the DRC (1998–2002), Liberia (2000–01), and the Balkans (1992)[13] and is now in jail in the United States. However, between 2003 and 2005, while there was an Interpol warrant out for his arrest, Bout ferried equipment, weapons, and ammunition into Iraq for the U.S. Department of Defense and a number of major U.S. defense contractors.[14]

Joe der Hovsepian has been an arms dealer for more than five decades. He started in the trade in post-war Germany with a company run by former senior Nazi officers, who were supported by German and U.S. intelligence to undertake covert arms deals in the early years of the Cold War. Klaus Barbie was among their senior operators in Latin America, as was Charles Taylor in Africa. Der Hovsepian himself has violated UN arms embargoes across the globe, selling to most sides in the Balkans conflict (1990–92), Yemen, Saudi Arabia, and Syria. When asked about his Nazi and neo-Nazi ties and whether they create difficulties for him in the trade, he suggested that they often won over Arab customers who believed that "if Hitler had finished off the Jews they wouldn't have all the problems they have today."[15] He then revealed that he works for the U.S. Department of Defense in Iraq and Afghanistan and for USAID in those two countries and Liberia.[16]

9.3. The Arms Trade and Genocide

Weapons and the arms trade do not cause conflicts, mass atrocities, or genocide. But the easy availability of weapons enables them, and makes it much more likely they will be violent, continue for longer, and claim more victims. Similarly, the massive size of defense budgets and the centrality of what has been described as "permanent war" make it far more likely that conflicts will be resolved violently rather than by diplomacy and negotiation.

The commission of mass atrocities and genocide requires the provision of weapons and other supplies and services. The suppliers are known as *enablers*,

---

[12] *Final Report of the Panel of Experts on the Illegal Exploitation of Natural Resources and Other Forms of Wealth in the Democratic Republic of Congo*, UN Security Council doc. S/2002/1146, October 16, 2002, www.securitycouncilreport.org/atf/cf/%7B65BFCF9 B-6D27-4E9C-8CD3-CF6E4FF96FF9%7D/DRC%20S%202002%201146.pdf.

[13] Dates indicate years that Bout sold weapons, rather than years of conflicts as such.

[14] Doug Farah and Stephen Braun, *Merchant of Death* (London: John Wiley & Sons, 2007), 219–234.

[15] *Shadow World*, 59.

[16] Interview conducted by the author with der Hovsepian, cited in *Shadow World*, 420.

and suppliers of weapons and ammunition are clearly the most important of these enablers because mass atrocities and genocide cannot occur without adequate arms and matériel.

For instance, in the case of Sudan, from at least 1990, small arms and ammunition were provided by a wide range of sources and included Brazilian and Ukrainian arms. Military aircraft, which were essential "in planning and carrying out atrocities" across the country, were supplied by Russia to the Sudanese government.[17] In the DRC, some companies involved in the extraction of minerals have also been complicit in ensuring supplies of weaponry to the protagonists.[18] A number of these companies have links to third parties in the United Arab Emirates, a growing hub for arms trading activities.[19] But perhaps the most explicit example of weapons' suppliers facilitating mass atrocities is that of the Rwandan genocide.

9.4.   The Case of Rwanda

The tragedy of Rwanda evokes traumatic images. We have a visceral sense of the mass use of machetes to slaughter. Machetes are weapons easily obtainable, cheap, and easy to use. But, crucially, there were numerous more conventional weapons used as well to create the environment for the genocide and to facilitate and contribute to the killing.

The question arises whether, if governments, international organizations, and monitoring groups had known more about the build-up of weaponry in preparation for the genocide, they might have reacted earlier or more effectively. Could there have been measures taken to stop the flow of weapons into the country, given knowledge of the sources?

Rwanda was carefully prepared for genocide, first by a massive and targeted propaganda campaign and second through the rapid militarization of Rwandan society between 1990 and 1994. Without this, it is unlikely that the genocide could have occurred on the scale it did.

In response to the Rwanda Patriotic Front (RPF) attacks in October 1990, the ruling elite implemented a "Civil Defense Plan." This Civil Defense would be created by providing military training and supplies to all corners of the country in order to build a ready-trained militia with leaders in each of Rwanda's communes and communities.[20]

---

[17] "Disrupting the Supply Chain for Mass Atrocities: How to Stop Third-Party Enablers of Genocide and Other Crimes Against Humanity," Human Rights First, July 2011, www.human rightsfirst.org/2011/07/07/disrupting-the-supply-chain-for-mass-atrocities/.

[18] "Final Report of the Panel of Experts on the Illegal Exploitation of Natural Resources and Other Forms of Wealth in the Democratic Republic of Congo," October 16, 2002, S/2002/1146, paras 12–24.

[19] *Shadow World*, 527–28.

[20] Linda Melvern, *Conspiracy to Murder: The Rwandan Genocide* (London: Verso, 2006), 21–32.

It was from this program that the infamous Interahamwe emerged, a youth militia that was part of President Habyarimana's ruling party and that would constitute the genocide's shock troops. At the same time, the Rwandan army was rapidly expanded from just under 10,000 troops in 1990 to 35,000 by 1993.[21] But these plans faced a major obstacle: a paucity of weapons.

Between 1980 and 1988, the Habyarimana regime spent a paltry $5 million on arms imports. Between 1990 and 1994, tons of arms and ammunition were bought and disbursed throughout the country. So large was the buying spree that Rwanda, a continental minnow in weapons terms, became Africa's third-largest importer of arms between 1992 and 1994, spending more than $112 million, twenty times what it spent in the entire decade of the '80s.[22]

In the four years from 1990, Rwanda spent 70 percent of its annual state budget on arms, increasing its national debt by more than 100 percent.[23] By 1994, an estimated 85 tons of arms and ammunition had been distributed throughout the country, a huge amount considering Rwanda had a population of only 7 million. Militia commanders in the countryside filled in requisition slips for AK-47s and ammunition; grenades required no paperwork at all. By 1994, grenades were so widely available that they could be purchased from local vegetable markets for $3 apiece.[24]

Rwanda had a number of sources for its weapons: South Africa's state-owned armaments company, Armscor, supplied arms and ammunition worth $5.9 million to the Habyarimana regime in 1992 and 1993.[25] Not only did the transfer of South African arms help Rwanda militarize on its path to genocide, but it was conducted in violation of the arms embargo placed on apartheid South Africa, which would only be lifted after democratic elections in the country in 1994. In addition to 3,000 R-4 automatic rifles and ammunition, the South Africans supplied SS-77 machine guns, heavier Browning machine guns, 1 million rounds of ammunition, 70 hand-held grenade launchers with 10,000 grenades, 100 60-mm mortars, and a further 10,000 M-26 fragmentation grenades.[26] Between October 1990 and June 1992, Rwanda bought $12 million worth of weapons from Egypt, including 6 powerful towed guns; 70 mortars of various calibers, including 10,000 shells; 2,000

---

[21] Ibid.

[22] Mel McNulty, "French Arms, War and Genocide," *Crime, Law and Social Change* 33(1–2): 105–129 (2000).

[23] Fruchart, "Case Study: Democratic Republic of Congo, 2003–2006," 5.

[24] Nelson Alusala, "The Arming of Rwanda, and the Genocide," *African Security Review* 13(2): 137–140 (2004), www.issafrica.org/Pubs/ASR/13No2/CAlusala.htm.

[25] *Arming Rwanda: The Arms Trade and Human Rights Abuses in the Rwandan War*, Human Rights Watch, January 1, 1994, www.hrw.org/reports/1994/01/01/arming-rwanda.

[26] Ibid., 16.

RPG rockets; 2,000 landmines; 450 Egyptian Kalashnikov rifles; 200 kg of plastic explosives; and 3.2 million rounds of ammunition.[27]

This entire arms-buying spree was directed from the Rwandan embassy in Paris, "a seven-floor building in the 17th *arrondissement*, on orders from Kigali."[28] France was not only the largest supplier to Habyarimana's regime, but also played a role in securing the arms from South Africa and Egypt. The Egyptian weapons were paid for with a bank guarantee from Crédit Lyonnais, and the French, who had been secretly supplying the apartheid regime for a long time, acted as an intermediary during the South African deal.[29]

Between February 1990 and April 1994, France, in pursuit of influence and profits, exported to Rwanda arms and ammunition worth a total of 136 million French francs (FF). They also made direct transfers of weapons (i.e., arms taken from existing French supplies and paid for by the French Ministry of Defense or the Ministry of Cooperation) at no cost to Rwanda. With fewer administrative obstacles, these transfers could take place quickly and more frequently. In the four years preceding the genocide, France undertook thirty-six direct transfers worth FF43 million.[30]

What was additionally transferred for free makes for sober reading: France agreed to transfer – and presumably delivered – the following weapons: 3 Gazelle helicopters; 6 Rasura radar systems; 1 Alouette II helicopter; 6 68-mm rocket launchers (with 1,397 68-mm rockets; for the helicopters); 2 Milan antitank missile launchers; 70 12.7-mm heavy machine guns (with 132,400 rounds of ammunition); 8 105-mm cannons (with 15,000 shells); 6 120-mm mortars (with 11,000 shells); 3,570 90-mm shells (for AML-90 armored vehicles already in service); 8,850 60-mm mortar shells; 4,000 81-mm mortar shells; and 2,040 rounds of 20-mm, 256,500 rounds of 9-mm, 145,860 rounds of 7.62–mm, and 1,256,059 rounds of 5.56-mm ammunition, as well as many small arms and spare parts for helicopters and armored vehicles.[31]

It was only in May 1994, a month after the genocide started, that the UN imposed a mandatory arms embargo on the country.[32] For the Rwandan genocidaires, however, this did not mean a reduction in the flow of arms. Instead, the government turned to the ever-present shadow world of arms dealers to fulfill its needs. In particular, a company based in Sussex, in the United Kingdom, was highly successful in breaking the arms embargo on

[27] Ibid., 15.

[28] *Conspiracy to Murder*, 57–58.

[29] Ibid.

[30] Fruchart, "Case Study: Democratic Republic of Congo, 2003–2006," 7.

[31] Ibid., 6.

[32] "UN arms embargo on Rwanda (Non-Governmental Forces)," Stockholm International Peace Research Institute, October 25, 2012, www.sipri.org/databases/embargoes/un_arms_embar goes/rwanda.

Rwanda's behalf. Mil-Tec supplied the Rwandan army with arms from mid-April 1994 until mid-July 1994 – the exact time that the genocide was being conducted. Mil-Tec was run by Anoop Vidyarthi, a Kenyan Asian, from a "dingy office above an aromatherapy shop" in the north London suburb of Hendon.[33] In total, the company transferred more than $5.5 million worth of arms to Rwanda during these three bloody months. Most were sourced from Bulgaria and Israel. Among the weapons delivered were ammunition worth $1.3 million, 2,500 AK- 47s, 2,000 mortar bombs, and 100 rockets for RPG-launchers.[34]

Vidyarthi went underground as soon as the story broke. But Mil-Tec had not violated any UK government rules because it was registered in the Isle of Man. Due to sloppy legislation, the United Kingdom had failed to extend the UN arms embargo to British crown protectorates, of which the Isle of Man is one. This was only done in December 1996, a month after the Mil-Tec story erupted in the international media. We know what the consequences were: 800,000 men, women, and children killed over the course of 100 days between April and July 1994.[35]

It is my view that whereas the popularized images of the Rwandan genocide suggest a primal orgy of slaughter, a frenzy of bloodlust and carnage, a different picture captures the full reality: the genocide was meticulously organized in order to kill as many people as efficiently as possible. The mountains of weapons that had been imported into the country were crucial to achieving this aim.

Guns and firearms, as opposed to just machetes, were used specifically to kill young men with community standing who could resist the genocidaires and to exterminate large numbers of people in quick massacres. The slaughter of thousands of Rwandans in schools and football stadiums was done almost exclusively with firearms and grenades in order to achieve the highest kill rate possible.[36]

---

[33] "Arming Africa: Who Is the Second Largest Supplier of Weapons in the World? China? France? Russia? No, it's Britain," *The Independent*, November 19, 1996, www.independent. co.uk/news/world/arming-africa-who-is-the-secondlargest-supplier-of-weapons-in-the-wor ld-china-france-russia-no-its-britain-1353105.html; "Bloody Trade that Fuels Rwanda's War," *The Independent*, November 23, 1996, www.independent.co.uk/news/world/bloody-trade-that-fuels-rwandas-war-1353751.html

[34] Ibid.; and Fruchart, "Case Study: Democratic Republic of Congo, 2003–2006," 8.

[35] *Report of the Independent Inquiry into the Actions of the United Nations during the 1994 Genocide in Rwanda*, UN Security Council doc. S/1999/1257, December 15, 1999, www.secu ritycouncilreport.org/atf/cf/%7B65BFCF9B-6D27-4E9C-8CD3-CF6E4FF96FF9%7D/POC% 20S19991257.pdf.

[36] Philip Verwimp, "Machetes and Firearms: The Organization of Massacres in Rwanda," *Journal of Peace Research* 43(1): 7 (2006), www.engagingconflict.it/ec/wp-content/uploads/2012/06 /Verwimp-Machetes-and-Firearms-The-Organization-of-Massacres-in-Rwanda.pdf.

The importation of arms into Rwanda may not have caused the genocide. But it certainly enabled and intensified it, militarizing the country's social conflicts in a devastating spiral of violence. Above all, the imported arms made the genocide exponentially more efficient. It can only prompt the question: how many hundreds of thousands of lives may have been saved if the tools for ruthless and efficient killing were not so easily acquired? And were there warning signs in the buildup of weaponry that could have been noticed and responded to sooner?

9.5.   Arms Trade Information as a Warning Sign for Prevention of Genocide

The UN Office of the Special Adviser to the Secretary-General for the Prevention of Genocide identifies the presence of arms as a risk factor in its current framework of analysis.[37] The Rwandan case, as well as others, raises a number of additional important points in relation to enhancing the use of arms trade information in predicting and preventing genocide:

- Many weapons buildups don't lead to genocide, but genocide requires the buildup of weapons.
- In addition to conflict, transitions and upheavals result in weapons becoming more easily available. The most obvious case was after the collapse of the Soviet Union, when Viktor Bout and many others made billions from the surplus stocks of Soviet weaponry, selling to anyone who could pay. More recently, the overselling of weapons to Moammar Gaddafi resulted in massive surpluses that were kept in warehouses that were far from impregnable. As instability came to Libya, these warehouses were looted, with all manner of weapons becoming available on the world's black markets within days.[38]
- In the case of the DRC today, we see many weapons sourced from Rwanda, Zimbabwe, Angola, Albania, the Czech Republic, Ukraine, and China.[39]
- Significant weapons buildups are not easy to conceal. Outsized imports based on national income (the Rwandan imports would have absorbed a massive portion of the national income if France had actually charged them) and, obviously, the political context are key indicators.
- Different weapons obviously have different uses; therefore, one could arguably identify the types of weapons most likely to be used in mass atrocities

[37] "Analysis Framework: A Guide for States," Office of the Special Adviser of the Secretary-General on the Prevention of Genocide, http://aipr.files.wordpress.com/2012/05/foa-for-states-english.pdf.

[38] Andrew Feinstein, "Where Is Gadaffi's Vast Arms Stockpile?" *The Guardian*, October 26, 2011, www.theguardian.com/world/2011/oct/26/gadaffis-arms-stockpile.

[39] *Shadow World*, 451.

depending on the circumstances and the context. In addition to the obvious (small arms and, importantly, low-skill equipment and explosives that allow shock troops to inflict maximum damage with the least training), the combination of a buildup of conventional weapons together with repressive and torture equipment and, possibly, in certain circumstances, chemical weapons, could indicate intentions.

- Further work is required on identifying the types of weapons used in different mass atrocities and genocides. Mass purchases of such equipment could then be used as an obvious risk factor.
- A further interesting dimension to consider is the nature of arms transactions – not just what is bought, but the levels of secrecy of weapons procurement, the nature of the procurements, and how widely and to whom they are distributed. The Rwandans and French maintained an even higher than ordinary level of secrecy, which obviously makes it more difficult to detect but also raises more questions.
- In instances of authoritarian rule, leaders often have a key arms dealer. Charles Taylor favored Ukrainian-Israeli Leonid Minin, then Viktor Bout, and finally a Dutchman, Guus Kouwenhoven. If the favored dealers are effectively tracked, the activities and intentions of the rulers might be clearer.
- These rulers and their arms dealers also often have favored financial enablers. So, for instance, Charles Taylor and his dealers utilized Barclays Bank, where his brother worked. Educating these enablers about the sorts of transactions to be alert to could be a useful strategy for gleaning crucial information.

With these points in mind, it is suggested that the following are explicit ways in which knowledge of the arms trade could be used to predict and prevent genocide:

- Improved arms control and monitoring would have a positive impact on prevention. This includes more stringent regulation and better management of weapons and ammunition. In this vein, the international arms trade treaty passed by the UN in mid-2013 could be significant if rigorously implemented.[40] Article 6 (3) specifically forbids the export of weapons if they could be used in the commission of mass atrocities and genocide. However, the treaty lacks enforcement mechanisms and is generally regarded as a fairly weak tool.
- The early application and proper enforcement of international and regional arms embargoes are extremely important for genocide prevention. This requires far greater attention from the UN and regional multilateral organizations whose enforcement is currently inadequate.

---

[40] Full text and related documents available at www.un.org/disarmament/ATT/.

- The creation of meaningful weapons monitoring capacity at international, regional, and national levels is crucial. Tracking technology in relation to weapons and ammunition is fast improving and should be utilized.[41]
- By being more knowledgeable about weapons transfers and the activity of individual arms dealers and companies, countries and regions can not only improve enforcement, but also equip themselves with additional preventative tools. A key challenge is that government information is highly restricted even within governments, and its reliability is sometimes questionable.

If knowledge about weapons transfers and the activities of arms dealers and companies is valuable to enhancing the prediction and prevention of mass atrocities and genocide, it is worth considering the development of a global virtual community that could pool information and make it available to appropriate authorities. Organizations such as the Stockholm International Peace Research Institute (SIPRI), Transparency International's Defence Programme, the Oslo Peace Research Institute (PRIO), International Peace Information Service (IPIS), and Amnesty International's Defense team, among others, all track aspects of arms transfers, dealers, and companies.

Such information could meaningfully contribute to preventative work while also providing an important resource for law enforcement authorities committed to reducing the damaging effects of the global arms trade. However, for this to become a reality, governments need to display the political will to vigorously reform this trade that currently operates with so much latitude.

---

[41] See, for example, Douglas Page, "Microstamping Calls the Shots: A Revolutionary Gun Identification Technology Finds Favor and Foes," *Law Enforcement Technology* 35(1) (January 2008).

10   The Individual Responsibility to Protect

Edward C. Luck and Dana Zaret Luck

> Beyond the legal responsibilities of the State, individuals have a moral responsibility to protect.   Secretary-General Ban Ki-moon[1]

> When people are in danger, everyone has a duty to speak out. No one has a right to pass by on the other side.   Secretary-General Kofi A. Annan[2]

10.1.   Introduction

This chapter[3] takes a fresh look at a dimension of the Responsibility to Protect (R2P) – individual responsibility – that has been underappreciated both in theory and in practice, despite the moving words from the last two United Nations Secretaries-General.[4] This reconceptualization of R2P begins with the premise that neither prevention nor the protection of vulnerable populations

---

[1] Report of the Secretary-General, *The Role of Regional and Subregional Arrangements in Implementing the Responsibility to Protect*, A/65/877-S/2011/393, p. 4, para. 13.

[2] Remarks by the Secretary-General, "Reflections on Intervention," Thirty-fifth Annual Ditchley Foundation Lecture, Ditchley Park, SG/SM/6613, June 26, 1998.

[3] Draft chapter in *Reconstructing Atrocity Prevention*, edited by Sheri Rosenberg, Tibi Galis, and Alex Zucker (Cambridge: Cambridge University Press, 2015).

[4] The seminal documents on the Responsibility to Protect include (1) the Report of the International Commission on Intervention and State Sovereignty, *The Responsibility to Protect* (Ottawa: International Development Research Centre, 2001), (2) paragraphs 138–140 of the Outcome Document of the 2005 World Summit, and (3) the Report of the Secretary-General, *Implementing the Responsibility to Protect*, A/63/677, January 12, 2009. The independent International Commission, convened by Canada and co-chaired by Gareth Evans and Mohamed Sahnoun, former foreign ministers of Australia and Algeria, respectively, introduced the principle and outlined its potential applicability to preventing and responding to mass atrocities, as well as to rebuilding afterwards The Outcome Document, the unanimous product of one of the largest gatherings of heads of state and government in history, was the first endorsement of the principle by the Member States of the United Nations. It was then adopted by the General Assembly in Resolution 60/1. The Security Council reaffirmed the principle in Resolution 1674 (2006) and has invoked it frequently since then. The three-pillar implementation strategy laid out in Secretary-General Ban Ki-moon's 2009 report remains the framework for the UN's policy and practice. The senior author of this chapter was the architect of the strategy and the primary author of the report.

can be realized without individuals taking responsibility and assuming risk. For if R2P is only about collective responsibilities – those of governments and institutions – then it will confront recurring and often disabling collective action dilemmas and a pervasive lack of accountability. This chapter introduces a less hierarchical and more interactive approach – the Individual Responsibility to Protect (IR2P) – that seeks to refine and complement the state- and institution-centric paradigm that has largely framed discussion of R2P to date.[5] IR2P is about the decisions people make before, during, and after atrocity crimes are committed.

This chapter introduces IR2P by identifying seven groups of critical decision makers, on the ground as well as in governments and international institutions. It calls for more focused attention on finding means of influencing their decisions – literally often fatal choices – in a way that could make such crimes less likely, less extreme, less sustainable over time, and less likely to reoccur. It posits, as well, that the making of policy at the national and international levels could be enriched by the insights from existing lines of interdisciplinary research, although currently there is remarkably little conversation between those who study the origins and nature of mass atrocities and those charged with finding ways to prevent them. Drawing on lessons from the UN's mixed experience in trying to protect populations by preventing such crimes, this chapter suggests a series of challenges and opportunities that an IR2P perspective could bring to policy making.

For at least ten reasons, this is a propitious time to turn attention to the IR2P:

- One, since the debates of the past decade about the limits of sovereignty and the responsibilities of the state have largely affirmed the validity of core R2P principles, it is time to turn to second-generation questions about what individuals and groups, as well as governments and international institutions, can do to implement these principles in practice. As the R2P debates in the UN General Assembly among governments and those outside among scholars have focused increasingly on implementation, there is a growing need to adjust the initial articulation of R2P to the lessons learned from its application in practice.[6]

---

[5] The Secretary-General's 2009 report contended that "one of the keys to preventing small crimes from becoming large ones, as well as to ending such affronts to human dignity altogether, is to foster individual responsibility. Even in the worst genocide, there are ordinary people who refuse to be complicit in the collective evil, who display the values, the independence and the will to say no to those who would plunge their societies into cauldrons of cruelty, injustice, hatred and violence." Ibid., p.14, para. 27. A few years earlier, there was a student-led and short-lived movement in the United Kingdom called the individual Responsibility to Protect (iR2P), that posted a genocide prevention pledge.

[6] In an intriguing, if not entirely convincing, analysis, Anne Orford has contended that R2P itself was less a conceptual breakthrough than an attempt to bring theory in line with changing

- Two, over the past half dozen years, operational experience has demonstrated that the critical question in most situations – Syria has been a big exception– is not how to overcome objections to international involvement based on sovereignty concerns, but how to make external engagement effective in preventing mass atrocities and protecting populations over both the short and long haul. Practice, not theory, is driving the need to re-emphasize the roles of individuals and groups in preventing mass atrocities and protecting populations.
- Three, some of the most effective efforts at prevention and protection have sought to remind individual leaders that they could be held politically and/or legally accountable for their actions. This has led to growing appreciation both of the role that the International Criminal Court (ICC) and regional tribunals have played in atrocity prevention and of the place for quiet interpersonal diplomacy in persuading leaders to take a different tack.
- Four, the original assumption that governments are the primary perpetrators of mass atrocities looks increasingly anachronistic in an era when transnational armed groups, such as the Islamic State (ISIS or ISIL), Boko Haram, al-Shabab, and the Lord's Resistance Army, among others, have incorporated the commission of vicious atrocity crimes into their very identity and sense of purpose. These groups have been immune to political or moral appeals, as flouting human rights, humanitarian, and human protection standards has been integral to their efforts to recruit disaffected and alienated individuals and groups. Since these groups have adopted the tactics of terrorism, the national and international responses have invoked the rhetoric and employed the tools of both counterterrorism and human protection. The implications of this uneasy mix for the integrity of R2P principles merit further reflection by governments and scholars alike.
- Five, it has become increasingly evident that responsibility and accountability are political matters. Unless individuals and groups demand an end to mass atrocities, governments and intergovernmental institutions will have little incentive to act. Moreover, if responsibility rests solely with large collective entities, such as governments and international institutions, then no one will be accountable. From the outset, R2P has sought to shape individual values and political priorities as the best route to moving governments and international institutions.
- Six, advancing prevention and protection objectives is never easy or quick, and they generally require local and national action by individuals and groups that complement steps taken by external actors. Experience has underscored the need for modesty on the part of those who would seek

administrative practice, especially at and by the United Nations. *International Authority and the Responsibility to Protect* (Cambridge: Cambridge University Press, 2011).

painless solutions from afar. Apparent "victories" in the short term rarely result in sustainable change in those conditions on the ground that permitted such atrocities to occur in the first place.[7] Without sufficient domestic buy-in, externally inspired and/or imposed "solutions" have proved unsustainable in a number of situations, such as in the Democratic Republic of the Congo (DRC), Libya, the Sudan, and South Sudan.[8]

- Seven, new technology is empowering vulnerable individuals and groups to engage in more immediate and interactive efforts at prevention and self-protection; to communicate more directly with national, regional, and international actors about possible assistance; and to develop more active and responsive social networks within and across national boundaries.[9] As a result, earlier hierarchical models of atrocity prevention and protection can now be supplemented by more nuanced iterations that incorporate horizontal group-to-group and bottom-up dimensions as well. Early warning and assessment are no longer the provinces solely of governments and intergovernmental organizations as information flows as quickly along cultural and civil society lines and while borders and distances are increasingly irrelevant to the streaming of data and the formation of interest and advocacy groups.[10]

- Eight, the opportunities presented by new technologies are also imposing new challenges for potential responders, both in the field and at headquarters. Pressures are likely to build for delegating the responsibility for decisions about when and how to respond from capitals and headquarters to civilian representatives and police and military commanders in the field. Established systems for command, control, communications, intelligence, and the

---

[7] As Amir Pasic and Thomas G. Weiss put it before R2P was first articulated, "Rescue in complex emergencies is problematic because it is triggered precisely when the autonomy of a society is in jeopardy. . . . The central paradox of rescue thus is that it seeks to restore a social order that has failed to protect its members from natural or man-made deprivations. . . . Populations in danger require sustained commitments that are different from the current approach of rescue." "The Politics of Rescue: Yugoslavia's Wars and the Humanitarian Impulse," in *Ethics and International Affairs: A Reader*, 2nd ed., edited by Joel H. Rosenthal (Washington, DC: Georgetown University Press, 1999), 321–322.

[8] This has certainly been true in Iraq as well, although the interventions there in 2003 and 2014 were not undertaken primarily for R2P or human protection reasons.

[9] On how technology and social networks have combined to change the dynamics of atrocity prevention, see Sarah E. Kreps, "Social Networks and Technology in the Prevention of Crimes against Humanity," in *Mass Atrocity Crimes: Preventing Future Outrages*, edited by Robert I. Rotberg (Washington, DC: Brookings Institution Press, 2010), 175–191.

[10] The international response to the kidnapping of hundreds of Nigerian school girls by Boko Haram in April 2014, for instance, was much quicker and deeper than that of the Nigerian government, compelling it to act, however belatedly, to try to secure their release. See, for instance, Adam Nossiter and Alan Cowell, "Nigerian Leader Cancels Visit to Village of Abducted Girls," *New York Times*, May 16, 2014. It has been less clear, however, whether international public interest generated in such a manner can be sustained sufficiently long or focused enough on practical policy options to make a difference in terms of outcomes.

assessment and curation of information are likely to prove inadequate as calls from the vulnerable for assistance multiply and reach publics and parliaments through social media and mobile communications devices, as has been the case in Syria.[11]

- Nine, to no one's surprise, experience in implementing R2P principles has been uneven. Too often, there has been a pronounced gap between words and deeds. So, sadly, a compelling reason to develop a deeper understanding of individual responsibility is that vulnerable populations cannot rely on governments and intergovernmental institutions to meet their protection obligations in a full, consistent, and timely manner.

- Ten, the United States and the UN will have new leaders in January 2017. There is no guarantee that they will support robust measures to curb atrocity crimes in distant places. Public opinion surveys in the United States and Europe, for instance, indicate a continuing, and perhaps deepening, reluctance to commit ground forces far from home for these or other purposes.[12] Efforts to provide protection for vulnerable populations from the air in

---

[11] As early as 2000, the Brahimi report on UN peace operations cautioned that "modern, well utilized information technology (IT) is a key enabler ... but gaps in strategy, policy and practice impede its effective use." Since then, progress in mobile communications has far outstripped reform in UN peacekeeping and rapid response capacities. In particular, efforts to delegate authority and responsibility to civilian and military officers in the field has been uneven, despite the assertion in the Brahimi report that "United Nations peacekeepers – troops or police – who witness violence against civilians should be presumed to be authorized to stop it, within their means, in support of basic United Nations principles." Capitals that provide peacekeeping contingents are still often reluctant to cede the degree of authority and autonomy to force commanders that the IR2P principles would expect and that the full utilization of the protection possibilities of new communications technologies would require. United Nations, *Report of the Panel on United Nations Peace Operations*, A/55/305, S/2000/809, 21 August 2000, xiv and x.

[12] Some encouragement could be derived from the results of a survey of American public attitudes released by the Chicago Council on Global Affairs in October 2014. Seventy-one percent of respondents favored using U.S. troops "to stop a government from committing genocide and killing large numbers of its own people." The same percentage approved of employing U.S. forces "to deal with humanitarian crises." This response, which has remained fairly steady over the past decade, was the highest percentage for any of the purposes for the use of force given in the survey. On the other hand, while, by a 58 percent to 41 percent margin, respondents preferred that the U.S. play "an active part" in world affairs instead of "staying out" of them, this margin has been declining since 2002. *Foreign Policy in the Age of Retrenchment: Results of the 2014 Chicago Council Survey of American Public Opinion and US Foreign Policy*, 24–25 and 6–7, respectively. In late 2013, moreover, Pew found Americans' perception of U.S. power in the world to be at a forty-year low and isolationist sentiment at the highest point since 1964. Pew Research Center for the People and the Press, *America's Place in the World 2013*. In September 2013, the German Marshall Fund reported that 62 percent of Americans and 72 percent of respondents from European Union countries opposed military intervention in Syria, up from 55 and 59 percent, respectively, in 2012. *Transatlantic Trends 2013*, September 18, 2013, 31–32. In the same annual survey in 2014, only 49 percent of Americans and 43 percent of respondents from EU countries agreed that NATO should be engaged in "military operations outside of the United States and Europe." *Transatlantic Trends 2014*, September 10, 2014, 46.

Kosovo, Libya, Iraq, and Syria have had, at best, mixed results. Given these factors, fresh approaches, such as IR2P, may be needed to sustain public support for and political commitments to R2P at a time of political transition.

As these points underscore, for all of the progress that has been made in raising the visibility of atrocity crimes and in redoubling efforts to prevent them, assured protection is not at hand. Nor has the growing acceptance of R2P principles led to simple scenarios or unambiguous answers. For instance, the assignment by the 2005 World Summit of specific R2P responsibilities to the diffuse and ill-defined "international community" raises stubborn collective action problems. A decade ago, Alex Bellamy warned that the assertion of "an *unassigned* duty to intervene" could lead to "disputes about where that responsibility lies."[13] In a similar vein, James Pattison pointed out that a requirement for Security Council authorization "identifies only a *procedure* that agents should follow when discharging the responsibility to protect. It does not identify which particular *agent* has this responsibility."[14]

Likewise, should the term "international community" be interpreted as encompassing individuals and groups, as well as governments and intergovernmental bodies? As Special Adviser, the senior author responded in the affirmative, and the Member States largely seemed to accept this broader interpretation. But how should responsibility be apportioned within societies, for instance, between leaders and the general population? Which individuals within a government or society should be held legally accountable for the failure to protect, particularly when there has been a breakdown of law and order or non-state actors control parts of the territory? Such questions, key to understanding responsibility and accountability, compel a concerted effort to deconstruct R2P from the perspective of individual capacity and responsibility.

Moreover, the original R2P paradigm pictured situations in which governments were "bad" and vulnerable populations were "good." This grossly simplified the kinds of moral and policy tradeoffs that have long confronted potential interveners in civil conflicts, from the Balkans to Sri Lanka to Syria, in which elements of the opposition had themselves committed atrocities even as the burden of repression and responsibility remained on the government side. In the Central African Republic (CAR),

---

[13] Alex Bellamy, "Responsibility to Protect or Trojan Horse? The Crisis in Darfur and Humanitarian Intervention after Iraq," *Ethics and International Affairs* 19(2): 33 (2005) (emphasis in the original).

[14] James Pattison, "Whose Responsibility to Protect? The Duties of Humanitarian Intervention," *Journal of Military Ethics* 7(4): 263 (emphasis in the original). Also see James Pattison, "Assigning Humanitarian Intervention and the Responsibility to Protect," in *Responsibility to Protect: From Principle to Practice*, edited by Julia Hoffmann and André Nollkaemper (Amsterdam: Pallas Publications-Amsterdam University Press, 2012), 173–184.

the weakness of the national government and the viciousness of the largely Christian–Muslim violence have made it very hard to identify any "good" guys, whereas there have been plenty of victims on both sides. The international moral outrage in the early years of this century over the mass atrocity crimes being committed in Darfur could not be regenerated over the subsequent failure of the government of an independent South Sudan to meet its responsibility to curb the atrocities and sectarian violence that engulfed the new country when its leadership split along tribal lines. Nor did a classic R2P mandate from the Security Council in July 2011 give the new UN peacekeeping mission in South Sudan much guidance on how to quell the violence against civilian populations.[15]

In each of these situations, the etiology of atrocity crimes was shaped by the perceptions, assessments, and judgments of key internal and external actors. The assumptions and choices of the vulnerable, of those who might consider committing such crimes, and of those who seek to prevent or end them are framed by distinct sets of values, psychosocial factors, and cultural norms. None of their positions is given or fixed. Individuals have rights and agency and, therefore, responsibility. Because they have the capacity to react, to learn, and, hopefully, never to forget, the interactions among individuals and groups prior to and even after the commission of such crimes may be critical to preventing or curbing further violence.

IR2P, therefore, does not view governments or international organizations as black boxes, opaque and impenetrable. They are made up of people whose perceptions, experiences, and biases affect the priorities, decisions, and actions of the governments and institutions that employ them.[16] The debates within governments and international institutions about how to implement global norms and standards are usually vigorous and sometimes partisan. An IR2P perspective thus calls for a layered approach to developing messages and policy

---

[15] Security Council resolution 1996 (2011) established the UN Mission in the Republic of South Sudan (UNMISS) and included in its mandate "advising and assisting the Government of the Republic of South Sudan, including military and police at national and local levels as appropriate, in fulfilling its responsibility to protect civilians, in compliance with international humanitarian, human rights, and refugee law." Although the language closely reflected the text of Pillar II of the Secretary-General's strategy for implementing R2P, the members of the Council apparently had consulted neither the UN secretariat nor the government about the content and form of any such advice and assistance. A May 2014 Council resolution on South Sudan again asserted that "the Government of South Sudan bears the primary responsibility to protect civilians within its territory and subject to its jurisdiction, including from potential crimes against humanity and war crimes." It further expressed "grave concern" over reports that such crimes had been committed by all parties to the conflict. Resolution 2155 (2014) of May 27, 2014.

[16] The lack either of will or a sense of accountability among American policymakers was cited by Samantha Power as among the key reasons for their not responding more robustly to unfolding mass atrocities. See the concluding chapter of her Pulitzer Prize–winning work, *A Problem from Hell: America and the Age of Genocide* (New York: HarperCollins, 2002).

steps tailored to influence at least seven sets of individuals when a society is under stress or at risk of atrocity crimes: (1) vulnerable populations who are likely to be targeted; (2) bystanders and would-be or actual perpetrators, including those who enable or incite such crimes; (3) group and community leaders; (4) national leaders, who can choose other paths; (5) leaders of influential foreign countries, who may face tough choices about whether, when, and how to intervene; (6) key officials and decision makers in international organizations; and (7) survivors – themselves physical and/or emotional casualties – whose narratives and lessons will shape the chances of recidivism.

IR2P is a subset of R2P. Their distinctions are tactical, not strategic. At its core, as a political project as well as a set of normative principles, the responsibility to protect aims – as does its IR2P iteration – to influence the decisions taken by individuals, both inside and outside of governments. The primary difference is one of emphasis, of how one thinks about and approaches the challenge of atrocity prevention. Where does one start, which questions come first, and where should one aim to make a difference? Who are the key actors, what measures and arguments could alter their choices, and when should one seek to apply suasion or dissuasion? As the debates about R2P shift from theory to practice, from the strategic to the operational level, and from the general to the specific, where should R2P advocates and analysts focus their energies next? What practical lessons can be gleaned from the growing number of cases in which R2P principles and perspectives have been applied? Has prevention worked? Where, how, and why? Is R2P still relevant when the members of the Security Council are hopelessly divided on how to handle a particular situation or when powerful governments are reluctant to intervene? How can we, as individuals and members of groups, make a difference?

10.2.   Actors

As noted earlier, from an IR2P perspective, efforts to prevent mass atrocity crimes or their escalation should take into account the interests, values, priorities, capacities, and perceptions of at least seven groups of individuals within a society under stress and within those governments and international institutions capable of responding in a constructive and timely manner. External, national, and local messaging should seek to influence how these individuals and groups understand the situation, their choices, and the likely consequences of those choices. Those considering or undertaking international engagement and/or intervention should weigh how such actions would be perceived by the following seven groups of actors:

10.2.1. *Vulnerable Populations*

The vulnerable include those who have been or are likely to be targeted for such crimes. In situations of one-sided violence, the vulnerable may be a distinct group or groups identified by race, religion, ethnicity, tribe, gender, sexual orientation, disability, age, or political-economic characteristics. Usually, the targeted are part of a minority, but, as in the cases of Syria and Iraq, this is not always the case. In cases of broader civil strife, particularly when sectarian divisions are prominent, intercommunal violence and acts of retribution may create vulnerabilities for a much wider range of groups, large and small. When the violence is one-sided, international sympathies for persecuted minorities, particularly under repressive regimes, may be relatively easy to generate. When the situation is more nuanced, however, international publics may find it more difficult to distinguish who are the perpetrators and who are the victims. This appears to have been one of the factors complicating the generation of an effective international response to the horrific atrocity crimes that have been perpetrated by the government in Syria, as support for a strong response faded markedly once the conflict began to look more like a civil war and more radical and brutal jihadist groups joined the fight against the repressive regime.

Too often, distant analysts and policymakers, fueled by rescue fantasies, have cast the vulnerable as little more than passive victims, with no options and no part in prevention and protection. This could be a fatal error because if R2P relies solely on timely and decisive external response, its prevention and protection record will be spotty at best. More often than not, the resulting measures will be too little, too late.[17]

Even with the impressive expansion of the rhetorical commitment to R2P around the world, the actual progress on prevention and protection has been mixed and modest. In many places, people, groups, and communities have turned to self-protection or, more often, have sustained well-established practices of self-protection.[18] However, these measures may also offer less

[17] Frédéric Mégret has commented on the danger of allowing the "international rescue" vision embodied in R2P to draw attention from the efforts that people and civil society under threat can and often have taken to protect themselves from atrocity crimes. An overemphasis on the international dimensions of R2P, he cautions, could reduce the agency ascribed to the victims. Frédéric Mégret, "Beyond the 'Salvation' Paradigm: Responsibility to Protect (Others) vs. the Power of Protecting Oneself," *Security Dialogue* 40(6): 575–595 (December 2009).

[18] For more on individual and community self-protection measures, see the report and case studies from the 2010 series cosponsored by the Brookings Institution and the United States Institute of Peace (USIP) on "Community Self-Protection Strategies," two 2010 studies by Casey A. Barrs for the Cuny Center on "How Civilians Survive Violence: A Preliminary Inventory" and on "Preparedness Support: Helping Brace Beneficiaries, Local Staff and Partners for Violence," Aditi Gorur, "Community Self-Protection Strategies: How Peacekeepers Can Help or Harm," for the Stimson Center (August 2013), and two 2013 reports for the Sentinel Project by Sean E. Langberg on "Localized Early Warning Systems: From Natural Disasters to Human Security,

than a panacea. For instance, self-protection efforts may lead to some unattractive tradeoffs among the R2P crimes being committed. In CAR, as elsewhere, massive ethnic cleansing has become a means of avoiding even greater violence. As Secretary-General Ban Ki-moon lamented in April 2014, "genocide was avoided in large measure because of the mass exodus of minorities to areas where they felt they were safe – with their own people."[19] With the commission of atrocity crimes in Syria and Iraq, the number of forcibly displaced people worldwide has swelled to record numbers.[20]

As discussed later, experience suggests that intervention is most likely to help when those threatened by such crimes have recognized what is under way and have already taken steps to deter, delay, ameliorate, or prevent them. Moreover, the chances that intervention will make things worse multiply when the decisions made in faraway capitals and headquarters are divorced from a deep and dynamic understanding of conditions on the ground and the interests, perspectives, and expectations of key local actors. Vulnerable individuals need to possess – and to be understood as possessing – some degree of agency over their lives and their futures, as well as those of their extended families and communities.[21] The IR2P dimension of R2P, with its emphasis on bottom-up, interactive decision making, seeks to add this missing dynamic to the original R2P paradigm.

Outside the corridors of power, ordinary people must decide whether they have an individual responsibility to try to prevent atrocity crimes and/or to protect those most immediately threatened. For them, their choices and the consequences of those choices may be a great deal starker, more immediate, and more personal. In places and times when tensions are high, the stakes involved in implementing the principles on which the responsibility to protect is based are likely to be acute, even existential for those most directly involved.[22] It is on the ground, in those situations that paragraph 139 of the

Leveraging a People-Centered Protection Network" and Danny Hirschel-Burns on "The Responsibility to Do What We Can: Understanding and Strengthening Local, Nonviolent Strategies for Civilian Self-Protection in the Context of Mass Atrocities."

[19] Remarks to the High-Level Meeting on the Central African Republic, Brussels, Belgium, 2 April 2014. Quoted in Somini Sengupta and Alan Cowell, "Chad, Amid Criticism, Will Pull Troops from Force in Central Africa," *New York Times*, April 4, 2014.

[20] In June 2014, the UN High Commissioner for Refugees (UNHCR) reported that, as of the end of 2013, the number of forcibly displaced people was at the highest level since the end of World War II. According to UNHCR's annual Global Trends Report, the worldwide number of refugees, asylum-seekers, and internally displaced had grown to 51.2 million, up 6 million from the year before, with the largest growth from those fleeing the war in Syria. UNHCR, *War's Human Cost: Global Trends 2013* (Geneva: UNHCR, June 2014).

[21] David Rieff, for instance, championed "the victims' access to their rights – that is, a construction that makes them subjects, not objects." "Humanitarianism in Crisis," *Foreign Affairs* 81(6): 111–121 (November–December 2002).

[22] See, for instance, Hugo Slim, "Values versus Power: Responsible Sovereignty as Struggle in Zimbabwe," *Global Responsibility to Protect* 2(1–2): 155–160 (2010).

Outcome Document called "states under stress," that the decisive steps toward or away from mass violence are usually taken. That is where an understanding of individual responsibility and of the options available to vulnerable populations – not just the broader historical, psychosocial, cultural, economic, and political factors that are beyond their immediate control – might make the most difference.

Those committing genocide often claim that their victims were in fact planning genocidal acts against them, so that their crimes are justified as preventive or pre-emptive acts of self-defense.[23] Whether the resort to such claims is affected by how passive or active the target population is in terms of taking preventive or self-protective measures is unclear, however. The perceptions and motivations underlying the actions of the perpetrators and the target populations, as well as their interactivity, are among the many topics raised in this chapter that require further study.

At the outset, it may not be entirely evident who will eventually be the targets of atrocity crimes. Will members of groups not yet directly threatened identify with those first targeted or with the perpetrators? If they see no chance of bargaining with those who threaten them or others, will they fight or flee? Will they take steps to counter bullying, incitement, and messages of hate and intolerance, whether directed at them or at others? Will they engage in self-protection measures and/or offer protection to those more vulnerable than they are, even as they seek to draw international attention to the signs of possible atrocities down the line? In other words, will they take the essential early preventive steps that will make international engagement both more likely and more likely to succeed?

The alerting mechanism of anticipatory anxiety in vulnerable groups may enable them to detect and respond to the earliest signs of potential threats, such as subtle precursors of hate speech or victimization, before they escalate. However, once an individual confronts an impending threat to his or her survival, a neurophysiological and hard-wired fight–flight response is activated, and, if no clear opportunity to fight or flee exists, then a paralyzing freeze state can ensue. Although this immobilizing state can buy time to further assess and hopefully avoid the risk of danger, it can also produce debilitating feelings of dissociation, depersonalization, and emotional distress that can have long-lasting post-traumatic effects. For some time, neuroscientists have paid a good deal of attention to the neurological substrates of the various aspects of

---

[23] In recent decades, such "it is either us or them" posturing has been heard both in the Balkans and in the Great Lakes region of Africa and more recently in Iraq and Syria. Benjamin A. Valentino has employed a "strategic" or "instrumental policy" perspective to frame mass killings as the rational policy choice of leaders determined to transform their societies in radical ways or to counter guerilla insurgencies. *Final Solutions: Mass Killing and Genocide in the 20th Century* (Ithaca, NY: Cornell University Press, 2004).

the fear response. However, only recently have clinicians begun to understand this process and to develop techniques and programs to address in a systematic and integrated fashion the varied mental health needs of individuals traumatized by atrocity and war.[24]

Finally, care needs to be taken so that the focus on mass crimes does not lead to desensitizing policymakers to the value and uniqueness of each human life. The concept of mass atrocities is impossible to appreciate in the aggregate on an emotional and empathic level. In a seminal article, Robert Jay Lifton coined the phrase "psychic numbing" to capture the way in which people individually and collectively respond to immense and overwhelming threats of danger – such as nuclear warfare – by shutting off their emotional responsivity and becoming emotionally withdrawn and detached.[25] By framing the psychic numbing associated with mass atrocities within the context of behavioral decision making, Paul Slovic et al. presented ways to deconstruct the "mass" and to repersonalize the focus onto individual victims.[26] They argue that the best way to combat the numbing effect of large numbers of losses is to re-engage compassionate reactions, to overcome flaws in moral intuition, to better utilize early warning signals, to establish effective human rights indicators, and to reconsider the meaning of "widespread and systematic" human rights violations so that the rights of individuals are not lost in aggregated numbers.

10.2.2. Perpetrators and Bystanders

For the purposes of this chapter, perpetrators include not only those planning or committing atrocity crimes, but also those aiding, abetting, and inciting such violence. External policy messaging and responses should also address those considering participating in such acts, which often entail the mobilization of large numbers of sympathizers or enablers.[27] Perpetrators may be agents of

---

[24] Richard F. Mollica, ed., *Textbook of Global Mental Health: Trauma and Recovery* (Cambridge, MA: Harvard Program in Refugee Trauma, 2011), and Myra Giberovitch, *Recovering from Genocidal Trauma: An Information and Practice Guide for Working with Holocaust Survivors* (Toronto: University of Toronto Press, 2014).

[25] Robert Jay Lifton, "Beyond Psychic Numbing: A Call to Awareness," *American Journal of Orthopsychiatrics* 52(4) (1982).

[26] Paul Slovic, David Zionts, Andrew K. Woods, Ryan Goodman, and Derek Jinks, "Psychic Numbing and Mass Atrocity," in *The Behavioral Foundations of Public Policy*, edited by Eldar Shafir (Princeton, NJ: Princeton University Press, 2013), 126–142.

[27] Several major studies have looked at the conditions under which large numbers of seemingly ordinary people become perpetrators of mass atrocity crimes. See, for instance, Daniel Goldhagen, *Hitler's Willing Executioners: Ordinary Germans and the Holocaust* (New York: Alfred Knopf. 1996); Scott Straus, *The Order of Genocide: Race, Power, and War in Rwanda* (Ithaca, NY: Cornell University Press, 2006); and James Waller, *Becoming Evil: How Ordinary People Commit Genocide and Mass Killing*, 2nd ed. (Oxford: Oxford University Press, 2007).

government, as the initial R2P paradigm assumed. But that often is not the case. Where governments are weak or unable to control territory, armed groups may be the worst perpetrators of mass atrocity crimes. Their first targets are often group and community leaders, those local figures and elders most respected by the population. To spur ethnic cleansing or to dominate the local population, armed groups try to break the ties of identity and legitimacy that have defined a sense of place, hierarchy, and community even in localities where national governments have seemed distant, ineffectual, and corrupt.

Employing the playbook of terrorism, perpetrators – whether or not sponsored by governments – may seek to intimidate, humiliate, and traumatize populations through mass rape, executions, and demonstrations of extreme violence, cruelty, and torture. Systematic rape, as in Bosnia, may be employed not only to degrade and brutalize women, but also as a genocidal tactic to force unwanted pregnancies and to discourage procreation of the target group. Armed groups may compel children to join their ranks. In an effort to destroy family units, perpetrators may force family members to witness and/or to participate in violent acts against each other. Through such extreme and degrading measures, they aim to undermine established social frameworks, values, and moral precepts while forcing whole neighborhoods and villages to flee their homes and abandon their livelihoods. Sometimes – recall the Revolutionary United Front's (RUF) tactic of severing limbs in Sierra Leone – they leave some of the scarred and wounded to remind others of their power, ruthlessness, and willingness to flout legal and moral standards at will. They may calculate, as well, that only a particularly large and/or vicious atrocity will gain the global notoriety they seek. Thus, ISIS/ISIL is quick to post videos of mass executions and beheadings.

It may well be, as Benjamin Valentino has posited, that "the impetus for mass killing usually originates from a relatively small group of powerful political or military leaders."[28] But the actual perpetrators form a substantially wider circle, and, they, in turn, depend on much of the population to look the other way, whether from intimidation, indifference, or tacit sympathy.[29] "Those who orchestrate mass violence," notes Laurel Fletcher, "are aided by the failure of spectators to intervene. In this context, 'doing nothing' is 'doing something' – bystanders are thus an integral part of the killing apparatus."[30] Yet post-atrocity policy and justice practices tend to leave them out of the equation. According to

---

[28] *Final Solutions*, op. cit., p. 2.

[29] The Holocaust, for instance, was carried out in tens of thousands of locations across Central Europe, with more being discovered with each passing year. The impetus may have sprung from the warped thinking of one leader, the strategic planning may have been carried out by a relative handful of high-level officials and officers, but the actual killing became a highly decentralized operation.

[30] Laurel E. Fletcher, "From Indifference to Engagement: Bystanders and International Criminal Justice," *Michigan Journal of International Law* 26: 1026–1027 (2004).

Fletcher, "transitional justice mechanisms do not engage bystanders directly – they are the audience for, but not the subjects of, courts and commissions."[31] As in counterterrorism, the saying "see something, say something" is most apt in the context of individual and group efforts to prevent atrocity crimes.

As international law has long recognized, individuals can and should be held accountable for their actions – or inaction – even when many of their peers participate in the commission of mass murder and sexual violence. People make choices. People take sides. Even in periods of great stress, individual volition remains. Different people act differently in such situations. The responsibility to provide protection, therefore, cannot rest solely with large, impersonal, and opaque institutions. Accountability must reach beyond a handful of top officials, just as preventive efforts at education, engagement, and bridge-building must reach those who would be called on and/or could be inclined to carry out the crimes. The core purpose of both R2P and its IR2P iteration is to prevent mass atrocity crimes, not just to react after they are committed.[32] Therefore, the focus should be on would-be perpetrators and likely bystanders, not just on those who have actually committed such horrific crimes.

Systematic war rape, gender-based violence, and murder on a massive scale are the accumulation of large numbers of individual acts of extreme violence. There is a growing body of research based on the differentiation between reactive aggression and instrumental aggression that is directed toward understanding the mechanisms by which combatants persist in committing acts of highly personalized brutality.[33] By studying the relationship between perpetrators' performance on measures of appetitive aggression and post-traumatic stress disorder (PTSD), the authors found that "appetitive aggression can inhibit PTSD and trauma-related symptoms in perpetrators and prevent perpetrators from getting traumatized by their own atrocities."[34] Moreover, they reported the chilling finding that "the victim's struggling can be

---

[31] Laurel E. Fletcher, "Facing Up to the Past: Bystanders and Transitional Justice," *Harvard Human Rights Journal* 20: 47 (2007).

[32] Although the 2001 ICISS report launching R2P is remembered more for what it had to say about the use of force, it devoted substantial attention to prevention as well. The Commission declared that "prevention is the single most important dimension of the responsibility to protect: preventive options should always be exhausted before intervention is contemplated, and more commitment and resources must be devoted to it." *The Responsibility to Protect*, op. cit., p. XI. Moreover, when the assembled heads of state and government made their R2P pledge at the 2005 World Summit, it was to protect populations by preventing the four crimes and their incitement.

[33] Thomas Ebert, Roland Weierstall, and Maggie Schauer, "Fascination Violence: On Mind and Brain of Man Hunters," *European Archives of Psychiatry and Clinical Neuroscience*, 260(suppl. 2): 100–105 (2010).

[34] Roland Weierstall, Susanne Schaal, Inge Schalinski, Jean-Pierre Dusingizemungu, and Thomas Elbert, "The Thrill of Being Violent as an Antidote to Posttraumatic Stress Disorder in Rwandese Genocide Perpetrators," *European Journal of Psychotraumatology* 2:6345 (2011).

an essential rewarding cue for perpetrators" that fuels their continued aggression. This syndrome may help to explain the zealotry of some armed groups and terrorist movements, for whom the exercise of violence and torture appears to be almost an end-in-itself. Governments intent on eliminating portions of their populations are hardly immune to such behaviors, as the excesses of the Holocaust, Cambodia, Rwanda, and Syria illustrate. As Barbara Harff and Helen Fein have noted, "perpetrators of genocide often are repeat offenders, because elites and security forces may become habituated to mass killing as a strategic response to challenges to state security."[35]

Yet, for all the impersonal statistics associated with mass atrocities, including the open question of when the number of victims reaches a "mass" level, it should never be forgotten that each victim is an individual, with a family, a history, and a future. Each act is purposeful. Each is a crime. The very use of mass graves may be calculated to have just such a blurring effect, as the enormity of the crimes becomes very hard to fully grasp and assess. "Following orders" is never an excuse because responsibility for such acts must not be depersonalized, with the blame shouldered by institutions rather than the individuals who populate and lead them. The mobilization of groups of people to commit mass atrocities can only succeed if there are enough individuals willing to respond to the call to violence and too few who have the courage to stand against the destructive tide. How to affect that balance will be a central challenge for IR2P and R2P strategies alike.

10.2.3. Group and Community Leaders

R2P was initially framed in a binary context, one in which governments and intergovernmental organizations were seen as the dominant, even sole, actors of consequence. It would be a grave mistake, however, to cast R2P either as a two-sided equation in which the only significant actors are government perpetrators and external saviors or as predominantly a hierarchical exercise in which the horizontal relationships among groups matter far less than the vertical ones between governments and intergovernmental organizations. In real-life scenarios, non-state actors, ranging from armed groups to civil society organizations to sectarian communities within or with ties to societies under stress, matter a great deal. As noted earlier, traditional, tribal, and village

---

doi:10.3402/ejpt.v2i0.6345, published online November 25, 2011. On appetitive aggression, see Roland Weierstall and Thomas Ebert, "The Appetitive Aggression Scale: Development of an Instrument for the Assessment of Human's Attraction to Violence," *European Journal of Psychotraumatology* 2:8430 (2011). doi: 10.3402/ejpt.2i0.8430, first published online November 25, 2011.

[35] Barbara Harff, noting an observation that Helen Fein had made, "No Lessons from the Holocaust?: Assessing Risks of Genocide and Political Mass Murder since 1955," *American Political Science Review* 97(1): 62 (February 2007).

leaders and elders are often among the first targeted by armed groups initiating a campaign of atrocity crimes, precisely because of the demoralizing and disorienting effect this may have on local society. Likewise, repressive governments intent on taming or eliminating opposing elements of the population will often begin with opinion leaders, teachers, and/or political representatives with moderate views and healing voices. Religious and civic leaders prone to reach across partisan lines and to mediate differences among groups will be similarly targeted.

On the one hand, civil society groups, including the private sector, can, and often do, play critical roles in persuading governments to start down one path or another. Their influence may be directed in healing, passive, or destructive ways. An active civil society does not make a country immune from the possibility of atrocity crimes because the content of their activities and the inclusiveness of the groups matter more than their existence.[36] On the other hand, messaging from national and external opinion leaders through traditional and social media may be able to affect the relative political weight of groups from civil and uncivil society, as well as the credence given to calls for tolerance and moderation versus those preaching hatred, revenge, and violence. Incitement and hate speech often cross borders or even oceans, a tendency likely to become more pronounced with the advent of social media and new communications technologies.

In that regard, it should be recalled that the notion of community, for both civil and uncivil society groups, is often transnational in scope. Intergroup relations usually transcend borders, with diaspora prone to taking sides and to invoking unresolved grudges and rekindling long-standing prejudices. Rarely are the effects of mass atrocities or the politics that produce or inflame them confined within a single state or society. Neighbors and neighborhoods make a difference, particularly where there have been forced mass movements of groups and populations in the past. In an era of global finance, trade, and communications, the attitudes and policies of major powers, former colonizers, and prime investors matter, even when they try to be above the fray. Given these dynamics, no two cases are identical. These are complicated and layered situations that call for tailored, nuanced, and flexible responses in which cooperative actions by governments are often necessary but not sufficient steps.

---

[36] In an article often caricatured as "bowling with Hitler," Sheri Berman contended that the combination of the abundance of civil society groups and the lack of strong and responsive political institutions in Weimar Germany actually gave the National Socialists an alternative path to building their political base and to undermining the Weimar democratic experiment. "Civil Society and the Collapse of the Weimar Republic," *World Politics* 49(3): 401–429 (April 1997).

10.2.4. National Leaders

This fourth group includes officials, parliamentarians, and influential opinion leaders in countries under stress or at risk of mass atrocity crimes. R2P's initial paradigm focused on situations in which national authorities were already determined to commit mass atrocities against a specific group or groups within the country's population. In such worst-case scenarios, international options are few and time is short. Prevention has failed or, more likely, has never been pursued vigorously, and there are relatively few choices left between verbal protest, diplomatic demarches, and vague threats of future action, on the one hand, and coercive sanctions and/or military intervention, on the other hand. These tend to be the classic too little-too late situations, in which intervention is inherently costly and risky, and the likelihood of success in offering effective protection is uncertain at best.

In most cases, however, there are opportunities to engage national authorities well before they take such a fateful decision. As discussed later, in recent years, there have been a number of situations in which timely warnings of international concern and reminders about international accountability have helped to convince national leaders in societies under stress to think twice about embarking on such a destructive path. Such messages carry greater weight if the national leadership's international patrons are willing to join in the anti-atrocity chorus. If the leaders of the country are divided or uncertain about how to proceed, then the chances of effective preventive efforts rise, particularly when the preparation for committing such crimes would have to entail the mobilization of large elements of the population. On the other hand, the deterrent and persuasive effects of international messaging aimed at preventing such crimes are weakened when it is evident that key actors in the international community would be very reluctant to intervene should efforts at prevention fail. Credibility matters in such situations.

To suggest that individuals also have responsibilities should in no way diminish the solemn obligations that states and international institutions assumed under the 2005 Outcome Document. As noted earlier, it is both understandable and appropriate that the study and practice of R2P has accorded primacy to the place of international and national institutions in advancing these goals. The 2005 World Summit Outcome Document was an agreement among heads of state and government. One of its most remarkable features was their unequivocal pledge in paragraph 138 to protect their populations by preventing genocide, war crimes, ethnic cleansing, and crimes against humanity, as well as their incitement. Today, the central challenge facing the responsibility to protect is getting those leaders (and their successors) to live up to those solemn commitments. This chapter contends that the incorporation of IR2P perspectives could provide fresh insights into how to hold national and international leaders accountable, as well as those who incite or commit violence at a local and/or national level.

10.2.5. Foreign Leaders

This set includes key officials and parliamentarians in neighboring countries and in those more distant capitals with the capacity to influence developments in a country under stress. In most cases, the level and number of concerned officials will be at a relatively modest level in the months leading up to a crisis, when early engagement and preventive action would have the most chance to make a difference. In part, this is because most atrocity crimes occur in countries that are not top priorities for the major powers, so their engagement beforehand may be sporadic and shallow. Those who know those societies best, usually regional officers in foreign ministries and intelligence services, are not well placed in decision-making circles. Likewise, few parliamentarians will pay much attention to a distant country situation that is not getting headlines in the media. Nevertheless, country officers, along with journalists and nongovernmental organization (NGO) representatives on the ground and independent experts on the country in question, are the most probable sources of early warning and early detection of possible precursors to mass atrocities. There may be no more than a handful of individuals with expertise and credibility on the troubling developments at this early stage, so their views matter, as does their will and capacity to project them in public and policy-making circles.

Once the violence begins to escalate, higher level officials start to focus more intensively on the situation, but the circle of those engaged remains quite compact. Although a larger number of officials will be expected to feed information into the decision-making process, relatively few officials, generally those with broader responsibilities, will actually be part of it. Their first-hand knowledge of the situation and of the dynamics of the society and culture in question is likely to be modest as well, raising the possibility that actions taken will cause as much harm as good. So, decisions about whether and how to respond to unfolding atrocity crimes are highly dependent on the values, priorities, and knowledge level of a remarkably small number of officials, as well as on their perceptions of the level of public and parliamentary support for robust action. Reaching and influencing them in a timely, targeted, and focused manner may be critical both to whether a timely response will be forthcoming and to whether that response will be designed and undertaken in a manner to maximize and sustain protection over time. As the immediate crisis begins to subside, the attention of top policymakers tends to move elsewhere.

An IR2P perspective suggests bearing three caveats in mind regarding decisions about possible foreign engagement or intervention.

- One, foreign advocates of forceful international intervention should be careful not to mislead vulnerable populations into believing that coercive international action is more likely either to occur or to be decisive than is actually the case. Some critics of R2P may have exaggerated its moral hazard dangers, but care should be taken in public messaging not to encourage risky action on the part of local groups that may be inclined to look for foreign saviors rather than to take self-protective measures within societies at risk.[37]
- Two, in most cases, for reasons of law, of gaining and sustaining public support and of burden sharing, even capitals with substantial economic and military capacities will look to partners to help carry out any intervention to curb unfolding atrocity crimes.[38] Generally, national leaders will seek authorization by the UN Security Council for any coercive intervention and collaboration with a regional body whenever possible, even for noncoercive interventions. All of this puts a premium on interpersonal relationships and skilled public and private diplomacy.
- Three, decisions about how to respond to early signs of possible atrocity crimes are rarely going to be clear-cut: information and assessment are generally uncertain or ambiguous, they can be manipulated by one side or another, the number of places under stress at any point may be large, the costs and consequences of different courses of action are always debatable, and there will be differences of view about who should take the lead and whether there is sufficient legal authority to act.[39] In such circumstances, individual judgment matters a great deal. Moreover, the relationship between national interests and international obligations may not always be self-evident in those countries with the means to most effectively and expeditiously respond.

---

[37] According to the Independent Inquiry into the Actions of the United Nations During the 1994 Genocide in Rwanda, three groups there – political leaders, civilian populations, and national staff of the UN peacekeeping mission – had reason to expect greater protection efforts on their behalf. S/1999/1257, December 16, 1999, 44–46. The moral hazard argument is developed in a number of writings by Alan J. Kuperman. See, for instance, "The Moral Hazard of Humanitarian Intervention: Lessons from the Balkans," *International Studies Quarterly* 52 (1): 49–80 (March 2008), "Rethinking the Responsibility to Protect," *The Whitehead Journal of Diplomacy and International Relations*, 19–29 (Winter/Spring 2009), and "Obama's Libya Debacle: How a Well-Meaning Intervention Ended in Failure," *Foreign Affairs*, 94 (2), 66-77 (March/April 2015).

[38] The major exception, exercised most recently and baldly by Russia in rationalizing its interventions in Georgia and the Ukraine, would be a unilateral effort to assist one's nationals in another country on the pretext of a larger humanitarian or R2P rationale.

[39] Gregory Brazeal has used a bureaucratic decision-making model to help explain the repeated failure of the U.S. government to mount a vigorous response to unfolding mass atrocity crimes. Gregory Brazeal, "Bureaucracy and the U.S. Response to Mass Atrocity," *National Security and Armed Conflict Law Review* 57(1) (2010–2011).

In the United States, for instance, there were significant divisions within the Bush Administration at the time of the 2005 World Summit about the potential effect of R2P on American decision-making sovereignty.[40] In 2009, the incoming Obama Administration, on the other hand, was populated with key officials, such as Samantha Power, Susan Rice, and Anne Marie Slaughter, who had been outspoken advocates of preventing atrocity crimes and of responding to them vigorously. Its National Security Strategy includes a paragraph on preventing genocide and mass atrocities. The Strategy endorses the responsibility to protect and pledges to work with others and to strengthen internal capabilities for prevention and response.[41] But choices about when and how to respond in specific situations have been subject to sharp debate and some partisanship. National interest is not a given, immutable for all time, but rather something whose interpretation has been and will continue to be contested by political and policy elites, as well as by the larger electorate. The question of whether to intervene to protect populations cannot be divorced from larger debates about how interventionist a country's foreign and military policy ought to be.[42]

The United States is hardly the only country in which the civic and governmental discourse on these matters appears unsettled and in considerable flux. In India, for instance, the government's stance toward R2P has varied markedly over time, but has been moving toward somewhat greater acceptance and understanding.[43] It appears that the Brazilian government has tried to reconcile its concerns for the protection of human rights and its worries

---

[40] For instance, the U.S. Permanent Representative to the UN, Ambassador John Bolton, who had only assumed his position weeks before the World Summit, argued that the responsibility to protect would compromise U.S. decision-making sovereignty by imposing preordained obligations. On the eve of the Summit, Ambassador Bolton sent a letter to the other Member States cautioning against language that would appear to equate the responsibilities of the state and of the international community for R2P, as these are "not of the same character." The Bush Administration, however, had already decided to support the negotiated text on R2P in the Outcome Document. See Letter from Ambassador John R. Bolton to UN Member States, August 30, 2005, cited in Edward C. Luck, "Sovereignty, Choice, and the Responsibility to Protect," Global Responsibility to Protect, vol. I, no. 1, p. 19.

[41] White House, *National Security Strategy*, May 2010, p. 48.

[42] For an insightful analysis of the persistent ambivalence that has characterized attitudes in both the Bush and Obama administrations toward R2P, see Julian Junk, "The Two-Level Politics of Support – US Foreign Policy and the Responsibility to Protect," *Conflict, Security & Development* 14 (2014), published online in July 2014: ISSN 1478-1174. As Tom Farer and Claudia Fuentes Julio have put it, "when the United States is not itself prepared to use force to end crimes against humanity, there is no effective alternative" and it "will remain very reluctant to risk casualties or even much treasure where only humanitarian interests are at stake." "Flesh on Doctrinal Bones?: The United States and R2P," in *Politics of Human Rights: Rallying to the R2P Cause?* edited by Mónica Serrano and Thomas G. Weiss (London: Routledge, 2014), 224–225.

[43] India's evolving stance toward R2P is traced in Madhan Mohan Jaganathan and Gerrit Kurtz, "Singing the Tune of Sovereignty?: India and the Responsibility to Protect." *Conflict, Security & Development* 14 (2014), published online in June 2014. Also see Kudrat Virk,

about the unauthorized use of force through its advocacy of the notion of "responsibility while protecting."[44] Even in less democratic China there has been a lively academic and, to a lesser extent, political debate about R2P.[45] Many governments appear to be behind the curve in terms of coming to grips with the implications of the pledges they made at the 2005 World Summit. By any standard of norm development, R2P is still at an early stage, and one of its primary functions has been to spur just such national, as well as international, soul-searching.[46]

10.2.6. International Officials

At the UN, the tendency to blame divisions among the Member States, especially among the five permanent members of the Security Council, for errors of judgment and lack of will within the secretariat is well-established. Nevertheless, as addressed in more detail later, the series of failures to respond to the mass atrocities in Rwanda, Srebrenica, and Sri Lanka has led to

"India and R2P's Burdens of Dissent and Accommodation," in Serrano and Weiss, op. cit., 129–147.

[44] The Brazilian concept paper on "responsibility while protecting" can be found as an Annex to Letter Dated 9 November 2011 from the Permanent Representative of Brazil to the United Nations Addressed to the Secretary-General, A/66/551-S/2011/701, 11 November 2011. Also see Thorsten Benner, "Brazil as a Norm Entrepreneur: The 'Responsibility While Protecting' Initiative," GPPi Working Paper (Berlin: Global Public Policy Institute, March 2013); Monica Herz, "Brazil and R2P: Responsibility While Protecting," in Serrano and Weiss, op. cit., 107–128; and Oliver Stuenkel and Marcos Tourinho, "Regulating Intervention: Brazil and the Responsibility to Protect," *Conflict, Security & Development* 14 (2014), published online June 2014.

[45] This debate is analyzed in Liu Tiewa, "Is China Like the Other Permanent Members?: Governmental and Academic Debates on R2P," in Serrano and Weiss, op. cit., 148–170 and in Liu Tiewa and Zhang Haibin, "Debates in China About the Responsibility to Protect as a Developing International Norm: A General Assessment," *Conflict, Security & Development* 14 (2014), published online July 2014. The reasons for Russian and South African caution toward R2P are also addressed in that special issue of the journal: Xymena Kurowska, "Multipolarity as Resistance to Liberal Norms: Russia's Position on Responsibility to Protect"; and Harry Verhoeven, C. S. R. Murthy, and Ricardo Soares de Oliveira, "'Our Identity Is Our Currency': South Africa, the Responsibility to Protect and the Logic of African Intervention."

[46] The Global Centre for the Responsibility to Protect and the International Coalition for the Responsibility to Protect (ICRtoP) publish useful summaries of the annual informal interactive debates in the General Assembly on the reports produced each year by the Secretary-General on different aspects of R2P. On the whole, these have shown wider acceptance and understanding of R2P principles and practice by the Member States. The Global Centre's website tracks the growing number of references to R2P in statements and resolutions of the Security Council. The frequency has accelerated, not diminished, since the controversial use of force to protect populations in Libya in 2011. For a range of assessments of progress over the first decade since the publication of the ICISS report, including one by the senior author of this chapter, see Special Issue, "Reflections on R2P: Ten Years On," *Global Responsibility to Protect* 3(4) (2011). Consideration is being given at the UN to the possibility of devoting the Secretary-General's 2015 R2P report to a review of progress over the decade since the 2005 World Summit endorsement and to possible priorities for the decade to come.

considerable soul-searching and institutional innovation. In August 2000, a year before the publication of the International Commission on Intervention and State Sovereignty (ICISS) report on the responsibility to protect, the Brahimi report underscored "the need to have more effective collection and assessment of information at United Nations Headquarters, including an enhanced conflict early warning system that can detect and recognize the threat or risk of conflict or genocide."[47] It also stressed the importance of individual responsibility, underlining "the necessity to provide field missions with high-quality leaders and managers who are granted greater flexibility and autonomy by Headquarters" and "the importance of holding individual officials at Headquarters and in the field accountable for their performance, recognizing that they need to be given commensurate responsibility, authority and resources to fulfill their assigned tasks."[48]

Four years later, in August 2004, Secretary-General Kofi Annan appointed the first Special Adviser for the Prevention of Genocide, Juan Méndez, with a mandate stressing catalytic and early warning roles.[49] When he took office in January 2007, Secretary-General Ban Ki-moon went further, making that post full-time, raising it to the Under-Secretary-General level, and appointing Francis Deng to succeed Méndez. In addition, he appointed the senior author of this chapter to the new post of Special Adviser for the Responsibility to Protect, with a mandate to lead the conceptual, political, and operational/institutional development of R2P. The office of the two Special Advisers has served since 2007 as the centerpiece of efforts to embed mass atrocity prevention in the systemwide work of the world organization.[50]

Noting that he had an obligation to serve as "the spokesperson for the vulnerable and the threatened," in his first report on R2P Secretary-General Ban underscored that he bore "a particular responsibility for ensuring that the international community responds in a 'timely and decisive' manner, as called for in paragraph 139 of the Summit Outcome." Echoing the Brahimi report, he acknowledged that "the Secretary-General has an obligation to tell the Security Council – and in this case the General Assembly as well – what it needs to know, not what it wants to hear."[51]

More recently, the Secretary-General publicly acknowledged his recurring efforts to get the rest of the bureaucracy on board with this message.

---

[47] *Report of the Panel on United Nations Peace Operations*, op. cit., p.1, para. 6 (d).

[48] Ibid., p.2, para. 6 (i) and (k).

[49] Letter from the Secretary-General to the President of the Security Council, S/2004/567, 1 August 2004. The Annex outlines the mandate.

[50] In July 2012, Adama Dieng was appointed to succeed Dr. Deng, and, a year later, Dr. Jennifer Welsh succeeded Dr. Luck.

[51] Report of the Secretary-General, *Implementing the Responsibility to Protect*, A/63/677, 12 January 2009, 26, para. 61.

At the commemoration of the Rwandan genocide in Kigali, in April 2014, he declared that:

I have sent my own signal to UN representatives around the world. My message to them is simply this: When you see people at risk of atrocity crimes, do not wait for instructions from afar. Speak up, even if it may offend. Act. Our first duty must always be to protect people – to protect human beings in need and distress.[52]

His "rights up front" initiative, spawned by the 2012 internal review of the shortcomings of the UN's performance in Sri Lanka, has sought to prioritize the reporting of concerns over escalating human rights violations even when political or diplomatic sensitivities suggest downplaying warnings of possible atrocities.[53] From an IR2P perspective, it is striking that the first step in the "rights up front" action plan is "integrating human rights into the lifeblood of staff so they understand what the UN's mandates and commitments to human rights mean for their Department, Agency, Fund or Programme and for them personally."[54] It is too early to gauge how successful these initiatives will prove to be in practice, but the fact that they are still needed within the UN bureaucracy seven years after the Secretary-General made atrocity prevention and R2P one of his top public and internal priorities speaks to how difficult it is to make the individual responsibility to protect stick, even in the world body that fostered it. Evidently, old habits do die hard.

10.2.7. Survivors

Survivors are themselves, directly or indirectly, casualties of mass violence. Post-atrocity, they must try to heal their physical and emotional wounds in environments with inadequate social and medical infrastructure and few, if any, mental health practitioners. Women who have survived war rape and children who have served, voluntarily or not, with armed groups that have committed atrocity crimes face particularly difficult challenges.[55] These gaps are often filled by independent groups who volunteer their services. For instance, for more than twenty years, the Bosnian women's health organization, Medica Zenica, has partnered with Medica Mondiale, a feminist women's rights and relief organization in Cologne, Germany, to provide comprehensive

---

[52] Remarks at the Commemoration of the 20th Anniversary of the Rwandan Genocide, Kigali, Rwanda, April 7, 2014.

[53] Report of the Secretary-General's Internal Review Panel on UN Actions in Sri Lanka, November 2012.

[54] UN Summary of "Rights Up Front," December 17, 2013. Also see press conference of Deputy Secretary-General Jan Eliasson, December 19, 2013.

[55] Theresa Stichick Betancourt et al., "Sierra Leone's Former Child Soldiers: A Follow-up Study of Psychosocial Adjustment and Community Reintegration," *Child Development* 81(4): 1077–1095 (July–August 2010).

psychosocial and medical support to women and children survivors of war and postwar trauma and victims of other forms of violence, and education and empowerment of women.[56]

Moreover, many survivors may have to live for years in vast camps for the displaced, where they remain vulnerable to extortion, bullying, and sexual violence, not to mention physical, medical, and cultural deprivations. In the camps, children often lack proper educational and recreational opportunities, whereas those preaching extremism or retribution have a captive audience. Other survivors have to try to build a new life in an unfamiliar country, where they are culturally distinct and never fully integrated. Those who return to their villages and homelands will never live without fear, nor see their neighbors, government, or homeland the same way again. Among the first victims of atrocities are safety, security, and confidence in the institutions of governance. Survivors may sense what the scholars tell us: the best predictor of genocide is past genocide.[57]

Survivors have important stories to tell. They should be accorded a more prominent place in R2P decision making, especially when it comes to attempts to translate the short-term results of R2P engagements and interventions into sustainable societal change.[58] Too often, international efforts to provide protection, whether consensual, as in Kenya, or coercive, as in Libya, have lacked sustainability. Leaders and publics in foreign countries may have short attention spans, as well as a financial and political interest in pushing survivors to reconcile with former perpetrators more quickly or fully than they are psychologically prepared for. Survivors are likely to have more existential and longer term perspectives than have external actors. It is their lives and those of their families and communities that have been brutally and tragically transformed for perpetuity.[59] In Rwanda, for instance, the survivors of the 1994 genocide have had to find ways of living with the Hutu majority, even though many thousands of them participated directly in the genocidal violence. Mass

---

[56] http://medicazenica.org/uk and www.medicamondiale.org.

[57] According to Barbara Harff, new episodes of genocide are more than three times as likely if there was a previous one. "No Lessons from the Holocaust?" op. cit., 66.

[58] As Secretary-General Ban Ki-moon put it in his 2009 report on implementing R2P, "in all of the discussions of global, regional and national institutions, care should be taken not to lose sight of the individual victims and survivors of such crimes. They need to be supported and encouraged to tell their stories candidly and fully, without fear of retribution or stigmatization. In that regard, women's non-governmental organizations have often played a critical role in engaging and assisting survivors of systematic sexual violence. They deserve our full support." Op. cit., 14, para. 26.

[59] Questioning the emphasis on truth and justice as "rallying cries for efforts to assist communities in (re)building in the aftermath of mass atrocities," Laurel E. Fletcher and Harvey M. Weinstein have asserted that such efforts "employ a paradigm that focuses on individuals who have been wronged (victims) and those who inflicted their wounds (perpetrators). Missing is an appreciation for the damage mass violence causes at the level of communities. Totalizing experiences necessitate totalizing responses." "Violence and Social Repair: Rethinking the Contribution of Justice to Reconciliation," *Human Rights Quarterly* 24: 639 (2002).

atrocity crimes usually have a political purpose, so the intent is to leave an indelible mark not only on the direct victims of the violence, but on their relatives, descendants, friends, and neighbors as well. In this, they inevitably succeed.

Survivors, however, can be empowered by the very potency of their stories, by bearing witness, and by their determination that such crimes should "never again" take place. They can help shape the future. Survivors have both the possibility and the imperative of framing the post-atrocity narrative. Their accounts may be dismissed or contested by those who seek to rewrite history and to whitewash their direct or indirect responsibility for the atrocities that were committed. Holocaust denial persists to this day, as do efforts to deny the extent of the genocide in Rwanda. Two generations later, many Cambodians are still reluctant to confront the horrors of the killing fields. Documentation of the mass killings in Guatemala and the Balkans is being painstakingly assembled to make it more difficult to forget or deny what transpired. This has become an important contribution of the various tribunals as they seek to set the historical record straight, as well as offer a modicum of justice and accountability. How these narratives are developed, documented, preserved, and disseminated matters immensely, not least because they could well affect the likelihood of a reoccurrence of mass violence.

What lessons will survivors draw for themselves, their children, their groups, and their societies? How will they choose to deal with generations of pain and loss? How will they seek accountability and justice? How will they view efforts, often promoted from abroad, at individual and social reconciliation and post-atrocity peacebuilding? How will they view policies and practices designed to prevent a recurrence of the violence, given the history of recidivism in many places, including Rwanda? In those societies that have suffered mass atrocities, as well as in neighboring countries, what will future generations be taught about the mass atrocities and the processes of justice, reconciliation, and accountability that followed?

In the aftermath of mass atrocities, relationships between national and international actors may be strained by divergent experiences, expectations, and narratives. For instance, Paul Kagame, president of Rwanda, recently commented that:

The genocide happened. Some members of the international community were involved with its happening and also the failure to prevent it or stop it. And they have failed to help manage the aftermath. So we as Rwandans have had to deal with this tragic history of ours. We have no alternative but to confront it, and we will. Even if there are so many responsible, we take full responsibility for ourselves.[60]

---

[60] Interview, "Rebooting Rwanda: A Conversation with Paul Kagame," *Foreign Affairs* 93(3): 48 (May/June 2014). For interdisciplinary assessments of progress there since the genocide,

The persistence of such gaps in understanding does not imply that survivors have a monopoly on wisdom about post-atrocity policy choices, but it does suggest that *outside* actors should appreciate that they are – in the short- and long-run – just that: external, not internal, players. They have a choice about the nature, degree, and sustainability of their involvement. Survivors know this, just as they know that they do not have the luxury of choice. They must face the aftermath every day, even as they work to build a better future.

10.3.   Lessons from Operational Experience

Since 2008, the UN, regional organizations, governments, and national and transnational civil society have tried to apply R2P principles in a wide range of situations in which mass atrocity crimes were threatened or under way. The results have been mixed, but generally encouraging. Diplomacy – whether global, regional, or bilateral, public and private – has achieved some success in Kenya (detailed later), Burundi, Guinea, and Kyrgyzstan, among other places. More robust responses have helped – at points – to curb mass atrocities in the Democratic Republic of the Congo (DRC), Mali, Somalia, and Libya. In Côte d'Ivoire, at earlier points, UN diplomatic efforts to curb incitement and the marking of opposition homes to identify ethnicity seemed to succeed, but in the end more forceful action was needed to protect populations.[61] The situation remains precarious in the CAR and South Sudan, and disastrous in Syria.[62] As discussed later, the UN and influential Member States failed to invoke R2P principles either in anticipation of or in response to the violent end of the civil war in Sri Lanka in 2009.

Although it is too soon to draw definitive conclusions about what works, where, and when, it appears that prevention and protection goals have been best served (1) when the international engagement has been early and sustained, (2) when global and regional actors pursued coordinated and collaborative efforts, (3) when external actors had some leverage over key players in the situation and were willing to exercise it, (4) when civil society in

---

see Scott Straus and Lars Waldorf, eds., *Remaking Rwanda: State Building and Human Rights after Mass Violence* (Madison: University of Wisconsin Press, 2011).

[61] In November 2004, Juan Méndez called on the leaders there to take steps to halt xenophobic hate speech, which then subsided. Statement by the Special Adviser on the Prevention of Genocide, November 15, 2004. Six years later, the Special Advisers on the Prevention of Genocide and on R2P expressed concern about the marking of houses there and the practice ceased. Statement by Special Advisers Deng and Luck on the Situation in Côte d'Ivoire, December 29, 2010. Acting under Chapter VII, on March 30, 2011, the Security Council imposed sanctions and recalled its authorization for the UN Operation in Côte d'Ivoire (UNOCI) "to use all necessary means" to protect the civilian population in resolution 1975 (2011).

[62] For an insightful and sober assessment, see Simon Adams, "Failure to Protect: Syria and the UN Security Council," Occasional Paper No. 5 (March 2015), Global Centre for the Responsibility to Protect.

countries under stress or at risk offered a moderating voice, and (5) when individuals in pivotal positions, as well as institutions, were targeted.[63]

One of the more comprehensive and successful applications of R2P and IR2P principles came in Kenya, in early 2008. There, in a rarity, the international strategy encompassed all of the seven groups addressed earlier. Ironically, this was accomplished before Secretary-General Ban had articulated his implementation strategy or even given his first speech on the subject. International observers were not surprised that there was some civil unrest following the disputed results of the December 27, 2007, presidential, parliamentary, and local elections in Kenya because there had been a history of postelection violence there, and this had been a bitter and closely fought contest. The rapid escalation of the violence and its increasingly sectarian character, however, had not been anticipated in one of Africa's more stable and democratic countries. Within days, a few key international officials and public opinion leaders had invoked R2P, decided to employ it as the lens through which to view the crisis, and began to articulate policy responses that addressed all seven of the groups noted earlier.[64] Given how contentious and underdeveloped the concept was at that point, this readiness to apply it to the worsening situation in Kenya was quite remarkable, as was the nuanced and differentiated strategy that emerged at both the regional/African Union (AU) and global/UN levels. The implementation efforts demonstrated the mutually reinforcing benefits of marrying individual, institutional, and state-centric approaches to R2P.

---

[63] Some would call these the "easy" cases and assert that R2P was intended to offer a strategy for dealing with the toughest situations, when governments are uncooperative and determined to commit atrocity crimes against elements of their population and where civil society is underdeveloped, weak, and/or co-opted. It is worth recalling, however, the emphasis that the ICISS report put on prevention and on seeking ways to influence governments without the ultimate resort to the use of force. Moreover, as noted earlier, experience has shown that in most situations of concern governments are not united and determined to commit such crimes and that, in many cases, non-state actors have been the worst perpetrators. Secretary-General Ban's implementation strategy, as prepared by the senior author of this chapter, has sought "early and flexible response, tailored to the circumstances of each situation," with the objective of trying to keep "easy" cases from becoming "hard" ones. In the most intractable situations, where governments are determined to follow the path to mass atrocities, such as in Syria and Sri Lanka, the most that international actors may be willing or able to do is to raise the political and economic costs of committing atrocity crimes and pledge to pursue individual accountability down the line.

[64] For a compilation of comments by public figures, see Meredith Preston-McGhie and Serena Sharma, "Kenya," *The Responsibility to Protect: The Promise of Stopping Mass Atrocities in Our Time*, edited by in Jared Genser and Irwin Cotler (Oxford: Oxford University Press, 2012), 291–297. Kofi Annan has stated on several occasions that he saw the Kenyan crisis from the outset through an R2P lens. See, for instance, Roger Cohen, "How Kofi Annan Rescued Kenya," *New York Review of Books* 55(2) (August 14, 2008). In his opening remarks at the Kenya National Dialogue and Reconciliation Conference: One Year Later, Annan commented that "urgent action was needed to resolve the crisis. Effective external assistance proves that the responsibility to protect can work." Kofi Annan Foundation, March 2009.

In retrospect, there has been a tendency to label this an easy case for R2P implementation, as though a relatively successful outcome must mean that the challenge was not too great and the political stars must all have been in alignment. At the time, however, none of this seemed assured. Within the UN secretariat, and undoubtedly among the Member States as well, for instance, there was widespread reluctance at the outset to see Kenya as an R2P situation. Among top UN officials, the Secretary-General and his two Special Advisers were pretty much alone in advocating that the crisis be seen through an R2P lens. The shadow of the UN's failures in Rwanda, however, hung heavily over the early deliberations, and, to the senior author of this chapter, at least, the situation offered a chance to demonstrate that R2P was about prevention as much as response. Less than a week after the election, the Secretary-General reminded "the Government, as well as the political and religious leaders of Kenya, of their legal and moral responsibility to protect the lives of innocent people, regardless of their racial, religious or ethnic origins and he strongly urges them to do everything within their capacity to prevent further violence."[65]

Throughout the crisis, the degree of coordination and mutually reinforcing action among the UN, the AU, and influential capitals was impressive, in part because only a handful of leaders were heavily involved, and they all sought pretty much the same end. The Chair of the AU, President John Kufuor of Ghana, recognized the risks of further escalation and consulted in the early days of the crisis with both the UN and with former UN Secretary-General Kofi Annan, also of Ghana. He persuaded Annan to lead a three-person high-level AU mediation team – the AU Panel of Eminent African Personalities – and President Mwai Kibaki and opposition leader Raila Odinga to accept their intervention.[66] The forty-one-day mediation effort, which had more than its share of ups and downs, produced a power-sharing agreement linked to a raft of governance, judicial, and constitutional reforms.[67] When Annan needed financial, logistical, and technical support, it was forthcoming from the UN, from interested Member States, and from NGOs with technical expertise. When he needed big capitals to put pressure on the government or the opposition, they obliged, including a mid-February visit by U.S. Secretary of

---

[65] Statement Attributable to the Spokesperson for the Secretary-General on the Situation in Kenya, January 2, 2008. The text sought to encourage civil society to speak out against the violence and to remind Kenyans that the obligations under R2P had both a moral and legal foundation.

[66] Joining Annan on the Panel were Graça Machel, the former First Lady of Mozambique, and President Benjamin Mkapa of Tanzania.

[67] For a detailed insider history of the mediation effort and its conclusions, see The Office of the AU Panel of Eminent African Personalities, *Back from the Brink: The 2008 Mediation Process and Reforms in Kenya* (Addis Ababa, Ethiopia: The African Union Commission, 2014). Also see Elisabeth Lindenmayer and Josie Liannan Kaye, *A Choice for Peace? The Story of 41 Days of Mediation in Kenya* (New York: International Peace Institute, 2009).

State Condoleezza Rice to reinforce the need for a peaceful settlement and to underscore the consequences for bilateral assistance and relations should the violence continue.[68]

At every level – regional, global, and bilateral – the message was consistent: that the leaders of Kenya had an inescapable responsibility to protect populations by stopping both acts of violence and their incitement and that impunity for serious crimes could no longer be expected. Annan repeatedly called for justice as well as for reconciliation, while national and then international investigations were launched to try to ensure some degree of accountability for the postelection violence.[69] Drawing from lessons learned painfully in Rwanda, the interlocutors put considerable emphasis on the need to curb hate speech and the incitement of further violence.[70] In their private meetings with Kibaki and Odinga, both Annan and Ban underscored the need for the Kenyan leaders to ensure that their followers stopped inciting further violence that could lead to even greater mass atrocities.[71] They were reminded of the limits of impunity in the age of international tribunals and the ICC. Cause and effect are hard to establish definitively in such situations, but incitement and hate speech did subside, as did the levels of violence.

These messages were reinforced by Kenyan and international civil society groups. Annan and his colleagues made a particular point to be as transparent as possible in their mediation efforts, visiting critical parts of the country, holding frequent press events, and cultivating and empowering more moderate and nonsectarian elements of the population.[72] Particular

---

[68] *Back from the Brink*, op. cit., 31–32.

[69] Ibid., chapter six, 101–122.

[70] For example, Graça Machel, who had headed the 2006 African Peer Review Mechanism (APRM) for Kenya, warned President Kibaki that the hate speech she heard in Kenya reminded her of that which had fueled the genocide in Rwanda. Ibid., 102. According to the AU Panel's Agenda, "The mass media in general must be encouraged to broadcast messages of peace, while the radio stations, especially those transmitting in vernacular languages, must stop broadcasting hate messages." Ibid., 254. The February 1, 2008, public statement of the AU Panel-moderated Kenya National Dialogue and Reconciliation called on public leaders to "refrain from irresponsible and provocative statements," while "hate and threatening messages, leaflets, SMS, or any other broadcasts of that nature must cease forthwith." Ibid., 258–259.

[71] Secretary-General Ban's comments at his press conference in Nairobi on February 1, 2008, gave the flavor of his message: "the people and leaders of Kenya, particularly political leaders, have the duty, and the responsibility, to wake up and reverse this tragic path before it escalates into the horror of mass killings and devastation we have witnessed in recent history." The previous day, he told the African Union summit in Addis Ababa that President Kibaki and opposition leader Rail Odinga "have the responsibility to do everything possible to resolve the sources of crisis peacefully." For his part, he declared that he would "spare no effort to operationalize the Responsibility to Protect." For a summary of Annan's initial meeting with the Kenyan leaders, see *Back from the Brink*, op. cit., 24–25. Also see Secretary-General Ban's comments on the crisis in *Implementing the Responsibility to Protect*, op. cit., 24, para. 55.

[72] See, among other sources, Lindenmayer and Kaye, op. cit., Preston-McGhie and Sharma, op. cit., 288–289, and *Back from the Brink*, op. cit., 29–31 and 237–238.

attention was given to women's groups and the private sector, both constituencies with a strong stake in peaceful settlement. For all its political and tribal divisions, Kenya had (and continues to have) a strong and active civil society, as well as traditions of pluralism and a relatively free press. Annan and the other AU panelists recognized that these assets could provide natural allies in their mediation efforts and potential checks on excesses by the country's political leadership.

At the time of the AU mediation effort, it appeared that most Kenyans appreciated the international political engagement, so sovereignty concerns did not present a barrier to be overcome in the early application of R2P principles (later, this picture darkened with the domestic and international political campaigns against the ICC indictments of top Kenyan leaders). Indeed, some participants in the process credited the emergence and growing acceptance of R2P for the relatively early and successful diplomatic mission. According to the Office of the AU Panel of Eminent African Personalities, "the African Union's willingness to engage, through the Panel, owed a good deal to growing political support in Africa for the responsibility to protect doctrine, as well as Article 4(h) of the African Union's Constitutive Act, transforming the Organization of African Unity to the African Union, which affirmed the right to intervene in the affairs of Member States under certain conditions."[73] Article 4(h) made the intervention's "legitimacy easier for national leaders to accept."[74] Looking back on the episode, the Office concluded that:

Kenya saw the best of R2P and its limits. The rapid convergence of an African and international consensus on the need to offer (and insist on) external mediation was very positive. The limits of R2P were revealed by the international community's subsequent inability to induce Kenya's political leaders to implement the reforms they had brought into being.[75]

Indeed, another, even broader-based, international and national effort was required to forestall pre- and postelection violence the next time around, in March 2013, under the new Constitution. Although the campaign against violence largely succeeded, it also demonstrated that the 2008 effort was better at short-term protection than at providing long-term answers to Kenya's core governance challenges. What the original ICISS report called postprotection "rebuilding" was incomplete.[76]

---

[73] *Back from the Brink*, op. cit., 21–22.
[74] Ibid., 234.
[75] Ibid., 244.
[76] This would appear to have been another example of a failure to exercise full responsibility after protecting.

This brief account also suggests that whereas individual responsibility played a critical role in ensuring the success of the immediate engagement to save Kenyan lives in 2008, over the longer term, efforts to transform societies to prevent a reoccurrence of mass atrocities will entail much more fundamental and collective campaigns over a number of years led by institutions, as well as by individuals, with the capacity to give sustained attention to the postprotection rebuilding process. In that sense, the difficulties that have been encountered in the UN system and elsewhere in integrating atrocity prevention, development, and postconflict peacebuilding efforts have been most telling.[77] Part of the problem has been a tendency in capitals, as well as in international institutions, to think of R2P as a short-term emergency response doctrine, not as a guide to the longer term development of societies and their governance mechanisms. In addition, as addressed in the Secretary-General's 2012 report on Pillar Three of his R2P implementation strategy, the distinction between prevention and response has often been drawn too sharply.[78] In practice, the senior author of this chapter found that, in most situations, there was a need at any point both to respond to certain developments and to seek to prevent other things from happening. There usually was an interactive process under way between prevention and response because both involved actions and reactions on various levels, with the prime actors on the local and national levels, not in foreign capitals or international institutions. In most situations, especially the more challenging ones, there was a need to sustain attention to both prevention and response over the course of many years, not just over those months when a crisis was the focus of international media coverage and NGO activism.

It is sobering, in retrospect, to recall that the relative success that the application of R2P principles gained in Kenya was followed just a year later with the utter failure to apply them to the large loss of civilian lives in Sri Lanka at the end of its long civil war.[79] Clearly, the international willingness to see

---

[77] The second pillar of Secretary-General Ban's 2009 implementation strategy, as conceived and drafted by the senior author of this chapter, was intended precisely to address this gap. *Implementing the Responsibility to Protect*, op. cit., 15–22. This pillar was addressed in the Secretary-General's sixth annual report on R2P, *Fulfilling Our Collective Responsibility: International Assistance and the Responsibility to Protect*, A/68/947-S/2014/449, July 11, 2014. It was the subject of an informal interactive dialogue in the General Assembly in September 2014.

[78] One of the examples cited by the Secretary-General was the establishment of an international commission of inquiry, such as in Guinea in 2009, to determine the facts of a situation and, in doing so, to ease tensions and point to ways of repairing strains within a society. Report of the Secretary-General, *The Responsibility to Protect: Timely and Decisive Response*, A/66/874-S/2012/578, July 25, 2012, 3–4, para. 8, 11, and 12.

[79] For a detailed account of the allegations and evidence about mass crimes committed by government and opposition forces, see *Report of the Secretary-General's Panel of Experts on Accountability in Sri Lanka*, March 31, 2011. Also see the Secretary-General's statement on the release of the report, SG/SM/13524, April 25, 2011, and Steven R. Ratner, a member of the Panel

crises through an R2P lens has been decidedly situation-specific, even though, as noted earlier, the broad understanding and acceptance of those principles have been growing and expanding geographically. Damien Kingsbury cites four principal reasons why R2P principles were not invoked in a timely manner in response to the situation in Sri Lanka: (1) international divisions "over whether or not RtoP is a legitimate form of international activity," with the government of Sri Lanka and "its main sponsor, China" among the opponents; (2) the government's armed opposition, the Liberation Tigers of Tamil Eelam (LTTE), "was widely classified as a proscribed terrorist organization," so "there was little international sympathy for the LTTE and considerable international support for the continued unity of the state of Sri Lanka"; (3) neither economic sanctions nor military intervention appeared to be feasible options, as either would have likely caused more harm than good; and (4) a divided UN Security Council took no action and, in fact, failed even to address the situation, thus providing no political authorization for the invocation of these principles.[80] "In the end," he lamented, "no country cared enough about Sri Lanka's Tamils to want to go to the trouble of invoking RtoP."[81]

There is much to Professor Kingsbury's arguments, but the dynamics of this case look more nuanced when viewed through an IR2P lens and when compared to the markedly more energetic response to the violence in Kenya the previous year. Surely, R2P principles were, if anything, even more controversial in early 2008 before the Secretary-General's first R2P speech had been given and his first report laying out his R2P implementation strategy had been published in January 2009. If anything, R2P's relative success in Kenya should have bolstered the case for its consideration the following year in Sri Lanka. Certainly, there was little international sympathy for the LTTE, but the victims of the violence were largely Tamil civilians caught in the middle of the struggle, used as human shields by the LTTE and indiscriminately shelled by government forces. Indeed, the classic R2P scenario of a minority group being persecuted by government forces fit the situation in Sri Lanka much better than that in Kenya. In neither case was the employment of coercive measures under Chapter VII of the Charter perceived as the most promising way to curb the violence. The Kenyan response had demonstrated the potential utility of applying diplomatic and political pressure on key leaders, along with offering some carrots, especially where similar messages could be elicited from global and regional bodies and from domestic and international civil society. In Kenya, members of the Security Council had been largely supportive of the

---

of Experts, "Accountability and the Sri Lankan Civil War," *American Journal of International Law* 106: 795–807 (October 2012). An unpublished paper by Alex Bellamy on R2P and the UN's handling of the situation contains much useful information and analysis.

[80] Damien Kingsbury, "Sri Lanka," in Genser and Cotler, op. cit., 312–314.

[81] Ibid., 314.

diplomatic efforts, but its role, which was more reactive than proactive, was of secondary importance. Neither Kofi Annan nor Ban Ki-moon looked to the Council for their cues.

There were several critical missing ingredients in Sri Lanka. Unlike in Kenya, there was no effective regional organization and no political consensus in the region about how to proceed. Civil society in Sri Lanka tended to be divided and weak, in part because of years of government suppression during the campaign against the violent tactics of the LTTE. The press was relatively tame. The UN system had few partners with which to work in Sri Lanka, and even those national staff and local groups involved in trying to deliver humanitarian assistance or monitor human rights conditions there were subject to harassment and disappearances. The Sri Lankan authorities had a reputation for being very sensitive about sovereignty and decidedly hostile toward the UN and its human rights and atrocity prevention agendas. None of this, however, either explains or excuses the secretariat of the UN for failing to speak out more forcefully and consistently for R2P principles in the waning months of the civil war, when the possibility of war crimes and crimes against humanity grew increasingly imminent.

Some seminal, but sobering, answers can be found in the *Report of the Secretary-General's Internal Review Panel on UN Actions in Sri Lanka*, mandated by Secretary-General Ban and released in November 2012.[82] They tend to illustrate the importance of the perceptions and decisions of a handful of high-level officials in shaping the response (or lack of it) from the world body. Indeed, the report's first recommendation is that "the Secretary-General should renew a vision of the UN's most fundamental responsibilities regarding large-scale violations of international human rights and humanitarian law in crises, with a particular emphasis on the responsibility of senior staff."[83]

The Policy Committee, the top advisory group to the Secretary-General in the secretariat, met to address the crisis only once during the last nine months of the civil war, on March 12, 2009.[84] The Special Adviser for the Responsibility to Protect was not invited to attend, although this had been the usual practice when the Committee considered other situations in which there were concerns about possible atrocity crimes being committed.[85] In this case, even more than in the Kenyan situation, R2P perspectives were not welcome in the policy-making process. The Special Adviser on the Prevention of Genocide initially

---

[82] The text of this report can be found online, but it was never formally published as a UN document and it lacks a UN number.
[83] Ibid., 31, para. 87 (a).
[84] Ibid., 22, para. 61.
[85] He was included in the June 2009 Policy Committee meeting that addressed the possibility of an international investigation, but not the one the following month on accountability.

"favored quiet diplomacy" and then "was not supported by UNHQ" when he tried to issue a public statement.[86] None of the UN's intergovernmental organs – not the Security Council, the Human Rights Council, or the General Assembly – met to formally address the situation in Sri Lanka during the months of escalating violence.[87]

According to the Report, "the concept of a 'Responsibility to Protect' was raised occasionally during the final stages of the conflict, but to no useful result. Differing perceptions among Member States and the Secretariat of the concept's meaning and use had become so contentious as to nullify its potential value. Indeed, making references to the Responsibility to Protect was seen as more likely to weaken rather than strengthen UN actions."[88] Attitudes toward R2P varied markedly at that time across the secretariat, with those responsible for humanitarian affairs, political affairs, and peacekeeping tending to be more skeptical and some in human rights doubtful of its added value. With the release of the Secretary-General's strategy for implementing R2P in January 2009, understanding and support from Member States actually began to build, but this period – between the publication of that initial report and the General Assembly's debate on it that summer – was certainly a sensitive time for the development and acceptance of the concept. It is quite possible that some top officials engaged in self-censorship at that point when it came to asserting R2P principles, mistaking the give-and-take leading up to the General Assembly debate as growing doubts about their validity. As the Internal Review Report notes, the secretariat failed to tell the Member States what they needed to know rather than what they wanted to hear – something that had been promised, as noted earlier, in the 2009 implementation report.[89] In any case, it is evident that R2P will lose its credibility if it is only invoked at politically convenient times.[90]

---

[86] Ibid., 23, para. 63. Later, on May 15, 2009, the Special Adviser on the Prevention of Genocide did issue a public statement that, in part, stated that "the two sides should be reminded that individuals can be held personally responsible for war crimes and other international crimes committed in the course of the conflict and which attract international jurisdiction." Two months earlier, on March 14, 2009, the Office of the High Commissioner for Human Rights had issued a similar statement about individual responsibility for war crimes and crimes against humanity. Ibid., 11–12, para. 26.

[87] Ibid., 24, para. 68.

[88] Ibid., 26, para. 74. Counterintuitively, the report then concluded that "although many Member States still have serious concerns regarding some interpretations and implications of the Responsibility to Protect, in practice possibly the greatest contribution of this concept could be as a process to help facilitate the emergence among Member States of early political consensus on human rights protection." Ibid., 31, para. 86. It also suggested that the Secretary-General use R2P as "a 'convening' initiative" for getting Member States to focus more on the human rights dimensions of a crisis situation. Ibid., 34, para. 87.

[89] Ibid., 27, para. 77.

[90] Edward C. Luck, "Foreword," in *The International Politics of Human Rights: Rallying to the R2P Cause?* edited by Monica Serrano and Thomas G. Weiss (London: Routledge, 2014), xvii.

Throughout its narrative and analysis, the Internal Review Report makes it abundantly clear that humanitarian assistance, not atrocity prevention, was the dominant concern in the UN secretariat during the closing months of the civil war in Sri Lanka. Policy making was led by the Emergency Relief Coordinator and the Chef de Cabinet. In a growing humanitarian emergency, priority was given to maintaining humanitarian access and space, both of which depended on some degree of cooperation from both parties to the conflict, but particularly from the government. At headquarters, there was a tendency to question the validity of estimates of growing civilian casualties made by human rights monitors on the ground and to downplay indications that most of these were the result of actions by government forces. These "cultural challenges," according to the Report, stemmed from the decision to frame the problem as one of humanitarian access rather than one of human rights or R2P.[91]

The decision to downplay the human rights and atrocity prevention dimensions of the crisis was not dictated by the Member States or by the Security Council. It was the choice of a handful of top UN officials, understandable but, in retrospect, flawed. Whether a different choice would have saved many lives cannot be known, and there was a risk that a more vocal stance on atrocity prevention would have alienated the government without changing its policy or that of detached external powers. However, the UN clearly lost an opportunity to draw international attention to a pending mass atrocity and to try to rally political support to trying to prevent it. That was the purpose of R2P; and the Internal Review underscores why individual responsibility is at the core of making R2P work in practice.

Tellingly, and again with the benefit of 20/20 hindsight, the internal culture of the UN secretariat and the perceptions and attitudes of top officials had also been highlighted in the candid reviews of the failures of the world body to prevent the mass killings in Srebrenica in 1995 and the horrendous genocide in Rwanda the previous year.[92] The 1999 Srebrenica report, which was prepared by Secretary-General Kofi Annan at the behest of the General Assembly, underscored "the pervasive ambivalence within the United Nations regarding the role of force in the pursuit of peace; an institutional ideology of impartiality even when confronted with attempted genocide."[93] Also published in 1999, the report of the Independent Inquiry into the Actions of the United Nations during the 1994 Genocide in Rwanda similarly criticized the secretariat, including

---

[91] *Internal Review Panel Report*, op. cit., 26–27, para. 75–76. As noted earlier, this finding has since led to the Secretary-General's "rights up front" initiative.

[92] It is telling that both mass crimes occurred in the presence of lightly armed UN peacekeepers and in the absence of prominent concerns about national sovereignty given the ongoing conflicts and peace negotiations in both places. So their circumstances did not fully explain the emphasis in the ICISS report that followed on sovereignty and rules for the use of force.

[93] Report of the Secretary-General pursuant to General Assembly resolution 53/35, *The Fall of Srebrenica*, A/54/549, November 15, 1999, 108, para. 505.

then Secretary-General Boutros Boutros-Ghali for their repeated "emphasis on a cease-fire, more than moral outrage against the massacres."[94] Moreover, "in the view of the Inquiry, the United Nations had an obligation to make absolutely clear to the members of the so-called Interim Government the individual responsibility which accompanies the commission of genocide and war crimes."[95] It further urged the Member States, as well as the secretariat, to "identify situations as genocide when warranted and assume the concomitant responsibility to act."[96] The reports, which helped to lay the political foundation for the launch of the ICISS commission the next year and for the establishment of the post of Special Adviser for the Prevention of Genocide in 2004, had a series of institutional and policy recommendations as well. Their candid findings about the cultural shortcomings of the secretariat, manifested in the misperceptions and misplaced priorities of key international officials, however, spoke to the need to view the principle of R2P through individual as well as institutional perspectives.[97]

10.4.   The Way Forward

The introduction (or reintroduction) of individual and group perspectives into the R2P narrative has both conceptual and operational implications. It should shape both way we think about stemming mass atrocities and the ways in which we go about this challenging task. There is no debate over the proposition that the primary responsibility for preventing mass atrocities and for protecting populations lies with the state because the protection of people within its borders is a state's sovereign responsibility (Pillar I of the Secretary-General's implementation strategy). There also is little debate about the parallel and concurrent responsibility of the international community to assist the state in meeting these duties (Pillar II of the strategy). Yet the fact that these first two pillars have stirred little

---

[94] Report of the Independent Inquiry into the Actions of the UN During the 1994 Genocide in Rwanda, op. cit., 41.

[95] Ibid., 39. The report did acknowledge that some UN personnel on the ground "performed acts of courage in the face of the chaos that developed in Rwanda, and did save the lives of many civilians, political leaders and United Nations staff, sometimes at the risk of their own lives" and that the Force Commander and contingents from Ghana and Tunisia remained throughout the genocide. Ibid., 30–31.

[96] Ibid., rec. 1, 55.

[97] According to Richard N. Barnett, even in the early days of the genocide in Rwanda, UN officials were still convinced that the best way to address the long-standing ethnic conflict was through a power-sharing agreement and supporting the Arusha Accords. Much like the Independent Inquiry, he concluded that "New York's reaction suggests that ignorance was rooted not simply in objective uncertainty or the absence of telltale indicators of genocide but also in the UN's culture." *Eyewitness to a Genocide: The United Nations and Rwanda* (Ithaca, NY: Cornell University Press, 2002), 157.

dissension among the Member States does not mean that they are well understood or that their attainment should be relatively easy to accomplish. They entail both structural prevention (longer term, more strategic, and more institutional and normative steps) and operational prevention (more immediate, more tactical, and more situation-specific measures).

Neither set of preventive measures – neither structural nor operational – is likely to be achieved without the active engagement of civil society locally, nationally, regionally, and internationally. They may be the responsibility of the state, but – like so many other areas of public policy – their achievement poses a sovereignty gap; that is, they can only be obtained with the collaboration of non-state actors. Their advancement may also be facilitated by the material, legal, and political cooperation of other states and international actors, including through the development and codification of related norms and standards, such as R2P, human rights, and humanitarian principles.

Fundamental questions of the relationship between states and the populations on their territory come into play here in ways that range far beyond the scope of this chapter. What should be underscored at this point, however, is that the assertion of the state's primary responsibility in no way excuses individuals and groups from their share of the responsibility to prevent mass atrocity crimes and protect populations. State and individual responsibility are not exclusive – if anything, they are interdependent because neither can be properly exercised in the absence of the other. State responsibility has little meaning distinct from the parallel responsibility of the society and its people to respect and promote these principles. It is very difficult, on the other hand, for individuals and groups to practice effective prevention in places where oppressive governments are determined to undermine those efforts.

It was agreed at the 2005 World Summit, as well, that the international community has a responsibility to respond "in a timely and decisive manner" when national authorities "are manifestly failing" to protect populations on their territory from the four agreed mass atrocity crimes (Pillar III of the strategy). How that third set of responsibilities ought to be carried out in practice, however, continues to generate debate in specific circumstances. Even when the Security Council authorizes enforcement action in such a situation, as in the case of Libya, implementation is likely to be left to ad hoc coalitions of the willing or to regional and/or subregional organizations. Traditionally, the Council has exercised relatively little oversight of military enforcement operations it has authorized, whether launched for humanitarian or other reasons. These matters, however, have received a great deal of scholarly and governmental attention, in part because of the Brazilian "responsibility while protecting" initiative noted earlier and the more recent

French efforts to foster agreement among the five permanent members of the Council not to employ the veto in such situations.[98]

Any attempt to articulate rules or guidelines for decision making in the Council, however, must confront not only constitutional objections, but also the immensely political nature of decisions regarding the use of coercive measures, whether through sanctions or, most pointedly, military intervention.[99] These are, for national leaders, political choices of the highest order, matters on which public and parliamentary sentiment is likely to become engaged. Rules cannot substitute for political judgment in such situations. In two respects, this is where IR2P perspectives come into play. One is in developing a more informed and differentiated understanding of who are the critical players on the ground, what motivates them, and what tools of suasion or coercion external actors have to influence their choices. The other is in developing better means of getting sharper, more specific, and timelier information and analysis to decision makers in external capitals and international bodies about the social, economic, and political dynamics in countries under stress. More targeted assessment is needed as well about the short- and long-term implications of different policy options, especially when coercive, Chapter VII measures are being considered. In the experience of the senior author, seasoned assessment tends to be a more critical shortcoming in generating effective policy responses than early warning in most cases.[100]

Over the past fifteen to twenty years, there has been a great deal of work undertaken at the UN, in capitals, and in academia about ways to sharpen and more precisely target sanctions, whether economic, financial, military, travel, diplomatic, or political. The initial impulse was to lessen the unintended effects on civilian populations, but then attention turned as well to how to

---

[98] In the words of the senior author, the situation in Libya illustrates, as well, the critical importance of exercising "responsibility before protecting (RBP)" and "responsibility after protecting (RAP)." More often than not, international actors have failed to demonstrate sufficient capacity for RBP and RAP in most interventions, in large part because of inadequate understanding of the situations on the ground and of the time and effort that would be required to make a sustainable difference. For the French initiative, see statement by President François Hollande, Opening of the 68th General Assembly, September 24, 2013, and op-ed by Foreign Minister Laurent Fabius, "A Call for Self-Restraint at the UN," *New York Times*, October 4, 2013. According to the proposal, the five permanent members of the Council would agree to "voluntarily regulate their right to exercise the veto" in the case of mass crime when fifty members of the General Assembly request the Secretary-General to determine the scope of the crime and she or he determines its serious nature. Foreign Minister Fabius commented, however, that "to be realistically applicable, this code would exclude cases where the vital national interests of a permanent member of the Council were at stake." Also see Edward C. Luck, "The Security Council at 70: Ever Changing or Never Changing?" in *The UN Security Council in the 21st Century*, edited by Sebastian von Einsiedel, David M. Malone, and Bruno Ugarte (Boulder, CO: Lynne Rienner Publishers, 2015).

[99] On the constitutional issues, see "The Security Council at 70," ibid.

[100] This point was made in the second R2P report of the Secretary-General, on early warning and assessment, in 2010 (A/64/864), of which the senior author was the primary drafter.

make sanctions a more effective tool for countering terrorism and the proliferation of weapons of mass destruction. The confluence between counterterrorism and human protection agendas noted earlier was manifested in the summit-level meeting of the Security Council in September 2014, chaired by U.S. president Barack Obama, on the movement of terrorist recruits across borders. The Chapter VII resolution it produced – as well as the rhetoric it featured – relied heavily on measures to be taken through the Council's existing counterterrorism machinery, although both agendas would be served.[101] Although arms embargoes, travel bans, and diplomatic steps have been authorized by the Council to deal with atrocity situations, more case studies are needed assessing their results and more analysis is needed of what kinds of sanctions might make a difference in dissuading individuals, groups, and leaders from participating in atrocity crimes in some of the tougher situations, such as Syria, CAR, and those involving various armed groups. The history of regional sanctions regimes has been thinner, but their prospects deserve further attention, whether undertaken in conjunction with Chapter VII measures or under Chapter VIII authorization.

The notion that individuals have responsibilities under international law related to atrocity crimes is well established. For the past seventy years, individuals – whether government officials or rebel leaders – have been prosecuted for their roles in committing the kinds of mass crimes that are proscribed under the principle of R2P. With the advent of regional tribunals and the ICC, such prosecutions have become more frequent and the defendants more diverse. As discussed earlier, in a number of situations, international officials seeking to persuade parties to respect R2P standards have found it useful to invoke the possibility of international prosecution of those leaders who fail to do so.

Understandably, most of the vast literature on the ICC, regional tribunals, and accountability has focused on legal and political matters. An IR2P perspective, however, would suggest the utility of devoting additional work to several topics. One would be how to avoid revictimizing those survivors who are willing to make the considerable sacrifice of serving as sources and witnesses in the investigations and trials relating to such traumatic events.[102] A second, related question would be to consider more fully and in a more differentiated manner what appropriate restitution would be in such cases. A third would be to examine accountability through a psychosocial lens, in

---

[101] Resolution 2178 (2014), September 24, 2014.

[102] One of the few treatments of this question can be found in Tod Lindberg, "The Responsibility to Respect: Victims and Human Dignity at the International Criminal Court," in *Human Dignity and the Future of Global Institutions*, edited by Mark P. Lagon and Anthony Clark Arend (Washington, DC: Georgetown University Press, 2014), 49–66.

part to get a better sense of how to frame and target international messages to national leaders about the need to avoid actions that could lead to the commission of such mass crimes. Related is the more specific question of how to convince the heads of armed groups and terrorist networks that accountability, much less law and international standards, should matter to them. Finally, there is the question of whether those who have knowledge of events leading to the commission of such crimes and the capacity to discourage those developments can be held accountable. The 2007 judgment of the International Court of Justice (ICJ) in the case of Serbia and the genocidal killings in Srebrenica seems to suggest that there is a responsibility to try, if not to succeed. More thought could be given to how such a due diligence standard could be measured and whether it might be applied to the leaders of more distant countries, including particularly of the veto-bearing permanent members of the Security Council, as Louise Arbour suggested when she was High Commissioner for Human Rights.[103]

Beyond questions of legal accountability, there is the matter of how to motivate national and international leaders to make human protection and curbing atrocity crimes a higher policy priority. Clearly, a number of the prime advocates for R2P have had personal experiences with situations of mass atrocity that have had lasting effects on their thinking about such matters: Gareth Evans from Cambodia, Lieutenant-General Romeo Dallaire from Rwanda, Kofi Annan from Rwanda and Srebrenica, Ban Ki-moon from Sri Lanka, Samantha Power from the Balkans, Bill Clinton and his Administration from Rwanda.[104] At an earlier point, of course, was Raphael Lemkin's extraordinary dedication to the idea and the norm of genocide prevention following the Holocaust. Bad experience, however, should not be the only way to educate future leaders on the importance of ending mass atrocity crimes and of taking a "not on my watch" stand against atrocities.

As of this writing, forty-three governments have appointed R2P Focal Points in recognition of the need to have an individual official take responsibility for these matters within their bureaucracies. Facilitated by the Global Centre for the Responsibility to Protect in New York, the focal points

---

[103] See Louis Arbour, "The Responsibility to Protect as a Duty of Care in International Law and Practice," *Review of International Studies* 34(3): 445–458 (2008); see page 453 on the particular responsibilities of the permanent members, as well as her interview at the Council on Foreign Relations, Washington Office, June 12, 2007. In the view of the senior author, her suggestion that the members of the Security Council could face legal consequences for how they vote in the Council, even on matters as grave as mass atrocities, would be inconsistent with the political role it was expected to play under the Charter. In his view, the R2P project has been aimed more at raising the political, not legal, costs of blocking Council action in such situations. Nevertheless, it is a provocative argument that speaks to the individual, as well as collective, responsibilities of leaders and representatives of the permanent members.

[104] See, on the latter, Mark Landler, "U.S. Envoys See a Rwanda Moment in Syria's Escalating Crisis," *New York Times*, May 14, 2014.

initiative is co-sponsored by the governments of Denmark, Ghana, Costa Rica, and Australia. In a 2012 press release, the four governments described a national R2P Focal Point as "a senior official who will facilitate the creation of national and sub-national mechanisms for atrocity prevention and who will promote international cooperation by participating in the global network."[105] In many ways, a Focal Point represents the personification and embodiment of a government's commitment to R2P principles. For colleagues in the government, public groups, and international partners, she or he provides an indispensable contact point for atrocity prevention matters. In addition, a number of countries have been considering or have instituted cross-agency groups to help coordinate national policy making on atrocity issues. One of the more elaborate is the Atrocity Prevention Board (APB), launched following a major address by President Obama in August 2011 and a subsequent Presidential Study (PSD 10). To date, the APB process has given the question of curbing atrocities greater and more sustainable attention than it might have otherwise received and has brought new bureaucratic players, such as USAID, into the atrocity prevention sphere. It has been less effective at generating additional funding for the effort and at reaching out to counterparts overseas.[106]

Although the International Parliamentary Union (IPU) has shown some interest in R2P, the challenge of sustaining the attention of legislators on atrocity prevention remains daunting, given that the link between distant atrocities and immediate national interests is not always apparent to those focused on day-to-day legislative and fiscal matters. Nevertheless, individual parliamentarians can – and often have – taken the lead in introducing legislation that would make incitement, recruitment, funding, and participation in mass atrocities at home or abroad illegal and/or that would provide political, logistical, or material support to international efforts to curb atrocities or enhance accountability. At the least, it is important that questions of national response to unfolding atrocities not get unnecessarily muddied in partisan politics.

Over time – and changing values and priorities is a long-term project – the key to reducing the incidence and severity of mass atrocities lies in education, training, and the embedding of principles of tolerance, pluralism, and human dignity deep into individual, community, and societal values.[107] This will require the full empowerment and equal participation of women in education,

---

[105] Global Centre for the Responsibility to Protect, September 29, 2012.
[106] For a useful and broad-ranging analysis, see James P. Finkel, *Atrocity Prevention at the Crossroads: Assessing the President's Atrocity Prevention Board after Two Years*, Center for the Prevention of Genocide, U.S. Holocaust Memorial Museum, Occasional Paper no. 2, September 2014.
[107] See, for instance, the work of the Global Centre for Pluralism in Ottawa, Canada.

governance, commerce, and post-atrocity reconstruction. Education of girls and boys on an equal basis should help to instill an appreciation of those who are different, along with recognition of the potential costs of intolerance and bigotry. Men and boys need to understand that there can be no higher priority than valuing and protecting women, girls, and other vulnerable populations.

Much like prohibiting the use of weapons of mass destruction, the commission of mass atrocities must be regarded, virtually universally, as simply unacceptable. It can no longer be regarded as a rational instrument of political choice, as an option for leaders seeking to gain power or silence opposition. This will require confronting the realities of past atrocities in all of their horror and acknowledging their lasting damage to individuals, families, groups, and societies, not to mention to established standards of morality and humanity. The larger R2P enterprise will only succeed to the extent that it persuades individuals, as well as governments and institutions, that they have choices and responsibilities when faced with hate speech, exclusion, ethnic politics, and the demonization of groups within society.

For these reasons, this chapter has called for the inclusion of an individual perspective on R2P not just alongside but integrated into the dominant national and international paradigms. It has not contended that the study of this individual iteration of R2P, which we have labeled IR2P, should supplant the examination of institutional and national patterns of prevention and response. Rather, it should inform them by providing fresh insights, by enriching our understanding of the psychosocial drivers of institutional and national behavior, and by raising new questions about the path ahead. It has contended that the further efforts to operationalize R2P move forward – the closer that the world comes to matching words with deeds – the more evident it will become that the individual dimensions of R2P matter in understanding the etiology of atrocity crimes and how they can be prevented, ameliorated, or curbed.

If the R2P project continues to maintain its remarkable early momentum, over time, the balance between the individual and the collective or institutional dimensions of atrocity prevention should shift toward the latter as values become embedded in legislation, practices, doctrines, and institutions. Regardless of whether or when this might occur, the need to improve the effectiveness of both dimensions and the productivity of their interplay is evident. As noted earlier, experience suggests that when the individual (IR2P) and collective (R2P) dimensions of atrocity prevention move in the same direction, the prospects for saving lives expand substantially. And that is the way forward.

11   Resource Predation, Contemporary Conflict, and the Prevention of Genocide and Mass Atrocities

Michael T. Klare

Ever since awareness of the Holocaust became widespread, at the end of World War II, people of goodwill have sought to devise strategies for preventing further episodes of genocide and mass atrocities. These efforts resulted in an early success in 1948, when the United Nations General Assembly adopted the Convention on the Prevention and Punishment of the Crime of Genocide (the Genocide Convention), the first international measure to outlaw acts defined as genocide and to devise procedures for identifying and punishing those responsible for committing such acts. When it became evident, over the ensuing decades, that additional measures were needed to deter genocide and mass killing, the UN and some of its Member States sought to bolster the Genocide Convention with other, more vigorous measures. On the punitive side, several conflict-specific tribunals were convened to try individuals accused of violating the Convention, including the International Criminal Tribunal for the former Yugoslavia (ICTY) and the International Criminal Tribunal for Rwanda (ICTR); these were supplemented, in 2002, by the establishment of a permanent tribunal, the International Criminal Court (ICC), to prosecute individuals for genocide, war crimes, and crimes against humanity. On the preventive side, the UN Security Council also voted to ban the supply of arms and other military equipment to governments and armed factions accused of aggression, war crimes, and mass atrocities.[1] When it was learned that some of those entities had engaged in the sale of diamonds and other valuable resources to finance clandestine arms purchases and otherwise sustain their operations, the Security Council also imposed sanctions on the export of such commodities by the groups involved.[2]

The imposition of sanctions on resource exports tied to outlawed military activities was part of a larger UN effort to develop "targeted sanctions" aimed

---

[1] For background on these measures, see David Cortright and George A. Lopez, *The Sanctions Decade: Assessing UN Strategies in the 1990s* (Boulder, CO: Lynne Rienner, 2000).

[2] Ibid.

at the groups and individuals responsible for war crimes and mass violence rather than the population of a country as a whole, as had been the case with earlier UN measures, such as the economic sanctions imposed on Iraq after its 1990 invasion of Kuwait. Initially, these targeted measures included arms embargoes and restrictions on the financial activities of the governments and organizations involved.[3] It soon became evident, however, that many of these actors were able to continue buying arms and paying their soldiers by selling valuable commodities – gems, rare minerals, old-growth timber, narcotics, and so on – via black market channels. Not only did these sales enable the outlawed parties to continue fighting and killing, but they also created a means by which military leaders and their business associates could accumulate significant wealth – thus eliminating any inclination they might have to end the violence and sign a peace accord.[4] To eliminate this source of revenue, the Security Council decided to ban such transactions and impose penalties on those who engaged in them.[5]

The development of sanctions aimed at curbing illicit resource transactions also provided the UN with a useful tool to address some of the distinctive characteristics of contemporary conflict in general and mass killing in particular. In contrast to earlier such episodes, which were largely conducted by the military and security forces of states, recent wars and atrocities have been conducted by some combination of state and non-state actors, including ethnic militias, insurgent forces, separatist groups, and criminal gangs. And while earlier episodes of genocide and mass killing generally took place in the context of conventional warfare between opposing armies, recent cases have largely occurred in the context of civil wars and ethnic clashes – wherein conventional force-on-force battles have been few and attacks on unprotected civilians legion.[6] Typically, the leaders of armed groups engaged in such attacks cite ethnic and religious grievances to justify their assaults on targeted populations; research suggests, however, that they are often motivated by the pursuit of personal or familial wealth. By portraying the targeted group as heretical, subhuman, demonical, and so forth, these leaders can mobilize their followers to engage in mass killing, rape, torture, mutilation, and other atrocities intended to depopulate an area and gain control over its

---

[3] Ibid.

[4] For background on this phenomenon, see David Keen, *The Economic Functions of Violence in Civil Wars*, Adelphi Paper no. 320 (Oxford: Oxford University Press and International Institute for Strategic Studies, 1998).

[5] For background, see David Cortright and George A. Lopez, *Sanctions and the Search for Security* (Boulder, CO: Lynne Rienner, 2002), 181–200.

[6] For background and discussion, see Ben Kiernan, *Blood and Soil: A World History of Genocide and Extermination from Sparta to Darfur* (New Haven, CT: Yale University Press, 2007); Paul Collier and Nicholas Sambanis, eds., *Understanding Civil War*, vol. 1 (Washington, DC: World Bank, 2005).

resource assets. So long as the leaders' private wealth can be enhanced in this fashion, they often persist in employing such means of violence, even in the face of approbation.[7] It is to impede this system of wealth accumulation – thereby (hopefully) reducing the level of violence – that the UN Security Council has imposed sanctions on illicit resource trafficking.

This approach was first applied, in the 1990s, to the National Union for the Total Independence of Angola (known as UNITA, from its initials in Portuguese), a militant faction long in conflict with the recognized government of Angola. During the Cold War, UNITA enjoyed the support of several foreign governments (including the United States) because of its unrelenting opposition to the Soviet-backed regime in Luanda; at the end of the Cold War, however, such support largely evaporated. Despite this, UNITA continued its violent campaign against the Luanda regime, often engaging in the systematic murder, torture, and displacement of civilians.[8] In response, the UN Security Council voted, under Resolution 864 of September 15, 1993, to prohibit the sale or transfer of arms and other military aid to UNITA. These sanctions were renewed in subsequent years, after UNITA violated its commitment to disband its forces and cease fighting under the Lusaka Protocol of October 31, 1994. When UN investigators discovered that UNITA was financing its ongoing operations through the clandestine sale of diamonds,[9] the Security Council voted, under Resolution 1173 of June 12, 1998, to ban such sales.[10] Significantly, this action was taken under Chapter VII of the UN Charter, which covers "threats to the peace" and is binding on all Member States. Furthermore, to ensure enforcement with Resolution 1173, the Council established a process for the systematic evaluation of its implementation.[11]

Evidently convinced of the utility of such measures, the Security Council went on to impose similar commodity restrictions on other organizations and governments it determined were engaging in unlawful aggression and mass atrocities. Following reports by human rights investigators of widespread killing, torture, mutilation, sexual slavery, and other atrocities by the Revolutionary United Front (RUF) in Sierra Leone[12] – many taking place as

---

[7] For background and discussion, see the essays in Mats Berdal and David M. Malone, *Greed and Grievance: Economic Agendas in Civil Wars* (Boulder, CO: Lynne Rienner, 2000).

[8] For details, see Human Rights Watch (HRW), *Angola Unravels* (New York: HRW, 1999), 52–82.

[9] The information was collected and published by a "Panel of Experts" appointed by the Security Council to investigate the situation in Angola. See "Report of the Panel of Experts on Violations of Security Council Sanctions against UNITA to the President of the Security Council," S/2000/203, March 10, 2000.

[10] UN Security Council Resolution 1173, Security Council doc. S/RES/1173, June 12, 1998.

[11] For discussion, see Cortright and Lopez, *Sanctions and the Search for Security*, 183–184.

[12] See, for example, Amnesty International, *Sierra Leone: 1998 – A Year of Atrocities against Civilians* (London: Amnesty, November 1, 1998).

part of a drive by the organization to gain control over Sierra Leone's diamond-producing areas[13] – the Security council voted in Resolution 1306 of July 5, 2000, to ban the import of rough diamonds originating in that country unless sold under the government's Certificate of Origin scheme. Later, when it was discovered that the government of Liberia – then headed by Charles Taylor – was selling smuggled Sierra Leonean diamonds on the international market and using the proceeds to finance military operations by the RUF, the Council adopted a second measure, Resolution 1343 of March 7, 2001, banning diamond exports by Liberia.[14]

Although armed groups have trafficked in a variety of commodities to obtain funds for their ongoing operations, diamonds were especially prized for this purpose because of their widespread availability in various conflict zones and their ease of concealment and transportation – a phenomenon encapsulated in the term "blood diamonds," used when describing such gems.[15] In addition to measures aimed at Angola, Liberia, and Sierra Leone, the Security Council again targeted diamonds in 2005, when armed factions in Côte d'Ivoire were accused of using them to finance activities resulting in serious violations of human rights and international humanitarian law; under Resolution 1643 of December 15, all diamond exports from that country were banned.[16]

Restrictions of this sort have been imposed on resource trafficking in other countries and extended to other commodities. On December 19, 2000, for example, the Security Council (under Resolution 1333) banned opium production by the Taliban in Afghanistan and enjoined others from supplying the Taliban with the chemical acetic anhydride (used to process poppy leaves into opium). Restrictions of various sorts have also been imposed on the export of raw timber from Liberia and of "conflict minerals" – primarily tin, tantalum, and tungsten – from the Democratic Republic of the Congo (DRC).

In recent years, the Security Council has also imposed sanctions on resource trafficking by certain terrorist groups, including Al Qaeda and its offshoots, which have been accused of mass killings and other crimes against humanity. On February 22, 2012, the Council voted (under Resolution 2036) to ban

---

[13] See John L. Hirsch, *Sierra Leone: Diamonds and the Struggle for Democracy*, International Peace Academy Occasional Paper (Boulder, CO: Lynne Rienner, 2001).

[14] For background, see Cortright and Lopez, *Sanctions and the Search for Security*, 184–88.

[15] On the attraction of diamonds as an illicit source of income for armed bands, see Michael L. Ross, "Oil, Drugs, and Diamonds: The Varying Roles of Natural Resources in Civil War," in *The Political Economy of Armed Conflict*, edited by Karen Ballentine and Jake Sherman (Boulder: Lynne Rienner, 2003), 47–70.

[16] See UN Security Council, Department of Public Information, "Security Council Renews Côte d'Ivoire Arms Embargo, Travel Restrictions until 15 December 2006, Unanimously Adopting Resolution 1643 (2005)" (December 15, 2005), www.un.org/News/Press/docs/2005/sc8585 .doc.htm.

exports of charcoal from Somalia, claiming that proceeds from these sales were being used to finance operations by al-Shabaab, a militant Islamic group accused of widespread violence against civilians.[17] (Although a seemingly mundane commodity – at least when compared to diamonds – charcoal made from acacia trees is a highly sought-after commodity in the Arabian Peninsula, where sales of Somali charcoal are believed to net al-Shabaab as much as $25 million per year.[18]) More recently, in 2014 and 2015 (under Resolutions 2161 and 2199), the Council imposed sanctions of various sorts on the Islamic State in Iraq and Syria (ISIS, also called the Islamic State in Iraq and the Levant, or ISIL) and the Al-Nusra Front for the People of the Levant, both of which have been accused of deadly assaults on civilians and religious minorities.

Although the UN has taken the lead in imposing sanctions of this sort, other organizations and some states have adopted similar measures aimed at curbing the trade in illicit materials from areas of conflict where mass atrocities are occurring. Following the global outcry over the phenomenon of "blood diamonds," for example, the international diamond industry joined with various governments and human rights organizations to establish the Kimberly Process Certification Scheme, a voluntary mechanism for excluding illicit stones from the legitimate diamond trade. Responding to similar concerns over efforts by armed bands in the eastern Congo to profit from illicit sales of gold, tin, tungsten, and columbite–tantalite ("coltan," a source of tantalum), the World Bank, the European Union (EU), the International Tin Research Institute (ITRI), and other organizations have taken steps to improve the monitoring of mineral exports from the DRC. The U.S. government has cooperated with these efforts through passage of the Clean Diamond Act of 2003, which prohibits the importation of rough diamonds that are not controlled through the Kimberley Process, and Section 1502 of the Dodd-Frank Wall Street Reform and Consumer Protection Act of 2010, which requires U.S. manufacturers to adopt measures to exclude "conflict minerals" – defined as minerals that "directly or indirectly finance or benefit armed groups in the Democratic Republic of the Congo" – from their products.[19] The United States has also worked behind the scenes to obstruct international financial transactions by ISIS and its business partners.[20] When first instituted, the sanctions on illicit

---

[17] See UN Security Council, Department of Public Information, "Security Council Requests African Union to Increase Troop Level of Somalia Mission to 17,700, Establish Expanded Presence in Keeping with Strategic Concept" (February 22, 2012), www.un.org/News/Press/docs/2012/sc10550.doc.htm.

[18] See Jeffrey Gettleman and Nicholas Kulish, "Somali Militants Mixing Business and Terror," *New York Times* (October 1, 2013).

[19] Public Law 111–203 (July 21, 2010).

[20] See Julie Hirschfield Davis, "Following the ISIS Money," *New York Times*, October 22, 2014.

resource trafficking imposed by the UN and other bodies were largely intended to bolster arms embargoes and related measures aimed at preventing outlawed combatants from engaging in warfare and mass atrocities by restricting their access to operating funds.[21] "Express[ing] its concern that illicit trade in diamonds constitutes a principal source of funding for UNITA," effective action was required to block that organization's access to the diamond market, the Security Council noted in Resolution 1295 of April 18, 2000.[22] As time went on, however, analysts at the UN and elsewhere concluded that the sale of natural resources had a much larger function in sustaining violence than the mere acquisition of operating funds; in many cases, such sales were found to be a motive for initiating combat in the first place or as an incentive for continuing the killing once hostilities had commenced. For example, resource predators have employed mass atrocities against civilians – including rape, torture, mutilation, and enslavement – to force targeted populations to abandon resource-rich areas or to undertake involuntary extractive activities. In Resolution 1857 of December 22, 2008, the Security Council declared that "the linkage between the illegal exploitation of natural resources [and the] illicit trade in such resources [are among] the major factors fuelling and exacerbating conflicts in the Great Lakes region of Africa," and so justified strict international regulation and oversight.[23] The use of sanctions, then, has come to take on increased significance in the struggle to prevent mass atrocities.

The imposition of such measures by the UN and other entities has been praised as a success in helping to curb conflict and violence against civilians. At the same time, questions have been raised as to their utility in prevention and about the effectiveness of efforts to implement the sanctions. These questions deserve close and serious attention. But, before turning to such as assessment, it is necessary to consider the context in which these measures were imposed, the nature of the combatants involved, and the role of resource predation in sparking acts of violence, including atrocity crimes.

11.1.   The Distinctive Features of Contemporary Conflict

That restrictions on the export of diamonds and other valuable materials from areas of conflict have come to assume such a significant role in efforts to curb

---

[21] For background, see Katherine Andrews and Tobias C. Berkman, "United Nations Mechanisms for Combating Illegal Trade in Regions of Conflict," Stimson Center Backgrounder (June 2005), www.stimson.org/books-reports/united-nations-mechanisms-for-combating-illegal-trade-in-regions-of-conflict/.

[22] UN Security Council Resolution 1295, Security Council doc. S/RES/1295 (April 18, 2000).

[23] UN Security Council Resolution 1857, Security Council doc. S/RES/1857 (December 22, 2008).

mass atrocities is due in large part to an improved understanding of the distinctive characteristics of contemporary conflict. All conflicts, of course, possess certain features in common, notably the use of violence to destroy, immobilize, and intimidate a perceived adversary. But the nature of conflict also changes over time, reflecting shifts in technology, political organization, economic conditions, and other aspects of human life. The conflicts of the post-Cold War era, in particular, have exhibited substantial differences from those of the previous epoch. And because prevention efforts can only prove effective if based on a thorough understanding of the conflict environment in which they occur, it has become essential for opponents of genocide and mass atrocities to illuminate these differences.

Among the most prominent differences between current and past conflicts is the degree to which they are now fought *within* countries rather than *between* them, with an accompanying shift from reliance on established, *professional* armies to irregular, *nonprofessional* military formations, such as ethnic militias, insurgent groups, and terrorist organizations. Of the seventy-three armed conflicts that took place between 2002 and 2011 in which the forces of an established state took part, the Uppsala Conflict Data Program (UCDP) reported in 2013, only four were conventional interstate wars involving the regular forces of two established states; all the rest, sixty-nine in total, were intrastate conflicts involving governmental and non-state parties. These episodes included civil wars (Sudan vs. South Sudan, Syria, Côte d'Ivoire), insurgencies (Chechnya, Colombia, Libya, Nigeria), and separatist struggles (Ethiopia, Kashmir, Kurdistan, Myanmar). In addition, the world experienced 223 conflicts in which non-state parties *alone* took part – in most cases, militias or insurgent groups allied with a particular ethnic or religious community. These contests included, for example, the fighting between the Nuer and the Dinka in South Sudan and among various tribal groups in Nigeria. In almost all of the conflicts occurring between 2002 and 2011, irregular forces of one sort or another performed the bulk of the fighting, and civilians were often the *intended* victims of attack.[24]

The causes and characteristics of internal conflicts vary, but most involve a struggle among contending groups and factions for control of state power (and the wealth and privileges such power confers) or efforts by a particular group in a multiethnic or multireligious society to break away from the existing state structure and establish its own independent state or autonomous region. Typically, these conflicts are driven by some combination of what analysts call "greed" and "grievance" – that is, they involve efforts by one or another

[24] See Lotta Themnér and Peter Wallensteen, "Patterns of Organized Violence, 2002–11," Stockholm International Peace Research Institute (SIPRI): *SIPRI Yearbook 2013: Armaments, Disarmament and International Security* (Oxford: Oxford University Press, 2013), 41–60.

group to overcome a history of exploitation and discrimination imposed by another group, as well as a desire to reap the economic benefits of seizing state power or establishing its own self-governing entity.[25]

The degree to which "greed" and "grievance" fuel such conflicts varies from case to case, but most exhibit some degree of both. The conflict in Biafra (1967–70) provides a good historical example of this reality: the Igbo people, long the dominant group in the southeastern quadrant of Nigeria, created the breakaway Republic of Biafra in part to escape their subordinate status in the federal government (which was largely dominated by the Hausa-Fulani and Yoruba peoples) and to gain control over Nigeria's oil fields, most of which were located in their territory but from whose presence they had previously received little economic benefit; federal authorities, furious at the upstart Igbo and alarmed over the potential loss of oil revenues, were unsparing in their brutal drive to restore control over the region. Low-level conflict has persisted in other oil-producing areas of southern Nigeria, with minority communities regularly complaining of the central government's failure to provide them with an equitable share of the nation's petroleum income.[26]

To a considerable degree, internal conflicts of this sort (and associated ethnic massacres) occur in less-developed, multiethnic states with few sources of wealth save agriculture and the extraction of natural resources. Often the product of imperial rule and lacking agreed-upon domestic and international borders, these states typically lack stable, well-functioning state institutions and representative leaders. More often than not, the top leaders of these states seek personal enrichment through the exploitation of the nation's exportable resources, rather than seeking broad-based economic development (which might result in the emergence of contending elites); the result, accordingly, is an environment of enduring poverty and resentment, especially among those ethnic and religious groups that feel particularly disadvantaged by the existing government's hold on power.[27]

Not surprisingly, the systematic use of violence by government officials to retain their hold on power – and thereby perpetuate their control over the

[25] For discussion of this point, see Michael L. Ross, *The Oil Curse: How Petroleum Wealth Shapes the Development of Nations* (Princeton, NJ: Princeton University Press, 2012), and Ross, "Oil, Drugs, and Diamonds." See also David Keen, *Complex Emergencies* (Cambridge, UK: Polity, 2008), 25–70, and the essays in Berdal and Malone, eds., *Greed and Grievance*.

[26] For background, see Annalisa Zinn, "Theory Versus Reality: Civil War Onset and Avoidance in Nigeria Since 1960," in *Understanding Civil War*, vol. 1, edited by Paul Collier and Nicholas Sambanis (Washington, DC: World Bank, 2005), 96–100.

[27] See William Reno, "Shadow States and the Political Economy of Civil Wars," in *Greed and Grievance: Economic Agendas in Civil Wars*, edited by Mats Berdal and David M. Malone (Boulder, CO: Lynne Rienner, 2000), 43–68, and Charles Cater, "The Political Economy of Conflict and UN Intervention: Rethinking the Critical Cases of Africa," in *The Political Economy of Armed Conflict*, edited by Karen Ballentine and Jake Sherman (Boulder, CO: Lynne Rienner, 2003), 19–46.

exploitation of the nation's natural resources – is a common feature of such states.[28] Commonly, moreover, the military and security forces of these countries contribute to the pervasive atmosphere of violence by using force – or the threat of force – to extract wealth and sexual favors from targeted populations, thereby augmenting their (usually meager) pay.[29] All this, in turn, frequently prompts targeted groups and business interests to establish their own militias and security organizations – typically along ethnic and sectarian lines. Under these circumstances, as William Reno of Northwestern University has noted, "the state's agents, and those who challenge them, find powerful incentives to consistently maximize their use of violence."[30]

With poverty, ethnic discord, and systematic violence inherent features of such states, the risk of dissolution and civil war is ever-present. As they slide into decay and conflict, the political and economic systems that prevailed during the preconflict period are frequently reconfigured to operate under wartime conditions. The various ethnic militias and security organizations that were established to acquire or protect valuable assets become the core of the various contending armies. Likewise, the long-term struggle for control over valuable natural resources continues unabated, with the territories harboring these resources becoming a major site of military confrontation. Rather than eliminate economic activity, as many might assume, the outbreak of conflict produces what has been termed a new "political economy of war" – an environment in which contending elites from all sides accumulate wealth through illicit trafficking in arms, gold, diamonds, ivory, narcotics, and other valuable commodities.[31] As a result, says conflict analyst David Keen, "the image of war as a contest has sometimes come to serve as a smokescreen for the emergence of a wartime political economy from which rebels and even the government (and government-affiliated groups) may be benefiting."[32]

This analysis has been given further support by research conducted by Paul Collier and his associates at the World Bank. After an extensive study of conditions in nations torn by internal conflict over the past few decades, he concluded that "economic opportunity" – as manifested by the presence of *Causal* diamonds, rare timber, and other "lootable" assets – is far more likely to be

---

[28] Ibid., 54–64.

[29] This is well exemplified by the case of the eastern Congo. For background, see U.S. Governmental Accountability Office (GAO), *The Democratic Republic of the Congo: U.S. Agencies Should Take Further Actions to Contribute to the Effective Regulation and Control of the Minerals Trade in Eastern Democratic Republic of the Congo*, Report GAO-10–1030 (September 2010), 16–17.

[30] Reno, "Shadow States and the Political Economy of Civil Wars," 55.

[31] For background and discussion, see ibid., 54–60, and Keen, *Complex Emergencies*, 25–49.

[32] David Keen, "Incentives and Disincentives for Violence," in *Greed and Grievance: Economic Agendas in Civil Wars*, edited by Mats Berdal and David M. Malone (Boulder, CO: Lynne Rienner, 2000).

Economic opportunity more imp tha political grievances

associated with such conflict than are social or political grievances. "Some societies are much more prone to conflict than others simply because they offer more inviting economic prospects for rebellion," he wrote in 1999. And since economic agendas are the primary driver of warfare, "it is likely that some groups are benefiting from conflict and that these groups therefore have some interest in initiating and sustaining it."[33]

This phenomenon is well illustrated by the situation in the DRC. Although an internationally recognized government holds sway in the capital, the eastern part of the country has been tormented for decades by fighting among various ethnic and political factions – with the regular army often behaving more like a private militia than the representative of an established government.[34] To make matters worse, senior officials of neighboring countries, including Rwanda, Uganda, and Zimbabwe, have forged alliances with various Congolese factions in order to benefit from the chaos. All these actors have professed to seek a negotiated outcome of one sort or another, but in most cases have been driven by a desire to reap economic benefits from the exploitation of the region's valuable gold, tin, and coltan deposits.[35] To sustain all of these activities, the various armed factions and their business partners have created "a self-financing war economy centered on mineral exploitation," according to the Panel of Experts on the Illegal Exploitation of Natural Resources and Other Forms of Wealth of the Democratic Republic of the Congo (the Panel of Experts on the DRC).[36]

A very similar situation has emerged in the areas of Iraq and Syria controlled by the Islamic State. In contrast to most other terrorist organizations, ISIS has sought to create a functioning state, or "caliphate," in these areas, with all the institutions of a functioning society. This, in turn, has required it to create a self-financing war economy like that entrenched in the eastern DRC. To fuel this economy, ISIS relies on multiple streams of income, including taxes,

---

[33] Paul Collier, "Doing Well Out of War: An Economic Perspective," in *Greed and Grievance: Economic Agendas in Civil Wars*, edited by Mats Berdal and David M. Malone (Boulder, CO: Lynne Rienner, 2000), 91–111.

[34] For background on the fighting in the Democratic Republic of the Congo, see Gérard Prunier, *Africa's World War* (Oxford: Oxford University Press, 2009), and Jason Stearns, *Dancing in the Glory of Monsters: The Collapse of the Congo and the Great War of Africa* (New York: Public Affairs, 2011).

[35] The best source of information and analysis on the motives of the combatants in eastern Congo is the *Final Report of the Panel of Experts on the Illegal Exploitation of Natural Resources and Other Forms of Wealth of the Democratic Republic of the Congo*, UN Security Council doc. S/2002/1146 (October 16, 2002; hereinafter cited as UN, *Final Report of the Panel of Experts on the DRC*), http://www.securitycouncilreport.org/atf/cf/%7B65BFCF9B-6D27-4E 9C-8CD3-CF6E4FF96FF9%7D/DRC%20S%202002%201146.pdf. For additional background, see Léonce Ndikumana and Kisangani F. Emizet, "The Economics of Civil War: The Case of the Democratic Republic of Congo," in *Understanding Civil War*, vol. 1, edited by Paul Collier and Nicholas Sambanis (Washington, DC: World Bank, 2005), 63–87.

[36] UN, *Final Report of the Panel of Experts on the DRC*, para. 12.

looting, extortion, and the covert sale of oil and archaeological relics obtained from areas under its control. According to a November 2014 UN report, ISIS was receiving as much as $1.6 million per day from black-market oil sales (this was before the United States and a number of other states began bombing oil facilities in ISIS-controlled areas). [37]

As noted by UN investigators and other outside observers, ethnic and religious animosities typically play a significant role in the conduct of these and other such conflicts, which are often accompanied by mass killings of targeted populations along with atrocities including large-scale rape, torture, mutilation, and forced expulsion from traditional lands ("ethnic cleansing"). Typically, leaders of the various fighting parties invoke historic grievances to justify the initiation of these actions, and the resulting conflicts are often portrayed in the Western press as expressions of "mindless" ethnic and religious hatred. But ethnic and religious anger is rarely the sole or principal cause of the fighting; rather, it often constitutes a tool employed by political and economic elites to mobilize mass support for actions intended to perpetuate their power and augment their wealth. [38] In the DRC, for example, various unscrupulous elites have exploited long-standing tribal animosities to justify the use of mass atrocities to drive members of targeted groups from their lands and/or force them to work as slaves in primitive mining operations. [39] Similar behaviors are also evident in Burundi, where contending Tutsi and Hutu elites have invoked long-simmering ethnic hostilities to spur violence against opposing groups; but, as suggested by Floribert Ngaruko and Janvier D. Nkurunziza, claims by Burundian elites that "they are fighting for an ethnic cause is pure demagogy." Rather, "they use ethnicity, a highly-charged issue, to mobilize the masses for private gain." [40] And although the core leadership of ISIS may be driven by religious zealotry, they have forged mutually convenient alliances with local business interests that profit from the illicit sale of petroleum products and plundered antiquities. [41]

---

[37] On the financing of ISIS, see UN Security Council, Report of the Analytical Support and Sanctions Monitoring Team on the Threat Posed by the Islamic State in Iraq and the Levant and the Al-Nusrah Front for the People of the Levant, Security Council doc. S/2014/815, November 14, 2014, 20–21. (Hereinafter cited as UN Analytical Support and Monitoring Team, Report on the Threat Posed by ISIL.)

[38] For discussion, see Keen, Complex Emergencies, 13–14, 71–73.

[39] See Léonce Ndikumana and Kisangani F. Emizet, "The Economics of Civil War: The Case of the Democratic Republic of Congo," in Understanding Civil War, vol. 1, edited by Paul Collier and Nicholas Sambanis (Washington, DC: World Bank, 2005), 63–87.

[40] Floribert Ngaruko and Janvier D. Nkurunziza, "Civil War and Its Duration in Burundi," in Understanding Civil War, vol. 1, edited by Paul Collier and Nicholas Sambanis (Washington, DC: World Bank, 2005), 57.

[41] See UN Analytical Support and Sanctions Monitoring Team, Report of the Threat Posed by ISIL, 20–24. See also Borzou Daragahi and Erika Solomon, "Fuelling ISIS Inc.," Financial Times, September 21, 2014.

[handwritten margin notes: "wartime politics" / "More valuable to sustain fighting"]

It follows from all this that the parties to these contests are likely to perceive a strong interest in sustaining the fighting, rather than achieving military victory or an acceptable peace settlement. So long as the conditions of war allow key elites to continue their profiteering – especially when leaders on all "sides" are benefiting from the situation – they are unlikely to pursue a conclusive outcome, whether through combat or peace negotiations. "A common assumption" of outside observers has been that "the aim in a war is to win it," Keen wrote in 2002. In many recent conflicts, however, the aim of key combatants has been to preserve the economic benefits they obtain from the wartime political economy. As a result, "some parties may be more anxious to prolong a war than to win it."[42] To a considerable degree, this explains why so many recent conflicts have proved so long lasting, lethal, and destructive.

The protracted nature of the fighting, the widespread invocation of ethnic grievances to justify pecuniary activities and a heavy reliance on sheer brutality to achieve the contending parties' objectives are largely responsible for the heavy toll among civilians in these conflicts and the pronounced incidence of killing, rape, torture, ethnic cleansing, and other mass atrocities. Here, again, the DRC provides an instructive example. "Population displacement is the outcome of frequent armed conflict, with the predictable consequences of food insecurity, malnutrition and high mortality rates for both the displaced and host populations," the UN Panel of Experts on the DRC reported in 2002.[43] The situation in areas controlled by ISIS is equally dire, with members of minority religious groups often forced to turn over all their possessions to the Islamic State in order to escape execution, while many young women from these groups have been abducted and sold into sexual slavery.[44]

11.2.   The Pivotal Role of Resource Commerce

What distinguishes contemporary conflicts from those of the past, then, is the largely intrastate nature of the fighting; a heavy reliance on irregular, nonprofessional forces (with government troops often assuming the role of private militias); the widespread invocation of ethnic and religious grievances to justify exploitative activities; and the emergence of a "self-financing war economy" that creates incentives for the prolongation of combat. In all of this, moreover, we see the pivotal function of resource exploitation in driving the

---

[42] David Keen, "Incentives and Disincentives for Violence," 26–27.
[43] UN, *Final Report of the Panel of Experts on the DRC*, para. 94.
[44] See UN, Independent International Commission of Inquiry on the Syrian Arab Republic, *Rule of Terror: Living under ISIS in Syria*, November 14, 2014, www.ohchr.org/Documents/HRBodies/HRCouncil/CoISyria/HRC_CRP_ISIS_14Nov2014.pdf.

fighting and the accompanying atrocities against civilians. As documented in reports commissioned by the UN Security Council and other bodies, the extraction and export of valuable commodities figures in many aspects of these contests and the unique economies they spawn. These range from the original impulse to initiate armed violence to the financing of arms purchases, the recruitment of soldiers, the enrichment of rebel leaders and their associates, the mobilization of subject populations for involuntary resource extraction, and the solicitation of foreign support.

The importance of resource predation in the outbreak and prolongation of conflict begins with its role as a motive for commencing hostilities. Resource extraction may not be the only, or the major, motive for war and interethnic conflict, but it has often been a factor. As noted earlier, the presence of diamonds and other easily "lootable" resources has been an especially powerful factor in the outbreak and prolongation of internal conflicts.[45] In Sierra Leone, for example, the rebellion initiated by the RUF in 1991 was intended as much to secure control over the country's diamond trade as anything else. "Underneath the political issue on the surface of the conflict are the economic factors that drove the war from the onset," noted John L. Hirsch, U.S. ambassador to Sierra Leone from 1995 to 1998. "The alluvial diamond fields of eastern Sierra Leone have been the main locus of fighting and the RUF's base of operations from the start."[46] Control over the diamond trade was also a powerful motive in the conflicts – all including atrocities – in Angola, Côte d'Ivoire, Liberia, and the DRC.[47]

Other valuable commodities have also played a significant role in spurring conflict marked by atrocity crimes. In the eastern Congo, for example, it is the presence of gold, tin, coltan, and tungsten that has sparked much of the violence by local armed factions and foreign governments. "With minor exceptions, the objective of military activity [in eastern Congo] is to secure access to mining sites or ensure a supply of captive labor," usually for illicit mining activities, the Panel of Experts on the DRC observed in 2002.[48] In addition to local bands, a number of external forces – including troops from Rwanda, Uganda, and Zimbabwe – entered into the fighting in order to benefit from illicit mineral operations. "Rwanda's military appears to be benefiting directly from the conflict," the UN Panel on the DRC reported in 2001. In several reported cases, Rwandan forces attacked villages that were believed to house large

---

[45] For discussion, see Michael L. Ross, "Oil, Drugs, and Diamonds: The Varying Roles of Natural Resources in Civil War," in *The Political Economy of Armed Conflict*, edited by Karen Ballentine and Jake Sherman (Boulder, CO: Lynne Rienner, 2003), 47–70.

[46] Hirsch, *Sierra Leone*, 15.

[47] For background and discussion, see Philippe Le Billon, *Wars of Plunder* (Oxford: Oxford University Press, 2013), 85–123.

[48] UN, *Final Report of the Panel of Experts on the DRC*, para. 93. See also GAO, *The Democratic Republic of the Congo*, 16–18.

supplies of coltan, seizing all the available supplies and then flying them to processing plants in Rwanda.[49] Forces from Uganda are reported to have engaged in similar operations.[50]

Often, foreign leaders were found to have participated in these operations in order to secure wealth for themselves and their relatives and cronies, as well as to obtain financing for their security forces and government ministries. For example, Charles Taylor, while president of Liberia, agreed to help the RUF evade UN sanctions on Sierra Leonean diamond exports in large part out of expectations of extracting a significant share of the proceeds for his own use. "The [Sierra Leonean] government's inability to regulate the diamond trade through official channels allowed Taylor and [RUF leader Foday] Sankoh to finance the war and reap huge gains by smuggling diamonds through Liberia and Côte d'Ivoire," Hirsch observed.[51]

From all of this, analysts have identified and described a "transnational war economy" in which wealth-seeking government officials collude with rebel leaders and international business interests to perpetuate illicit resource trading schemes.[52] As Keen and others have noted, this system possesses many tentacles, including the ethnic militias and rebel forces involved in procuring the commodities, entrepreneurs involved in smuggling them out of the war zone, corrupt border protection and customs officers, and government officials involved in laundering illicit materials so they can be sold on legitimate international markets. Together, these actors have a common interest in expanding and preserving the war economy.[53]

Once these trade patterns have been established, combat commanders use the proceeds from illicit resource sales to acquire arms, pay their troops, and ensure the continuing assistance of foreign governments. This practice became especially vital after the end of the Cold War, when the United States and the Soviet Union ceased funding insurgent organizations as a way of subverting regimes linked to their adversary. To make up for this lost aid, rebel groups turned to resource trafficking as a source of funds.[54] This was especially the case in Angola, where UNITA had once enjoyed significant international financing but was forced, after 1990, to rely on illicit diamond sales to finance its operations. As observed by the UN Panel of Experts on Violations

---

[49] UN, *Report of the Panel of Experts on the Illegal Exploitation of Natural Resources and Other Forms of Wealth of the Democratic Republic of the Congo* (April 12, 2001), para. 126–134, 177–179.

[50] Ibid., para. 135–142, 180.

[51] Hirsch, *Sierra Leone*, p15. See also UN, *Report of the Panel of Experts on Sierra Leone Diamond and Arms*, Security Council doc. S/2000/1195, para. 98. (Hereinafter cited as UN, *Report of the Panel of Experts on Sierra Leone*.)

[52] Keen, *Complex Emergencies*, 49.

[53] Ibid., 31–49.

[54] See Reno, "Shadow States," 43–44.

of Security Council Sanctions against UNITA (Panel of Experts on UNITA), diamond trafficking became essential to all aspects of UNITA's operations. "[D]iamonds had a uniquely important role within UNITA's political and military economy," the panel noted. "UNITA's ongoing ability to sell rough diamonds for cash and to exchange rough diamonds for weapons provide the means for it to sustain its political and military activities." Moreover, "diamonds have been and continue to be an important component of UNITA's strategy for acquiring friends and maintaining external support."[55]

In addition to providing the funds needed to support ongoing combat operations, diamond sales were used to ensure the cooperation of leaders in neighboring states – an essential prerequisite for such activities as the clandestine acquisition of arms, ammunition, and other military materiél. "The Panel received corroborated evidence that [UNITA leader Jonas] Savimbi has used diamonds selectively to buy or to strengthen existing political relations," it reported in 2000. "It is clear, for example, ... that large quantities of diamonds and cash were given by Savimbi to the former President of Zaire, Mobutu Sese Seko, in exchange for favors to UNITA."[56] Similar gifts were given to the leaders of Burkina Faso and Togo, the panel noted. To secure the cooperation of President Gnassingbé Eyadema of Togo, for example, a top UNITA official "gave to Eyadema a 'passport sized' packet of diamonds on Savimbi's behalf."[57] Similar gifts were reportedly given to the president of Burkina Faso, Blaise Compaoré.[58]

In addition, it is evident that Savimbi – like many other rebel leaders – viewed illicit diamond sales as a means of acquiring wealth for himself and his close associates and their family members. According to the UN Panel of Experts on UNITA, at least some of the diamonds trafficked by Savimbi through UNITA's international networks were used "for the payment of salaries and stipends for senior UNITA personnel and their families living abroad."[59] The accumulation of private wealth from illicit diamond sales was also a significant motive for Foday Sankoh's 1991 invasion of Sierra Leone and for Charles Taylor's enthusiastic support for the attack.[60]

The centrality of resource predation is also evident in another, especially significant aspect of contemporary conflict: the high incidence of civilian

---

[55] *Report of the Panel of Experts on Violations of Security Council Sanctions Against UNITA*, UN Security Council doc. S/2000/203 (March 10, 2000), para. 77. (Hereinafter cited as UN, *Report of the Panel of Experts on UNITA*.)

[56] Ibid., para. 100.

[57] Ibid., para. 33.

[58] Ibid., para. 103.

[59] Ibid., para. 118.

[60] See Hirsch, Sierra Leone, 31–32. See also UN, *Report of the Panel of Experts on Sierra Leone Diamond and Arms*, Security Council doc. S/2000/1195, para. 98. (Hereinafter cited as UN, *Report of the Panel of Experts on Sierra Leone.*)

casualties and mass atrocities. This follows from the nature of resource predation itself. In many of these countries, the most prolific deposits of valuable materials – alluvial diamond fields, gold mines, old-growth forests, coltan deposits, and so forth – are located in remote areas that are occupied by minority or indigenous peoples with little allegiance to the government or the rebels. To secure control over these deposits and drive away (or enslave) the local inhabitants, the contending parties often resort to mass atrocities – typically including systematic rape, torture, mutilation, and ethnic cleansing.

Typically, the first objective of atrocities against civilians is to clear the resource-rich area of its inhabitants. In Sierra Leone, Keen observed, "notorious atrocities sometimes served an economic function in depopulating resource-rich areas with minimal military resources."[61] Extreme violence has also been employed by various factions to expel the existing inhabitants of mineral-rich areas in the DRC. In some areas, the UN Panel of Experts reported, forces aligned with Rwanda "have attacked and burned villages to seize coltan mined by some Hutu groups or local villagers. The Panel has taken testimony from villagers who have been forced to leave their villages following attacks."[62] In areas of Syria controlled by ISIS, mass executions and threats of violence have been used to force religious minorities, including Christians, Kurds, and Yezidis, to abandon their homes and villages, allowing systematic looting of their property by the Islamic State.[63]

The second goal of atrocities is to mobilize the vast armies of laborers needed to work the diamond fields and mineral deposits – a task often accomplished by forcing defenseless local populations to perform these functions for little or no pay. In Angola, for example, the Panel of Experts found evidence that UNITA had acquired diamonds by exploiting the labor of "people requisitioned for this purpose."[64] Similarly, in the eastern Congo, groups associated with the Rwandan army have been accused by a UN panel of conscripting resident Hutus "to carry out mining under forced labor conditions."[65] To intimidate local populations and ensure their compliance with their demands, rebel groups often employ severe brutality. "[E]xtreme violence, such as massacres of villages, rapes, and mutilations of civilians, may also result from efforts of the illegal armed groups and some units of the Congolese national military to generate fear and consolidate control over economic activities, including mining activities," the U.S. Government Accountability Office (GAO) reported in 2010.[66]

---

[61] Keen, *Complex Emergencies*, 27.
[62] UN, *Final Report of the Panel of Experts on the DRC*, para. 93.
[63] See Independent International Commission of Inquiry, *Rule of Terror*, pp. 5–7.
[64] UN, *Report of the Panel of Experts on UNITA*, para. 78.
[65] UN, *Final Report of the Panel of Experts on the DRC*, para. 93.
[66] GAO, *The Democratic Republic of the Congo*, 15.

From all this, it should be evident that resource predation plays a critical role in almost every aspect of contemporary conflict, including the mass atrocities that often characterize these conflicts. By imposing sanctions on such transactions, then, the UN Security Council and other concerned bodies seek not only to impede military operations, but also to eliminate the conditions under which aggression and mass atrocities arise in the first place.

11.3.   Tackling the Trafficking Networks

Imposing sanctions on the underground trade in resources is one thing; ensuring their successful implementation is something else altogether. Ever since the Security Council adopted Resolution 1173 of 1998, banning the sale of diamonds by UNITA, proponents of sanctions have had to grapple with the obstacles to their implementation embedded in the international war economy. In particular, they have to contend with the durability of the transnational networks established by rebel leaders and their business associates to manage illicit trafficking activities, along with the desire of some government officials in nearby countries to enhance their private wealth by colluding in these transactions.

The creation of these networks is a natural outcome of the trafficking process. To transport illicit commodities from areas of conflict to foreign markets and conceal their original source (and thereby evade sanctions), rebel leaders and their business associates must recruit a transnational cadre of collaborators – brokers, shippers, financiers, diamond cutters, customs officials, and so on – to assist with various aspects of the operation. These networks are cemented, of course, by their mutual partaking of the assorted benefits extracted from this commerce. As indicated by the panels of experts established by the Security Council to assess the implementation of UN sanctions on UNITA, the RUF, and other rebel groups, all sanctioned organizations have established networks of this sort to facilitate their illicit resource exports.[67]

The UN Panel of Experts on the DRC was especially revealing of the nature and composition of these "elite networks" in its 2002 report to the Security Council. "The networks consist of a small core of political and military elites and business persons and, in the case of the [conflict] areas, selected rebel leaders and administrators," it noted. To conduct their illicit operations, "the elite networks form business companies or joint ventures that are fronts through which members of the networks carry on their respective commercial activities." Most ominously, "The elite networks ensure the viability of their economic activities through control over the military and other security forces

---

[67] See, for example, UN, *Report of the Panel of Experts on Sierra Leone*, para. 81–89.

that they use to intimidate, threaten violence, or carry out selected acts of violence."[68]

In addition to support from these networks, rebel commanders require access to an intermediate site – one located somewhere between the war zone and major international markets – in which to launder illicit commodities for sale elsewhere. As noted by the Panel of Experts on UNITA, a key reason for Savimbi's success in circumventing UN sanctions was his ability to gain access "to locations where diamond deals can be transacted."[69] Such locales are needed because commodities originating in the sanctioned country cannot legally be exported to foreign markets and so must first be sent to another country whose officials are willing to attest that the materials originated *there*, rather than in the conflict zone. Similarly, it is illegal for sanctioned organizations to acquire arms directly, and so they must persuade a friendly state to acquire them on their behalf, using false "end-user certificates" saying the arms were for their own use and no one else's. In providing such services, the leaders of these intermediary states, or "third countries," are usually motivated by some combination of sympathy for the rebels and the receipt of personal rewards, whether in the form of cash, diamonds, gold, or some other inducement.[70]

As noted, Jonas Savimbi of UNITA devoted considerable effort to the establishment and maintenance of such alliances, paying particular attention to his relationship with President Mobutu of Zaire (the name given by Mobutu to the present-day DRC). "Until the overthrow of Mobutu in May 1997, UNITA used Zaire as a base for the stockpiling of weapons, and it used Zairian end-user certificates as the means by which arms brokers working for UNITA were able to obtain the weapons Savimbi wanted," the UN Panel of Experts on UNITA reported. "Mobutu provided Savimbi with the Zairian end-user certificates, and in exchange Savimbi gave Mobutu diamonds and cash."[71] After Mobutu's demise in 1997, UNITA established these sorts of ties with the leaders of Burkina Faso, Rwanda, Togo, and other states.[72]

In much the same fashion, leaders of the RUF in Sierra Leone maintained close ties with Charles Taylor in Liberia. Before the RUF invasion of Sierra Leone, Liberia was a minor diamond producer, capable of producing no more than 100,000 carats per year; once the RUF cemented its alliance with Charles Taylor, Liberian diamond exports to Belgium jumped to an astonishing level of

---

[68] UN, *Final Report of the Panel of Experts on the DRC*, para. 21.
[69] UN, *Report of the Panel of Experts on UNITA*, para. 80.
[70] See ibid., para. 82–86.
[71] UN, *Report of the Panel of Experts on UNITA*, para. 20.
[72] Ibid., para. 22, 33, 83, 103.

6.8 million carats per year.[73] Similarly, leaders of the various DRC factions established close relations with senior military officials in Rwanda and Uganda.[74] By establishing and preserving such ties, rebel groups have been able to circumvent the various sanctions on illicit commodities.

As members of the UN Security Council became aware of these obstacles to the implementation of the sanctions they had approved, they began to take steps to eliminate such barriers by crafting new measures – including additional sanctions – aimed at the dissolution of the international trafficking networks. After being informed by the UN Panel of Experts on Sierra Leone that "the bulk of RUF diamonds leave Sierra Leone through Liberia, and that such illicit trade cannot be conducted without the permission and involvement of Liberian government officials at the highest levels," the Security Council voted, under Resolution 1343 of March 7, 2001, to ban all diamond exports from *that* country – the first to penalize a nation-state for helping a rebel organization evade UN sanctions.[75] To ensure effective implementation of this resolution, the Council also established a Panel of Experts to monitor diamond trafficking in Sierra Leone and to identify individuals and companies deemed to be in violation of the measure.[76]

Steps have also been taken to ensure the implementation of sanctions on Angola, Côte d'Ivoire, and the DRC. When it was found that UNITA was continuing to export diamonds in violation of Resolution 1173 by trafficking them through neighboring states, the Council, on April 18, 2000, adopted a new measure, Resolution 1295, calling on Member States "to take immediate steps to enforce, strengthen, or enact legislation making it a criminal offence under domestic law for their nationals or other individuals operating on their territory to violate the measures imposed by the Council against UNITA."[77] To further enhance the implementation of sanctions, the Council voted to replace the panel of experts with a "monitoring mechanism" charged with the tasks of investigating compliance with the sanctions and informing the Secretary-General of any violations.[78]

Similarly, when it was discovered that rebel groups in eastern Congo were employing comparable techniques to finance their operations, the Council adopted several measures aimed at curbing such activities. Under Resolution 1896 of November 30, 2009, the Council called on Member States to observe Security Council guidelines for monitoring the trade in minerals and excluding any acquired from war zones in the DRC. A follow-up measure, Resolution

---

[73] UN, *Report of the Panel of Experts on Sierra Leone*, para. 112, 122.
[74] See UN, *Final Report of the Panel of Experts on the DRC*, para. 12–16.
[75] UN Security Council Resolution 1343, Security Council doc. S/RES/1343 (March 7, 2001).
[76] UN Security Council Resolution 1395, Security Council doc. S/2002/470 (February 27, 2002).
[77] UN Security Council Resolution 1295, Security Council doc. S/RES/1295 (April 18, 2000).
[78] Ibid.

1952 of November 29, 2010, requires the DRC government and neighboring states to take further steps in this direction. These measures are particularly noteworthy in that they reveal the lengths to which the Council has been prepared to go in establishing mechanisms for curbing the illicit flow of resources. Resolution 1952, for example, calls on Member States "to exercise due diligence" in procuring imported materials by "strengthening company management systems, identifying and assessing supply chain risks, designing and implementing strategies to respond to identified risks, conducting independent audits, and publicly disclosing supply chain due diligence and findings." To ensure compliance with this measure, the resolution also enjoined the existing Group of Experts on the DRC to oversee its implementation and to report on any future violations.[79]

More recently, the Security Council, under Resolution 2161 of June 17, 2014, has sought to impede the Islamic State's financial operations by requiring all Member States to freeze the economic assets of any individuals or companies found to be cooperating with ISIS. A second measure, Resolution 2199 of February 12, 2015, specifically banned all forms of oil commerce with ISIS and called on Member States to seize the assets (including tanker trucks and refinery gear) of those found to be in violation of this ban. This measure also called on Member States to take steps to combat the illegal trade in antiquities from Iraq and Syria.

In implementing these and similar measures, the UN and other interested parties have run into a recurring obstacle to their efforts: the fact that it can be very difficult to distinguish "conflict diamonds" and "conflict minerals" (commodities derived from an area of conflict under UN sanctions) from those acquired elsewhere. As a result, rebel groups and their government allies have been able to label commodities acquired from combat zones as having originated somewhere else. This was, for example, the strategy employed by Charles Taylor and the RUF to traffic stones from Sierra Leone on the international diamond market. Resolution 1343 of 2001 was intended to impede that approach by banning diamond sales from Liberia, but subsequent research revealed that smugglers were able to traffic their gems through other nearby countries, including Guinea and Côte d'Ivoire.[80] Similarly, it has proved relatively easy to disguise gold, coltan, and cassiterite from eastern Congo as being from Rwanda and Uganda.[81]

---

[79] UN Security Council Resolution 1952, Security Council doc. S/RES/1952 (November 29, 2010).

[80] See UN, *Report of the Panel of Experts on Liberia*, Security Council doc. S/2003/937 (October 28, 2003), para. 131, 133.

[81] For discussion of this phenomenon, see UN, *Final Report of the Group of Experts on the Democratic Republic of the Congo*, Security Council doc. S/2014/42 (January 23, 2014), para. 161–224.

These experiences have led to the construction of more rigorous measures – some established outside of the UN system (but with its approval) – to exclude illicit commodities from international markets. Of these measures, the most elaborate and well established is the Kimberley Process for controlling the diamond trade. First envisioned at a conference in Kimberley, South Africa, in May 2000, and finally adopted on November 5, 2002, the Kimberley Process Certification Scheme (KPCS) requires participating governments to establish import and export control regimes for managing transfers of rough stones and to employ a common documentation system for all such transactions. The process incentivizes states to join the process by banning all diamond imports from countries that fail to adopt these measures and by allowing those that do to claim that their imports and exports are "conflict free." As of December 2013, the KPCS had fifty-four participants (including governments, trade organizations, and interested nongovernmental organizations [NGOs]), and its members accounted for an estimated 99.8 percent of the worldwide production of rough diamonds.[82]

Since its inception, the Kimberley Process has enjoyed widespread international endorsement. In Resolution 1459 of January 28, 2003, the UN Security Council voiced its support for the process and called on all diamond-trading Member States to join. In the United States, moreover, Congress voted under the Clean Diamond Trade Act of 2003 to prohibit "the importation into, or exportation from, the United States of any rough diamond, from whatever source, that has not been controlled through the Kimberley Process Certification Scheme."[83] Many other states have adopted similar measures, and most of the world's industrial associations, such as the World Diamond Council, are participants.

Similar measures have been undertaken to prevent the export of "conflict minerals" from the eastern Congo. As we have seen, Security Council Resolution 1952 of 2010 requires that the DRC government and neighboring states adopt strict guidelines to exclude illicit commodities from their mineral exports. As part of these efforts, personnel from the UN Stabilization Mission in the Democratic Republic of the Congo (MONUSCO) have worked with DRC mining and customs officials to exercise improved oversight of commodities experts.[84] Several international organizations are assisting in this effort. The World Bank, for example, has undertaken Operation PROMINES to enhance the technical capacity of DRC mining oversight personnel, and the Organization for Economic Cooperation and Development (OECD) has issued "Due Diligence Guidance for Responsible Supply Chains

---

[82] "About," Kimberley Process Certification Scheme, www.kimberleyprocess.com/en/about.
[83] Public Law 108–19, 108th Congress (April 25, 2003).
[84] GAO, *The Democratic Republic of the Congo*, 4.

on Minerals" for companies extracting materials from the eastern DRC and other conflict areas.[85] The EU is considering legislation that would establish a certification scheme in accordance with the OECD due-diligence guidelines.[86]

Various governments have also taken a hand in these efforts. In accordance with the Dodd-Frank Act of 2010, the United States is preparing to assume a particularly significant role. Under Section 1502 of the Act, U.S. companies are required to take steps to exclude "conflict minerals" from their manufacturing activities and to report on the measures they are taking to "exercise due diligence on the source and chain of custody of" suspect commodities acquired from the DRC.[87] The actual steps companies must take in accordance with this measure were spelled out in a rule announced by the Securities and Exchange Commission (SEC) in August 2012. This rule requires that all U.S. manufacturers that incorporate certain minerals – tin, tantalum, tungsten, and gold – in their products must report on the origin of these materials and, if any were acquired from the DRC or neighboring countries, must demonstrate that vigorous action is being taken to exclude minerals tied to armed factions; if they are unable to provide such documentation, they must publicly state which of their products are not "DRC conflict free."[88] The U.S. Chamber of Commerce, the National Association of Manufacturers, and the Business Roundtable have filed suit to block implementation of the 2012 rule, but, as of this writing, the courts have ruled in the SEC's favor.[89]

In consonance with such measures, various trade organizations and governments are collaborating in efforts to establish mineral supply chains that can be reliably deemed "conflict-mineral-free." In 2011, for example, the State Department launched its Public-Private Alliance (PPA) for Responsible Minerals Trade, intended to support efforts to establish mineral supply chains from the DRC area that are verifiably free of conflict minerals.[90] One such project is the Conflict-Free Smelter Program, a clearinghouse for information on smelters servicing the computer and electronic industry maintained by the Global e-Sustainability Initiative (GeSI) and the Electronics Industry

---

[85] Ibid., 29–30.

[86] GAO, *Conflict Minerals: Stakeholder Options for Responsible Sourcing Are Expanding, but More Information on Smelters Is Needed*, Report to Congressional Committees, report GAO-14–575 (Washington, DC: GAO, June 2014), 10.

[87] Public Law No. 111–203, signed into law on July 21, 2010.

[88] Securities and Exchange Commission, "Conflict Minerals," 17 CFR Parts 240 and 249b, Release no. 34–67716, file no. S7-40–10 (August 22, 2012), http://www.sec.gov/rules/final/2012/3467716.pdf.

[89] For background on this matter, see GAO, *Conflict Minerals: Stakeholder Options for Responsible Sourcing Are Expanding*, 15–16 and footnote 30.

[90] U.S. Department of State, "Public-Private Alliance for Responsible Minerals Trade" (November 15, 2011), www.state.gov/r/pa/prs/ps/2011/11/177214.htm.

Citizenship Coalition (EICC).[91] Similar endeavors have been undertaken by the International Tin Research Institute, the London Bullion Market Association, and the Responsible Jewellery Council; in general, these efforts aim to identify and "certify" raw materials that have been deemed "conflict free" and to exclude from international trade any commodities of suspect origin.[92]

Efforts are also under way at the regional level to adopt and implement such schemes. In 2010, the International Conference on the Great Lakes Region (ICGLR), an intergovernmental organization of central African states, began working with NGOs to develop a certification program to ensure that conflict minerals are excluded from regional trade. Like the Kimberley Process, the ICGLR certification scheme will identify mines and smelters that are found to operate in accordance with the organization's conflict-free requirements. The group issued its first certificate in November 2013, to a mine in Rwanda, and the program was expected to be extended to Burundi, Tanzania, and the DRC in 2014.[93]

In addition, various advocacy and NGOs have taken steps to curb the trade in conflict minerals. For example, the Enough Project, an NGO based in Washington, DC, has put pressure on major manufacturers, including Intel and Apple Computer, to exclude such materials from their resource imports.[94] In response, Apple agreed in February 2013 to adopt effective measures for this purpose. "Apple suppliers are using conflict-free sources of tantalum, are certifying tantalum smelters, or are transitioning their sourcing to already certified tantalum smelters," the company noted on its website.[95] Intel followed suit in January 2014, announcing that it will not use minerals procured from conflict zones in any of its microprocessors. "We felt an obligation to implement changes in our supply chain to ensure that our business and our products were not inadvertently funding human atrocities," Intel CEO Brian Krzanich declared at the Consumer Electronics Show (CES) in Las Vegas.[96]

11.4.   Successes, Concerns, and Recommendations

The use of sanctions on resource trafficking to prevent conflict and mass atrocities is a work in progress. From its initial application in 1998, in

---

[91] For further information on this endeavor, see www.conflictfreesmelter.org.

[92] See GAO, *Conflict Minerals: Stakeholder Options for Responsible Sourcing Are Expanding*, 21–30.

[93] Ibid., 27.

[94] See Enough Project, "Conflict Minerals," www.enoughproject.org/conflict-minerals.

[95] Apple, "Sourcing Conflict-Free Materials," www.apple.com/supplierresponsibility/labor-and-human-rights.html on February 19, 2013.

[96] Joe Miller, "Intel Vows to Stop Using 'Conflict Minerals' in New Chips," BBC News (January 7, 2014), www.bbc.co.uk/news/technology-25636001.

Resolution 1173 on diamond sales by UNITA, this approach has undergone significant development. From simply banning illicit diamond exports, as in the initial Security Council action, to the introduction of complex oversight mechanisms, as in Resolution 1952 of 2010 on the DRC, the UN and its partners have developed sophisticated tools to ensure compliance with such measures. Many other organizations have contributed their vigor and expertise to this effort. Clearly, a great deal has been accomplished – but it is equally obvious that more work is needed to ensure the utility of this approach.

Recognizing this, what can be said about the effectiveness of these measures up until now?

Many observers believe that the earliest UN measures, on Angola, Liberia, and Sierra Leone, proved relatively effective in curbing the flow of funds to rebel groups, thus constraining their ability to fight – and, by extension, reducing the incidence of atrocities. In an assessment of the sanctions on UNITA, for example, the UN Panel of Experts determined that pressures brought on Savimbi's allies in neighboring states to sever their ties with UNITA had achieved considerable success, draining the rebel faction of operating funds and slowing the pace of its military operations.[97] Shortly after the death of Savimbi in 2003, a top UNITA official, Alcides Sakala, indicated that in the previous few years, "we found communicating more difficult with our outside supporters because of them [the sanctions] and some of our friends became more cautious."[98]

The sanctions on Liberia and Sierra Leone also proved effective in curbing rebel military activities. As most of the RUF's diamonds were smuggled through Liberia, the embargo on exports from that country effectively denied the RUF of a significant share of its operating funds. "The diamond embargo in particular resulted in an almost complete halt to the traffic in illicit diamonds from Sierra Leone to Liberia," Alex Vines observed in a 2003 assessment of UN action. Events in Sierra Leone in late 2000 and 2001 "also show that the threat and the imposition of sanctions on Liberia probably contributed to the RUF's decision to sign an unconditional ceasefire in November 2000 and its reaffirmation in the agreement of May 2001."[99]

Most observers have been less inclined to see success in the case of sanctions on rebel groups in the DRC. Although some progress has been made in establishing "conflict-free" mining operations in the eastern Congo, rebel

---

[97] See UN, *Final Report of the Monitoring Mechanism on Angola Sanctions*, Security Council doc. S/2000/1225 (December 21, 2000), esp. para. 65–71, 219–223.

[98] Interview with Alex Vines, Washington, DC, June 2002, as cited in Alex Vines, "Monitoring UN Sanctions in Africa: The Role of Panels of Experts," in *Verification Yearbook 2003*, edited by Trevor Findlay (London: Verification Research, Training and Information Centre, 2003), 253.

[99] Vines, "Monitoring UN Sanctions in Africa," 256.

groups continue to control some areas and to smuggle gold and other ores through clandestine networks of the sort described earlier. As noted, these groups have established close ties with friendly officials in neighboring states who have shown little inclination to surrender their profits from the lucrative trade. It has also proved much harder to monitor the flow of gold and mineral ores than of diamonds, which trade in a highly centralized and regulated market. For all these reasons, the UN Group of Experts on the DRC determined in January 2014 that far more progress would be needed to ensure the effective implementation of UN sanctions and similar measures adopted by Member States. Despite efforts to curb the trade in conflict minerals, "Many armed groups in eastern Democratic Republic of the Congo have derived funding from the production of and trade in natural resources," the group noted.[100]

In all fairness, it should be noted that UN officials are aware of the weaknesses in the DRC sanctions regime and have undertaken vigorous efforts to correct them. The problem of distinguishing illicit from legal materials in mineral exports from the affected countries, for example, is being addressed by the World Bank's measures to enhance regional monitoring capabilities. Similarly, the measures contained in the Dodd-Frank Act and the OECD guidelines on due diligence, only now being implemented, will result in additional monitoring endeavors. How effectively all these new initiatives will work in practice may not be known for several years.

At the same time, many doubts have arisen about the effectiveness of measures aimed at impeding the financing of conflict, and specifically conflict marked by mass atrocities, especially when these measures are unaccompanied by others of a political, diplomatic, and military nature. This was especially evident in the eastern DRC, where the ongoing violence made it extremely difficult for government officials (and their international advisers) to gain access to some mining areas in order to ascertain whether or not the minerals produced there could be deemed "conflict free" in accordance with the Dodd-Frank Act.[101] Security in the region only began to improve in the summer and fall of 2013, after the UN Security Council, under Resolution 2098 of March 28, 2013, established a new "intervention brigade" within MONUSCO to conduct "targeted offensive operations, with or without the Congolese national army, against armed groups" in the eastern Congo.[102] Vigorous action by this unit, composed of 3,000 seasoned peacekeepers, is

---

[100] UN, *Final Report of the Group of Experts on the Democratic Republic of the Congo*, 3.

[101] See GAO, *SEC Conflict Minerals Rule: Information on Responsible Sourcing and Companies Affected*, Report GAO-13–689 (Washington, DC: GAO, July 2013).

[102] UN News Centre, "Security Council Approves Intervention Force to Target Armed Groups in DR Congo," Press Release (March 28, 2013), www.un.org/apps/news/story.asp?NewsID=44523#.Us71ZbTvzx4.

credited with demolishing one of the most aggressive of the rebel factions, the M-23 (named after March 23, 2009, the date of a failed peace accord), and helping to bring a degree of calm and restored economic activity to the region.[103] Further success in curbing the trade in conflict minerals, the UN Group of Experts on the DRC noted in 2014, will require additional efforts to provide security in mineral-producing areas, enhance the capacity of local government institutions, and promote employment in legal commercial activities.[104]

Objections have also been raised to the implementation of the Kimberley Process. In December 2011, the advocacy group Global Witness – one of the principal founders of the process – withdrew from the operation after members gave their approval to a diamond-exporting scheme proposed by Zimbabwe. Leaders of Global Witness had been complaining of flaws in the process for some time, but claimed that approval of the Zimbabwe operation was the "last straw," by certifying exports by mining firms with close ties to the government of Robert Mugabe. Not only had these firms acquired the mining concessions after government forces used armed violence to drive off artisanal miners, resulting in an estimated 200 deaths, but they were also diverting some of their profits to state agencies widely held responsible for egregious human rights abuses. "Nearly nine years after the Kimberley Process was launched, the sad truth is that most consumers still cannot be sure where their diamonds come from, nor whether they are financing armed violence or abusive regimes," said Charmian Gooch, a founding director of Global Witness.[105]

In addition, concern has been expressed over the adverse impact of sanctions on noncombatant populations in affected areas. Even if successful in curbing the trade in illicit resources, it has been argued, such measures often penalize artisanal miners and their families who depend on such activities for their livelihood. In recognition of these concerns, the UN Security Council, in Resolution 2021 of November 29, 2011, enjoined the Group of Experts on the DRC to assess social and economic conditions in the eastern Congo. In its report of November 2012, the group indicated that the imposition of tougher controls on mineral exports had led to a decline in family income of miners engaged in illicit production, as ores from such mines fetched a lower price than those mined in accordance with officially approved schemes, but that most

---

[103] See Nicholas Kulish, "After Outside Pressure, Rebels in Congo Lay Down Their Arms," *New York Times* (November 6, 2013).

[104] UN, *Final Report of the Group of Experts on the Democratic Republic of the Congo*, para. 239–251.

[105] Global Witness, "Global Witness Leaves Kimberley Process, Calls for Diamond Trade to Be Held Accountable," Press Release (December 5, 2011), www.globalwitness.org/library /global-witness-leaves-kimberley-process-calls-diamond-trade-be-held-accountable.

miners quickly adapted to the new trading regime or switched to other income-producing activities.[106]

As of this writing, it is impossible to assess the impact of UN sanctions on the Islamic State, especially as these have been accompanied by U.S. air strikes against economic targets (including oil refineries) in ISIS-controlled territories. Some observers have reported a contraction in the Islamic State's economic resources as a result of both sanctions and air strikes, producing some defections and internal dissension.[107] Nevertheless, ISIS remains a potent military force and continues to mount periodic offensives against government forces in both Iraq and Syria.

On balance, then, it can be said that these measures have achieved some success, but remain imperfect in many respects. It follows, then, that greater effort should to be taken to improve the implementation of these measures – as, in fact, the UN and associated bodies are attempting to do. At the same time, it has become evident that such measures must often be accompanied by more vigorous steps, such as the deployment of specialized peacekeeping forces (akin to the "intervention brigade" employed in the DRC) and the provision of increased employment opportunities in legal occupations. But aside from the question of their effective implementation per se, and in the light of the subject of this book, there is a larger question: is the imposition of sanctions on illicit resource trafficking a useful strategy for preventing genocide and mass atrocities?

If the test of this question is whether or not the adoption of such measures has succeeded in preventing outbreaks of mass atrocities, then the answer must be "No." Too many such events have occurred in recent years despite the introduction of sanctions. But perhaps that is setting the bar too high. If we ask instead whether the adoption of these measures has made it *harder* for potential perpetrators to initiate and sustain mass atrocities, then the answer might be "Yes, but only when the international community has demonstrated relative unity in its determination to curb illicit resource trafficking and to couple sanctions with other measures, such as the provision of security and supply-chain oversight." This is most evident in the DRC, where combined action by the UN Intervention Brigade and Congolese government forces has resulted in the eradication of some armed bands (or their absorption into government forces) while assorted international efforts have facilitated the emergence of conflict-free mining operations. When and if such conditions can be replicated in the future, sanctions on illicit resource trafficking can help

---

[106] UN, *Report of the Group of Experts on the Democratic Republic of the Congo*, Security Council doc. S/2012/843 (November 15, 2012), para. 220–239.

[107] Helene Cooper, Anne Bernard, and Eric Schmitt, "Battered but Unbowed, ISIS Is Still on the Offensive," *New York Times*, March 14, 2015.

deprive violent groups of operating funds and so reduce the risk of mass atrocities.

However imperfect in execution, sanctions on resource trafficking speak to two of the most fundamental characteristics of contemporary conflict and mass violence: first, that many of these episodes are driven by a desire on the part of their perpetrators to profit from the export and sale of valuable commodities; and second, that the original perpetrators of the violence are often aided by elaborate networks of "enablers" – smugglers, corrupt officials, and witting entrepreneurs – in conducting these operations. By seeking to impede these exports, the sanctions not only deprive the perpetrators of operating funds but also expose and "shame" the assorted enablers, thereby reducing their ability and inclination to engage in further such activities. On top of this, the measures being put in place to implement Section 1502 of the Dodd-Frank Act require that major U.S. manufacturers engage in due diligence to avoid the incorporation of conflict minerals in their products, thus mobilizing some of the world's most powerful entities in the struggle to prevent mass atrocities. Once individual firms agree to abide by such measures, moreover, they have a vested interest in persuading others to do likewise – thereby expanding efforts to isolate traffickers. When announcing his company's decision to exclude conflict minerals from its products at the 2014 Consumer Electronic Show, Intel CEO Brian Krzanich exhorted the "entire industry" to follow in its footsteps.[108]

Only time will tell if these and other such endeavors will succeed in having a lasting effect in reducing the incidence and magnitude of genocide and mass atrocities. Unforeseen developments of many kinds can alter the current world order, producing a more permissive environment for systematic, large-scale violence against targeted populations. In the meantime, however, the introduction and continuing refinement of sanctions on illicit resource trafficking offers the international community a useful tool that – in conjunction with other measures – can help reduce the level and frequency of mass atrocities.

[108] As quoted in Miller, "Intel Vows to Stop Using 'Conflict Minerals' in New Chips."

12   Deconstructing Risk and Developing Resilience: The Role of Inhibitory Factors in Genocide Prevention

Deborah Mayersen

12.1.   Introduction

"'Genocide' Charge in Rwanda" blared the headline in The *Times*; a few days later it was "Rwanda Policy of Genocide Alleged."[1] This was not, however, April 1994, when genocide erupted in Rwanda with unprecedented ferocity, but rather January 1964. After a ragtag group of Tutsi refugees, displaced to neighboring countries during the decolonization process, launched the Bugesera invasion in December 1963, fear and panic led to the outbreak of massacres of Tutsi, resulting in 10,000 to 14,000 deaths in December and January.[2] At first it seemed as though the worst fears of many would be realized. Just two years earlier, United Nations Commissioner Majid Rahnema, sent to Rwanda as part of a UN Visiting Commission in response to unrest there, had reported back that the tiny nation was at grave risk of genocide.[3] Yet, before news of the massacres had even reached Western newspapers, they were over. UN Commissioner Max Dorsinville subsequently reported, "There is no question of a systematic elimination or extermination of the Tutsi, or of what some sources have hastened to call genocide."[4] If the risk of genocide was real, however – as the comments of observers such as Rahnema and the subsequent 1994 genocide both suggest – what stopped the December 1963–January 1964 massacres from escalating into genocide? Why did the violence remain much more limited?

The central goal of this chapter is to explore the role of factors that inhibit genocide, even in circumstances of grave risk. The case of the 1963–64 ethnic

---

[1] The Times, Wednesday January 29, 1964, 8; The Times, Monday February 3, 1964, 10.

[2] René Lemarchand, *Rwanda and Burundi* (New York: Praeger Publishers, 1970), 219–227; Aaron Segal, *Massacre in Rwanda*, Fabian Research Series 240 (London: Fabian Society, 1964).

[3] United Nations, *Question of the Future of Ruanda-Urundi: Statement Made by Mr. Majid Rahnema, United Nations Commissioner for Ruanda-Urundi, at the 1265th Meeting of the Fourth Committee*, A/C.4/525 (January 23, 1962), 17–18.

[4] "The United Nations' Findings on Rwanda and Burundi," *Africa Report* 9(4): 7 (1964).

[handwritten in left margin: Burundi 2015.6?]

massacres in Rwanda is not isolated. In modern history, many examples can be identified where there appeared to be serious risk of genocide, yet eruptions of violence against targeted minorities remained far more limited in scope and intent. Some of these minorities, such as the Tutsi in Rwanda and the Armenians in the late Ottoman Empire, were ultimately targeted in genocides that occurred decades later. In other societies, such as the Dominican Republic in the 1930s, multiple preconditions for genocide can be identified, massacres were perpetrated against the targeted group (ethnic Haitians), but the violence never escalated into genocide.[5] Currently, however, there is only very limited knowledge available as to what prevents the eruption of genocide in high-risk situations. The vast majority of scholarship within comparative genocide studies has focused on cases of genocide where this escalation *has* occurred. Numerous models have been developed that identify the preconditions for genocide. Yet far less is known about factors that can arrest or reduce risk. In this chapter, I argue that the absence of genocide in high-risk situations is not simply attributable to the lack of necessary preconditions. Rather, in many cases, stabilizing and mitigating factors can be identified that actively limit and reduce risk. Furthermore, a greater understanding of the role of these factors can suggest new pathways for preventing genocide.

For the purposes of this chapter, genocide will be defined in accordance with the UN Convention on the Prevention and Punishment of the Crime of Genocide (Genocide Convention) as acts, such as killing or causing serious harm to members of a group, "committed with intent to destroy, in whole or in part, a national, ethnical, racial or religious group."[6] Political groups will also be included as potential victim groups, as is common in genocide studies.[7] Additionally, genocide will be understood as "the crime of crimes," involving large-scale attempts to destroy victim groups rather than outbreaks of violence more limited in scope and intent.

The chapter is divided into three sections. In the first section, I will examine how risk has been conceptualized within the fields of genocide studies and genocide prevention. I will then consider the relationship between risk factors and mitigating factors in influencing the risk of genocide and discuss

---

[5] Edward Paulino, "Anti-Haitianism, Historical Memory, and the Potential for Genocidal Violence in the Dominican Republic," *Genocide Studies and Prevention* 1(3): 265–288 (December 2006); Jared Diamond, *Collapse: How Societies Choose to Fail or Survive* (Melbourne: Penguin, 2005); David Howard, *Coloring the Nation: Race and Ethnicity in the Dominican Republic* (Oxford: Signal Books, 2001); Richard Turits, "A World Destroyed, A Nation Imposed: The 1937 Haitian Massacre in the Dominican Republic," *Hispanic American Historical Review* 82(3): 589–635 (2002).

[6] *Convention on the Prevention and Punishment of the Crime of Genocide*, www.preventgenocide .org/law/convention/text.htm (accessed January 7, 2014).

[7] For example, Barbara Harff, "No Lessons Learned from the Holocaust? Assessing Risks of Genocide and Political Mass Murder since 1955," *American Political Science Review* 97(1): 57–73 (February 2003).

alternative methodological approaches that can offer fresh insight in this area. The second section of the chapter will focus directly on the role of mitigating factors in arresting and reducing the risk of genocide. Utilizing several high-risk but nongenocidal case studies as examples, I propose that mitigating factors can be grouped into three broad categories arranged around perpetrator, bystander, and victim agency. Finally, I will conclude by considering how greater knowledge of the role of factors that stabilize and reduce risk of genocide can offer practical insights for the field of genocide prevention.

12.2.   Deconstructing Risk

In the past three decades, genocide studies scholars have made great strides in identifying and understanding the role of factors that increase the risk of genocide. There is fairly broad agreement around several key preconditions:

- A plural and divided society, in which there are one or more disadvantaged "outgroups," typically subject to discrimination and persecution[8]
- Internal strife, such as war, economic crisis, political crisis, or other real or perceived difficulties that substantially impact upon the at-risk nation[9]
- The emergence of a genocidal ideology[10]
- Propaganda, inciting violence against the target group, and/or attempts to dehumanize the target group (e.g., depicting them as vermin or subhuman)[11]

A number of additional risk factors have been identified by scholars examining risk from a range of disciplinary and theoretical perspectives, and these provide a nuanced understanding as the field has developed over time. These include the role of political systems, formidable leaders, a context of wider war, perceptions of the victim group as posing an existential threat to mainstream

---

[8] Leo Kuper, *Genocide: Its Political Use in the Twentieth Century* (New Haven, CT: Yale University Press, 1981), 57–58;Helen Fein, *Accounting for Genocide: National Responses and Jewish Victimisation during the Holocaust* (New York: The Free Press, 1979), 9; Florence Mazian, *Why Genocide? The Armenian and Jewish Experiences in Perspective* (Ames: Iowa State University Press, 1990), ix; Gregory Stanton, "Could the Rwandan Genocide Have Been Prevented?" *Journal of Genocide Research* 6(2): 213–214 (2004).

[9] Fein, *Accounting for Genocide*, 9; Mazian, *Why Genocide?* ix.; Ervin Staub, *The Roots of Evil: The Origins of Genocide and Other Group Violence* (Cambridge: Cambridge University Press, 1989), 17.

[10] Kuper, *Genocide*, 84; Fein, *Accounting for Genocide*, 9; Mazian, *Why Genocide?* ix–x; Stanton, "Could the Rwandan Genocide Have Been Prevented?" 214–216.

[11] Kuper, *Genocide*, 84; Fein, *Accounting for Genocide*, 9; Mazian, *Why Genocide?* ix; Stanton, "Could the Rwandan Genocide have been Prevented?" 214–216; Israel Charny, "Genocide Early Warning System (GEWS)," in *Encyclopaedia of Genocide*, edited by Israel Charny (Santa Barbara: ABC-CLIO, 1999), 257–259.

typical methodology
process evidence →

society, and an escalating cycle of violence and impunity.[12] Qualitative research into the risk factors for genocide has been complemented by quantitative approaches that have sought to examine antecedents statistically.[13] Although different approaches have sometimes yielded very different findings, collectively, this research has vastly expanded our understanding of the factors that lead to genocide.

One of the reasons for this success has been the effectiveness of the dominant methodology, which involves identifying historical cases of genocide, then examining events in the period leading up to them. Qualitative scholars have typically selected one to four case studies, such as the Holocaust and the Armenian genocide, for comparative analysis. Quantitative scholars, by contrast, have worked with a larger number of cases, utilizing more expansive definitions of genocide (including politicide and other forms of mass killing), but have similarly examined their antecedents comparatively to identify cross-situational preconditions.

Yet, perhaps because this approach has proven very effective in advancing knowledge of risk, there has been little consideration of its methodological limitations – namely, that this approach both constrains and distorts our understanding of the processes that may culminate in genocide. In particular, limiting the selection of cases to those in which genocide has taken place limits the resulting analyses to situations in which escalatory factors were the dominant influence, while factors that contributed to resilience – stabilizing or reducing risk – ultimately failed completely, thus rendering them insignificant for analytical purposes.[14] As a result of this constraint in case study selection, both qualitative and quantitative research examining the path to genocide has strongly focused on escalatory factors. We know much more about risk and escalation than we do about resilience and mitigation.

In fact, genocide is rarely the culmination of a linear risk/escalation process, as many of the models of risk of genocide imply. Rather, even in cases that culminate in genocide, there are very often pre-genocidal cycles of violence, in

---

[12] See, e.g., Matthew Krain, "State-Sponsored Mass Murder: The Onset and Severity of Genocides and Politicides," *Journal of Conflict Resolution* 41(3): 332 (June 1997); Harff, "No Lessons Learned from the Holocaust?" 57–73; Staub, *The Roots of Evil*, 17; Charny, "Genocide Early Warning System," 257–259.

[13] For example, Harff, "No Lessons Learned from the Holocaust?" 57–73; Krain, "State-Sponsored Mass Murder: The Onset and Severity of Genocides and Politicides," 332; Ben Goldsmith et al., "Forecasting the Onset of Genocide and Politicide: Annual Out-of-Sample Forecasts on a Global Dataset, 1988–2003," *Journal of Peace Research* 50(4): 437–452 (July 2013).

[14] Stephen McLoughlin and Deborah Mayersen, "Reconsidering Root Causes: A New Framework for the Structural Prevention of Genocide and Mass Atrocities," in *Genocide, Risk and Resilience: An Interdisciplinary Approach*, edited by Bert Ingelaere, Stephan Parmentier, Jacques Haers, and Barbara Segaert (New York: Palgrave MacMillan, 2013).

which risk rapidly escalates, followed by partial resolution, in which there is a temporary amelioration of risk.[15] There can also be long periods of stability, even in the presence of multiple risk factors for genocide.[16] Moreover, the vast majority of cases in which there are some risk factors for genocide present do not result in genocide at all. Genocide is an extreme and relatively rare outcome. Far more common than outbreaks of genocide are incidents of civil war, forced displacement, repeated outbreaks of limited targeted violence, and situations in which minorities experience ongoing persecution but are not targeted for annihilation. A major limitation of the current methodological approach is that it excludes from analysis these case studies in which some risk factors for genocide are present but genocide has not occurred.

In the past six or seven years, the consequences of this omission have become particularly significant as research examining risk of genocide has been utilized increasingly by anti-genocide advocates and policymakers alike. For the first time, knowledge of risk factors for genocide has been used not just reflexively, to understand the antecedents of past genocides, but prospectively, that is, to identify countries and peoples at risk of future genocide. Several "risk lists" are now regularly published by civil society organizations. One of the most well-known is Genocide Watch's "Countries at Risk of Genocide, Politicide or Mass Atrocities," which utilizes an ascending scale of risk factors, based on founder Gregory Stanton's eight-stage model of genocide, to determine the level of risk in countries around the world.[17] The factors are classification (into groups based on ethnic, religious, national, or other type of identity), symbolization (giving names or symbols to these classifications), dehumanization (one group denying the humanity of another group), organization (of the genocide), polarization (extremists driving the groups apart), preparation (for the genocide through acts such as separation of the victim group), extermination, and denial (including attempts to hide evidence of the genocide).[18] Another widely cited risk list is the "Country Risks of Genocide and Politicide" list, originated and developed by political scientist Barbara Harff, one of the pioneers of genocide studies.[19] Harff's list denotes risk level through a numerical Risk Index Score calculated based on seven factors that influence risk of genocide and/or politicide as determined by Harff's quantitative research. These factors are prior genocides and politicides, ethnic character of the ruling elite, ideological character of the

[15] Deborah Mayersen, "On the Timing of Genocide," *Genocide Studies and Prevention* 5(1): 20–38 (April 2010).

[16] Ibid.

[17] Available at www.genocidewatch.org/alerts/countriesatrisk2012.html (accessed February 14, 2013).

[18] Full details of each category are available at www.genocidewatch.org/alerts/countriesatrisk2012.html (accessed December 16, 2013).

[19] Available at www.gpanet.org/webfm_send/120 (accessed February 14, 2013).

ruling elite, type of regime, trade openness, state-led discrimination, and instability risks.[20] Other lists include those by Minority Rights International, which identifies "Peoples Under Threat" and focuses on risks to groups rather than states, and lists that identify risk of intrastate violence more broadly, such as the Failed States Index.[21]

Risk lists for genocide and mass atrocities, however, have evolved from models of risk factors utilizing the dominant methodological approach. That is, they denote risk by identifying the presence of escalatory factors that were also present prior to the advent of genocide (or other mass atrocities) in the sample of case studies from which each model was developed. Thus far, they have not, however, utilized a parallel sample of high-risk but nongenocidal case studies from which equivalent information on the role of factors that promote resilience might be gleaned. This is a crucial omission given that the risk analysis is being conducted on nations in precisely this category. They therefore do not adequately incorporate the role of mitigating factors in reducing or arresting the risk of genocide. As a result, current risk lists overestimate the risk of genocide and mass atrocities, thus limiting their utility. Genocide Watch's "Countries at Risk Report – 2012" (the most recent available at the time of writing), for example, identifies forty-eight at-risk nations – a sizeable portion of the 196 nations globally.[22] Even at the highest risk level there are ten nations currently listed. This lack of precision in turn severely challenges the limited resources currently allocated to genocide prevention.

12.3.   The Role of Mitigating Factors in Reducing Risk of Genocide

The small numbers of studies that have explored the role of inhibitory factors in averting genocide have yielded some valuable findings. Chirot and McCauley, for example, have proposed three factors that contribute to limiting violence in many nations at risk of genocide and politicide. The first is that "competing groups ... can work out rules of conflict and conciliation that dampen violence and make the complete destruction of any of the competing parties less likely."[23] Second, "exchanges are worked out between competing groups that

[20] Barbara Harff, "Assessing Risks of Genocide and Politicide: A Global Watch List for 2012" [Electronic Version], in *Peace and Conflict 2012*, edited by J. Joseph Hewitt, Jonathan Wilkenfield, and Ted Robert Gurr (Boulder, CO: Paradigm, 2012), www.gpanet.org/webfm_send/120 (accessed October 12, 2011).

[21] Available at www.minorityrights.org/11337/peoples-under-threat/peoples-under-threat-2012.html; www.foreignpolicy.com/failed_states_index_2012_interactive (accessed February 14, 2013).

[22] Genocide Watch, "Countries at Risk Report – 2012," www.genocidewatch.org/images/Countries_at_Risk_Report_2012.pdf (accessed December 16, 2013).

[23] Daniel Chirot and Clark McCauley, *Why Not Kill Them All? The Logic and Prevention of Mass Political Murder* (Princeton, NJ: Princeton University Press, 2006), 96.

give them an interest in maintaining rules of conflict to limit damage."[24]
Finally, they cite the lack of extreme ideology. Both Leo Kuper and Manus
Midlarsky have analyzed multiple examples of at-risk but nongenocidal
societies to understand the role of constraints in inhibiting genocide.
Kuper's research into South Africa under apartheid, for example, concluded
that even though many of the risk factors for genocide were present in this
case, the overwhelming demographic majority of the underprivileged black
population and the white dependence on black labor were powerful
restraints.[25] Hamburg's more recent analysis of this case identified the
importance of individual leadership, most particularly that of Nelson
Mandela, in preventing crises from escalating; the nonviolent approach
adopted by the leadership in its struggle for freedom from oppression; and
the role of the international community, both in condemning apartheid and
supporting South Africa's transition to democracy.[26] Midlarsky's analyses
have identified two cross-situational factors that promote resilience in at-risk
but ultimately nongenocidal societies. The first is the "absence of loss."
According to Midlarsky, therefore, the behavior of Bulgaria and Finland in
refusing to cede their Jewish populations to Nazi control in World War II, in
contrast to other European nations in this respect, can be explained through
"the absence of territorial loss and its accompanying refugee influx."[27] The
second feature of such societies Midlarsky defines as the "affinity condition."
Potential victim populations may be protected by "large affine populations
or governments (ethnoreligiously similar or ideologically sympathetic,
frequently in neighbouring countries) with substantial political and/or
military influence."[28] Additional scholarship, some of which is discussed
further later, has centered on understanding the dynamics of risk reduction in
specific conflicts. Overall, however, the volume of scholarship in this area is
very limited.

Research into at-risk but nongenocidal case studies offers substantial
benefits but also presents new methodological challenges. In particular,
the identification of suitable cases requires well-defined parameters, such
as a clearly demonstrable risk of genocide. Current risk lists provide
contemporary examples, but their recent inception limits their utility for
examination of longer term factors. To guide case study selection for this
analysis, therefore, I have used the presence of indicators of risk of genocide

---

[24] Ibid.
[25] Kuper, *Genocide*.
[26] David Hamburg, *Preventing Genocide: Practical Steps Toward Early Detection and Effective Action* (Boulder, CO: Paradigm Publishers, 2008), 72–96.
[27] Manus Midlarsky, *The Killing Trap: Genocide in the Twentieth Century* (Cambridge: Cambridge University Press, 2005), 328–329.
[28] Ibid., 335.

that are well-recognized in the scholarship (as outlined earlier), but the absence of genocide itself (during the time period of analysis) to identify appropriate examples.[29] Present indicators of risk of genocide are a persecuted outgroup, internal strife, fears expressed by expert observers regarding the possible extermination of the group, outbreaks of limited targeted violence against the group, a genocide/politicide experienced by the group in the period prior to or subsequent to the period under examination, a time of crisis in which the risk of genocide appears to be heightened, an exclusivist ideology espoused by the dominant power, and propaganda presenting the vulnerable group as posing some kind of existential threat to the dominant power. Although not all case studies exhibit all of these risk factors, the case studies each exhibit several of them, collectively demonstrating clear risk of genocide. This method of case study selection also facilitates analysis of case studies at multiple points on the spectrum of risk of genocide. The role of factors that promote resilience can be examined at different levels of risk, both on the cusp of genocide and well before that crisis point. The case studies I examine in the remainder of this chapter are the Hamidian massacres in Ottoman Armenia (1894–96), the massacre of Tutsi in Rwanda discussed in the opening paragraph of this chapter (1963–64), the crisis in East Timor (1999), Bulgaria's treatment of its Jews during the Holocaust, the persecution of the Bahá'í minority in Iran (1979–present), and the treatment of Jews in Iraq and Yemen (1900–1952).

The results of my analysis are presented through the conceptual prism of agency. In any genocide or potential genocide, three primary categories of actors can be identified: persecutors/perpetrators, bystanders, and victims/targeted groups. Typically, in cases of genocide perpetrators possess a high degree of agency – that is, capacity to act in a range of ways – whereas the agency of bystanders and victims is severely circumscribed. The relative agency of persecutors, bystanders, and targeted groups can vary in several ways that contribute to nongenocidal outcomes, however. For example, the agency of potential perpetrators may be circumscribed, bystanders or targeted groups may have a greater capacity to respond to their circumstances, or there may be a combination of these factors working together. Yet the implications from each may be quite different for understanding the factors that promote resilience to genocide and for developing practical strategies that promote genocide prevention. In the following section, therefore, I examine in turn the impact of persecutor/perpetrator agency, bystander agency, and victim agency – utilizing historical cases for each – to carefully identify the specific factors involved in mitigating the risk of genocide.

---

[29] See earlier "Deconstructing Risk" section for scholarship utilized to identify indictors of risk of genocide.

12.3.1. Persecutor/Perpetrator Agency as an Inhibitory Factor: The Armenians in Ottoman Turkey and the Tutsi in Rwanda

Genocide is a crime of considerable magnitude. Regimes and their leaders marshal substantial resources for its perpetration and must have sufficient control of government, military, and territory to render it feasible. In addition, regimes must manage any threat of international intervention. In two historical cases, that of the Armenians in the Ottoman Empire during the Hamidian massacres in the 1890s and that of the Tutsi in Rwanda during the massacres in 1963–64, there is evidence that limits to persecutor agency functioned as a strongly inhibitory factor.[30]

Under Ottoman rule, the Armenians were a persecuted minority, with the reduced status of *ghiaours* (infidels) as Christians in a Moslem land. Following the Treaty of Berlin in 1878, however, in which the Ottoman government ostensibly committed to their protection, they were increasingly targeted through discriminatory laws and practices, onerous taxation, and through attacks from Kurdish brigands allowed to operate with impunity. Missionaries, consular officials, and observers remarked on the vulnerability of the minority to extermination and believed the government's practices demonstrated its malign intent.[31] The sultan, however, was constrained by the political weakness of the Empire, its dire economic situation, and the threat of Great Power intervention, as had happened following earlier government-sanctioned massacres of Christians in Bulgaria in 1876.[32] Nevertheless, in 1894, in the district of Sassoun, escalating tensions erupted into massacre when a Kurdish attack on the Armenians of Sassoun was supported by the Turkish army. During a period of three weeks, massacres swept through the region, more than half of the sixty villages there were destroyed, and more than 5,000 Armenians killed.[33] When Great Power protests about the massacre quickly lost momentum, a much larger outbreak of massacres occurred across Anatolia in 1895, mostly in regions in which the

---

[30] Deborah Mayersen, "Intermittent Intervention: Europe and the Precipitation of the Armenian Massacres of 1894-1896," in *Terror, War, Tradition: Studies in European History*, edited by Samuel Koehne and Bernard Mees (Unley, SA: Australian Humanities Press, 2007), 247–270.

[31] See, for example, M. G. Rolin-Jaequemyns, *Armenia, The Armenians, and the Treaties* (London: John Heywood, 1891), 70; Ohan Gaidzakian, *Illustrated Armenia and the Armenians* (Boston, n.p., 1898), 205.

[32] Deborah Mayersen, *On the Path to Genocide: Armenia and Rwanda Reexamined* (New York: Berghahn Books, 2014).

[33] E. Hodgetts, *Round about Armenia: The Record of a Journey across the Balkans through Turkey, the Caucasus and Persia in 1895* (London: Sampson Low Marston, 1896), 111–112; Edwin Bliss, *Turkey and the Armenian Atrocities* (Boston: H. L. Hastings, 1896), 374; W. Spry, *Life on the Bosphorus – Doings in the City of the Sultan: Turkey Past and Present, Including Chronicles of the Caliphs from Mahomet to Abdul Hamid II* (London: H. S. Nichols, 1895), 281, reprinted in Vatche Ghazarian (ed.), *Armenians in the Ottoman Empire: An Anthology of Transformation 13th–19th Centuries* (Waltham: Mayreni Publishing, 1997), 624.

Powers had demanded reform. According to the German Protestant pastor and missionary, Johannes Lepsius, writing at the time of the events:

It is beyond question that the Turkish people, the military and the Kurds, knew that they were acting, not only under the direction of subordinate officials, who had promised them exemption from punishment, but by the command and in the name of the Sultan himself.[34]

In 1896, there was renewed violence, this time in Constantinople. Yet this massacre, "occurring under the very eyes of the Ambassadors and the European residents," roused the attention of Europe in a way that the previous massacres had not done, and "a cry of horror arose in England."[35] For a short time at least, the Ottoman government had a real fear of European intervention.[36] This was almost certainly a decisive factor in the cessation of large-scale massacres. Although the government continued with less aggressive tactics of persecution, it did not have the power to pursue continued massacres or escalate the violence in the face of potential European intervention.

During the crisis sparked by the Bugesera invasion in Rwanda in December 1963, substantial constraints on the agency of the government there also appear to have reduced the risk of targeted massacres escalating into genocide. At the time of the invasion, Rwanda had been independent for just eighteen months. For the first time, the country was ruled by democratically elected leaders from the Hutu majority, following the previous rule of the Belgian colonial authorities, who had utilized the pre-existing Tutsi monarchical system to cement their power. During the decolonization process, political parties had campaigned heavily along what were then perceived as racial lines, and political differences erupted into violence.[37] Hutu and Tutsi leaders and ordinary citizens were targeted in racially motivated murders, assassinations, and widespread incidents of arson. By the time of independence, some 100,000 of the Tutsi minority had fled Rwanda as refugees.[38] When a group of these refugees invaded from Burundi in December 1963, there was an atmosphere of panic and great fear among the Hutu of a return to Tutsi rule.[39] Although the

---

[34] Johannes Lepsius, *Armenia and Europe: An Indictment* (London: Hodder and Stoughton, 1897), 83.

[35] James Bryce, *Transcaucasia and Ararat: Being Notes of a Vacation Tour in the Autumn of 1876*, 4th ed., revised (London: MacMillan and Co, 1896), 517.

[36] Ibid., 518.

[37] Deborah Mayersen, "'Deep Cleavages that Divide': The Origins and Development of Ethnic Violence in Rwanda," *Critical Race and Whiteness Studies* 8(2): 1–17 (December 2012).

[38] John Webster, *The Political Development of Rwanda and Burundi*, Occasional Paper No. 16 (Syracuse, NY: Syracuse University Maxwell Graduate School of Citizenship and Public Affairs), 1966, 84.

[39] United Nations, Press Services Office of Public Information, "The Situation in Rwanda and Burundi," SG/SM/24 (March 3, 1964), in *Chronique de politique étrangère* XVI (Nos. 4–6), July–December 1963, 705.

invasion was easily repelled, retaliatory massacres erupted in which Hutu targeted the Tutsi in Rwanda, claiming 10,000–14,000 lives over the following weeks.[40]

Despite the presence of many risk factors for genocide – such as the presence of an outgroup, internal strife, and observers noting the dangers inherent in the situation – the crisis abated relatively quickly. Within weeks, calm was restored and further refugee incursions did not provoke renewed violence.[41] The government simply did not have the capacity to consider a centrally driven escalation of the violence. Rwanda's military consisted of only 1,000 poorly equipped soldiers who were wholly occupied protecting the nation's borders from further incursions.[42] A secondary contributing factor to this de-escalation was that the government was particularly mindful to avoid provocative action due to a real (although not necessarily accurate) fear of external intervention. The Tutsi "government-in-exile," which had formed in protest to the Hutu victory, had found a sympathetic audience at the UN and were keen to discredit the Hutu-led government and promote a need for international involvement. In response to what the Rwandan government perceived as a "neo-colonialist" threat, the government was focused on highlighting its moderation to the UN and international community.[43] Together, these factors substantially reduced the risk of genocide.

12.3.2. Bystander Agency as an Inhibitory Factor: The East Timorese and Bulgaria's Jews

In the case of East Timor in 1999, external groups campaigning on behalf of the East Timorese were a crucial factor in averting potential genocide. The nation had already experienced politicide, with more than 100,000 people dying from targeted violence and politically induced famine in the years after Indonesia's invasion in 1975.[44] In August 1999, the East Timorese people were given the opportunity to choose a future of autonomy or independence from Indonesia. After almost 80 percent of voters chose independence, massive violence erupted, with Indonesian-sponsored militias perpetrating

---

[40] Segal, *Massacre in Rwanda*, 15; Lemarchand, *Rwanda and Burundi*, 225.

[41] UN, Press Services Office, "The Situation in Rwanda and Burundi," 705.

[42] Fred Wagoner, "Nation Building in Africa: A Description and Analysis of the Development of Rwanda" (PhD diss., The American University, 1968), 298. There were no militia such as those that played an important role in fomenting violence prior to the 1994 genocide.

[43] Rwanda, Ministère des Affaires Étrangères, *Toute la vérité sur le terrorisme "Inyenzi" au Rwanda: une mise au point du Ministère des Affaires Étrangères du Rwanda* (Kigali: Service d'Information, 1964), particularly Annexe XI.

[44] Clinton Fernandes, *The Independence of East Timor: Multi-Dimensional Perspectives – Occupation, Resistance, and International Political Activism* (Brighton: Sussex Academic Press, 2011).

"systematic, widespread and flagrant violations of international humanitarian and human rights law."[45] The Indonesian military perpetrated a campaign of forced displacement of East Timorese into West Timor.[46] There was wanton destruction, with the majority of buildings in the country destroyed, along with vital infrastructure such as electricity and water supplies.[47] As an advisor to the Australian government later commented, there were fears that "very large numbers of East Timorese were being killed ... [and] that the killing could reach genocidal proportions."[48]

Outside of East Timor, intense media coverage of the violence "generated widespread outrage among ordinary citizens, and provided the basis for mobilizing protests and demands for international action."[49] Public outrage in Australia was particularly strong.[50] Ordinary Australians contacted their parliamentary representatives and demanded that the government take action.[51] Although the Australian government had outlined a policy earlier in the year that sought to avoid placing large numbers of peacekeeping troops in East Timor, public opinion compelled a policy reversal.[52] Australia signaled its willingness to lead a multilateral force and pressured the United States for support. The resulting diplomatic pressure on Indonesia from the United States, including economic pressure, along with other international pressure, led to Indonesia begrudgingly acquiescing to a multilateral peacekeeping force in East Timor.[53] The Australian-led INTERFET, the International Force for East Timor, was very rapidly deployed in a highly successful mission to quell the violence. In this case, international public opinion was instrumental in leading to an intervention that averted further mass atrocities in East Timor.

The experience of Bulgaria's Jews during the Holocaust suggests that far more localized bystander agency can also be instrumental in averting genocide.

---

[45] United Nations Security Council, Resolution 1264 (September 15, 1999); John Blaxland, "Information Era Manoeuvre: The Australian-Led Mission to East Timor," *Journal of Information Warfare* 1(2): 94 (2002); James Cotton, "Against the Grain: The East Timor Intervention," *Survival* 43(1): 127–142 (2001).

[46] Clinton Fernandes, "The Road to INTERFET: Bringing the Politics Back In," *Security Challenges* 4(3): 93 (2008).

[47] Ibid.

[48] Hugh White, "The Road to INTERFET: Reflections on Australian Strategic Decisions Concerning East Timor, December 1998–September 1999," *Security Challenges* 4(1): 81 (2008).

[49] Geoffrey Robinson, *"If You Leave Us Here, We Will Die": How Genocide Was Stopped in East Timor* (Princeton, NJ: Princeton University Press, 2010), 200.

[50] Fernandes, "The Road to INTERFET," 93.

[51] Interview with the Hon Bruce Baird, AM, Former Member of the House of Representatives, Australia (October 11, 2012).

[52] White, "The Road to INTERFET," 75; Blaxland, "Information Era Manoeuvre," 96.

[53] Fernandes, "The Road to INTERFET," 93–95; White, "The Road to INTERFET," 83; Cotton, "Against the Grain," 132.

Bulgaria was an ally of Nazi Germany during World War II. Although historically there had not been high levels of anti-Semitism there, German racial laws were introduced in Bulgaria as they had been elsewhere. In early 1943, the Bulgarian government made secret plans to begin deporting Bulgaria's Jews to German territories.[54] Deportations were to commence in March; however, the day before their commencement Dimitar Peshev, a prominent politician and member of the Bulgarian parliament, was alerted to the plan by an old school friend – part of a Jewish delegation who were desperately seeking intervention to prevent the Jews from their region of Bulgaria from being deported.[55] Peshev immediately intervened. Gathering some colleagues from the parliament, Peshev approached the Minister of the Interior, who agreed to postpone the deportation order after a dramatic argument.[56]

Yet the danger remained. Peshev prepared a letter for Bulgaria's prime minister, in which he stated: "[The measure to deport the Jews] is inadmissible not only because these people, while not deprived of their Bulgarian citizenship, cannot be banished from Bulgaria, but also because ... it would put on Bulgaria's face an undeserved stigma."[57] Peshev convinced forty-two of his parliamentary colleagues, across political boundaries, to join him in signing the letter.[58] Many of these parliamentarians, while not necessarily anti-Semitic, had up until that point been willing to quietly ignore the issue and allow the Jews to be deported to Poland.[59] (Although it was not revealed at the time, we now know the intended destination of the deportations were the Nazi death camps.) Peshev's intervention proved crucial. By making the deportations so public, the letter forced the government to reconsider its plans. Public protests were galvanized. Although the Jews of the Bulgarian-occupied territories of Thrace and Macedonia were deported, Jews from Bulgaria proper, who were Bulgarian citizens, were not.[60] Their position remained precarious for some months, but, ultimately, the intervention of Peshev and his fellow deputies was instrumental in saving more than 48,000 Jewish lives. It is important to also acknowledge the wider factors that contributed to the success of Peshev and his colleagues in saving Bulgaria's Jews, including the broader lack of anti-Semitism in Bulgaria, the role of

---

[54] Republic of Bulgaria National Assembly, *Dimitar Peshev*, 2011–2092, Yad Vashem Archives, 38.
[55] Ibid.
[56] Israel Gutman et al., *The Encyclopedia of the Righteous Among the Nations: Rescuers of Jews during the Holocaust, Europe (Part II)* (Jerusalem: Yad Vashem, 2011), 19.
[57] Bulgaria National Assembly, *Peshev*, 7.
[58] Record Group P.37, File 171, Benjamin Arditti Archive, Yad Vashem Archives, Jerusalem, Israel.
[59] Bulgaria National Assembly, *Peshev*, 14.
[60] Bulgaria National Assembly, *Peshev*, 26.

the Bulgarian Orthodox church in leading protests against anti-Jewish discrimination, the prudence of King Boris III in managing Bulgaria's relationship with Nazi Germany, and the turning of the tide of the war as these events unfolded.[61] Yet this bystander intervention by individuals working together proved pivotal in preventing the extermination of Bulgaria's Jewish population.

12.3.3. *Victim Agency as an Inhibitory Factor: The Bahá'í in Iran and the Jews in Yemen and Iraq*

In a number of high-risk but nongenocidal examples, potential victim groups have been able to leverage their own agency to mitigate the risk of genocide by securing the support and resources of what Midlarsky has referred to as *affine groups* – that is, ethnoreligiously similar or ideologically sympathetic populations or nations able to exert substantial influence.[62] The case of the Bahá'í in Iran is an ongoing example of a vulnerable minority campaigning vigorously for its own protection in response to government persecution. Genocide Watch, other nongovernmental organizations, and scholars alike have recognized and documented the vulnerability of the Bahá'í, a religious group, to potential genocide in Iran.[63] Present indicators of risk include their status as an "outgroup," legal discrimination against them, and repeated incidents of targeted violence against Bahá'í. Although the group has been a long-standing target in Iranian society, since the Islamic revolution in 1979, it has been at particular risk. After assuming power, the fundamentalist government systematically targeted the Bahá'í minority with executions, political imprisonment, prohibitions against religious activities, exclusion from government employment, exclusion from access to education, and a range of additional discriminatory measures. Concerted efforts from the global Bahá'í community, however, led to strong international awareness and condemnation of the Iranian government's actions.[64] Katherine Bigelow has suggested that this effort "helped prevent a massacre of the Iranian Bahá'í community."[65] The campaign has contributed to an ongoing focus on the human rights of the Bahá'í within the UN, with resolutions on the issue

---

[61] Midlarsky, *The Killing Trap*, 326–330.

[62] Ibid., 335.

[63] Genocide Watch, "Countries at Risk Report–2012"; Katharine Bigelow, "A Campaign to Deter Genocide: The Bahá'í Experience," in *Genocide Watch*, edited by Helen Fein (New Haven, NJ: Yale University Press, 1992).

[64] Bigelow, "A Campaign to Deter Genocide," 192.

[65] Ibid. Similarly, according to Leo Kuper, "The international surveillance initiated by the Bahá'ís would seem to have restrained the large-scale massacres that earlier appeared imminent" (Leo Kuper, "Reflections on the Prevention of Genocide," in *Genocide Watch*, 139).

almost every year since 1980.[66] Sustained international pressure appears to have been a contributing factor to the reduction in levels of persecution in the late 1980s, although social, economic, and cultural restrictions continued.[67] In recent years, there has been a resurgence in levels of persecution, and the Bahá'í in Iran remain an at-risk minority.[68] Nevertheless, evidence suggests that the Bahá'í have been able to reduce their vulnerability to genocide in Iran through a judicious campaign of international publicity to protect their human rights.

The ability of persecuted Jews to emigrate to Israel since its establishment in 1948 also appears to have reduced the risk of genocide in at least two countries. The Jews of Yemen, for example, experienced discrimination and the forced conversion of orphaned children to Islam in the nineteenth and twentieth centuries.[69] In 1947, an Arab riot against the Jewish community of Aden led to a pogrom that killed more than eighty Jews.[70] Over the following years, however, the vast majority of the community emigrated to the newly established Israel. In Operation Magic Carpet, British and American transport planes facilitated the evacuation of around 49,000 Yemenite Jews to Israel. This averted the potential for further or escalating violence, although the few remaining Jews in Yemen have continued to suffer persecution. The experience of the Jewish community in Iraq has many parallels.[71] Under Ottoman rule, the Iraqi Jewish community suffered some discrimination and persecution, but the population grew steadily. After a period of peace and prosperity under the British Mandate, conditions deteriorated in independent Iraq in the 1930s, both from the influence of Nazi propaganda and growing tensions in British Palestine. Discrimination escalated through the 1930s and 1940s, and, in 1941, a pogrom erupted in Baghdad.[72] By the end of 1948, Jews in Iraq suffered severe persecution, being dismissed from their jobs, forbidden to engage in many industries, and subject to arbitrary arrest and seizure of property.[73] In 1950, a law banning Jewish emigration was temporarily relaxed,

---

[66] For a summary of these resolutions, see Bahá'í International Community (BIC), *The Bahá'í Question: Cultural Cleansing in Iran* (New York: BIC, 2008), appendix II.

[67] Iran Human Rights Documentation Center (IHRDC), *A Faith Denied: The Persecution of the Bahá'ís of Iran* (New Haven, CT: IHRDC, 2006), 48; BIC, *The Bahá'í Question*, 4.

[68] BIC, *The Bahá'í Question*, 4–6.

[69] Isaac Hollander, *Jews and Muslims in Lower Yemen: A Study in Protection and Restraint, 1918–1949* (Boston: Brill, 2005); Tudor Parfitt, *The Road to Redemption: The Jews of the Yemen, 1900–1950* (New York: E. J. Brill, 1996).

[70] Parfitt, *The Road to Redemption*, 167.

[71] Nissim Rejwan, *The Jews of Iraq: 3000 Years of History and Culture* (Boulder, CO: Westview Press, 1985); Marina Benjamin, *Last Days in Babylon: The Story of the Jews of Baghdad* (London: Bloomsbury, 2007); Moshe Gat, *The Jewish Exodus from Iraq, 1948–1951* (London: Frank Cass, 1997).

[72] Gat, *The Jewish Exodus*, 17–25.

[73] Rejwan, *The Jews of Iraq*, 233–242.

and the ongoing persecution, combined with a series of bombings, convinced most of the community to leave. Between 1948 and 1951, the vast majority of the Iraqi Jewish community emigrated to Israel, many in a massive airlift, Operation Ezra and Nehemiah. Those Jews who stayed suffered continuing persecution, ultimately fleeing later. There is now no Jewish community left in Iraq at all. The ability of this group to emigrate to Israel most likely averted continuing and escalating violence against them.

12.4.   Inhibitory Factors and Genocide Prevention

The case studies presented in the preceding sections demonstrate that a range of stabilizing and mitigating factors have actively reduced the risk of genocide in at-risk nations in the past and can potentially be utilized for doing so in at-risk nations in the future. Utilizing the prism of agency, in particular, highlights the value of engaging with a full spectrum of potential approaches for promoting resilience in at-risks nations. Increasing the agency of targeted groups, for example, is an area that has been relatively overlooked. It must be recognized, of course, that potential victim groups are inherently vulnerable and do possess limited agency. Nevertheless, the case studies of the Bahá'í in Iran and the Jews in Iraq and Yemen demonstrate that, with the assistance of affine nations or groups, targeted communities can be empowered in ways that substantially reduce their vulnerability. Midlarsky, as noted earlier, has previously highlighted the role of affine governments or groups in protecting vulnerable minorities through threatening reprisals against potential perpetrators. There is potential for strategies to be developed that empower targeted groups as a means to ameliorate risk of genocide. Civil society organizations, for example, might undertake case-by-case analysis of potential pathways for empowerment. In some cases, it might be possible to foster a strong relationship between a vulnerable minority in an at-risk nation and outside groups or nations with the capacity to offer assistance or protection. Further research in this area may identify a range of approaches to pursue.

A broad conceptualization of bystander agency also offers new pathways for genocide prevention. Commonly, *bystander intervention* has been narrowly defined as military intervention on the cusp of genocide, akin to the events in East Timor. Such intervention can be highly effective (although it can also cause new problems), but the international political will required for it is often lacking. Even with the substantial resources currently dedicated to building political will, the prospect of multilateral intervention to curb or prevent genocide in any given circumstance is tenuous. The East Timor case demonstrates the importance of a particular nation being willing to take the leading role in an intervention, and, in many cases, there is no willing leader.

Examining the concept of bystander agency more broadly through a range of nongenocidal case studies, however, suggests the potential value of focusing on the role of less traditional actors in this process. The case study of Bulgaria during the Holocaust highlights that bystanders within a regime, rather than external to it, can make a critical difference. It suggests that, in high-risk nations, a concerted campaign to educate as many government officials as possible through a tailored program focusing on genocide prevention and the role of "upstanders" can have a real impact. Such a campaign could be organized by nongovernmental organizations or as part of an international aid program. Currently, such education is well-established in many Western countries, through organizations such as the Holocaust Educational Trust in the United Kingdom and Courage to Care in Australia, although it tends to target students and the wider community rather than government officials specifically. Organizations such as the Auschwitz Institute for Peace and Reconciliation in the United States are leading the way, targeting such education toward members of the U.S. military who may be deployed in at-risk nations and government officials and diplomats globally. Yet specifically offering such programs as widely as possible within all levels of government of at-risk nations could vastly increase its impact.

The role of constraints on perpetrator agency in reducing risk of genocide is already widely recognized. A credible threat of international intervention can be a highly effective means of curbing the genocidal aspirations of a belligerent regime.[74] Yet such a threat can be difficult to maintain. Regimes often pursue aggressive wars as part of their ideology, and international warfare facilitates conditions in which genocide can be pursued with impunity. Careful consideration of the role of perpetrator agency can suggest alternative approaches through which it may be limited. The valuable research of Barbara Harff, for example, has highlighted the protective role of international trade in reducing risk of genocide. The economic interdependence of trading partners limits each partner's ability to commit egregious violations of human rights without concern for the consequences. The political scientist Rudolph Rummel has explored the protective role of democracy in genocide prevention, arguing that democratic rulers typically lack sufficient agency to pursue genocidal goals, which requires higher levels of control over media, civil society, and government than are usually acceptable within democracies. This analysis suggests that there may be further scope for considering new ways in which the agency of potential perpetrators can be limited in at-risk nations.

---

[74] Vahakn Dadrian, *Warrant for Genocide: Key Elements of Turko-Armenian Conflict* (New Brunswick, NJ: Transaction Publishers, 1998), 160.

12.5.   Conclusion

For the field of genocide prevention, knowledge of factors that inhibit genocide is crucial. Certainly, knowledge of risk factors for genocide enables identification of at-risk nations, but knowledge of factors that promote resilience has the greatest potential for actually preventing genocide. A scholarship directly focused on identifying the role of stabilizing and mitigating factors, therefore, has a great deal to contribute. Furthermore, it offers the potential for an evidence-based approach to genocide prevention. Currently, we have a broad knowledge of some factors that may promote stability and long-term risk reduction. However, there are many examples of at-risk but nongenocidal nations that have yet to be analyzed for the role mitigating factors have played. Additional research, using these cases, into factors that promote resilience would increase the likelihood of identifying new strategies for genocide prevention.

13   Military Means of Preventing Mass Atrocities

Dwight Raymond

13.1.   Introduction: Prevention in Context

A recent military doctrinal publication describes mass atrocities as "widespread and often systematic acts of violence against civilians by state or non-state armed groups, including killing, causing serious bodily or mental harm, or deliberately inflicting conditions of life that cause serious bodily or mental harm." The document also defines mass atrocity response operations (MARO) as "military activities conducted to prevent or halt mass atrocities."[1] Most policymakers accept, at least in theory, that preventing mass atrocities is preferable to responding to them – not only because it saves lives, but also because even a modest commitment of resources to prevention may avoid the need for much larger outlays to repair the damage once atrocities have occurred.[2] As asserted in the 2001 International Commission on Intervention and State Sovereignty (ICISS) report, *The Responsibility to Protect*, the international community must "change its basic mindset from a 'culture of reaction' to that of a 'culture of prevention.'"[3]

Mass atrocity prevention is an important complement to the protection of civilians (POC), which consists of "efforts that protect civilians from physical violence, secure their rights to access essential services and resources, and create a secure, stable, and just environment over the long term."[4] It is also an

---

This chapter reflects the author's personal opinions and is not the official view of any U.S. governmental organization.

[1] U.S. Department of Defense, *Peace Operations*, Joint Publication 3-07.3 (Washington, DC: Joint Chiefs of Staff, August 1, 2012), B-1 and GL-4, www.fas.org/irp/doddir/dod/jp3-07-3.pdf.

[2] On the other hand, it may be pointed out that undertaking effective preventive efforts in every single country at risk of mass atrocities may also be quite costly in monetary terms.

[3] *The Responsibility to Protect*, Report of the International Commission on Intervention and State Sovereignty (Ottawa: International Development Research Centre, 2001), 27, http://responsibilitytoprotect.org/ICISS%20Report.pdf.

[4] *Protection of Civilians Military Reference Guide* (Carlisle, PA: U.S. Army Peacekeeping and Stability Operations Institute, 2013), 6, http://pksoi.army.mil/PKM/publications/collaborative/collaborativereview.cfm?collaborativeID=15. Also see Geneva Convention (IV) Relative to the Protection of Civilian Persons in Time of War (August 12, 1949), 75 UNTS 287, www.icrc.org/applic/ihl/ihl.nsf/INTRO/380?OpenDocument.

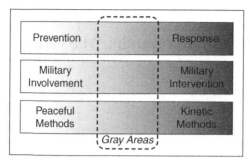

Figure 13.1: Military Prevention "Gray Areas"

integral component of the Responsibility to Protect (R2P) as conceived in the prevent-react-rebuild framework of the 2001 ICISS report[5] and the "three pillars" of R2P as defined by United Nations Secretary-General Ban Ki-moon in 2009.[6]

Although military forces are often viewed as actors of last resort with limited utility for mass atrocity prevention,[7] there are several ways in which they can be employed to shape a preventive environment and deter would-be perpetrators from committing atrocities. Indeed, in some situations, it may be appropriate to involve the military earlier rather than later, albeit in conjunction with other nonmilitary efforts. This chapter discusses a range of ends, ways, and means for the use of military forces to prevent mass atrocities, as well as criteria for their use and the potential risks. Unless otherwise stated, the discussion applies not only to international military forces, but also to the forces of countries at risk, both of which can be effective in preventing mass atrocities.

As depicted in Figure 13.1, it is often difficult to categorize the use of military force within precise boundaries, and there are gray areas between the extremes of a preventive peaceful military involvement, on the one hand, and a responsive kinetic military intervention, on the other. As this chapter discusses, these gray areas can result in a slippery slope to conflict escalation, protracted commitments, or other second-order effects.

---

[5] *The Responsibility to Protect*, xi *et passim*.

[6] The three pillars are: (1) "... the enduring responsibility of the State to protect its populations, whether nationals or not, from genocide, war crimes, ethnic cleansing and crimes against humanity, and from their incitement." (2) "... the commitment of the international community to assist States in meeting those obligations." (3) "... the responsibility of Member States to respond collectively in a timely and decisive manner when a State is manifestly failing to provide such protection." See *Implementing the Responsibility to Protect: Report of the Secretary-General*, UN General Assembly (January 12, 2009), A/63/677, www.unhcr.org/refworld/docid /4989924d2.html.

[7] For example, discussion of military prevention measures in *The Responsibility to Protect* is limited to stand-off reconnaissance, consensual preventive deployments, and the threat to use force. *The Responsibility to Protect*, 25.

> **"Do No Harm"**
> - Adhere to legal codes
> - Do not undermine nonmilitary efforts
>
> **Deliberate Actions**
> - Provide information
> - Protect vulnerable civilians
> - Influence potential perpetrators
> - Support positive actors

Figure 13.2: Military Protection of Civilians

Although it is tempting to try to make a clear distinction between "prevention" and "response," in practice the two overlap. Any individual activity, such as deploying a force to a location, may be classified either way, depending on the context or objective. Action may be taken in response to developments that presage mass atrocities[8] or, conversely, after violence has begun, to prevent a situation from worsening. Moreover, military actions often evolve incrementally, further blurring the distinction between prevention and response. Preventive considerations will also likely apply during the "rebuilding" phase after mass atrocities have occurred, as the risk of subsequent outbreaks of violence, with a renewal of atrocities, typically persists.

Some preventive military actions, and most response actions, fall under the rubric of "humanitarian intervention," a frequently used term, albeit one that is rejected by those who view the notions of "humanitarian" and "military" as mutually exclusive.[9] "Military involvement," in this chapter, is not assumed to be synonymous with "military intervention,"[10] although it is inevitable that a gray area also exists between these two terms, as it does between peaceful and kinetic military activities.

Whether preventing or responding to mass atrocities, domestic or international military forces can protect civilians in two ways, as shown in Figure 13.2. The first, which may be described as "do no harm," consists of

---

[8] For examples of such indicators, see the risk factors in the Analysis Framework of the Office of the UN Special Adviser on the Prevention of Genocide (OSAPG), www.un.org/en/preventgenocide/adviser/index.shtml.

[9] Alternative terms include "military intervention for human protection (or humanitarian) purposes," "humanitarian military intervention," and "armed intervention in response to serious breaches of human rights and of international humanitarian law." See Anne Ryniker, "The ICRC's Position on 'Humanitarian Intervention,'" *International Review of the Red Cross* 83(842): 527–532 (June 2001) and "Humanitarian Intervention: A Contested Concept" in *Humanitarian Intervention*, 2nd ed., edited by Thomas G. Weiss (Cambridge, UK: Polity Press, 2012), 6–15.

[10] Intervention is often understood as interference in another nation's affairs through the threat or use of military force, but it may also consist of diplomatic or economic measures.

adherence to international humanitarian law/law of armed conflict, international human rights law, *jus in bello* precepts, and applicable codes of military justice and national laws. "Do no harm" also implies that military forces do not undermine any vital nonmilitary efforts to prevent atrocities, such as the improvement of governance, rule of law, or social well-being. Obviously, when domestic militaries in vulnerable states "do no harm," the likelihood of mass atrocities is greatly reduced. International militaries conducting routine peacetime activities, such as training, exercises, and presence missions, should also abide by this maxim.

The second consists of deliberate actions to enhance civilian well-being, such as providing a safe and secure environment for the population. While the overall purpose of the effort may be human security (e.g., preventing or responding to mass atrocities), such an operation may be pursuing other strategic objectives at the same time, such as defeating an aggressor, regime change, quelling an insurgency, ending a civil war, or peacekeeping. In situations such as these, atrocities and other forms of civilian harm may be collateral consequences, with their mitigation an important supporting task for military forces.[11] Whether civilian protection is a primary mission objective or a supporting consideration for other objectives, military forces can be used to provide situational information, protect vulnerable civilians, influence (i.e., reform, deter, or if necessary defeat and/or neutralize) potential perpetrators and negative actors, or support positive actors. Both domestic and international militaries can be employed to these ends.

Peacetime operational environments are likely to be complex, with military forces employed for other purposes in addition to mass atrocity prevention. These may include training, exercises, peace support missions, or other operations typically carried out as part of a regional presence. Such activities may be part of a steady-state pattern or intended to be of short duration. By adding a "mass atrocity prevention lens"[12] while conducting their operations, military forces can provide a secondary benefit to whatever their primary objectives may be. For example, they can help monitor conditions on the ground with an eye to risk indicators, thus enhancing early awareness of potential mass atrocities. Military forces may also help prevent mass atrocities by highlighting relevant issues during multinational and other engagements that are primarily intended to support other objectives. For example, a unit providing training to military forces in an at-risk country

---

[11] In some situations, action on behalf of victims will require an impartial force, such as a peacekeeping mission, to take sides.

[12] See Alex J. Bellamy, "Mass Atrocities and Armed Conflict: Links, Distinctions, and Implications for the Responsibility to Prevent," Policy Analysis Brief, Stanley Foundation (February 2011), 8–9, www.stanleyfoundation.org/resources.cfm?ID=445.

could add topics such as civil-military relations and human rights to the curriculum.

13.2.   Military Support of Mass Atrocity Prevention

Most analysis of atrocity prevention policy distinguishes between "root cause/structural" prevention and "direct" prevention.[13] Structural prevention addresses long-term grievances attributable to systemic shortcomings in a safe and secure environment, good governance, the rule of law, social well-being, and a sustainable economy.[14] In general, military forces support structural prevention with activities that constructively shape the operational environment to address systemic concerns. Direct prevention is more short-term and situational in nature, related to emerging crises and their proximate triggers. Military forces usually support direct prevention with activities intended to deter, impede, or punish potential perpetrators. Deterrence depends on a combination of credibility and capability to convince perpetrators that they will incur unacceptable costs if they take action resulting in, or likely to result in, mass atrocities.[15] Direct prevention may also include actions to stop perpetrators when deterrent measures have failed.

13.2.1. Ends

Strategy entails choices regarding ends, ways, and means. With respect to mass atrocity prevention, military ends are (or should be) derived from higher level policy goals, which may include:[16]

- Obtaining early awareness of potential mass atrocities
- Mitigating conditions that could increase the likelihood of mass atrocities
- Preventing the resumption and/or escalation of violence

---

[13] See, for example, *The Responsibility to Protect*, 22–25, and Bellamy, "Mass Atrocities and Armed Conflict," 4 *et passim*. Other studies use the categories of "structural" and "proximate" prevention.

[14] These areas are discussed in, for example, *Guiding Principles for Stabilization and Reconstruction* (Washington, DC: United States Institute of Peace, 2009), www.usip.org/pub lications/guiding-principles-stabilization-and-reconstruction; *Considerations for Mission Leadership in United Nations Peacekeeping Operations*, International Forum for the Challenges of Peace Operations (Stockholm: Edita Västra Aros AB, 2010); and *Protection of Civilians Military Reference Guide*.

[15] Different deterrent measures may be appropriate for different levels of perpetrators (i.e., architects, facilitators, and foot soldiers).

[16] Based on Dwight Raymond, Cliff Bernath, Don Braum, and Ken Zurcher, *Mass Atrocity Prevention and Response Options (MAPRO): A Policy Planning Handbook* (Carlisle, PA: PKSOI, 2012), 57 and 82, http://pksoi.army.mil/PKM/publications/collaborative/collaborati vereview.cfm?collaborativeID=11. Some policy goals have direct implications for military forces; others have, at best, marginal relevance for the military.

- Avoiding spillover of a conflict into the surrounding region
- Exposing perpetrators and their enablers[17] to international scrutiny
- Establishing the credibility and capability of the at-risk country or the international community to prevent or respond to mass atrocities
- Ensuring effective and timely provision of humanitarian assistance
- Protecting the rights of displaced and other vulnerable populations
- Protecting potential victims
- Furthering the at-risk country's political stability, legitimate governance, and rule of law
- Dissuading, stopping, isolating, or punishing perpetrators and/or their enablers
- Diminishing perpetrator motivation or capability to conduct mass atrocities
- Building and demonstrating international resolve
- Convincing bystanders and other actors not to support perpetrators and to take constructive action to mitigate mass atrocities

Political leaders decide whether and how military forces will be used to prevent mass atrocities and should provide requisite guidance in the form of policy goals or objectives that clarify the formulation of military ends. These decisions will likely derive from international authorization (such as a UN Security Council Resolution or an invitation by the host government) and include an act of national policy establishing that a nation's use of its military is legitimate under its own laws.

13.2.2. Ways

Internationally deployed military forces and those of an at-risk country may help prevent mass atrocities in six general ways:

- Improve situational understanding of mass atrocity conditions
- Shape a stable environment with capable and legitimate security institutions
- Support and enable other, nonmilitary efforts (e.g., diplomacy and humanitarian assistance)
- "Rattle sabers" to intimidate and deter potential perpetrators
- Plan and prepare for future contingencies, including coercive action against perpetrators
- Conduct limited operations to protect victims or neutralize perpetrators (including peace support operations or preemptive actions)

---

[17] "Enablers" are third parties that provide material, monetary, moral, political, or other support to perpetrators. They may be indispensable to perpetrators and also be susceptible to outside pressure. For a comprehensive analysis of the role of third-party enablers and ways to influence them, see Human Rights First, "Disrupting the Supply Chain for Mass Atrocities: How to Stop Third-Party Enablers of Genocide and Other Crimes against Humanity" (July 2011), www.humanrightsfirst.org/2011/07/07/disrupting-the-supply-chain-for-mass-atrocities/.

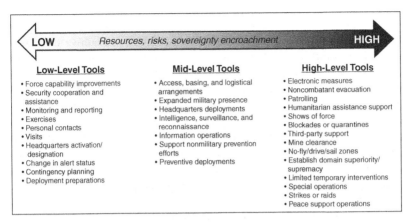

Figure 13.3: Military Prevention Tools

13.2.3. Means

The "prevention toolbox" discussed later comprises the military means or instruments available to shape a positive environment, deter perpetrators, or support both functions.[18] Some tools are suitable for domestic military forces, some for international forces, and many apply to both. Military efforts should be integrated into a comprehensive approach that may also include political/diplomatic, informational, and economic measures. These options invariably incur a cost in time and resources and have potential risks that are discussed later in the chapter. Many options may impinge, to some degree, on the sovereignty of the at-risk country. Some could easily transit from prevention, through the gray areas discussed earlier, into the domains of response, intervention, and kinetic methods. Figure 13.3 loosely groups potential military tools into three categories based on the associated level of resources required, risk incurred, and degree to which they encroach on sovereignty.

The categorization in Figure 13.3 is subjective and not fixed, as many of the tools fall into different groups depending on the circumstances. Additionally, the tools are not necessarily mutually exclusive, and, in all likelihood, a combination of measures will need to be considered.

---

[18] Based on Sarah Sewall, Dwight Raymond, and Sally Chin, *Mass Atrocity Response Operations (MARO): A Military Planning Handbook* (Cambridge, MA: President and Fellows of Harvard College, 2010), 120–127, www.hks.harvard.edu/centers/carr/programs /mass-atrocity-response-operations/publications/military-planning-handbook, and *MAPRO Handbook*, 69–70 and 103–115.

13.2.3.1. Low-Level Tools

- **Force Capability Improvements:** Military forces can improve their own internal capabilities related to mass atrocity prevention, including the ability to deploy rapidly. Doctrine, training, exercises, and leader education can provide qualitative improvements in a unit. Capability may also be enhanced by modifying units and staffs or adding equipment. For example, a unit may be allocated specialists to assist with the investigation of mass atrocity sites, or light infantry may be provided vehicles to improve their ability to patrol wider areas. If the "force" in question is some sort of multinational or other composite organization, the improvements are likely to be particularly needed, and the procedures to achieve them are apt to be especially complex and time-consuming.

- **Security Cooperation and Assistance:** Military forces can help improve the capabilities of security forces in the at-risk country, the region, and in international forces or their troop-contributing countries (TCCs). Assistance may include training, equipment, facility development, resources, logistics, intelligence, or communications. In addition to focusing on traditional areas such as marksmanship, staff training, and operational exercises, assistance programs may also address human rights, civil-military relations, protection of civilians, legal training, and other topics to help decrease the likelihood that forces being trained will take part in mass atrocities.

- **Monitoring and Reporting:** Military assets can help clarify the risk of a mass atrocity situation. In some cases, dedicated teams may be dispatched to the at-risk country or region to conduct surveys and assessments, or military personnel may augment civilian teams formed for that purpose. Military units that are already present for other purposes, such as training, may incorporate a "mass atrocity prevention lens" and add this function to their primary responsibilities.

- **Exercises:** Military forces frequently conduct exercises, and mass atrocity scenarios may be particularly beneficial because they represent complex, worst-case situations. They are also likely to gain the interest and participation of key nonmilitary organizations. Previously scheduled exercises may be recast with a view to preventing mass atrocities. New exercises specifically aimed at a potential threat can also be conducted. Media emphasis on the exercises can send a deterrent message to potential perpetrators. Although it is obviously better if these exercises include units that will actually participate in any subsequent operation, there may still be a deterrent benefit if other units are involved.

- **Personal Contacts:** Transnational personal military relationships often exist and, in some cases, may be utilized to help emphasize atrocity prevention.

Communications between military counterparts may be beneficial, but care should be taken that they do not undermine civilian authority.

- **Visits:** It may be helpful for military delegations or units to visit the at-risk country and the surrounding region. Visits may be conducted to ascertain facts, mediate disputes, convey messages, establish presence, or to conduct reconnaissance and preparations for future activities. Visits by senior military personnel, naval vessels, or aircraft are the most likely candidates for these efforts. Port visits by ships may be particularly visible and influential and, in some situations, may provide an appropriate venue for negotiations with officials from the host state or parties to a conflict. Such meetings may help defuse the situation while conveying a deterrent message to potential perpetrators.

- **Headquarters Activation/Designation:** Meaningful planning and preparation cannot occur until the units to be deployed are identified. Once a headquarters and its subordinate components have been designated or activated, commanders and staffs can focus on their assigned and implied tasks and anticipated challenges. This measure may not require any actual movement, but it will probably require the units in question to disengage from their existing responsibilities and devote greater attention to the impending operation. This is a necessary early step for any actual employment of a military force and, if made public, sends a strong message to perpetrators. If the headquarters is a multinational organization, this step should be accomplished as early as possible.

- **Change in Alert Status:** Readiness postures of designated units can be heightened (e.g., by limiting the number of personnel on leave or preparing to deploy within a shortened timeframe). The designated units will also have to divert their focus from other activities and take tangible steps to respond if ordered, including orientation training for mission personnel and promulgation of plans and orders at all levels. With sufficient media attention, even a low investment of resources may result in significant public information benefits, while units will be better prepared for the operation.

- **Contingency Planning:** Military forces can develop contingency plans for potential scenarios, thus increasing the likelihood of effectiveness if in fact they are employed to prevent or respond to mass atrocities. Additionally, planning can be used to provide decision makers with informed assessments and policy options. Planning may be especially complicated for multinational headquarters or peacekeeping missions that are still being formed, particularly if adequate guidance is lacking. Contingency planning should address a range of potential scenarios but may be constrained if the contingencies are politically sensitive.

- **Deployment Preparations:** Units can begin preparations for short-notice deployment. Area-specific and cultural training should be considered if time permits. Again, media coverage can help signal resolve without demanding an irrevocable commitment, while still having a potential deterrent effect on perpetrators. Units will require maps, immunizations, supplies, and, in some cases, additional equipment suitable for the region. Predeployment survey parties and advance parties may be formed and deployed and equipment prepared for shipment by air, sea, or land. One requirement that may be problematic is interpreter support, which may be provided either by out-of-country native speakers or, once the force is established in the region, by local citizens. Interpreter recruiting efforts may help prepare for this contingency while at the same time providing a messaging benefit.

13.2.3.2. Mid-Level Tools

- **Access, Basing, and Logistical Arrangements:** If the existing military presence in the region is minimal, political authorities may need to negotiate basing and/or access arrangements in neighboring countries. Negotiations should begin as early as possible, preferably as part of regional contingency planning. Equipment and supplies may be prepositioned, airspace and maritime transit permissions arranged, logistical systems established, and support units deployed to the region. Airfields may be expanded to ensure they can handle military transport planes, and tanker bridges established to extend aircraft range. Sea-basing may augment land bases or provide limited early-basing capability if regional land bases are not feasible. This will improve the military force's capability for subsequent operations, expand the ability to maintain situational awareness, and potentially have a deterrent effect on perpetrators.
- **Expanded Military Presence:** Existing military presence in the region may be reinforced with additional forces. For example, ground forces may be increased, air force and aviation units may be added to a regional air base, or a naval group may be repositioned in the region. Any air and maritime forces that are already in the region may operate close to the at-risk country's boundaries and territorial waters and in regional chokepoints to assert freedom of navigation. This will familiarize forces with the area of operations, permit additional intelligence gathering, and, again, potentially have a deterrent effect on perpetrators.
- **Headquarters Deployments:** The force headquarters and subordinate command echelons may be deployed to the region, accept operational control of existing forces, and begin directing operations. This may be accompanied by public information efforts such as press conferences, news releases, and embedded media. These deployments may provide a head start for future operations, acclimatize the force to the region, and have a deterrent effect on would-be perpetrators.

- **Intelligence, Surveillance, and Reconnaissance:** Intelligence, surveillance, and reconnaissance (ISR) activity focused on a country at risk may be deployed or additional resources added to regional capability. These can include ships and aircraft capable of surveillance and intercept, unmanned aerial systems (UASs), satellites, and analytical capability. Increased surveillance may have a deterrent effect on perpetrators and their enablers if they believe their actions are likely to be monitored. Accordingly, results of ISR activities may be selectively released to reinforce diplomatic and informational efforts to prevent mass atrocities. If human intelligence (HUMINT) capability is deficient, collection networks may be developed or expanded. Although establishing a complete HUMINT network is likely to be time-consuming, early efforts may generate dividends later. In order to gather evidence of atrocities and assist in developing targets for a potential intervention, additional ISR assets may be committed to around-the-clock coverage of vulnerable populations or activities of armed actors in the at-risk country. This option requires reprioritization and a substantial redistribution of high-demand, low-density ISR assets, and there must be a careful analysis to gauge the impact on other intelligence efforts.

- **Information Operations:** Military information operations, including public affairs and psychological operations,[19] can support broader efforts to heighten awareness of a situation, gain support for policies, and influence perpetrators and their supporters. Effective information operations enhance the impact of other efforts, and successful employment of other measures often provides informational benefits as well. Whether preventive or responsive in nature, a military operation requires a dedicated information operations effort that effectively integrates audiences, messages, and means of delivery. Information operations are critical to atrocity prevention and should not be addressed as an afterthought. Any military force should include trained public affairs with the experience and media contacts to promulgate messages effectively. Military camera teams can document atrocities as well as prevention and response efforts. These teams may operate in a variety of risk environments, and their recordings may be used to support information operations, rebut deniers, and provide evidence. Psychological operations may include leaflet drops, jamming, and radio or television broadcasts, as well as covert efforts to affect the perceptions and actions of regime members, security forces, and the population at large. These efforts may dissuade mass atrocities, foment distrust within the perpetrators' ranks, weaken their morale, and reduce popular support for perpetrators and their actions. Potential perpetrators may be reminded that they have the option of

---

[19] In U.S. military doctrinal terminology, "Psychological Operations (PSYOP)" has been replaced by "Military Information Support Operations (MISO)."

behaving responsibly or suffering the consequences, which may include lethal targeting, financial and travel sanctions, or criminal prosecution.

- **Support Nonmilitary Prevention Efforts:** Military forces may provide support to nonmilitary organizations involved in atrocity prevention efforts. For example, a unit might be tasked to provide support to a civilian team on a fact-finding mission. Potential support areas may include security, logistics (e.g., basing, supplies, transportation, or other services), staff augmentation, or communications.
- **Preventive Deployments:** An international or domestic military force may be deployed preemptively to an area at risk in order to provide a stabilizing presence. A successful international example was the UN Preventive Deployment Force (UNPREDEP) established in Macedonia in 1995.[20] This measure might be considered when forcible entry is not required and it seems likely to defuse rather than ignite a volatile situation. The deployment may be intended as a show of force, to conduct peace support operations as discussed later, or to provide support to local police and civil authorities.

13.2.3.3. High-Level Tools

- **Electronic Measures:** Electronic measures may be conducted against telecommunications networks to disrupt communications, gain intelligence, or conduct psychological operations. For example, jamming radio stations may be effective in reducing incitement to commit atrocities, although jammers must be available in sufficient quantities and locations to be effective. Perpetrator communications may be disrupted to cause confusion; alternatively, perpetrators may refrain from conducting atrocities if they are unable to communicate with adequate secrecy.
- **Noncombatant Evacuation:** Military forces normally conduct noncombatant evacuation operations (NEO) in support of political agencies. Emphasis may be placed on evacuating foreigners, nongovernmental organization (NGO) personnel, or potential local victims from high-risk areas. Evacuation may remove civilians from potential danger, clear the way for subsequent operations by removing potential hostages, or prevent perpetrators from retaliating against civilian populations if higher intensity operations commence.
- **Patrolling:** Ground, air, maritime, and special operations forces may conduct patrols in a region or country at risk to improve awareness of vulnerable populations, perpetrators, or other aspects of the operational environment.

---

[20] See Henryk J. Sokalski, *An Ounce of Prevention: Macedonia and the UN Experience in Preventive Diplomacy* (Washington, DC: USIP Press, 2006).

They may also be used to extend the military force's presence and serve as an important preliminary step to future operations. Some patrols, such as ambushes and interdiction patrols, serve combat or other functions with a direct impact on other actors.

- **Humanitarian Assistance Support:** Military forces may conduct short-duration missions to support humanitarian assistance or provide transportation and distribution support for other organizations engaged in this activity. This may provide not only critically needed support but also a public relations benefit. As with many other options, any advantage to announcing the mission in advance must be balanced against the need for security. Military involvement in humanitarian assistance should be done in close consultation and coordination with humanitarian agencies and in accordance with the Oslo Guidelines on the use of military assets in humanitarian activities.[21] If air superiority is ensured, air drops or air-landing of humanitarian supplies may be conducted for needy civilians. This may, however, cause a chaotic situation if insufficient supplies are provided and should be a measure of last resort conducted in close coordination with humanitarian agencies.

- **Shows of Force:** Shows of force provide visible, but restrained, displays of military power. They convey the message that the force can operate with impunity and could inflict severe damage if desired. Once deployed to a region, forces may begin aggressive patrolling close to the nation's borders. Maritime forces may operate close to or inside territorial waters, air forces may approach or transit a country's airspace, and land forces may be positioned on the borders or conduct short-duration missions into inadequately defended parts of the nation in question. In situations where there is limited threat of air defense, low-altitude aircraft runs may intimidate potential perpetrators. Whereas an aggressive posture may produce a sobering effect on would-be perpetrators, it must be balanced against the risk of unintended escalation, accidents, or loss of military personnel or equipment to hostile fire. Additionally, if a show of force is actually a bluff, there is a possibility the bluff will be called. Early shows of force may be useful as deception efforts that draw the adversary's attention away from any potential future operations by the military force.

- **Blockades or Quarantines:** A blockade (which may constitute an act of war) or quarantine can be implemented to isolate the at-risk country or prevent the transit of selected items (e.g., weapons) and illicit trade (such as drug or human trafficking) that provides finances to perpetrators and their

---

[21] "Guidelines on the Use of Foreign Military and Civil Defence Assets in Disaster Relief," UN Office for the Coordination of Humanitarian Affairs (November 2007), www.unocha.org /what-we-do/coordination-tools/UN-CMCoord/publications.

enablers. Blockades may intercept all shipments, selected shipments, or simply entail the stop and search of carriers as a form of harassment. This measure may be implemented in conjunction with economic sanctions. The risk of straining relations with countries that are engaged in trade with the perpetrators or that own the transportation assets needs to be taken into account.

- **Third-Party Support:** Military forces may provide supplies, training, intelligence, and services such as logistical support to other actors playing a more direct role in preventing atrocities. Depending on the circumstances, the recipients of this support may be national security forces, rebel groups, self-defense groups from targeted populations, international or regional peace support missions, or other organizations. Domestic military forces may provide these types of support to police forces to improve local security. In contrast to generalized security assistance, this support specifically focuses on enabling immediate operational efforts to prevent mass atrocities.

- **Mine Clearance:** A military force may conduct mine-clearing operations on the borders of the at-risk country, within the country itself, or in its coastal waters. In addition to removing a potential hazard to civilians, this may enable subsequent operations or support a deception plan, and it may include the destruction of perpetrator capabilities to lay additional mines. In addition, the fact that a military force is taking active measures to prepare for an intervention may dissuade perpetrators from committing mass atrocities.

- **No-Fly/Drive/Sail Zones:** In some situations, military force may be used to contain perpetrator movements that threaten civilians. This presumes capability advantages that either deter perpetrators from taking unwanted actions or physically stops them from doing so. Although it may have limited effectiveness in some environments, airpower will probably be instrumental in the enforcement of any zone, and it will require significant resources. This measure may also be effective in setting appropriate conditions for any subsequent military operations. An effective no-fly zone will likely require neutralizing ground-based air defenses, and the imposition of any zone will probably require the will and capability to take kinetic actions. Such zones may not be sufficient by themselves, as perpetrators may seek alternative methods to target their victims. Zones should allow for the option of accommodating deliveries of humanitarian assistance to civilian populations.

- **Establish Domain Superiority/Supremacy:** Military forces may be employed to establish superiority (when resistance is not prohibitive) or supremacy (when resistance is ineffective) over the air, sea, or land. A fourth domain, cyberspace, is not as definitively bounded or controllable, but may also be worth considering. This may enable other efforts such as no-fly zones. It may be preferable to establish superiority/supremacy over a local area if resources are limited, the area of operations is too big, or the risk of conflict escalation is too great.

- **Limited Temporary Interventions:** A military force may conduct a limited intervention to provide local protection for civilians at great risk. Perpetrators in the area may be incapable of opposing the force or may be deterred from attacking them because of the implied threat of expanded intervention. Such actions may be announced in advance along with clear threats to perpetrators not to interfere.

- **Special Operations:** Special Operations Forces (SOF) may be inserted to conduct unconventional warfare or other operations. SOF forces are quickly deployable, flexible, easily acclimated to other environments, and occupy a small footprint while requiring minimal logistical support. SOF operations can organize resistance forces to undermine a complicit government, give potential victims the means to defend themselves, or divert the adversary's focus from other areas. SOF may conduct reconnaissance or direct action missions to disrupt perpetrators, attack key targets, direct air strikes, or enable future operations by other forces. They may also undermine perpetrator perceptions that atrocities can be concealed. Last, SOF may be used for nonlethal actions such as relief. For example, in 1991, during Operation Provide Comfort, SOF personnel deployed to Kurdish displaced persons camps to conduct advance preparations for the delivery of humanitarian assistance.[22]

- **Strikes or Raids:** Strikes or raids may be conducted against key military or perpetrator leadership targets in an at-risk country. In addition to degrading perpetrator capabilities, this may create a sense of vulnerability and dissuade adversaries from conducting atrocities. In some situations, initial targets may be primarily of symbolic importance, with an implied threat of escalation if necessary. Air and maritime assets may be employed, as well as land-based missile systems or artillery in adjacent countries if they are within range. With sufficient targeting data, cruise missiles provide precision and long-range standoff with limited threat to the firing platform. Unmanned aerial systems, if available and capable, also provide relatively low-yield and precise strike capability. In some situations, indirect fire systems may temporarily displace forward to extend their reach. Helicopters may be employed from adjacent countries or from ships to strike targets or provide surveillance. Raids by SOF or other ground forces

[22] See Gordon W. Rudd, *Humanitarian Intervention: Assisting the Iraqi Kurds in Operation Provide Comfort, 1991* (Washington, DC: Department of the Army, 2004).

can disrupt or confuse the adversary with a multifront conflict, attack critical assets, rescue hostages, or support deception plans.

- **Peace Support Operations:** Military forces may be employed in or assist peace support operations (peacekeeping, peace enforcement, peacemaking, peacebuilding, and conflict prevention). Peacekeeping operations are undertaken with the consent of all major parties to a dispute and are designed to monitor and facilitate implementation of an agreement. Peace enforcement is designed to compel compliance with resolutions or sanctions and, within the UN, is generally understood to occur under Chapter VII of the UN Charter. Military support to peacemaking may include military-to-military relations, security assistance, or other activities to influence parties in dispute to seek a diplomatic settlement. Peacebuilding consists primarily of postconflict diplomatic and economic measures to strengthen and rebuild infrastructure and institutions to avoid relapse into conflict. Conflict prevention efforts monitor and identify the causes of conflict and take timely efforts to prevent it from occurring, escalating, or resuming. A military force can support peace operations even if it is not formally participating in them. Existing peace support operations should include measures to assess and address risk of mass atrocity.

As previously mentioned, some combination of all of the measures listed here may be used, in most cases synchronized with diplomatic, informational, and economic tools.[23] Some of the measures are quite provocative, and many straddle an ambiguous boundary between the involvement of military forces in peaceful prevention and intervention entailing a war-like response.

13.3.   Criteria and Potential Risks for Use of Military Forces

The use of military force in support of mass atrocity prevention poses a wide range of potential issues, even when it is employed in ways that fall far short of coercive intervention. It is invariably divisive. Whereas some favor more proactive use of military forces to protect civilians, reservations on the use of the military, both in general and in specific cases, are reflected in two broad points of view. The first tends to be deontological, reflecting an aversion to militaristic policies, reservations about neo-imperialism, or a concern for state sovereignty and/or international law. The second is more teleological and centers on the reluctance to commit blood and treasure in distant lands to a dubious mission with no vital national interests at stake (as Bismarck famously stated, "the whole of the Balkans is not worth the bones of a single Pomeranian grenadier").

---

[23] See *MAPRO Handbook*, 84–120, for additional discussion of nonmilitary measures.

When military efforts are contemplated, the debate should surround several questions:

- **Are military measures really needed?** Nonmilitary measures may be more appropriate, particularly if political solutions will be necessary in the end. However, military efforts can contribute to both structural and direct prevention by supporting diplomatic and political initiatives and addressing military-related gaps.
- **Will military measures be legitimate (internationally and domestically)?** Legitimacy is largely based on perceptions of the legality, motivations, and effectiveness of military action. Some suggest that certain actions may not be technically legal, but could still be "legitimate."[24]
- **Will military measures be worth the cost and effort?** This question matters in different ways to different audiences. Citizens in a country contemplating the deployment of its military forces may be more risk-averse than people in the country at risk of being targeted for mass atrocities. Other relevant audiences include neighboring countries that may be affected by military action or lack thereof.
- **Would the use of military force be effective?** Military forces are sometimes committed in a hasty or token effort to take action, addressing symptoms in the short term but subsequently failing to solve the underlying problems. Overhasty involvement can easily lead to mission creep and a commitment that transcends what was originally envisioned. An implied circular political-military debate also underpins this question:

POLICYMAKER:	What can the military do?
MILITARY PLANNER:	What is the mission?
POLICYMAKER:	I can't tell you the mission until I know what you can do.
MILITARY PLANNER:	I can't tell you what I can do until I know what the mission is.

- **What new problems will be created if military force is used?** Military efforts pose a variety of risks, as I discuss later, including the possibility of unintended consequences. If preventive efforts focus on symptoms rather than root causes, the same problems that led to atrocities are likely to re-emerge in the future.

There are two sets of criteria that may be helpful in working through the debate on these matters. The first is taken from the 2001 ICISS report and

---

[24] This was, for example, the conclusion reached by the Independent International Commission on Kosovo regarding the 1999 NATO intervention in Kosovo, which was not approved by the UN Security Council. See *The Kosovo Report: Conflict, International Response, Lessons Learned* (New York: Oxford University Press, 2000), 4, http://reliefweb.int/report/albania/kosovo-report.

generally tends to guard against the perils of aggressive or militaristic action.[25] This set is of particular interest to stakeholders in the international community. Although designed to guide military intervention under the R2P framework, it is also useful when considering many preventive military efforts.

13.3.1. ICISS Criteria

- **Right Authority:** Most observers agree that the preferred body for authorization of military force is the UN Security Council, although views differ about the legality and legitimacy of alternative authorities if the Security Council is unable or unwilling to make a decision.[26] On the other hand, this still sidesteps the question of whether or not the decision to take action by any single nation's political leadership is legal under their own laws.
- **Just Cause:** Action is reserved for extreme situations to prevent large-scale loss of life or ethnic cleansing resulting from deliberate state action, neglect, or inability to act.
- **Right Intention:** The primary objective of an operation should be to halt or avert human suffering. If other objectives exist, they should be subordinated to this purpose.
- **Last Resort:** Opinions differ as to whether every possible nonmilitary measure must be tried and exhausted before military means are employed. At a minimum, less extreme measures should be considered and judged insufficient.
- **Proportional Means:** Military efforts should be restrained, conducted on a minimum scale, with limited duration and restricted intensity.
- **Reasonable Prospects of Success:** Military efforts should be feasible, and the anticipated consequences of the action should be acceptable.

The second set of criteria, based on the Weinberger Doctrine, primarily applies to a nation considering the employment of military force abroad. It is generally intended to lessen the possibility that military forces will be hastily committed to noncritical endeavors that are apt to fail, become quagmires, and/or incur casualties. Like the ICISS criteria, it is focused on the commitment of troops to combat but is also applicable to any use of military forces to prevent mass atrocities. It differs from the ICISS criteria

---

[25] *The Responsibility to Protect*, 32–37.

[26] The 2005 World Summit Outcome Document, which is the most widely accepted conception of R2P, stresses the necessity of a UN Security Council resolution. See, however, "When the Security Council Fails to Act," in *The Responsibility to Protect*, 53–55.

in several ways; most notably, it does not emphasize the reduction of human suffering above all other interests. Additionally, it does not state that military force, if used, should be restrained in the interests of proportionality or other concerns. Rather, it suggests that overwhelming force should be used as a hedge against risks and to overcome the inevitable friction of war.[27]

13.3.2. Weinberger Criteria

- **Vital Interests:** The nation should not commit forces to combat unless the vital national interests of the nation or its allies are involved.
- **Commit to Win:** Troops should only be committed wholeheartedly and with the clear intention of winning.
- **Clear Objectives and Adequate Capacity:** Combat troops should be committed only with clearly defined political and military objectives and with the capacity to accomplish those objectives.
- **Continual Reassessment and Adjustment:** The relationship between the objectives and the size and composition of the forces committed should be continually reassessed and adjusted as needed.
- **Public Support:** Troops should not be committed to battle without a reasonable assurance of the support of public opinion and the legislature.
- **Last Resort:** The commitment of troops should be considered only as a last resort.

It should be noted that the Powell Doctrine is similar to the Weinberger Doctrine, except that it also requires having an exit strategy, understanding the action's consequences, and broad international support. Figure 4 combines the ICISS, Weinberger, and Powell criteria into a set of guidelines for decision-making on the use of military force to mitigate mass atrocities. These guidelines, together with the ICISS-Weinberger-Powell criteria, should be considered by any policymaker contemplating the use of even modest (low-level) preventive military measures. They should certainly be a factor when higher-level actions are posited.[28]

---

[27] Modified here to apply to other nations in addition to the United States. See "The Uses of Military Power: Remarks Prepared for Delivery by the Hon. Caspar W. Weinberger, Secretary of Defense, to the National Press Club, Washington, DC, Wednesday, November 28, 1984," www.pbs.org/wgbh/pages/frontline/shows/military/force/weinberger.html.

[28] In August and September 2013, some countries contemplated military action against Syria over its use of chemical weapons against civilians. Collectively, the ICISS-Weinberger-Powell criteria and the guidelines in Figure 13.4 would have provided weak grounds for kinetic action. They may have been more supportive of shows of force and measures such as strong diplomatic language to help deter the further use of chemical weapons against civilians.

• **Compelling Interests**: Military forces should be used to pursue important international and national interests, which include the reduction of serious threats to civilians and the prevention of conflict.

• **Legitimacy and Support**: Military efforts should have sufficient domestic and international support/authorization, and be supported by responsible stakeholders in the host nation.

• **Clear, Attainable Objectives and Adequate Resources**: Military forces should be employed with clearly defined political and military objectives and with the capacity to accomplish those objectives. The integration of ends, ways, and means should be frequently reassessed throughout planning and implementation.

• **Civil-Military Integration**: Military measures should be integrated with nonmilitary international and domestic efforts and actors.

• **Risk Mitigation**: The risks, costs, and potential negative consequences of military actions should be clearly understood and mitigated as much as possible.

• **Exit Strategy**: A comprehensive and feasible exit strategy should address relevant military and nonmilitary concerns, avoid endless entanglement, and minimize the likelihood of future mass atrocity situations.

Figure 13.4: Guidelines for Military Mass Atrocity Prevention and Response

13.3.3. Risks

Military efforts entail numerous risks (i.e., things that can go wrong), even if they are intended to be low-key and nonkinetic. Indeed, the reason so many experienced military leaders are cautious about using military force is because they know how easily risks can become reality. Risks may be either "accepted" or mitigated; mitigation includes efforts to make risk less likely, reduce its impact, and react to it if it materializes. Although each situation is unique, the following is a list of the most common risks in using force to prevent mass atrocities:

• **Ineffectiveness:** Preventive efforts may fail. The measures may be too benign, inadequately resourced, or too late to achieve the desired outcome. If the intent is to apply graduated measures, the time it takes to incrementally escalate pressure on perpetrators may offer a window of opportunity for mass atrocities to occur or go on occurring. Leaders of national governments or international organizations have to determine that atrocities are imminent or occurring, decide on a course of action, and mobilize and deploy the neces- sary assets. Each of these steps can be time-consuming and result in actions that are too late. By themselves, military actions will have limited impact on structural grievances such as governance, rule of law, economic instability or inequality, territorial disputes, and other root causes of conflict. Lack of progress on these issues may generate resentment among stakeholders who were originally supportive of the preventive efforts. In addition to being ineffective, empty threats and failed efforts may also weaken the credibility of the national government or international organization undertaking the preventive action, which may encourage – rather than discourage – future perpetrators. The effectiveness of any military force will be hampered to the extent that the guidance, mandate, or strategy under which it operates is tardy, vague, incomplete, overly restrictive, or conflicting.

- **Unintended Escalation:** Preventive action may ignite a volatile situation. Perpetrators may accelerate atrocities because they perceive that a window of opportunity is closing or because the military effort is perceived as merely a bluff. Military involvement may fuel conflict by inspiring opposition groups to intensify activities that contributed to the situation. This in turn could prompt a harsh perpetrator response or intervention by other external parties. The introduction of a military presence may change the nature of a conflict, inspiring resistance due to nationalism or other motivations. Perpetrators and other adversaries may attempt to retaliate within and outside the at-risk country against the military force or others. Many military commanders instinctively try to maintain the initiative, defeat adversaries by multiple means, and continually press for advantages, all of which may contribute to unforeseen escalation.

- **Collateral Damage:** Even when carefully conducted to be discriminate and proportional, military "kinetic" actions may result in unintended civilian casualties.[29] Even a force with a relatively benign mission, if on a heightened force-protection status, may engage innocents without being aware of their status or intentions. Vehicle, aviation, and other accidents may result in civilian harm. Civilian well-being may also be jeopardized by crimes committed by soldiers, environmental damage, diseases brought in by foreign troops, and distortion of wages and commodity prices. Finally, military forces may overstress or soak up local infrastructure, resources (such as water), and skilled labor to the detriment of the population and other actors such as humanitarian workers. For example, armored vehicles can quickly tear up roadways and make them virtually impassable for civilian traffic.

- **Losses and Costs:** Military action may result in casualties or equipment loss due to accidents or hostile contact. The bombing of U.S. Marine and French paratrooper barracks in Lebanon (1983), the Blackhawk Down incident in

---

[29] A report of the UN Human Rights Council concluded that during its 2011 operations in Libya, "NATO conducted a highly precise campaign with a demonstrable determination to avoid civilian casualties. For the most part they succeeded." See *Report of the International Commission of Inquiry on Libya*, A/HRC/19/68 (New York: United Nations, March 2, 2012), 197. The report concluded that sixty civilians were accidentally killed and fifty-five wounded during NATO's 17,939 armed sorties (17).

Somalia (1993), and the brutal murder of Belgian paratroopers in Rwanda (1994) provide just a few examples of the risks associated with military missions for humanitarian purposes and explain part of the reluctance to conduct such missions.[30] If there is insufficient military force to cover a wide area, small and dispersed elements, such as patrols and outposts, may be easily overwhelmed by a larger adversary. Over time, the force may become a convenient target for a variety of spoilers. In an extreme situation, an entire committed force may be at risk if placed in a situation beyond its capability. Nonmilitary resources, such as humanitarian workers, embassy personnel, and private citizens, may also be put in jeopardy as a result of military efforts. Military operations also incur budgetary costs as well as opportunity costs regarding other potential commitments.

- **Quagmire/Mission Creep:** Military efforts may result in an extended commitment due to the complex environment, the need to address root causes, the desire to build capacity in a fragile state, and a variety of challenges and second-order effects that develop over time. Some situations are so intractable that they cannot be resolved under the best of circumstances, and certainly not if military forces are committed in a limited effort. A realistic exit strategy may help, but this does not automatically mean the effort will be quick or cheap. In most cases, it is desirable to achieve an end state with minimal likelihood that future intervention will be needed.

- **Fissures:** Military activities will likely be part of an integrated effort by an international organization, coalition, and other stakeholders, including those within the at-risk country. In addition to inevitable politicization of the effort and fundamental controversies about whether military means should even be used, partners[31] may disagree about goals, methods, needs, priorities, agendas, burden-sharing, mandate interpretation, and other issues, as well as having their own internal divisions. Some actors may contend that efforts should be limited to humanitarian assistance or to peacekeeping duties consisting of monitoring events in a relatively secure environment. Others may be influenced by their domestic populations who are skeptical about the effort, particularly if there are setbacks. Some partners may have questionable legitimacy; for example, a rebel group opposed to a government committing mass atrocities may itself be committing human rights violations. Efforts to neutralize perpetrators may even result in empowering other

---

[30] U.S. Marines returned to Lebanon in September 1982 in part to provide a stabilizing presence after the massacre of Palestinian civilians at the Sabra and Shatila refugee camps. In Somalia, military forces were deployed to support and enable humanitarian assistance. The Belgian paratroopers were part of the UN Assistance Mission for Rwanda (UNAMIR), a peacekeeping mission with a restricted mandate.

[31] A variety of host state and international actors may play a role in atrocity prevention. Although the term "partners" is used here, it should be noted that many actors (such as some NGOs) strongly object to being considered as partners of any military or political entity.

perpetrators. In many cases, the key question is whether the host government is primarily a partner or an adversary in the effort to prevent atrocities. Host-state security forces may be part of the problem, but, at some point, they will have to become part of the solution. Humanitarian actors will likely be critical, but if perpetrators perceive that humanitarian assistance efforts are an arm of external intervention, there may be restrictions imposed on humanitarian relief to victims and endangered populations, and aid providers themselves may be targeted, leading to the reduction of humanitarian access. Concerns about this possibility, and their instinctive preference for neutrality, may dissuade NGOs from cooperating with military forces and their political sponsors or partners.

- **Unintended Negative Consequences:** Unintended consequences are likely whenever a simplistic solution is applied to a complex problem. Moreover, fog and friction are inevitable in military operations and will also contribute to the unexpected unfolding of events. Military efforts may contribute to new problems: expanded civil war, insurgency, terrorism, military coups, regime and/or societal collapse, regional spillover, influx of foreign fighters, or loss of credibility by the UN and other actors. A failed or overly costly effort may result in reluctance to intervene in mass atrocity situations in the future. Failure may also encourage future perpetrators by reducing the likelihood of intervention and accountability.

- **Risks of Inaction:** The risks just listed are daunting and may provide justification for passivity. However, there are also risks involved in not acting (or merely conducting token efforts). These include the possibility that a situation may deteriorate even further, requiring a more robust – and costly – effort in the future. Overemphasis on the principle of last resort could lead to excessive appeasement of perpetrators. Additionally, inaction may embolden perpetrators elsewhere.

In addition to the risks outlined here, a preventive effort is likely to have to contend with three underlying challenges: corruption in the host state, constraints on operations, and weak unity of effort. While a military force typically has limited authority, ability, and responsibility to address these issues, they may negate any positive effect a military effort might otherwise have.

13.4.   Conclusion

Despite widespread and understandable reluctance to use military measures, they can help shape the environment and deter or impede perpetrators from committing mass atrocities. Military efforts can and should complement diplomatic and political efforts and should be integrated with them. They may be supportive or threatening, but, in either case, they involve risks that must be balanced against the risk of doing nothing or waiting until it is too late.

There are certainly good reasons to avoid the use of military force: concerns about encroaching on state sovereignty, about the legitimacy of military action, about humanitarian intervention as nothing but neo-imperialism in disguise, about the selectiveness of such measures (i.e., who is a "worthy" victim and who is not), and about whether military measures will result in causing more suffering rather than ending it.[32] Especially within the nation contemplating use of its military, there will also be reservations about whether compelling national interests are at stake, the potential costs and losses, and whether it might result in a protracted commitment.

The 2008 Genocide Prevention Task Force stated that there is "a wide range of options between the extremes of doing nothing and sending in the Marines" (i.e., employing force in a coercive intervention).[33] Military measures to shape and deter are part of this wide range, although the military sword is indeed double-edged. Military tools alone seldom comprise a panacea and include risks of conflict escalation, losses, ineffectiveness, and other contents of the proverbial Pandora's box. However, military tools, applied with clear guidance of what they are intended to achieve, can be potent in supporting both direct and structural prevention, thus precluding the need for a costly kinetic intervention later.

[32] See Ramesh Thakur, "R2P after Libya and Syria: Engaging Emerging Powers," *The Washington Quarterly* (Spring 2013), 61–76, and Rajon Menon, "It's Fatally Flawed," *The American Interest* (July/August 2013), 6–16.

[33] *Preventing Genocide: A Blueprint for U.S. Policymakers* (Washington, DC: The United States Holocaust Memorial Museum, the American Academy of Diplomacy, and the Endowment of the United States Institute of Peace, 2008), xvii.

Part III

Acting Out Prevention

14 Performing Prevention: Civil Society, Performance Studies, and the Role of Public Activism in Genocide Prevention

Kerry Whigham

The explosion of popular social movements in the past four years – beginning with the so-called Arab Spring and echoing across the diversity of movements that followed it, including the Indignados in Spain and Portugal, Yo Soy 132 in Mexico, and Occupy Wall Street in the United States and beyond – demonstrates that large segments of the population around the globe find the state to be failing in the way it is dealing not only with the physical violence of mass atrocities, but also with the structural, legal, and economic violence that typically precedes or follows them. This phenomenon is not new, of course. Popular, grassroots movements have developed throughout modern times in societies where a segment of the population has felt the state to be acting improperly or insufficiently in the face of violence or inequality. History has shown that the transformation of violent or unjust state policies is often born from the grassroots efforts of those most affected by that violence, specifically when they rally together in collective resistance to it. These movements and the group practices that they generate in a citizenry serve as acts of truth-telling – courageous confrontations whereby a disempowered populace stands up to the strength of an oppressive state in order to change the way that state power operates and to reclaim some of the power that has been taken from them.

Despite the visible power of civil society movements in the face of mass violence, much of the discussion in the mass atrocity prevention community remains focused solely on the role of the state. In recent years, for example, there has been a great deal of debate regarding new global norms like the principle of the Responsibility to Protect (R2P), a concept that places primary emphasis on the obligation of states both to protect their populations and to ensure the protection of populations whose states are failing in this responsibility. Although the implementation of this concept is important and potentially paradigm-shifting when it comes to the way the world thinks about

The author would like to thank Tibi Galis, Deborah Kapchan, and Diana Taylor. Without their support and counsel, these ideas would not exist.

prevention, it often gets mired in disputes over the legality and morality of military intervention, a debate that is completely state-centric and that distracts from the power and efficacy of nonviolent and long-term means of prevention that do not necessarily emanate from state policy.

This chapter will take a broad view of genocide prevention, building on the belief that the societal processing of past genocidal violence is preventive of its recurrence. The cases used in this chapter are also quite broad, united neither by chronology nor geography; rather, this chapter discusses popular movements that have arisen within multiple *perpetrator regimes*. I employ the term "perpetrator regime" to signify any government or governing regime that has committed genocide, taking my definition of genocide from Raphael Lemkin, who coined the term in 1944, in his *Axis Rule in Occupied Europe*:

> Generally speaking, genocide ... is intended ... to signify a coordinated plan of different actions aiming at the destruction of essential foundations of the life of national groups, with the aim of annihilating the groups themselves. The objectives of such a plan would be the disintegration of the political and social institutions, of culture, language, national feelings, religion, and the economic existence of national groups, and the destruction of the personal security, liberty, health, dignity, and even the lives of the individuals belonging to such groups.[1]

I use Lemkin's definition, rather than the one contained in the 1948 United Nations Convention on the Prevention and Punishment of the Crime of Genocide – the most established *legal* definition – because the UN definition fails to include political groups. By using Lemkin's definition, the ideas of this chapter will also be applicable to the violence of perpetrator regimes in places like Latin America and Cambodia, for example, where a large proportion of state violence was directed against "political subversives," as defined by the perpetrator regimes. Furthermore, Lemkin's definition highlights the numerous ways in which a group can be destroyed that do not involve killing or other physical violence at all; for instance, he cites the prohibition of cultural practices and language, as well as economic restrictions, as potentially genocidal.

Additionally, I refer in this chapter to perpetrator regimes as authoritarian or totalitarian. I categorize all perpetrator regimes as falling somewhere on the spectrum of authoritarianism and totalitarianism. According to the political scientist Juan J. Linz, regimes are authoritarian when they seek to decrease political diversity or pluralism, limit political participation, and legitimate themselves through shared values (like nationalism or modernization).[2] Linz

---

[1] Raphael Lemkin, *Axis Rule in Occupied Europe: Laws of Occupation, Analysis of Government, Proposals for Redress* (Washington, DC: Carnegie Endowment for International Peace, 1944), 79.

[2] Juan J. Linz, *Totalitarian and Authoritarian Regimes* (Boulder, CO: Lynne Rienner Publishers, 2000).

and Hannah Arendt describe totalitarianism as an even more aggressive form of authoritarianism, in which the state controls every aspect of life, promotes a totalizing ideology, and not only limits but completely eliminates political diversity and participation.[3] In the sense that perpetrator regimes seek extreme control over the lives (and deaths) of their citizens, or at least of selected victim groups within that citizenry, restricting their political access and diversity, every perpetrator regime can be defined as authoritarian, and some particularly radical ones cross the line to totalitarianism.

In contrast to many of the chapters in this volume, which necessarily focus on the role of government in the prevention of genocide and other mass atrocities, this chapter looks more closely at the grassroots social movements that have developed in response to genocide and what the practices that emerged from these movements have contributed to the recovery from genocide and the prevention of future atrocities. I argue that a deeper theory of prevention also calls for, at its core, a new performative theory of the violence of mass atrocity and how that violence "performs" over time. After outlining this theory, I offer examples of several genocidal and postgenocidal communities in which social movements have emerged, working both in collaboration and in contestation with the state. By looking at the practices of these movements alongside this new model of violence, I propose a novel understanding of how societies refigure genocidal violence – potentially in a preventive mode – both in opposition to and in concert with the state. To conduct this analysis, I turn to the interdisciplinary field of performance studies, which can offer a framework and a diverse set of theories for understanding the described "interventions" of civil societies across multiple contexts as both performative and preventive.

14.1. Genocide Prevention and Performance Studies

If there is one driving force that motivates the field of performance studies, it is the notion that the way the body operates and the things the body does represent a mode of knowledge production that deserves equal value or emphasis in the understanding and study of people. This assertion is at the heart of Diana Taylor's *The Archive and the Repertoire: Performing Cultural Memory in the Americas*.[4] In this work, Taylor distinguishes between two different categories of the transmission of knowledge and memory: the *archive*, which encompasses all written and documented information, and the *repertoire*, a far more tenuous form of transmission that centers on the acts of the body.

---

[3] Ibid.; Hannah Arendt, *The Origins of Totalitarianism* (New York: Harcourt, 1968).
[4] Diana Taylor, *The Archive and the Repertoire: Performing Cultural Memory in the Americas* (Durham, NC: Duke University Press, 2003).

Western traditions and academia in general tend to prize archival information because it is far more easily identifiable, collectable, and verifiable. But, as Taylor argues, this tendency serves to undervalue all the modes of memory and knowledge transmission that take place without the meeting of pen to paper, including oral histories, public rituals, group protest and activism, and more overt modes of performance, such as dance, theater, and folk song, not to mention the numerous performances of the body in daily interaction. A favoring of the archive over the repertoire also serves to discount the value of nonliterary cultures or societies that place more or equal weight on transmitting knowledge through the body than through the written word.[5]

Performance studies as a field extends two contributions to this reality that serve to redress the traditional academic imbalance between the archive and the repertoire. First, performance studies offers a lens through which to view and analyze these acts of the repertoire. Richard Schechner, one of the founders of the field, writes, "Certain events are performances and other events less so. There are limits to what 'is' performance. But just about anything can be studied 'as' performance."[6] Looking at political, cultural, religious, and even quotidian interactions *as a performance* highlights the constructed nature of these events. In the same way that scholars deconstruct the historical and cultural context under which each archival document is created, viewing acts of the repertoire as a performance emphasizes that they, too, have a history, a context, a genealogy, and a highly constructed nature.

Second, performance studies cares little about analyzing a performance as a success or a failure. (A performance studies theorist is not the same thing as a theater critic, whose reviews of a play advise readers whether the performance is worth attending or not.) Instead, the question at the heart of every performance analysis asks what the performance *does* or *enacts* through its existence. For instance, historically, the 1943 Warsaw Ghetto Uprising – the month-long historic revolt of ghettoized Polish Jews against German Nazi forces – could be categorized as a failure, given that the rebellion was suppressed and nearly everyone involved in it was killed. Even if it failed in its initial purpose of liberating the ghetto, however, it was a performative event because it enacted many other things. For instance, it sparked new levels of commitment and hope in the Polish underground. It is also remembered as one of the more important and inspiring moments of the Holocaust – a moment of light in a vast expanse of darkness – which demonstrates that the effects of this "performance" are still felt today. A performance studies analysis of this event asks not *if* it succeeded, but *what* it succeeded at doing. This level of scrutiny calls for "big picture" thinking – a real meta-analysis of an event – that is

---

[5] Ibid.

[6] Richard Schechner, *Performance Studies: An Introduction* (London: Routledge, 2002), 30.

consistent with the level of analysis and thinking necessary for developing a comprehensive theory of mass atrocity prevention. But to understand what specifically performance studies has to offer to thinking about genocide and its prevention, it is important to review briefly the current thinking on the perpetration of and recovery from genocide.

14.2.   Genocide and Its Aftermath as Process and Performance

Current thinking in the field of genocide studies emphasizes genocide's nature as a *process*, rather than as an event. Beginning with Arendt's *The Origins of Totalitarianism* and Raul Hilberg's *The Destruction of the European Jews*, scholars have articulated the processual nature of genocide in numerous ways, but one of the more recent and influential models is that provided by genocide studies pioneer Gregory Stanton in his "8 Stages of Genocide," first presented as a briefing paper to the U.S. Department of State in 1996, then published as a book twelve years later.[7] In this document, Stanton demonstrates that the actual killing of individuals is only one step in a much larger process that begins with more mundane acts – for instance, the classification of individuals into specific social groups and the marking of those groups through processes of symbolization.[8] These earlier stages, if not addressed immediately, can continue to advance gradually toward mass killing and other atrocities. The idea of process is also central to the concept and practice of *transitional justice*, which emerged relatively recently yet has grown incredibly quickly, especially in response to the end of Eastern Bloc Communist dictatorships after the fall of the Soviet Union and the demise of the numerous military dictatorships in Latin America, all of which occurred in and around the same period. Transitional justice refers to measures taken by a state to deal with and make amends for past mass atrocities committed by that state. Although the term nominally seems to refer solely to judicial modes of dealing with the past, transitional justice may in fact consist of both juridical and nonjuridical components. The International Center for Transitional Justice (ICTJ), for instance, classifies transitional justice strategies into four different categories: (1) the criminal prosecution of perpetrators, (2) material and symbolic reparations for victims, (3) institutional reforms, and (4) truth commissions.[9] Past experience attests that the implementation of only one of these strategies is usually insufficient for addressing past abuses; rather, like genocide itself, transitional justice is a

---

[7] Gregory H. Stanton, *The 8 Stages of Genocide*, Briefing Paper for United States Department of State (1996); Gregory H. Stanton, *Eight Stages of Genocide* (Los Angeles: Sage, 2008).

[8] Stanton uses the term "symbolization" to describe acts that solidify the classification of individuals into groups through the use of symbols. For instance, the Third Reich used symbolization when it forced all Jews to wear the six-pointed Star of David in public.

[9] See www.ictj.org/about/transitional-justice.

process with multiple stages and multiple levels of implementation. It is largely a political process, however, and is left mainly to the state to execute – an ironic twist given that it is usually the state itself that has perpetrated the crimes it seeks to redress through transitional justice. Transitional justice may contribute to the healing of individual trauma, but its central purpose is the consolidation of a more durable and (most often) more democratic regime.[10] As the ICTJ website states, "[S]tates have duties to guarantee that the [systematic human rights] violations will not recur, and therefore, a special duty to reform institutions that were either involved in or incapable of preventing the abuses."[11] So, as the ICTJ stresses, dealing with the past through transitional justice is essential for preventing the re-emergence of violence. Still, although it can serve to stabilize a government, it can only do so much to heal the emotional and social trauma experienced by a postgenocidal society on an individual or collective basis (especially given that this is not its main purpose).

In addition to being processes, genocide and transitional justice can also be viewed as performances that enact certain things through the process of their implementation. First, they are performances of power, whereby the state exerts its authority over a population either through violent means (in the case of genocide) or through legal, economic, and structural reforms (in the case of transitional justice). Second, they are, or at least they require, performances of citizenship and personhood. As perpetrator and victim groups are defined and modified throughout the process of a genocide, states and their subjects decide who counts as a citizen and, in many cases, what it means to be, as Giorgio Agamben puts it, "life worthy of life."[12] Likewise, during transitional justice processes, these roles are redefined as victim groups are reclaimed by the state and perpetrators are either punished or forgiven by that same state.

Both of these performances highlight the role of the state in performing and recovering from genocide, thus maintaining traditional conceptions of power that frame the state as the key actor in genocide and transitional justice alike. The effects of genocidal violence, however, far exceed the reach of the state, infiltrating every aspect of daily life. The violence of genocide involves much more than the physical violence of torture and killing. It also manifests in a rapidly shifting social environment through which neighbor is turned against neighbor, and, as historian Marion A. Kaplan puts it, the abnormal is

---

[10] Tibi Galis, "Keeping the Wolves at Bay: Transitional Justice and Reform in Argentina, South Africa and Hungary" (PhD diss., Clark University, 2015).

[11] http://ictj.org/about/transitional-justice

[12] Giorgio Agamben, *Homo Sacer: Sovereign Power and Bare Life*, translated by Daniel Heller-Roazen (Stanford, CA: Stanford University Press, 1998).

normalized.[13] Similarly, transitions out of a period of genocide not only entail the reform of state structures, but must also involve the mending of the social fabric that has been left rent by state violence. This social component of recovery cannot be addressed solely through the installment of a new regime or the passage of new laws. The collective trauma experienced during and after genocide has long-lasting, persistent effects. Therefore, a more complex understanding of the performance of genocide and transitional justice would acknowledge that the state is not the only, or even necessarily the most important, player in these processes.

Because the performance of genocide so clearly exceeds the bounds of the state, a complex conceptualization of recovery from genocide and the prevention of its recurrence should also look outside the framework of the state to non-state actors and their role in processing past atrocities and preventing them in the future. Although many methods of prevention necessarily serve to address the *structural* violence that has allowed genocide to occur, or to end the *physical* violence of illegal detainment, displacement, torture, and murder, the *affective* or *shared, emotional* aspects of genocidal violence may have even more long-lasting effects and therefore must be engaged by any effective prevention strategy. If we accept the proposition of the ICTJ, as well as of scholars such as Barbara Harff,[14] Alexander Mayer-Rieckh, and Pablo de Greiff, that dealing with the past is a key aspect of preventing future genocide,[15] then this new concept of affective violence can help reframe what prevention looks like, broadening the scope of who is able to perform the act of prevention and how. This theory would understand violence, similar to genocide and transitional justice, as a process rather than an event, acknowledging that even though the physical aspects of violence may be evental, existing only in the moment, its emotional or affective effects can extend far into the future. Furthermore, the violence of genocide is felt not only by its direct victims (i.e., those who experience the physical violence of torture or murder), but by the entire society they belong to, people whose daily lives are transformed and whose interrelationships are reconfigured by the affective force of this enduring violence.

Affect – by which I mean the shared, social force of emotion – is, at its very core, a group phenomenon. It is not, however, something that can be completely managed through government structures and institutional reforms

---

[13] Marion A. Kaplan, *Between Dignity and Despair: Jewish Life in Nazi Germany* (New York: Oxford University Press, 1998), 9.

[14] Political scientist Barbara Harff's influential model for assessing risk of genocide places "prior genocides and politicides" as the number one risk factor for future genocides and politicides (Harff 2005, 58).

[15] Alexander Mayer-Reickh and Pablo de Grieff, eds., *Justice as Prevention: Vetting Public Employees in Transitional Societies* (New York: Social Science Research Council, 2007).

or through the psychological mastery of the individual. It is a shared experience that travels among individuals and exists largely through this process of transfer. In *Political Affect: Connecting the Social and the Somatic*, John Protevi offers a conception of the subject that attempts to bridge past notions that frame the subject as either a purely rational being or a purely social one. Protevi argues that, instead, subjects are formed through the felt experience of affect, which almost always bypasses the cognitive reach of the subject but subsequently shapes the cognitive patterns through which that subject operates.[16] Furthermore, he writes that because affect is "the imbrication of the social and the somatic," it only makes sense to analyze subjectivity as something formed in collectivities, throughout which affect is distributed and felt.[17] Thus, he offers the notion of "bodies politic" to describe the collection of individual, sensual bodies that are collectively formed through "politically shaped and triggered affective cognition."[18] It is one of the forms of subjectivity-shaping affect that I take on here by offering the concept of *resonant violence*.

Resonant violence is the term I use to describe the affective energy of large-scale, genocidal violence that, once performed on an individual or a population, continues to resonate within that individual or social body-politic, undergoing various stages of amplification and intensification until or unless it is processed, transformed, or, to continue the sonic metaphor, recomposed through acts that allow this energy to resonate less or differently. Resonant violence describes the violence that exists in between individual psychic trauma and the systemic violence of the state. It describes the *felt* experience of violence that affects daily social interaction and that continues to perform long after physical and structural violences have ceased.

The affective phenomenon I am attempting to conceptualize through the term "resonant violence" is marked by several important characteristics. First is the idea that a violent act performed on an individual or group has an affective force. Although it may or may not be brought about by a physical act, the affective quality of a violent act far supersedes its physical quality. In *The Cultural Politics of Emotion*, British scholar Sara Ahmed develops a theory of "affective economics," which describes how affect or emotions do not necessarily reside within subjects or objects but circulate among them. Rather than viewing emotions as something that individual subjects possess, Ahmed sees them as a social force that possesses subjects and plays a large role in shaping groups. They do this principally through their ability to "stick to" or "saturate" an object; when an object becomes saturated with emotion, it

---

[16] John Protevi, *Political Affect: Connecting the Social and the Somatic* (Minneapolis: University of Minnesota Press, 2009), xii.
[17] Ibid., xiv.
[18] Ibid., 33.

transforms and shapes the world around it based on how that world now relates to it. In a similar way, resonant violence can be thought of as violence that inundates the individual or collective subject, treating that subject as an object (a receiver of violence), filling it with the affective force that comes with any violent act – rejection, anger, hate, disdain – and, in so doing, transforming that subject and its relationship to the world around it. This affective force resides within the subject. In the case of genocide, the residual effects of this force can be horrifying. For instance, as genocide scholar Ervin Staub points out, often perpetrators of genocide carry within them the residual violence of past victimization – for instance, the Serbs, who were ruled for half a millennium by the Turks, and the Hutus of Rwanda, who were subjugated by Tutsis decades prior to the 1994 genocide in that country.[19]

These examples illustrate how the affective force of violence not only remains within the body, but continues to perform upon the body in a way that does not simply replicate the initial moment of violence, but may also amplify it. Inspired by the work of several theorists,[20] I refer to this phenomenon as *resonance*. The affective force of resonant violence moves the body, creating oscillations that affect not only the individual subject but everyone and everything surrounding her. The resonant violence trapped within the body politic is constantly vibrating, oscillating, constricting, and expanding in a way that is difficult for the subject to control. Resonance has a life of its own.

Furthermore, this resonance has the quality of being able to feed off other vibrations. Nothing can resonate on its own; it must resonate *with* something else. Although this can mean that the violent affect resonates with the individual body, it can also mean that this affect resonates across bodies. As Viet Erlmann writes of aural resonance in *Reason and Resonance*, "[R]esonance entails adjacency, sympathy, and the collapse of the boundary between perceiver and perceived."[21] Resonance actually breaks down (or, perhaps better, shakes down) boundaries, causing things to resonate together. And so, when resonant violence acts across bodies, its vibratory power grows. It amplifies. In *Capitalism and Christianity, American Style*, William E. Connolly describes what he calls a "resonance machine," a phenomenon that is created when different ideas, discourses, or affective energies meet and complement each other in specific ways. Through this

---

[19] Ervin Staub, "The Origins and Prevention of Genocide, Mass Killing, and Other Collective Violence," *Peace and Conflict: Journal of Peace Psychology* 5(4): 303–336 (1999).

[20] William E. Connolly, *Capitalism and Christianity, American Style* (Durham, NC: Duke University Press, 2008); Veit Erlmann, *Reason and Resonance: A History of Modern Aurality* (Brooklyn: Zone Books, 2010); Jean-Luc Nancy, *Listening*, translated by Charlotte Mandell, 4th ed. (New York: Fordham University Press, 2007).

[21] Erlmann, *Reason and Resonance*, 10.

process, these affects can intensify, "recoil back" upon the initial energies, or transform into something else altogether through their power to reinforce and feed off the subject's "existential orientation" to the world and to others.[22] Importantly, Connolly points out that the elements that resonate do not necessarily have to be the same as long as they are similarly oriented. So, with resonant violence, the affective force of violence experienced by different individuals does not need to be identical for them to resonate with each other. But the ability for different violences to resonate means that subjective experiences of violence can grow exponentially in instances of the group, so that the mass experience of resonant violence is much greater than the sum of its parts.

Resonant violence is also performative; as Joseph Roach asserts in *Cities of the Dead*, "all violence is performative" because it does things.[23] What makes resonant violence differently performative is, first, the persistent quality of its performance, in that it does not end with the initial act of violence but continues to perform affectively both inside the body of the victim and through affective transmission to others. Second, it is different because of how exactly it performs. Resonant violence's most destructive performance is in its ability to destroy social bonds and atomize individuals. It works specifically through its ability to break down collectivities, even if the violence is being experienced collectively. It is most powerful when felt by individuals as not having a social component because resonant violence ultimately works toward complete social atomization. Agamben offers a supreme description of resonant violence's performativity in *Homo Sacer: Sovereign Power and Bare Life*. During the Holocaust, according to Agamben (and Primo Levi, from whom he takes the term) prisoners of concentration camps developed the term *Muselmann* (literally "Muslim") to label the prisoner who had completely given up hope, opting instead for total apathy and a life apart from humanity. Agamben writes:

> He no longer belongs to the world of men in any way; he does not even belong to the threatened and precarious world of the camp inhabitants who have forgotten him from the very beginning. Mute and absolutely alone, he has passed into another world without memory and without grief.[24]

I argue that it is resonant violence that produces the *Muselmann*, a figure who can be literally surrounded by others undergoing the same terror as he is, yet still disconnects completely from real human (read: communal) existence.

In characterizing the various totalitarian regimes of her time, political philosopher Hannah Arendt describes "terror" as "the form of government

---

[22] Connolly, *Capitalism and Christianity, American Style*, 42.

[23] Joseph Roach, *Cities of the Dead: Circum-Atlantic Performance* (New York: Columbia University Press, 1996), 41.

[24] Agamben, *Homo Sacer*, 185.

that comes into being when violence, having destroyed all power, does not abdicate but, on the contrary, remains in full control."[25] The supreme consequence of this perpetual reign of violence is the increased atomization of society, brought about mainly by what Arendt describes as "the ubiquity of the informer," or what could be characterized in more general terms as a belief that the enemy is everywhere.[26] Similarly, when all opposition to resonant violence falls away, society atomizes, and the individual is forced to experience the shared affect of resonant violence alone. This is the terrifying paradox of resonant violence: it works through transmission between individuals exactly by making those individuals feel that they are not connected.

Finally, and most importantly, because resonant violence is an affective force that resonates within and among "bodies," a central way to curtail it is through practices that transform that violence through performances *of* the body that convert it into new modes of agency and power that allow it to resonate differently. In her 1969 essay "On Violence," Arendt takes on theorists of the early twentieth century (most specifically Max Weber), their definitions of power, and their overriding tendency to conflate it with violence. For Arendt, power is not something endowed upon an individual or institution through its ability to exert violent force on others. Instead, power can only exist within the context of a group and that group's ability to empower an individual or a governing body. It is within this social contract of acting in concert, then, where true power lies.[27] Violence, on the other hand, describes the coercive force used when the consent of the group does not allow for true power. Although violence can indeed destroy power through its ability to atomize society, power can never grow out of violence because the group is being forced to submit, rather than submitting willingly.[28] In Arendt's view, then, violence and power are complete opposites. As she writes, "[W]hen the one rules absolutely, the other is absent."[29]

I take issue with Arendt's definitions in one key way: I argue that it *is* possible for power to emerge from violence, albeit through unexpected processes of recomposition, whereby resonant violence undergoes a transubstantiation of sorts that transforms it into a new form of affective power or that reorients existing relations of power to favor or solidify new subjectivities. The affective force of this power can then transform others through transmission across new bodies and entities. Ahmed alludes to this when she discusses reparative or reconciliatory practices in nations dealing

[25] Hannah Arendt, *On Violence* (New York: Harcourt, Brace, Jovanovich, 1970), 55.
[26] Ibid.
[27] Ibid., 44.
[28] Ibid., 53.
[29] Ibid., 56.

with a history of injustice. She challenges the truism that a "good scar" is one that is invisible, writing:

A good scar is one that sticks out, a lumpy sign on the skin. It's not that the wound is exposed or that the skin is bleeding. But the scar is a sign of the injury: a good scar allows healing, it even covers over, *but the covering always exposes the injury, reminding us of how it shapes the body.*[30]

Ahmed describes a process whereby past violence is externalized from the body and transformed in such a way that it actually strengthens the body rather than diminishing it. In this manner, the violence does not disappear without a trace but instead leaves visible marks on and through the body. These processes of recomposition are not only backward-looking, attempting to amend the injuries of the past. They can also be preventive of future violence because productive memory practices also look forward in their ability to shape and influence social relations.

The remainder of this chapter focuses on one specific performative mode of transforming resonant violence that has spontaneously emerged (usually without the consent or encouragement of the state) in the aftermath of genocide and state terror, leaving behind its own "scars" to be seen and confronted by the larger public. These visibilized scars, however, serve to reinforce new forms or relations of power that appear through the processes of recomposition that make the scars visible. They demonstrate potential strategies of prevention that can influence or exceed the framework of the state, calling into question the very notion of who is able to "perform" the act of prevention.

14.3.   Processing Resonant Violence Through Co-embodied Practice

Co-embodied practice is the term I use to describe ritual acts performed by a collection of individual bodies coming together in public space and acting in concert. These performances are immensely varied in their manifestations, but they are alike in one central way: they bring together multiple people who derive their power purely through the public presence of their physical bodies. Perhaps most importantly, unlike other strategies for addressing genocidal violence, they do not necessarily require the consent of the state; indeed, some of the most well-known examples of co-embodied practice as a mode of processing genocidal violence have emerged while the perpetrator regime was still in power. Co-embodied practices are not inherently beneficial or positive; acts of genocide could themselves be viewed as co-embodied

---

[30] Sara Ahmed, *The Cultural Politics of Emotion* (New York: Routledge, 2004), 201; emphasis in original.

practices because they represent the public presence of multiple bodies acting toward a shared goal. When they have been put to the positive and productive overcoming of shared trauma, however, they have been central in the processing of resonant violence in numerous cultural contexts. From the Madres de Plaza de Mayo (Mothers of the Plaza de Mayo) in Argentina to the annual ritual burials in Bosnia to the 1969 occupation of Alcatraz Island in the United States, co-embodied practices have played an essential role in the transformation of resonant violence into more productive modes of power and affect. By looking at these practices through a performance studies lens, links can be made to deepen and complicate theories of genocide and mass atrocity prevention, expanding current notions of what it means to prevent genocide and who is able to perform such acts of prevention. To accomplish this goal, I will offer the beginnings of a comparative study of several co-embodied practices across a series of cultural and historical contexts. In examining these cases, I will outline six things these practices do to help societies deal with the past in order to construct a present and a future free of genocide and other mass atrocities: (1) refigure public space, (2) undo social atomization, (3) break down the public-private divide, (4) produce new forms of agency and citizenship, (5) create spaces for affective transmission, and (6) motivate the transformation of state structures.

14.3.1. Refiguring Public Space

One of the most important and central things that co-embodied practices do is refigure public space. During periods of genocide and state terror, public space almost always goes through a process of restriction and control. For example, in *Memorias en la Ciudad*, a book that examines nearly three hundred sites of memory in Buenos Aires, created in response to the military dictatorship of 1976–83, the authors write:

Urban space has always been a terrain for expression of social conflicts, and the State has taken numerous opportunities to intervene, seeking to design that space as a means of control and discipline, structuring not only the space itself but how it is used, and thus regulating the practices and modes of inhabiting it.[31]

Although certain privileged segments of a given population may enjoy unrestricted access to the city, public spaces typically become so restricted by authoritarian regimes that they can no longer be considered truly public. As such, space is used as a tool for repression through the creation of what Steve

---

[31] Memoria Abierta, *Memorias En La Ciudad: Señales Del Terrorismo de Estado En Buenos Aires* (Buenos Aires, Argentina: Eudeba, 2009), 67; my translation.

Pile calls "geographies of domination."[32] Pile uses this term to describe any number of methods – including the division or cordoning off of space, as well as the direction of movement within it – to produce a spatial manifestation of a regime's authority.[33] Although these geographies of domination work to reinforce certain power relations, they also open up the possibility for alternative spatialities that Pile calls "geographies of resistance," within which dominating power relations can be evaded or transgressed.[34] Within genocidal regimes, there is not much space left open, so resistance must create its own space by insinuating itself into spaces of domination, appropriating that space for itself.[35] By doing so, public space is opened and refigured, establishing new or alternative power relations; this phenomenon is one of the performative aspects of co-embodied practice.

As group acts that happen out in the open and for all to see, co-embodied practices resist constraints on public space and, in so doing, actually reverse violent forces of control. In her study on social, racial, and sexual normativity, Ahmed writes about how, in daily life, bodies are directed in some ways more than others; they are asked to follow certain figurative paths, and, as these paths are followed again and again, they become deeply ingrained to the point that they seem innate. They become norms, and the body that follows these paths, reproducing their lines, is a normative body.[36] Under an authoritarian regime, the constructed nature of norms becomes a bit more pronounced because bodies are asked to follow certain "paths" – to be normative – or else risk horrifying punishments ranging from imprisonment to torture to death. These paths can be figurative (e.g., some authoritarian regimes require individuals to wear specific clothing or maintain their physical appearance in a certain way) or literal (e.g., authoritarian regimes often restrict public space and the actual paths through which people are allowed to walk through that space). When people resist these normative paths, however, opting instead for paths that lead them into geographies of resistance, new paths are created, and the possibility for alternative norms is highlighted. Co-embodied practices represent an example of how these paths can be reinscribed, thus refiguring how public space functions under authoritarian regimes.

During Argentina's last genocidal military dictatorship of 1976–83 (Argentineans refer to it as "the last dictatorship" because it was the most

---

[32] Steve Pile, "Introduction: Opposition, Political Identities and Spaces of Resistance," in *Geographies of Resistance*, edited by Steve Pile and Michael Keith (London: Routledge, 1997), 2.

[33] Ibid., 3.

[34] Ibid., 1, 14.

[35] Ibid., 16.

[36] Sara Ahmed, *Queer Phenomenology: Orientations, Objects, Others* (Durham, NC: Duke University Press, 2006).

recent in a long line of twentieth-century dictatorships in that country), public space was so tightly controlled that some public squares were redesigned so they could only be used as transitory spaces allowing people to pass through them to get from one place to another, rather than as public gathering spots, which could have allowed for conspiration and the sort of congregation of individuals the dictatorship hoped to avoid.[37] It was in this environment that a group of mothers whose children had been "disappeared" by the regime began to gather in the Plaza de Mayo, the central square of the capital. This public square – the site of the country's declaration of independence from Spain – is surrounded by the presidential offices, the national bank, and the city's cathedral. By occupying this space, the Madres de Plaza de Mayo petitioned all the various forms of power that conspired in the policies of the regime – political, economic, and clerical – for the return of their missing children.[38] By electing to march every Thursday afternoon (rather than on weekends), the Madres also ensured that their performance was not only for these centers of power, but also for the wider public who passed by the square during their workday. Through their defiant occupation of the square, the Madres demonstrated to others the possibility for resistance. Moreover, they reminded the country of the true nature of "public" space. In her study of this important group, Marguerite Guzman Bouvard writes:

During the time of the junta, which categorized all public demonstrations and gatherings as subversive, the Mothers defied physical assault and their own fear by gathering in its vast empty spaces. The Plaza became a sacred area where they could assume their dignity, the right to think and act as human beings against a repressing government. Defying death threats, the Mothers marched straight into the seat of power, demanding government accountability. Because the junta ultimately was unable to eject them from that space, except for brief periods, the Mothers felt that it belonged to them.[39]

This sense of belonging is even more poetically articulated in one interview with a member of the Madres, who told Bouvard, "The Plaza is in my skin. It's in my body . . . It is a space that is ours."[40] Here, this mother demonstrates exactly how co-embodied practices like the marches of the Madres de Plaza de Mayo work to refigure controlled public space, making it public once again to the point that this mother feels that space in her own skin. This conflation of the mother's own body with the Plaza itself shows how these practices create geographies of resistance not only in the concrete landscape; rather, the body

[37] Memoria Abierta, *Memorias En La Ciudad: Señales Del Terrorismo de Estado En Buenos Aires*, 67.
[38] Marguerite Guzman Bouvard, *Revolutionizing Motherhood: The Mothers of the Plaza de Mayo* (Wilmington, DE: Scholarly Resources, 1994), 2.
[39] Ibid., 254.
[40] Quoted in ibid., 254.

of every individual citizen can become a geography of resistance, a manifestation of refigured space in a repressive or repressed public sphere.

14.3.2. Undoing Social Atomization

Co-embodied practices like the marches of the Madres around the Plaza de Mayo not only refigure public space by refusing to accept the strictures of regulation and control. They also serve to undo one of the most dangerous and preeminent phenomena of any society suffering under a genocidal or totalitarian regime: the atomization, fragmentation, and isolation of its citizens.

In her elaboration of the genocidal regimes of Nazi Germany and the Stalinist Soviet Union in *The Origins of Totalitarianism*, Arendt writes, "It has frequently been observed that terror can rule absolutely only over men who are isolated against each other and that, therefore, one of the primary concerns of all tyrannical government is to bring this isolation about."[41] They do this largely by generating in each citizen a sense of loneliness which, in turn, leads to a deep dependency, the only viable answer to which is the oppressive regime itself. As such, the regime at once breaks down the population's reliance on other citizens while increasing its reliance on the authoritarian state.[42] If, as Arendt asserts, the greatest power of state terror is the individualization and atomization of society, then every act of co-embodied practice works against that cause. The *co* of co-embodied practice is where its true power lies. Terrorized individuals act *in concert* and thus undo resonant violence's atomizing power. Because co-embodied practices are, by their very nature, group acts, they performatively accomplish this goal of uniting a fragmented society through the mere fact of their existence.

The aforementioned Madres de Plaza de Mayo are, of course, one example of this power; an alternate example comes from another family group in Argentina known as H.I.J.O.S., which stands for *Hijos y hijas por la Identidad y la Justicia contra el Olivido y el Silencio* (Sons and Daughters for Identity and Justice against Forgetting and Silence). This group, formed in the late 1990s by sons and daughters of people disappeared during the last military dictatorship, is best-known for the creation of a unique form of street activism known as the *escrache*, a term that comes from the Spanish slang word *escrachar*, meaning "to uncover" or "reveal something hidden." In response to the culture of impunity toward past perpetrators, *escraches* were events where protesters gathered in front of the houses of unprosecuted criminals to make the

---

[41] Hannah Arendt, *The Origins of Totalitarianism* (New York: Harcourt, 1968), 474.
[42] Ibid., 476.

neighborhood aware that a perpetrator was living in their midst and to call on the state for formal justice. Although H.I.J.O.S. was founded by the children of those directly victimized by the violence of the dictatorship, thousands of people participated in *escraches*, including those with no direct history of victimization. Indeed, H.I.J.O.S. encouraged the participation of anyone, especially any young person. In their official description of "Who We Are," the H.I.J.O.S. website states:

H.I.J.O.S. is an organization ... formed by children of those who were disappeared, assassinated, politically imprisoned, and exiled during the military dictatorship and in the years prior; *and moreover by young people that, without having suffered in their own family the direct repression of the last military dictatorship, understand that we are children of the same history.*[43]

Whereas the violence of the dictatorship was working to atomize society, H.I.J.O.S. worked to undo this atomization, not only by gathering with others who had suffered directly from this violence, but also by offering to share this space of suffering with anyone who would join their cause.

When resonant violence goes unprocessed, it can last for many years. For instance, the United States committed genocide against the vast populations of American Indians beginning in the eighteenth century and manifesting in mass killings, relocation, the appropriation of children, and forced assimilation projects that sought to destroy native cultures. To this day, these genocides remain, at least officially, unrecognized by the state, and only minimal efforts have been made by the government to repair the damage. As a result, American Indians still face countless economic, social, and legal hardships. For example, according to the U.S. Census Bureau, American Indians have the highest poverty rate (27 percent) of any ethnic or racial group in the country,[44] and, according to the Centers for Disease Control and Prevention, they have the second-highest infant mortality rate of any group (nearly 50 percent greater than that of children born to white mothers).[45] Years of anti–American Indian policy and sentiment served not only to annihilate native populations, but also to fragmentize them. Toward the end of the 1960s, however, a large group of American Indians from many tribal groups joined in a mass movement to begin to address the resonant violence perpetrated against them.

---

[43] "Quiénes Somos," H.I.J.O.S. (accessed July 28, 2013), available at www.hijos-capital.org.ar /index.php?option=com_content&view=article&id=20&Itemid=399. My translation, emphasis added.

[44] "Poverty Rates for Selected Detailed Race and Hispanic Groups by State and Place: 2007–2011," United States Census Bureau (accessed November 11, 2013), available at https://www.census .gov/prod/2013pubs/acsbr11-17.pdf.

[45] "American Indian & Alaska Native Populations," Centers for Disease Control and Prevention (accessed November 11, 2013), available at www.cdc.gov/minorityhealth/populations/REMP /aian.html.

One example of this group undoing social atomization through co-embodied practice comes from the 1969 Occupation of Alcatraz Island in California. In response to the continuing economic and social violence against American Indians in the United States, a group of American Indians (mostly college students) representing multiple tribal groups formed an organization called Indians of All Tribes. Citing a nineteenth-century treaty signed by the U.S. government with the Sioux people, which stated that any decommissioned federal land formerly held by the Sioux would automatically revert to Sioux ownership, Indians of All Tribes invaded and occupied the decommissioned island prison in the San Francisco Bay for one and a half years, petitioning the U.S. government for the return of the land. Although the occupation itself ultimately failed, it led to the birth of the modern American Indian Rights Movement (or Red Power Movement), which went on to have resounding effects on the way the U.S. government dealt with Native Americans. One of the main ways it succeeded in this was by creating a union of diverse and previously disconnected populations. As Lenny Foster, a member of the Navajo tribe and one of the original participants, writes in his account of the occupation:

John Trudell [a spokesman for the occupation] named this group Indians of All Tribes because, although the people were from all parts of the country, a sense of unity and brotherhood was evolving. Alcatraz was a place where urban and reservation Indians were coming together and examining the U.S. government's failure to honor its treaties and its obligations to Indian people. We were becoming Indian activists, and it was time to reclaim our Indian dignity. The Indian Nation had awakened.[46]

Foster's description exemplifies the power of co-embodied practices to undo the atomizing power of resonant violence. The group practice of the occupation brought together people from across the country in order to address the continuing effects of a genocide (or multiple genocides of each tribal group) that had "ended" more than a century prior. The first step in processing the violence committed against them was to create an inclusive union that highlighted the shared qualities that brought everyone together, which in turn rejected the force of the resonant violence that had been working to divide and separate American Indians for over a century.

14.3.3. Breaking Down the Public-Private Divide

In *The Structural Transformation of the Public Sphere*, Jürgen Habermas describes the public sphere as the realm where private individuals gather to

---

[46] Lenny Foster, "Alcatraz Is Not an Island," in *American Indian Activism: Alcatraz to the Longest Walk*, edited by Troy Johnson, Joane Nagel, and Duane Champagne (Urbana: University of Illinois Press, 1997), 138.

engage in a dialogue about and with the forces governing their lives, especially those involving the state and the market. The notion of a public sphere developed largely alongside the notion of a market economy, according to Habermas, as a means to "put the state in touch with the needs of society."[47] The existence of this sphere is essential in open, democratic societies because, as Clara Ramírez-Barat writes, "[t]he public sphere is the space in which citizens are conceived not as mere recipients of the state's actions nor in terms of their private relations as individuals, but rather as political agents with a say in the processes that affect them."[48]

Of course, in perpetrator regimes, the state has no interest in giving individuals a say in how they are governed. As such, the public sphere is narrowed to the point of nonexistence by the forces of authoritarianism, shutting out any voices that criticize the project of the regime. The closed nature of these regimes, along with their intent to atomize individuals within a society, works to push much of life as a whole out of the streets, obscuring it from public view by confining it within the walls of the home, where people are left to process and manage their fear or trauma alone. Within the context of Argentina's military dictatorship, Pilar Calveiro, an Argentine scholar who was herself imprisoned and tortured during this period, writes of this sequestration of society. During the junta, the general public opted not to acknowledge most of the crimes happening around them – a phenomenon Diana Taylor has referred to as "percepticide"[49] – both as a result of the regime's privatizing forces and as a form of self-preservation. As Calveiro writes:

[T]he society as a whole accepted the incongruence between the discourse and the political practice of the military, between public life and private life, between what was said and what was kept quiet, between what was known and what was ignored as a form of preservation.[50]

Calveiro describes how this pretending not to see what is so plainly visible, pretending not to know what is so widely known, can become so intense that it creates a kind of schizophrenia in the population that has grave consequences, including the reconciliation of the nonexistence of a public sphere as a bearable or even necessary fact of life.[51]

---

[47] Jürgen Habermas, *The Structural Transformation of the Public Sphere: An Inquiry into a Category of Bourgeois Society,* translated by Frederick G. Lawrence (Cambridge, MA: MIT Press, 1991), 31.

[48] Clara Ramírez-Barat, "Introduction: Transitional Justice and the Public Sphere," in *Beyond Outreach: Transitional Justice, Culture and Society,* edited by Clara Ramírez-Barat (New York: SSRC, 2013), 32.

[49] Diana Taylor, *Disappearing Acts: Spectacles of Gender and Nationalism in Argentina's "Dirty War"* (Durham, NC: Duke University Press, 1997), 123.

[50] Pilar Calveiro, *Poder y desaparición: los campos de concentración en Argentina* (Buenos Aires: Colihue, 1998), 151.

[51] Ibid.

Both during times of genocide and in periods of transitional justice following it, co-embodied practices can offer an opportunity to revive the public sphere.[52] Across a diverse set of cultural contexts (including the former Yugoslavia, Argentina, Chile, Peru, and Rwanda), some groups have attempted to accomplish this task through a clever contradiction: when the oppressive state has forced the individual out of the public realm and into the private sphere almost completely, groups of united individuals have responded by taking what, for many, seems the most endemically private of phenomena – personal emotion – and transforming it into a public act.

In perpetrator regimes, victimized populations have much death to mourn. Whereas most Western societies typically practice mourning in the private sphere, many instances of co-embodied practice have worked to break down the barriers between private and public when it comes to the act of mourning. By making their mourning public, these groups use personal pain as a form of activism that transforms the resonant violence that both led to and results from death.[53] This sort of activism works to create what Douglas Crimp has called an "intimate public sphere," within which "these practices counter the invisibility of and indifference to feelings of loss by making them extravagantly public as well as building collective cultural practices that can acknowledge and showcase them."[54] By creating an intimate public sphere in a place where little or no public sphere exists at all, these groups call into question the very idea of a public-private divide and challenge the constructed nature of the regime's status quo.

One example of a group that has broken down the public-private divide through mourning is the Association of the Mothers of Srebrenica. This group of women from Bosnia and Herzegovina was formed in the wake of the 1995 genocide in the UN Safe Area of Srebrenica. Although their families are gone forever, the mothers, sisters, and widows of those killed continue to fight for truth and justice as they petition their own government and the world to recognize and be held responsible for the role they played in the atrocity. Each year, on July 11, the Mothers of Srebrenica hold a mass burial of the remains of victims found and identified through forensic evidence over the

---

[52] Ramírez-Barat, "Introduction: Transitional Justice and the Public Sphere."

[53] The most obvious example of these public mourning practices may be the Madres de Plaza de Mayo. The Madres themselves, however, do not necessarily frame their activism as a form of mourning, especially since their central demand is and always has been "*Aparición con vida*," a statement that emphasizes the desire to have their children back alive. This refusal to acknowledge the death of the children is especially prominent in the Madres. By refusing the deaths of their children, the Madres ensure that the state does not close the door so easily on the past, emphasizing that it still has much for which it must answer.

[54] Quoted in Ann Cvetkovich, *An Archive of Feelings: Trauma, Sexuality, and Lesbian Public Cultures* (Durham, NC: Duke University Press Books, 2003), 263.

previous year. This annual funeral is not only an act of memorialization; it is also part of an effort to keep the event alive in the present so that it is not forgotten.[55] The Mothers of Srebrenica have also taken their struggle to the world stage by filing a lawsuit against the UN and the Dutch government for their role in the genocide.[56] In 2013, their efforts contributed to a ruling that held Dutch peacekeeping forces responsible for the massacre, forcing the Dutch government to pay reparations to the victims.[57] The acts of the group serve to turn the private performance of mourning into a public display that reinvigorates a public sphere that was left severely damaged by the perpetrator regime, and the maintenance of a vibrant public sphere can serve as a strong deterrent against modes of authoritarianism that could lead to future genocide.

14.3.4. Producing New Forms of Agency and Citizenship

The resonant violence of genocide constructs certain forms of agency and citizenship that are deemed acceptable. During genocide, the social and legal category of "citizen," with all of the rights it entails, narrows significantly to disallow unwanted segments of the population by deeming them noncitizens (and, in many cases, "nonhuman"), thus revoking the political agency of these subjects. For example, the Nuremberg Laws of 1930s Germany were designed to take away the rights of citizenship from German Jews. Another example comes from General Jorge Rafael Videla, one of the leaders of the first military junta in Argentina's last dictatorship, who explained that the junta was not repressing society as a whole, but only "a minority which we do not consider Argentine."[58] This quote encapsulates the approach used by many genocidal regimes to justify actions against a group, claiming the government has no responsibility to that group in the first place.

In *Pasado y Presente*, Argentine scholar Hugo Vezzetti likens this shift in the role of citizenship to the aforementioned privatization of the public sphere; after all, a person's role as citizen is defined through her presence in the public sphere, where she can be in dialogue with the state. To add to this notion,

---

[55] Lisa DiCaprio, "The Betrayal of Srebrenica: The Ten-Year Commemoration," *The Public Historian* 31(3): 73–95 (Summer 2009); Sabina Cehajic, Rupert Brown, and Emanuele Castano, "Forgive and Forget?: Antecedents and Consequences of Intergroup Forgiveness in Bosnia and Herzegovina," *Political Psychology* 29(3): 351–367 (June 2008); Alma Brnicanin, "Remembering Srebrenica," *Al Jazeera* (July 11, 2013), available at www.aljazeera.com /indepth/features/2013/2013/07/201371171716868343.html.

[56] *Mothers of Srebrenica v. The State of the Netherlands and the United Nations* (Dutch Supreme Court 2012).

[57] *The State of the Netherlands v. Hasa Nuhanović* (Supreme Court of the Netherlands), September 6, 2013.

[58] Quoted in Rita Arditti, *Searching for Life: The Grandmothers of the Plaza de Mayo and the Disappeared Children of Argentina* (Berkeley: University of California Press, 1999), 8.

Vezzetti references the work of another Argentine scholar, Guillermo O'Donnell, who actually calls this closure of the public sphere *desciudadanización*, or "de-citizen-ization."[59] Although these two scholars are writing specifically of the Argentine experience, processes of de-citizen-ization are evident in almost every case of genocide, as certain segments of a society are labeled pure and good, while others are defined as the impure element that, as Arjun Appadurai argues, prevent the majority group from reaching "the horizon of an unsullied national whole, a pure and untainted national ethos."[60]

In the face of processes that reduce the individual's role and power when it comes to matters of the state, co-embodied practices can provide a means for restoring lost forms of agency. Furthermore, in the aftermath of genocide, they can offer new avenues for active citizenship that were not exercised prior to the violence. In fact, as Emily Klein argues, it is difficult even to conceive of the notion of citizenship today without thinking of it as an embodied practice – one that often uses the tools of spectacle to assert itself. She writes, "Distinct from traditional definitions of legal and political citizenship that entail obeying laws and helping to craft them, these new brands of embodied and engaged citizenship promote the broader values of critical reflection and, when necessary, active and spectacular expressions of dissent."[61] This use of spectacular embodied performance to express dissent and, in the same moment, construct new potential modes of being for the political subject has manifested across cultural contexts and has proved key in reinvigorating political or civil agency in postgenocidal or totalitarian societies.

The Red Power Movement, which began with the Occupation of Alcatraz Island in 1969, featured a variety of protests and demonstrations, but perhaps the most climactic of these was the Longest Walk of 1978, in which hundreds of American Indians gathered in San Francisco, site of the Alcatraz Occupation, and began a cross-country walk to Washington, DC, to deliver a list of demands to then President Carter. The walk took five months. According to Troy Johnson, Duane Champagne, and Joane Nagel, "The Longest Walk was intended to symbolize the forced removal of American Indians from their homelands and to draw attention to the continuing problems of Indian people and their communities."[62] It was a larger

---

[59] Hugo Vezzetti, *Pasado y Presente: Guerra, Dictadura y Sociedad En La Argentina* (Buenos Aires: Siglo Vientiuno, 2002), 53.

[60] Arjun Appadurai, *Fear of Small Numbers: An Essay on the Geography of Anger* (Durham, NC: Duke University Press, 2006), 8.

[61] Emily Klein, "Spectacular Citizenships: Staging Latina Resistance through Urban Performances of Pain," *Frontiers: A Journal of Women Studies* 32(1): 102 (2011).

[62] Troy Johnson, Duane Champagne, and Joane Nagel, "American Indian Activism and Transformation," in *American Indian Activism: Alcatraz to the Longest Walk*, edited by Troy Johnson, Joane Nagel, and Duane Champagne (Urbana: University of Illinois Press, 1997), 37.

recreation of an earlier protest known as the Trail of Broken Treaties (1972), a reference to the infamous Trail of Tears of the 1830s, in which thousands of native peoples were forced to relocate from the eastern United States to the west; many died during the arduous trek.[63]

Although the Longest Walk was meant to highlight the failed promises of the United States, as a co-embodied practice it also created a new form of agency for the participants and those they represented. Moving in the opposite direction of the Trail of Tears, an act of forced relocation from east to west, the Longest Walk was a voluntary act of migration from west to east. As such, it could be viewed as a performative undoing of the Trail of Tears, an act of resistance whereby the participating American Indians reclaimed the agency that had been taken from them by marching back to the place their ancestors were forced to leave. Furthermore, by ending the walk in Washington, DC, and petitioning the government directly for policy changes, the participants also used the practice to emphasize their role as citizens and to claim all of the rights that come with that designation, thus undoing some of the processes of de-citizen-ization that they had been experiencing for years.

Another example comes from Rwanda, where, in 1994, between 500,000 and 1 million Rwandans were killed during one hundred days of ethnic violence primarily targeting the Tutsi minority. One of the key tools perpetrators used during the genocide in Rwanda was the national radio station, Radio Télévision Libre des Mille Collines (RTLM), to broadcast racist ideology that helped to incite genocide, including the public pronouncement of addresses where listeners were encouraged to go and kill the families living there. In 2011, in Berlin, the International Institute of Political Murder created a theater production/artistic installation called *Hate Radio* about the role that RTLM played in the genocide. During the production, actors performed transcripts from actual RTLM broadcasts word-for-word in a reconstructed radio studio, as audiences sat listening and watching. The text was performed in the original French and Kinyarwanda, with subtitles projected so the German-speaking audience could understand. No changes were made to the actual transcripts of the radio broadcast, but during "station breaks," video testimonies of survivors were projected onto the studio walls, which helped to frame the performance in a specific mode.[64]

---

[63] Ibid., 33; Ward Churchill, "The Bloody Wake of Alcatraz: Political Repression of the American Indian Movement During the 1970s," in *American Indian Activism: Alcatraz to the Longest Walk*, edited by Troy Johnson, Joane Nagel, and Duane Champagne (Urbana: University of Illinois Press, 1997), 246, 260.

[64] *Press Kit: Hate Radio: The Re-Enactment of an RTLM Genocide Radio Show* (Berlin: Augustin PR, 2011), available at http://international-institute.de/wp-content/uploads/2011/10/Press-Kit_Hate-Radio_11_08_02.pdf.

What was especially interesting about the performance was that the actors performing the roles of the RTLM hosts were all Rwandan survivors of the genocide. By performing these roles, these actors were speaking the words that, for some of them, led to the deaths (either directly or indirectly) of their own families, friends, and neighbors. Although the act of inhabiting the role of a perpetrator may seem morbid, it may also be seen as a co-embodied practice whereby survivors of genocidal violence claim a new form of agency by taking the words of the perpetrators and, rather than reusing them for their original intent, reframing them for the exact opposite purpose. *Hate Radio* is a piece of theater meant to make people understand the power of malicious propaganda to incite genocide in order that it not be used in such a way again. The words of perpetrators are being used to do exactly the opposite of what the perpetrators would have wanted. Moreover, this act is being carried out by the people those perpetrators wanted to exterminate. As such, it represents a moment wherein the survivors transform the agency of the perpetrator into their own form of agency in a paradoxical act that reverses the direction of power relations that allowed the Rwandan genocide to happen in the first place.[65]

14.3.5. Creating Spaces for Affective Transmission

Because co-embodied practice is by its nature social and public, one important thing it creates is a space for the transmission of affect to others. Many understand the transmissibility of affect as an irrational and therefore dangerous phenomenon due largely to the tendency to understand affective transmission in terms of notions like "mob mentality" and "groupthink," which emphasize the dangerous or unruly side of affective transmission. Indeed, the transmission of negative affect by a repressive regime through tools like propaganda and hate speech can be a key instrument in the commission of massive human rights violations, up to and including genocide. Nevertheless, affective transmission within a group can also have positive and productive effects, and co-embodied practices are often central in opening a space for this to occur. The affect transferred through these practices almost always has both positive and negative qualities; both shades of affect, however, can ultimately be productive when it comes to the recomposition of resonant violence.

First, co-embodied practices can create a space where the negative affect of participants is shared. This sharing of negative affect (like grief or anger)

---

[65] It is worth noting that, given the strict laws in Rwanda regulating how the genocide is remembered and discussed, *Hate Radio* could not be performed in Rwanda itself. It was created and performed in Germany.

can be connected to the de-atomizing power of co-embodied practice; it allows trauma to be experienced in a communal rather than isolated way. As Ann Cvetkovich writes in her seminal work *The Archive of Feelings*, shared affect, "including the affects associated with trauma, serves as the foundation for the formation of public cultures."[66] In other words, the same affects that may be difficult or unpleasant to experience alone can provide a rallying point around which new communities can gather and from which new sources of power and agency can emanate.

Second, co-embodied practice can spread and create positive affect as well. Ahmed writes that a common result in the transmission of affect between individuals is its conversion into new forms of affect.[67] As a case in point, what often happens through co-embodied practices that develop as a response to genocide is the conversion of negative affect into more positive affect. For example, when asked about her political activism in response to her son's disappearance, Taty Almeida, a member of the Madres de Plaza de Mayo-Linea Fundadora, says, "Actually, that pain, that rage, what they did to us did not leave us with hate. No! We transformed it into love for our children and into a fight – a peaceful fight."[68] With this statement, Almeida acknowledges the conversion of her negative affect into a positive force that propelled her and the other Mothers forward in an energizing and productive way.

Third, co-embodied practices may not only allow for the transmission of affect among those directly involved, but also among spectators of the events. In this way, sites of co-embodied practice can become what Alison Landsberg terms "transferential spaces," or spaces where even those who did not experience trauma directly can encounter and begin to understand the trauma of others.[69] If these transferential spaces make tragedy, as she writes, "imaginable, thinkable, and speakable to us,"[70] perhaps they can also produce new commitments toward the prevention of future tragedy. For instance, the public nature of the marches of the Madres de Plaza de Mayo led to international recognition of the human rights abuses in Argentina. This global support served both to protect the Madres within

---

[66] Cvetkovich, *An Archive of Feelings*, 10.

[67] Sara Ahmed, "Happy Objects," in *The Affect Theory Reader*, edited by Melissa Gregg and Gregory J. Seigworth (Durham, NC: Duke University Press, 2010), 38.

[68] "Porque justamente, ese dolor, esa rabia, ese que nos hicieron no nos quedamos con el odio. ¡No! Lo transformamos en amor a nuestros hijos, y en lucha – lucha pacífica." Taty Almeida, interview with author (July 17, 2013).

[69] Alison Landsberg, *Prosthetic Memory: The Transformation of American Remembrance in the Age of Mass Culture* (New York: Columbia University Press, 2004), 139.

[70] Ibid.

Argentina and to contribute to the dismantling of the military junta's power, leading to its demise in 1983.[71]

14.3.6. *Motivating the Transformation of State Structures*

A final and important performative possibility for co-embodied practices is their ability to create a social environment that either forces or convinces the state to modify its policies in dealing with past and present crimes and abuses. Michel Foucault, in the final series of lectures before his death, discussed at length the ancient Greek concept of *parresia*, which he defined as a very specific mode of truth-telling whereby a citizen presents himself to an unjust ruler in order to tell that ruler he is wrong about something.[72] However, not every act of truth-telling by a citizen to the state counts as *parresia*; Foucault wrote that true parrhesiasts "are those who undertake to tell the truth at an unspecified price, which may be as high as their own death."[73] Although the person who tells the truth to the state may risk her life, she may also succeed in persuading the state to change its ways.

Whereas, for Foucault, the spoken word is central to the act of *parresia*, I would argue that some co-embodied practices represent parrhesiatic acts of the body – truth-telling mechanisms in which the central means of "speaking" truth to power is the insertion or amplification of the body in public space. This mode of *parresia*, in which the truth-telling device *is* the corporal act, is especially powerful because, during times of repression, the body is often the entity that feels the effects of repression most directly. Likewise, if parrhesiasts risk punishments up to and including death, it is the body that receives that punishment as it is transformed from body to corpse.

When co-embodied practices function as parrhesiatic events, however, it does not always result in punishment and death. They may also succeed in their efforts to tell the truth and, thus, persuade a change in the ruling body. When this happens – when the parrhesiasts succeed – they must then decide how to move forward. Do they continue their bodily acts of truth-telling by finding new missions, new aspirations, new truths to be told? Or do they consider their task complete, their truth told, and revert to less vocal (although not necessarily less participatory) modes of citizenship?

This decision describes one that two of the different Argentine activist groups discussed in this chapter had to make in the recent past. By the early

---

[71] Marguerite Guzman Bouvard, *Revolutionizing Motherhood: The Mothers of the Plaza de Mayo* (Wilmington, DE: Scholarly Resources, 1993).

[72] Michel Foucault, *The Government of the Self and Others: Lectures at the College de France, 1982–1983*, edited by Frédéric Gros, translated by Graham Burchell (New York: Palgrave Macmillan, 2010).

[73] Ibid., 56.

2000s, both branches of the Madres de Plaza de Mayo were still marching every week in the central square, while H.I.J.O.S. was still making *escraches* to call for justice for the perpetrators of the genocide. For years, the Argentine government refused to take an active stance toward dealing with the history of the dictatorship, but this changed in 2003, with the election of Nestor Kirchner as president. Kirchner made memory of the past a huge focus of his presidency. Soon after his election, the laws that prevented the prosecution of crimes during the dictatorship were declared unconstitutional, and trials for perpetrators resumed in 2005.

All along, the rallying cry of the H.I.J.O.S.' *escraches* had been "*Si no hay justicia, hay escrache!*" ("If there is no justice, there is *escrache!*") Now that perpetrators were being put on trial again, the formal justice for which H.I.J.O.S. had been protesting was a reality. As such, in large part, H.I.J.O.S. stopped organizing *escraches*. Although the group still exists today, the most visible manifestation of the group has disappeared. Many former participants have even gone on to work in public office for the government. The parrhesiatic act of H.I.J.O.S., the *escrache*, contributed to changing the tides of the state, and, when it succeeded, most of its participants celebrated their success and the new, more memory-conscious government.

The Madres, on the other hand, chose not to discontinue their weekly marches in the main square. These women, who began marching nearly fifteen years before H.I.J.O.S. was even formed, contributed immensely to the shift in memory policy by the Argentine government. Even though the murderers of their children were finally being brought to justice, however, both groups of Madres have adapted to the current political climate by modifying and broadening the scope of their activism. For instance, the Asociación Madres de Plaza de Mayo started the Universidad Popular Madres de Plaza de Mayo (People's University Mothers of the Plaza de Mayo), which trains Argentine youth in political activism. Madres de Plaza de Mayo-Linea Fundadora, on the other hand, has several programs that serve underprivileged or incarcerated youth, offering them artistic and musical training in the hopes of inspiring in them visions of a brighter future. Although these modes of activism are quite different from the initial mission of the Madres, both groups frame these new paths as continuing the political fight that their disappeared children were fighting. These programs serve as new parrhesiatic acts; they highlight to the state neglected populations or demographic groups by serving these populations themselves, and thus they contribute to the transformation of resonant violence by creating a more vibrant public sphere and a less atomized society. As such, the Madres have conceived of their mission as parrhesiasts as expanding, rather than as having been completed, when the trials resumed in 2005.

14.4.   Conclusion

On December 17, 2010, the single embodied act of a twenty-five-year-old Tunisian setting himself on fire led to an unprecedented and sudden boom of social movements throughout North Africa and the Middle East. As a result, several authoritarian governments fell completely, and the power of others was severely shaken. This renewed fervor of social movements could not be geographically contained, either. Since the end of 2010, the world has seen an enormous growth of similar movements worldwide, including Occupy Wall Street in the United States, Yo Soy 132 in Mexico, and the Indignados in Spain and Portugal. Although these movements have had varying levels of success in the extent of change they have effected, the co-embodied practices they have generated are representative of a larger reality that the world and, more specifically in relation to this text, the community working toward the prevention of genocide and mass atrocity must take into account: the state is not the only or even the most important source of power when it comes to thinking about prevention, at least when it comes to affecting actual change in the way a society handles physical, structural, or economic violence.

This chapter outlines one particular category of practice that has emerged spontaneously, across a variety of cultural contexts, as a means of addressing genocidal violence and its resonating effects in a manner independent of state processes. A brief survey, it is only the beginning of what I hope will be a much more extensive engagement with these practices and what they are able to do. I challenge the academic and activist communities to deepen this research by finding other practices that support or challenge these theories. I especially hope it leads to the discovery of even more performative capacities for such practices as people test these theories in other cultural contexts.

As a conclusion, I do feel the need to offer a few caveats. First and most importantly, I am not in any way asserting that co-embodied practices like those detailed in this chapter are events that can be forced into existence. Unlike many of the chapters in this volume that seek to offer practical suggestions for the prevention community, these co-embodied practices are not an item on the "to do" list of a state that is interested in preventing genocide. In fact, the power of these practices largely stems from the fact that they emerge spontaneously and independently of any state influence.

Second, I am not asserting that co-embodied practices, by their very nature, are positive. As stated earlier, genocide itself is a co-embodied practice. Moreover, the same societies that have developed positive and productive social movements that work toward the processing of resonant violence and thus the prevention of future violence have also generated other groups with their own set of co-embodied practices that work toward the perpetration and continuation of resonant violence. For every march during the Civil Rights

Movement, there was likely a cross-burning by the Ku Klux Klan. Both are examples of co-embodied practice; only one was working toward the positive transformation of resonant violence.

Finally, given that these practices cannot be forced, how can they be helpful when it comes to thinking about prevention? What purpose does it serve to analyze them? More than anything, what I hope to offer with this chapter is a reminder that prevention is not something that only involves the state. Rather, it is a societal process that ultimately involves every citizen. Co-embodied practices like those mentioned in this chapter are an example of the influence that individual citizens with little political clout can have in preventing genocide, stopping genocide, and addressing past genocide so that it does not happen again. It becomes the role of states and the prevention community, then, to observe the practices that do emerge and to listen to the specific demands and assertions being made by those practices. As such, positive co-embodied practices can serve as guideposts for prevention strategy.

Given that every society must forge its own path in dealing with a violent past and preventing a violent future, it is particularly important to pay attention to the co-embodied practices emerging within a population because they can give the clearest picture of the needs and desires of a specific citizenry. Rather than structuring transitional justice and prevention strategies that come from the top and are designed to "trickle down" to the rest of the population, these practices can provide guidance in the formation of strategies that more clearly represent the society they are created to serve. Furthermore, they can help to remind state powers that perhaps the most important feature of a functioning society that upholds its responsibility to protect its own people is that it allows for an accessible public sphere where dissent can be expressed peacefully and openly.

Bibliography

Agamben, Giorgio. 1998. *Homo Sacer: Sovereign Power and Bare Life. Translated by Daniel Heller-Roazen*. Stanford: Stanford University Press.

Ahmed, Sara. 2004. *The Cultural Politics of Emotion*. New York: Routledge.

Ahmed, Sara. 2006. *Queer Phenomenology: Orientations, Objects, Others*. Durham, NC: Duke University Press.

Ahmed, Sara. 2010. "Happy Objects." In *The Affect Theory Reader*, edited by Melissa Gregg and Gregory J. Seigworth, 29–51. Durham, NC: Duke University Press.

Appadurai, Arjun. 2006. *Fear of Small Numbers: An Essay on the Geography of Anger*. Durham, NC: Duke University Press.

Arditti, Rita. 1999. *Searching for Life: The Grandmothers of the Plaza de Mayo and the Disappeared Children of Argentina*. Berkeley: University of California Press.

Arendt, Hannah. 1970. *On Violence*. New York: Harcourt, Brace, Jovanovich.

Arendt, Hannah. 1968. *The Origins of Totalitarianism*. New York: Harcourt.

Bouvard, Marguerite Guzman. 1994. *Revolutionizing Motherhood: The Mothers of the Plaza de Mayo*. Wilmington, DE: Scholarly Resources.

Brnicanin, Alma. July 11, 2013. "Remembering Srebrenica." *Al Jazeera*. Available at www.aljazeera.com/indepth/features/2013/2013/07/201371171716868343.html.

Burke, Sara. 2013. "Introduction: Time to Press the Reset Button on Representative Democracy? (Or Do We Need a Whole New Operating System?)." In *"The Future We the People Need: Voices from New Social Movements in North Africa, Middle East, Europe & North America*, edited by Werner Puschra and Sara Burke, 5–11. FES International Policy Analysis. New York: Friedrich Ebert Stiftung.

Calveiro, Pilar. 1998. *Poder y desaparición: los campos de concentración en Argentina*. Buenos Aires: Colihue.

Cehajic, Sabina, Rupert Brown, and Emanuele Castano. June 2008. "Forgive and Forget?: Antecedents and Consequences of Intergroup Forgiveness in Bosnia and Herzegovina." *Political Psychology* 29(3): 351–367.

Churchill, Ward. 1997. "The Bloody Wake of Alcatraz: Political Repression of the American Indian Movement During the 1970s." In *American Indian Activism: Alcatraz to the Longest Walk*, edited by Troy Johnson, Joane Nagel, and Duane Champagne, 242–284. Urbana: University of Illinois Press.

Connolly, William E. 2008. *Capitalism and Christianity, American Style*. Durham, NC: Duke University Press.

Cvetkovich, Ann. 2003. *An Archive of Feelings: Trauma, Sexuality, and Lesbian Public Cultures*. Durham, NC: Duke University Press Books.

DiCaprio, Lisa. Summer 2009. "The Betrayal of Srebrenica: The Ten-Year Commemoration." *The Public Historian* 31(3): 73–95.

Erikson, Kai. 1976. *Everything in Its Path: Destruction of Community in the Buffalo Creek Flood*. New York: Simon and Schuster.

Erlmann, Veit. 2010. *Reason and Resonance: A History of Modern Aurality*. Brooklyn: Zone Books.

Foster, Lenny. 1997. "Alcatraz Is Not an Island." In *American Indian Activism: Alcatraz to the Longest Walk*, edited by Troy Johnson, Joane Nagel, and Duane Champagne. Urbana: University of Illinois Press, 136–139.

Foucault, Michel. 2010. *The Government of the Self and Others: Lectures at the College de France, 1982–1983*. Edited by Frédéric Gros. Translated by Graham Burchell. New York: Palgrave Macmillan.

Galis, Tiberiu. 2015. "Keeping the Wolves at Bay: Transitional Justice and Reform in Argentina, South Africa and Hungary." PhD diss., Clark University.

Habermas, Jürgen. 1991. *The Structural Transformation of the Public Sphere: An Inquiry into a Category of Bourgeois Society*. Translated by Frederick G. Lawrence. Cambridge, MA: MIT Press.

Harff, Barbara. 2005. "Assessing Risk of Genocide and Politicide." In *Peace and Conflict: A Global Survey of Armed Conflicts, Self-Determination Movements, and Democracy*, edited by Monty G. Marshall and Ted Robert Gurr. College Park, MD: University of Maryland, 57–61.

Johnson, Troy, Duane Champagne, and Joane Nagel. 1997. "American Indian Activism and Transformation." In *American Indian Activism: Alcatraz to the Longest Walk*, edited by Troy Johnson, Joane Nagel, and Duane Champagne. Urbana: University of Illinois Press, 9–44.

Kaplan, Marion A. 1998. *Between Dignity and Despair: Jewish Life in Nazi Germany.* New York: Oxford University Press.

Klein, Emily. 2011. "Spectacular Citizenships: Staging Latina Resistance through Urban Performances of Pain." *Frontiers: A Journal of Women Studies* 32(1): 102–124.

Landsberg, Alison. 2004. *Prosthetic Memory: The Transformation of American Remembrance in the Age of Mass Culture.* New York: Columbia University Press.

Memoria Abierta. 2009. *Memorias En La Ciudad: Señales Del Terrorismo de Estado En Buenos Aires.* Buenos Aires: Eudeba.

Mothers of Srebrenica v. The State of the Netherlands and the United Nations (Dutch Supreme Court 2012).

Nancy, Jean-Luc. 2007. *Listening*, 4th ed. Translated by Charlotte Mandell. New York: Fordham University Press.

Pile, Steve. 1997. "Introduction: Opposition, Political Identities and Spaces of Resistance." In *Geographies of Resistance*, edited by Steve Pile and Michael Keith. London: Routledge,1–32.

Press Kit: Hate Radio: The Re-Enactment of an RTLM Genocide Radio Show. 2011. Berlin: Augustin PR. Available at http://international-institute.de/wp-content/uploads/2011/10/Press-Kit_Hate-Radio_11_08_02.pdf.

Protevi, John. 2009. *Political Affect: Connecting the Social and the Somatic.* Minneapolis: University of Minnesota Press.

"Quiénes Somos." H.I.J.O.S. (Accessed July 28, 2013). www.hijos-capital.org.ar/index.php?option=com_content&view=article&id=20&Itemid=399.

Ramírez-Barat, Clara. 2013. "Introduction: Transitional Justice and the Public Sphere." In *Beyond Outreach: Transitional Justice, Culture and Society*, edited by Clara Ramírez-Barat. New York: SSRC.

Roach, Joseph. 1996. *Cities of the Dead: Circum-Atlantic Performance.* New York: Columbia University Press.

Schechner, Richard. 2002. *Performance Studies: An Introduction.* London: Routledge.

Stanton, Gregory H. 2008. *Eight Stages of Genocide.* Los Angeles: Sage.

Stanton, Gregory H. 1996. *The 8 Stages of Genocide.* Briefing Paper for United States Department of State. www.genocidewatch.org/images/8StagesBriefingpaper.pdf

Taylor, Diana. 1997. *Disappearing Acts: Spectacles of Gender and Nationalism in Argentina's "Dirty War."* Durham, NC: Duke University Press.

Taylor, Diana. 2003. *The Archive and the Repertoire: Performing Cultural Memory in the Americas.* Durham, NC: Duke University Press.

Vezzetti, Hugo. 2002. *Pasado y Presente: Guerra, Dictadura y Sociedad En La Argentina.* Buenos Aires: Siglo Vientiuno.

15 Early Warning for Mass Atrocities: Tracking Escalation Parameters at the Population Level

Jennifer Leaning

15.1. Introduction

Since the end of the Cold War, the international community has intensified its commitment to reduce instances of conflict and mass atrocities. To this end, over the past twenty-five years, the United Nations and the International Criminal Court have established principles, statutes, commitments, and frameworks to ascertain and respond to situations of sustained attack on civilian populations.[1] The major actors and implementing agencies have formulated and debated the relative utility and applicability of concepts and approaches such as risk assessment, conflict prevention, responsibility to protect, humanitarian early warning, and prevention of genocide and mass atrocities.[2]

Now, there is a need to apply these understandings to the practical realm of policy so that national governments can ascertain and productively react to imminent and medium-term challenges to peace and stability within their own societies. At the same time, it is widely acknowledged that the capacity to raise such alerts at international and regional levels must also be strengthened and refined.[3]

The discussion in this chapter has a narrow intent: to identify ways to support the "alert" phase of early warning for mass atrocities. This intent pushes off

---

[1] UN Security Council, Final Report of the Commission of Experts Established Pursuant to Security Council Resolution 780 (1992), S/1994/674 (May 27, 1994), www.icty.org/x/file/Abo ut/OTP/un_commission_of_experts_report1994_en.pdf.

[2] UN General Assembly, Draft Resolution Referred to the High-Level Plenary Meeting of the General Assembly by the General Assembly at Its Fifty-Ninth Session: 2005 World Summit Outcome (September 15, 2005), http://responsibilitytoprotect.org/worldsummitout comed202005(1).pdf.

[3] UN Security Council, Report of the Secretary-General on the Protection of Civilians in Armed Conflict, S/2012/376 (May 22, 2012); UN Security Council, Report of the Secretary-General on the Protection of Civilians in Armed Conflict, S/2010/579 (November 11, 2010); UN Security Council, Report of the Secretary-General on the Protection of Civilians in Armed Conflict, S/2009/277 (May 29, 2009).

from the substantial work that has already been done to identify underlying risk factors.[4] At the same time, it acknowledges the essential prior and parallel activities of national governments to establish the key underpinnings of peace and stability: good governance, the rule of law, economic development and reduction of inequality, protection of human rights, and adequate health and *long-term* education, among other elements.[5] The discussion implicitly recognizes as well, *v.* however, that national attention to these longer term measures may prove fitful *short term* or inadequate and cannot substitute for capacities to alert government officials to divisive trends or events in their own society that require a fast response in order to prevent a slide into unrest or outright violence.

Early action, in response to alerts, may take a multitude of paths. Options with practical success have been tabulated and organized in several important recent UN documents and civil society reports.[6] Although ~~early~~ warning and early action inevitably take place as part of a policy continuum, for analytic purposes, there is value in looking closely at the process of early warning in itself. From this perspective, early warning can be understood as what is termed here a *complex mode of ascertainment*, the effort to scan and assess shifts in social, political, and economic dynamics that might signal the likelihood of a situation escalating into mass atrocities.

15.2.   Early Warning in the Humanitarian Context

Humanitarian early warning can be seen as the capacity to provide accurate and actionable information to relevant policymakers about impending escalation in a situation that threatens a large civilian population. Definitions from the International Federation of Red Cross and Red Crescent Societies emphasize the potential to galvanize community action: "An EWS [early warning system] represents the set of capacities needed to generate and disseminate timely and

---

[4] See Alex J. Bellamy and Stephen McLoughlin, "Preventing Genocide and Mass Atrocities: Causes and Paths of Escalation," Asia-Pacific Centre for the Responsibility to Protect (June 2009), www.r2pasiapacific.org/docs/R2P%20Reports/Causes%20and%20Paths%20of%20Escalation%20Report%20June%202009.pdf; see also European Peacebuilding Liaison Office, "Model Early Warning Matrix Country Report" (July 2012), www.eplo.org/assets/files/2.%20Activities/Civil%20Society%20Dialogue%20Network/Policy%20Meetings/EEAS%20Early%20Warning%20Tools/_Model_Early_Warning_Risk_Matrix.pdf and Global Centre for the Responsibility to Protect, "Populations at Risk" (accessed August 31, 2014), www.globalr2p.org/regions/.

[5] The World Bank Group, Worldwide Governance Indicators (WGI) Project (accessed August 31, 2014), http://info.worldbank.org/governance/wgi/index.aspx#home.

[6] See Asia Pacific Centre for the Responsibility to Protect, "Operationalizing the Responsibility to Prevent," APC R2P Brief 2.2 (2012); also Barbara Harff, "How to Use Risk Assessment and Early Warning in the Prevention and De-Escalation of Genocide and other Mass Atrocities," *Global Responsibility to Protect* 1(4): 506–531 (2009), and Gareth Evans, "The Responsibility to Protect: Ending Mass Atrocity Crimes Once and for All," *Irish Studies in International Affairs* 20(1): 7–13 (2009).

meaningful warning information that enables at-risk individuals, communities and organizations to prepare and act appropriately and in sufficient time to reduce harm or loss (adapted from UNISDR 2009 and others)."[7] From the perspective of the UN Special Adviser on the Prevention of Genocide, early warning is defined as "the collection, analysis and communication of information about escalatory developments in situations that could potentially lead to genocide, crimes against humanity or massive and serious war crimes, far enough in advance for relevant UN organs to take timely and effective preventive measures."[8]

The rationale for developing early warning in the general context of humanitarian crises (disaster, armed conflict, economic collapse, state failure, mass atrocities) has three elements:

1. These crises, once full-blown, exact extremely high human and economic costs over long periods of time. Many of these crises provoke or lead to extensive population flight and regional instability, wars of all kinds persist for years, and postcrisis phases are characterized by their protracted duration.
2. The baseline risks and escalation patterns for these crises are relatively well understood; in many settings, they are empirically discernible, and new technologies offer new discernment capacity.
3. To some extent, strategies for prevention, mitigation, and intervention have been defined and historically tested.

The rationale for early warning in the more specific context of mass atrocities is arguably even stronger because it is widely recognized that the social, psychological, economic, and political consequences of mass atrocities extend with perceptible negative power over generations and even centuries.[9]

15.2.1. Alerts at the Population Level

The notion of "alert" is embedded in the overall concept of early warning. It implies calling notice (usually in a negative sense, as in "alarm") to an observed

[7] International Federation of Red Cross and Red Crescent Societies, "Community Early Warning Systems: Guiding Principles" (Geneva, 2013), 13, www.ifrc.org/PageFiles/103323/1227800-IFRC-CEWS-Guiding-Principles-EN.pdf.

[8] Lawrence Woocher, "Developing a Strategy, Methods and Tools for Genocide Early Warning," Office of the Special Adviser to the UN Secretary-General on the Prevention of Genocide (New York: Center for International Conflict Resolution, Columbia University, September 26, 2006), www.un.org/en/preventgenocide/adviser/pdf/WoocherEarlywarningreport,2006-11-10.pdf

[9] See Marianne Hirsch, "The Generation of Postmemory," *Poetics Today* 29(1): 103–128. (2008), in Mieke Bal, Jonathan V. Crewe, and Leo Spitzer, eds. *Acts of Memory: Cultural Recall in the Present* (UPNE, 1999); Jenny Edkins, *Trauma and the Memory of Politics* (Cambridge: Cambridge University Press, 2003).

departure from average trend lines or to an incident that, because of its qualitative import, is known to require immediate attention.

In public health surveillance,[10] systems for establishing background trends in disease and illness are established. Using reporting protocols, now strengthened by technology that interrogate these background trends, an abrupt departure from data on average daily incidence of illness or another condition signals the possible onset of a new threat. For instance, in the Northern Hemisphere, a sudden surge during the late fall and early winter in visits to physicians and emergency departments for "influenza-like illness (ILI)" (fever $\geq 100°F$ plus cough or sore throat)[11] suggests the arrival of influenza season. This surge is identified through large statistical increases over the baseline number of visits routinely tracked over time. The cause is investigated, and, if the increase in patient visits persists and the complaints fit the case definition of influenza, the authorities announce the onset of flu season and notify all providers and the general population about the need to institute flu-specific preventive and treatment measures.

In refugee settings, the report of a single documented case of measles is treated as a sentinel event, a warning of impending risk of epidemic disease among a densely settled population, which requires an immediate emergency response. *sentinel alerts* Here, it is the known deadly contagion of measles in crowd settings that provokes such a strong response; this alert is based not on statistical variation, but on the qualitative import of the information. Years of empirical investigation have provided the knowledge that measles spreads very rapidly and with more virulence in emergency crowd settings where many children are unvaccinated.[12]

15.2.2. Case Definition

Central to this discussion of "alerts" is the concept of *case definition*. Every parameter of interest, such as a particular disease, requires a clear, unambiguous, and succinct definition. The definition may vary depending on the level of specificity and certainty required for making a diagnosis. In emergency settlements of displaced people, experience has shown there are five main conditions that contribute to mortality: measles, diarrhea, upper respiratory infections, malaria, and malnutrition.[13] Health workers in these settings must

[10] World Health Organization. "Public Health Surveillance," www.who.int/topics/public_health_ surveillance/en/
[11] Case definition for influenza: Centers for Disease Control and Prevention. "Interim Guidance on Case Definitions to Be Used For Investigations of Influenza A (H3N2)v Virus Cases," www.cdc .gov/flu/swineflu/case-definitions.htm
[12] Medicins sans Frontieres, *Refugee Health: An Approach to Emergency Situations* (London: Macmillan, 1997), 172–177.
[13] Mike J. Toole et al., "Famine-Affected, Refugee, and Displaced Populations: Recommendations for Public Health Issues. Recommendations and Reports," *Morbidity*

work rapidly because of the need to screen many people per day. By assuming this underlying prevalence pattern, they can maximize their efficiency and, as first priority, screen for these five conditions. Because diagnostic facilities are limited and the tests take time, health teams rely primarily on observation and physical examination. Hence, the case definitions for diseases of potential epidemic or high mortality concern are kept to the bare minimum required for rapid identification and application of proven first-line response or therapy.

15.2.3. Early Warning as Complex Ascertainment

Tracking population-level parameters to strengthen early warning for issues beyond epidemic surveillance requires developing an integrated set of analytic processes here referred to as *complex ascertainment*. The parameters of interest here, however, are not just trends in disease or mortality but in social or political issues, such as poverty, crime, income, education, migration, or employment. Some of the most powerful explanatory models of serious health conditions come from the work of social epidemiologists who analyze the social determinants of health through aggregation and cross-correlation of many lines of evidence and trend data developed in the social sciences.[14]

The approach termed "complex ascertainment" differs, however, from social epidemiology in that its aim is to warn, not to explain. Its task is to conduct surveillance, not explore relationships. And it is constrained by the practical imperative to provide warning at a population scale in as close to real time as possible.

Data that can be gleaned from major annual or quarterly reports on economic issues, for instance, are integrated with data from satellite surveillance, crowd sourcing, and social media. The complexity of this mixed form of ascertainment is that it involves gathering and making sense of different kinds of data and trends in differing geographic, political, and social conditions, as well as observations relating to human behavior. This information is iteratively analyzed based on known, assumed, or hypothesized relationships between and among these different data streams. The underlying assumptions and hypotheses deployed in these analytic moves have been derived from what has been learned from years of empirical and historical research into the drivers and escalation scenarios that lead to mass atrocities.

What is suggested here, in other words, is a merger of techniques of social epidemiology with what can be ascertained through crisis mapping technologies. This merger is already taking place in many commercial and

and Mortality Weekly Report (July 24, 1992/41 [RR-13];001), www.cdc.gov/mmwr/preview /mmwrhtml/00019261.htm

[14] Michael Marmot and Richard Wilkinson, *Social Determinants of Health* (Oxford: Oxford University Press, 1999).

military sectors, from marketing analyses and supply-chain management to urban planning and military game development. Work along these lines is well under way in the civilian disaster space. As applied to mass atrocities, the discussion is still notional but put forth here to invite engagement from these sectors in an effort to strengthen our capacity to discern impending signs of what is proving to be the most prevalent international crime of this new century.

15.2.3.1. Data in Complex Ascertainment

The concept of early warning in the social space thus builds on the notion of disease tracking, where the sudden occurrence of statistical variation in trend lines or the appearance of a sentinel event may suggest a need for heightened scrutiny or new action. A set of baseline conditions needs to be established and systems then put in place to highlight shifts in trends or occurrence of sentinel events.

[handwritten margin note: need baseline conditions]

In the social space of humanitarian crises or mass atrocities, however, baseline conditions could be seen as all those tracing the ebb and flow of human existence – not a feasible starting point for mass atrocity early warning. Furthermore, in this context, case definitions, although definitive, are not qualitatively or quantitatively precise.

Humanitarian crises include wars and disasters that threaten the life or welfare of a large noncombatant population and require outside help; the term itself has acquired a stability relatively unsecured by a more specific or empirically assembled definition.[15] The case definition for mass atrocities is grounded in analysis of historical experience[16] and encapsulated in international legal treaties.

Several requirements for data gathering and data analysis underscore the complexity attached to this kind of early warning:

- Historical and legal understanding of multifaceted case definitions (disaster, war, forced migration, mass atrocities) determines the kinds of data that are sought and the relationships that are assumed or hypothesized.
- Data gathering must be omnivorous, real-time, and continuous (to the greatest extent possible), as well as limited in time frame of interest and geographic scope, since it must incorporate and, in many cases, rely predominantly on remote observation.
- Data analysis must be tethered tightly to geographical and visual display because people act in space as well as time, and human analytic capacities are usually most strongly employed in visual modes.

---

[15] See http://humanitariancoalition.ca/info-portal/factsheets/what-is-a-humanitarian-crisis.
[16] Geoffrey Robertson, *Crimes Against Humanity: A Struggle for Global Justice* (New York: The New Press, 2000).

- Data analysis, to be robust and persuasive in the diplomatic and political realm, must rely on aggregation and modeling derived from accepted methods of epidemiology and social science inference.[17]
- Hypotheses are generated and validated in an ongoing analytic process that aims for speed as well as accuracy – resulting at its best in a trenchant but transient simplification.
- These processes are repeated on a daily, weekly, or monthly basis, depending on the underlying dynamics of the parameters of interest and on what kinds of trends or sentinel events have been discerned.

15.2.3.2. Technological Support The advent of mobile phone technologies and web-based data gathering capacity permits the assembly of a vast array of data. Satellite mapping equipped with capacities for high-resolution imagery and infrared tracing are technologies now more available in the civilian space. Diffusion of drones for civilian use may immensely accelerate the capacity for remote observation at closer and more precise resolution in small areas than satellite surveillance.

Many sources of information are now accessible from the internet (websites, email, online situation reports, blogs, pictures, video, audio, social media such as Twitter and Facebook).

Mobile phones increasingly come with GPS chips, and communication costs will continue to plummet. Location-aware applications for mobile technologies are becoming rapidly popular around the world, and this trend is only going to increase. Mobile technology allows users to capture ambient information and targeted information. Communication of information can range from radio or SMS broadcasting to dissemination via cell or satellite uplink.

Crisis mapping technologies deployed now in a range of disaster settings[18] will prove helpful in identifying, recording, or tracking events and indicators that occur on a population scale and geo-locating these events and indicators on a map.

Current applications of crisis mapping technologies include:

- Mobile technology (communications and locations)
- Satellite imaging (Satellite Sentinel)[19]

---

[17] Gary King, Robert O. Keohane, and Sidney Verba, *Designing Social Inquiry: Scientific Inference in Qualitative Research* (Princeton, NJ: Princeton University Press, 1994).

[18] See discussion of 2010 Haiti earthquake in S. Brophy-Williams, N. Segaren, and J. Leaning, "Humanitarian Norms and the Use of Information," in *World Disaster Report 2013* (Geneva: International Federation of the Red Cross and Red Crescent Societies, 2013), 163–193. Also see role played by Open Street map in identifying small towns and roads throughout areas of West Africa hit by Ebola epidemic; http://wiki.openstreetmap.org/wiki/2014_West_Africa_Ebola_Response#Daily_updates

[19] Satellite Sentinel, www.satsentinel.org/

structural aspects

escalation scenarios

- Crowd sourcing (Ushahidi plus)[20]
- Internet trolling (spiders, etc.)
- Ground mapping (Open Street map)[21]
- Remote seismic and toxic gas sensing (explosions, toxic gases)
- Social networking platforms (communications and social relationships)
- Civilian drones[22]

15.3.   Early Warning for Mass Atrocities: From Data to Information to Patterns

Our understanding of mass atrocities as a complex social phenomenon that moves through time and space allows us to consider the potential opportunities for early warning arising from shifts in observable or ascertainable dynamics and inflection points.

All international frameworks for conflict or mass atrocity prevention make the distinction between fundamental structural aspects of a given society (such as history of previous genocide or marked disparities in income) that have been found to increase the risk of potential mass atrocities – and the escalation scenario that sets an at-risk society on an escalation path toward actual occurrence of mass atrocities.[23]

The escalation scenarios for a given society, let alone for a general framework, have not yet been developed to support an actionable and reliable platform for early warning. A number of historical instances of mass atrocities have been analyzed from the standpoint of escalation steps, however. It is these steps that analysts of at-risk societies now look for when assessing escalation paths.

It is argued here that the application of complex ascertainment for early warning in humanitarian crises might permit the development of more systematic prototypes for assessing mass atrocity escalation paths.

What follows in this section is first the elaboration of the case definition of mass atrocities and then the application of complex ascertainment to the challenge of discerning mass atrocity escalation pathways.

---

[20] Ushahidi, www.ushahidi.com/

[21] See Openstreet map web site and current map development for Ebola in West Africa, www .openstreetmap.org/

[22] Civilian drones now used for weather forecasting, traffic patterns, law enforcement, and other functions. See Global Research. Center for Research on Globalization, www.globalresearch.ca /unmanned-aerial-vehicles-uav-drones-for-military-and-civilian-use/5374666

[23] UN Office for Genocide Prevention and the Responsibility to Protect, "A Framework of Analysis for Mass Atrocity Crimes: Risk Factors [draft]" (Summer 2014).

15.3.1. Case Definition

The accepted case definition of mass atrocities includes genocide and other forms of violence against targeted groups, but also crimes against humanity and war crimes.[24] A more fine-grained appreciation of the nature and process of mass atrocity involves looking more closely at the three main categories of crime it encompasses.

The term "mass atrocity" derives from the legal definition of atrocity crimes as developed in international law and now enshrined in the Rome Statute of the International Criminal Court.[25] Atrocity crimes encompass three separate categories: genocide, crimes against humanity, and war crimes.

The elements to watch for in the legal definitions of these crimes provide the definitional framework for mass atrocity early warning.

15.3.1.1. Genocide
Genocide, as defined in the 1948 Convention on the Prevention and Punishment of the Crime of Genocide, is the deliberate targeted attempt to annihilate in whole or in part a group identified by nationality, race, ethnicity, or religion. Past instances of genocide have involved systematic and widespread assault against a group so identified. The acts include killings, rapes, and extensive destruction of conditions that support life.[26]

The intent to commit these acts is an essential element of the crime. Establishing intent has proved very difficult, particularly in sufficient real time to mobilize that aspect as grounds for intervening. However, recent efforts to argue a presumption of intent, based on observations of the scale and organization of the acts, may prove fruitful.[27]

15.3.1.2. Crimes against Humanity
Crimes against humanity are systematic acts of extreme violence against civilian populations – such as killings, rapes, and ethnic cleansing – that violate the dignity and rights of populations, whether in peace or in war. Kidnapping, experimentation, torture, and other murderous and degrading acts are covered under this category.

---

[24] European Union Task Force on the EU Prevention of Mass Atrocities, *The EU and the Prevention of Mass Atrocities: An Assessment of Strengths and Weaknesses*, 2013. Foundation for the International Prevention of Genocide and Mass Atrocities. http://massatrocitiestask force.eu/Report_files/

[25] David Scheffer, "Genocide and Atrocity Crimes," *Genocide Studies and Prevention* 1(3): 229–250 (2006).

[26] UN General Assembly, Convention on the Prevention and Punishment of the Crime of Genocide, 78 UNTS 277/ [1951] ATS 2 / UN Doc. A/RES/260 (December 9, 1948), www.un .org/ga/search/view_doc.asp?symbol=a/res/260(III).

[27] Jennifer Leaning, "Diagnosing Genocide – The Case of Darfur," *New England Journal of Medicine* 351: 735–738 (August 19, 2004).

Individual authorities with some knowledge of the acts, acting on behalf of a state or state-like entity, can be charged with these crimes.[28]

15.3.1.3. War Crimes War crimes are those defined in the Rome Statute as grave violations of the Four Geneva Conventions and other laws and customs of the international law of armed conflict.

15.3.2. Complex Ascertainment in Mass Atrocity Escalation

The assessment of trends by complex ascertainment methodologies enables the establishment of a background baseline regarding ordinary or normal fluctuations in conditions of interest, as well as the addition of solid confirmatory or cautionary understanding against which to assess changes in trends, insertion of new players, or other factors.

Background data metrics of focused interest in mass atrocity early warning involve tracking baseline and shifting conditions that will intensify underlying stresses in a community or country. These metrics include sudden internal shifts in population movement or settlement, anticipatory signs of how and where people will move when they are attacked, or departures from normal group behavior, such as marketplace gatherings.

With these considerations in mind, development of relevant background conditions for mass atrocity escalation would aim to provide data on ecological or social context and data on relevantly independent variables known empirically to be pivotal in escalation scenarios.

15.3.2.1. Baseline Information Baseline information would thus be collected in the following categories and subcategories:

- Geography, human and natural

  - Access to water
  - Natural obstacles to flight (wide rivers, mountains)
  - Forests and tree cover

- Demography, current and past trends

  - Population growth
  - Migration from rural to urban settlement
  - Population density

[28] Larry May, *Crimes Against Humanity: A Normative Account* (Cambridge: Cambridge University Press, 2005).

- Human settlement

  - Farms, urban areas
  - Periurban informal congregations
  - Neighborhoods (heterogeneous or homogeneous by ethnicity, race, religion, language, etc.)
  - Schools (heterogeneous or homogeneous by ethnicity, race, religion, language, etc.)

- Agricultural and livestock impacts on land, forest cover, and water
- Fuel and transportation routes
- Human mobility routines

  - Travel/commuter routes
  - Market days
  - Holiday travel routes and destinations
  - Religious or ceremonial gatherings

- Use of mobile phones (steady state)
- Previous behavior of authorities, assailants, and perpetrators

  - Methods of assault, oppression, and infliction of terror
  - Identification and forced settlement of target population

- Past behavior of victims from previous instances of mass atrocities or conflict

  - Modes and routes of early and late flight
  - Range of survival strategies
  - Manifestations of desperation, revenge, grief, fear

15.3.2.2. Identification of Trend Shifts or Sentinel Events   Information would also be collected on sudden shifts from background trends or steady-state dynamics that we know from past experience to have been useful in signaling significant trend departures or possible sentinel events (often termed "triggers" or "red flags" in mass atrocities parlance).[29]

- Meteorological trend shifts

  - Rainfall, drought, unusual weather conditions
  - Recent major natural disasters
  - Seasonally imposed variation in access and exit routes

---

[29] Geoff Loane et al., "Civilian Protection and Humanitarian Assistance – Report of the 2009 Civilian Protection Working Group," *Prehospital and Disaster Medicine* 24(S2): s197–s201 (2009). Situational awareness measures are described to warn humanitarians that the local area is under threat.

- Worsening market and trade and financial dynamics
- Agrarian distress signs, such as sale of next year's seeds, failure to plant next season's crops, sale of livestock, male migration to towns, entire families leaving for cities under burden of drought or debt or scattered hostile armed attack
- Signs of rising friction in social relationships among hostile or stigmatized groups

  - Identity group separation, such as increases in communally segregated settlements or schools
  - Sudden influx of unfamiliar or alien communally defined groups
  - Appearance and growing intensity of hate speech (media, graffiti, posters)

- Changes in observed group and individual behavior known to shift under various kinds of stress

  - Absence of usual social gatherings or sudden appearance of new street crowds
  - Increase in abandoned or deserted homes in stressed neighborhoods
  - Changes in activity at hospitals, clinics, pharmacies, markets
  - Shifts in road traffic (speed, vehicles, trucks)
  - Pedestrian behavior (no greetings on streets, crossing streets when other people draw near)
  - Imposition of curfews
  - Signs of new and growing numbers of fresh graves
  - Escalation in social and behavioral responses to social friction, such as increase in passport applications, uptick in one-way travel out of the country, bank withdrawals, stock market sell-off

- Military and civilian weapons, installations, transport

  - Military and police presence; specific units, equipment; evidence of effective command structure
  - Kinds of weapons carried by officials, military, civilians, including children
  - Presence of and discipline at checkpoints
  - Hardening of roads, new airfields

- Time frames in which these metrics are expressed

  - Rapid clustering of observations
  - Rapid sequencing along plausible causal pathways (military influx, appearance of fresh graves)

15.3.2.3. Information-Gathering Methods   The information features just outlined demand multiple and various mechanisms for data acquisition. To the extent that we have acquired experience with complex ascertainment in early warning for disasters, it appears that the following methods might be the most powerful in acquiring data to use in anticipating trends or identifying sentinel events for mass atrocities:

- Observation of daily social behaviors (remotely or from observers in area)
- Interviews with key stakeholders and policy experts, targeted individuals, vulnerable groups (structured, open-ended focus groups)
- Assessments of local civil society leaders, historians, human rights experts, social scientists with expertise relevant to the region and the societies in question
- Analysis of media content and tone (particularly hate speech and incitement to violence; much can be gleaned from web-based sources)
- Targeted or random survey interviews of people in defined population areas (qualitative and quantitative)
- Study of maps (topographical, seasonal, political, social-demographic)
- Interrogation or analysis of existing digitized and nondigitized databases (sequential reports from major agencies on economics, climate change, population growth, landmine datasets, photographs, past satellite imagery – Google and Digital Globe)

15.3.2.4. Early Warning for Mass Atrocities: From Information to Patterns   Whether something of significance is transpiring in a given area requires a seasoned understanding of what to look for and which questions to ask. This understanding springs from the recognition of patterns based on analysis of past experience. Pattern recognition can bolster crucial attention to changes in qualitative details (substantive changes in content of speech, for instance, or introduction of new armed elements), shifts in trend lines, and apprehension of sentinel events.

15.3.2.4.1. Patterns   It is now well understood that human beings best absorb complex information when it can be expressed in a visual format.[30] People think most generatively about a particular situation when the presentation of information permits visualization of context (often through maps) and depicts data adjacencies and connections. These relationships may derive from displays of statistical analyses (such as trend lines, scatter plot diagrams, tables), organized static or dynamic geospatial graphics

---

[30] Edward R. Tufte, *The Visual Display of Quantitative Information* (Cheshire, CT: Graphics Press, 1983).

(such as spread of assaults against communities through time and across varying terrain), or categories of qualitative associations and contextual understandings observed in many different empirical fact pictures that have proved robust through time.

Visualization supports the process of simplification – an essential activity of human intelligence[31] – and allows people to make sense of their world. Visualization proves particularly helpful in sense-making as incoming data and information become increasingly diverse and voluminous.[32] Such visual depictions of many bits of data and information are helpful in themselves to promote understanding of the big picture and its many interlocking variables. Those positioned as policy or academic analysts of mass atrocities may find these depictions particularly useful because the context in question may call up data and information that otherwise their brains, operating in routine modes, would find strange or not immediately self-explanatory.

The most significant aspect of this understanding derived from visual simplifications, however, is that the visual platform provides the critical stimulus for further inquiry. Visualizing data promotes much more than a better appreciation of a particular fact picture. The very process of seeing phenomena in relationship to space, time, or other variables drives a deeper cognitive process of interrogation. As Tufte said, "At their best, graphics [visual displays] are instruments for reasoning about quantitative information."[33] Why are groups of people in the midst of the rainy season fleeing along these dry season paths, even as they must know the route is already starting to flood? (In Angola, check the landmine dataset maps for this area.) Why are these street demonstrations always going along the same avenues in this city? (In the Balkans, northern Ireland, and Hungary, check last census for ethnic/religious population by street map, or check for historical routes of previous mass demonstrations.) Why has this large weekly market been apparently deserted for the last month? (In Liberia, check for infiltration of hostile militias; check for trade in small arms, drugs, or humans by volume of small plane traffic at adjacent borders; or check for new disease outbreak.)

Repeat visualizations and interrogations of the same situation, matched against repeat visualizations or detailed fact descriptions from other contexts, define the process of pattern recognition. We navigate our familiar world through a library of pattern recognitions. In the fraught and unstable world of impending mass atrocities, early warning will require the development of

---

[31] Mann L. and I. L. Janis, "Emergency Decision-making: A Theoretical Analysis of Responses to Disaster Warnings," *Journal of Human Stress* 3(2): 35–47 (1977).

[32] Jennifer Leaning, "The Use of Patterns in Crisis Mapping to Combat Mass Atrocity Crimes," in *Mass Atrocity Crimes: Preventing Future Outrages*, edited by Robert I. Rotberg (Washington, DC: Brookings Institution Press, 2010), 192–219.

[33] Edward Tufte, *The Visual Display of Quantitative Information*, 9 (introduction).

similar libraries, comprised of very different patterns. And, as our process of pattern formation and recognition matures, in any particular setting our capacity to identify a parsimonious set of highly relevant indicators will become increasingly more effective.[34]

15.3.2.4.2. The Emerging Role of Big Data

Building patterns and libraries of patterns for mass atrocity early warning requires amassing and aggregating data and information from a very rich array of sources. This effort requires major technical supports. Twenty years ago, computational capacities had not yet established deep connections to the Internet and information-communication technologies were in their infancy. Information sources related to mass atrocities could be found in the general literature on human rights violations, including books, journal articles, conference proceedings, reports from human rights groups, legal documents and court findings, various annual reports by UN and international institutions, and laboriously constructed purpose-built databases for use by academic social scientists and government agencies.[35] Aside from this last information source, which lived on individual and non-networked computers,[36] all reports were in printed form only, and even learning that they existed, let alone gaining access to them, took significant time and effort.

Yet efforts at early warning for crises of various sorts (famine, armed conflict) were under way. Spurred by recurrent famines and refugee crises[37] and by the atrocity-laden wars of the early 1990s (above all the Rwandan genocide),[38] analysts and scholars debated issues of indicators and sequences of key human behaviors, relying on their close reading of historical events and their in-depth experience in trying to mount a response to particular (and often repeated) instances of social distress in one geographic setting, such as the Horn of Africa or the African Great Lakes. The entire international political edifice of early warning for armed conflict and atrocities was constructed

---

[34] For instance, Russell Schimmer at Yale has analyzed GIS data of vegetation growth to reveal patterns about the genocide/displacement in Darfur. See also Patrick Meier, "Tracking Genocide by Remote Sensing," iRevolution (accessed August 31, 2014), http://irevolution.wordpress .com/2008/06/12/tracking-genocide-by-remote-sensing/.

[35] Hans Thoolen, "Information Aspects of Humanitarian Early Warning, in *Early Warning and Conflict Resolution*, edited by Kumar Rupesinghe and Michiko Kuroda (London: St Martins Press, MacMillan Press, 1992), 166–179.

[36] Philip A. Strodt, "Pattern Recognition of International Crises Using Hidden Markov Models, in *Synergy in Early Warning: Conference Proceedings*, edited by Susanne Schmiedl and Howard Adelman (Toronto: University of Toronto, March 15–18, 1997).

[37] Peter Walker, "Famine Early Warning and Local Knowledge: The Possibilities for Pro-active Responses to Stress," in *Early Warning and Conflict Resolution*, edited by Kumar Rupesinghe and Michiko Kuroda (London: St Martins Press, MacMillan Press, 1992), 87–104.

[38] Mark Levene, "Connecting Threads: Rwanda, the Holocaust, and the Pattern of Contemporary Genocide," in *Genocide: Essays toward Understanding, Early Warning, and Prevention*, edited by Roger W. Smith (Williamsburg, VA: Association of Genocide Scholars, 1999), 27–64.

during these past twenty years, building almost entirely on anecdotal reports or generalized themes gleaned from the writing of academic and policy authorities whose findings were published or, with varying degrees of difficulty, reported in the gray literature.[39]

The great majority of these analyses of early warning for mass atrocities took the form of detailed examination of one specific instance linked to a discussion of comparative themes emerging from the literature on other mass atrocities. In other words, inherent in the process was a *forme fruste* of pattern formation and recognition.

Since 2009, crisis early warning for disasters has begun to make use of crowd sourcing, social media, and satellite technologies in order to map terrain, cities, and population flows to support humanitarian efforts, including the sounding of early alerts.[40] Not yet realized, however, is the potential for Big Data to support a capacity for complex ascertainment and pattern formation in early warning of mass atrocities.

The promising challenge ahead is to marshal and organize the massive amounts of information and data (now existing in many places and formats, across historical, social, political, and environmental sectors, much of it not digitized) into structured and searchable information. The aim would be to enable an end user to analyze the urgency and leverage points in a specific escalation scenario within a time frame when action will make a difference. What makes this aim possible is the sophisticated deployment of information technologies on the Web and the exponentially expanding prowess of Big Data to acquire, sort, and aggregate data from diverse sources (digitized and nondigitized, structured or nonstructured).

With this aim in mind, the approach to Big Data requires two related but very distinct analytic efforts. The first involves intense engagement with content experts – academics in the social and statistical sciences and policy analysts, some with practical field experience in assessments of armed conflict and mass atrocities. They must take the lead in finding user-friendly ways to document and classify patterns of relevant escalation scenarios. The main task is to specify the categories, metrics, measures, and indicators of known or hypothesized relevance to the building of background patterns, and patterns of departures, in trends and occurrence of sentinel events.

For instance, it is well understood that hate speech is an important parameter to track for prevention of mass atrocities, both as a background risk factor and a

---

[39] See, e.g., the notes and background readings assembled to support the report of the Independent International Commission on the Responsibility to Protect, International Commission on Intervention and State Sovereignty, *The Responsibility to Protect: Report of the International Commission on Intervention and State Sovereignty* (Ottawa: International Development Research Centre, December 2001), http://responsibilitytoprotect.org/ICISS%20Report.pdf.

[40] International Network of Crisis Mappers, www.un-spider.org/book/export/html/5099.

trend indicator (through mounting intensity, frequency, and volume) that signals a possible escalation path.[41] Beyond that understanding, however, policymakers and analysts working on mass atrocities have not addressed the nested set of precise and specific components of hate speech that would allow Big Data to conduct a rational and useful search. To draw out the problem, one could say that the category is hate speech while the metric is the volume, frequency, and intensity of hate speech in a specified period of time and via a specified medium (such as radio). But the measure of volume, frequency, or intensity has not yet been discussed in any detail: how would one quantitatively or qualitatively specify these components? Furthermore, we recognize that what is deemed hate speech in one culture may not necessarily be deemed as such in another and that what has the most pernicious effect in some societies is hate radio, whereas, in others, the peak incitement may be driven by the hate-filled speeches of political leaders.

This example reveals the gap between what the atrocity prevention community would seek from Big Data experts and what our current fuzzy definitions would allow them to do. It will require major effort on the part of content experts to bridge that gap and dogged efforts on the part of data analysts to create programs sophisticated enough to search for what we have not yet been able to comprehensively specify.

The second analytic effort requires the enlistment of computer scientists familiar with Big Data analytics. Once strong approximations (or, better yet, the specific categories, metrics, measures, and indicators) have been defined by content experts, the ICT capacities[42] can be marshaled and programmed to develop a real-time taxonomy of mass atrocity escalation patterns. These patterns, over time iterated to create libraries of patterns, will permit end users in rapid real time to recognize an escalation scenario and issue early warning based on key indicators. The patterns may be sufficiently rich to support the identification of guidance for effective response.

Steps can be taken in the absence of such precise and specific delineation of these components. It would be possible to make rough approximations based on what we know to be significant factors in hate speech (use of insect terminology; commands to identify, segregate, deport, or annihilate a particular

---

[41] Office of the UN Special Adviser on the Prevention of Genocide, Analysis Framework (2009) at 1. United States Peacekeeping and Stability Operations Institute, *Mass Atrocity Prevention and Response Options (MAPRO): A Policy Planning Handbook* (Carlisle, PA: March 2012), 14–15.

[42] Necessary functionalities include data animation over time and space, high-resolution satellite imagery overlays (updated regularly), human and automated change-detection analysis over space and time, applied geostatistics for pattern analysis based on mass atrocity metrics, drag-and-drop mapping analysis widgets for customization, scenario building based on pattern analysis, simulation for alternative response options, and online/offline capability with synchronization (derived from discussions with Patrick Meier at the Harvard Humanitarian Initiative, Harvard University, in the years 2008–10).

group; or charges that a particular stigmatized group has aided and abetted an enemy of the state). Armed with these approximations, it would be possible to request, for example, a search for these terms in the Hungarian press (and in the few listservs that manually compile instances of hate speech in Hungary) to monitor possible escalations in hate speech against the Roma (see example in Section 5.2). And, as the section that follows attempts to demonstrate, the atrocity prevention community is already making good use of its current fund of knowledge and current technological capacities.

15.4. Early Warning for Mass Atrocities: From Patterns to Understanding

Over decades, historians and social scientists collectively have amassed and organized a prodigious amount of information relevant to armed conflict, genocide, crimes against humanity, and war crimes. This effort has also resulted in powerful consensus on the key elements and relationships among these elements that could, were an "atrocity prevention lens"[43] applied, allow us to identify critical inflection points along a possible escalation scenario.

15.4.1. Basic Understandings

The background information and pattern dynamics developed from this collective endeavor support a few basic understandings. The first is that human beings are caused to suffer and react to suffering in fairly predictable ways. Despite the infinite diversity in how humans experience suffering, the assaults on their well-being can be generally catalogued and their behavior in the face of these assaults can be largely observed and qualitatively described.

The second is that every society on earth is capable of committing mass atrocities, and virtually all of them have – in remote or recent pasts. Armed conflict or colonial conquest, as a recurrent feature in human social existence, provides the incentives and capacities for many of the mass atrocity crimes documented over the centuries. Fissures within societies can split open under the stress of war or economic collapse, often aggravated by factors such as fear, deprivation, and malignant leadership.[44]

The third understanding is that mass atrocities (i.e., genocide, crimes against humanity, and war crimes) follow distinct patterns of perpetrator escalation and population response. The original conception of this comes

---

[43] Alex J. Bellamy, "Mass Atrocities and Armed Conflict: Links, Distinctions, and Implications for the Responsibility to Prevent," Policy Analysis Brief, Stanley Foundation (February 2011), www.stanleyfoundation.org/resources.cfm?id=445.

[44] Ben Kiernan, *Blood and Soil: A World History of Genocide and Extermination from Sparta to Darfur* (New Haven, CT: Yale University Press, 2007).

from Raul Hilberg's painstaking reconstruction of the process of the destruction of the Jews in the Holocaust.[45]

As a geospatial application of early warning, this understanding could have illuminated the initial phases of more recent mass atrocities, such as the 1994 genocide in Rwanda. Government policies of forced migration, forced evacuation, or enforced mobility also have been shown to create fertile ground for infliction of mass atrocities, as in the Greek-Turkish population transfers following World War I,[46] ethnic cleansing strategies during the wars in the former Yugoslavia,[47] or in occupation regimes such as the West Bank and Gaza.[48]

15.4.2. Escalation Pathways

The following is a very simplified summary of known patterns in crisis escalation, all of which apply to escalation paths for mass atrocities. These dynamics (background conditions, shifts in trends, and triggers or sentinel events) are gleaned from analyses of current and historical instances.[49]

Complex ascertainment systems, using multiple methods and enlisting Big Data capacities where possible, would strengthen analysis of these patterns, permitting deployment of early warning as tensions intensify. These escalation scenarios and tipping points can be observed and reported on from a number of different perspectives and layers of society. Leaders and activists within a particular society and culture are likely to be able to perceive and interpret these behaviors more deeply and precisely than can outside actors. On the other hand, international and regional observers can provide important information to affirm or confront the assessments of local actors, since local leaders and activists may become inured to tipping or escalation points in chronic and long-standing situations of disparity and distress.

---

[45] Raoul Hilberg, *The Destruction of the European Jews* (New Haven, CT: Yale University Press, 2003).

[46] Bruce Clark, *Twice a Stranger: The Mass Expulsions that Forged Modern Greece and Turkey* (Cambridge, MA: Harvard University Press, 2009).

[47] Report of the Commission of Experts to the President of the UN Security Council on Grave Breaches of the Geneva Conventions. S/1994/674 (May 27, 1994), para. 129–150, www.icty .org/x/file/About/OTP/un_commission_of_experts_report1994_en.pdf

[48] See discussion on freedom of movement in Human Rights Committee, General Comment 27, Freedom of Movement (Art.12), U.N. Doc CCPR/C/21/Rev.1/Add.9 (1999). General Comment No. 27 * Freedom of movement, Article (12) Liberty of movement and freedom to choose residence (para. 1), http://www1.umn.edu/humanrts/gencomm/hrcom27.htm.

[49] See, e.g., Office of the UN Special Adviser on the Prevention of Genocide, Analysis Framework (2009), www.un.org/en/preventgenocide/adviser/pdf/osapg_analysis_framework.pdf. Also, UN Development Programme, *The Changing Nature of Conflict: Priorities for UNDP Response* (New York: UNDP, July 2013).

1. Background conditions of disparity/denial: Large segment of very poor; minorities who are heavily stigmatized; growing numbers disenfranchised or left behind; large numbers left behind in the modernizing project (illiterate, unaware, not easily teachable, not easily reached by nuanced argument; not schooled in problematic national pasts).

2. Background dependencies and constraints: Reliance on foreign aid to meet operating budget; great power–client state relationships; income from one resource; dependence on one staple export crop; monopolitical culture (party, state economy, state press); dominant religion active in political discourse; disruptive characteristics of neighboring states, including presence of ancient related peoples.

3. Escalation via disjunctions in trends: Breakdown of social habits; signs of increasing communal mistrust; growing popular recognition of these gaps; rising expectations dashed by disappointment (globalization); change in economic relationships, market prices; increased traffic and insecurity at border areas; heavier use of private airports; new influx of arms.

4. Escalation via distress/disparities: A sense of isolation and no options and no recourse; growing anger at gaps in rule of law, administrative regularity and probity, public services, corrupt or incompetent judiciary; rise in hate speech; perceived sense of no access, no way out, no path toward moderate improvement; deep discontent linked to and interpreted through past histories of grievances and humiliation, aggravated by outside spoilers (criminal, regional communal ties, diaspora agitation and influence); a general brittleness in terms of crowd and press reactions, easy swings of mood.

5. Escalation via triggers or sentinel events: Anniversaries of disputed events; occasions prompting large crowds/riots/demonstrations, such as hotly contested elections or victory of polarizing party, sudden deaths or killings of prominent figures, or uproar over abrupt shift in market prices for essential foodstuffs or energy.

6. Escalation at most acute phases: Patterns of perpetrator assaults and target population behaviors in the most acute escalation phases can be discerned and analyzed using existing methodologies (direct reports by observers in the field, interviews with those who have fled, and satellite surveillance relying on background patterns for interpretation):

- Escalation can be gauged by population fear behaviors (flight, congregation, hiding)
- Escalation can be tracked by perpetrator behaviors (influx of heavy weapons and new infrastructure development; convoys massing at borders or military groups surrounding an urban area; mass riots linked to violent attacks on specific homes, buildings; invasions and plunder of villages)

- People with ties to land are more difficult to force to flee than are urban populations (farmers and peasants with built and fixed assets such as irrigation and prepared fields, livestock, and stored food or seed)
- People will flee in predictable directions by previously used routes (under acute threat, people resort to habits and seek known paths, riverbeds, or hiding places)
- Flight is a dangerous time, especially for women and children (women are slowed down by child responsibilities and are often separated from male family members, so can be easily overtaken in any mode of flight by assailants)
- Timing of acute outbreaks or sudden state attacks on populations remains difficult to predict precisely (a consistent finding in all studies, complicating the pace and communication of early warning)

15.5.   From Understanding to Action

Opportunities to test or apply the concepts and methods of early warning for mass atrocities are unfortunately abundant. Complex ascertainment will certainly be vastly improved as the early-warning community moves into more active and enduring engagements with Big Data. Yet, in this transition period, it is now possible to discern through brief examples how what we already know about early warning might be, or might have been, very useful in averting or mitigating mass atrocities.

15.5.1.   Time Frame, Sequence of Events, and Information Reliability

The following brief examples taken from the past ten to fifteen years highlight the major constraints and variables to be dealt with when considering the applicability of mass atrocity early warning. Timing of onset and duration of events of interest always prove pivotal to the quality and relevance of information acquired. Some mass atrocity events erupt with great rapidity, as in Kenya in 2008, when communal violence flared and spread immediately after deeply disputed election returns were released. Long periods of rising tensions that then subside, only to rise again, provide good baselines and opportunities for very specific pattern formations to bolster early warning, as perhaps might be the case in the election cycles of violence and relative passivity witnessed in Zimbabwe.

Reliability of information always enters into any process that involves assessment of the external world. For early warning, the topic of information is vast and relatively undertheorized. We do know that a crucial element in triangulating any kind of information received indirectly is to have trusted observers in place who can manage to report out. Yet we also know that long-time residents of an area in recurrent or steady-state turmoil can be lulled into mistaking trees for forests. Much attention is turning to the information derived from the wisdom of crowds (crowdsourcing can identify hot spots and trends – Twitter is proving its power in this domain), but perpetrators and their allies may undermine the reliability of information by inserting high volumes of plausible false data.

Closely related to reliability of information is protecting the security of the source. In oppressive regimes with tight controls on social media and email or in settings of rapid deterioration of normal conditions, intrepid individuals have learned techniques to breach firewalls and get the word out to family or the press in the global context of the Internet. Their personal safety may be placed in jeopardy, however. To triangulate these messages with information from known and trusted sources in the region, analysts may request coded information delivery to a password-protected platform, including encrypted geo-location data. Once this information is transmitted to the protected platform, the information can then be decoded and displayed on a dynamic map in space and time. In these times, only very competent police states can effectively delay or defeat information transfer.

These situations, which tend to be long-lived, demand the full potentialities of satellite and crowdsourcing resources, as well as imaginative exploitation of guarded communications from field-based observers and more expansive interviews with those who have fled the country.

15.5.2. Examples

Early warning opportunities arise in all phases of the unfolding of mass atrocities. In advance of acute escalation, early warning attempts to forestall the outbreak of mass violence. In the midst of mass atrocities, early warning calls attention to new targets, new peaks, or new methods in the infliction of brutality. As this period of mass atrocity abates or is halted, early warning looks back and forward in order to build local, regional, and international capacity to institutionalize in that society the needed mechanisms for anticipatory early warning for the future.

15.5.2.1. Early Warning as Prevention   One brief vignette serves to capture the potential of complex ascertainment to warn in advance of the potential outbreak of widespread and targeted mass violence.

15.5.2.1.1. Roma in Hungary   A current example is the situation of the Roma in Hungary, where crisis mapping could prove instrumental in sounding a targeted early warning of impending mass atrocities. The background conditions include centuries-long discrimination against the Roma population in Hungary and the historical genocide of 1944–45, wherein the fascist Hungarian government collaborated with the Third Reich in sending 500,000 Jews and tens of thousands of Roma to the Nazi death camps.[50] In the past five years, accelerating trends in hate speech and physical violence directed at the Roma in Hungary are beginning to generate international attention.[51] The rise of extremist political groups in Hungary, with hostile rhetoric directed against the Roma – and, increasingly, against Jews – has also raised alarm.[52] During this period, the right-wing Jobbik party has gained a foothold in the Hungarian parliament, and the Hungarian government has revised its constitution and judiciary to limit democratic challenges to its laws and deliberations.[53] Racist paramilitary groups have proliferated and are allowed by the state to flourish.

The options for early warning are myriad, and some are now being deployed: UN, EU, and local actors are monitoring trends in hate speech in terms of quantity, intensity, and mode of delivery (radio, TV, newspapers, internet, speeches). No website currently tracks anti-Roma indicators specifically, although the website of the No Hate Speech Movement noted intense hate speech surfacing within the country on International Roma Day in April 2014.[54] Content analysis of photos and editorials in news media would provide further information, particularly on references to segregation and expulsion of the Roma population. The international community is watching for trigger events such as mass rallies and targeted killings. Because the situation is so polarized, it is important now to zone in on specific language of hate speech calling for segregation, expulsion, and elimination (an occasional theme in the Hungarian right-wing discourse). Ongoing international scrutiny is essential, with the development of plans for appropriate intervention when necessary.[55]

---

[50] Michael Stewart, "The 'Gypsy Problem': An Invisible Genocide," in *Forgotten Genocides: Oblivion, Denial, and Memory*, edited by Rene LeMarchand (Philadelphia: University of Pennsylvania Press, 2011), 137–156.

[51] European Union Agency for Fundamental Rights, "EU-MIDIS (European Union Minorities and Discrimination Survey): Main Results Report" (2009), http://fra.europa.eu/sites/default/files/fra_uploads/664-eumidis_mainreport_conference-edition_en_.pdf.

[52] Amnesty International, "Violent Attacks against Roma in Hungary: Time to Investigate Racial Motivation" (November 10, 2010), www.amnesty.org/en/library/info/EUR27/001/2010.

[53] "Constitutional Reforms: Hungary Steps away from European Democracy," *Spiegel Online International* (March 11, 2013), www.spiegel.de/international/europe/hungary-constitutional-reforms-signal-drift-away-from-democracy-a-888064.html.

[54] See, e.g., this youth-based reporting platform for hate speech in the EU: see www.nohate speechmovement.org/hate-speech-watch.

[55] FXB Center for Health and Human Rights, "Accelerating Patterns of Violence against Roma in Hungary" (February 2014); report delivered to the UN Special Adviser on the Prevention of Genocide, http://fxb.harvard.edu/report-growing-patterns-violence-roma-hungary-sound-alarms/

15.5.2.2. Early Warning as Mitigation Many examples exist of the potential for mass atrocity early warning during an acute event. Mass atrocities are a process, so the sooner accurate, precise, and new information can be marshaled about the evolving nature and patterns of the attacks, targets, and perpetrators, the sooner policymakers can be mobilized to formulate and implement appropriate responses.

15.5.2.2.1. Darfur 2003–2005 The key early warning dilemma in the first three years of the war in Darfur was how to document the extensive and targeted attacks by Sudanese forces on black African villages in Darfur. Human rights observers were not permitted into Darfur, whereas humanitarian organizations were under close scrutiny by the government to hew closely to their narrow (and very difficult) mission of relieving the suffering of those who were immediate casualties of the conflict. Early human rights reports gathered by interviewing refugees in Chad along the Darfur border found that the pattern of documented attacks suggested either ethnic cleansing or genocide.[56] These reports were constrained by sampling issues, however, given that access to the affected region was restricted at the time.

Primitive use of satellite data on village destruction in Darfur allowed for time-stamped photos documenting the growing extent and intensity of the Sudanese/janjaweed assaults and scorched-earth attacks. The core problem was that this mapping data could not be tethered to data on the ethnic makeup of villages (black African Darfuri – such as Fur – or Arab Darfuri). No recent maps or census existed that could permit geo-locating villages according to satellite coordinates or to document village settlement patterns by communal identity.

Had current crisis mapping capacities been available, gathering near real-time satellite data on the systematic destruction of black African Darfuri villages and forced population movement into internally displaced persons (IDP) areas or as refugees and providing this information in a composite-labeled and time-sequenced mode, it would have revealed the scope, scale, and probably even intent of atrocities committed.[57] Whether the information would have prompted a robust intervention at this relatively early but very intense phase of the conflict is beyond the remit of this discussion. However, it certainly would have strengthened the argument presented to the international

---

[56] See John Heffernan and Jennifer Leaning, *Darfur: Assault on Survival: A Call for Security, Justice, and Restitution* (Cambridge, MA: Physicians for Human Rights, January 2006), http://physiciansforhumanrights.org/library/reports/darfur-assault-on-survival-report-sudan-2006.html.

[57] Jennifer Leaning, "The Crime of Genocide: The Case of Darfur," in *Public Health and Human Rights: Evidence-Based Approaches*, edited by H. Pizer and C. Beyer (Baltimore, MD: Johns Hopkins University Press, 2007).

policy community, buttressing the evidence delivered to the UN Fact-Finding Mission to the Sudan in 2004–05.[58]

15.5.2.3. Early Warning to Forestall   Much has been written about the value of postconflict processes involving truth and reconciliation and the pursuit of justice.[59] In the immediate aftermath of violence that may have amounted to atrocity crimes, the UN has commissioned independent commissions of inquiry or, through its Office of Human Rights, set up fact-finding investigations. Independent human rights organizations, from various perspectives, have also attempted in the immediate postcrisis period to examine events while evidence may still be available and accessible.[60]

Some of these reports emphasize the roles of various actors and institutions that may be strengthened or created to change the underlying conditions that led to the crisis. Often, these reports highlight observed shifts in trends or sentinel events in the crisis under investigation in order to help structure more informed and immediate early warning for future outbreaks. Other reports examine the evidence that can be gathered to determine whether a case may be made for establishing a judicial process. During and upon publication of these reports, interested parties, often governments, have always launched intense campaigns of criticism, in which they dispute the facts, themes, interpretations, and overall conclusions.

All of these endeavors would find their attempts to amass the relevant fact pictures accelerated by sophisticated deployment of complex ascertainment methodologies – whether deployed during the crisis or mobilized as part of the aftermath assessment. The verdict of history is much served by vigorous efforts to gather as much information as possible. This quest is best undertaken before the evidence is destroyed, survivors scattered or dead, and memories distorted by time.

As the ruins were still smoldering from the carpet-bombing of cities during World War II, the U.S. and allied Strategic Bombing Surveys were conducted in Japan, Nazi Germany, and the European theater of war. The aim was to see whether intensive bombing of important infrastructure and sites of industrial strength would dampen civilian morale and diminish support for the war. In all instances, the findings suggested that such bombing had an opposite effect. Yet, although launched with one aim in mind, the effort amassed such a weight of

---

[58] "Report of the International Commission of Inquiry on Darfur to the UN Secretary-General," Geneva (January 25, 2005), www.un.org/news/dh/sudan/com_inq_darfur.pdf

[59] For an incisive review of these matters, see Martha Minow, *Between Vengeance and Forgiveness: Facing History after Genocide and Mass Violence* (Boston: Beacon Press, 1998).

[60] UN Office of the High Commissioner for Human Rights, *International Commissions of Inquiry and Fact-Finding Missions on International Human Rights Law and International Humanitarian Law: Guidance and Practice* (Geneva: UN Office of the High Commissioner for Human Rights, 2013).

evidence from ordinary survivors that it served to contribute, in advance of the Fourth Geneva Convention, an invaluable contemporaneous account of the appalling impact of aerial bombardment on civilian life.[61]

15.6.   Conclusion

It is well understood that it is a great challenge to mobilize the skills, manpower, and other resources needed to promote effective prevention of and early intervention in mass atrocities. That mobilization requires multinational political will.

Yet, behind that challenge is the problem of effective knowledge. All reasonable actors, at all levels of governance, now recognize that to move swiftly and productively to forestall these major crises it is essential to know as soon as possible what is happening to whom, in what locations, and in what time frame. Crafting a comprehensive strategy for early warning and early intervention demands the dynamic curating of knowledge as it accumulates – a knowledge system – to bring to life the capacity for complex ascertainment.

In the past ten years, the political and technological grounds have been laid to support this grand idea. The disaster, genocide, and conflict communities have created common language and common understandings about the roles of prevention, early warning, and early intervention. Disaster, conflict, and atrocity escalation scenarios are well understood – at the small-group and population level. Crisis mapping has now become a basic descriptive tool used by governments and major international agencies alike as they seek to assess their reach and outstanding gaps in response operations.

What is still lacking is the capacity to obtain information in an actionable time frame. Only some form of knowledge system – such as the one described in Section 2.3 – would have the analytic power to capture data and distill an escalation pathway to the scale and extent of reliability required for timely and effective prevention or intervention.

A necessary component of this knowledge system is a technological capacity for scanning, gathering, digitizing, sifting, analyzing, and portraying data from the universe of sources now available. But the process is essentially a cognitive one, integrating usable information, background knowledge, and associational thinking supported by pattern recognition. Much of the principal work to build this knowledge system must be done by authorities and practitioners in the early-warning community. It begins by specifying the escalation elements more precisely, such as hate speech in its various dimensions of content, intensity,

---

[61] The U.S. Strategic Bombing Survey, Summary Report (European War), September 30, 1945, www.anesi.com/ussbs02.htm. Summary Report (Pacific War), July 1, 1946, https://archive.org /details/summaryreportpac00unit.

frequency, source, and target. It continues by interrogating the initial graphs and patterns that technical partners begin to produce. In the iterations, we will gain valuable new knowledge about dynamics not yet discerned through the study of historical cases, and we will also hone our capacity for real-time early warning. As we learn more about our world, this system will also tell us in simpler and faster ways when it is about to turn deadly.

16 Mobilizing Economic Sanctions for Preventing Mass Atrocities: From Targeting Dictators to Enablers

George A. Lopez

16.1. The Sanctions and Rights Protection Linkage

Over the past four decades, economic sanctions and human rights protection have become increasingly interconnected. During the Cold War, the United States undertook various embargo actions against the Soviet Union and its allies to protest abuses of civil and political rights in those countries. U.S. policy took on new and stronger dimensions during the Carter Administration as Congress supported the suspension of military and foreign aid to a number of Latin American regimes that had been traditional U.S. allies. This was followed by the significant policy debate in the United States and Europe regarding the efficacy of sanctions for bringing about human rights improvements, if not a full regime change, in the apartheid government of South Africa.[1]

During the post-Cold War decade, human rights advocacy and advancement grew into a more globalized and powerful force against repressive governments and extended quite logically to addressing the perpetration of mass atrocities.[2] It became fully operationalized in the work of numerous nongovernmental organizations (NGOs), through far-reaching policy principles derived from the

Portions of this paper are drawn from various memos and concept papers developed by the author with staff members of Human Rights First in the formation of their work on enablers and crimes against humanity in 2010. That collaboration, especially formed with Ann-Louise Colgan, now of the U.S. Institute of Peace, and Julia Fromholz, now of the U.S. Department of State, in the formulations explored in this chapter is gratefully acknowledged.

[1] For an overview of these U.S. pro-rights sanctions actions in the past and the present, see George A. Lopez, "Matching Means with Intentions: Sanctions and Human Rights" in *The Future of Human Rights: U.S. Policy for a New Era*, edited by William F. Schulz (University of Pennsylvania Press, 2008); and George A. Lopez, "Enforcing Human Rights Through Economic and Other Sanctions" in *The Handbook of International Human Rights Law*, edited by Dinah Shelton (New York: Oxford University Press, 2013).

[2] Jackie Smith and Ron Pagnucco, with George A. Lopez "Globalizing Human Rights: The Work of Transnational Human Rights NGOs in the 1990s," *Human Rights Quarterly* 20(2): 379–412 (May 1998); and especially, David Forsythe, ed., *Encyclopedia of Human Rights* (New York: Oxford University Press, 2009)

expansion of international human rights law and has ultimately been enforced in new courts engaged in prosecutions of individuals for mass atrocities and genocide. These developments have led one prominent scholar to label this human rights evolution as "the justice cascade."[3]

Significant changes have also occurred in the sanctions realm. Historically, sanctions involved a nation-against-nation general trade embargo, often paired with reduction of foreign and military assistance to the target government. By the end of the 1990s, however, sanctions had abandoned trade measures in favor of a diverse set of specialized, targeted coercive measures involving finances, travel, arms, and selective commodities, most often imposed by multilateral organizations to achieve a wide array of goals. In addition to sanctions to protect human rights, these goals included ending international and civil wars, protecting innocents caught in war, extraditing international fugitives, controlling the spread of international terrorism, deterring the proliferation of weapons of mass destruction, and restoring democratically elected governments. Indicative of the expanded resort to sanctions and their diverse aims, some analysts labeled the 1990s as a "sanctions decade," while others worried the trend had become a "sanctions epidemic."[4]

The most pronounced change linking sanctions and rights abuses occurred in its operational form. Since the late 1990s, multilateral organizations, the United Nations Security Council, the European Union, the British Commonwealth, and ad hoc coalitions of states have imposed targeted sanctions against individuals and entities to punish or constrain their specific role in human rights abuses and political killings. This use of these refined, precision targeted, "smart sanctions" has been increasingly advocated by transnational human rights NGOS, and their imposition and enforcement has occupied an increasingly prominent place in the coercive tool kit of policymakers.[5]

In this chapter, I argue that to have any realistic hope of halting or especially in preventing mass atrocities through the imposition of smart sanctions requires a significant change in policy thinking and action. Decision makers must expand their thinking beyond the targeting of the dictators and the few perpetrators of atrocities, most of whom are identified after the fact. I urge a focus on the immediate elite supporters of a killing regime as those who directly or indirectly support and authorize mass atrocities. So, too, I urge the use of in-depth intelligence to focus our resources on constraining the less

---

[3] Kathryn Sikkink, *The Justice Cascade: How Human Rights Prosecutions Are Changing World Politic* (New York: Norton & Co, 2011). Also relevant is Dinah Shelton, ed., *The Handbook of International Human Rights Law* (New York: Oxford University Press, 2013).

[4] David Cortight and George A. Lopez, *The Sanctions Decade: Assessing UN Security Council Sanctions in the 1990s* (Lynne Rienner Publishers, 2000); and Richard N. Haass, "Sanctioning Madness," *Foreign Affairs* (November/December, 1997).

[5] George A. Lopez, "Tools, Tasks and Tough Thinking: Sanctions and R2P," A Policy Brief, Global Centre for the Responsibility to Protect (Summer 2013).

visible actors and especially on those processes and products that significantly *enable* these abuses to occur and sustain the direct perpetrators' violence over time. Such action requires a more rapid and deeper analysis of the tools and techniques that are being – or soon will be – used to kill large numbers of people. It also demands some risk-taking by policymakers to cast a wider net of controls and sanctions quickly on material and actor targets than has been the case in the past.

16.2. How Smart Sanctions Should Assist Atrocity Prevention

The development and institutionalization of "smart sanctions" provides an array of coercive measures to the international community that have proved somewhat effective in particular cases of massive rights abuses and ongoing atrocities. As such, they provide a basis for scrutinizing how they can be further mobilized to attain prevention goals. Sanctions measures are precisely targeted or "smart" in two ways. First, they take aim at specific subnational and transnational actors deemed most responsible for the policies or actions considered by the imposer as illegal or abhorrent. Rather than punishing the society generally through trade sanctions, smart sanctions aim to constrain identifiable, culpable perpetrators. Generally, in human rights sanctions, these are the abusive government institutions and leaders who authorize and, when identifiable, the individuals who perpetrate the killings. But a deeper probing of the abuses should indicate their connection to specific products, companies that supply them, asset holding entities, and a wider array of individuals and entities than are visible on early analysis.

Second, smart sanctions isolate discrete areas of economic coercion to a specific microlevel economic activity that can be identified as contributing to increased human rights violations. Most often, such sanctions aim at the flow of weapons into a country, even as these have been the most difficult sanctions to enforce effectively.[6] The measures listed here comprise the sanctions most readily available to constrain or end large-scale rights abuses and killing. They include:

- freezing financial assets held outside the country of (a) the national government, (b) regime members in their individual capacity, or (c) those persons designated as key supporters or enablers of the regime;
- suspending credits, aid and loans available to the national government, its agencies, and those economic actors in the nation who deal with monies involving international financial institutions;

---

[6] See George A. Lopez and David Cortright, eds., *Towards Smart Sanctions: Targeting Economic Statecraft* (Boulder, CO: Rowman & Littlefield, 2002).

- denying access to overseas financial markets, often to the target government's National Bank and other governmental entities, as well as to designated private banks and investors and individual designees;
- restricting the trade of specific goods and commodities that provide power resources and revenue to the norm-violating actors, most especially highly traded and income-producing mineral resources;
- banning aid and trade of weapons, munitions, military replacement parts, and dual-use goods of a military nature;
- banning computers, cell phones, and satellites, as well as related communications technologies, especially of a "jamming" and discovery of user nature;
- banning flight and travel of individuals and/or specific air and sea carriers;
- denial of visa, travel, and educational opportunities to those individuals on the designee list;
- denying import of or otherwise access to goods labeled as "luxury items" for the entities and individuals on the designated list.

One advantage of these smart sanctions lies in how they make the political action undertaken by individuals and entities of engaging in atrocities a matter for which their wrong-doing becomes a more direct, personal responsibility. Thus, "personal" assets used in these wrong-doings and, more fundamentally, various assets used to sustain their functioning are constrained. Thus, with many sanctions, the overseas funds held by dictators become inaccessible to them and their relatives. Their children lose travel visas and access to tuition monies to attend elite Western schools and universities.

When time is of the essence in responding to unfolding mass atrocities, some targeted sanctions are likely to be more appealing and effective than others. Due to economic circumstances, some sanctions imposers are likely to be more versatile in targeting certain entities than others. But, in all cases, as I illustrate herein, sanctions' effectiveness in stifling atrocities demands a convergence of factors anchored in tracing the people and products associated with atrocities and the willingness of sanctions-imposing actors to unite behind a collection of sanctions to be levied. In addition, imposers should be continually aware of the ways in which violence perpetrators, and especially their enablers, grow in number as atrocities continue. This should lead to an expanding list of those to be sanctions' targets.

16.3.   Cases Involving Sanctions and Rights Abuses

Prior to imposing sanctions on Iraq for its invasion of Kuwait in August, 1990, the UN's Permanent Five powers and a sufficient number of rotating Security Council members reached agreement on sanctions only twice in the UN's first forty-five years of existence. Significantly, each time involved a racial human rights case: Southern Rhodesia (1966) and South Africa (1977). In the nearly quarter-century since the Iraq resolution, many UN sanctions cases have had some dimensions of rights concerns reflected in the mandates.[7] At the same time, these sanctions have been fraught with inconsistencies regarding their design and "clout," thus limiting their human rights impact. Put in its best light, over time, the international community, acting through the UN Security Council, has made only limited progress in more narrowly defined rights protection cases. And these were guided by two themes – some would call them "global norms" – that developed since the late 1990s: the protection of innocent civilians in armed conflict (Protection of Civilians [POC]) and the responsibility to protect civilians faced with mass atrocities (Responsibility to Protect [R2P]).

In at least four cases – Yugoslavia, Rwanda, Liberia (until 2001), and Sudan/ Darfur – UN sanctions resulted in little or no reduction in the killing because the Council acted late and then imposed a limited and weakly enforced arms embargo that was not integrated with other more powerful financial or other sanctions.[8] Similarly, the limited measures imposed in Afghanistan prior to 2001 also had no discernible impact on the policies of the Taliban regime regarding treatment of cultural artifacts or women's rights.

Despite protestations of "never again," the failure of the international community to use sanctions or other means to prevent ethnic cleansing in Bosnia in 1992 or genocide in Rwanda in 1994 was repeated regarding Darfur a decade later. Without question, the Darfur case serves as a glaring example of too few sanctions imposed too late and without the broad targeting of a substantial number of elites that would maximize their effectiveness. Despite near global condemnation of the Sudanese regime for its and its agents' actions against the citizens of the Darfur region from 2003 through 2008, a rather watered-down set of financial asset freezes and travel restrictions were imposed against a small number of Sudanese officials in a series of Security Council Resolutions.

Most, but not all, of this backtracking was due to the unwillingness of the Chinese and Russians to support extensive sanctions. A draft Security Council resolution targeting more than thirty persons responsible for killings and brutal actions in the region faced serious opposition, and ultimately the final resolution designated only four individuals for sanctions. The UN debate

---

[7] Regarding the historic dimensions of human rights in UN sanctions resolution see Andrew Clapham, "Sanctions and Economic, Social and Cultural Rights," in *United Nations Sanctions and International Law*, edited by Vera Gowlland-Debbas (The Hague: Kluwer Law International, 2001).

[8] See Michael Brzoska and George A. Lopez *Putting Teeth in the Tiger: Improving the Effectiveness of Arms Embargoes* (London: Emerald Press, 2009).

over sanctions continued for so long prior to their adoption that whoever was finally targeted to face financial penalties surely avoided them.[9]

The Libyan case, February–September 2011, serves as the most definitive situation of prevention of mass atrocity via sanctions and the related measures that followed them. The Security Council expressed this directly by noting in its Resolutions 1970 and 1973 that the concept of R2P was the guiding framework for both the sanctions and later for the imposition of the no-fly zone. Without question, national sanctions imposed by the United States and the European Union locked down the bulk of the identifiable assets of the Gaddafi regime and gave a needed boost to the UN targeted financial sanctions, asset freeze, travel ban, and arms embargo imposed in Security Council Resolution 1970 passed just days later.

By cutting off nearly half of Gaddafi's usable monies – about $36 billion in Libyan funds were locked down in the first week of sanctions – the international community immediately denied the dictator the monies needed to import heavy weapons from various sellers, to hire foot soldier mercenaries from Chad, or to contract with elite commando units from South Africa and elsewhere. These constraints prevented the Libyan war from being longer and deadlier had they not been successfully imposed and enforced. Tripoli, for example, was not destroyed in an all-out battle, and Libyan cities were spared the terrible death, destruction, and massive population displacements that was inflicted on Syrian cities by Assad's tanks and air force.

That this sanctions episode also included massive NATO bombing as an enforcement action ultimately helped the Libyan rebels overthrow the Gaddafi government. But this final end to the brutal Gaddafi regime was not a simple case of stifling mass atrocities and opening the way for safe and secure governance that respected human rights. On the contrary, various forces in Libya resisted with military force the emergence of a central government, which itself made strategic errors and resorted to its own use of force to resolve disputes. The likelihood that Libya was a failed state became a reality by 2014.

Moreover, within the UN Security Council, what appeared to be the success of targeted sanctions to constrain mass-killing by Gaddafi became discounted by some Security Council members – most notably Russia – during their opposition to the military enforcement of the no-fly zone and its extension by NATO to topple Gaddafi. Because these actions were legitimized by invoking the R2P principle in the Council, the backlash against the bombing extended to the R2P principles and – at least for a time – any Security Council actions, such

---

[9] For an analysis of such patterns of sanctions preparation, see Michael Brzoska and George A. Lopez "Sanctions Design and Security Council Dynamics," in *UN Targeted Sanctions as Instruments of Global Governance*, edited by Thomas Biersteker and Sue Eckert (forthcoming).

as sanctions, that might interfere in internal conflicts. Thus, Council inaction – of sanctions or otherwise – to ongoing atrocities in Syria and later very limited response to massive violence in Central African Republic and South Sudan occurred.

16.4.   Using More Advanced Sanctions Concepts and Tools for Atrocity Prevention

Rather than concluding that the backlash to the Libya case means that sanctions are irrelevant as an international tool and will have limited utility in meeting the imperative of mass atrocity prevention, I suggest that sanctions strategy and tactical application adapt and advance more deliberately. Specifically, we need to move beyond targeting the "leader" and the "killer-on-the-ground" in imposing sanctions (although these must indeed continue) and cast a broader and deeper net guided by both what we know about how mass killings and displacements unfold and, as available, evidence-based findings about products and people linked to atrocities. The aim here is to change the basic dynamics when atrocities are under way and expand who and what we stifle and thwart as violence against civilians unfolds. I argue that a social science contribution to the development of these tools can be the definition and new conceptualization that labels particular activities and actors as foci for effective policy action. Such actions would be seen in a new light and serve as a new data-gathering and human rights monitoring category. In turn, this category of actors – the *enablers* – and the materials they provide to the mass atrocity equation can become the focus of targeted sanctions.

Embedded in the notion of enabler is accepting the notion that while locking down the assets of dictators is necessary for atrocity prevention, it is seldom sufficient. By exploring the scope and examples of enabling here, I offer a new, earlier, and certainly lower level focus for sanctions targeting. One potentially effective approach is to focus on the means used to commit mass atrocities and on those who provide them. Because mass atrocities are organized crimes, crippling the means to organize and sustain them – money, communications networks, and other resources – can disrupt their execution. A key element of their organization that is particularly relevant to international responses is the role of third parties. The cases of recent history have taught that perpetrators are seldom able to carry out these crimes on their own. Rather, they are dependent on direct or indirect support from external actors – governments, commercial entities, and individuals – whose goods and services enable them to wage attacks against civilians.

Although atrocities vary in cause and method, and perpetrators are generally both creative and resourceful, we can identify a core set of activities that enable and sustain the violence. By developing the correct categories to target the third parties engaged in those activities, it may prove possible to decrease or interrupt the perpetrators' access to the necessary means. This may, in turn, alter their calculus for committing atrocities against civilians. Targeting the enablers is not a panacea, but it should lead to a better understanding of the dynamics of atrocities and present a practical lever with significant untapped potential to halt the world's worst crimes.

16.5.   Positing and Operationalizing the Definition

In 2010, a working group of Human Rights First and U.S. Institute of Peace personnel struggling with this enabler concept identified three essential elements to enabling. First, a third party provides resources, goods, services, or other practical support – directly or indirectly – to the perpetrator of ongoing atrocities. Second, this support is a critical ingredient that enables or sustains the commission of the atrocities, without which the atrocities would not have taken place to the same extent. Third, the third party knew – or clearly should have known – about the atrocities and about the ways in which its goods or support were likely to contribute to the commission of these crimes.

The type of support identified in the first element might take the forms listed here:

(A) Providing the means that are used to commit the atrocities directly, including:

- weapons (small arms and light weapons; heavy weapons; chemical and biological weapons)
- ammunition
- military equipment
- personnel (private security forces; paramilitary forces)
- other instruments (heavy vehicles; bulldozers)

(B) Offering goods and services that indirectly facilitate or sustain atrocities, including:

- transportation by air or sea of products used to commit or coordinate violence
- vehicles (trucks and other land vehicles)
- fuel
- technology and communications equipment (satellite phones; cell phones; computer hardware and software)
- air support
- facilities (buildings; warehouses; training stations)
- technical assistance

  – information sharing (tip-offs; target lists)
  – safe-havens, communications routes, and other geographical support

(C) Providing general support that materially builds or sustains the capacity of
    the perpetrator to commit atrocities. This includes the large financial
    reserves accumulated by violent actors, with special attention to the
    diverse form that such assets now take, from sovereign wealth funds to
    shadow holding companies. Often, such enterprises are linked to substan-
    tial networks of illicit extraction or trafficking of natural resources that
    generate revenue for the perpetrator.

In this formulation, I chose to limit "enabling" to a focus on material
resources. For now, I do not extend to the provision of moral support or
"political cover," however real and significant those realities are in the
enabling of those who brutalize their own citizens. Because these realities do
not constitute practical support, as described earlier, and they are more difficult
to quantify and interdict, for now, they stand outside the parameters of our work.

Countries, commercial entities, and individuals may all be enablers. In the
case of countries, examples include the situation in Darfur, Sudan, where
transfers of arms by China, Russia, Chad, and other governments or state-
owned entities to government and rebel forces have helped sustain the violence
against civilians for six years. There are many other examples in the recent
past in which third-party governments provided weapons to their allies or
proxies even when it was clear that they were being used to commit crimes
against humanity. Countries involved in questionable trading chains or opaque
transshipment practices involving weapons, vehicles, or other forms of
equipment may also be enabling atrocities in less direct ways.

In the case of commercial entities, the range of enabling activities is potentially
very broad. In Nigeria, multinational oil companies have faced lawsuits after
being accused of hiring abusive security forces in the Niger Delta. In Darfur, the
supply of Toyota trucks accessed by rebel groups has been essential to their
capacity to commit widespread attacks on civilians. The most recent UN Panel of
Experts on Sudan reported that Al-Futtaim Motors Company, the official Toyota
dealership in the United Arab Emirates (UAE), was, along with second-hand
dealers in UAE, the source of "by far the largest number of vehicles that were
documented as part of arms embargo violations in Darfur."[10] That dealership
"declined or replied . . . in a perfunctory manner" to three requests by the Panel
for information about buyers of the trucks identified in Darfur.

State and commercial actors both may also function as go-betweens, thus
playing an important indirect role as enablers. During the Rwandan genocide,

---

[10] Report of the Panel of Experts established pursuant to Resolution 1591 (2005) concerning the
Sudan (S/2009/562), 158.

even after a UN arms embargo sought to stop the flow of weapons into that country, arms continued to arrive routed through nearby countries and facilitated by international corporations. A 2009 Stockholm International Peace Research Institute (SIPRI) study revealed that more than 90 percent of air cargo carriers used by international organizations and humanitarian agencies to transport crisis response supplies were also named in open source reports on arms trafficking. Individual business people can be instrumental as suppliers or middlemen: international arms merchant Viktor Bout is a famous example, but others include the Dutch businessman convicted of providing chemical components that Saddam Hussein's regime used against Kurdish civilians.

Countries and commercial actors also act as enablers when they are engaged in the exploitation of natural resources that generate revenues for the perpetrators and thereby sustain their capacity to abuse civilian populations. Examples include eastern Congo, where windfalls from the illicit mineral trade fuel the rebels' pursuit of arms and thus contribute to atrocities against civilians. In Burma, during their period of repressive rule that may now be drawing to a close, the country's military rulers derived massive export earnings from their gem mines, which help to finance their brutal repression of that country's citizens.

Rightly, those interested in preventing mass atrocities most often focus on the ineffectiveness of arms embargoes as the major failure of sanctions, the UN, or others who attempt to limit such trade or illicit movement of these tools of murderers. This point is well taken, but it is also worth noting that changes in the arms smuggling networks must be better understood in order to stifle not only the flow of arms, but also the new, often unwitting group of enablers that now typify the chain of arms smuggling. For example, various sanctions analysts, especially the UN Panels of Experts assigned to monitor sanctions effectiveness, have testified since the mid-2000s to the increased complexity of sophisticated arms smuggling via resort to air transport. First, over the past decade, the air transport of military equipment suspected of being ultimately destined for a region or a group subject to a UN or other arms embargos – and which are the material of mass atrocities – is now seldom flown directly from the source location to its ultimate destination. Rather, it is first intentionally exported to destinations not subject to the arms embargo.

Second, in quite a number of cases like Sudan, many of those actors involved in the supply chain did not fit the Victor Bout-like stereotypical profile of arms smugglers. Some air carrier companies may be completely unaware of the ultimate and intended destination of the military equipment they transport because the documentation submitted in support of any export license application is partial or falsified. This process involves respectable companies linked to governments via long-term contractual relationships. Often, the movement of goods involves private security companies, with links to air cargo companies that also had logistics contracts to supply goods in support of U.S. and NATO-led operations in Iraq and Afghanistan.

Most interesting about this recent trend is that none of the aircraft and very, very few of the air cargo companies involved in the international transfer across European airspace had ever been identified in any open source report as involved in illicit or even suspect transfers. Where such cases exist, the aircraft will have been re-registered under a different registration number and a different company name. They may be flying under an air-operating certificate or a call sign of a perfectly respectable air cargo company about which there is no suspicion.

Finally, of particular significance has been the use of small, private aircraft involved in illicit or unauthorized flows of valuable minerals and natural resources such as cobalt, cassiterite, and gold, which continue to finance both the arms trade and brutal wars in sub-Saharan Africa. In the case of gold, diamonds, and the corresponding hard currency transfers intended to purchase them, modern, Western-manufactured executive jets, leased in a manner similar to hired cars, appear to be the new vehicle of choice for moving arms and technologies useful to repressive governments. Although some of the activities and flight patterns of ruling elites from Libya and Cote D'Ivoire who are subject to embargos and who were flying in Gulfstream and Falcon luxury jets have been documented by various reporting agencies, no action has been taken against these enabling air services or companies.

16.6.   New Approaches for Halting Enablers

Various efforts to halt or punish enablers – without calling them by that name or viewing them as a distinct set of actors – already exist. New approaches, therefore, must take those efforts into account and build on them. At the same time, understanding the growing complexity of illicit networks that supply materials used in mass atrocities and acting more aggressively with sanctions and related tools to stifle such enablers is clearly in order. Most amenable to taking new actions – or even to taking greater risks in imposing sanctions on targets that occasionally may prove quickly that they are not enablers – should be the UN; regional organizations, such as the European Union (EU) and African Union (AU); and, finally, central governments themselves. Commercial actors will likely be sensitive to approaches from those governments and international and regional organizations, too, as well as from consumers and other market-based forces, whether acting on their own, through guideline initiatives, or through NGOs.

The softest existing approach available for halting the reach of enablers emphasizes information: in situations in which enablers are involved unwittingly or are particularly susceptible to concerns about negative publicity, shining a critical spotlight on their role may be sufficient to get their attention. Some entities – particularly multinational corporations with strong presences in the United States or Europe – may then be open to new commitments to transparency and due diligence standards to protect human rights.

For example, at least one company investigated and discussed in the October 2009 Panel of Experts report on violations of the arms embargo in Darfur was willing to cooperate and fully disclose its relationships in Sudan in order to ensure compliance with UN sanctions. On the other hand, as we have seen through the ongoing role of countries such as China and Russia in the crisis in Darfur, even in the face of public protest in the United States and internationally, public attention alone is often insufficient. Although this approach might be a useful first step, overreliance on it may risk oversimplifying complex situations, thereby limiting success.

A stronger and more concerted approach, but one that pertains only to commercial actors, involves the range of mechanisms that has emerged over the past decade to engage corporations in more responsible practices that protect human rights. A number of these efforts involve the U.S. and other governments, and civil society actors have played a key role in each case. One example is the Kimberley Process, which brings together governments, corporations, and civil society in an effort to regulate the diamond trade. Others include the Voluntary Principles, the Organization for Economic Cooperation and Development (OECD) Guidelines, and the UN Global Compact.

The work being done by the UN Special Representative on Business and Human Rights is also noteworthy in this regard. Efforts by nongovernmental actors to provide guidelines to businesses include the Red Flags project, which identifies potential legal liabilities in high-risk situations. This investigative and regulatory work can be augmented by bridging to the work of other agents who share the need for or desire to expose such behavior. These certainly include the UN Panels of Experts, but also Lloyd's Registry and INTERPOL. These and other initiatives may provide a foundation and entry points for addressing commercial enablers of atrocities.

A still tougher set of approaches to both state and non-state actors involves the myriad political, economic, or legal mechanisms that can be used against countries, commercial entities, or individuals to deter or dissuade their actions. In its bilateral relationships, the United States can bring pressure to bear on enabling governments through public or private condemnations, by suspending business or cultural exchange programs, by withdrawing diplomatic representation, by reducing aid and other forms of support, or by implementing a wide range of other tools.

The United States can also pursue broad or targeted bilateral sanctions or work through the UN Security Council to impose multilateral sanctions against countries or commercial actors. Enforcement of sanctions is a separate challenge, at least as important as their imposition, as we have seen in the case of the Darfur arms embargo. New regulations specifically targeted at certain commercial entities or activities may be useful. In situations in which there is evidence that enablers are engaged in illegal behavior or have violated international law (including human rights law), it may be possible to pursue international criminal sanctions and other legal measures against them.

Whether addressing commercial actors or states in a given situation, information about who the third parties are and what role they are playing is critical. By enhancing its intelligence gathering and analysis related to enablers, the U.S. government should be able to better assess the levers that can be employed to target them. The use of crowdsourcing methodology and what is called "Big Data" in data analysis on potential enabling parties or products has unexplored potential. Including information on third-party actors in intelligence reports on atrocity situations and in interagency discussions about policy options may be a useful approach. The United States could also seek to engage international partners in information sharing to supplement its own intelligence sources on enablers and to help enlist others in the effort to halt enablers of mass atrocities.

The short overview of recent trends in destabilizing arms transfers via air noted earlier reveals the very different landscape confronting UN Member State governments and international organizations concerned with monitoring and enforcing UN and other arms embargoes. A growing portion of military equipment that ultimately reaches embargoed destinations and designated listed groups may very well have begun its journey as a legitimate arms transfer. As such, it was subject to a proper arms export licensing procedure. Government officials authorizing this transfer may have received genuine – or at least very authentic looking – supporting documentation and issued an export license in good faith. However, at some stage subsequent to the departure of the cargo from its point of origin, the transfer becomes illicit.

This reality – I would argue – warrants greater government scrutiny of military transfers to conflict zones. International aviation authorities must continually update lists of new carriers in the arms marketplace and ensure their law-abiding activity. Suspicious transfers and company cargo for which there is doubt regarding its sanctions-busting status should be seized for inspection and promptly permitted to depart if found without contraband and if all of its paperwork checks out as legitimate. Such actions simply are not undertaken in the contemporary order, and thus enablers continue to thrive.

16.7. Conclusion

Even as a greater consensus among citizens and policymakers alike emerged that confronting and stifling mass atrocities should be a foreign policy priority, the range of tools for so doing and the creative, aggressive application of them has lagged behind this recognition. The poor record of the international community in addressing atrocities in practice makes clear the complexity of the problems to mounting a successful response. One challenge is the need to have practical tools that can change quickly the basic dynamics of killing "on the ground" when atrocities are predicted or under way and that contribute to efforts to halt such violence against civilians.

Past efforts have seen mixed results due to the absence of a coordinated and coherent approach and the insufficient understanding of the role of third-party enablers in the killings. Although renewed efforts to stop arms flows or to embargo conflict minerals enhance a government's ability to prevent or halt genocide, a systematic effort to establish a common theme and approach to address the range of enablers is lacking. In this chapter, I articulated a definition and new conceptualization that labels particular activities and actors as enablers and thus the foci for more effective policy action, especially the application of targeted economic sanctions techniques. Progress in this area must be made if atrocity prevention is to become the norm, rather than the rarity.

17 Corporate Behavior and Atrocity Prevention: Is Aiding and Abetting Liability the Best Way to Influence Corporate Behavior?

Owen C. Pell and Kelly Bonner

17.1. Introduction

The corporation has been and remains an elusive figure under international law. A legal fiction created at least 400 years ago under domestic law, it remains unclear to what extent the "corporate person" has under international law the rights and duties of a natural person. Yet, as recognized thirteen years ago in the United Nations Global Compact, corporations are vitally important not only to any discussion of human rights, but to the more specific discussion of mass atrocity prevention. As societies have developed economically and world trade and commerce have become increasingly coordinated and interdependent, multinational corporations (MNCs) have become central players in international affairs, occupying roles traditionally filled by governments. In contrast to what might be called "macro" principles of human rights (i.e., broad aspirational principles aimed at society as a whole) embodied in multilateral treaties such as the Convention on the Prevention and Punishment of the Crime of Genocide of 1951 (hereinafter Genocide Convention)[1] or the more recently established Rome Statute of the International Criminal Court (ICC) (hereinafter Rome Statute),[2] corporations increasingly serve as the principal point for developing and implementing "micro" principles of human rights – that is, human rights as applied on a day-to-day basis to individuals.

Yet, despite their growing importance, and with limited and intensely personal exceptions, for much of the twentieth century corporations played

Mr. Pell is a partner at White & Case LLP, where Ms. Bonner is an associate. The authors extend special thanks to Spencer Willig, Harold Williford, Lynn Kaiser, and Peter Radulescu of White & Case LLP for their considerable assistance and contributions.

[1] Convention on the Prevention and Punishment of the Crime of Genocide, December 9, 1948, 102 Stat. 3045, 78 UNT.S. 277, enacted as U.S. law at 18 U.S.C. § 1091 (1987).

[2] Rome Statute of the International Criminal Court, UN Doc. A/CONF.183/9 (July 17, 1998).

an ignoble role in preventing mass atrocities. During the 1930s, multinational corporations operating in Germany and Eastern Europe failed to address the rising tide of anti-Semitism and the atrocities of the Holocaust. During World War II, many firms profited from the use of forced or slave labor by concentration camp inmates or prisoners of war,[3] whereas other corporations have been accused of indirectly profiting through the operations of German subsidiaries.[4] Not until the end of the Cold War did corporations begin to look self-critically at their actions and compliance with human rights abuses.

Within the past thirty years, corporations have assumed a larger role in promoting international human rights. Beginning with the Sullivan Principles in 1977, which were developed by the Rev. Leon Sullivan and General Motors to constructively engage with South Africa's apartheid regime,[5] corporations have moved to incorporate corporate social responsibility (CSR) initiatives into their organizational frameworks. Over time, some of these initiatives have yielded industrywide adherence to specific human rights standards, thereby helping to develop multilateral human rights principles.[6] Collectively, through their flexibility, size, financial acumen, and cross-border influence, MNCs have become indispensable partners at the intersection of human rights and civil society, in what can only be described as the next generation in CSR, a kind of "CSR 2.0."

Accompanying this transition has been an evolutionary shift in municipal law relating to corporate transparency and disclosure. Since 9/11 and the corporate accounting and financial debacles that occurred around and since that time, the U.S. government and federal regulators have required corporations not only to maintain books and records reflecting compliance with increasingly more laws relating to what might be called business ethics,

---

[3] For further discussion, see *infra* at Section 17.3.

[4] For example, in 2001, IBM was forced to respond to allegations that it aided the Nazi government during the Holocaust by providing Hollerith punch-cards through its German subsidiary, used to identify and track ethnic minorities for deportation and extermination. IBM Press Release, *Statement on Nazi-Era Book and Lawsuit* (February 14, 2001), www-03.ibm.com/press/us/en/pressrelease/1388.wss.

[5] Ken Silverstein, "Sullivan Principles: Corporations Must Contribute to the Culture of Peace and Help End Gun Violence," Forbes (December 25, 2013), www.forbes.com/sites/kensilverstein/2012/12/25/sullivan-principles-corporations-must-contribute-to-the-culture-of-peace-and-help-end-gun-violence/.

[6] Broadly, the concept of "corporate social responsibility" explores the link between corporations and the social consequences of their actions and suggests a corporate responsibility not only to shareholders but to other stakeholders such as workers, customers, investors, governments, and local communities. For a more in-depth discussion of corporate social responsibility, see Michael E. Porter and Mark R. Kramer, "Strategy and Society: The Link Between Competitive Advantage and Corporate Social Responsibility," *Harvard Business Review* 84, 12 (December 2006).

but also to disclose when those compliance systems break down.[7] Most well known are examples relating to anticorruption laws which, since 9/11, have become virtually universal, but this trend extends to environmental rules, diversity-in-hiring rules, and know-your-customer rules designed to thwart terrorism and/or organized crime and/or ensure compliance with trade-related sanction regimes aimed at countries that support or finance terrorists. Faced with aggressive prosecution and sanctions, corporations have adopted comprehensive internal compliance regimes on how to act in legally murky situations and how to protect themselves from employee malfeasance and inadvertent violations. In fact, the propagation of detailed internal compliance programs has led to an interesting phenomenon in which companies routinely exceed the specific requirements of domestic law based on the perceived cost-effectiveness of avoiding even minor transgressions and ease of administration.[8]

In contrast to the well-defined legal regimes surrounding anticorruption or conflict of interest regulations, international law relating to the prevention of

---

[7] See, e.g., Sarbanes Oxley Public Company Accounting Reform and Investor Protection Act of 2002 ("Sarbanes-Oxley"), 15 U.S.C. §7262 (2002) (requiring chief executive and chief financial officers of U.S. publicly owned corporations, their wholly owned subsidiaries, and all foreign-owned corporations whose shares are registered with the Securities Exchange Commission [SEC] to certify the accuracy of periodic filings presenting the company's financial condition); Uniting and Strengthening America by Providing Appropriate Tools Required to Intercept and Obstruct Terrorism Act of 2001 (PATRIOT Act), P.L. No. 107–56, §§312 and 352, 115 Stat. 272 (2001) (imposing due diligence and enhanced due diligence requirements on U.S. financial institutions that maintain correspondent accounts for foreign financial institutions for private banking accounts for non-U.S. persons and requiring the establishment of anti-money laundering programs including internal policies and controls); and Dodd-Frank Wall Street Reform and Consumer Protection Act, Pub. L. No. 111–203, §1502, 124 Stat. 1376, 2223 (2010) (requiring all issuers to disclose use of conflict minerals and supply chain due diligence reports). The United States is not the only nation to adopt similar transparency measures. New regulations promulgated under the UK Companies Act 2006 would require corporations to report nonfinancial information, including disclosures on human rights where such information is necessary for an understanding of the business. The Companies Act 2006 (Strategic Report and Directors' Report) Regulations 2013 No. 1970 (October 1, 2013); see also Linklaters, "New UK Annual Strategic Report and Requirements to Disclose Human Rights, Diversity and Greenhouse Emissions" (June 20, 2013), www.linklaters.com/Publications/Publication1005Newsletter/UK-Corporate-20-June-2013/Pages/New-UK-annual-strategic-report-disclose-human-rights-diversity-greenhouse-gas-emissions.aspx. Meanwhile, in April 2013, the European Commission circulated a draft directive to require large and listed corporations to include additional information on anticorruption and bribery matters, information on risks regarding nonfinancial matters, and additional information on diversity. Ibid.

[8] For example, even though the U.S. Foreign Corrupt Practices Act (FCPA) allows for small so-called *grease payments* to facilitate minor bureaucratic actions to which someone is otherwise entitled, most companies routinely prohibit these payments as part of fostering a uniform culture of anticorruption compliance. See 15 U.S.C. §§78dd-1 (b) and (f) (3) [Section 30A of the Securities & Exchange Act of 1934] (excepting facilitating payments for "routine governmental action … which is ordinarily and commonly performed by a foreign official" including for "obtaining permits, licenses, or other official documents to qualify a person to do business in a foreign country" and "processing governmental papers, such as visas and work orders").

"atrocity crimes" – war crimes, genocide, crimes against humanity, and the still-developing crime of aggression – remains largely unexplored.[9] The international community is developing comprehensive sovereign responses to atrocity crimes while they are occurring and stresses the importance of deterring atrocities.[10] Genocide scholars Barbara Harff and Gregory Stanton have articulated the most widely accepted risk assessment and chronological models for anticipating states with the potential for outbreaks of atrocities or genocide.[11] In identifying triggers such as ethnic control over economic opportunities, discrimination against minorities, or resource conflict, the international community has been able to begin fostering the development of identifiable goals for corporations that want to assist in atrocity crime prevention.[12] Moreover, atrocity crime prevention models conceptualizing genocide as a process, with identifiable transition events (albeit not linear) from stability to the onset of violence, may enable corporations to operate with greater insight into how atrocities happen and how to manage their investment and operations so as to minimize the risk of heightening intergroup tensions.[13]

Nonetheless, international actors have struggled to frame specific norms of prevention.[14] This situation poses tremendous risks for MNCs, particularly

[9] By "atrocity crimes," we adopt the term and criteria articulated by David Scheffer in his 2006 article, encompassing genocide, war crimes, ethnic cleansing, and crimes against humanity. David Scheffer, "Genocide and Atrocity Crimes," *Genocide Studies and Prevention* 1, 3: 229–250 (December 2006); and "The Future of Atrocity Law," *Suffolk Transnational Law Review* 25: 389–432 (2002).

[10] See Gareth Evans, *The Responsibility to Protect: Ending Mass Atrocity Crimes Once and for All* (Washington, DC: Brookings Institution Press, 2008), 79; see also Madeleine K. Albright and William S. Cohen, *Preventing Genocide: A Blueprint for U.S. Policymakers* (U.S. Holocaust Memorial Museum, The American Academy of Diplomacy, and the Endowment of the United States Institute of Peace [USIP], 2008) at xxiii. (emphasizing the need for early, decisive action as mass atrocities loom or begin to unfold) and Newt Gingrich and George Mitchell, *American Interests and UN Reform: Report of the Congressional Task Force on the United Nations* (Washington, DC: USIP, 2005), 28 ("The United Nations must create a rapid reaction capability among UN member-states that can identify and act on threats before they fully develop").

[11] Barbara Harff, "No Lessons Learned from the Holocaust? Assessing Risks of Genocide and Political Mass Murder since 1955," *American Political Science Review* 97(1): 57–73 (February 2003) (identifying six factors for assessing the risk of genocide, including the occurrence of a previous genocide in the same polity, autocracy, ethnic minority rule, political upheaval during war or revolution, exclusionary ideology, closure of borders to international trade, and discrimination) and Gregory H. Stanton, "8 Stages of Genocide," Genocide Watch (1998), http://genocidewatch.net/genocide-2/8-stages-of-genocide/.

[12] A number of major MNCs have actually implemented many of these preventative goals through equal opportunity hiring practices, local hiring preferences, skills training programs, and community investment funds through CSR initiatives, discussed more fully in Section 17.2.

[13] See Sheri P. Rosenberg and Everita Silna, "Genocide by Attrition: Silent and Efficient," in *Genocide Matters*, edited by Joyce Apsel and Ernesto Verdeja (Abingdon: Oxon Routledge, 2013), 106, 106–126.

[14] Peter J. Katzenstein, "Introduction," in *The Culture of National Security: Norms and Identity in World Politics*, edited by Peter J. Katzenstein (New York: Columbia University Press, 1996), 5

those engaged in extractive industries. In the past two decades alone, battles over natural resources have become entangled with ethnic conflict in the Democratic Republic of Congo (DRC), Indonesia, Myanmar, the Niger Delta, and South Sudan, raising the specter of atrocity crimes. Through their operations in these conflict zones, MNCs may be perceived as complicit in the commission of atrocities by delegating to and/or contracting services from private or public security providers, thus exposing corporations, and possibly their directors and officers, to legal liability. Yet, as we discuss more fully later, existing international legal standards of indirect liability do not provide an effective guide to corporate behavior, and, in the absence of clear standards, corporations have adopted ad hoc and inconsistent approaches to forestalling and reacting to human rights abuses. This creates the dual problem of balancing legitimate and important corporate behavior (including behaviors that might further civil society) against conduct that should be avoided.

This chapter considers the problems of companies implicated in atrocity crimes (Section 17.2) and how inconsistent international law and, for example, U.S. aiding and abetting standards, do not incentivize better compliance (Section 17.3). Alternative options are considered with respect to providing a basis for atrocity crime prevention compliance to become a realistic consideration for companies doing business in conflict regions around the world; such options suggest that mandatory disclosure regimes based on precedents like the anticorruption regimes now in wide use may offer the best means for deterring improper corporate behavior by allowing corporations to protect themselves from complicity in human rights abuses while pursuing legitimate corporate goals (Section 17.4).

Theses mand- atory discl- osure

17.2.   Industry Risks and Responses

History shows that, again and again, corporations confronted with human rights abuses act responsively rather than attempting to act prophylactically, and although an ounce of prevention may be worth a pound of cure, for corporations engaged in conflict zones, systematic preventative measures have been extremely hard to come by.

17.2.1. Talisman Energy

From 2001 through 2003, Canadian-based Talisman Energy came under fire for allegedly aiding and abetting the forced displacement of non-Muslim Sudanese

(defining norms as a broader category of behavior expectations than law, insofar as not all norms are legally obligatory).

civilians in South Sudan.[15] The company was accused of complicity in extrajudicial killings, torture, rape, and the destruction of villages in conjunction with these displacements.[16] After a sustained nongovernmental organization (NGO) lobbying campaign, legislation was introduced in the U.S. Congress that, if passed, would have delisted Talisman shares from the New York Stock Exchange.[17] Talisman also faced a billion-dollar class action lawsuit in the United States stemming from the alleged human rights abuses. Although the suit was dismissed in 2009, Talisman ceased operations in Sudan and has since adopted a policy of consultation with both NGOs and the U.S. and Canadian governments before investing in conflict areas.[18] More recently, Talisman voluntarily agreed to disclose payments to governments on a country-by-country basis in connection with the Publish What You Pay (PWYP) campaign and later became a signatory to the Extractive Industries Transparency Initiative (EITI).[19] Talisman has also developed an internal security policy premised on the Voluntary Principles on Security and Human Rights (hereinafter Voluntary Principles), a multistakeholder initiative involving governments, companies, and NGOs to promote the implementation of guiding principles for oil, gas, and mining corporations in conducting risk assessments and engaging

[15] See "Sudan: Talisman Energy Must Do More to Protect Human Rights," Human Rights Watch (May 1, 2001), www.amnesty.org/en/library/asset/AFR54/010/2001/en/a40a4dfd-fb35-11dd -9486-a1064e51935d/afr540102001en.pdf (outlining human rights abuses by government forces in Talisman-involved areas of Sudan); Caroline Kaeb, "Emerging Issues of Human Rights Responsibility in the Extractive and Manufacturing Industries: Patterns and Liability Risks," *Northwestern Journal of International Human Rights* 6: 327, 342–343 (2008).

[16] Kaeb, *supra* note 16.

[17] Sudan Peace Act, H.R. 2052, 107th Cong. § 9 (2001) (prohibiting "any entity engaged in the development of oil or gas in Sudan. . . from trading its securities . . . in any capital market in the United States"); Sudan, Oil, and Human Rights, Human Rights Watch (2003). See Bernard Simon, "Oil Company Defends Role in Sudan," *New York Times*, October 17, 2001, www.nytimes.com/2001/10/17/business/oil-company-defends-role-in-sudan.html? ref=talismanenergyinc.

[18] *Presbyterian Church of Sudan v. Talisman Energy, Inc.*, 582 F.3d 244 (2d Cir. 2009) (affirming plaintiff's summary judgment to Talisman because the Sudanese did not establish that the company acted with the purpose of assisting the Sudanese Government to violate international law); see Talisman Energy Inc., News Release (Form 6-K) (March 12, 2003) (announcing the completion of Talisman's sale of its indirectly held interest in the Sudan project to ONGC Videsh Limited for $771 million). Talisman announced its plans to sell its Sudan assets in October 2002, while stating that "Talisman's presence in Sudan has been a force for good." Talisman Energy Inc., News Release (Form 6-K) (October 31, 2002). See also "Talisman to Sell Its Stake in Company in Sudan," *New York Times*, October 31, 2002, www.nytimes.com/2002/ 10/31 /business/talisman-to-sell-its-stake-in-company-in-sudan.html.

[19] The EITI is a multistakeholder initiative seeking to stamp out resource-fueled corruption (and the ethnic tensions that arise from such resources) by standardizing publication of revenues paid by extractive companies and received by governments in connection with natural resource development. See Extractive Industries Transparency Initiative, "What Is the EITI," http://eiti.org/.

with private and public security to ensure operational security in a manner most respectful of human rights.[20]

17.2.2. ChevronTexaco

ChevronTexaco has also faced issues in connection with its operations in the Niger Delta.[21] Chevron faced accusations of complicity with the 1998 shooting of protestors at the company's offshore drilling rig and construction barge and in the subsequent detention and torture of a protest leader by Nigerian authorities.[22] Chevron was also accused of participating in a 1999 incident involving the killing of several people after Nigerian forces opened fire on two villages from helicopters leased from a company subsidiary.[23] Although Chevron continues to operate in the Niger Delta, the company founded the Niger Delta Partnership Initiative in 2011 to address socioeconomic challenges in Southern Nigeria[24], and it supplements U.S. foreign aid to the region.

17.2.3. Total and Unocal

In Myanmar, France-based Total and U.S.-based Unocal Corporation faced allegations of forced labor provided by the then-Burmese government in connection with constructing a $1.2 billion natural gas pipeline during the 1990s and complicity in the attendant murder, rape, and torture of local residents by Burmese security forces.[25] In 2005, Myanmar nationals and Unocal settled a nine-year case pending in U.S. federal and California state

---

[20] "Corporate Responsibility: Human Rights," Talisman Energy, www.talisman-energy.com/re sponsibility/human_rights.html; "Corporate Responsibility: Transparency," Talisman Energy, www.talisman-energy.com/responsibility/transparency.html.

[21] See Kaeb, *supra* note 16, at 339–340 (discussing factual allegations against ChevronTexaco Corporation).

[22] *Bowoto v. Chevron Corp.*, 557 F. Supp. 2d 1080, 1082–83 (N.D. Cal. 2008) (outlining the incidents alleged, but ultimately not holding Chevron liable). It is alleged that these government forces were transported on a Chevron subsidiary's leased helicopters and that at least one company representative was present during the shootings. Ibid. See also *Bowoto v. Chevron*, EarthRights International, www.earthrights.org/legal/bowoto-v-chevron (making available the complaint and court documents from the case in which EarthRights International was co-counsel, representing the plaintiffs); Ashby Jones, "Breaking News: Jury Finds for Chevron in Nigeria Human-Rights Case," *Wall Street Journal* (December 1, 2008), http://blogs.wsj.com /law/2008/12/01/breaking-news-jury-acquits-chevron-in-nigeria-human-rights-case.

[23] See *Bowoto*, 557 F. Supp.2d at 1082–83; EarthRights, *supra* note 23.

[24] "Nigeria Fact Sheet," Chevron (April 2013), 3, www.chevron.com/documents/pdf/nigeriafact sheet.pdf (outlining Chevron's involvement in Nigeria).

[25] See *Doe v. Unocal Corp.*, 395 F.3d 932, 937–44, 952 (9th Cir. 2002) (summarizing the allegations against Unocal and the prior proceedings in lower courts and noting that "the evidence … supports the conclusion that Unocal gave practical assistance to the Burmese Military in subjecting Plaintiffs to forced labor"); see also Kaeb, *supra* note 16, at 340–342.

court stemming from these allegations.[26] Total settled a similar case in France and established a solidarity fund to compensate victims.[27] Total has also made human rights performance an integral part of its CSR policies, subscribed to the Voluntary Principles, and become a member of the Global Business Initiative on Human Rights.[28] However, Total has resisted involving Myanmar in EITI and ignored recommendations from the French government to freeze its Myanmar investments, stating that "[f]ar from solving Myanmar's problems, a forced withdrawal would only lead to our replacement by other operators probably less committed to the ethical principles guiding all our initiatives."[29]

17.2.3. Rio Tinto

The Anglo-Australian mining conglomerate Rio Tinto was implicated in gross human rights violations and atrocities in connection with its mining activities in Papua New Guinea (PNG), where allegations that the government violently suppressed employee protests over environmental damage and racially discriminatory hiring practices by Rio Tinto on the island of Bougainville contributed to the Bougainville separatist crisis in 1988 and, ultimately, civil war.[30] By 1997, the PNG government was alleged to have killed more than 10,000 people, sometimes using Rio Tinto helicopters and vehicles.[31] As discussed later, a nearly thirteen-year-old lawsuit against Rio Tinto was only recently dismissed following the Supreme Court's decision in *Kiobel v. Royal*

---

[26] See *Doe*, 395 F.3d at 944 (reversing the District Court's summary judgment on the major ATS claims); Bloomberg News, "Unocal Settles Rights Suit in Myanmar," *New York Times*, December 14, 2004, www.nytimes.com/2004/12/14/business/14unocal.

[27] See Kaeb, *supra* note 16, at 341. A Belgian case against Total from 2002 that was reopened in 2007 was dropped once again in 2008. "Belgium Drops Myanmar Rights Case Against Total," AFP (March 5, 2008), http://afp.google.com/article/ALeqM5g03FLW0Ks50sU4W gQuGU-Gay-P-w.

[28] "Ethical Business Conduct," Total, www.total.com/en/our-challenges/ethical-business-con duct/upholding-human-rights/initiatives-to-promote-human-rights-201667.html.

[29] Total S.A., "Sharing Our Energies 2006: Corporate Social Responsibility Report 24" (2006), www.total.com/static/en/medias/topic1606/Total_2006_CSR_en.pdf.

[30] See *Sarei v. Rio Tinto, PLC*, 487 F.3d 1193, 1198 (9th Cir. 2007) (describing the environmental damage from the mining operations and the human rights abuses that occurred in the ten-year struggle of the Bougainville civil uprising); "Rio Tinto: A Shameful History of Human and Labour Rights Abuses and Environmental Degradation Around the Globe," London Mining Network (April 20, 2010), http://londonminingnetwork.org/2010/04/rio-tinto-a-shameful-his tory-of-human-and-labour-rights-abuses-and-environmental-degradation-around-the-globe/ (outlining the allegations against Rio Tinto in connection to its Panguna Mine operation on Bougainville Island).

[31] See *Sarei*, 487 F.3d at 1198; see also *Bougainville: Our Island, Our Fight* (Ipso Facto Prods Pty. Ltd. 1998) (documenting the indigenous population's fight against the mining companies and PNG government). This film is notable as one of the few examples of Western media reporting on the Bougainville conflict.

Dutch Petroleum Co.[32] As of 2012, Rio Tinto has ceased mining activities in PNG, but, as of May 2012, appears to be contemplating a reopening.[33] In the years since the Bougainville crises, Rio Tinto has acceded to the Voluntary Principles, signed the UN Global Compact, and published a guide for integrating human rights into corporate practice.[34]

17.2.4. Voluntary Corporate Initiatives

As noted, a frequent response of corporations implicated in gross human rights violations has been to accede to voluntary principles ensuring respect for human rights. These initiatives include the Voluntary Principles[35], comprising a multistakeholder initiative involving governments, corporations, and NGOs to promote implementation of "a set of principles [guiding] oil, gas and mining companies on providing security for their operations in a manner that respects human rights"; the EITI, a multistakeholder initiative focused on the resource extraction industry and discussed above;[36] and the UN Guiding Principles on Business and Human Rights (hereinafter UN Guiding Principles")[37], which is the first set of UN-endorsed global guidelines aimed at providing a framework for actors to strengthen their respective approaches to business and human rights.

Voluntary initiatives may provide an alternative to the risks of piecemeal and protracted litigation and may be a way for corporations to engage on human rights issues while fostering consensus around standardized and workable principles.[38] Increasingly, these initiatives also serve as a basis for

---

[32] *Sarei v. Rio Tinto*, 722 F.3d 1109, 1110 (9th Cir. 2013) (affirming lower court's dismissal in light of *Kiobel*).

[33] Andrew Topf, "After Bougainville Black Eye, Rio Tinto Wading Back into PNG," Mining.Com (May 11, 2012), www.mining.com/after-bougainville-black-eye-rio-tinto-wading-back-into-png/; James Regan, "Rio Tinto Considers Restarting Papua New Guinea Copper Mine," Reuters (February 7, 2013), www.reuters.com/article/2013/02/07/riotinto-australia-bougainville.

[34] Rio Tinto, "Human Rights," www.riotinto.com/ourcommitment/human-rights-4800.aspx

[35] "Voluntary Principles on Security and Human Rights," www.voluntaryprinciples.org/.

[36] See EITI, *supra* note 20.

[37] Report of the Special Representative of the Secretary-General on the issue of human rights and transnational corporations and other business enterprises, John Ruggie, *Guiding Principles on Business and Human Rights: Implementing the United Nations "Protect, Respect and Remedy" Framework*, UN Doc. A/HRC/17/31 (March 21, 2011).

[38] See, e.g., Michael Goldhaber, "The Global Lawyer: Marty Likes It," *American Law Daily* (December 20, 2010), http://amlawdaily.typepad.com/amlawdaily/2010/12/globallawyer1220.html (reporting Martin Lipton's, of Wachtell, Lipton, Rosen & Katz, endorsing the Guiding Principles as "eminently reasonable" and a "potentially significant blueprint" that "insightfully marries aspirations with practicality") and Stephen Greenhouse, "Major Retailers Join Bangladesh Safety Plan," *New York Times* (May 13, 2013), www.nytimes.com/2013/05/14/business/global/hm-agrees-to-bangladesh-safety-plan.html?_r=0 (discussing major corporate initiatives to improve employee safety and working conditions in the wake of the Rana Plaza disaster).

government-sponsored implementation plans and multilateral initiatives to ensure compliance.[39] Rather than salutary schemes with little practical influence, these initiatives represent significant efforts to identify goals and challenges, routinize corporate human rights policies, and create a generation of executives who think deeply about human rights.

Yet even these initiatives have their drawbacks. For example, they often are cast broadly and generally fail to provide clear guidance or binding requirements as to what corporations should do when confronted with the imminent risk or reality of atrocity crimes.[40] They also are primarily reactive in that they were developed to respond to existing abuses such as corruption or unfair hiring practices. Finally, they do not identify or systematically address specific triggers that may lead to atrocity crimes and, to the extent that they are narrowly drawn to address particular industries or regions, may not mesh with broader voluntary initiatives.

17.3.   Existing Law Does Not Currently Incentivize Corporations to Develop Atrocity Crime Prevention Guidelines

Assuming voluntary atrocity crime prevention guidelines could be schematized, the question is whether MNCs would then have any guidance as to what behaviors they should avoid or any incentive to devote significant corporate assets toward developing and implementing compliance regimes. That is, the international legal community has not yet articulated standards sufficient to impose clear and predictable liability on corporations for indirect conduct relating to atrocity crimes, let alone impose direct legal liability on corporate directors or officers for failing to supervise subordinates or subsidiaries within conflict zones.

---

[39] In the case of the Guiding Principles, Great Britain became the first state to promulgate a national action plan implementing the Guiding Principles. See "Good Business: Implementing the UN Guiding Principles on Business and Human Rights," presented to Parliament by the Secretary of State for Foreign and Commonwealth Affairs (September 4, 2013), https://www.gov.uk/government/uploads/system/uploads/attachment_data/file/2369 01/BHR_Action_Plan–final_online_version_1_.pdf. The United States has expressed similar commitments toward implementing EITI. See Barack Obama, U.S. Pres., "Opening Remarks on Open Government Partnership" (September 20, 2011), www.whitehouse.gov /the-press-office/2011/09/20/opening-remarks-president-obama-open-government-partners hip and "U.S. Open Government National Action Plan" (September 20, 2011), www.open govpartnership.org/country/united-states/action-plan (stating that the U.S. Government "is Hereby Committing to Implement the EITI to Ensure that Taxpayers are Receiving Ever Dollar Due for Extraction of Our Natural Resources").

[40] See Chris Albin-Lackey, "Without Rules: A Failed Approach to Corporate Accountability," in World Report 2013, *Human Rights Watch*, 32–33 (2013).

enterprise
liability

17.3.1. International Law

As yet, international law does not definitively impose civil or criminal liability on corporations for violations of international law.[41] Although the Nuremberg Trials following World War II spurred recognition of natural persons' liability for criminal violations of international law, neither the charters for the International Military Tribunals (IMTs) for Nuremburg[42] or the Far East[43] recognized criminal liability for corporate violations of international law.[44] Treaties codifying certain international crimes such as genocide, war crimes, and acts constituting so-called "crimes against humanity" also did not recognize corporate liability,[45] and statutes establishing international courts

not express

[41] See, e.g., Brief of Amicus Curiae Professor James Crawford in Support of Conditional Cross Petitioner at 9, *Presbyterian Church of Sudan et al v. Talisman Energy, Inc.*, No. 09–1418 (2d. Cir., June 23, 2010); International Comm'n of Jurists, 2 *Report of the Int'l Commission of Jurists Expert Legal Panel on Corporate Complicity in Int'l Crimes* 56 (2008) and John Ruggie, *Report of the Special Representative of the Secretary-General on the Issues of Human Rights and Transnational Corporations and Other Business Enterprises*, UN Doc. A/HRC/4/035, ¶ 44 (February 9, 2007) ("In conclusion, it does not seem that the international human rights instruments discussed here currently impose direct liabilities on corporations").

[42] Although the Charter of the IMT (Nuremberg) (October 6, 1945), 81 UNT.S. 284 (1954) authorized the tribunal to "try and punish persons who . . . whether as individuals or members of organizations," Ibid. at 286 (Art. 6) "committed certain crimes or were members of so-called "criminal organization[s]," Ibid. at 290 (Art. 9), the effect was not enterprise liability but to make membership in such an organization a punishable offense—a recognition of "the right to bring individuals to trial for membership [in the criminal organization]." Ibid. (Art. 10). Even where the organization was ostensibly involved in the commission of war crimes, the Nuremberg prosecutions proceeded against the individuals who owned or operated the firm; the firm itself was not the subject of the prosecution. See *United States v. Krauch*, 8 Trials of War Criminals Before the Nuremberg Military Tribunals Under Control Council Law No. 10 ("I. G. Farben Case") 1081, 1152–53 (1952) and *In re Tesch and Others* ("Zyklon B Case"), *excerpted in* Ann. Digest and Reports of Public International Law Cases, Year 1946 (H. Lauterpacht ed., 1951).

[43] Charter of the International Military Tribunal for the Far East, January 19, 1946, *as amended*, April 26, 1946, art. 5, T.I.A.S. No. 1589 ("The Tribunal shall have the power to try and punish Far Eastern war criminals who as individuals or as members of organizations are charged with offense").

[44] *Flores v. S. Peru Copper Corp.*, 414 F.3d 233, 244 n.18 (2d Cir. 2003) (noting "the major legal significance of the (Nuremberg) judgments lies . . . in those portions of the judgments dealing with the area of personal responsibility for international law crimes") (quoting Telford Taylor, Chief of Counsel for War Crimes, *Final Report of the Secretary of the Army on the Nuremberg War Crimes Trials Under Council Law No. 10*, at 109 [August 15, 1949; 1997 ed.; emphasis in court opinion]).

[45] See, e.g., Genocide Convention, December 9, 1948, art. 4, 78 UNT.S. 277 (1951) (only "constitutionally responsible rulers, public officials, or private individuals" can be punished for genocide); Geneva Convention for the Amelioration of the Condition of the Wounded and Sick in Armed Forces in the Field ("Geneva Convention I"), August 12, 1949, art. 49, 75 UNT.S. 31 (1950) (providing penal sanctions "for persons committing, or ordering to be committed, any of the grave breaches of the present Convention defined," i.e., war crimes); and Protocol Additional to the Geneva Convention of 12 August 1949 and Relating to the Protection of Victims of Non-International Armed Conflicts, June 8, 1977, art. 6, 1125 UNT.S. 609 (1978) (same regarding internal armed conflict); and the Convention Against Torture and

[margin handwriting: Viol. by corp itself]

[margin handwriting: ICC Statute]

[margin handwriting: IMT]

and tribunals equally fail to establish this principle.[46] Most recently, Article 25 of the Rome Statute confirms the principle of "[i]ndividual criminal responsibility" as the limit of the ICC's authority, noting that "[t]he Court shall have jurisdiction over natural persons pursuant to this Statute."[47] Indeed, efforts to impose liability on corporations failed to obtain the requisite support during negotiations of the Rome Statute.[48]

Efforts to impose criminal liability on corporate executives for participation in war crimes or crimes against humanity have proved more successful. For example, during World War II, German and Japanese corporations directly used forced labor in their own factories and operations as part of total mobilization effort by the Axis powers during the war.[49] Their direct participation in certain war crimes and crimes against humanity led to the prosecution and conviction of Nazi industrialists for forced labor before the IMT at Nuremberg[50] and to the

---

Other Cruel, Inhuman, or Degrading Treatment or Punishment ("CAT"), December 10, 1974, arts. 4 and 6, 1465 UNT.S. 85 (1987) (extending liability only to natural persons).

[46] Statute of the International Criminal Tribunal for the Former Yugoslavia (ICTY), S.C. Res. 827, Art. 7(1), UN Doc. S/RES/827 (May 25, 1993) (conferring jurisdiction on the ICTY only to try natural persons) and Statute of the International Criminal Tribunal for Rwanda (ICTR), S.C. Res. 955, Art. 6(1), UN Doc. S/RES/955 (Nov. 8, 1994) (same). Although the Statute for the Special Court of Sierra Leone (SCLC) did not expressly confine jurisdiction to natural persons, "there is no doubt that so far actual prosecutions under the statute 'have been confined to natural persons.'" William A. Schabas, The UN Int'l Criminal Tribunals: The Former Yugoslavia, Rwanda & Sierra Leone at 139 (2006) (internal citation omitted).

[47] Rome Statute, art. 25(c)(1) (2002); see also Kai Ambos, Article 25, in *Commentary on the Rome Statute of the International Criminal Court: Observers' Notes, Article by Article* at 477–78 (2d ed. 2008) (noting that "common standards for corporate liability; in fact, the concept is not even recognized in some major criminal law systems").

[48] See Per Saland, "International Criminal Law Principles," in *The International Criminal Court: The Making of the Rome Statute*, edited by Roy Lee (The Hague: Kluwer Law International, 1999), 189, 198–199 (discussing the decision to link criminal responsibility to individuals but not other legal entities under Rome Statute). ICC drafters also resisted the inclusion of conspiracy liability, which is explicitly contained within the Genocide Convention and instead adopted liability for "contributing to a common purpose." See Jonathan A. Bush, "The Prehistory of Corporations and Conspiracy in International Criminal Law: What Nuremberg Really Said," *Columbia Law Review* 109(5): 1099–1100 (2009).

[49] Anita Ramasatry, "Corporate Complicity: From Nuremberg to Rangoon – An Examination of Forced Labor Cases and Their Impact on the Liability of Multinational Corporations," *Berkeley Journal of International Law* 20: 91, 105, and n.50 (2002) (discussing the Krupp, Flick, and I. G. Farben cases and to a lesser extent, the Hermann Goering Works (HGW) and Dresdner Bank cases).

[50] *United States v. Flick* ("The Flick Case"), 6 Trials of War Criminals Before the Nuremberg Military Tribunals Under Control Council Law No. 10, at 11 (1952) [hereinafter "Nuremberg Trials"], www.loc.gov/rr/frd/Military_Law/NTs_war-criminals.html (setting forth the indictment of steel magnate and five principal associates); *United States v. Krupp* ("The Krupp Case"), 9 Nuremberg Trials, *supra*, at 7 (indicting and convicting industrialist and eleven top aids for war crimes and crimes against humanity with respect to plunder and spoliation of civilian property and factories in occupied territories and deportation and use of prisoners of war and concentration camp inmates as forced laborers); *United States v. Carl Krauch* ("The I. G. Farben Case"), 7 Nuremberg Trials, *supra*, at 10 (indicting twenty-four directors and officers of I. G. Farben-Industrie A.G. and convicting five for war crimes and crimes against

prosecution and conviction of Japanese mining executives before the British War Crimes Court in Hong Kong for abuses committed at the Kinkaseki Mine in Formosa.[51] More recently, business officials were convicted for direct and public incitement to commit genocide and crimes against humanity in connection with hate propaganda disseminated by the *Radio Télévision Libre des Mille Collines* (RTLM) radio station and the *Kangura* newspaper during the Rwandan genocide[52] to supplying arms to Liberian strongman Charles Taylor.[53]

Yet even these cases provide only limited guidance for corporate actors not engaged in direct abuses. First, there are limited fora in which corporate actors may be prosecuted for complicity in atrocity crimes and even fewer courts in which victims may initiate claims or seek civil remedies. Second, these tribunals have produced limited guidance on indirect or inadvertent participation by corporate supervisors or managers. In the German industrialists cases, the respective officials either directly supervised war crimes in the case of I. G. Farben officials[54] or "purposefully availed itself

humanity for plunder, slavery, and complicity in aggression and mass murder); *United States v. von Weizsaecker* ("The Ministries Case"), 12 Nuremberg Trials, *supra*, at 13, 18 (indicting but failing to convict, *inter alia*, Karl Rasche, chairman of the Dresden Bank for his actions as a private banker in facilitating slave labor where providing money or credit to finance criminal activity did not constitute a violation of customary international law, even where the bank had knowledge of the purpose for such financing). See also *Prosecutor v. Delalic and Others*, Case No. IT-96-21-A, Judgment, ¶¶ 261–263 (February 21, 2001) (discussing the French Nuremberg-style criminal trial and conviction of civilian superiors of Roechling Iron and Steel Works owners and managers for ill-treatment of deportees forced to labor).

[51] Ramasatry, *Corporate Complicity, supra* note 50, at 114 (indicting nine and convicting eight civilian managers and supervisors of the Japanese Nippon Mining Company accused of mistreating prisoners of war forced to labor in the Kinkaseki Mine).

[52] *Prosecutor v. Ferdinand Nahimana, Jean-Bosco Barayagwiza, Hassan Ngeze*, Case No. ICTR-99-52-T, Judgment and Sentence (December 3, 2000).

[53] Recent criminal trials of individuals for business-related international crimes include the domestic Dutch prosecutions of Guus van Kouwenhoven, who was convicted of smuggling arms to Liberia in 2006 but had his conviction overturned on appeal, and Franz van Anraat, who was convicted and sentenced to fifteen years in prison – later raised to seventeen years – for complicity in war crimes committed by Saddam Hussein. See Marlise Simons, "8-Year Sentence for Businessman Who Smuggled Arms to Liberia," *New York Times* (June 8, 2006), at A8 (reporting Kouwenhoven's conviction); Marlise Simons, *Arms Ruling Overturned by Dutch*, *New York Times* (March 11, 2008), at A10 (reporting Kouwenhoven's conviction overturned); Marlise Simons, "Vendor Tied to Gas Attack Is Convicted," *New York Times*, December 24, 2005, at A5 (van Anraat's conviction); Marlise Simons, "World Briefing Europe: The Netherlands: Stiffer Sentence for Iraq Poison Gas," *New York Times* (May 10, 2007), at A14 (reporting increase in van Anraat's sentence).

[54] *The IG Farben Case, supra* note 51, at 1185–87 ("the defendants most closely connected with the Auschwitz construction project bear great responsibility with respect to the workers. They applied to the Reich Office for Labor ... Responsibility for taking the initiative in the unlawful employment was theirs, and, to some extent at least, they must share the responsibility for mistreatment of the workers with the SS and the construction contractors camp labor ... at Auschwitz with the initiative displayed by the officials of Farben in the procurement and utilization of such labor, is a crime against humanity").

of slave labor" in the case of the Krupp firm.[55] In *Prosecutor v. Ferdinand Nahimana, Jean-Bosco Barayagwiza, Hassan Ngeze and the South* and the Kinkaseki Mine cases, where defendants were held to have not participated directly in the atrocities, evidence still proved direct control over the perpetrators, knowledge of the abuses, and either a failure to supervise or failure to take reasonable steps to prevent abuses.[56]

17.3.2. U.S. Law

Absent clear international standards and fora, victims typically have sought recourse in domestic courts. For example, U.S. federal courts, which until recently imposed relaxed pleading requirements,[57] supplied aggressive discovery mechanisms by which human rights abuse plaintiffs could substantiate claims or compel disclosure of potentially embarrassing corporate information and offered the possibility of higher damages awards.[58] But these remedies do not provide clear standards.

Federal statutes providing for jurisdiction and substantive rights of action for victims of human rights abuses and atrocities, including the U.S. Alien Tort Statute (ATS) and Torture Victims Protection Act (TVPA), do not provide reliable coverage with respect to corporate or corporate officer liability. Plaintiffs alleging aiding and abetting under the ATS must satisfy a high standard of intent, which they have typically been unable to do. Moreover, following the U.S. Supreme Court's decision in *Kiobel*, ATS claims must now "touch and concern" activities occurring in the "territory of the United States" in order to survive a motion to dismiss, and it is likely that many ATS claims

---

[55] *The Krupp Case, supra* note 51, at 1412 (noting that when the SS offered concentration camp inmates as free labor to armament firms in 1944, many firms refused whereas the Krupp firm "sought concentration camp labor because of the scarcity of manpower then prevailing in Germany").

[56] See *Prosecutor v. Ferdinand Nahimana* at ¶970-977A (RTLM's senior managers had direct supervisory control over the station's content, actual knowledge that RTLM's racial vehemence generated concern within Rwandan Ministry of Information, and, in the case of Barayagwiza, active engagement in the management of the station and failure to take "necessary and reasonable measures to prevent the killings ... instigated by RTLM") and Ramasatry, *Corporate Complicity, supra* note 50, at 114–115 (although two of the defendants did not directly participate in beatings or mistreatment of prisoners, there was evidence that the managers were "entirely responsible for the safety and welfare of the POW laborers at the mine" and that the managers failed to supervise conditions at the mine or report abuses).

[57] See, e.g., *Bell Atlantic Corp. v. Twombly*, 550 U.S. 544 (2007) (abandoning the "conceivability" standard previously articulated in *Conley v. Gibson*, 355 U.S. 41 (1957) for a stricter "plausibility" standard, requiring "enough fact[s] to rise a reasonable expectation that discovery will reveal evidence") and *Ashcroft v. Iqbal*, 556 U.S. 662 (2009) (extending *Twombly's* heightened pleading standards to all federal court cases).

[58] See Sarah Joseph, "Corporations and Transnational Human Rights Litigation" (Oxford: Hart Publishing, 2004), 17.

will fail this test.[59] The TVPA has been infrequently used by courts to impose liability against civilian superiors for human rights violations committed within a supervisor's areas of responsibility;[60] however, courts have held that the TVPA does not apply to organizational entities, including corporations,[61] and may not provide for aiding and abetting liability.[62] Finally, heightened U.S. pleading standards (i.e., the types of supporting facts that a claimant must allege to state a claim) mean that alleging human rights violations in U.S. federal courts is harder because it is difficult to plead facts sufficient to establish knowledge or substantial assistance on the part of a supervisor.[63] Plaintiffs must allege facts plausibly suggesting that supervisors aided and abetted human rights violations committed by their subordinates and not merely consistent with the truth of the allegations asserted.[64] Similarly, recourse to state aiding and abetting law – even

[59] *Kiobel v. Royal Dutch Petroleum Co.*, No. 10–1491, slip op. at 14 (April 17, 2013).

[60] See, e.g., *Ford v. Garcia*, 289 F.3d 1283, 1288 (11th Cir. 2002) (noting that plaintiff must demonstrate under the TVPA that Salvadorian officials failed to take "all reasonable steps to prevent or repress" the murders of American churchwomen, noting that "[a]lthough the TVPA does not explicitly provide for liability of commanders for human rights violations of their troops, legislative history makes clear that Congress intended to adopt the doctrine of command responsibility from international law as part of the Act") and *Doe v. Liu Qi*, 349 F. Supp. 2d 1258, 1331–1333 (N.D. Cal. 2004) (Chinese mayor and deputy provincial government liable under the ATS and the TVPA for violations of Falun Gong practitioners' human rights under command responsibility doctrine where the mayor "held the power not only to formulate all important provincial policies and policy decisions, but also to supervise, direct and lead the executive branch of the city government ... including the operation of the Public Security Bureau" and where the deputy provincial governor did not have lone authority to authorize conduct but was "a high ranking municipal and provincial official who 'actively participated in the governing bodies that supervised the acts of repression and played a major policy-making and supervisory role in the policies and practices that were carried out'").

[61] See *Mohamad v. Palestinian Authority*, 132 S. Ct. 1702, 1707 (2012) (only natural persons can be held liable for violations of the TVPA).

[62] *Compare Hilao v. Estate of Marcos*, 103 F.3d 767, 779 (9th Cir. 1996) (noting that TVPA imposes liability on individuals responsible for acts of torture or summary execution even if they did not personally perform or order the abuses at issue) *with Stoneridge Inv. Partners LLC v. Scientific-Atlanta, Inc.*, 552 U.S. 148, 158 (2008) (cautioning against judicial creation of causes of action absent congressional action, potentially calling into question right to assert implied aiding and abetting claims under TVPA).

[63] See *Ashcroft v. Iqbal*, 556 U.S. 662, 678 (2009) (a complaint will not satisfy the pleading requirements if it offers only "labels and conclusions" or "a formulaic recitation of the elements of a cause of action," and does not "suffice if it tenders 'naked assertion[s]' devoid of 'further factual enhancement'"); see also id. ("[A]complaint must contain sufficient factual matter, accepted as true, to 'state a claim to relief that is plausible on its face.' A claim has facial plausibility when the plaintiff pleads factual content that allows the court to draw the reasonable inference that the defendant is liable for the misconduct alleged.' The plausibility standard is not akin to a 'probability requirement,' but it asks for more than a sheer possibility that a defendant has acted unlawfully. Where a complaint pleads facts that are 'merely consistent with' a defendant's liability, it 'stops short of the line between possibility and plausibility of entitlement to relief.'" (quoting *Bell Atlantic Corp. v. Twombly*, 550 U.S. 544, 564 (2004) (internal citations omitted))).

[64] *Twombly*, 550 U.S. at 557.

if applicable – not only requires "actual knowledge of the underlying [offense]" and "substantial assistance" on the part of the alleged wrongdoer, but also requires plaintiff's injury to be "'a direct or reasonably foreseeable result' of the complained of conduct ... '[b]ut-for' causation does not suffice; the breach must proximately cause the loss."[65]

17.3.2.1. U.S. Federal Statutory Law   Case-by-case adjudication under the ATS[66] and TVPA[67] has resulted in only limited corporate liability for human rights violations. The ATS, enacted as part of the Judiciary Act of 1789, grants U.S. district courts "original jurisdiction of any civil action by an alien for a tort only, committed in violation of the law of nations or a treaty of the United States."[68] Prior to the Second Circuit's decision in *Filártiga v. Peña-Irala*, the ATS existed as a kind of "legal Lohengrin," without attribution or explanation. Following *Filártiga*, which extended the jurisdiction of U.S. federal courts to certain human rights violations committed extraterritorially by a non-U.S. citizen, initial ATS cases targeted government officials for violations of international law, but attention quickly shifted to individuals or companies acting under color of state law, as evidenced in *Kadic v. Karadžić*, or companies operating under state license who allegedly aided and abetted violations of international law, such as in *Doe v. Unocal*.

From the outset, plaintiffs alleging aiding and abetting under the ATS must satisfy a high standard of intent, which plaintiffs are typically unable to do. For example, in *Doe v. Unocal*, the first major ATS lawsuit against a private corporation, the plaintiffs contended that Unocal, an American company, "knowingly [took] advantage of and profit[ed] from [the Burmese Government's] practice of using forced labor and forced relocation, in concert with other human rights violations including rape and torture, to further the interests of [its] gas pipeline project."[69] The district court granted summary judgment for lack of requisite intent, but the Ninth Circuit reversed, noting that the intent requirement for aiding and abetting is "actual or constructive (i.e., reasonable) knowledge that the accomplice's

---

[65] *Kolbeck*, 939 F. Supp. 240 at 249; see *Edwards & Hanly v. Wells Fargo Sec. Clearance Corp.*, 602 F.2d 478, 484 (2d Cir. 1979); *J. P. Morgan Chase Bank v. Winnick*, 406 F. Supp. 2d 247, 256 (S.D.N.Y. 2005).

[66] 28 U.S.C. § 1350 (2006) (hereinafter "ATS").

[67] Torture Victim Protection Act of 1991 (TVPA), Pub. L. No. 102–256, 106 Stat. 73 (1992) (codified at 28 U.S.C. § 1350 (note)). The TVPA was codified as a note to the ATS.

[68] ATS § 1350; see also *Filártiga v. Peña-Irala*, 630 F.2d 876 (2d Cir. 1980) (extending the jurisdiction of U.S. courts to wrongful acts outside the U.S. committed by non-U.S. citizens).

[69] *Doe v. Unocal*, 963 F. Supp. 880, 883–84, 895 (C.D. Cal. 1997) (finding that corporations could be held liable under the ATS for aiding and abetting sovereign states that were committing human rights violations).

actions will assist the perpetrator of the crime."[70] The case then settled before a Ninth Circuit's rehearing.[71]

The Second Circuit then held in *Presbyterian Church of Sudan v. Talisman Energy, Inc.* that, applying international law, "the [intent] standard for aiding and abetting liability in [ATS] actions is purpose rather than knowledge alone."[72] In granting summary judgment, the court determined that the Sudanese plaintiffs could not satisfy this high intent standard, and the court concluded that "there were insufficient facts or circumstances suggesting that Talisman acted with the purpose to advance violations of international humanitarian law."[73]

Although not addressing intent, the recent Supreme Court decision in *Kiobel* will make it even harder to bring corporate aiding and abetting human rights violations cases in the U.S. against non-U.S. entities or for non-U.S. conduct.[74] Similar to *Filártiga*, the conduct at issue in *Kiobel* occurred entirely abroad, and there were no U.S. defendants – although Royal Dutch Shell had a U.S. office and was listed on the New York Stock Exchange. In *Kiobel*, twelve Nigerian citizens sued Royal Dutch Shell under the ATS for allegedly aiding and abetting the Nigerian government in committing violations of the law of nations in the Niger Delta during its crackdown on anti-oil company protests.[75] On interlocutory appeal, the Second Circuit dismissed the entire complaint on the grounds that the law of nations did not recognize corporate liability. The case subsequently underwent two rounds of briefing before the U.S. Supreme Court, first addressing whether corporations could be sued under international law and then whether the ATS provided jurisdiction claims for extraterritorial violations of international law.

Ultimately, the Supreme Court affirmed the lower court's dismissal based on a holding that the ATS cases, although purely jurisdictional (i.e., creating no

---

[70] *Doe v. Unocal*, 395 F.3d 932, 953 (9th Cir. 2002).

[71] Ibid. at 953; *Doe v. Unocal*, 395 F.3d 978 (9th Cir. 2003) (granting a rehearing by the en banc court); Bloomberg News, "Unocal Settles Rights Suit in Myanmar," *New York Times* (December 14, 2004), www.nytimes.com/2004/12/14/business/14unocal.

[72] *Presbyterian Church of Sudan v. Talisman Energy, Inc.*, 582 F.3d 244, 259 (2d Cir. 2009). The district court in this case initially imposed the intent requirement. See *Presbyterian Church of Sudan v. Talisman Energy, Inc.*, 453 F. Supp. 2d 633 (S.D.N.Y. 2006). Before this case, "no court had ever required plaintiffs alleging an aiding and abetting theory of liability to satisfy a criminal law intent requirement." Stephens et al., *International Human Rights Litigation in U.S. Courts* 319 (2d ed.) (Leiden: Koninklijke Brill NV, 2008). The plaintiffs in this case were Sudanese nationals alleging that Talisman Energy, a Canadian company, aided and abetted in the forced displacement of non-Muslim Sudanese from its oil extraction area in southern Sudan and the related extrajudicial killings, torture, rape, and destruction of property by the Sudanese government.

[73] Ibid. at 264.

[74] *Kiobel v. Royal Dutch Petroleum Co.*, 569 U.S. ___, No. 10–1491, slip op. at 1 (April 17, 2013).

[75] Ibid. at 1.

causes of action under U.S. or international law), were subject to the general federal statutory presumption against extraterritoriality.[76] In light of this decision, ATS claims must now "touch and concern" activities occurring in the "territory of the United States" in order to survive a motion to dismiss, and the mere presence of a corporation in the country is not enough to rebut the presumption.[77] Since *Kiobel*, a number of pending ATS cases have been dismissed on extraterritorial grounds, including *Giraldo v. Drummond*, No. 09cv1041 (N.D. Ala. 2013), dismissing claims that Drummond, a U.S.-based mining concern, and its employees (including its corporate president) aided and abetted extrajudicial killings and other human rights violations committed by paramilitary groups in Colombia; and *Sarei v. Rio Tinto PLC* No. 02-cv-56256 (9th Cir. 2013).[78]

By contrast, courts have applied the TVPA to impose liability against civilian superiors for human rights violations committed within those supervisors' areas of responsibility.[79] The TVPA provides a civil cause of action for U.S. nationals and aliens for torture and/or extrajudicial killing.[80] Unlike the ATS, the TVPA provides a substantive cause of action, whereas the ATS is jurisdictional in nature.[81] The legislative history supports liability in a situation in which those "with higher authority ... authorized, tolerated or knowingly ignored" violations.[82] These decisions have typically looked to international criminal and humanitarian law to define the scope of command

---

[76] Ibid. at 6–7 ("But to rebut the presumption, the ATS would need to evince a 'clear indication of extraterritoriality. It does not"; citation omitted). See *Morrison v. Nat'l Austl. Bank Ltd.*, 561 U.S. 247, 255 (2010) (reflecting the Court's continuing skepticism regarding extraterritorial application of U.S. law).

[77] *Kiobel*, No. 10–1491, slip op. at 14 (April 17, 2013) ("[E]ven where the claims touch and concern the territory of the United States, they must do so with sufficient force to displace the presumption against extraterritorial application. Corporations are often present in many countries, and it would reach too far to say that mere corporate presence suffices."). So-called "F-cubed" cases, involving a suit by a foreign plaintiff against a foreign defendant for conduct occurring wholly outside of the United States are now barred from bringing suit under the ATS.

[78] A third *Daimler AG v. Bauman*, 134 S. Ct. 746 (2014) recently was dismissed for lack of personal jurisdiction.

[79] See, e.g., *Doe v. Liu Qi*, 349 F. Supp. 2d 1258 (N.D. Cal. 2004) (holding the former Mayor of Beijing liable in a default judgment for overseeing the torture, arbitrary detention, and sexual assaults that occurred surrounding the preparation for the 2008 Beijing Olympics, where he had authority to formulate the security policy and to supervise and discipline the police forces). The TVPA Senate Report states "a higher official need not have personally performed or ordered the abuses in order to be held liable." S. Rep. No. 102–249, at 8 (1991).

[80] TVPA § 3.

[81] For a comparison of the ATS and the TVPA, see Ekaterina Apostolova, "The Relationship Between the Alien Tort Statute and the Torture Victim Protection Act," *Berkeley Journal of International Law*, 28: 640 (2010).

[82] S. Rep. No. 102–249, at 8–9 (1991). For a discussion of command responsibility under the ATS and TVPA, see Stephens, *supra* note 73 at 86–87, 257–264.

responsibility.[83] This application of command responsibility was recently reaffirmed by the Supreme Court.[84]

Significantly, however, courts have held that the TVPA does not apply to corporations.[85] In *Mohamad v. Palestinian Authority*, the Supreme Court unanimously affirmed the District of Columbia Circuit's dismissal of the suit on the ground that the TVPA does not authorize suits against organizations.[86] The TVPA also may not provide for aiding and abetting liability because the Act does not explicitly grant a cause of action for aiding and abetting.[87] Moreover, there are only two bases for standing under the TVPA: (1) the plaintiff is a direct victim of alleged torture, or (2) the plaintiff brings a claim on behalf of a deceased torture victim.[88] Further limiting the TVPA is its application to only individuals acting in an official capacity, under color of law,[89] and the requirement to exhaust local remedies or at least to show that such remedies are inadequate or unavailable.[90] Although no cases have yet

---

[83] See Stephens, *supra* note 75 at 261–264 (noting that courts have looked to the international criminal tribunals for the ICTR, ICTY and the ICC among others); see, e.g.,*Ford v. Garcia*, 289 F.3d 1283, 1290–99 (11th Cir. 2002) (referring to the ICTR and the ICTY).

[84] *Mohamad v. Palestinian Authority*, 132 S. Ct. 1702, 1709 (2012).

[85] Ibid.

[86] Ibid. at 1708. Justice Sotomayor, writing for the Court, stated that the TVPA's reference to potential defendants as "individuals" denotes only natural persons. Ibid. This case involved a suit against the Palestinian Authority and the Palestinian Liberation Organization, among others, for the alleged arrest, torture, and murder of a naturalized U.S. citizen, Azzam Rahim, during his visit to the West Bank. Ibid. at 1703.

[87] The provision in the statute for liability for any individual who "subjects" another to torture or extrajudicial killing is potential evidence that Congress intended for the statute to encompass aiding and abetting, but this issue remains unclear. See 28 U.S.C. § 1350 (note), §§ 1(A)(1), 1(A)(2);*Wiwa v. Royal Dutch Petroleum Co.*, No. 96 Civ. 8386, 2002 U.S. Dist. LEXIS 3293, at *50 (S.D.N.Y. February 22, 2002) (TVPA language and legislative history supported liability for "individuals who cause someone to undergo torture or extrajudicial killing, as well as those who actually carry out the deed").

[88] TVPA § 2(a). See Apostolova, *supra* note 82, at 651 ("The TVPA provides that for an extrajudicial killing claim a legal representative of the victim or 'any person who may be a claimant in an action for wrongful death' shall have standing to sue"; quoting TVPA § 2(a)(2)). In order to determine who has standing in such a case, the court should look to the law of the forum state. H.R. Rep. No. 102–367, at 4 (1991). However, there is "no requirement that the individual or the representative be either a U.S. citizen or an alien, or that the plaintiff or the acts have any connection to the United States." Stephens, *supra* note 73 at 85.

[89] The TVPA provides in relevant part a cause of action against "[a]n individual who, under actual or apparent authority, or color of law, of any foreign nation." TVPA § 2(a). See, e.g., *Schneider v. Kissinger*, 310 F. Supp. 2d 251, 267 (D.D.C. 2004) (dismissing TVPA claims because defendant was not acting "'under actual or apparent authority, or color of law, of any foreign nation'"; quoting TVPA § 2(a)).

[90] The claimant is required to exhaust all "adequate and available remedies in the place in which the conduct giving rise to the claim occurred." TVPA § 2(b). The House Report explains the rationale behind this limitation: "This requirement ensures that U.S. courts will not intrude into cases more appropriately handled by courts where the alleged torture or killing occurred. It will also avoid exposing U.S. courts to unnecessary burdens, and can be expected to encourage the development of meaningful remedies in other countries." H.R. Rep. No. 102–367, at 5 (1991),

been dismissed for failure to exhaust domestic remedies,[91] applying the TVPA only to individuals acting in an official capacity has been a bar to potential plaintiffs. These limitations, in addition to a ten-year statute of limitations,[92] present additional hurdles to potential plaintiffs.

Finally, heightened U.S. pleadings standards mean that alleging human rights violations in U.S. federal courts under either the ATS or TVPA will be even more difficult because it is difficult to plead facts sufficient to establish knowledge or substantial assistance on the part of a supervisor.[93] Plaintiffs must allege facts plausibly suggesting that supervisors aided and abetted human rights violations committed by their subordinates and not merely consistent with the truth of the allegations asserted.[94]

17.3.2.2. U.S. State Common Law Absent a showing of actual knowledge and substantial assistance, state common law does not provide aiding and abetting liability for corporations. To state a claim for aiding and abetting under U.S. state common law (specifically, New York law as representative of domestic common law standards for aiding and abetting), a plaintiff must allege (a) the existence of an underlying tort, (b) that the defendant had actual knowledge of the tort, (c) the defendant provided substantial assistance in carrying out the tort, and (d) the defendant proximately caused damages to the plaintiff as a result.[95]

To satisfy the knowledge requirement of aiding and abetting, a plaintiff must allege that the defendant "had actual knowledge" of the underlying tort."[96] Anything less – including allegations of constructive knowledge or that the

(margin note: State law A&A)

(margin note: packed jury instruction re: tort ⊗)

---

[91] *reprinted in* 1992 U.S.C.C.A.N. 84, 87–88. For a discussion of the exhaustion requirement under the TVPA, see Stephens, *supra* note 73 at 402–07.

See Stephens, *supra* note 73 at 405–407 (stating that courts generally presume that the "filing of a lawsuit in the United States indicates that domestic remedies are probably unavailable" and that "'torture victims bring suits in the United States against the alleged torturer only as a last resort'"; quoting S. Rep. No. 102–249, at 9–10 (1991); *Enahoro v. Abubakar*, 408 F.3d 877, 892 (7th Cir. 2005) ("[T]o the extent that there is any doubt ... both Congress and international tribunals have mandated that ... doubts [concerning exhaustion are to] be resolved in favor of the plaintiffs").

[92] 28 U.S.C. § 1350 (note), § 2(c) ("No action shall be maintained under this section unless it is commenced within 10 years after the cause of action arose").

[93] *Ashcroft v. Iqbal*, 129 S. Ct. 1937, 1949–50 (2009).

[94] *Twombly*, 550 U.S. at 557.

[95] See New York Pattern Jury Instructions, Pattern Jury Instructions 3:20; see also *Kolbeck v. LIT Am*, 939 F. Supp. 240, 246 (S.D.N.Y. 1996), *aff'd mem.*, 152 F.3d 918 (2d Cir. 1998) (noting that "general suspicion" of a tort "is not enough"). See *In re Refco Securities Litig.*, 2012 WL 996910 (S.D.N.Y.2012) (*citing Armstrong v. McAlpin*, 699 F.2d 79, 91 (2d Cir. 1983)). See also *Official Comm. of Unsecured Creditors of Hydrogen, L.L.C. v. Blomen* ("In re Hydrogen, L.L.C."), 431 B.R. 337, 352 (S.D.N.Y. 2010).

[96] *Kolbeck*, 939 F.Supp. at 246 ("New York common law ... has not adopted a constructive knowledge standard for imposing aiding and abetting liability. Rather, New York courts and federal courts in this district have required actual knowledge").

defendant was on notice as to the underlying misconduct – is insufficient.[97] Some courts, however, have held that conscious avoidance may also satisfy the knowledge requirement. *Conscious avoidance* is deemed to occur when "it can almost be said that the defendant actually knew" because he or she suspected a fact and realized its probability but refrained from confirming it, so that, at a later time, he or she could deny knowledge.[98] Furthermore, New York courts have held that alleging knowledge without pleading underlying facts to support the allegation is fatal to an aiding and abetting claim.[99]

To adequately plead "knowing inducement," the complaint must allege that the defendant advised or encouraged a fiduciary to act in instances where the induced conduct is known to be tortious.[100] To adequately plead "knowing participation," the complaint must allege that the defendant furnished "substantial assistance" to the primary wrongdoer. Substantial assistance is found where a defendant "(1) affirmatively assists, help conceals, or by virtue of failing to act when required to do so enables the fraud to proceed; and (2) the actions of the aider/abettor proximately caused the harm on which the primary liability is predicted."[101] Aiding and abetting liability arises only when the plaintiff's injury was "'a direct or reasonably foreseeable result' of the complained-of conduct... '[b]ut-for' causation does not suffice; the breach must proximately cause the loss."[102] New York courts have held that "[c]onduct that merely creates a condition that made the resulting injury possible"[103] is "too remote to constitute legal cause."[104]

---

[97] See *Fraternity Fund v. Beacon Hill Asset Mgmt., LLC*, 479 F. Supp. 2d 349 (S.D.N.Y. 2007) ("pleading knowledge for the purposes of an aiding and abetting claim requires allegations of facts that give rise to 'a strong inference' of 'actual knowledge'") (*citing Lerner v. Fleet Bank, N.A.*, 459 F.3d 273 (2d Cir. N.Y. 2006).

[98] See *United States v. Nektalov*, 461 F.3d 309, 315 (2d Cir. 2006). Lower courts disagree whether conscious avoidance is legally equivalent to actual knowledge. *Compare In re Refco Secs. Litig.*, 759 F.Supp.2d 301, 334 (S.D.N.Y. 2010) and *Fraternity Fund Ltd.*, 479 F.Supp.2d at 368 with *Pension Comm. of Univ. of Montreal Pension Plan v. Banc of Am. Secs.*, LLC, 446 F. Supp.2d 163, 202, n. 273 (S.D.N.Y. 2006).

[99] See *Lerner*, 459 F.3d at 293 (dismissing aiding and abetting fraud claim where "plaintiffs conclusorily allege that the banks had actual knowledge [but] ... failed to plead facts with the requisite particularity to support that claim").

[100] *In re Sharp*, 302 B.R. at 774–75.

[101] *Kolbeck*, 939 F.Supp. 240 at 247. "Substantial assistance exists where '(1) a defendant affirmatively assists, helps conceal, or by virtue of failing to act when required to do so enables the fraud to proceed, and (2) the actions of the aider/abettor proximately caused the harm on which the primary liability is predicated.'" *UniCredito Italiano*, 288 F.Supp.2d at 502 (*quoting McDaniel v. Bear Stearns & Co., Inc.*, 196 F.Supp.2d 343, 352 (S.D.N.Y. 2002)).

[102] Ibid. at 249; see *Edwards & Hanly v. Wells Fargo Sec. Clearance Corp.*, 602 F.2d 478, 484 (2d Cir. 1979); *JP Morgan Chase Bank v. Winnick*, 406 F. Supp. 2d 247, 256 (S.D.N.Y. 2005).

[103] *In re Parmalat Sec. Litig.*, 421 F. Supp. 2d 703, 722 (S.D.N.Y. 2006) (citation omitted).

[104] Ibid. See also *Cromer Fin. Ltd. v. Berger*, 137 F. Supp. 2d 452, 472 (S.D.N.Y. 2001) (dismissing aiding and abetting claim, where "the Ponzi scheme may have only been possible because of Bear Sterns' actions, or inaction, [but] Bear Sterns' conduct was not a proximate cause of the Ponzi scheme").

As shown by this, absent specific intent, whether under federal or state law, it will be difficult to hold supervisors and senior executives liable for negligent or even reckless failures of oversight and control. Applying state common law principles, supervisors could be held liable for aiding and abetting human rights violations committed by their subordinates only if facts can be shown demonstrating (1) the existence of a human rights violation that under state common law constituted an identifiable tort; (2) that the supervisor knowingly and substantially assisted the wrongdoer in committing the human rights violation by either assisting, concealing, or failing to act when required; and (3) that the supervisor's actions proximately caused the plaintiff's damages.

17.4.   Possible Alternatives

Existing legal standards as applied via international law or U.S. federal statute or state aiding and abetting liability fail to provide corporations with a predictable standard by which to balance legitimate corporate activities occurring in places where governments commit atrocity crimes against behavior by a corporation or its personnel that actually furthers atrocities. Absent specific intent on the part of corporate executives to engage in abuses, it will be difficult to hold corporations or their executives liable for negligent, or even reckless, failures of oversight and control under existing law. Assuming the goal is to create clear atrocity crime prevention norms against which forward-looking compliance may be structured and measured, it is worth considering whether existing corporate standards might be adopted to incentivize supervision and control.

17.4.1.   Nonvoluntary Government Regulation

One possible response is a nonvoluntary regulatory scheme, in which government agencies with existing authority over MNCs compel maintenance of books and records demonstrating corporate compliance with specific regulations and commensurate sanctions for failing to disclose lapses in compliance and/or for making misleading disclosures based on erroneous books and records. This type of scheme has the benefit of broad-based corporate adherence to a some kind of guiding standard; the backing of regulatory agencies that can develop supplemental rules, disclosure requirements, and penalties around the standard; and the potential for costly legal liability for noncompliant companies to the extent that they are publicly traded – which most MNCs are.

This kind of scheme is best evidenced by corporate compliance regimes developed in the United States in response to the Sarbanes-Oxley Act, which forced corporations to institute complaint procedures for accounting issues and contained a number of disclosure requirements,[105] and even more so in the Dodd-Frank Act, with its implications for foreign-based corporations.[106] Sarbanes-Oxley and Dodd-Frank created powerful incentives for corporations to disclose malfeasance or unethical business conduct to regulators and shareholders via public filings.[107] Sarbanes-Oxley required corporate disclosures relating to compliance breakdowns, raising additional issues should a corporation fail to comply, whereas Dodd-Frank imposes a requisite level of knowledge of corporate malfeasance on corporate officials through the signing of mandatory disclosure forms and makes the disclosed information "material," such that nondisclosure may raise issues under the securities laws, including potential securities fraud. Through these provisions, shareholders, NGOs, and government officials can monitor a corporation's disclosures and engage in public relations campaigns, shareholder action, or sanctions against corporations that continually engage in unethical business conduct.

The clearest example of a nonvoluntary regulatory regime addressing human rights abuses is Section 1521 of the Dodd-Frank Act regarding so-called "conflict minerals." In eastern DRC, profits from conflict minerals – the ores of gold, coltan, casserite, and wolframite (used to produce tantalum, tin, and tungsten – have been used to finance a decade-long armed conflict that has resulted in an estimated 3.7 million casualties and an internationally acknowledged crisis of rape and gender-based violence.[108] Section 1521 required the U.S. Securities and Exchange Commission (SEC) to issue regulations requiring all "issuers," as defined under the 1934 Securities Exchange Act, dealing in certain conflict minerals to conduct supply chain scrutiny to determine whether the metals originated in the DRC or neighboring

---

[105] Sarbanes-Oxley Act of 2002, 15 U.S.C. §§ 78f(m)(4), 7264.

[106] Dodd-Frank Wall Street Reform and Consumer Protection Act, Pub. L. No. 111–203, 124 Stat. 1376–2223 (2010).

[107] See Rachel Louise Ensign, "SEC Hands Out Second-Ever Dodd-Frank Whistleblower Award," Wall Street Journal (June 14, 2013), http://stream.wsj.com/story/latest-headlines/SS-2–63399/SS-2–253855/ ("The most significant aspect of the second [whistleblower] award is that it continues to validate the idea that having an award that incentivizes people to come forward is gaining traction"; quoting Sean McKessy, chief of the SEC's Office of the Whistleblower) and Emmanuel Olaoye, "Companies Will Be Treated Favorably If They Report Violations First, SEC Enforcer Tells Lawyers," Thomson Reuters (October 12, 2012), http://blog.thomsonreuters.com/index.php/companies-will-be-treated-favorably-if-they-report-violations-first-sec-enforcer-tells-lawyers/ ("Companies who come forward and self-report on the findings of an internal investigation stand a better chance of receiving lenient treatment from enforcement agencies than those who don't").

[108] "Conflict Diamonds: Did Someone Die for That Diamond?" Amnesty International, www.amnestyusa.org/our-work/issues/business-and-human-rights/oil-gas-and-mining-industries/conflict-diamonds; see also Blood Diamond (Warner Bros. 2006).

countries.[109] If so, that entity will be required to complete due diligence checks on whether, at any step along their supply chain, their purchase of the minerals has furthered the conflict in that region and disclose this information in public filings beginning in 2014.[110] Section 1521's use of the term "issuers" is crucial in that it is not restricted to U.S.-based companies but reaches even foreign companies that issue shares on U.S. stock exchanges.

Although there are certainly benefits to mandatory regulation in assuring broad-based adoption of compliance regimes and ensuring some level of compliance with a basic standard, mandatory regulation has significant drawbacks. As demonstrated by the SEC's prolonged efforts to promulgate rules implementing Section 1502 and the subsequent litigation in U.S. federal court by corporate interest groups challenging the new rules, the regulatory process is time-consuming, onerous, and not least of all contentious.[111] In a developing area such as atrocity crime prevention, any final regulatory scheme might lag far behind corporate- or NGO-led initiatives that are much more collaborative efforts that involve far fewer corporate lawyers. Once implemented, regulations also can be blunt instruments that can't always take into consideration circumstances requiring flexibility or adaptation. One of the chief arguments against the SEC's conflict mineral rules was that the rules were so broadly designed that smaller issuers with negligible dealings in conflict minerals would be unduly burdened by due diligence costs or that savvier participants would sidestep reporting costs altogether by seeking minerals from outlying areas, thus impoverishing small-scale suppliers in eastern DRC whose mines or smelting concerns legitimately source the ores at issue. Finally, once implemented, regulations risk calcification in the developing area of atrocity crime prevention – especially given the time and effort it would take to amend them. Regulations also can and will remain in place long after they may have outlived any utility, creating frustration among corporations and resistance to further regulations (and the costs associated with implementation).

There is also the possibility of government-sponsored interdiction of goods within a trade-based or World Trade Organization (WTO) framework from countries at risk for atrocities. Under this scenario, states could impose tariffs or other duties or charges on imports from countries deemed at risk for atrocities,

---

[109] "Legislation," Global Witness, www.globalwitness.org/campaigns/conflict/conflict-minerals/legislation.

[110] Ibid.

[111] See *Nat'l Assoc. of Mfg. v. SEC*, 748 F.3d 359 (D.C. Cir. 2014) (upholding SEC rules imposing conflict mineral disclosure requirements, but disallowing SEC requirement that issuers state whether their products were not "DRC conflict free" as compelled speech violating the First Amendment); see also *Am. Petr. Inst. v. SEC*, 953 F. Supp.2d 5 (D.C. Cir. 2013) (vacating SEC rules requiring public disclosure of payments made to foreign governments in connection with commercial development of natural resources).

or they could interdict goods deemed to be affiliated with conflict, such as so-called conflict minerals or "blood diamonds." One example would be the Clean Diamond Trade Act of 2003[112] and accompanying Executive Order 13312[113], which prohibit, subject to certain waiver authorities, importation into and exportation from the United States of any rough diamond, from whatever source, not controlled through the Kimberley Process (discussed later).[114] The Rough Diamond Trade Controls provide for criminal penalties of $50,000 per count for corporations and individuals and/or ten-year imprisonments for individuals and provide compelling disincentives for corporations to trade in conflict materials.[115] However, such penalties must be harmonized with international trade agreements such as the General Agreement on Tariffs and Trade (GATT) and may well require some type of waiver under that agreement.[116] Moreover, sanction regimes and interdictions, without interpretative guidance from regulatory agencies and the possibility of a waiver, provide limited guidance to corporations seeking to do business in conflict areas.

17.4.2. Compulsory Industry-Imposed Transparency Initiatives

A second option looks to industry-based voluntary initiatives that create at least the possibility for fostering compliance through shaming. The chief example here is the Kimberley Process Certification Scheme, which emerged out of civil conflict in Angola and Sierra Leone, where the fight to control diamond supplies resulted in human rights abuses by warring factions.[117] In the late 1990s, NGOs led by Global Witness spearheaded efforts to link diamond sales to conflict funding and developed the concept of "blood diamonds" to generate consumer awareness of brutalities resulting from the

---

[112] Clean Diamond Trade Act, 19 U.S.C. §§ 3901–3913 (2003).

[113] Exec. Order No. 13,312, 68 Fed. Reg. 45,151–52 (July 31, 2003).

[114] 31 C.F.R. 592, *as amended*, 69 C.F.R. 56936 (September 23, 2004) (implementing Executive Order 13312).

[115] Ibid.

[116] Section XI of the General Agreement on Tariffs and Trade (GATT) outlaws all "prohibitions or restrictions other than duties, taxes or other charges, whether made effective through quotas, import or export licenses or other measures" on the trade between WTO members. GATT, arts. I:1, XI:I and XIII:1, October 30, 1947, 55 UNT.S. 194; Tracey Michelle Price, "The Kimberley Process: Conflict Diamonds, WTO Obligations, and the Universality Debate," *Minnesota Journal of Global Trade* 12(1): 53 (2003); see also Daniel Pruzin, "WTO Members Approve Waiver For 'Blood Diamonds' Agreement," *International Trade Reporter* (March 6, 2003).

[117] The Kimberley Process is a joint initiative by governments, industry, and civil society to stem the flow of conflict diamonds by requiring its participants to undertake extensive reporting and transparency measures before certifying and shipping rough diamonds as "conflict-free." See David Beffert and Thorsten Benner, *Stemming the Tide of Conflict Diamonds: The Kimberley Process* (Hertie School of Governance Teaching Case, February 2005).

diamond trade.[118] Although major corporate interests and some governments initially opposed the NGOs, public outrage threatened to damage the market and cause economic injury even to those who did not trade in so-called blood or conflict diamonds. Recognizing that the diamond industry as a whole had to address the human rights abuses, in 2002 national, corporate, and NGO stakeholders built a process that forced all stakeholders to implement certification programs in exchange for participation in the global diamond trade, thus restoring industry reputation by ensuring that shipments of diamonds were certified "conflict-free."[119]

Yet this option also has drawbacks. Although the Kimberley Process and others of its ilk are laudable initiatives with significant accomplishments, they require the existence and agreement of small, centrally located groups of corporations whose compliance may be schematized. Furthermore, as noted earlier concerning all voluntary regimes, these initiatives produce fact-intensive guidelines dependent on industry or geographically specific concerns and cannot be replicated across disparate industries or global regions.[120] Finally, initiatives like the Kimberley Process do not address atrocity prevention so much as they react to one trigger of some atrocities (i.e., a key source of conflict funding as to one specific conflict; the concept of blood diamonds developed out of the sale of diamonds to fund conflicts in specific parts of Africa) and, as such, attack symptoms as opposed to a root cause of atrocities.

17.4.3. Control Person Liability

Finally, it is worth considering whether other binding legal standards already applicable in certain commercial settings might better incentivize corporations

---

[118] Ian Smillie, Lansana Bgerie, and Ralph Hazelton, "The Heart of the Matter: Diamonds and Human Security," Partnership Africa Canada (January 2000), www.pacweb.org/Documents /diamonds_KP/heart_of_the_matter_summary-Eng-Jan2000.pdf.

[119] See "The Kimberley Process," Global Witness, www.globalwitness.org/campaigns/con flict/conflict-diamonds/kimberley-process, and Global Witness, "A Rough Trade: The Role of Companies and Governments in the Angolan Conflict" (December 1998), www.globalwitness.org/sites/default/files/pdfs/A_Rough_Trade.pdf; see also "Kimberley Process," www.kimberleyprocess.com/. Global Witness left the Kimberley Process in 2011, citing flaws and loopholes that have not been fixed. "Global Witness Leaves Kimberley Process, Calls for Diamond Trade to be Held Accountable," Global Witness, www.globalwitness.org/libr ary/global-witness-leaves-kimberley-process-calls-diamond-trade-be-held-accountable.

[120] The Kimberley Process has encountered difficulties in translating its work to Zimbabwe, where diamonds from the Marange region, which are mined by the Zimbabwean government and the locus of many government human rights abuses, do not meet the criteria for the "conflict diamond" classification (i.e., by funding rebel groups engaged in conflict). See John Eligon, "Global Witness Quits Group on 'Blood Diamonds,'" *New York Times* (December 5, 2011), www.nytimes.com/ 2011/12 /06/world/africa/global-witness-quits-group-on-blood-diamonds.html.

to develop supervision and control mechanisms beyond the incentives created by aiding and abetting liability. One example might be a standard with which corporate compliance officers have dealt for years, one based on Section 20 of the Exchange Act, 15 U.S.C. § 78t(a).

The Exchange Act of 1934 and the Securities Act of 1933 were enacted under the impetus provided by the stock market crash of 1929.[121] With these two securities laws, Congress sought to restore confidence in the U.S. securities market and to address the public outrage that stemmed from the fact that many who engaged in the most egregious conduct leading up to the crash were perceived to be insulated from liability by the limited liability associated with corporate entities.[122] In the hearings preceding the passage of the Securities Act, Congress specifically referred to its desire to correct the "dangerous and unreliable system of depending upon dummy directors" that lack any accountability or responsibility for their actions.[123] Congress, consequently, sought to establish a comprehensive regulatory framework to regulate more stringently the capital markets and also to impose greater accountability on those involved in corporate and market fraud.[124]

17.4.3.1. Section 20(a) of the Exchange Act   Section 20(a) of the 1934 Act imposes liability on "[e]very person who, directly or indirectly, controls any person liable under any provision of this title," with a caveat that the controlling person may subsequently avoid liability by proving that he or she "acted in good faith and did not directly or indirectly induce" the violation. The broad language of this section and the absence of a definition of control – Congress explained that it would be difficult, if not impossible, to predict the

---

[121] See H.R. Rep. No. 73-1383, 6 (1934). The 1934 Act is much broader than the 1933 Act, which regulates only the new issues of securities to the public, whereas the 1934 Act governs the secondary trading of securities. John M. Wunderlich, "Bankruptcy's Protection for Non-Debtors from Securities Fraud Litigation," *Fordham Journal of Corporate & Financial Law* · 16: 375, 383 (2011). Because of the broad reach of the 1934 Act, Congress created the Securities and Exchange Commission (SEC) to enforce the statute. Brian Morgan, Note and Comment, *United States v. O'Hagan: Recognition of the Misappropriation Theory*, 13 BYU J. Pub. L. 147, 148 (1998).

[122] Loftus C. Carson, "The Liability of Controlling Persons Under the Federal Securities Acts," Notre Dame Law Review 72: 263, 266 (1997).

[123] S. Rep. No. 73-47, at 5–6 (1933). See Stock Exchange Practices: Hearing on S. Res. 84 (72nd Cong.) and S. Res. 56 and 97 (73rd Cong.) Before the Senate Comm. On Banking and Currency, 73rd Cong., 1st Sess. 6556 (1934) (remark of Sen. Alben W. Barkley).

[124] See H.R. Rep. No. 73-1383, at 5 (1934). Quoting President Woodrow Wilson, Chairman Rayburn stated: "Society cannot afford to have individuals wield the power of thousands without personal responsibility. It cannot afford to let its strongest men be the only men who are inaccessible to the law. Modern democratic society, in particular, cannot afford to constitute its economic undertakings upon the monarchial or aristocratic principle and adopt the fiction that the kings and great men thus set up can do no wrong which will make them personally amenable to the law which restrains smaller men; that their kingdom, not themselves, must suffer for their blindness, their follies, and their transgressions of right." Ibid.

many ways in which control may be exerted[125] – has resulted in competing views among the federal circuit courts of appeals regarding what elements must be plead for a prima facie case of controlling person liability.[126]

17.4.3.2. Determining "Control Person"   U.S. district courts have essentially applied two distinct standards in determining who is a control person.[127] Under the "potential control" standard, adopted (with varying permutations) by the Fifth, Sixth, Seventh, Eighth,[128] Ninth, Tenth, and Eleventh Circuits – and to an extent in the Second Circuit[129] – a plaintiff must show "the power to control the transaction underlying the alleged securities violation and not the exercise of that power."[130] In other words, the "potential control" standard requires a plaintiff to allege that the defendant "had the power to direct or cause the direction of the management and policies" of the company, regardless of whether he or she exercised such control. Accordingly, by interpreting Section 20[131] to require only (1) a showing that a "subordinate committed a predicate violation" and (2) that the defendant was a "control" or "controlling" person, it is possible to establish a prima facie section 20(a) claim without any showing as to the superior's intent.

This standard has proved controversial because other circuits – namely, the Second, Third, and Fourth Circuits – have adopted the "culpable participation"

---

[125]   H.R. Rep. No. 73–1383 (1934) at 26 ("In this section and in section 11, when reference is made to 'control', the term is intended to include actual control as well as what has been called legally enforceable control. See *Handy & Harmon v. Burnet* 284 U.S. 136 (1931). It was thought undesirable to attempt to define the term. It would be difficult if not impossible to enumerate or to anticipate the many ways in which actual control may be exerted. A few examples of the methods used are stock ownership, lease, contract, and agency. It is well known that actual control sometimes may be exerted through ownership of much less than a majority of the stock of a corporation either by the ownership of such stock alone or through such ownership in combination with other factors").

[126]   Erin L. Massey, "Control Person Liability Under Section 20(a): Striking A Balance Of Interests For Plaintiffs And Defendants," *Houston Business and Tax Law Journal* 6: 109, 111 (2005).

[127]   The U.S. Supreme Court has yet to resolve this split in authority.

[128]   *Lustgraaf v. Behrens*, 619 F.3d 867 (8th Cir. 2010) *citing Metge v. Baehler*, 762 F.2d 621 (8th Cir. 1985) (which determined that culpable participation by an alleged controlling person in the primary violation is not an element of the claim, but rather is reserved as an affirmative defense, and thus need not be pleaded to establish a prima facie case for controlling person liability).

[129]   The Second Circuit, in a 1996 opinion, stated that culpable participation is an element in proving the prima facie case of control. *SEC v. First Jersey Secs., Inc.*, 101 F.3d 1450 (2d Cir. 1996). However, because this case did not overrule previous cases that omitted culpable participation as a part of the prima facie case, it has not ended the debate on the issue in the Second Circuit. See also *Berks County Employees' Ret. Fund v. First Am. Corp.*, 734 F. Supp. 2d 533, 537 (S.D.N.Y. 2010); *Vladimir v. Bioenvision Inc.*, 606 F. Supp. 2d 473, 496 (S.D.N.Y. 2009).

[130]   See, e.g., *Maher v. Durango Metals Inc.*, 144 F.3d 1302, 1305 (10th Cir. 1998).

[131]   *Berks County Employees' Ret. Fund v. First Am. Corp.*, 734 F. Supp. 2d 533, 537 (S.D.N.Y. 2010) and *Vladimir v. Bioenvision Inc.*, 606 F. Supp. 2d 473, 496 (S.D.N.Y. 2009).

standard of Section 20(a), requiring that the control person either intend to aid the subordinate in the commission of his violation through "deliberate" or "intentional" inaction or was "in some meaningful sense" a "culpable participant" in the primary violation requirement – more analogous to an aiding and abetting standard.[132] Under "culpable participation," a plaintiff must plead and prove that "the control person was in some meaningful sense a culpable participant in the primary violation."[133] In other words, the § 20(a) standard becomes highly analogous to the aiding and abetting standard.[134]

---

[132] See, e.g., *Aldridge v. A.T. Cross Corp.*, 284 F.3d 72, 85(1st Cir. 2002) ("unless there are facts that indicate that the controlling shareholders were actively participating in the decision-making processes of the corporation, no controlling person liability can be imposed"); *Ganino v. Citizens Utils. Co.*, 228 F.3d 154, 170 (2d Cir. 2000) ("to make out a prima facie case under §20(a) of the Exchange Act, a plaintiff "must show a primary violation . . . by the controlled person . . . and control of the primary violator by the targeted defendant . . . and show that the controlling person was in some meaningful sense a culpable participant in the fraud perpetrated by the controlled person"); *Rochez Bros. v. Rhoades*, 527 F.2d 880, 885 (3rd Cir. 1975) (rejecting secondary liability for a "controlling person" corporation under section 20(a) of the Exchange Act where the corporation had "no knowledge of [fraudster's] acts and did not "consciously intend to aid [fraudster] in his scheme . . . [t]he appellant would have been required to show that the [corporation's] inaction was deliberate and done intentionally to further the fraud"); *In re Monster Worldwide, Inc. Sec. Litig.*, No. 07–2237, 2008 WL 623339, at *3 (S.D.N.Y. March 4, 2008) ("[a]s for the alleged violation of Section 20(a), in order to establish a prima facie case of liability under Section 20(a) a plaintiff must show: "(1) a primary violation by a controlled person; (2) control of the primary violator by the defendant; and (3) that the controlling person was in some meaningful sense a culpable participant in the primary violation"); *In re Parmalat Sec. Litig.*, 497 F. Supp. 2d 526, 532 (S.D.N.Y. 2007) (describing intradistrict split in rejecting culpable participation requirement); *In re Refco, Inc. Sec. Litig.*, 503 F. Supp. 2d 611, 660 & n.43 (S.D.N.Y. 2007) ("Unlike § 15, § 20(a) requires that the plaintiff must also 'allege culpable participation "in some meaningful sense" by the controlling person in the fraud'").

[133] *Boguslavsky v. Kaplan*, 159 F.3d 715, 720 (2d Cir. 1998).

[134] See, e.g., *Aldridge v. A.T. Cross Corp.*, 284 F.3d 72, 85(1st Cir. 2002) ("unless there are facts that indicate that the controlling shareholders were actively participating in the decision making processes of the corporation, no controlling person liability can be imposed"); *Ganino v. Citizens Utils. Co.*, 228 F.3d 154, 170 (2d Cir. 2000) ("to make out a prima facie case under §20(a) of the Exchange Act, a plaintiff "must show a primary violation . . . by the controlled person . . . and control of the primary violator by the targeted defendant . . . and show that the controlling person was in some meaningful sense a culpable participant in the fraud perpetrated by the controlled person"); *Rochez Bros. v. Rhoades*, 527 F.2d 880, 885 (3rd Cir. 1975) (rejecting secondary liability for a "controlling person" corporation under section 20(a) of the Exchange Act where the corporation had "no knowledge of [fraudster's] acts and did not "consciously intend to aid [fraudster] in his scheme . . . [t]he appellant would have been required to show that the [corporation's] inaction was deliberate and done intentionally to further the fraud"); *In re Monster Worldwide, Inc. Sec. Litig.*, No. 07–2237, 2008 WL 623339, at *3 (S.D.N.Y. March 4, 2008) ("[a]s for the alleged violation of Section 20(a), in order to establish a prima facie case of liability under Section 20(a) a plaintiff must show: "(1) a primary violation by a controlled person; (2) control of the primary violator by the defendant; and (3) that the controlling person was in some meaningful sense a culpable participant in the primary violation"); *In re Parmalat Sec. Litig.*, 497 F. Supp. 2d 526, 532 (S.D.N.Y. 2007) (describing intradistrict split in rejecting culpable participation requirement); *In re Refco, Inc. Sec. Litig.*, 503 F. Supp. 2d 611, 660 & n.43 (S.D.N.Y. 2007) ("Unlike § 15, § 20(a) requires that the

Even where the "potential control" standard has been adopted, the approach is not without potential drawbacks. Adhering to the "potential control" standard, if a defendant is found to have controlled the primary violator, that defendant will not be liable if it can establish the "good faith" affirmative defense. To prove good faith, a defendant must show that "he exercised due care in his supervision of the primary violator's activities in that he maintained and enforced a reasonable and proper system of supervision and internal controls."

However, by pegging liability to "control of the primary violator by the targeted defendant," as suggested by the plain language of Section 20, this same section provides a compelling vehicle for assessing command responsibility, placing the burden on the controlling person to establish good faith and functional – not merely hierarchical – distance from the subordinate's wrongdoing. Applied in this manner, such a standard could incentivize more robust compliance and prevention programs targeting senior leadership, and corporate compliance experience in the securities fraud context might be transferable to programs and infrastructure directed toward preventing human rights violations by corporate subordinates. Nowhere is this better illustrated than through prosecution of Foreign Corrupt Practices Act cases, which may provide additional guidance to developing atrocity prevention regimes.

17.4.3.3. Section §20(a), the Foreign Corrupt Practices Act, and Beyond

In 2009, in one of the few cases of this type, the SEC brought an action against Nature's Sunshine Products, Inc., in which the commission alleged that the company's CEO and chief financial officer were liable as control persons in connection with the company's alleged violations of the Foreign Corrupt Practices Act (FCPA).[135] According to the SEC's allegations, Nature's Sunshine violated the FCPA by paying bribes to employees of the

---

plaintiff must also 'allege culpable participation "in some meaningful sense" by the controlling person in the fraud").

[135] The SEC's complaint charged Faggioli and Huff with control person liability for NSP's primary violation of the FCPA's books and records and internal controls provisions. Under Section 13(b)(2)(A) of the Exchange Act (15 U.S.C. § 78m(b)(2)(A)), an issuer is required to "make and keep books, records, and accounts, which in reasonable detail, accurately and fairly reflect the transactions and dispositions" of the issuer's assets. Section 13(b)(2)(B) of the Exchange Act (15 U.S.C. § 78m(b)(2)(B)) requires issuers to devise and maintain a system of internal accounting controls sufficient to provide reasonable assurances that books and records are accurate and that transactions are taken pursuant to management direction. In civil cases, these provisions impose strict liability on issuers, but are usually read to require scienter for individuals; that is, requiring that individuals knowingly evaded or failed to implement internal controls or falsified books and records. The SEC brought charges against Faggioli and Huff based on their status as control persons under the control person liability provision of the Exchange Act, Section 20(a).

company's Brazilian subsidiary and by failing to keep accurate books and records in connection with those payments. The SEC alleged that the company's CEO and CFO were liable as control persons for the company's FCPA violations. Even though the CEO and CFO were not involved in the underlying misconduct, the SEC's theory was that the CEO had overall responsibility for the company's international operations, whereas the CFO had supervisory responsibility for the management of and policies concerning the company's books and records. The company and its officers eventually settled with the SEC and paid fines, although without admitting or denying liability.[136]

The SEC's embrace of "control person" liability for FCPA violations raises the interesting question of the broader interaction between the FCPA and a policy aimed at preventing corporate complicity in atrocities. Support for the idea of a substantial overlap is provided by the fact that Congress originally enacted the FCPA in 1977 to specifically promote democratic values across the world through international business.[137] And it is in furtherance of that purpose that the FCPA makes it a criminal act for a U.S. corporation to bribe foreign officials while conducting business abroad.[138] The Act also requires companies to meet certain accounting practices,[139] as well as to maintain proper mechanisms to prevent any illegal payments.[140]

More specifically, the antibribery provisions of the FCPA make it unlawful to offer to pay or pay any foreign official in order to influence decisions or gain an advantage in business affairs or to retain business.[141] Given the recognized connection between many atrocity crimes and government corruption,[142] it not

---

[136] But see *Christine Johnson v. Siemens AG*, No. 1:09-cv-05310 (E.D.N.Y. 2009) (dismissing for failure to plead a claim where the amended complaint failed to allege facts giving rise to a strong inference of scienter as required under the Private Securities Litigation Reform Act and because an individual defendant cannot be held liable as a control person in the absence of an alleged violation of § 10(b) of the Securities Exchange Act or Rule 10b-5 promulgated thereunder).

[137] See Daniel Patrick Ashe, Comment, "The Lengthening Anti-Bribery Lasso of the United States: The Recent Extraterritorial Application of the U.S. Foreign Corrupt Practices Act," *Fordham Law Review* 73: 2897, 2903 (2005) (Congress believed that "American businesses would benefit from the good will [that came] with upright [business] practices" as well as the integrity and skill that developed as it learned to compete using lawful means).

[138] 15 U.S.C. §§ 78dd-1(a), 2(a), 3(a) (2006).

[139] 15 U.S.C. § 78m(b)(2)(A) (2006).

[140] 15 U.S.C. § 78c(8)(a) (2006). The proper mechanisms include accurate books and records, which are meant to ensure that any illegal payments cannot be kept hidden from auditors.

[141] § 78dd-1(a)(1).

[142] The link between government corruption and the risk of the commission of atrocity crimes has been documented. See, e.g., The Secretary General, *Report of the Secretary-General on Responsibility to Protect: State Responsibility and Prevention*, ¶ 45, delivered to the Security Council and the General Assembly, UN Doc. S/2013/399, A/67/929 (July 9, 2013) (noting that policies aimed at reducing corruption can mitigate grievances that create instability and constitute risk factors for atrocity crimes); Jonas Claes, "Atrocity Prevention at the State

difficult to see the FCPA rubric being applied to human rights issues.[143] Importantly, in 1998, Congress further amended the FCPA and greatly expanded its scope by allowing claims against foreign businesses and foreign nationals for bribery of public officials in their own countries.[144] Adopting a broader conceptual understanding of corruption could yield a definition that would include complicity in atrocities and genocide, which might allow companies to fold atrocity crime prevention into their existing FCPA compliance structures.

In this context, it is important to note that FCPA compliance is one of the most rapidly growing practice areas of the past decade, as compliance-training opportunities abound and firms develop specialty FCPA practice groups. The rise of this industry is due in large part to the U.S. Department of Justice's proven record of using the FCPA to obtain and collect substantial settlements against multinational companies – amounts totaling tens or hundreds of millions of dollars and, on occasion, even surpassing $1 billion.[145] Placing a policy tool aimed at preventing atrocities in such a fertile and thriving compliance environment, in and of itself, could have a transformative impact.

Level: Security Sector Reform and Horizontal Equality," United States Institute of Peace (April 23, 2013), www.usip.org/publications/atrocity-prevention-the-state-level (noting that reducing corruption is particularly relevant to mitigating the risk of mass violence) and Michaela Wrong, *It's Our Turn to Eat: The Story of a Kenyan Whistleblower* (2009) (documenting the link between Kenyan municipal graft and ethnic resentments that culminated in atrocities following the disputed December 2007 presidential election).

[143] U.S. federal prosecutors and regulators have already applied the FCPA to human rights issues in the case of Chiquita's activities in Colombia in the early 2000s. In March 2007, Chiquita admitted that, from 1997 to 2001, it made approximately $1.7 million in corrupt payments to the United Self-Defense Forces of Colombia (known by its acronym in Spanish, AUC), a paramilitary organization that the U.S. government had designated a terrorist group. Chiquita pleaded guilty to FCPA violations and agreed to pay $25 million. See Laurie P. Cohen, "Chiquita under the Gun," *Wall Street Journal* (August 2, 2007), http://online.wsj.com/news/articles/SB118601669056785578. Chiquita was later sued by relatives of those tortured and killed by the AUC for ATS and TVPA violations and state common law and Colombian claims. These cases are pending. See *In re: Chiquita Brands Int'l, Inc. Alien Tort Statute and Shareholder Derivative Litig.*, Case No. 08–01916 (S.D. Fla. 2008).

[144] See 15 U.S.C. § 78dd-3; see also Ned Sebelius, "Foreign Corrupt Practices Act," *American Criminal Law Review* 45: 579, 587 (2008) (describing the SEC's and DOJ's ability to prosecute someone even if he does not do business in the United States). Prior to the 1998 amendments, the OECD Convention on Combating Bribery of Foreign Public Officials in International Business Transaction was implemented by more than thirty nations. *Convention on Combating Bribery of Foreign Public Officials in International Business Transactions*, December 17, 1997, S. Treaty Doc. No. 105–43 (1998), 37 I.L.M.

[145] See The FCPA Blog, "Who Will Crack the Top Ten?" (August 3, 2012), www.fcpablog.com/blog/2012/8/3/who-will-crack-the-top-ten.html.

17.4.4. Dodd Frank

A control and influence approach also was applied by the SEC in its Final Rule on Section 1502 of the Dodd-Frank Act, which mandated that the SEC adopt rules requiring public companies to provide certain information (even if that information normally would not have been viewed as "material") relating to specified minerals used in consumer electronics and that have been associated with violence and human rights abuses in the DRC and adjoining countries. SEC guidance ties the question of whether an issuer should file a report regarding its having made a "contract to manufacture" a DRC-related product to "the degree of influence [the issuer] exercises over the materials, parts, ingredients, or components to be included in any product that contains conflict minerals or their derivatives."[146] An issuer will not be considered to "contract to manufacture" a product if it does no more than take certain enumerated actions including (1) specifying or negotiating contractual terms with a manufacturer that does not directly relate to the manufacturing of the product (unless it specifies or negotiates taking these actions so as to exercise a degree of influence over the manufacturing of the product that is practically equivalent to contracting on terms that directly relate to the manufacturing of the product); (2) affixing its brand, marks, logo, or label to a generic product manufactured by a third party; or (e) servicing, maintaining, or repairing a product manufactured by a third party.[147] The power of the Dodd-Frank approach is that, like the FCPA, even activity of little financial value becomes material based on its connection to particular places in the world where atrocities have occurred due to trade in certain minerals. The activity is then monitored, and compliance focuses on monitoring, rather than interdicting the behavior.

17.4.5. OECD

In contrast to the SEC's approach, the OECD's Due Diligence Guidance for Responsible Supply Chains of Minerals from Conflict-Affected and High-Risk Areas on supply chain verification (which are nonbinding and advisory) do not adopt a supervisory obligation, but instead appear to take an approach more akin to "constructive engagement" with respect to encouraging supply chain responsibility. The OECD Guidelines recommend that companies in a supply chain should seek to influence their suppliers to commit to responsible supply chain policies and, where necessary, take steps to build leverage over suppliers

---

[146] Conflict Minerals, Exchange Act Release No. 34–67716; File No. S7-40–10 regarding 17 CFR parts 240.13 and 249b (August 22, 2012) at 21, www.sec.gov/rules/final/2012/34–67716.pdf.
[147] Ibid.

that can most effectively prevent or mitigate identified risks.[148] Significantly, no disclosures are required.

Similarly, the 2011 OECD Guidelines for Multinational Enterprises suggested that "enterprises can also influence suppliers through contractual arrangements such as management contracts, pre-qualification requirements for potential suppliers, voting trusts, and license or franchise agreements. Other factors relevant to determining the appropriate response to the identified risks include the severity and probability of adverse impacts and how crucial that supplier is to the enterprise."[149]

17.5.   Conclusion

Examining the described options, there are no clear answers as to which model best ensures corporate compliance with atrocity crime prevention standards, not least because any focused and aggressive legal remedy runs the risk of calcification and obsolescence as standards evolve and events – and ways of conducting business – unfold and change. The law is a blunt instrument, and in evolving areas of law such as atrocity crime prevention, its utility as a means of shaping future behavior – as opposed to punishing past wrongs – is uncertain. Yet, as atrocity crime prevention standards develop, governments and corporations should examine corporate disclosure models that encourage transparency while imposing a requisite level of knowledge and supervision on corporate officers. Based on the FCPA and SEC conflict mineral rules, it appears that transparency-based models are comparatively easier to develop and implement because they focus on knowledge channels tied to those often making legally required disclosures under the securities laws (i.e., corporate executives already sensitive to having knowledge about specific corporate matters). Also, knowledge-creating disclosure models probably cause a faster reaction in terms of the development of internal corporate compliance processes because key executives are extremely sensitive to the risk of exposure should compliance systems break down. In this vein, it is worth considering whether governments should study adopting special designations for countries at risk for atrocity crimes, similar to state sponsor of terror designations, and then link those designations to enhanced disclosure obligations of some kind. The goal would be to balance the desire to foster reasonable development policies and corporate investment with the desire to impede the dysfunctional societal processes that may lead to atrocity

---

[148] OECD (2011), *OECD Due Diligence Guidance for Responsible Supply Chains of Minerals from Conflict-Affected and High-Risk Areas: Second Edition*, 18, 73, OECD Publishing, http://dx.doi.org/10.1787/9789264185050-en

[149] OECD (2011), *OECD Guidelines for Multinational Enterprises*, 24, OECD Publishing, http://dx.doi.org/10.1787/9789264115415-en

crimes. If compliance-based models aimed at preventing atrocity crimes could be developed akin to those in successful compliance regimes in other areas, then corporations doing business in at-risk countries could be held to higher yet attainable standards, which, in turn, could encourage still better compliance programs that could reduce possible corporate involvement in atrocity crimes.

R2P

18   A Short Story of a Long Effort: The United Nations and the Prevention of Mass Atrocities

Ekkehard Strauss

In retrospect, all instances of mass atrocities had early warning signs.[1] Thus, the idea expressed in the slogan "Never Again" appears to be simple and straightforward: take preventive measures against mass atrocities[2] "in order to liberate mankind from such an odious scourge."[3] This notion, however, is based on a set of assumptions and perceptions that remain largely unarticulated and unexamined in discussions about prevention.

One of the most widespread and deeply held beliefs is that there exists, in every case of mass atrocities, a chain of events leading up to it, logically and chronologically, and that therefore prevention consists of identifying the links in the chain and disrupting the connections between them. Despite the fact that this understanding, based on a few popularly favored cases of genocide,[4] has been refuted by more recent research, the language of mass atrocity prevention literature – and, more significantly, of policy itself – continues to reinforce the perception of a linear development over time, one whose main stages and related causes are sufficiently known.[5] Looking back at historical cases, this

---

[1] See, e.g., David A. Hamburg, *No More Killing Fields: Preventing Deadly Conflict* (Lanham, MD: Rowman & Littlefield, 2004), 17 et seq.

[2] The term "mass atrocities" in this chapter is understood to be synonymous with "atrocity crimes," encompassing exceptional cases of the three categories of crimes listed in paragraphs 138 and 139 of the 2005 World Summit Outcome Document, defining and delineating the "responsibility to protect" (commonly referred to as R2P): www.un.org/en/ga/search/view_doc.asp?symbol=A/RES/60/1. With a view to the origins of R2P, beyond the definition of these crimes in international law, relevant acts must involve the persecution of large parts of the population based on identities applied by the perpetrators.

[3] United Nations General Assembly, *Convention on the Prevention and Punishment of the Crime of Genocide*, 78 UNTS 277/ [1951] ATS 2/UN Doc. A/RES/260, December 9, 1948, preamble, para. 3.

[4] The Armenian genocide (1915), the Holocaust (1939–45), the Rwandan genocide (1994), and the Srebrenica genocide (1995).

[5] See UN Human Rights Council, *Report of the United Nations High Commissioner for Human Rights and Reports of the Office for the High Commissioner and the Secretary-General: Prevention of Genocide*, A/HRC/10/25 (March 9, 2009), http://daccess-dds-ny.un.org/doc/UN DOC/GEN/G09/118/26/PDF/G0911826.pdf?OpenElement; and UN Human Rights Council, *Annual Report of the United Nations High Commissioner for Human Rights and Reports of the Office for the High Commissioner and the Secretary-General: Efforts of the United Nations system to prevent genocide and the activities of the Special Adviser to the Secretary-General on*

gives rise to the conclusion that if only the causes had been addressed earlier, the progression toward mass atrocities would have been prevented – painting over the fact that there have been just as many situations where the same causes were present and yet no mass atrocities occurred. The truth is, it remains impossible to predict, on the basis of today's methodologies, which direction any particular situation may evolve in, no matter how many causal factors are present. At the same time, it has proven politically impracticable to agree on preventive policy measures if there is no demonstrable link to anticipated mass atrocities, unless such measures support already ongoing efforts to prevent human rights violations or conflict, provide humanitarian protection, or promote development.

Notwithstanding its failures in the past, the prevention of mass atrocities remains an important objective of the international community, with strong ethical and emotional positions involved, often nourished by perceptions of parallels with preventive efforts in public health and environmental and criminal law, as I will discuss later. Following the inclusion of the Responsibility to Protect (R2P) in the 2005 World Summit Outcome Document,[6] the discussion on prevention of mass atrocities has gained considerable momentum within the United Nations, but it has not yet been able to overcome the historical, political, and legal hurdles of implementation.

This chapter provides a short summary of the challenges in each of these three dimensions and attempts to outline how implementation of R2P at the international level could contribute to the prevention of not only genocide, but all mass atrocities, by reviving and effectively implementing the legal obligations deriving from the Genocide Convention.

18.1. The Historical Dimension

Since long before the UN was created, throughout the history of mankind in fact, there have been instances of mass atrocities, including the Thirty Years' War, the killings of Native Americans, and the killings of Herero and Namaqua in German West Africa.[7] Within the UN, however, the collective memory of mass atrocities begins with the 1915 massacres of Armenians in the Ottoman Empire.

Provoked by the lack of response to reports of the Armenian massacres in 1915 and the skepticism he encountered in the United States regarding his

---

the Prevention of Genocide, A/HRC/10/30 (February 18, 2009), http://daccess-dds-ny.un.org /doc/UNDOC/GEN/G09/114/42/PDF/G0911442.pdf?OpenElement.

[6] UN General Assembly Resolution A/RES/60/1 (September 16, 2005), para. 138–140, www.un.org /en/ga/search/view_doc.asp?symbol=A/RES/60/1.

[7] See Ben Kiernan, *Blood and Soil: A World History of Genocide and Extermination from Sparta to Darfur* (New Haven, CT: Yale University Press, 2007).

interpretation that Nazi persecution of Jews extended beyond the aim of gaining territory to exterminating the group as a whole, Raphael Lemkin, in the early 1940s, began to advocate for the adoption of an international treaty to prevent and punish the killing of a group of people with shared identity. Lemkin's own thinking on genocide – a term he coined to describe a crime that did not yet exist – was more comprehensive than the definition and preventive measures finally encoded in the Genocide Convention of 1948:

> Generally speaking, genocide does not necessarily mean the immediate destruction of a nation, except when accomplished by mass killings of all members of a nation. It is intended rather to signify a coordinated plan of different actions aiming at the destruction of essential foundations of the life of national groups, with the aim of annihilating the groups themselves. The objectives of such a plan would be the disintegration of the political and social institutions, of culture, language, national feelings, religion, and the economic existence of national groups, and the destruction of the personal security, liberty, health, dignity, and even the lives of the individuals belonging to such groups.[8]

The Genocide Convention was drafted mainly with the Holocaust in mind as a reference for future scenarios. When discussing the question of the obligation to prevent in the draft text, states referred to the preparations undertaken by the Nazi Germans years before the Holocaust, including the testing of gas chambers and the development of procedures for the industrial production of soap from human bones.[9] In general, states referred to the obligation to prevent mainly in the context of the definition of genocide and in rather abstract terms.

The Universal Declaration of Human Rights and the UN Charter itself were also influenced heavily by the perceived causes of World War II, including the relationship between a state's internal repression and external aggression.[10] When anti-Semitism resurfaced in various countries during the 1960s, the drafting of the Convention on the Elimination of All Forms of Racial Discrimination considered additional preventive measures, again with a view to the events that led to the Holocaust, as understood at the time.[11]

In this context, the conviction that the Holocaust was "unique," as claimed by the survivors and the Allied powers alike, had the unintended effect of transforming genocide from an international crime into an impossible standard

---

[8] Raphael Lemkin, *Axis Rule in Occupied Europe: Laws of Occupation, Analysis of Government, Proposals for Redress* (Washington, DC: Carnegie Endowment for International Peace, 1944), 79.

[9] E/794, May 24, 1948, in Hirad Abtahi and Philippa Webb, eds., *The Genocide Convention: The Travaux Préparatoires* (Leiden, the Netherlands: Martinus Nijhoff, 2008), 1110.

[10] See, e.g., Mary Ann Glendon, *A World Made New: Eleanor Roosevelt and the Universal Declaration of Human Rights* (New York: Random House, 2001).

[11] Michael Banton, *International Action Against Racial Discrimination* (Oxford: Oxford University Press, 1996), 50 et seq.

of comparison for instances of mass killing. As a result, the Convention was not applied to subsequent situations of mass atrocities, such as Cambodia (1975–79), Ethiopia (1977–78), and Iraq (1987–88). Two things had to happen in order for that to change: the first was the end of the U.S.–Soviet Cold War, in which the Holocaust was used by both sides, whenever convenient, as an ideological tool for the denunciation of the other, as Germany was divided and transformed from an enemy to be defeated into an ally needed to stop the advance of the opposing superpower. The second was a discussion among Holocaust survivors themselves that resulted in a shift away from the idea of "uniqueness" toward the notion of "unprecedentedness."[12] This meant that the word "genocide" could at least be mentioned by officials and policymakers in connection with events in Rwanda (1994) and Bosnia-Herzegovina (1995). Yet, in both instances, the UN Secretary-General subsequently termed the international response a "collective failure."[13]

With regard to Rwanda and Bosnia-Herzegovina, the permanent members of the UN Security Council carefully avoided invoking the Genocide Convention, because their understanding, as well as that of the media and civil society, was that any official use of the term "genocide" would carry an obligation to intervene. Nevertheless, these situations entered into the collective memory of the UN, replacing the Holocaust as primary reference points in the subsequent discussion on genocide prevention. As such, they informed the decision of U.S. Secretary of State Colin Powell in September 2004, when he characterized the situation in Darfur as genocide but rejected the idea that it implied any legal obligation on the part of the United States to act.[14]

Given the importance of the Holocaust in the drafting of the UN Charter, it is surprising that "mass atrocity prevention" – described explicitly in those words – has not appeared as an item on the agenda of relevant UN bodies. In the past, the General Assembly has addressed situations of ongoing mass atrocities in special sessions or under the item "human rights situations and reports of special rapporteurs and representatives"[15] or "emergency

---

[12] Yehuda Bauer, "Contemporary Research on the Holocaust," in *Contemporary Responses to the Holocaust*, edited by Konrad Kwiet and Jürgen Matthäus (Westport, CT: Praeger Publishers, 2004), 3 et seq.

[13] "'Risk of Genocide Remains Frighteningly Real,' Secretary-General Tells Human Rights Commission as He Launches Action Plan to Prevent Genocide," Press Release SG/SM /9197 AFR/893, HR/CN/1077 (April 7, 2004), www.un.org/News/Press/docs/2004/sgs m9245.doc.htm.

[14] For details on the considerations within the administration, see Rebecca Hamilton, "Inside Colin Powell's Decision to Declare Genocide in Darfur," *The Atlantic* (August 17, 2011), available at www.theatlantic.com/international/archive/2011/08/inside-colin-powells-deci sion-to-declare-genocide-in-darfur/243560/?single_page=true.

[15] See, e.g., UN General Assembly Resolutions A/RES/49/205, December 23, 1994 (former Yugoslavia); A/RES/49/206, December 23, 1994 (Rwanda); and A/RES/66/176, December 19, 2011 (Syria).

assistance,"[16] although, following its long-standing practice of considering gross violations of human rights within a state a threat to international peace and security, the item "prevention of armed conflict" has been used as well.[17] Since 2009, the General Assembly has discussed the R2P on an annual basis, in varying formats and from a different perspective each year.[18]

The General Assembly decided, in 2006, that the Human Rights Council should address situations of violations of human rights, including gross and systematic violations, and make recommendations and respond promptly to human rights emergencies.[19] Since then, the Human Rights Council has held sixteen country-related special sessions to address situations of ongoing violence causing human rights violations and has characterized them using the following terms, with no apparent standard of classification: "massive," "massacres,"[20] "atrocities,"[21] "gross and systematic,"[22] "some may amount to crimes against humanity," "grave and systemic,"[23] and "widespread, systematic and gross."[24]

The Security Council, for its part, has referred to "massive flows of refugees towards or across international frontiers"[25] and "the consequences for the countries of the region"[26] when authorizing outside intervention in situations of mass atrocities. Regarding some situations, including Somalia (1990), Iraq (1991), and, most recently, Libya (2011), the language that Council members have used in their resolutions has been "the unique character of the present situation,"[27] "the magnitude of the humanitarian crisis,"[28] and "the gross and systematic violations of human rights."[29]

Notwithstanding the lack of agenda items dealing explicitly with prevention of mass atrocities, discussions of related issues – prevention of armed conflict, protection of civilians (POC), and protection of human rights – have, over time,

---

[16] See, e.g., UN General Assembly Resolution A/RES/45/253, December 21, 1990 (Liberia).

[17] See UN General Assembly Resolution A/RES/66/253, August 3, 2012 (Syria).

[18] July 29, 2009 (informal interactive dialogue and debate), August 9, 2010 (informal interactive dialogue), July 12, 2011 (informal interactive dialogue), September 5, 2012 (informal interactive dialogue).

[19] UN General Assembly Resolution A/RES/60/251 (March 15, 2006).

[20] UN Human Rights Council Report A/HRC/S-2/2 (August 17, 2006).

[21] UN Human Rights Council Report A/HRC/S-14/1 (December 23, 2010).

[22] UN Human Rights Council Report A/HRC/S-15/1 (February 25, 2011), para. 2.

[23] UN Human Rights Council Resolution A/HRC/RES/S-17/1 (July 22, 2011), para. 1, 2.

[24] UN Human Rights Council Resolution A/HRC/RES/S-18/1 (December 2, 2011), para. 2.

[25] UN Security Council Resolution 688, S/RES/688 (April 5, 1991).

[26] UN Security Council Resolution 713, S/RES/713 (September 25, 1991).

[27] UN Security Council Resolution 794, S/RES/794 (December 3, 1992); similar res. 929 (1994) on Rwanda.

[28] UN Security Council Resolution 929, S/RES/929 (June 22, 1994).

[29] UN Security Council Resolution 1970, S/RES/1970 (February 26, 2011).

led to a number of reports and resolutions offering useful considerations on mass atrocity prevention and R2P.[30]

Moreover, all of the Secretaries-General have addressed mass atrocity prevention as a challenge deserving unique attention in response to key events during their tenures. Much progress has been made, in particular during the past twenty years, in understanding the social and political conditions leading to genocide. Efforts by Javier Perez de Cuellar (1982–91) ended the Nicaraguan Civil War in 1990, leading to the formation of a UN Observer Group, which later became the model for the UN Observer Mission in El Salvador that monitored human rights and investigated alleged violations.[31] In 1992, responding to a request from the Security Council for proposals to strengthen peacemaking and peacekeeping in the post–Cold War era, Boutros Boutros-Ghali (1992–96) outlined in his "Agenda for Peace" a range of preventive diplomacy measures the international community could use in situations where peacekeeping and peacemaking might not be successful.[32] For Kofi Annan, the inability of the UN to take action in Kosovo in 1999 was one of his defining moments. This experience led him to initiate the development of the R2P [33] and its integration into the UN in 2005, as well as the 1999 reviews of UN action in Rwanda and Srebrenica[34] and their consequences for the future of UN peacekeeping. On a parallel track, he strengthened the early-warning capacity of the UN regarding genocide by creating the Office of the Special Adviser on the Prevention of Genocide (OSAPG) in 2004, in the broader context of his five-point action plan on

[30] See UN Security Council, *Report of the Secretary-General on the Protection of Civilians in Armed Conflict*, S/2012/376 (May 22, 2012), http://daccess-dds-ny.un.org/doc/UNDOC/GEN/N12/328/94/PDF/N1232894.pdf?OpenElement; and *Prevention of armed conflict: Report of the Secretary-General*, A/55/985–S/2001/574 (June 7, 2001), http://daccess-dds-ny.un.org/doc/UNDOC/GEN/N01/404/64/PDF/N0140464.pdf?OpenElement.

[31] UN Security Council Resolution 693, S/RES/693 (May 20, 1991).

[32] UN Secretary-General, *An Agenda for Peace: Preventive Diplomacy, Peacemaking and Peacekeeping*, A/47/277 (June 17, 1992), www.unrol.org/doc.aspx?n=A_47_277.pdf.

[33] Independent International Commission on Kosovo, *The Kosovo Report: Conflict, International Response, Lessons Learned* (New York: Oxford University Press, 2000), http://reliefweb.int/sites/reliefweb.int/files/resources/F62789D9FCC56FB3C1256C1700303E3B-thekosovoreport.htm; *Prevention of Armed Conflict: Report of the Secretary-General*, A/55/985–S/2001/574 (June 7, 2001), http://daccess-dds-ny.un.org/doc/UNDOC/GEN/N01/404/64/PDF/N0140464.pdf?OpenElement; *In Larger Freedom: Towards Development, Security and Human Rights for All: Report of the Secretary-General*, A/59/2005 (March 21, 2005), www.un.org/en/events/pastevents/in_larger_freedom.shtml.

[34] UN Security Council, *Report of the Independent Inquiry into the Actions of the United Nations during the 1994 Genocide in Rwanda*, S/1999/1257 (December 16, 1999), http://daccess-dds-ny.un.org/doc/UNDOC/GEN/N99/395/47/IMG/N9939547.pdf?OpenElement; *Report of the Secretary-General Pursuant to General Assembly Resolution 53/35: The Fall of Srebrenica*, A/54/549 (November 15, 1999), http://daccess-dds-ny.un.org/doc/UNDOC/GEN/N99/348/76/IMG/N9934876.pdf?OpenElement.

genocide.[35] Toward the end of his tenure, however, his harsh public statements on the situation in Darfur – where Arab militia allied with the government in Khartoum chased hundreds of members of African tribes away from their villages by means of killing, rape, and pillage – suggested he may have concluded that there had been no meaningful progress.[36]

Ban Ki-Moon made important pledges to uphold the R2P at the beginning of his tenure[37] but was unable to make significant headway in bringing an end to the Darfur conflict, where atrocities declined mainly because there were so few villages left to attack. Although he has invoked the R2P in a variety of situations, the underlying criteria and consequences for UN action remain unclear.[38] Thus, for Ban, Sri Lanka and Syria appear to be his defining moments. The internal review of UN action in Sri Lanka, undertaken at his initiative in 2012, broadened the perspective on UN action in situations of mass atrocities to situations beyond the peacekeeping context.[39] Although the recommendations that emerged from that review have been integrated into the 2013 "Rights Up Front" initiative,[40] what happened during the twenty-six years of civil war in Sri Lanka may be too little known among UN Member States, civil society, and the media to easily enter the collective memory of past failures in situations of mass atrocities, and, as a result, implementation of the recommendations could be difficult, even though many of them repeat findings from the review reports on Rwanda, Srebrenica, and Kosovo.[41] Ban declared 2012 the "Year of Prevention," with the aim of fulfilling the commitment made in the 2005 World Summit Outcome Document to assist states under stress before crises and conflicts break out.[42] The prioritization of early warning and early action to prevent violent conflict and advance the preventive

---

[35] "'Risk of Genocide Remains Frighteningly Real,' Secretary-General Tells Human Rights Commission as He Launches Action Plan to Prevent Genocide," Press Release SG/SM/9197 AFR/893, HR/CN/1077 (April 7, 2004), www.un.org/News/Press/docs/2004/sgsm9245.doc.htm.

[36] See, e.g., "New York, 11 September 2006 – Secretary-General's remarks to the Security Council on the situation in Darfur," www.un.org/sg/statements/?nid=2197.

[37] UN Secretary-General, "United Nations Has Moral Duty to Act on Lessons of Rwanda, Says Secretary-General in Message to Mark Fourteenth Anniversary of 1994 Genocide," SG/SM /11495 AFR/1674 (April 4, 2008), www.un.org/News/Press/docs/2008/sgsm11495.doc.htm.

[38] In 2012, Edward Luck, the former Special Adviser on the Responsibility to Protect, stated, "We've applied R2P in probably nine or ten different cases already." See www.unric.org/en /responsibility-to-protect/26988-the-responsibly-to-protect-on-a-case-by-case-basis.

[39] *Report of the Secretary-General's Internal Review Panel on United Nations Action in Sri Lanka* (November 2012), www.un.org/News/dh/infocus/Sri_Lanka/The_Internal_Review_Panel_rep ort_on_Sri_Lanka.pdf.

[40] See "Resources" at www.un.org/sg/rightsupfront/.

[41] Independent International Commission on Kosovo, The Kosovo Report (2000), http://relief web.int/sites/reliefweb.int/files/resources/6D26FF88119644CFC1256989005CD392-thekoso voreport.pdf.

[42] "Address to Stanley Foundation Conference on the Responsibility to Protect," (January 18, 2012), www.un.org/apps/news/infocus/sgspeeches/search_full.asp?statID=1433.

approach to human rights was also part of Ban's five-year action agenda for his second term as Secretary-General.[43]

While the cases of failure seem quite obvious, the cases where prevention might have succeeded remain much less clear; apart from the former Yugoslav Republic of Macedonia (1995), Burundi (1994), and, more controversial, Kenya (2007, 2013), hardly any examples are discussed. The assessments in each case have applied different methodologies, mainly deriving from a set of causes related to armed conflict rather than comparing actual events to anticipated outcomes. Some observers have even claimed that worse was prevented in situations where massive human rights violations were ongoing, such as the Central African Republic at the time of this writing (2014) or the military intervention in Libya in 2011.[44]

Reviewing this history demonstrates the lack of an agreed genocide and mass atrocity theory within the UN as well as within academia. Such a theory would include the distinguishing elements of these crimes, in particular the persecution of a group based on its identity as perceived by the potential perpetrators, and their main causes and consequences as a basis for early warning, early action, and subsequent impact assessments. Bureaucratic reforms, designed primarily to revise procedures and mechanisms in light of past failures, are no substitute.

Interestingly, in a parallel historical development since the early 1970s, international environmental law has evolved into a highly dynamic and innovative field. Treaties have moved from agreements on fishing rights, the boundaries of rivers, and the protection of individual species toward the prevention of pollution and harm of the common good. The precautionary principle has been adopted as an integral aspect of every measure affecting the environment, with the aim of preventing irreparable damage even when scientific uncertainties prevail about the exact cause-and-effect relationships.[45]

Since the 1980s, public health has grown into a recognizable concern at the UN, which has broadened its focus beyond individual behavior and risk factors to encompass population health and population-level issues such as inequality, poverty, and education. The discussion now centers around the prevention and management of disease and injuries through monitoring of at-risk cases and the promotion of healthy behaviors, habits, and environments. It is now a matter of common knowledge, and

[43] The Secretary-General's Five-year Action Agenda" (January 25, 2012), www.un.org/sg/priorities/.

[44] Bernard-Henri Lévy, "Sur Dieudonné, Valls a eu raison," *Le Parisien* (January 5, 2014), accessed March 13, 2014, www.leparisien.fr/politique/bernard-henri-levy-sur-dieudonne-valls-a-eu-raison-05-01-2014-3463669.php.

[45] See, e.g., Philippe Sands and Jacqueline Peel with Adriana Fabra and Ruth MacKensie, *Principles of International Environmental Law*, 3rd ed. (New York: Cambridge University Press, 2012).

internationally accepted, that diseases are often preventable through simple, nonmedical methods.[46]

In the early 1990s, crime prevention became the center of increased international attention based on research undertaken by the World Health Organization.[47] Governments were encouraged to go beyond law enforcement and criminal justice to tackle the risk factors that cause crime, an approach that is not only more cost-effective but also leads to greater social benefits than standard methods of responding to crime.

Although many elements of these seemingly unrelated preventive agendas appear occasionally in the context of genocide and mass atrocity prevention, little in the way of cross-references or systematic review has occurred with a view to transferring potentially relevant concepts.[48] Over time, in the absence of an agreed genocide and mass atrocity theory, the distinction between structural and direct prevention, adopted from the slightly older field of conflict prevention, has been translated into an understanding of genocide and mass atrocities as processes that unfold in a linear fashion, accompanied by an almost obsessive classification of measures and approaches to address each phase, which may support systematic thinking but fails to reflect reality on the ground. (In the context of the R2P, it takes the form of the three-pillar approach.[49])

By and large, the discussion on mass atrocity prevention still clings to the perception of past situations rather than developing a more abstract and distinguishable set of causes and scenarios. Consequently, prevention policy tends to follow rather than anticipate the development of situations over time. New procedures and mechanisms have been created in reaction to historical events and have remained primarily at the level of reactive punishment rather than proactive prevention.

Notwithstanding claims to the contrary, the R2P has yet to be applied in a way that distinguishes it from past humanitarian interventions and regime changes. It can offer a way forward, however, if applied as a political approach, one based on existing legal obligations that derive mainly from the Genocide Convention to respond to exceptional situations identified as at-risk on the basis of a distinguishable set of causes and scenarios within an agreed

---

[46] See, e.g., Michael H. Merson, Robert E. Black, Anne J. Mills, eds., *International Public Health: Diseases, Programs, Systems, and Policies*, 2nd ed. (Sudbury, MA: Jones and Bartlett Publishers, 2006).

[47] *World Report on Violence and Health*, edited by Etienne G. Krug, Linda L. Dahlberg, James A. Mercy, Anthony B. Zwi and Rafael Lozano (Geneva: World Health Organization, 2002), www.who.int/violence_injury_prevention/violence/world_report/en/.

[48] An example is David A. Hamburg, regarding the application of principles of public health to genocide prevention; see David A. Hamburg, *Preventing Genocide* (Herndon, VA: Paradigm Publishers, 2008), 5.

[49] www.un.org/en/preventgenocide/adviser/responsibility.shtml

genocide and mass atrocity theory. We will now look at the legal basis to support this approach.

18.2. The Legal Dimension

The Nuremberg indictments of Hermann Göring et al. reflected the difficulty of addressing the particular nature of genocide advocated by Lemkin on the basis of contemporary international law. While the indictments of the International Military Tribunal subsumed genocide within murder and ill-treatment of the civilian population of occupied territories as a war crime, the acts of seizing and retaining control of the German State, including persecution and deportations of religious and ethnic minorities, were considered as constituting part of the crime of foreign aggression.[50] In their verdict, the judges did not refer to the crime of genocide.[51]

Although the Genocide Convention succeeded in closing some of the legal gaps left by the Nuremberg principles, it has proven inadequate to prevent intentional mass murder. The prevention of genocide in the Convention is defined much more narrowly than it was in Lemkin's conception and rests almost exclusively on criminal law. Yet the Convention has never been applied to a significant number of individual cases so as to demonstrate its deterrent impact; instead, it has been limited to exceptional cases of state-organized murder. The preventive effect of criminal law requires adequate penalties and effective sentencing. Punishment is expected to deter future crime based on a rational decision by the perpetrator. According to the underlying theory of crime, perpetrators make rational choices, and increasing the potential costs of a crime far beyond its expected gains will deter potential perpetrators, while those already punished in the past will be deterred from committing the crime again.

Yet this theory explains mainly crimes involving rational planning, whereas individual perpetrators of acts of genocide are typically motivated by many other factors.[52] In any case, this approach requires a strong and functioning legal system, which is lacking in many states. It also fails to take into account other, often more effective, mechanisms for a society to secure compliance with its rules, including traditional means of shaming. The creation of ad hoc

---

[50] *Trial of the Major War Criminals before the International Military Tribunal: Nuremberg, 14 November 1945–1 October 1946* (Nuremberg: International Military Tribunal, 1947), Count One, D, p. 33–34; Count Four, B, 3, d, p. 66 et seq. Also http://avalon.law.yale.edu/imt/count1. asp.

[51] Principles of International Law Recognized in the Charter of the Nürnberg Tribunal and in the Judgment of the Tribunal, *Yearbook of the International Law Commission* (New York: United Nations, 1950), vol. II, para. 97.

[52] See, e.g., James Waller, *Becoming Evil: How Ordinary People Commit Genocide and Mass Killing*, 2nd ed. (New York: Oxford University Press, 2007).

tribunals for Yugoslavia and Rwanda, followed by the International Criminal Court, and the adoption in some countries of legislation establishing universal jurisdiction, indicates a willingness on the part of some states to establish accountability under the Genocide Convention, but, owing to a lack of capacity and political will, prosecution has been limited to a small number of cases, leaving the majority of alleged perpetrators unpunished.[53]

To compensate for the shortcomings of an approach built on criminal punishment, additional elements have been incorporated into the theory and practice of genocide prevention, building on developments in related areas of international law. The term "prevention" appears, inter alia, in the title, the preamble, and the substantive articles of various human rights conventions.[54] Most treaty bodies have interpreted the obligation to prevent as a general obligation to avoid the repetition of similar violations in the future,[55] but some of these conventions include the obligation to implement specific legal, administrative, or other means to prevent violations or their causes. This includes the obligation to monitor abstract risk situations (e.g., the monitoring of compulsory labor to prevent it turning into slavery) and the obligation to investigate any suspicion. Legal measures include the reform of national provisions that have proven to be inadequate. In this context, some conventions include the obligation to collect systematically information on violations. Other measures include the provision of educational, health, economic, or social services to potential victims or perpetrators. A third approach includes educational measures for potential perpetrators, victims, or the population at large. These measures are obligatory for the state party even before any violation has occurred.

Some treaty bodies have developed special early-warning and early-action procedures not necessarily connected directly with the legal obligation to prevent established in the respective convention. In 1993, the Committee on the Elimination of Racial Discrimination formulated a procedure to address

---

[53] See, e.g., Article 23.4 of the Spanish Judicial Power Organization Act (LOPJ) of 1 July 1985; the Crimes Against Humanity and War Crimes Act of Canada, S.C. 2000, c. 24; the Law on universal jurisdiction of Belgium of 1993.

[54] See, e.g., preambular para. 10 CERD: "Resolved . . . to prevent and combat racist doctrines and practices"; preambular para. 5 CSPCA, A/Res/3068 (XXVIII), 30. November 1973; preambular para. 3 CAAS, A/Res./40/64, December 10, 1985: "Observing that, . . .; Undertake to prevent, prohibit and eradicate all practices of this nature". art. 3 CERD: "prevent, prohibit and eradicate all practices of this nature," art. 3 Convention against Discrimination in Education (CADE) vom 14. Dezember 1985: "eliminate and prevent discrimination"; art. 2 Slavery Convention (SIC), 25 September 1926, A/Res/794 (VIII) vom 23. Oktober 1953: "prevent and suppress the slave trade"; art. 3 Supplementary Convention on the Abolition of Slavery, the Slave Trade, and Institutions and Practices Similar to Slavery (SupISIC, 7 September 1956: "to prevent ships and aircraft"; art. 2 CAT: . . . measures to prevent acts of torture."

[55] See, e.g., Bradley McCallum v. South Africa, A/66/40, Vol. II (2011), Part I, Annex VI, sect. WW, 559–67.

serious, massive, or persistent pattern of racial discrimination, in some cases with genocidal dimensions.[56] The committee conducted field visits to two states in the context of the procedure. Other sources of information include UN field presences and national nongovernmental organizations (NGOs). The procedure leads to a formal decision expressing the views of the committee, which often include detailed recommendations to halt further human rights violations and to initiate a dialogue with the victims. Based on almost identical provisions, country visits can also be carried out confidentially by the Committee on the Prevention of Torture and its Subcommittee, by the Committee on the Elimination of Discrimination against Women, and by the Committee on Economic, Social, and Cultural Rights.[57]

In a parallel development in environmental law, initially drafted in response to catastrophe, awareness of the far-reaching consequences of pollution led to the acceptance of prevention as the fundamental notion behind legislation on the transport, production, and storage of materials known to be hazardous. The precautionary approach, as stated in Principle 15 of the 1992 Rio Declaration on Environment and Development, requires states to take precautionary measures even if scientific certainty is lacking.[58] This uncertainty must not be used to postpone measures.[59]

As in public health and environmental protection, the cause-and-effect relationship between risk and occurrence in mass atrocities is still neither fully understood empirically nor agreed upon. However, the integration of a general precautionary principle into the prevention of genocide and mass atrocities would go beyond the limits of the Genocide Convention.[60] However, as in environmental law and public health, the obligations to prevent and punish genocide were interpreted by some as elements of a broader strategy for the mitigation of risk rather than the overambitious objective of eradicating the crime.

Over the past twenty years, the methodology and mechanisms for genocide prevention have developed significantly beyond an exclusive reliance on the deterrent effect of criminal punishment. As now conceived, it aims to generate political will and build the capacity of governments and other stakeholders to implement and enforce existing legal obligations and normative principles. In his speech to the Stockholm International Forum on January 26, 2004, then

---

[56] *Report of the Committee on the Elimination of Racial Discrimination* (A/48/18 annex III) (September 15, 1993).

[57] Articles 8, 9 CEDAW; article 11 OP CESCR.

[58] Rio Declaration on Environment and Development, UN General Assembly A/CONF.151/26 (vol. I) (August 12, 1992), www.un.org/documents/ga/conf151/aconf15126-1annex1.htm.

[59] See, e.g., Joakim Zander, *The Application of the Precautionary Principle in Practice: Comparative Dimensions* (Cambridge: Cambridge University Press, 2010), 33 et seq.

[60] See for this proposal Richter, "The Precautionary Principle: Environmental Epidemiology's Gift to Genocide Prevention," Epidemiology 17 (6), 340 et seq.

Secretary-General Kofi Annan stressed the need for states to take additional action to prevent genocide, opening with the words "There can be no more important issue, and no more binding obligation, than the prevention of genocide."

Referring to the fact that the Genocide Convention was the first human rights document adopted by the General Assembly, even before the Universal Declaration on Human Rights, he continued, "Indeed, this may be considered one of the original purposes of the United Nations."[61] A few months later, on April 7, 2004, the tenth anniversary of the start of the Rwandan genocide, Annan outlined a five-point action plan for preventing genocide: (1) the prevention of armed conflict, (2) the protection of civilians in armed conflict, (3) judicial action in national and international courts to end impunity, (4) the systematic gathering of information and the set up of an early warning system, and (5) a commitment on the part of states to take swift and decisive action in a range of areas, including military action, to halt ongoing genocide.[62] Later that year, he appointed his first special adviser on the prevention of genocide as an early warning instrument.[63] Building on an analysis of past instances of genocide, the first special adviser, Juan E. Méndez (2004–07), developed an initial Analysis Framework, which was expanded by his successors to comprise eight categories of factors to determine risk of genocide in a given situation.[64] The framework builds on a range of other early warning systems developed by genocide scholars, think tanks, and human rights organizations based on quantitative and qualitative indicators.[65] The second special adviser, Francis Deng (2007–12), interpreted genocide as an identity-based conflict and sought to address it chiefly by means of education and local capacity building.[66]

With regard to genocide and mass atrocities, prevention today is often differentiated into structural and operational dimensions. This approach appears to build on different models of crime prevention derived from theories of crime and applied without further clarification. Other approaches

---

[61] "Genocide Is Threat to Peace Requiring Strong, United Action, Secretary-General Tells Stockholm International Forum," Press Release SG/SM/9126 (January 26, 2004), www.un.org/News/Press/docs/2004/SGsm9126.doc.htm.

[62] "'Risk of Genocide Remains Frighteningly Real', Secretary-General Tells Human Rights Commission as He Launches Action Plan to Prevent Genocide," Press Release SG/SM/9245 (April 7, 2004), www.un.org/News/Press/docs/2004/sgsm9245.doc.htm.

[63] www.un.org/en/preventgenocide/adviser/

[64] "Analysis Framework: A Guide for States," Office of the Special Adviser on the Prevention of Genocide, http://aipr.files.wordpress.com/2012/05/foa-for-states-english.pdf.

[65] See, e.g., Barbara Harff, "No Lessons Learned from the Holocaust? Assessing Risks of Genocide and Political Mass Murder since 1955," *American Political Science Review*, 97(1): 57–73 (2003), www.gpanet.org/webfm_send/29.

[66] Francis Deng, "Keynote Speech: Genocide, Risk, Resilience and Responsibility," Conference of the International Association of Genocide Scholars (IAGS), Siena, Italy (June 19, 2013), www.genocidescholars.org/sites/default/files/document%09%5Bcurrent-page%3A1%5D/documents/Key%20note%20speech_IAGS%20conference_Siena_19June2013.pdf.

seem guided by a public health model, which distinguishes between primary, secondary, and tertiary prevention, gradually moving down in scale from the more general level of public education to the more focused levels of, first, risk groups and, then, individuals.[67]

It took until 2006 for the content of the legal obligation to prevent genocide to be clarified for the first time, in a ruling of the International Court of Justice (ICJ). The ICJ developed the obligation of states to prevent genocide into a substantive legal concept, finding that the obligation to prevent had a "separate legal existence of its own," as well as its own, well-defined scope. The court held that

[t]he obligation to prevent the commission of the crime of genocide is imposed by the Genocide Convention on any State party which, in a given situation, has it in its power to contribute to restraining in any degree the commission of genocide. [T]he obligation to prevent genocide places a State under a duty to act which is not dependent on the certainty that the action to be taken will succeed in preventing the commission of acts of genocide, or even on the likelihood of that outcome.[68]

Although the obligation to prevent is only breached when genocide is actually committed, a serious prevailing risk of genocide is sufficient to trigger the obligation. As part of the primary norm, intent is considered a necessary element of state responsibility.

However, there remains a disconnect between the interpretation of the legal obligation to prevent genocide under the Convention and the mandate of the mechanisms and institutions tasked with responding to mass atrocity risks.

One possible solution to this dilemma would be to draft additional legal instruments. Past proposals have sought to introduce specific preventive measures or clarify the interpretation of the Genocide Convention as it stands; for example, through an extension of the definition of genocide to political groups, an Optional Protocol on genocidal intent, an Optional Protocol on prevention,[69] the establishment of a treaty body for implementation of the Convention,[70] or a revised mandate for the OSAPG. However, none of these proposals has met with either much interest or success.

---

[67] See, e.g., Hamburg, *Preventing Genocide*, and Gareth Evans, *The Responsibility to Protect: Ending Mass Atrocity Crimes Once and for All* (Washington, DC: Brookings Institution Press, 2008).

[68] ICJ, Application of the Convention on the Prevention and Punishment of the Crime of Genocide (*Bosnia and Herzegovina v. Serbia and Montenegro*), Judgment, I.C.J. Reports 2007, para. 461.

[69] UN Economic and Social Council, Commission on Human Rights, Sub-Commission on Prevention of Discrimination and Protection of Minorities, *Revised and Updated Report on the Question of the Prevention and Punishment of the Crime of Genocide Prepared by Mr. B. Whitaker*, E/CN.4/Sub.2/1985/6 (July 2, 1985), www.armenews.com/IMG/whitaker.pdf.

[70] Office of the United Nations High Commissioner for Human Rights, "Views of States parties to the Convention on the Prevention and Punishment of the Crime of Genocide on the Secretary-General's Proposal That They Consider Setting up a Committee on the Prevention of Genocide:

There is a need for a genocide and mass atrocity theory that could serve as the basis for a legal interpretation of the Convention that is both distinct and limited with regard to the obligation to prevent genocide. I propose that this theory be based on the "criminal spin" theory of crime while taking into account the specific criminological explanations for the crime of genocide and the situational circumstances of the respective country.[71] The criminal spin theory also offers useful insights into the dynamics of mass violence once it has begun to unfold, explaining group behavior as the product of (1) individuals' choices, (2) individuals' perception of decisions made previously, and (3) individuals' sense of belonging to a group. Step by step, this behavior unwinds into a "criminal spin," resulting in acts that the individual would not have chosen initially but that, at their conclusion, appear to have been inevitable. Moreover, a genocide theory based on the criminal spin theory would allow for different theories of crime to be used to explain the contribution of different perpetrators and variances during the genocidal process.[72] Compared with the Holocaust, tomorrow's genocides will include factors much better explained on the basis of multiple crime theories. The contribution of different perpetrators might be explained by different crime theories[73] and so could be different sequences of events. Furthermore, once events have begun to unfold and become visible, the criminal spin theory offers important insights into the dynamics of mass violence[74]

The development of a model based on these elements would serve as a new guide to interpretation of the legal obligation to prevent genocide. Although some have proposed to interpret genocidal intent according to the status and role of the perpetrator,[75] full implementation of the obligation to prevent requires establishing genocide as an offense of specific endangerment – as expressed in *all* the acts defined as genocide in Articles II and III of the Convention: not only killing members of the group, but also causing serious bodily or mental harm to members of the group or deliberately inflicting on the

Note by the Secretariat," E/CN.4/2005/46 (December 10, 2004), http://daccess-dds-ny.un.org/doc/UNDOC/GEN/G04/168/93/PDF/G0416893.pdf?OpenElement.

[71] S. Kai Ambos, "Criminologically Explained Reality of Genocide, Structure of the Offence and the 'Intent to Destroy' Requirement," in *Collective Violence and International Criminal Justice*, edited by Alette Smeulers (Antwerp: Intersentia, 2010), 153 et seq.

[72] Alette Smeulers, "Perpetrators of International Crimes: Towards a Typology (January 22, 2014)," in *Supranational Criminology: Towards a Criminology of International Crimes*, edited by A. Smeulers and R. Haveman (Antwerp: Intersentia, 2008), 233 et seq.

[73] Ibid.

[74] Natti Ronel, "The Criminal Spin: Towards an Alternative Criminological Theory," in *International Perspectives on Crime and Justice*, edited by K. Jaishankar (Newcastle upon Tyne: Cambridge Scholars Publishing, 2009), 142 et seq.

[75] Kai Ambos, "What Does 'Intent to Destroy' in Genocide Mean?" *International Review of the Red Cross* 91: 833–858 (2009).

group conditions of life calculated to bring about its physical destruction in whole or in part. Yet, based on the scenario of the Holocaust, the application of the Convention has so far been limited to the obligation to prevent applying only to those acts that evidently presented a risk of death to members of the group in question. By adapting the interpretation of genocidal intent to the risks in advance of mass killings, the Convention will respond to the reality of mass murder after the Holocaust.[76] The violation of obligations to protect and prevent certain human rights violations, then, can help establish when there is real risk of genocide and mass atrocities in a particular situation. Real risk occurs if, based on the available evidence, the genocide prevention theory can establish a potential group of victims, a potential group of perpetrators, and concrete scenarios of mass violence.[77] Although the elements for consideration may vary according to the situation, the following violations would certainly all be relevant: killings; torture; mutilation; rape and sexual violence; abduction; forced population movement; expropriation; destruction of property; looting; lack of freedom of speech, press, assembly, or religion; destruction of subsistence food supply; denial of water or medical attention; manmade famine; redirection of aid supplies; discrimination in access to work and resources; political marginalization; restricted movement; discrimination in education; and lack of access to justice and redress.

The R2P could be an effective instrument for fulfilling the legal obligations of the Genocide Convention based on the theory just outlined – assuming it is understood as a *political concept*, applicable in *exceptional* situations of violence against individuals or groups within a country with the aim of their extermination. As defined in the 2005 World Summit Outcome Document and drawing on lessons learned from past failures, the R2P offers a continuum of steps that national governments and the international community may take to prevent or halt such violence based on existing obligations under international law. The implementation of agreed-on steps would establish whether a government was "manifestly failing" to protect its own population and, consequently, whether the international community was legally obligated by the Genocide Convention, human rights, and humanitarian law to take measures to protect individuals and groups from the specifically identified risks to their physical integrity.

However, this brings us to the reality that one of the main obstacles to making genocide prevention more operational is political resistance from states themselves.

---

[76] See Ekkehard Strauss, "Reconsidering Genocidal Intent in the Interest of Prevention," *Global Responsibility to Protect* 5: 129 et seq. (2013).

[77] See Sheri P. Rosenberg, "A Common Standard for Applying the Responsibility to Protect," Global Centre for the Responsibility to Protect (October 7, 2013), www.globalr2p.org/resources/468.

18.3.   The Political Dimension

In the UN, situations of mass atrocities are addressed in an essentially schematic fashion that still reflects the response of the League of Nations to the early twentieth-century massacres of the Armenians: following media reports and pressure by civil society, senior government and UN officials and the Secretary-General denounce the atrocities. In most cases, the Human Rights Council and the Security Council discuss the situation, calling for the protection of civilians and respect for humanitarian and human rights law. When it fails to improve, a fact-finding mission, targeted sanctions, and, in some cases, referral to the ICC or the establishment of a peace mission follows.

It needs to be recognized that the UN has hugely improved compared to its passivity in the past. Still, the Secretariat, the Human Rights Council, and the Security Council only take up a small number of situations under the premise of preventing extraordinary violence from turning into mass atrocities, as opposed to the more common and more numerous cases of human rights violations and humanitarian protection. Historically, it has only been in the aftermath of atrocities that these bodies have recognized the exceptional nature of the violence, sometimes leading to organizational reviews and recommendations for operational reforms that have been implemented only partially and with declining enthusiasm over time.

For the most part, political concerns about genocide and mass atrocity prevention center around the possibility that the legal obligation to prevent may be used as a pretext for regime change via military intervention by stronger states in weaker ones. The original conception of R2P, in 2001, included a catalogue of principles for "military intervention for human protection purposes" in order to distinguish it from humanitarian intervention.[78] However, negotiations on the 2005 Summit Outcome and subsequent discussion on implementing the R2P largely skirted the question, concentrating instead on prevention and capacity building, in order to avoid political resistance.

The year 2011 witnessed the first case of military intervention sanctioned under the aegis of the R2P, when members of the Security Council agreed on preventive action to save the people of Benghazi in Libya from mass atrocities. In Resolution 1973, Council members tried to define a sequence of measures, an improvement over the past, when measures were not applied in any particular order and lacked conditionality. Yet the text of the resolution reveals that there is still a dearth of tools at the Council's disposal to define a continuum of steps underpinned by benchmarks and timelines.[79] This lack of

---

[78] *The Responsibility to Protect: Report of the International Commission on Intervention and State Sovereignty* (Ottawa: International Development Research Centre, December 2001), xii, http://responsibilitytoprotect.org/ICISS%20Report.pdf.

[79] UN Security Council Resolution 1973, S/RES/1973 (March 17, 2011).

conceptual clarity translated into a lack of guidance regarding military operations on the ground, and the action quickly fell into the pattern seen in Kosovo in 1999: air raids against military assets, government infrastructure, and key industries until the government was deposed, with no particular features distinctive from past humanitarian interventions.

To channel the increasing political differences among Security Council members on the scope and objectives of the military operation in Libya, in November 2011, Brazil presented a paper outlining what it termed the "responsibility while protecting."[80] The document, partly built on the principles for military intervention spelled out in the 2001 conception of the R2P, emphasized that the use of force "must ... be carried out in strict conformity with international law, in particular international humanitarian law and the international law of armed conflict," but placed impractical conditions on the application of military force and undermined future application of the R2P by demanding that "[t]he three pillars must follow a strict line of political subordination and chronological sequencing."

There has yet to be a more comprehensive discussion on the implementation of the R2P in the context of the Brazilian proposal, although Brazil's letter was included in the July 2012 report of the Secretary-General on the R2P, probably in an attempt to neutralize general political opposition to it.[81] The outcome of such a discussion, when and if it does take place, could determine the future of R2P as a political concept to respond to mass atrocities.

If the R2P is to overcome current political resistance, its application must be limited to the physical protection of populations. There are signs that the UN is moving in the direction of a limited interpretation of mass atrocity, as indicated in comments made by Deputy Secretary-General Jan Eliasson at a special event commemorating the twentieth anniversary of the genocide in Rwanda:

We need look no further than South Sudan today for an example of dedication and innovation in protecting people. In spite of a tragically great number of people being killed in the conflict, thousands of civilians are alive today because they have sought shelter inside United Nations facilities and have been provided with protection and assistance. Conditions there are trying and difficult, and the situation remains volatile. But, for the moment, people are largely safe and the United Nations is doing its utmost to see to their needs while promoting a peaceful resolution of the conflict.[82]

---

[80] "Letter dated 9 November 2011 from the Permanent Representative of Brazil to the United Nations addressed to the Secretary-General," A/66/551–S/2011/701 (November 11, 2011), www.un.org/ga/search/view_doc.asp?symbol=A/66/551.

[81] "Responsibility to Protect: Timely and Decisive Response: Report of the Secretary-General," A/66/874–S/2012/578 (July 25, 2012), para. 49 et seq., www.un.org/ga/search/view_doc.asp?symbol=A/66/874.

[82] "Deputy Secretary-General's remarks at event on the Rwandan Genocide" (January 15, 2014), www.un.org/sg/dsg/statements/index.asp?nid=481.

In addition to the politically divisive question of military intervention, there are political challenges to the concept of R2P deriving from its relationship to (1) the prevention of human rights violations and (2) the protection of civilians in armed conflict.

With regard to the relationship between the R2P and the prevention of human rights violations, the special sessions of the Human Rights Council, as noted in Section 18.1, illustrate the lack of conceptual clarity and the reluctance to distinguish genocide prevention from other human rights violations, as well as the continued reliance on a linear model to understand the development of events. The policy of mainstreaming human rights into the activities of a variety of UN funds and agencies has led the Human Rights Council to promote a broad approach to mass atrocity prevention. However, institution building and economic development as such are not conducive to mass atrocity prevention as long as they sustain existing power structures based on majority–minority considerations. Instead, the Human Rights Council should promote the integration of the principles relating to the R2P into each culture and society without hesitation or condition, as a reflection of not only global but also local values and standards.[83]

From the outset, there has been a close connection between the R2P and the concept of POC. The Secretary-General referred to R2P already in his report on the protection of civilians immediately following the 2005 World Summit,[84] and the Security Council reaffirmed the provisions of the World Summit Outcome Document in its thematic resolution on the protection of civilians.[85] Subsequent periodic debates on the protection of civilians for a long time referred to the R2P without clarification of the legal, operational, or methodological similarities and differences between the two.[86] In addition, discussion of the coercive elements of the R2P and its possible application by the Security Council has caused considerable political and operational challenges for humanitarian actors on the ground – in Darfur, Afghanistan, and Somalia, among other places – with regard to access to vulnerable populations and related negotiations with state and non-state actors who

---

[83] UN General Assembly, "Implementing the Responsibility to Protect: Report of the Secretary-General," A/63/677 (January 12, 2009), para. 20, http://daccess-dds-ny.un.org/doc/UNDOC /GEN/N09/206/10/PDF/N0920610.pdf?OpenElement.

[84] UN Security Council, "Report of the Secretary-General on the Protection of Civilians in Armed Conflict," S/2005/740 (November 28, 2005), 15, http://daccess-dds-ny.un.org/doc/UNDOC /GEN/N05/610/43/PDF/N0561043.pdf?OpenElement.

[85] UN Security Council Resolution 1674, S/RES/1674 (April 28, 2006), http://daccess-dds-ny.un. org/doc/UNDOC/GEN/N06/331/99/PDF/N0633199.pdf?OpenElement. For details on the discussion, see Strauss, n. 8, 50.

[86] See Asia-Pacific Centre for the Responsibility to Protect, "The Responsibility to Protect and the Protection of Civilians: Asia-Pacific in the UN Security Council," Update No. 1 (February 10, 2009).

began to question their neutrality. These developments have led to increasing demands to distinguish the R2P from POC.[87]

Past instances of violence are an important risk factor for recurrence. This is why addressing national and international myths about past situations of genocide is an important part of prevention. In this regard, the development and implementation of comprehensive transitional justice processes in countries with experience of mass atrocities represents an important contribution to prevention. At the same time, the desirability of accountability for past atrocities within the framework of peace negotiations is still a subject of controversy. Overall, there remains a lack of international consensus on the relationship between peace and justice.[88]

The establishment of historical knowledge owned by the society in question is often undermined by mainstream narratives based on international media reports during a conflict, which are determined by external political interests. In addition, the concept of transitional justice, at least in its most common and broadly promoted form, is based on the false assumption that there is only one truth and that that truth resides solely with the victims.[89]

The Secretary-General's new plan to place "rights up front," based on the recommendations from the 2012 Internal Review Panel on UN Action in Sri Lanka, has been "received positively" by Member States.[90] The Panel characterized UN efforts in the last stages of the Sri Lankan Civil War as a "systemic failure" and recommended a list of changes to UN action on the ground in situations of gross human rights violations and mass atrocities. The Secretary-General's decision to translate these recommendations into policy has been an important political signal because it reiterates the commitment of the UN and its Member States to the protection of human rights as a minimum commitment in a world increasingly divided by religion, ethnicity, and wealth. In addition, the decision led to a process of reflection and discussion within the UN system about the prevention of mass atrocities

---

[87] See, e.g., Vesselin Popovski, "Siblings, but Not Twins: POC and R2P," *United Nations University* (November 1, 2011), http://unu.edu/publications/articles/siblings-but-not-twins-po c-and-r2p.html; Global Centre for the Responsibility to Protect, "The Relationship between the Responsibility to Protect and the Protection of Civilians in Armed Conflict," Policy Brief (Updated) (May 9, 2011), http://responsibilitytoprotect.org/The%20Relationship%20Between %20POC%20and%20R2P-%20Updated.pdf.

[88] See, e.g., Louise Arbour, "Are Freedom, Peace and Justice Incompatible Agendas?" Address by the Hon. Louise Arbour, President and CEO of the International Crisis Group, on the occasion of the Inaugural Roland Berger Lecture on Human Rights and Human Dignity (February 17, 2014), Oxford, www.crisisgroup.org/en/publication-type/speeches/2014/arbour-are-freedom-peace-and-justice-incompatible-agendas.aspx.

[89] See Chapter 8 of this volume, "Historical Dialogue and the Prevention of Atrocity Crimes," by Elazar Barkan.

[90] "Deputy Secretary-General's remarks at event on the Rwandan Genocide" (January 15, 2014), www.un.org/sg/dsg/statements/index.asp?nid=481.

that, unfortunately, did not take place after the adoption of the R2P at the 2005 World Summit.

On their own, however, neither Ban's decision nor the report of the Secretary-General will be able to create the political momentum to put "rights up front." Similar to previous reports introducing change, it should be expected that only about half of the recommendations will be implemented. Some of them are repeating recommendations from the Rwanda and Srebrenica reports, which were not implemented in almost twenty years. Furthermore, again, the report is linked to a specific country situation and, given the long duration of the conflict and the complex regional and international interests involved over time, will have difficulties entering the collective memory of the UN as yet another case of mass atrocities. Even though the UN system can concentrate on the implementation of those recommendations within its control, the transferability of the findings in the Sri Lanka report to other country situations requires a joint theory of genocide as a basis for an assessment of the risk of mass atrocities in every country where the UN is present. This could take away the internal and external political sensitivities around the issue and allow a more technical approach to prevention.

The recommendations also put the Office of the High Commissioner on Human Rights (OHCHR) largely in charge of coordinating UN efforts regarding early warning and early action on mass atrocities. Previous deliberations led to the realization that the mandate to protect and promote human rights led to difficulties in addressing situations at risk in the interest of the long-term relationship with the respective government and society required for its human rights work. Although special mechanisms have been able to provide early warning, including in the case of Rwanda, apparently, the UN human rights system was not able to set preventive action into motion. These considerations led to the creation of the separate OSAPG. Should increased responsibility be placed on OHCHR, it would require some clarification of how its previous weaknesses will be addressed.

The application of the R2P still requires a precedent to demonstrate its distinct objective and comparative contribution. Such a precedent would be comprised of the identification of a genocide risk; a continuum of steps, including benchmarks and timelines; and efforts to resolve the conflict locally and without regard to whether the outcome is favorable to the political and strategic interests of intervening powers. This sets the bar for the application of R2P very high, which should serve as a corrective factor to its overambitious use.

18.4.   Conclusion

The R2P offers a historic opportunity to implement the obligation to prevent genocide as established by the Genocide Convention. To this end, the causes and scenarios of future genocide must be separated from past historic events to identify specific and distinguishable elements for exceptional situations. These causes and scenarios should lead to a comprehensive theory on genocide and mass atrocities, one that allows the analysis of specific country situations. Based on this theory, genocide should be applied as an individual crime at all levels of responsibility based on a reinterpretation of "intent" in the interest of prevention. The real-risk standard offers a distinguishable element of proximity of events to the elements of the crime of genocide. Politically, the R2P requires a limitation to the physical protection of people as far and as long as the government is substantively failing to protect its own population. Translated into operational guidance, the conflict as such would be solved at the local level, while international involvement would ensure neutralizing genocide or mass atrocity as a policy option.

19 The Practical Use of Early Warning and Response in Preventing Mass Atrocities and Genocide: Experiences from the Great Lakes Region

Ashad Sentongo

19.1. Summary

The transnational impact of violent conflicts and of the 2004 Genocide in Rwanda led to various national and regional-level initiatives by states and civil society to work toward mass atrocity early warning and response (EWR) in the Great Lakes Region. However, the region remains without a well-developed and coherent EWR system, a system that would include information gathering and analytical and reporting functions to support mass atrocity and genocide prevention. Experiences from Kenya, South Sudan, and the Republic of Congo are marked by early warning initiatives at regional, national, and communal levels that have not always produced early responses. This is partly due to enduring grievances that run deep in target communities, deeper than existing initiatives are designed to deal with. These initiatives put into place disjointed, uncoordinated, and ineffective responses to complex issues. They highlight capacity gaps at state and civil society levels in terms of knowledge, skills, and resources to conduct effective analysis and warning. To respond to these challenges, this chapter recommends a robust national and regional advocacy agenda, strengthening the capacity of EWR structures, resource mobilization, creation of awareness, domestication of international instruments, and institutional linkages for information sharing around best practices and prevention-sensitive policies and local programs. It is essential to promote local responsibility and ownership through broad community participation in EWR initiatives. After all, communities are in the best position to understand conditions pertinent to mass atrocities prevention and to develop confidence-building measures through response options and programs.

19.2.   Introduction

Article II of the 1948 Convention on the Prevention and Punishment of the Crime of Genocide states that:

In the present Convention, genocide means any of the following acts committed with intent to destroy, in whole or in part, a national, ethnical, racial or religious group, as such: Killing members of the group; Causing serious bodily or mental harm to members of the group; Deliberately inflicting on the group conditions of life calculated to bring about its physical destruction in whole or in part; Imposing measures intended to prevent births within the group; Forcibly transferring children of the group to another group.

Thus, "genocide is the deliberate destruction of a national, ethnical, racial or religious group, in part or in whole,"[1] and it often occurs where conditions of discrimination and inequality in opportunities to access to power and resources for development are perceived to manifest particularly along ethnic, religious, or racial differences between groups. EWR aims to prevent and/or transform conditions that cause and/or escalate these conditions by identifying and alerting responsible decision makers to constructively deal with situations that contain indicators of potential mass atrocities. In this case, the terms "early," "warning," and "response" are operational concepts, each associated with a set of timely activities and various tools often deployed in sequence or in combination to help draw predictive conclusions about the potential for violence and to help generate options to prevent its occurrence or escalation.

Jonathan Whittall (2010) defines early warning as "initiatives that focus on systematic data collection, analysis and/or formulation of recommendations, including risk assessment and information sharing." The goal is to generate or attract "early response," that occurs in the latent stages of a predicted violent conflict, seeking to prevent, reduce, resolve, or transform conditions that may escalate into violence (Austin 2004). Some of the activities necessary during early warning include data collection and verification, analysis, mapping and monitoring, evaluation and assessment of risks, reporting, advocacy, monitoring, and evaluation.

"Warning" occurs when predictive conclusions and the evidence to support them are generated and shared with the parties involved in the conflict and with actors responsible for taking corrective steps toward prevention. It therefore includes advocating for timely and appropriate corrective actions as "response options" for prevention and transformation before the conflict escalates. This

---

[1] Office of the United Nations Special Adviser on Prevention of Genocide, www.un.org/en/pre ventgenocide/adviser/genocide_prevention.shtml

view assumes a reliable, timely, and consistent process, one in which inputs and decision processes about the information that is shared are clear and flexible enough to generate timely responses. Practical experiences, however, reveal the opposite, in which decisions to intervene in situations of potential violence are often subjected to concerns over group interests or sovereignty of states or are delayed due to uncertainties over who should actually respond and under what mandate. Most often, therefore, early warning does not necessarily produce "early responses." Instead, most challenges to early warning systems manifest through the failure to attract early responses to transform conditions that are predicted to lead to violence.

EWR can be conducted at local, national, and regional levels, and associated systems can be managed within or outside conflict areas. At each level, most systems use mixed methods of qualitative and quantitative research to forecast the possibility of violence or its escalation and to be able to focus responses toward preventing violence or its escalation, such as the Conflict Early Warning and Response Mechanism (CEWARN) (Christensen 2009)[2] and the Integrated Conflict and Early Warning System (ICEWS) (James, D'Orazio, and Schrodt 2011).[3] The methods are combined during information gathering and verification and the analyses of data. For example, ICEWS employs mathematical formulas to predict future situations of concern for early response.

This chapter examines experiences in EWR for the prevention of mass atrocities, to combat and contain atrocity crimes and genocide in the Great Lakes Region. Examples from Kenya, South Sudan, and the Democratic Republic of Congo (DRC) are discussed to explain successes and challenges for EWR systems. The term "system" is used here to refer to initiatives purposefully organized and maintained to collect relevant data, analyze and assess risks, and to share that information with recommendations on possible responses to the situation (Keyserlingk and Kopfmüller 2006). Although there is no comprehensive regional system with broader prevention aims, various EWR initiatives by intergovernmental bodies, business companies, and civil society organizations (CSOs) provide an understanding of regional- and national-level efforts that work toward the prevention of mass atrocities and genocide.

---

[2] Christensen H. Katja, "Conflict Early Warning and Response Mechanism in the Horn of Africa: IGAD as a Pioneer in Regional Conflict Prevention in Africa. A Field Study in Ethiopia" (October 2009), sponsored by the Swedish International Development Cooperation Agency in collaboration with the Department of Peace and Conflict Research at Uppsala University.

[3] James E. Yonamine, Vito D'Orazio, and Philip A. Schrodt, "Predicting Intra-State Conflict Onset: An Event Data Approach Using Euclidean and Levenshtein Distance Measures." Paper prepared for delivery at the Annual Meeting of the Midwest Political Science Association, Chicago, March 31–April 3, 2011.

19.3.   Great Lakes Region[4] Experiences: The International Conference on the Great Lakes Region and the Intergovernmental Authority on Development

The International Conference on the Great Lakes Region (ICGLR) Pact on Security, Stability, and Development in the Great Lakes Region (2006), as amended on November 24, 2012, after the Summit approved the application for membership by South Sudan, is composed of twelve core Member States. These are Angola, Burundi, Central African Republic (CAR), the Republic of Congo, the DRC, Kenya, Rwanda, South Sudan, Sudan, Tanzania, Uganda, and Zambia. Of these, four countries are also members of the Inter-Government Authority on Development (IGAD) that was established in 1996. They are Kenya, Sudan, Uganda and South Sudan, which was admitted in 2011. Other IGAD Member States include Djibouti, Eritrea, Ethiopia, and Somalia.

The East African Community (EAC)[5] is composed of Uganda, Kenya, Tanzania, Rwanda, and Burundi. South Sudan is about to be admitted into the Community, and its president has attended every meeting since the country gained independence. EAC has also drafted a protocol on EWR. The draft protocol aims to establish a mechanism to alert and develop responses within the EAC around interstate security issues, defense, pastoral conflicts, illegal trade, abuse of human rights, management of natural resources and the revenue generated from these, and aspects affecting economic relations between the Community's Member States. Although the draft outlines an institutional mechanism for EWR operations and implementation, it still has a long way to go before it is signed off as a binding document by the heads of state in the region.

Throughout the past fifty years, Member States of the ICGLR and IGAD region were constantly battered by violent conflicts, often mobilized along ethnic lines. The nature of these conflicts can be explained through colonial legacies, politics of exclusion, discrimination, economic disparities, and deprivation of freedoms. During this period, various communities committed genocides and mass atrocities among themselves, although there is a remarkable emerging commitment in working toward prevention activities. The agreements establishing IGAD and ICGLR indicate a common agenda to promote development, peace, and security in Member States, with approaches

---

[4] A region composed of Central and Eastern Africa states located around Lake Kivu, Lake Tanganyika, Lake Albert, Lake Nyasa, Lake Victoria, and Lake Turkana. San Tshiband, *Transnational Actors and the Conflicts in The Great Lakes Region of Africa* (2008), unpublished master's degree thesis, Department of Politics and International Relations, Lancaster University, UK.

[5] Workshop on Early Warning & Early Response Practice: Sharing the WANEP Experience & Strategy Planning. August 7–9, 2007. Accra, Ghana. Organized by the West Africa Network for Peacebuilding (WANEP) and the European Centre for Conflict Prevention/GPPAC Global Secretariat.

to conflict prevention and management that carry EWR mandates to terminate cycles of violence, genocide, and mass atrocities. Governments also recognize that the region's abundant wealth of natural and human resources is sufficient to spur regional development, but also that it remains unutilized or poorly managed because of "protracted conflicts" (Ramsbotham 2005).

However, over the years, the security and development agendas of the intergovernmental bodies have been fraught with practical concerns, and two perspectives stand out to suggest a very narrow approach taken by these bodies to deal with the complexity of violence and hostility in the region (Sandole 1999):

1. The pursuit of national or regional security has led to militarization of governance to maintain political regimes in power but is yet to produce conditions in which the right to life and conditions and opportunities to meet the needs and interests of individuals and communities are guaranteed and predictable.
2. Development is often pursued through corrupt approaches that discriminate along tribal lines or political orientation of the individual or group and not through merit and reward for hard work to improve the lives of all citizens.

These concerns continue to undermine peacebuilding and other efforts to intervene and stabilize the region.

The IGAD was established with a mandate to create an economic block to expand trade markets and to better organize resources for development in its Member States.[6] Under the agreement, some of the functions of the Council of Ministers, composed of representatives from all Ministries of Foreign Affairs, is prevention and management of conflicts that put a stop to development within and between Member States:[7]

1. Promotion of peace and security in the subregion and making recommendations to the IGAD Assembly.
2. Monitoring and enhancing humanitarian activities.
3. Following up on political and security affairs in the region, including conflict prevention, management, and resolution, as well as postconflict peacebuilding.

Under the IGAD Protocol on the establishment of a Conflict Early Warning and Response Mechanism (CEWARN) (2012),[8] a system was created to operate at both regional and national levels. A Council of Ministers head IGAD, and the CEWARN Unit is its technical arm and Secretariat. Under the

---

[6] Agreement Establishing the Inter-Government Authority on Development (IGAD). IGAD/SUM-96/AGRE. Nairobi, March 21, 1996.
[7] Article 10. Follow-up political and security affairs include conflict prevention, management, and resolution, as well as postconflict peace building.
[8] http://cewarn.org/attachments/article/58/The%20CEWARN%20Protocol.pdf

Secretariat, National Conflict Early Warning and Response Mechanisms (CEWERUs) were established at a country level in Member States, each consisting of a steering committee, a focal point, and local committees. Each CEWERU collaborates with civil society organizations to collect information at all levels up to the grassroots, undertake preliminary analysis for early warning, recommend response strategies for early response, and communicate to decision makers. According to the Protocol, information collected and shared through this process should be concerned with livestock rustling, conflicts over grazing land and water points, smuggling and illegal trade, nomadic movements, refugees, landmines, and banditry. To this end, IGAD has the most well-developed and functional EWR system, although it was designed to handle mostly land and pastoral conflicts in the Horn of Africa.

A report evaluating CEWARN in 2007–11 (Kassa 2011) states that the system "successfully developed a primary source of early warning information and data base that has been replicated by the African Union (AU)'s Continental Early Warning System (CEWS) and the Regional Economic Communities (RECs)." This success was built through twenty capacity-building and conflict intervention projects implemented by CEWARN during this time. Of these, three were conducted in Uganda, eight in Ethiopia, one in Djibouti, and eight in Kenya. However, successful collection and sharing of information did not generate timely and adequate responses that worked toward preventing the escalation of conflicts in the region. The report also observed that "although there has been some effort by Member States to mitigate the cross-border conflicts, the response structures have been weak and lacked a well designed system linking cross-border efforts and local actors. As a result the responses to the early warning information have been largely disjointed, uncoordinated and ineffective." From this perspective, the CEWARN system is inadequate to deliver effective prevention of genocide and mass atrocity.

The ICGLR was formed to respond to the transnational impact of the Rwanda Genocide of 1994 and other conflicts in the region on communities and governments beyond the IGAD region. Heads of State from the eleven most affected countries signed the Pact on Security, Stability, and Development in the Great Lakes Region in 2006.[9] Concerning the mandate to implement EWR specifically in the prevention of mass atrocities, as defined in Article 2 of the United Nations Convention, CEWARNs' mandate is lacking. The ICGLR protocol presents a more purposeful mandate consistent with the work of the UN, even including references to the Responsibility to Protect (R2P). It also opens a unique opportunity for prevention based on the political will expressed by heads of Member States through the signing of a legally binding pact. The

[9] www.internal-displacement.org/8025708F004BE3B1/%28httpInfoFiles%29/60ECE277A8ED A2DDC12572FB002BBDA7/$file/Great%20Lakes%20pact_en.pdf.

stress on the political will to act was reaffirmed by Decision 37 at the 5th Joint Summit of Heads of State and Government of the ICGLR on January 15, 2014.[10] The Regional Committee was henceforth mandated to undertake audits in South Sudan[11] and CAR[12] and report as soon as possible.

The Protocol on Prevention and the Punishment of the Crime of Genocide, War Crimes and Crimes against Humanity, and All Forms of Discrimination is one of the ten protocols in the Pact. Comparable to the Council of Ministers under the IGAD agreement, the Protocol establishes a Regional Committee with twelve members, from the twelve ICGLR Member States. Article 38 of the protocol outlines a number of functions for the Regional and National Committees that also contain early warning responsibilities, whereas the Summit, composed of all heads of state and governments, retained the early response responsibilities as the supreme decision-making organ of the ICGLR. The functions of the committees are to:

1. Regularly review situations in each Member State.
2. Collect and analyze information.
3. Alert the Summit of the Conference in due time to take urgent measures to prevent potential crimes.
4. Suggest specific measures to effectively fight impunity for these crimes.
5. Contribute to raising awareness and education on peace and reconciliation through regional and national programs.
6. Recommend policies and measures to guarantee the rights of victims.
7. Monitor, where applicable, national programs on Disarmament, Demobilization, Rehabilitation, Repatriation, and Reinstallation (DDRRR).

To implement this mandate at national and community levels in each Member State, National Committees are currently being established country by country. The membership of each committee includes government officials, academics, and civil society representatives. Of the twelve ICGLR Member States, Tanzania, Kenya, Uganda, Zambia, the Republic of Congo, and South Sudan have formed and operationalized National Committees to implement the Protocol by initiating and implementing national and grassroots programs for

---

[10] Declaration by Heads of State and Governments of the International Conference on the Great Lakes Region on the Promotion of Peace, Stability and Development in the Great Lakes Region. 5th Ordinary Summit of Heads of State and Government. Luanda, Angola (January 15, 2014), http://ikazeiwacu.unblog.fr/files/2014/01/200038991-joint-communique-of-the-declaration-of-the-summit-of-heads-of-state-and-government-of-the-international-conference-on-the-great-lakes-region-icglr-o.pdf

[11] Daniel Sullivan, "Not on the Agenda: The Humanitarian Crisis on the Two Year Anniversary of South Sudan's Referendum" (January 9, 2013), http://endgenocide.org/not-on-the-agenda-on-the-two-year-anniversary-of-south-sudans-referendum/

[12] Tom Watkins, "Humanitarian Groups: Don't Let CAR Devolve into Genocide" (May 1, 2014), http://edition.cnn.com/2014/05/01/world/africa/central-african-republic/

the prevention and punishment of genocide and mass atrocities. Rwanda established a Genocide Commission prior to the Protocol, and this is the body through which the Protocol can be implemented at the national and local levels. The ICGLR Secretariat hopes that, by the end of 2014, all the remaining states will have formed national committees to conduct and synergize various regional and local programs and projects.[13] Numerous operational and capacity challenges notwithstanding, the emerging structures enjoy a more precise mandate to provide EWR for the prevention and punishment of genocide, crimes against humanity, and mass atrocities.

However, as Wulf and Debiel (2009) observe, "regional organizations often fail to respond in time to prevent violent conflict not because of a lack of information on an emerging conflict but due to several barriers or weaknesses, namely the political differences and lack of common values within organizations, the hesitation to overrule the principle of non-interference in internal matters of the state, the lack of capacity to intervene, and the unclear and competitive mission and geographic reach of regional organizations. " Because of all these reasons, no direct engagement has been made by the Regional and National Committees to operationalize their mandate and intervene in situations taking place in the DRC, CAR, South Sudan, Burundi, and other Member States despite demands raised especially by the ICGLR partners (e.g., the AU and Office of the Special Adviser on Prevention of Genocide).

Currently, in South Sudan, competing missions and obligations of IGAD and ICGLR could undermine EWR possibilities. Decision processes are not clear as to how, for example, one of the organizations can intervene in a conflict when the affected country is a member of both organizations. In the case of the ongoing IGAD-mediated peace talks in Addis Ababa to end the fighting South Sudan and to implement the Secession of Hostilities Agreement[14], ICGLR's path to also fulfill its obligations remains unclear, particularly since the ICGLL Regional Committee of Genocide Prevention is mandated to conduct country assessments and recommend corrective actions that the Summit can take. On the other hand, it can be argued that the ICGLR has been consistent in its involvement in the conflict between the DRC government and M23 rebel group because its mandate was clear in terms of the obligation to engage with parties, given that the DRC is not a member of IGAD.

The lack of capacity, in terms of knowledge, skills, resources, and experience to intervene in such delicate situations and to handle the sensitive issue of genocide and mass atrocities, also remains a challenge. Members of ICLGR

---

[13] The 4th Ordinary Meeting of the ICGLR Regional Committee for the Prevention of Genocide. Kampala, Uganda. October 18–19, 2012.

[14] "South Sudan Action Network on Small Arms (SSANSA) Welcomes Secession of Hostilities Agreement in South Sudan," https://groups.google.com/forum/#!msg/wanabidii/klYKUoOn MXg/HErTaplGn6QJ

structures are not subject experts on the prevention of mass atrocities – the structures are themselves new, and there are no structures allowing for lessons to be learned at either regional or national levels. In the case of CEWARN, IGAD established the Rapid Response Fund to strengthen the rapid response capacity of the early response mechanisms by making resources readily available to address pastoral and related conflicts at the local, national, and cross-border/regional levels in the region.[15] In the case of ICGLR, the protocol is also clear that national governments are to fund the work of the Regional Committee,[16] which includes National Committees. However, all funding is currently obtained from organizations partnering with the committees because line ministries have not created relevant budget lines for them, with the exception of Tanzania. Some of the key partners include the Office of the Special Adviser on Prevention of Genocide (OSAPG), the Office of the High Commissioner for Human Rights (OHCHR), the Auschwitz Institute for Peace and Reconciliation, and the George Mason University Genocide Prevention Program.

EWR processes require tailored and professional skills to produce convincing reports that attract relevant interventions, especially at governmental and intergovernmental levels. ICGLR structures still lack skills in facilitating discussions about possible threats, operating a data collection and verification system, processing and analyzing information, report writing to communicate early warnings, and mapping developments and circumstances that could increase the risk of genocide and mass atrocity crimes. The skills and associated processes are also key to developing relevant responses; monitoring and evaluation to, for example, determine effectiveness prevention initiatives; or mobilization and application of the necessary resources to support these activities. The OSAPG[17] and the OHCHR have supported and conducted a series of training seminars for the Regional and National Committees on understanding the process of genocide and the OSAPG's Framework for Early Warning for the Prevention of Genocide and Mass Atrocities. Other activities supported by partners included, *inter alia*, developing the structure and functions of committees, developing terms of reference and rules of procedure, and country visits to provide technical support to National Committees in developing and implementing local programs.

---

[15] "The Regional Steering Committee of CEWARN's Rapid Response Fund (RRF) Convenes to Review Local-Level Peace Building Projects," www.cewarn.org/index.php?option=com_con tent&view=article&id=188:the-regional-steering-committee-of-cewarns-rapid-response-fund-rrf-convenes-to-review-local-level-peace-building-projects&catid=1:latest-news&Itemid=82

[16] Article 26 (2) "Member States shall provide the Committee with sufficient resources to carry out its work effectively."

[17] "Supporting Genocide Prevention in East Africa: The GP Project," http://ac4.ei.columbia.edu /2012/03/01/supporting-genocide-prevention-in-east-africa-the-gpp-project/

Beyond the skills gap, the structures are yet to develop country plans with relevant indicators for EWR at national and communal levels that can assess country situations effectively and, accordingly, report and make recommendations to the Summit, as required by the Protocol. Until now, there are almost no efforts working toward interaction between the structures and communities in terms of information collection, analysis, and dissemination that can determine readiness for prevention or responses to indicators and threats of genocide and mass atrocities.

19.4.   Country-Level Experiences

Competition for power and control of the same local resources and other local disputes between families, local leaders, or their communities underlie a number of conflicts that occur at the communal level in the Great Lakes Region. At this level, issues are often framed as existential and shared experiences across groups, where any form of inequality or injustice is perceived to threaten culture, religion, identity, and the recognition and security of individuals or their community (Burton 1993). Unfortunately, with CEWARN focusing mostly on land and pastoral conflicts and ICGLR still in the formative stages of what promises to become a regional EWR system, many conflicts do not receive due attention, particularly by the state, because of lack of capacity for effective early warning. Yet, in the context of EWR, Bates (2008) and Scott (1985) have argued that these forms of interactions and hostilities between groups contain patterns of resistance that characterize various social conflicts and disclose the culture, depict purposes, and reveal points of friction, intentions, and values that condition mobilization and readiness to fight. During EWR, such elements can help to predict and explain possible eruptions or escalation of hostilities into mass violence. One example of this is when language and behaviors are constructed for purposes of differentiation and exclusion of the "Other" from the group (Horowitz 1985). Such a condition can be aggravated and nationalized by leaders with political differences or ambitions who mobilize communities in their constituencies to win elections or instigate insurgence activities to gain political power. Examples of EWR initiatives in Kenya, the DRC, and South Sudan are discussed here to highlight experiences and challenges and to form a basis for the recommendations provided at the end of the chapter.

19.4.1.   Kenya

The most recent successful experience in translating early warning into early response to prevent violence in the Great Lakes Region can be discussed by comparing the 2008 postelection violence and the 2013 peaceful elections in

Kenya. Admittedly, prior to this experience, Kenya had a longer EWR history with regard to land and pastoral conflicts. For example, the Livestock Information Network and Knowledge System (LINKS), established by the Global Livestock CRSP Livestock Early Warning System, collaborated with the Famine Early Warning Systems Network (FEWS NET) to provide early warning on forage and drought conditions to help livestock keepers cope with drought. Another example is the Arid Lands Resource Management Project (ALRMP), which also provides early warning services aimed at mitigating the risk posed by arid conditions through strengthening management of natural resources during drought.[18]

According to the International Criminal Court (ICC), the devastating effects from the 2008 postelections violence included the commission of mass atrocities and crimes against humanity (Halakhe 2013). Babaud and Ndung'u (2012) have argued that experiences from the 2008 postelections informed, among others, EWR initiatives that contributed to violence-free 2013 elections in Kenya. Kenya also adopted devolution structures that distribute power and resources to broader levels of society, thus seeking to dismantle political units that developed in ethnically dominated constituencies and reduce the problem of elite ethnic mobilization characterized by stereotyping and hate speech between tribes. Other initiatives included:

1. Dealing with the question of local impunity in the face of indictment from the ICC through local tribunals
2. Reforms to improve the rule of law within the police and justice sectors
3. Neutralization of criminal gangs that terrorize opponents of their candidates
4. Security-sector reforms
5. Resolving enduring community grievances over the distribution and ownership of land and other local resources (Human Rights Watch 2013)

The following two EWR examples explain how technological innovation, along with corporate, national, and grassroots practices, produced multilevel and multidimensional approaches that contributed to more peaceful elections. The initiatives were collaborated on early enough among government institutions, business corporations, humanitarian agencies, civil society groups, and technology companies to generate timely responses to prevent a recurrence of the 2008 postelection violence.

As a first example, Dirosa (2013) describes innovative technological platforms, such as Ushahidi's crisis-mapping technologies, that were utilized to monitor Short Message Service (SMS) messages for hate speech, corruption, voter suppression, and other indicators of possible violence. The reports that

---

[18] Report on the Workshop on Early Warning Systems in Kenya. Africa Advanced Level Telecommunications Institute, Nairobi, Kenya. October 4, 2006.

were generated were used by government agencies and civil society to support conflict prevention practices and interventions, particularly at the grassroots level. This was consistent with Anderson's (2001) view that, "ultimately, solutions to violence are found at the local level, and strengthening initiatives at the local level must be done in order to prevent the outbreak of violence." Dirosa also reports that, in the Kenyan Rift Valley area, the Local Empowerment for Peace (LEAP) coordinated an EWR system through 600 trained peace monitors. These worked with civil society organizations, the police, and local government officials to observe, alert, and generate early responses to indications of violence. Coordination was conducted through two Early Warning Hubs designed to analyze and respond to cell phone and other forms of alerts from peace monitors. Analysis was done in partnership with various civil society organizations, including Mercy Corps.

As a second example, Safaricom worked with the Communications Commission of Kenya (CCK) to develop its own code of conduct in vetting bulk SMS content that political parties, politicians, and aspirants wished to send in the run-up to the 2013 elections. This followed a case study on the 2013 Kenyan presidential elections on corporate responses to hate speech.[19] The study concluded that lack of data on hate speech and other indicators in 2007 hindered any possible efforts that would have helped prevent violence. Safaricom scrutinized the language used in campaigns by politicians, political parties, and aspirants during 2012–13 to prevent divisive messages reaching grassroots communities. The study concluded that although hate speech did not disappear from public rhetoric, it was not disseminated through SMS messages, and it found a new home on the web. This was contrary to the negative role the media largely played during the 2008 postelectoral violence in Kenya.[20] This time around, media outlets and stations largely broadcast positive messages of peace, and commercial and government-run stations were deeply involved in educating voters on the issues, focusing on civic education, preaching restraint and tolerance, and avoiding any and all political incitement.

However, successful early responses that contributed to prevent electoral violence in 2013 should not be understood to have addressed or resolved the underlying grievances that fueled the escalation of claims of irregularities in the 2008 election and caused the descent into violence. Oucho (2011) argues that "simply dangled ethnic violence by both Kenyan and international media, the violence that almost brought Kenya to a standstill after the 2007 general

---

[19] "Corporate Responses to Hate Speech in the 2013 Kenyan Presidential Elections," Case Study Number 1 (November 2013). Institute for Human Rights and Business, London.

[20] Maureen Syallow, "Media Played a Major Role in the 2007/2008 Post Elections Violence in Kenya," http://maureensyallow.hubpages.com/hub/Media-Played-a-major-Role-in-the-20072008-Post-Elections-Violence-in-Kenya

election is a manifestation of longstanding issues which the country previously paid little attention to, and which it must address to avoid their recurrence and undesirable repercussions in future." As Oucho further explains, the issues in this long-term agenda concern the long-standing disparities in resource allocation for development across regions, access to and ownership of land, historical political grievances, and enduring cultural stereotypes that spur ethnic differentiation and animosity. These issues persist as warning signs that have constantly generated hostilities and violence in the country since Kenya's independence in 1963. According to Human Rights Watch (2013), the country continues to have trouble grappling with appropriate responses to these enduring problems. Accordingly, the Initiative for Peacebuilding recommended that, "effective early warning models in Kenya should contribute to building long-term peace and reinforcing state-society relations" (Babaud and Ndung'u 2012).

19.4.2. Democratic Republic of the Congo

The DRC's seemingly never-ending instability has been referred to as "The World's Worst War" (Gettleman 2012) and "Africa's World War" (Prinier 2009),[21] particularly given that it managed to draw all nine nations that border the country into the conflict as supporters of either government forces or rebels (the countries are Angola, Burundi, CAR, Republic of the Congo, Rwanda, Sudan, Tanzania, Uganda, and Zambia). With almost 5 million deaths from violence, poverty, and disease since the 1994 Rwanda Genocide – when Hutu refugees flooded the Eastern part of the DRC – efforts working toward EWR and prevention of mass atrocities have not yielded any noticeable success. Two attempts to provide EWR will be discussed to highlight experiences from the DRC. Both examples are explained from a civil society perspective because there are no national-level initiatives in place for EWR.

The first example is an initiative of the American Bar Association (ABR), the ABR Rule of Law Initiative (ABA ROLI). ABA ROLI, through its community-based network of legal service providers, operates an early warning system aimed at combating gender-based violence, especially in the North and South Kivu provinces of Eastern DRC.[22] The system, among its other aims, collects and shares information that would help interrupt the practice of using rape and similar practices as weapons of war by armed groups and individuals from the Congolese national army, the police, and civilians. In 2012 and 2013, ABA ROLI monitoring

---

[21] Gerald Prinier, *Africa's World War: Congo, the Rwandan Genocide, and the Making of a Continental Catastrophe* (New York: Oxford University Press, 2009).

[22] "Combating the Rape Crisis in Eastern Democratic Republic of Congo" (May 2009), www .americanbar.org/advocacy/rule_of_law/where_we_work/africa/democratic_republic_congo /news/news_drc_combating_the_rape_crisis_0509.html

teams reported to the government about planned attacks in the villages of Borobo and Buabo by the Mai Mai and Nyatura rebels, respectively. In both cases, according to the ABR (2013), Congolese armed forces were deployed early enough to provide safe passage to fleeing residents and were also able to protect the villages and force the rebels to withdraw their armies.

As a second example, the nongovernmental organization Invisible Children operated an Early Warning Radio Network in the DRC and CAR (Moore 2011). The organization operates a high-frequency radio notification and response system to deliver long-distance radio messages twice daily to areas at risk of possible attacks, especially in Rwanda Liberation Army (LRA)-affected remote locations, towns, and villages. The network connected communities with one another to share information and develop local responses that limited the LRA's ability to covertly commit mass atrocities without local actors being aware of what is going on. The system managed to prevent a repeat of what occurred in 2009 during the Makombo Christmas massacre, when the LRA troops killed more than 345 and abducted at least 250 civilians.

In spite of these successes, Githaiga (2011) observes that despite early warning signs of escalating tensions over allegations of electoral fraud following the November 2011 presidential and parliamentary elections, such systems failed to attract any early response to prevent the violence that followed. Instead, as Githaiga further noted, "the violence put into question the capacity of all stakeholders to translate early warning into early response to prevent violent conflict." Although the violence indicated weaknesses in the influence and strength of the mandate of systems like the Early Warning Radio Network and ABA ROLI, failure to translate early warning into early response was largely manifested among state leaders and political actors who instead instigated violence through extreme political views, claims of electoral fraud, and demands to invalidate the results.

Worse still, the tensions and hostilities explained here had already been predicted (Gettleman 2011) to be the tipping point for political instability and communal and state-based violence in the DRC. Political grievances that were carried over from the contentious 2006 elections, which many in the opposition boycotted, and the atrocities committed by armed groups from Uganda, Rwanda, and Tanzania within the DRC, continued through the 2011 elections. A number of Congolese within the DRC, in addition to those in Belgium, South Africa, and France, demonstrated their displeasure over a possible victory by the incumbent, Joseph Kabila. This occurred many months before the elections and also during the week running up to announcing the eventual winner. For example, the Institute for Security Studies (2011) in Nairobi warned before the elections that "with the existing tension, it is highly probable that at least in some parts of the country the announcement of the results will spark more public demonstrations." Although these and other conditions indicated the possibility for postelectoral violence – not the least of which being the mobilization of communities to take the law into their own hands in order to protect themselves and their interests – there were no appropriate responses to prevent the violence that followed.

The heavy-handedness of the security sector in responding to collective action from groups of disgruntled voters inspired by reports and statements from the opposition and international observers about electoral fraud contained signs of violence that were ignored by all parties. For example, opposition leader Etienne Tshisekedi announced himself as the winner of the November 2011 elections and asked his supporters not to accept any other outcome. This was before the Independent National Electoral Commission (CENI) released the official results. Although the AU, the ICGLR, and the UN Stabilization Mission in Congo (MONUSCO) called for pacifying measures, the calls were short of the required mandate and political authority to effectively prevent the violence.

Indiscriminate political and economic disparities across the country, poor social service infrastructure, and high levels of poverty and unemployment despite plentiful natural resources further complicated any possible translation of EWR into effective prevention. According to the World Bank[23], 71 percent of the 65.7 million people in the DRC live below the national poverty line, despite huge natural reserves of copper, timber, diamond, colton, tin, gold, and zinc. Ideally, the failure of EWR to prevent mass atrocities in the DRC cannot be explained by a lack of resources, but rather by the activities of self-seeking political entrepreneurs and illegal exploiters. Grievances during elections were therefore symptomatic of a larger systemic problem with governance in the DRC, and the violence was an escalation of enduring grievances among citizens over economic and political conditions worsened by the lack of promise from the electoral process that it was working toward improvement.

In the DRC, therefore, practical use of EWR does not fail due to lack of resources or timely information on threats and indicators for violence but because of the absence of political will from government, weaknesses in structure and enforcement of mandates among international organizations, and the inability of civil society organizations to effectively advocate for appropriate response options concerning prevention. Kron and Gettleman (2010)[24] reported that on July 30, 2010, the UN peacekeeping mission in the DRC was warned about an invasion and possible rape crimes by the Democratic Forces for the Liberation of Rwanda (FDLR) in the town of

---

[23] https://www.cia.gov/library/publications/the-world-factbook/fields/2046.html
[24] Josh Kron and Jeffrey Gettleman, "U.N. E-Mail Shows Early Warning of Congo Rapes" (August 31, 2010), www.nytimes.com/2010/09/01/world/africa/01congoweb.html?_r=3&ref=global-home&

Mpofi. Despite it being one of the largest UN peacekeeping missions in the world (costing more than $1 billion per year), the UN peacekeepers only responded on August 2, 2010. This was after a delay of three days, during which at least 179 women were raped and many civilians were killed.

19.4.3. South Sudan

The civil strife taking place in South Sudan since December 2013 is based on a continuation of very salient features that have long presented early warning signs of violence but did not attract viable responses from the state, regional organizations, or local actors. These include ethnicization of the national army, corruption, mismanagement of oil revenues, nepotism, abject poverty, illiteracy, contradictions in the 2011 Transitional Constitution, and transgenerational ethnic differentiation along tribal lines in competition for power and control of local resources like grazing land. Although these causes and drivers of the conflict existed before the country gained independence, the 2005 Comprehensive Peace Agreement (CPA) that contained South Sudan's road map to independence was silent about how they would be managed in the new nation. Currently, most of these same conditions seem to be missing from the agenda of the ongoing IGAD-led peace process in Addis Ababa.

At the national level, attempts at EWR started in March 2013, when the government adopted IGAD's Conflict Early Warning and Response Mechanism (CEWARM) under the South Sudan Peace and Reconciliation Commission (SSPRC). The decision was taken as part of the commission's seven-year strategy (2012–19) to help the government of South Sudan detect and respond to internal conflicts. This was after similar efforts had been tested at the local level since 2009 in the counties of South Kapoeta, North Kapoeta, Narus, Budi, and Ikwotos in the Eastern Equatorial state. Although CEWARN is designed to respond to land and pastoral conflicts in IGAD Member States, its former Vice President, Dr. Riek Machar, observed while launching the system that it was to provide "a new approach to governance in relation to conflict prevention"; particularly, he added, because the country "continued to grapple with multiple internal and regional security challenges which necessitate a nation-wide capacity to anticipate, and act pro-actively to prevent violent conflicts" (Uma 2012). Recognizing that the country is bordered by unstable states (i.e., CAR, DRC, Kenya, Sudan, and Uganda), the commission's approach was to expand on the geographical areas of reporting beyond the five counties mentioned earlier, to also include these five bordering states over issues of land and territorial-related disputes.

In May 2013, President Salva Kiir also established the National Committee on Reconciliation (NCR) chaired by Archbishop Daniel Deng Bul, predominantly composed of religious leaders.[25] The committee sought to consolidate all ongoing processes, including the work of the SSPRC, into a national reconciliation agenda to be managed at one central point. The functions included adopting a road map for national reconciliation; mapping conflicts, their causes, and drivers in all counties of South Sudan; and training peace mobilizers from all states. While launching the committee, the president recognized the divisive and devastating effects of the long civil war and the complex relationships between factors and actors in the country's conflicts that were affecting peace and stability. With all national processes managed under one roof, the government expected to be able to monitor how conflicts and processes evolve, identify the root causes and drivers in each situation, and direct responses toward reconciliation efforts at community, county, and state levels.

However, inadequate resources and overwhelmingly poor communications and other infrastructures and facilities constantly troubled the SSPRC and NRC in executing their mandates[26]. Allegations of a close allegiance to the central government[27] cast a shadow of doubt on both of these entities' activities, causing suspicion among the public and generating perceptions of political bias regarding their work. For example, in the Jonglei state, members of the Murle tribe accused the NRC of siding with the native Dinka tribe during the peacebuilding exercise. Despite signing the May 2012 peace agreement, peace broke down shortly afterward, and communal violence increased over cattle and land disputes. While launching the NRC, the president emphasized the pursuit of reconciliation at all levels to avoid the high costs involved in trying to recover from violent conflicts.

However, the SSPRC and NRC lacked the mandate and capacity to predict that this same president would fire his own vice-president over their efforts to develop strategies to prevent the violence that followed. This experience is consistent with Diaz and Sunita's (2012) conclusion reached after analyzing gender-sensitive early warning. The writers concluded that "one of the many challenges of early warning as a tool is that our ability to anticipate impending mass atrocities in a defined timeframe and context is more limited than our ability to identify populations, communities, or countries at risk over a longer period of time. Proximate and immediate causes are more unique to a particular situation, and more random in nature, than the typical set of factors or preconditions of instability that we encounter in most indices, rendering them tentative and diminishing their predictive power." In the same way, in South

---

[25] "South Sudan's Newly Appointed National Reconciliation Committee Takes Over," JUBA (May 5, 2013), www.sudantribune.com/spip.php?article46472
[26] Ibid.   [27] Ibid.

Sudan, despite the mandate of the SSPRC and NRC, no EWR system predicted the decision that the president was to take and the level of violence it produced.

On the other hand, warnings of the causes and drivers of the ongoing violence had been given in a study conducted by Partners in Development (Kuch and Ayul 2012) to guide the activities of the CEWARN in South Sudan. The study analyzed linkages, causes, drivers, and perpetrators of violent conflicts and examined the structural context of the conflicts in the country. The report warned of a number of threats to stability in the country, including patterns of destabilization and militarization from incursions between Sudan Armed Forces (SAF) and opposition armed groups, which were mostly tribal based. In addition, cattle rustling within and across international borders, climate change, intertribal and intercommunal conflicts over land and water, inadequate political representation, poor socioeconomic conditions, and weak state institutions all combined to generate hostility and drove people take up arms to improve their conditions.

19.5.   Recommendations

The preceding discussion highlights significant regional and country-level EWR initiatives that have produced minimal successes in states of the Great Lakes Region. Shortcomings include the failure of these initiatives to contribute information that would work toward preventing conflicts against vast political odds, plus capacity and resource gaps that constrained the generation and communication of warnings. That said, progress is being made in the region to develop and implement EWRs through local and regional initiatives that promote local responsibility and ownership through community participation. This is consistent with recommendations from a report from a global survey on early warning systems (United Nations 2006). The report observed that, to be effective, the systems must be people-centered and must integrate knowledge of the risks faced at the local level, provide technical monitoring and warning service, disseminate meaningful warnings to those at risk, and ensure public awareness and preparedness to act.

The following recommendations are consistent with these views and aim to increase attention to and gains from the EWR initiatives by increasing knowledge about and better application of associated mechanisms in the Great Lakes Region. The focus here is on increasing advocacy, strengthening the institutional linkages and the capacity of actors in ERW systems, improving resource mobilization, and fostering the domestication of international instruments and protocols as necessary steps toward developing effective EWR systems for the Great Lakes Region. Despite challenges that may persist, such as the ethnicization of politics and resource distribution, the recommendations raise the possibility of knowing when situations will lead to violence and how this violence can be prevented. The goal is to achieve timely dissemination of information and improve the preparedness of decision makers to understand warnings and adopt responses for the prevention of genocide and mass atrocity crimes in the Great Lakes Region of Africa.

19.5.1. Increased Advocacy

Intensive local and international advocacy is required to reach out to stakeholders to gain sufficient buy-in from them, and to encourage ICGLR heads of state to act more proactively to invest time, resources, and their political capital in EWR. Once this has been achieved, advocacy can then address the challenge of developing tailored EWR as a necessary process in preventing and managing conflicts in the region.

The earlier discussion on the state of EWR in the Great Lakes Region outlines the contributing factors to the challenge this recommendation is meant to tackle. These factors include the "reactionary culture" that persists within governments that only thinks of early warning after conflicts have already escalated, the lack of adequate resources, and the insufficient empirical evidence for effectiveness of EWR. A reactive approach has thus far produced poor early warning in the Great Lakes Region, thus making implementation of early response for prevention difficult. Legacies of violence are inadequately addressed due to lack of or poor early warning, and victim communities are stuck between working tirelessly to rebuild their lives and healing from past atrocities.

EWR is not very fashionable, especially among politicians, because of the technical nature of the elements involved, which require lots of time before the system produces tangible results. Recommendations may not produce immediate political gains for leaders who, for example, may be targeting winning the next election. This fact notwithstanding, advocates of EWR should avoid focusing on delivering short-term and immediate gains for politicians and instead work on building trust with actors at all levels in the system to share information and analysis. This will build confidence in EWR systems, information sources, and response decisions among various actors and will particularly stress the fact that the system is not functioning to serve political agendas but the collective needs and interests of all people. For example, trust by government and international actors is necessary for the development of policies and allocation of resources to build the capacity to manage and facilitate effective EWR systems. Persistent experiences of impunity, corruption, and violence in the Great Lakes Region undermine trust building for EWR, especially among victim communities and among organizations with similar initiatives for vulnerable sectors of the population (i.e., among women and children).

Advocacy for EWR must also speak to the realities of states, communities, victims, and also perpetrators in vulnerable and postconflict environments. There ought to be evidence of immediate and long-term incentives (e.g., creating a peaceful public market as a strategic investment), trust in information-gathering processes (protection for sources, focal points, and target groups), trust in government, trust in international and local organizations, and enhanced trust in institutions for effective response. In the latter case, this can take the form of community members observing effective response from those with the capacity to intervene and/or prevent. International actors should increase their focus on the local level because this is where information is generated and effective response is needed.

19.5.2. Strengthening the Capacity of Key Actors

Key actors in EWR can vary from one context to another, and each system may require unique competencies. Strengthening the operational capacity of such actors to function effectively in their own circumstances can improve the warning and responsive quality of systems developed for particular situations. This also involves conducting deep and comprehensive analyses of country situations and having the ability to effectively communicate findings to relevant decision makers involved in early response. In the Great Lakes Region, for instance, cultural and religious leaders, local governments, CSOs, and community-based organizations (CBOs) are well placed to collaborate with ICGLR structures to deliver appropriate early warning that can attract the right early response. Increasing the capacities of such stakeholders, along with policymakers, military, police, intelligence services, and formal justice systems, will inevitably help the region reap the benefits of EWR. Building the capacity of such actors to participate in data gathering and analysis and the sharing of early warning information can also expand the scope of the system and open more opportunities to implement relevant responses. In this way, strengthening measures should also include regularly updating the systems so that they remain responsive to changing social, political, and economic experiences related to violence and creating linkages with sets of responses determined by various initiatives in the conflict area.

Capacity building in this case involves skills training and exposure to practical experiences for key local actors to tailor processes and elements of EWR to conditions pertinent to the region. This approach will also improve steps already taken by states and CSOs that currently continue to fall short of effective implementation and generate appropriate options to respond to identified threats. The capacity of local actors can determine the difference between success or failure of EWR because they understand their environments far better than any international actor or those at the national level. System experts should be the ones to determine how local actors in communities can better locate where to gather information. Babaud and Ndung'u (2012) also concluded during the Kenya case study that one way to address conflict dynamics is by empowering people to identify their own security issues and to address them through community security projects. To be effective in this approach, local actors in communities need to believe in the utility of EWR, which reinforces their confidence in the system and allows them to participate more efficiently. Because most focal points or information providers at local levels are volunteers, their efforts and the risks associated with their roles must be offset by tangible and immediate improvements in how they deal with the various situations in which they find themselves. Efforts to this end should also:

1. Provide guidelines for information collection, its management, and preliminary analysis in a format and language that local people understand
2. Clearly frame EWR objectives and practices in ways that are identifiable with local conditions so that, in turn, local actors can identify with the rationale and add value to processes and activities working toward the goal the system seeks to achieve
3. Aim to create a shared language, understanding, and ability to define threats in ways so that actors at all levels of the EWR system understand the implications of the failure to report and respond appropriately
4. Ensure that clear management systems and instructions are conflict-sensitive among operators of the system at all levels
5. Improve neutrality during collection, analysis, and reporting activities

19.5.3. Creating Awareness

Creating awareness is a complex equation in the context of EWR. As a result of years of violent conflict, there is an explicit level of mistrust at local, national, and regional levels. Governments and civil society are capable of preventing mass atrocities, but this requires that a variety of sources gather information through various locally developed checks and balances to ensure that it is verified and can inform possible responses. In this way, the indicators of broader prevention systems will not be perceived as impositions on one's way of life, and local focal points will ideally be known by communities for the important work they do to minimize potential threats to individuals, groups, and the state as a whole. Therefore, how we create awareness is tantamount to the success of an EWR system. It is recommended that awareness be raised about how EWR systems function in respective contexts and as frameworks for effective response to threats to local peace without compromising the confidential quality of the systems because focal points may become the target of the acts they are working to prevent.

19.5.4. Institutional Linkages

Strengthening institutional linkages is crucial for effective EWR. There are many different actors gathering information and responding to specific issues of concern (e.g., CEWARN on land and pastoral disputes, Invisible Children on sexual and gender-based violence, and the ICGLR on genocide, mass atrocities, and crimes against humanity). These systems are relevant to and fit within the broader prevention agenda. Consolidating and sharing gathered information will deepen the knowledge base to guide policymaking, program development, and implementation at regional, national, and local levels.

Development of policies in this case involves determining who and defining how to respond to specific situations of concern, which in turn will also help to avoid a duplication of efforts, provide suitable responses to particular indicators and/or triggers, and synergize and reinforce mass atrocity prevention as a collective agenda in the region. Toward this synergy, it is recommended that the following areas be strengthened:

1. The maintenance of three-way information sharing and feedback systems involving local, national, and international actors
2. Collaboration of analyses and responses to capture all levels and dimensions of conflict situations
3. Sufficient facilitation to ensure that early warning processes are satisfactorily concluded and that early response activities are concluded and duly evaluated to determine their effectiveness

19.5.5. Resource Mobilization

Governments and international and local donors must take a step back and restructure their priorities. Prevention has been found to be cheaper than intervention in terms of cost, is capable of producing enduring solutions, and is more manageable especially when responses are implemented under low-intensity conditions during conflict situations. There is, therefore, important to interest EWR resource providers to allocate to these systems the necessary resources for achieving such gains *before* situations escalate beyond what early response can achieve. Bellamy (2011) also recommends that early warning analysis pay due attention to the circumstances that give rise to peacetime atrocities and not fixate on armed conflict. Because many of the EWR systems in the Great Lakes Region are built on the cooperation and goodwill of local volunteers, the costs associated with information gathering and early warning are much less than those for early response. As such, resource providers should increase financial support to early warning to benefit from the low costs of prevention, as opposed to the high costs of intervention to stop already occurring violence. This may involve building incentive structures and options in funding for governments and civil society with the goal of investing more time and effort on early warning, with requirements that all response options should carry strong early warning agendas to avoid recurrence.

19.5.6. Domestication of International Instruments and Protocols

There are several legal frameworks that can reinforce and contribute to the prevention of mass atrocities. Internationally, the Rome Statute of the ICC – which has been ratified by twelve states in the Great Lakes Region – and the principles of the R2P norm can reduce the risks of atrocity crimes, help develop a culture of accountability rather than impunity, and demonstrate the ability and willingness of respective states to hold perpetrators of genocide, war crimes, and crimes against humanity criminally accountable.

Regionally, the ICGLR Pact on Security, Stability, and Development in the Great Lakes Region includes ten protocols. All the protocols, if domesticated (i.e., given a force equivalent to domestic laws in Member States), can contribute to the prevention of mass atrocities because they all work toward finding peaceful resolutions, increasing personal security, and promoting prosperous economies. Of these ten protocols, three are crucial to EWR in the prevention of mass atrocities, genocide, and crimes against humanity:

1. The Protocol on the Prevention and Suppression of Sexual Violence Against Women and Children
2. The Protocol Against the Illegal Exploitation of Natural Resources
3. The Protocol for the Prevention and the Punishment of the Crime of Genocide, War Crimes, and Crimes against Humanity and All Forms of Discrimination

In the context of the prevention of conflict and the crimes of genocide and mass atrocities, the protocols are considered most important because the first of the three responds to a history of grave human rights abuses against women and children as the most vulnerable groups and introduces response and accountability measures. The second addresses control of resources as a key area of interest. The third directly speaks to mass atrocities, crimes against humanity, and genocide. All the protocols contain important initiatives and processes that, once domesticated and implemented by all Member States, will contribute to the achievement of peace, stability, and development in the region.

In such a complex mix of conditions and mechanisms, strategies for early warning and assessments to craft early responses should ensure that progress in, for example, the prevention of sexual and gender-based violence, is not emphasized at the expense of similar attention to other aspects of the system (e.g., the prevention of mass atrocities). However, taken together, the ICGLR protocols demonstrate that programmatic approaches to EWR need be multilevel and multidimensional with regard to dealing with the causes of conflict and the conditions under which these causes often escalate into violence and mass atrocities. Such a complex environment also suggests that a common prevention agenda for the region, best suited for peacetime implementation, be created before threats that give rise to mass atrocities escalate. In the Great Lakes Region, therefore, the idea is not to construct a new mandate for the EWR to function, but instead to manage existing opportunities into an organized agenda with clear roles that different stakeholders in the system can implement with sufficient legitimacy and mandate.

Genocide and mass atrocity prevention structures under the ICGLR are currently dedicated to, among other activities, the domestication of the Protocol in all twelve Member States. By establishing a Regional Committee, each Member State committed to developing a national committee to help domesticate the Protocol, whose functions include the coordination of early warning and early response, and to implement prevention activities at the national and local levels. EWRs are essentially the heartbeat of these committees, necessary components to implement the Protocol and fulfill its respective mandates.

Ideally, each Member State should have an EWR system in place, one recognized by domestic laws and with its actions respected and perceived as binding; this would commit the state to preventing mass atrocities and to punishing identified perpetrators. Such work should then feed into the Regional Committee's EWR system, which can play more of a coordinating role as opposed to duplicating efforts locally and nationally. From this perspective, the potential of this unprecedented regional network to operate an effective and efficient early warning and early response system at regional and national levels is encouraging. However, the complexities involved in its structures, capacity gaps, and enduring legacies of violence pose challenges. It is recommended that the international community, regional actors, and national and local stakeholders turn their efforts toward strengthening the ICGLR Genocide Prevention Program through the regional and national committees.

Bibliography

Austin, Alexander. 2004. *Early Warning and the Field: A Cargo Cult Science?* Berghof Handbook. Berlin: Berghof Research Center for Constructive Conflict Management. Available at www.berghof-handbook.net/articles/section-ii-analysing-conflict-and-assessing-conflict-transformation

Agreement Establishing the Inter-Government Authority on Development (IGAD). 1996. IGAD/SUM-96/AGRE. Nairobi, March 21, 1996.

American Bar Association. July 2013. "Early Warning System Helps to Thwart Attacks on Remote Villages in the Democratic Republic of Congo." Available at www.amer icanbar.org/advocacy/rule_of_law/where_we_work/africa/democratic_republic_ congo/news/news_drc_early_warning_system_helps_thwart_village_attacks_0713. html

Anderson, B. Mary. 2001. *Early Warning, Early Response and Conflict Analysis.* Cambridge, MA: Local Capacities for Peace Project (LCPP) and Hiroshima Peacebuilding Center. Cambridge, MA

Babaud, Sébastien, and James Ndung'u. 2012. *Early Warning and Conflict Prevention by the EU: Learning Lessons from the 2008 Post-Election Violence in Kenya* (March 2012). Initiative for Peacebuilding. Available at www.saferworld.org.uk/downloads /pubdocs/IfPEW_Kenya.pdf

Bates, Robert. 2008. *When Things Fall Apart: State Failure in Late Century Africa.* New York: Cambridge University Press.

Bellamy, J. Alex. 2011. *Mass Atrocities and Armed Conflict: Links, Distinctions, and Implications for the Responsibility to Prevent.* Policy Analysis Brief: *Innovative Approaches to Peace and Security.* Muscatine, IA: The Stanley Foundation.

Burton, John W. 1993. *Conflict Resolution as a Political Philosophy – Conflict Resolution Theory and Philosophy.* Manchester and New York: Manchester University Press.

Combating the Rape Crisis in Eastern Democratic Republic of Congo. May 2009. Available at www.americanbar.org/advocacy/rule_of_law/where_we_work/africa/d emocratic_republic_congo/news/news_drc_combating_the_rape_crisis_0509.html

"Corporate Responses to Hate Speech in the 2013 Kenyan Presidential Elections." November 2013. Case Study Number 1. London: Institute for Human Rights and Business.

Christensen, H. Katja. October 2009. "Conflict Early Warning and Response Mechanism in the Horn of Africa: IGAD as a Pioneer in Regional Conflict Prevention in Africa. A Field Study in Ethiopia, 2009." Sponsored by the Swedish International Development Cooperation Agency in collaboration with the Department of Peace and Conflict Research at Uppsala University. www.pcr.uu.se /digitalAssets/67/67531_1conflict_early_warning__igad_as_pioneer_in_regional_ conflict_prevention_in_africa__katja_h._christensen__mfs__2009.pdf

Christian, Gozzi (2012). Supporting Genocide Prevention in East Africa: The GP Project. Advanced Consortium on Cooperation, Conflict and Complexity (AC[4]). New York. http://ac4.ei.columbia.edu/2012/03/01/supporting-genocide-pre vention-in-east-africa-the-gpp-project/

"Declaration by Heads of State and Governments of the International Conference on the Great Lakes Region on the Promotion of Peace, Stability and Development in the Great Lakes Region." January 15, 2014. 5th Ordinary Summit of Heads of State and Government. Luanda, Angola. Available at http://ikazeiwacu.unblog.fr/files/2014/01/20 0038991-joint-communique-of-the-declaration-of-the-summit-of-heads-of-state-and-go vernment-of-the-international-conference-on-the-great-lakes-region-icglr-o.pdf

Diaz, Castillo Pablo, and Sunita Caminha. 2012. *Gender Responsive Early Warning: Overview and How-to Guide.* United Nations Entity for Gender Equality and

Empowerment of Women. October 2012. Available at http://cu-csds.org/wp-content /uploads/2009/10/unwomen2012vdk.pdf

Dirosa, Anthony. 2013. "Case Study for GenPrev." Auschwitz Institute Blog. June 25, 2013. Available at https://aipr.wordpress.com/tag/early-warning/

Gettleman, Jeffrey. 2011. "Killings and Intimidation Mar Elections in Congo." *New York Times*. November 28, 2011. Available at www.nytimes.com/2011/11/29/world/africa/co ngo-votes-amid-expectations-of-fraud-and-fears-of-violence.html?_r=0

Gettleman, Jeffrey. 2012. "The World's Worst War." *New York Times*. December 23, 2012. Available at www.nytimes.com/2012/12/16/sunday-review/congos-never-end ing-war.html?_r=0

Githaiga, Nyambura. 2011. *Tension Over DRC-Elections a Failure of Early Warning*. Institute for Security Studies – Nairobi, Kenya. http://www.issafrica.org/iss-today /tension-over-drc-elections-a-failure-of-early-warning

Halakhe, Abdullahi Boru. 2013. "R2P in Practice: Ethnic Violence, Elections and Atrocity Prevention in Kenya." Global Centre for the Responsibility to Protect. Occasional Paper Series. No. 4, December 2013, New York.

Horowitz, Donald. 1985. *Ethnic Groups in Conflict*. Berkeley and Los Angeles: University of California Press.

Human Rights Watch. 2013. "High Stakes: Political Violence and the 2013 Elections in Kenya." February 2013. Available at www.hrw.org/sites/default/files/reports/ken ya0213webwcover.pdf

James E. Yonamine, Vito D'Orazio, and Philip A. Schrodt. 2011. "Predicting Intra-State Conflict Onset: An Event Data Approach Using Euclidean and Levenshtein Distance Measures." Paper prepared for delivery at the Annual Meeting of the Midwest Political Science Association, Chicago, March 31–April 3, 2011.

Kassa, Kebede Girma. 2011. "Final Evaluation Report of the Rapid Response Fund of CEWARN." November 2011. Available at http://cewarn.org/attachments/061_CEW ARN%20RRF%20Evaluation%20Report.pdf

Keyserlingk, N. V., and S. Kopfmüller. 2006. Conflict Early Warning Systems: Lessons Learned from Establishing a Conflict Early Warning and Response Mechanism (CEWARN) in the Horn of Africa. www.beyondintractability.org/internal-biblio/9204

Kron, Josh, and Jeffrey Gettleman. 2010. "U.N. E-Mail Shows Early Warning of Congo Rapes." August 31, 2010. Available at www.nytimes.com/2010/09/01/world/africa/ 01congoweb.html?_r=3&ref=global-home&

Kuch, Priscilla Joseph, and James Thubo Ayul. 2012. *A Feasibility Study on South Sudan Conflict Early Warning and Response Mechanisms*. Juba, South Sudan: Partners in Development.

Moore, Meghan. 2011. "A New Chapter: Early Warning Radio Network. Pulitzer Center on Crisis Reporting." April 12, 2011. Available at http://pulitzercenter.org/articles /congo-lra-prevention-early-warning-radio-network

Oucho, O. John. 2011. "Undercurrents of the Post-Elections Violence in Kenya: Issues in the Long-Term Agenda." In *Democratic Gains and Gaps: A Study of the 2007 Kenyan General Elections*. Edited by John O. Oucho. Warwick, UK: University of Warwick.

Prinier Gerald. 2009. *Africa's World War: Congo, the Rwandan Genocide, and the Making of a Continental Catastrophe*. New York: Oxford University Press.

Ramsbotham, Oliver. 2005. "The Analysis of Protracted Social Conflicts: A Tribute to Edward Azar." *Review of International Studies* 31: 109–126. British International Studies Association

"Report on the Workshop on Early Warning Systems in Kenya." 2006. Africa Advanced Level Telecommunications Institute, Nairobi, Kenya. October 4, 2006.

Sandole, J. D. Dennis. 1999. *Capturing the Complexity of Conflict: Dealing with Violent Ethnic Conflicts of the Post-Cold War Era.* New York: Pinter.

Scott, James C. 1985. *Weapons of the Weak: Everyday Forms of Peasant Resistance.* New Haven, CT: Yale University Press.

"South Sudan's Newly Appointed National Reconciliation Committee Takes Over." May 5, 2013. JUBA. Available www.sudantribune.com/spip.php?article46472

Syallow, Maureen. January 2011. "Media played a major Role in the 2007/2008 Post Elections Violence in Kenya." Available at http://maureensyallow.hubpages.com/hub/Media-Played-a-major-Role-in-the-20072008-Post-Elections-Violence-in-Kenya

"The Regional Steering Committee of CEWARN's Rapid Response Fund (RRF) Convenes to Review Local-Level Peace Building Projects." November 2012. Available at www.cewarn.org/index.php?option=com_content&view=article&id=188:the-regional-steering-committee-of-cewarns-rapid-response-fund-rrf-convenes-to-review-local-level-peace-building-project&scatid=1:latest-news&Itemid=82

Uma, N. Julius. 2012. "South Sudan Launches Conflict Early Warning and Response Unit." Available at www.sudantribune.com/spip.php?article42544

United Nations. 2006. *"Global Survey of Early Warning Systems: An Assessment of Capacities, Gaps and Opportunities towards Building a Comprehensive Global Early Warning System for All Natural Hazards."* A report prepared at the request of the Secretary-General of the United Nations. September 2006. www.unisdr.org/2006/ppew/info-resources/ewc3/Global-Survey-of-Early-Warning-Systems.pdf

Watkins, Tom. May 1, 2014. "Humanitarian Groups: Don't Let CAR Devolve into Genocide." Available at http://edition.cnn.com/2014/05/01/world/africa/central-african-republic

Whittall, Jonathan. 2010. "Humanitarian Early Warning Systems: Myth and Reality." *Third World Quarterly* 31(8): 1237–1250.

Workshop on Early Warning & Early Response Practice: Sharing the WANEP Experience & Strategy Planning. August 7–9, 2007. Accra, Ghana. Organized by the West Africa Network for Peacebuilding (WANEP) and the European Centre for Conflict Prevention/GPPAC Global Secretariat.

Wulf, Herbert, and Tobias Debiel. 2009. "Conflict Early Warning and Response Mechanisms: Tools for Enhancing the Effectiveness of Regional Organizations." A Comparative Study of the AU, ECOWAS, IGAD, ASEAN/ARF and PIF. Crisis Working Papers Series No. 2, May 2009.

20 The Argentinean National Mechanism for the Prevention of Genocide: A Case Study in Contemporary Preventive Institution-Building

Ramiro Riera

National mechanisms for the prevention of genocide and mass atrocities are one of the most important measures that United Nations Member States can implement to promote the prevention of genocide and crimes against humanity and to facilitate the enforcement of the different pillars of Responsibility to Protect (R2P). In this context, the capacity development of the national mechanisms becomes an essential challenge that governments must address when turning into reality the prevention of mass atrocities and genocide.

National mechanisms are institutional public policy tools that states can use to effectively implement the prevention of genocide and mass atrocities in compliance with their international obligations. In general, these mechanisms require coordination among different agencies with different competences. Through these mechanisms, they cooperate to seek to meet the goals of preventing discrimination and violence, providing early warning, and helping to raise awareness against genocidal practices.

20.1. The Importance of Capacity Development for National Mechanisms

Capacity development is one of the numerous elements that make up the broader picture of institutional development. In broad terms, institutional development seeks to improve the effectiveness of an organization in a sustainable way by developing the capacities of the institution and its members, as well as through improving the political and legislative context within which an institution is situated. As such, capacity development can be understood as both a basic technical project of improving skills and systems as well as a political process that seeks to better situate a mechanism vis-à-vis the other branches of government.

Capacity development is relevant to all mechanisms and is a persistent, ongoing effort. The process is perhaps most obvious with regard to newly established mechanisms, which have to build institutional and individual capacity from scratch. It is a process that is, however, equally applicable to well-established mechanisms as they seek to maintain, improve, and adapt their capacities in the face of changing environments.

Nonetheless, capacity development is important for all institutions that function within the realm of general human rights and related issues. First, it is important for those affected by human rights violations that complaints and systemic issues be addressed in an efficient and effective manner. Second, effective national mechanisms help the government to better identify problems and better deal with them, thus contributing to a better-run state output toward citizens on these policies that are essential to them. Thus, capacity development is important for (1) improving the functioning of national mechanisms, (2) assuring that complaints are effectively and efficiently addressed, and (3) ensuring that national mechanisms contribute to effective and accountable early warning and information sharing among governmental institutions.

In the case of the capacity development of mechanisms that link up different parts and levels of government, it must not be exclusively an internal process, undertaken by a national mechanism alone or solely within the national context. This process must also take place through sharing and imparting members' good practices with other, nonparticipating institutions, both governmental or nongovernmental.

I would like to pause here to explain why, although the term "capacity building" is widely used, I choose to use the term "capacity development" in this chapter. I prefer the term "development" over "building" because the building metaphor suggests a step-by-step, linear process. "Development," on the other hand, suggests a process whereby people, organizations, and societies strengthen, create, and adapt capacity over time (OECD 2006: 12). Looking at the concept within this frame, I argue that capacity development has both a technical dimension and a power dimension. The technical dimension relates to elements such as skills, rules, expertise, techniques, procedures, and management found in a national mechanism. The power dimension relates to elements such as interests, resistance, or willingness of other actors to cooperate; incentives; conflicts; and coalitions.

To capture both dimensions, I propose that the study of the capacity development of national mechanisms for genocide prevention focuses on three mains issues: (1) the aims of capacity development, (2) the process of capacity development, and (3) the challenges and opportunities for capacity development.

20.2.   The Aims of Capacity Development

National mechanisms are an essential part of the national policies for the prevention of genocide. As coordination mechanisms among different governmental and nongovernmental institutions, they play a crucial role in preventing mass atrocities and responding to general and systematic human rights abuses.

By coordinating policies and receiving complaints, as well as through reporting on thematic questions and systemic problems, national mechanisms can have an important impact on both individuals and on the administrative sector and legislative environment as a whole. In this context, the aim of capacity development is to improve the effectiveness and efficiency of national mechanisms in fulfilling this role in a sustainable way. This process aims to (1) foster institutional learning and development within national mechanisms; (2) help national mechanisms to adapt to changing environments/new tasks and challenges; (3) enhance the ability of national mechanisms to handle complaints, conduct thematic research, and manage outreach activities; (4) increase the expertise and specialization of members; and (5) improve the credibility of national mechanisms.

This list makes it explicit that the process of capacity development is not only about technical support, but also about creating and enabling a favorable political environment for the institution to function effectively.

20.3.   The Process of Capacity Development

Before discussing the process of capacity development in more detail, it is worth noting that this process must be based on principles that respect the integrity and credibility of the mechanism: capacity development should be guided by the principles of local ownership, impartiality, gender sensitivity, and an acknowledgment that capacity development is a long-term process (UNDP 2003: 13). Capacity development should not only target the office holder and members of the national mechanism themselves, but also focus on a range of other relevant actors. These include parliaments, relevant agencies and members of the executive, civil society and human rights advocacy organizations, the media, other national mechanisms, and international actors or fora (such as the Special Adviser of the UN Secretary-General for Genocide Prevention and Responsibility to Protect).

20.3.1.   The Phases of Capacity Development

As with any public policy, capacity development consists of four phases: (1) needs assessment, (2) decision making and planning, (3) implementation, and (4) evaluation. Each one of these phases is essential for the success of capacity development.

20.3.1.1. Needs Assessment Capacity development is an ongoing process. However, because each government has its own purposes and realities, the national mechanisms will each have different needs. The first step in developing capacity is identifying these needs. For both new and future mechanisms, these needs will flow from the overall strategic goals of existing institutions, as well as from an assessment of what is happening on the ground. For newly formed institutions, an important early task will also be to identify the expected number and types of competencies. This will then help in determining the necessary funding required, in hiring appropriate numbers of personnel, and in properly allocating other resources.

One important needs assessment tool is the use of *mapping studies*. Such studies may involve research and analysis of relevant stakeholders and the environment within a state, as well as the identification of similar institutions at home and abroad that may offer examples of good practice that can be applied. Such studies enable institutions to identify strengths, weaknesses, opportunities, and threats and to integrate this knowledge into their capacity development plan. Furthermore, a comprehensive mapping study may provide national mechanisms with a useful baseline against which to measure the success of later capacity development processes.

20.3.1.2. Decision Making and Planning Upon determining the specific needs of a national mechanism, it is important to develop a plan to address these needs. It is possible to develop a blueprint or multiyear plans with measurable benchmarks. These serve to focus institutional goals and allow the chairperson of the mechanism to determine how successful he or she has been in achieving these goals. Some officeholders have implemented thematic mandates during their term in office. These can be particularly effective at giving focus to the work of a national mechanism and at addressing specific areas that are in need of greater attention.

For new and future national mechanisms, the identification of achievable short- and long-term goals (e.g., one- and five-year plans) can help guide the progress of an institution through what may be difficult early years. Such goals may include technical issues (such as setting up an electronic system of information sharing) as well as more abstract issues (such as increasing awareness about the institution and its powers among the agencies of the executive and legislative). Planning should be a long-term endeavor.

Another key element at the planning stage is the development of in-house regulations governing the way the mechanism will function. Such regulations might cover, for example, internal guidelines for information sharing and the number and means of notifications that the mechanism will send to each member. These rules ensure that information is handled in a standardized way.

20.3.1.3. Implementation   Some types of capacity development can be difficult to implement. In particular, large-scale reforms, such as legislative amendments or increases in budget or powers, may take a long time to achieve. Small-scale capacity development can, however, be both easy and relatively inexpensive. Specific capacity development activities can include seminars and workshops, regular staff meetings, training events, technical assistance, legal advice, needs assessments, technical support, organizing meetings with relevant stakeholders, and policy advice, as well as contributing to setting international standards and identifying good practice.

Capacity development can be both external (involving or relying on contributions from third parties) or internal (generated from within a mechanism itself). Ideally, both external and internal processes will occur together and contribute to the same goal. Capacity development cannot be externally forced upon people or institutions. In other words, external partners cannot "do" capacity development; at best, they can support capacity development processes.

20.3.1.4. Evaluation   Annual or thematic reports play a key role in capacity development by providing an opportunity for self-evaluation and performance review while also establishing goals for the following year. Many institutions also use them as a way of pushing for progress in achieving their goals (e.g., legislative reform, increasing cooperation with the military). These also can be useful in identifying successes and failures and focusing efforts for the following period. Indicators are essential for evaluation. They allow a mechanism to measure its progress against benchmarks that have been set in the past (e.g., time taken for early warning, satisfaction of those who approach the mechanism).

Unfortunately not everything can be measured in a useful way. Consequently, evaluation should also take into account intangible factors and involve qualitative as well as quantitative research. In a comparative perspective, little is known about when and how the work of national mechanisms is evaluated in terms of aims, benchmarks, methodology, and type of measurement. It would be beneficial for capacity development to exchange experiences and viewpoints between national mechanisms about how their work is evaluated. Indeed, without measurement of capacities against agreed-upon benchmarks, it would be difficult to decide which capacities need to be developed.

20.4.   Challenges and Opportunities for Capacity Development

20.4.1.   Challenges

Some of the challenges for the capacity development of national mechanisms for the prevention of genocide are environmental in nature and relate to the legal and political context; these include patronage, party politics, low levels of accountability, authoritarian government, and weak parliamentary scrutiny of government. National mechanisms may also face strong resistance to change from certain sectors of the society, local governments, some federal administrative agencies, or even from members within the national mechanism itself. Cooperation between the government and/or civil society is essential to successful capacity development of a mass atrocity prevention mechanism, given that its goal is to normalize the relationship between these two societal environments.

Staffing is a more practical challenge to capacity development. In particular, many institutions do not have much flexibility in hiring staff and rely on transfers from within the government's civil service. This issue is essential because the majority of existing national genocide prevention mechanisms don't have their own structure and staff, and member agencies provide these. As a result, in some cases, they may end up with unmotivated or uninterested individuals. These problems may be compounded in some states by poor public service conditions (such as low salaries), which can lead to high turnover among qualified staff. High turnover is a problem that is particularly relevant in the case of the chairperson of the national mechanisms because it is her responsibility to produce the annual report and to elaborate the action plans. There is a need for policies that govern the transfer of power from one chairperson to the next in a way that ensures that institutional knowledge is not lost and, especially, that there is no disruption in the functioning of the mechanism.

A related problem is funding. Many institutions that are members of national mechanisms face unpredictable funding or an overall lack of financial resources, particularly to pay for necessary infrastructure and appropriate numbers of qualified staff. The most recent international economic crisis has negatively affected the capacities of national mechanisms.

It may also be difficult for national mechanisms to identify capacity development needs. As noted earlier, effective assessments and evaluations can be difficult. Feedback is often skewed, depending on the outcome of information sharing, and it may be difficult to separate these issues and identify areas that need strengthening. When establishing a new mechanism, it may also be very difficult to foresee future needs, especially when the needs assessment process that leads to creation of the mechanism is superficial.

Consequently, it may be very difficult to start the national mechanism's activity with sufficient physical (e.g., staff, funding, office space) and technical resources (e.g., staff with appropriate knowledge or experience). It is very important not to forget that, in many cases of national mechanisms for mass atrocity prevention, the situation is further complicated by the reality that they don't have their own structure because they are principally a coordination organism among federal administration agencies and civil society organizations.

A final challenge to the capacity development of a national mechanism on genocide and mass atrocity prevention is the simple fact that this process of capacity development must inevitably take place in addition to fulfilling the missions and competencies of the new mechanism. Given the funding and staffing shortages that many institutions face, this may be a formidable obstacle.

20.4.2. Opportunities

A number of different situations can provide openings for a capacity development process to begin. In the case of the establishment of a national mechanism, capacity development can be driven by strong demand from nongovernmental organizations or local authorities. International or bilateral support can also provide a useful opportunity for capacity development. The Special Adviser to the UN Secretary-General for the Prevention of Genocide is a useful institution in this regard. It provides an opportunity to network with other institutions, share good practices, and learn about different models and approaches to information sharing and early warning capacity development. International and regional networks like the Latin American Network for Genocide and Mass Atrocity Prevention can also serve as a useful capacity development tool in that international practices can be used back home to demonstrate that certain proposed changes are not extraordinary and are in line with international norms. Some national mechanisms also find it reassuring to learn that other mechanisms are facing similar problems. This kind of regional fora may also serve a useful role as a platform for capacity development through, for example, the setting up of bilateral/twinning arrangements (e.g., exchange of personnel, interns) and regional or thematic initiatives (e.g., seminars on specific topics).

Capacity development is important for a number of different reasons. The process fosters institutional learning, makes national mechanisms better able to adapt to changing environments, and improves their credibility, efficiency and effectiveness. Capacity development is relevant to all institutions, both those in their infancy, as well as those that have existed for some years. As such, it is a persistent, ongoing effort. For it to be successful and sustainable, capacity development should be an endogenous process, one supported by external actors. Although external actors can support capacity development, they cannot take over ownership from the national mechanisms: local ownership is not simply a yes/no question, but is also a matter of process, trends, and dialogue.

Currently, capacity development activities among mechanisms appear to take place in an isolated, ad hoc, and reactive manner, replying to specific requests by states. Capacity development could be much more effective if it was coordinated, involved the pooling of resources, and included systematic follow-up of initial contacts, requests, and activities. As a forerunner to better coordinated capacity development, there is a clear need for a more systematic and comprehensive mapping study of the work of national mechanisms that would outline their needs and current state of affairs, as well as allow us a better understanding of national and regional contexts.

20.5. Some Experiences of National Mechanisms for the Prevention of Genocide

From a comparative perspective, there are three different models of national mechanisms: (1) those that have an external monitoring function, (2) those that have an internal monitoring function, and (3) those that have a mixed monitoring function, both internal and external. I describe the U.S. mechanism as representative of the first type. African experiences define the second type, and I briefly describe a few of these. I describe at length the Argentinean initiative as characterizing the third type.

20.5.1. *The National Mechanism of the United Sates*

According to the information provided to the UN Secretary-General in his report to the General Assembly and to the Security Council on State Responsibility and Prevention of March 13, 2013, in the United States, the establishment of the interagency Atrocities Prevention Board in 2012 was preceded by a thorough review of existing capacities and gaps and led to a series of recommendations that are now being implemented (United Nations 2013: para. 58). Basically, this mechanism monitors emerging threats, focuses U.S. government efforts, and develops new tools and capabilities. As an example, as a result of the Atrocities Prevention Board's activities, in January 2013, the president signed expanded war crimes rewards legislation, thus giving the State Department a new tool to promote accountability for the worst crimes known to humankind in different parts of the world.

The Board includes senior representatives of the Departments of State, Defense, Treasury, Justice (DOJ), and Homeland Security (DHS); the Joint

Staff; the U.S. Agency for International Development (USAID); the U.S. Mission to the UN, the Office of the Director of National Intelligence; the Central Intelligence Agency: the Office of the Vice President; and the National Security Staff. The Board identifies and addresses emerging atrocity threats by scanning the horizon for critical developments, assessing the risk of mass atrocities in particular situations, and supplementing existing efforts or catalyzing new efforts to ensure that atrocity threats receive adequate and timely attention. Likewise, the mechanism also coordinates the development of new policies and tools to enhance the capacity of the United States to effectively prevent and respond to atrocities (U.S. Government 2013). Agencies represented on the Board have all taken steps, including the creation of dedicated "alert channels," to help ensure that information related to atrocities and atrocity threats is appropriately collected, evaluated, and disseminated within the U.S. government.

The mechanism is exclusively focused on genocide and mass atrocity prevention efforts in societies other than the Unites States.

20.5.2. The African Committees

In Africa, since 2010, Kenya, Rwanda, Uganda, Zambia, the United Republic of Tanzania, South Sudan, and the Central African Republic have established national committees on the prevention and punishment of the crime of genocide, war crimes, crimes against humanity, and all forms of discrimination; this work is based on the Protocol of the International Conference on the Great Lakes Region (ICGLR) and builds on the Genocide Convention and the Rome Statute of the International Criminal Court (Bartoli and Ogata 2013).

As a consequence of the 1994 genocide in Rwanda, twelve countries of Africa founded the ICGLR in 2000. It is an intergovernmental organization of countries in the African Great Lakes Region and was established based on the recognition that political instability and conflicts in these countries have a considerable regional dimension and thus require a concerted effort to promote sustainable peace and development. In response to UN Security Council Resolutions 1291 and 1304, this group of African countries called for an International Conference on peace, security, democracy, and development in the Great Lakes Region. The Conference addresses cross-cutting issues such as gender, environment, human rights, HIV/AIDS, and human settlements. The countries of the ICGLR have adopted a protocol on genocide and mass atrocities prevention (Article 8 of the Covenant on Security, Stability, and Development in the Great Lakes Region). This international instrument aims to promote genocide prevention policies in each Member State. In order to ensure the rightful implementation of its projects and protocols, the ICGLR brings together experts and authorities from its member countries to meet on a regular basis. And every two years, the Regional Inter-Ministerial Committee (RIMC), the executive board of the ICGLR, assesses the progress that has been made. The Regional Committee for the Prevention of Genocide, War Crimes, Crimes against Humanity, and All Forms of Discrimination is the only committee whose composition is endorsed by all the heads of state and ministers of Member States. The Regional Committee is the first intergovernmental body in history politically mandated by twelve Member States of ICGLR to operationalize genocide prevention. Given the confluence of local, national, regional, and international linkages of the ICGLR structure, it is now possible to imagine a dedicated, long-term, collective effort to establish a genocide prevention system in the territories of ICGLR. This exploration makes sense if (1) local ownership of the project is ensured and maintained; (2) knowledge is made available, verified, and renewed; and (3) results are measured through meaningful processes. The functioning of the Regional Committee serves as a mechanism that helps to ensure the local ownership of the genocide prevention approach in each of the ICGLR member states.

On the other hand, some countries of the ICGLR have created their own committees and policies, complementary to the regional initiatives. All twelve Member States of the regional body have committed to establishing similar committees. While still in the process of development, these committees could pave the way for the creation or strengthening of national early warning mechanisms (United Nations 2013: para. 59).

In particular, the Republic of Tanzania created its own prevention committee in 2012. The National Committee for the Prevention of Genocide, War Crimes, Crimes against Humanity, and All Forms of Discrimination brought together ten focal point representatives of government ministries and civil society organizations. With the assistance of the Office of the Special Adviser of the UN on the Prevention of Genocide (OSAPG) and experts, the National Committee members produced their own Work Plan, identifying a set of risk factors to monitor and laying out a time table to institute their secretariat in the Ministry of Constitutional and Legal Affairs. They also developed their own rule of procedure.

The case of the Zambian National Committee is interesting because it illustrates the difficult processes of capacity development. The main challenge to establishing a national committee was principally budgetary. In addition, the need to further sensitize policymakers and remove the stigma attached to the possible creation of a committee was great. Some of the obstacles to the development of capacity in the field of genocide and mass atrocities prevention were related to the fact that new government officials had not been associated with ICGLR processes, and the term "genocide" is a sensitive one, perceived as suggesting its possible occurrence in Zambia instead of focusing on the preventive mandate of the initiatives. This aspect shows that a good communication and media strategy is necessary for the establishment and strengthening of new national bodies on this issue.

Another important experience is the one of the Kenyan National Committee on the Prevention and Punishment of Genocide, Crimes against Humanity, War Crimes, and All Forms of Discrimination. This national body began to develop its own early warning and coordination mechanism for preventing and responding to genocide and related atrocity crimes. The creation of the Kenyan national committee draws from the ICGLR Protocol for the Prevention and Punishment of the Crime of Genocide, War Crimes, and Crimes Against Humanity, and All Forms of Discrimination by taking into account the causes and dynamics of genocide as well as strategies and methodologies to build an effective early warning system for atrocity crimes. Also, the nascent National Committee developed a draft national action plan for early warning and early response.

In 2012, the Ugandan National Committee on the Prevention and Punishment of Genocide and Mass Atrocities was launched. The first steps to set up the new national body were preliminary genocide prevention training for Uganda's National Committee members, the development of a six-month Work Plan for the National Committee, and the discussion and agreement on subsequent steps for the implementation of the National Committee Work Plan. The Ugandan National Committee comprises representatives from the Office of the Prime Minister, the Ministry of Foreign Affairs, the Ministry of Justice, the Ministry of Internal Affairs, the Ministry of Defense, the Ministry of Gender, the Uganda High Commission, the Uganda Human Rights Commission, the Uganda Police Force, Care International, the International Refugee Rights Initiative, the Uganda Law Reform Commission, the Uganda Civil Society Fund, Regional Associates for Community Initiatives, and other civil society groups and human rights organizations. The National Committee also formed a bureau composed of a Chair from the Ministry of Justice and Constitutional Affairs, a Vice Chair from the Ministry of Foreign Affairs, and a Rapporteur from the Uganda Human Rights Commission. The main emphasis for the design of national policies and capacity development was on early warning and genocide prevention mechanisms and methodologies. The policies developed in Uganda address an analysis of genocide and mass atrocities risk, a framework for responding to the possibility of genocide, and strategies and methodologies for effective early warning systems for genocide prevention. It is important to mention that the Ugandan National Committee Work Plan outlines policy and operative features, identifies the responsibilities of partnering institutions and organizations, and provides a time frame for application.

20.5.3.   The National Mechanism of Argentina

In 2012, after the launch of the Latin American Network for Genocide and Mass Atrocity Prevention, the Republic of Argentina set in motion several measures meant to comply with the need to develop policies for the prevention of genocide. In this regard, the government adopted concrete measures that are worth highlighting and that are essential to the actions that have been carried out in different fields to support the prevention of genocide.

In this context, and based on a proposal presented by the National Human Rights and International Humanitarian Law Direction of the Ministry of Defense to create an institutional body responsible for the implementation of policies to prevent genocide, different national bodies with human rights competences started a dialogue meant to lead to a common effort and to the development of a National Mechanism for the Prevention of Genocide. This new initiative aims to coordinate policies related to the prevention of genocide in order to achieve more efficient and more effective results in this regard at the governmental level.

20.5.3.1.   Legal Framework   Since 1956, the Argentinean state is party to the Convention on the Prevention and Punishment of the Crime of Genocide adopted by the UN General Assembly Resolution 260 (III) A on December 9, 1948, and approved by Decree-Law 6286/56 on the April 9, 1956.

In this regard, it is important to mention that, after the Amendment to the Constitution in 1994, said Convention is recognized therein according to the stipulations of Article 75 Section 22 of the Constitution, which means that it has the highest level of relevance within the Argentinean legal system. Therefore, the Convention is included as part of Argentina's legal system, and the government of Argentina has the responsibility for enforcing the rules and international obligations contained therein.

It is common knowledge that the prevention of genocide is one of the international obligations stipulated in the Convention. In this sense, Article 1 of the Convention on the Prevention and Punishment of the Crime of Genocide states that:

The Contracting Parties confirm that genocide, whether committed in time of peace or in time of war, is a crime under international law which they undertake to prevent and to punish.

In addition, Article VIII establishes that:

Any Contracting Party may call upon the competent organs of the United Nations to take such action under the Charter of the United Nations as they consider appropriate for the prevention and suppression of acts of genocide or any of the other acts enumerated in Article III.[1]

In this regard, in the Argentine Republic, the punishment of the crime of genocide has been regulated with the ratification of the ICC statute. Still, there is a pending matter related to the development of specific and effective measures for the prevention of genocide. On this topic, and in compliance with the international obligations accepted by the government of Argentina, it was proposed in 2012 to create a National Mechanism for the Prevention of Genocide. This mechanism shall be established by an Executive Order with its main purpose being to coordinate actions of the pertinent governmental national and provincial bodies entitled to work in the prevention of genocide.

20.5.3.2. Background   On April 7, 2004, during his address to the Commission on Human Rights on the occasion of a special meeting to observe the International Day of Reflection on the 1994 Genocide in Rwanda, the UN Secretary-General outlined a Five Point Action Plan to prevent genocide:

1. Preventing the armed conflict that usually provides the context for genocide
2. Protecting civilians in armed conflict, including a mandate for UN peace-keepers to protect civilians
3. Ending impunity through judicial action in both national and international courts
4. Undertaking information gathering and early warning through a UN Special Adviser for Genocide Prevention making recommendations to the UN Security Council on actions to prevent or halt genocide
5. Taking swift and decisive action along a continuum of steps, including military action (United Nations 2006)

On that occasion, with regard to the development of a capacity within the UN system for early and clear warning of potential genocide, UN Secretary-General Kofi Annan announced his decision to create the new post of Special Adviser on the Prevention of Genocide, reporting through him to the Security Council.

Further contributing to an environment favorable to genocide prevention capacity development, on March 2012, an event was organized by Argentina's Ministry of Foreign Affairs; Ministry of Justice, Security, and Human Rights; the Secretariat for Human Rights of the Presidency of Brazil; and the

---

[1] The following acts shall be punishable: (a) Genocide; (b) Conspiracy to commit genocide; (c) Direct and public incitement to commit genocide; (d) Attempt to commit genocide; (e) Complicity in genocide.

Auschwitz Institute for Peace and Reconciliation (AIPR), with the support of the UN Office of the Special Advisers on Prevention of Genocide and Responsibility to Protect to launch the Latin American Network for Genocide and Mass Atrocity Prevention. The Network created through this event is an initiative directed at the prevention of future atrocities and is based on the Latin American experience in the matter; it is implemented through the development of a community of civil servants with expertise on the subject. In addition, it is committed to include, through training and regional cooperation, the concept of education for the prevention of genocide and mass atrocities as a priority in the Latin American regional agenda.

20.5.3.3. Action at the Local Level   In this context, the Republic of Argentina is working on the development of a National Mechanism for the Prevention of Genocide with the goal of making possible interinstitutional coordination of actions among different national and provincial governmental bodies with responsibility in the field of genocide prevention.

The National Mechanism will have the mission of establishing a communication and information sharing network that includes different competent bodies that will gather and process information and, if necessary, submit this information to the pertinent bodies at the UN level. It also aims to develop a training curriculum for government officials in the area of genocide prevention. In addition, the National Mechanisms shall have the following competences:

20.5.3.3.1. To Assess Potential Threats and Give Early Warning   To achieve this goal, the National Mechanism will develop:

- Mechanisms for communication and information sharing about cases and related situations
- Cooperation with nongovernmental organizations interested in the matter and with scholars in the field of human rights and international humanitarian law

20.5.3.3.2. To Prevent Systematically and Build Awareness   To achieve this goal, the National Mechanism will:

- Organize conferences, seminars, and training activities in the field of human rights and international humanitarian law (responsibility to protect, international criminal law, collective security, nondiscrimination, etc.)
- Develop a training curriculum, including minimum contents required for the elimination of discrimination and the prevention of genocide, for both the

private and public education systems and also for the ongoing training of public servants of the offices and bodies involved

• Develop standards and assessment criteria for mass communication and advertising

20.5.3.3.3. To Foster Cooperation and Information Sharing To achieve this goal, the National Mechanism will establish procedures to collect and process information and to share information with competent UN and regional organizations (OAS, UNASUR, MERCOSUR, etc.), as well as with the Special Adviser to the Secretary-General on the Prevention of Genocide, the Commission on Human Rights, Special Rapporteurs, the Inter-American Commission on Human Rights, the Human Rights Institute of the MERCOSUR.

The National Mechanisms of Argentina will include a Coordination Committee entitled to:

1. Request information from the different offices of the National Government when deemed necessary
2. Develop research on the matter
3. Consult with experts, organizations, governmental bodies, and any other person or organization that could cooperate on the matter
4. Give advice on the matter at the level of national or provincial bodies or bodies of the Ciudad Autónoma de Buenos Aires if required.

The Coordination Committee will have as members representatives of the Ministry of Defense; Ministry of Foreign Affairs; Ministry of Security; Ministry of Education; Ministry of Justice and Human Rights through the Secretariat for Justice and the Secretariat for Human Rights; the National Institute against Discrimination, Xenophobia and Racism (INADI); the Council of Ministers through the Secretariat for Public Information; and the Secretariat for Institutional Reform and Consolidation of Democracy. The Coordination Committee will be chaired by one of the member institutions, with all of them taking turns each year. The body chairing the Committee will consolidate and submit to the authorities of each member the Annual Working Plan and the Annual Report. In addition, the chairing body will call for the meeting of the Committee and develop the agenda.

In addition, there are plans to create a Council for the Prevention of Genocide that will act as an advising and coordinating body to work in close cooperation with civil or national governmental agencies that could be important in achieving the goals of the National Mechanism. The Council for the Prevention of Genocide will have as members representatives of agencies that the Coordination Committee considers relevant for the satisfactory achievement of the goals of the National Mechanisms.

Finally, the Mechanism will be completed through the establishment of a Federal Network for the Prevention of Genocide that will organize the participation of national or provincial bodies or bodies of the Ciudad Autónoma de Buenos Aires in the federal framework to coordinate national and provincial governmental policies related to mass atrocity prevention issues.

Meetings for the creation of the National Mechanism, with the participation of all parties involved, were held in July 2012 and February 2013. In November 2012, the Republic of Argentina, the Auschwitz Institute for Peace and Reconciliation, and the Office of the Special Adviser to the Secretary-General on the Prevention of Genocide of the UN organized a training program for all the members of the National Mechanism. During this training program, the members discussed the organization and creation of the National Mechanism.

The National Mechanism will begin functioning once the pertinent Executive Order is issued in this regard.

20.6.   Conclusion

The protection of human rights and the prevention of mass atrocities have entered a new stage: the development of national and international systems for the prevention of genocide. There is a "new generation" of mechanisms that contribute in different ways to protect and safeguard the lives of human beings around the world. It is true that the prevention of genocide was within the horizon of action very soon after the approval of the Convention for the Prevention and Punishment of the Crime of Genocide. However, it was not until the progressive development of International Criminal Law, the principles of R2P, and the main lines of the Additional Protocol to the UN Convention against Torture and Other Punishment and Cruel, Inhuman and Degrading Treatment that effective measures for the prevention of genocide and mass atrocities began to be implemented.

Regional and local policy initiatives are beginning to complement and improve the effectiveness of prevention measures. To further this process, it is necessary to have adequate guidelines and information on good practices relevant to capacity development on the prevention of genocide and mass atrocities.

National bodies for the prevention of genocide, the latest development in this field, are crucial to carrying out a preventive mandate, given the policy complexity of a national preventive agenda.

The success of achieving a national mechanism's tasks depends on the ability and efforts of the people who set it up, design its policies, propose ideas for its growth, implement new measures, and evaluate its results. Based on the analysis of current national mechanisms, early warning systems, proper articulation with other national and international bodies, bureaucratic training, and general awareness campaigns against discrimination and violence contain the essential keys to success for these bodies.

Of course, the fact that national mechanisms are recent phenomena offers a particular challenge for their analysis. Although they are still developing governmental institutions, their strengthening and capacity development is necessary and indispensable for the construction of an environment prepared to prevent all forms of genocide and mass atrocity.

References

Bartoli, Andrea, and Tetsushi Ogata. 2013. "Supporting Regional Approaches to Genocide Prevention: The International Conference on the Great Lakes Region (ICGLR)." Available at www.gpanet.org/content/supporting-regional-approaches-genocide-prevention-international-conference-great-lakes-regi

OECD. 2006. "The Challenge of Capacity Development: Working Towards Good Practice." DAC Guidelines and Reference Series. Paris: OECD. Available at www.fao.org/fileadmin/templates/capacitybuilding/pdf/DAC_paper_final.pdf

United Nations. 2006. "Report of the Secretary-General on the Implementation of the Five-Point Action Plan and on the Activities of the Special Adviser of the Secretary-General on the Prevention of Genocide–Commission on Human Rights." E/CN.4/2006/84 March 9, 2006. Available at www.responsibilitytoprotect.org/files/Report%20on%20SAPG%20to%20CHR%202006.pdf

United Nations Secretary-General. 2013. "Responsibility to Protect: State Responsibility and Prevention." A/67/929–S/2013/399. Available at www.un.org/en/ga/search/view_doc.asp?symbol=A/67/929

UNDP. 2003. "Ownership, Leadership and Transformation." Available at www.undp.org/content/dam/aplaws/publication/en/publications/capacity-development/drivers-of-change/leadership/ownership-leadership-and-transformation-executive-summary/Ownership-Leadership-Transformation-Can-We-Do-Better_executive%20summary.pdf

U.S. Government. 2013. "Fact Sheet: The Obama Administration's Comprehensive Efforts to Prevent Mass Atrocities over the Past Year." Available at www.whitehouse.gov/sites/default/files/docs/fact_sheet_administration_efforts_to_prevent_mass_atrocities5.pdf

Index

CPSIA information can be obtained
at www.ICGtesting.com
Printed in the USA
LVOW03*1106101115

461870LV00004B/17/P